WHITEAKER MIDDLE SCHOOL
Keizer, Oregon

SAFETY SYMBOLS	HAZARD	PRECAUTION	REMEDY
Disposal	Special disposal required	Dispose of wastes as directed by your teacher.	Ask your teacher how to dispose of laboratory materials.
Biological	Organisms that can harm humans	Avoid breathing in or skin contact with organisms. Wear dust mask or gloves. Wash hands thoroughly.	Notify your teacher if you suspect contact.
Extreme Temperature	Objects that can burn skin by being too cold or too hot	Use proper protection when handling.	Go to your teacher for first aid.
Sharp Object	Use of tools or glassware that can easily puncture or slice skin	Practice common sense behavior and follow guidelines for use of the tool.	Go to your teacher for first aid.
Fumes	Potential danger from smelling fumes	Must have good ventilation and never smell fumes directly.	Leave foul area and notify your teacher immediately.
Electrical	Possible danger from electrical shock or burn	Double-check setup with instructor. Check condition of wires and apparatus.	Do not attempt to fix electrical problems. Notify your teacher immediately.
Irritant	Substances that can irritate your skin or mucous membranes	Wear dust mask or gloves. Practice extra care when handling these materials.	Go to your teacher for first aid.
Chemical	Substances (acids and bases) that can react with and destroy tissue and other materials	Wear goggles and an apron.	Immediately flush with water and notify your teacher.
Toxic	Poisonous substance	Follow your teacher's instructions. Always wash hands thoroughly after use.	Go to your teacher for first aid.
Fire	Flammable and combustible materials may burn if exposed to an open flame or spark	Avoid flames and heat sources. Be aware of locations of fire safety equipment.	Notify your teacher immediately. Use fire safety equipment if necessary.

Eye Safety
This symbol appears when a danger to eyes exists.

Clothing Protection
This symbol appears when substances cou

Animal Safety
This symbol appears whenever live animals
safety of the animals and students must be

D1065344

GLENCOE

SCIENCE VOYAGES

Exploring the Life, Earth, and Physical Sciences

NATIONAL GEOGRAPHIC SOCIETY

Glencoe McGraw-Hill

New York, New York   Columbus, Ohio   Woodland Hills, California   Peoria, Illinois

A Glencoe Program

Glencoe Science Voyages

Student Edition
Teacher Wraparound Edition
Assessment
    Chapter Review
    Standardized Test Practice
    Performance Assessment
    Assessment—Chapter and Unit Tests
    ExamView Test Bank Software
    Performance Assessment in the Science
        Classroom
    Alternate Assessment in the Science Classroom
Study Guide for Content Mastery, SE and TE
Chapter Overview Study Guide, SE and TE
Reinforcement
Enrichment
Critical Thinking/Problem Solving
Multicultural Connections
Activity Worksheets

Laboratory Manual, SE and TE
Science Inquiry Activities, SE and TE
Home Involvement
Teaching Transparencies
Section Focus Transparencies
Science Integration Transparencies
Spanish Resources
Lesson Plans
Lab and Safety Skills in the Science Classroom
Cooperative Learning in the Science Classroom
Exploring Environmental Issues
MindJogger Videoquizzes and Teacher Guide
English/Spanish Audiocassettes
Interactive
    Lesson Planner CD-ROM
Interactive CD-ROM
Internet Site
Using the Internet in the Science Classroom

The "Test-Taking Tip" and "Test Practice" features in this book were written by The Princeton Review, the nation's leader in test preparation. Through its association with McGraw-Hill, The Princeton Review offers the best way to help students excel on standardized assessments.

The Princeton Review is not affiliated with Princeton University or Educational Testing Service.

Glencoe/McGraw-Hill

A Division of The McGraw-Hill Companies

Send all inquiries to:
Glencoe/McGraw-Hill
936 Eastwind Drive
Westerville, OH 43081

ISBN 0-02-828579-4
Printed in the United States of America.
2 3 4 5 6 7 8 9 10 058/043 06 05 04 03 02 01 00 99

Series Authors

Alton Biggs
Biology Instructor
Allen High School
Allen, Texas

John Eric Burns
Science Teacher
Ramona Jr. High School
Chino, California

Lucy Daniel, Ph.D.
Teacher, Consultant
Rutherford County Schools
Rutherfordton, North Carolina

Cathy Ezrailson
Science Department Head
Oak Ridge High School
Conroe, Texas

Ralph Feather, Jr., Ph.D.
Science Department Chair
Derry Area School District
Derry, Pennsylvania

Patricia Horton
Math and Science Teacher
Summit Intermediate School
Etiwanda, California

Thomas McCarthy, Ph.D.
Science Department Chair
St. Edwards School
Vero Beach, Florida

Ed Ortleb
Science Consultant
St. Louis Public Schools
St. Louis, Missouri

Susan Leach Snyder
Science Department Chair
Jones Middle School
Upper Arlington, Ohio

Eric Werwa, Ph.D.
Department of Physics and Astronomy
Otterbein College
Westerville, Ohio

National Geographic Society
Educational Division
Washington D.C.

Contributing Authors

Al Janulaw
Science Teacher
Creekside Middle School
Rohnert Park, California

Penny Parsekian
Science Writer
New London, Conneticut

Gerry Madrazo, Ph.D.
Mathematics and Science Education
  Network
University of North Carolina, Chapel Hill
Chapel Hill, North Carolina

Series Consultants

Chemistry

Douglas Martin, Ph.D.
Chemistry Department
Sonoma State University
Rohnert Park, California

Cheryl Wistrom, Ph.D.
Associate Professor of
   Chemistry
Saint Joseph's College
Rensselaer, Indiana

Earth Science

Tomasz K. Baumiller, Ph.D.
Museum of Paleontology
University of Michigan
Ann Arbor, Michigan

Maureen Allen
Science Resource Specialist
Irvine Unified School District
Laguna Hills, California

Connie Sutton, Ph.D.
Department of Geoscience
Indiana University
Indiana, Pennsylvania

Physics

Thomas Barrett, Ph.D.
Department of Physics
The Ohio State University
Columbus, Ohio

David Haase, Ph.D.
Professor of Physics
North Carolina State
   University
North Carolina

Life Science

William Ausich, Ph.D.
Department of Geological
   Sciences
The Ohio State University
Columbus, Ohio

Dennis Stockdale
Asheville High School
Asheville, North Carolina

Daniel Zeigler, Ph.D.
Director
Bacillus Genetic Stock Center
The Ohio State University
Columbus, Ohio

Reading

Nancy Farnan, Ph.D.
School of Teacher Education
San Diego State University
San Diego, California

Gary Kroesch
Mount Carmel High School
San Diego, California

Safety

Mark Vinciguerra
Lab Safety Instructor
Department of Physics
The Ohio State University
Columbus, Ohio

Curriculum

Tom Custer, Ph.D.
Maryland State Department of
   Education
Challenge/Reconstructed
   Schools
Baltimore, Maryland

Series Reviewers

Jhina Alvarado
Potrero Hill Middle School
for the Arts
San Francisco, California

Richard Cheeseman
Bert Lynn Middle School
Torrance, California

Linda Cook
Rider High School
Wichita Falls, Texas

John B. Davis
Niagara-Wheatfield
Central School
Sanborn, New York

Shirley Ann DeFilippo
Timothy Edwards
Middle School
South Windsor, Connecticut

Janet Doughty
H J McDonald Middle School
New Bern, North Carolina

Jason Druten
Jefferson Middle School
Torrance, California

Lin Harp
Magellan Middle School
Raleigh, North Carolina

Doris Holland
West Cary Middle School
Raleigh, North Carolina

Deborah Huffine
Noblesville Intermediate
School
Noblesville, Indiana

Paul Osborne
DeValls Bluff High School
DeValls Bluff, Arkansas

Erik Resnick
Robert E. Peary Middle School
Gardena, California

Robert Sirbu
Lowell Junior High School
Oakland, California

Michael Tally
Wake County
Public Schools
Raleigh, North Carolina

Cindy Williamson
Whiteville City Schools
Whiteville, North Carolina

Maurice Yaggi
Middlebrook School
Wilton, Connecticut

Donna York
Anchorage School District
Anchorage, Alaska

Activity Testers

Clayton Millage
Science Teacher
Lynden Middle School
Lynden, Washington

Science Kit and Boreal Laboratories
Tonawanda, New York

Contents in Brief

Contents

Contents

Contents

Contents

Contents

Contents

Contents

Contents

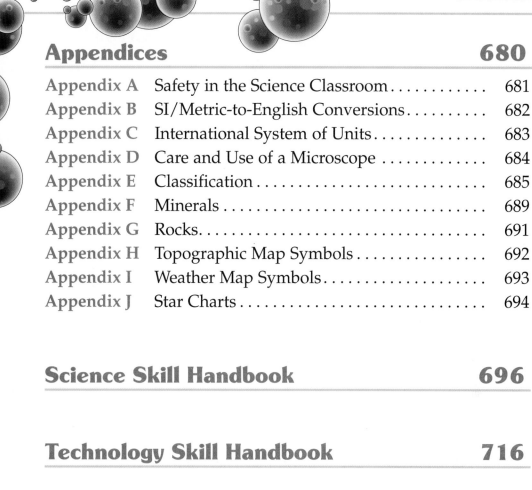

Contents

Appendices   680

History of Science

How it Works

Reading & Writing in Science

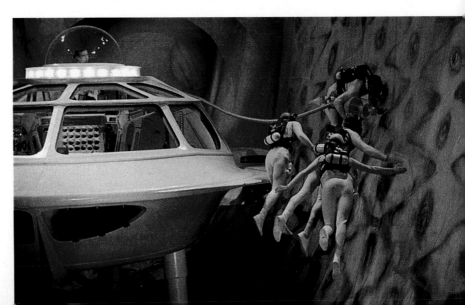

Science & Math

Science & Society

Activities

Activities

Mini Lab

Try at Home

Mini Lab

Whorl

Arch

Loop

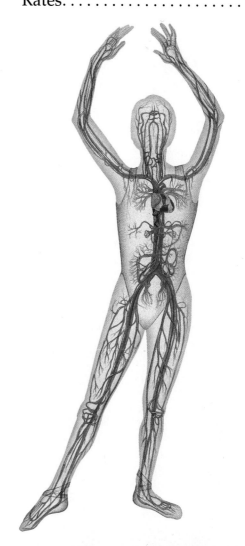

Explore Activities

Problem Solving

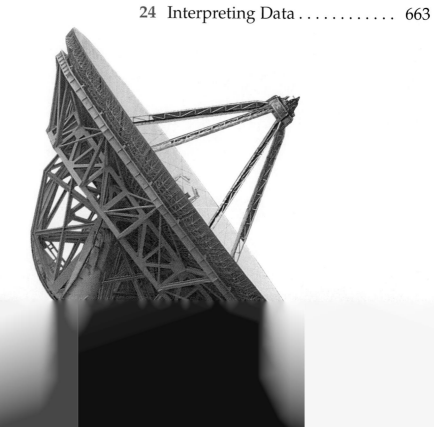

Skill Builders

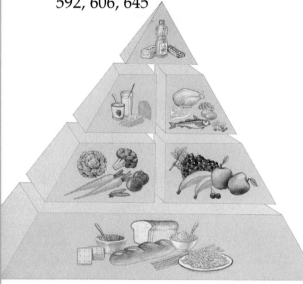

Skill Activities

The Nature of Matter

NATIONAL GEOGRAPHIC

What's Happening Here?

As wondrous as this winter scene in Yellowstone National Park (left) appears, beneath the scenic variety there is a sameness. The hanging icicles and sculpted snow, the plunging cascade, the mist hovering above the stream are solid, liquid, and gaseous forms of water. Regardless of these outer forms, the molecules of water are all identical. Beads of mercury (below) create a shimmering galaxy—but, within the element mercury, each atom is the same. Yet, how dynamic is the hidden world of the atom! The molecules of water locked into blocks of ice, the atoms within the shiny mercury, and even the particles that make up this page of your science book are in constant motion. Why are some substances solids, while other are liquids or gases? These are some of the questions explored in this unit.

interNET CONNECTION

Explore the Glencoe Science Web Site at **www.glencoe.com/sec/ science** to find out more about topics found in this unit.

3

The Nature of Science

Chapter Preview

Skills Preview

Skill Builders
- Communicate
- Hypothesize

Activities
- Design an Experiment
- Make and Use a Table

MiniLabs
- Compare and Contrast
- Observe and Infer

Reading Check ✔

As you read about the nature of science, use the headings and subheadings to make an outline. Under each subheading, write a few important points.

Explore Activity

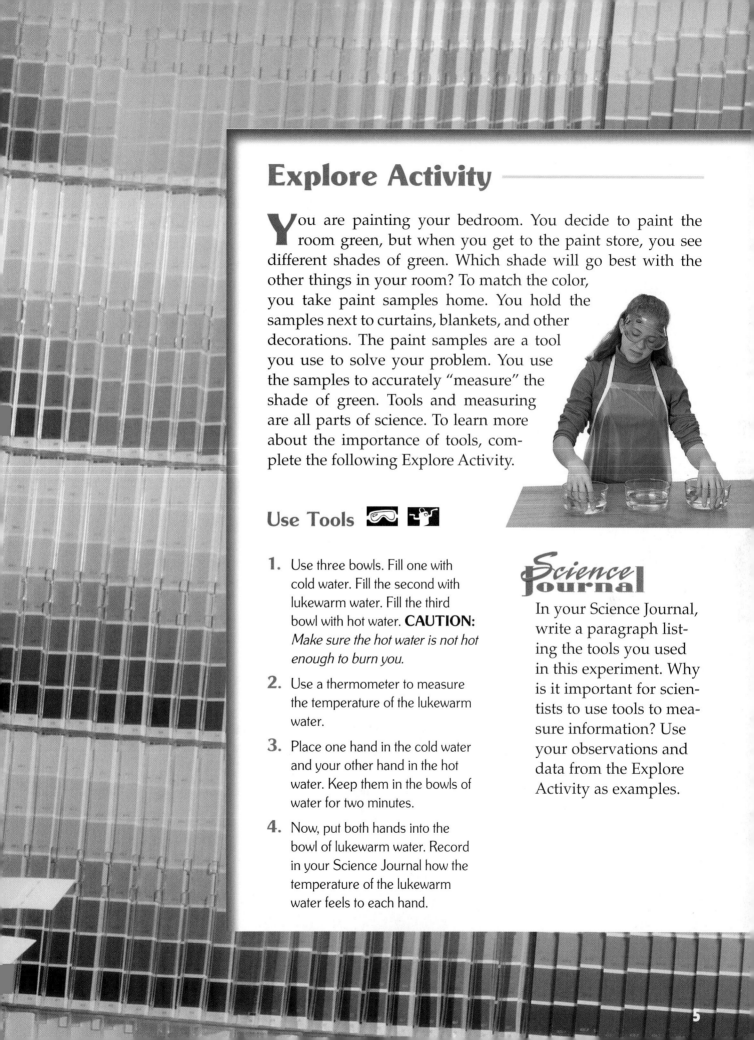

You are painting your bedroom. You decide to paint the room green, but when you get to the paint store, you see different shades of green. Which shade will go best with the other things in your room? To match the color, you take paint samples home. You hold the samples next to curtains, blankets, and other decorations. The paint samples are a tool you use to solve your problem. You use the samples to accurately "measure" the shade of green. Tools and measuring are all parts of science. To learn more about the importance of tools, complete the following Explore Activity.

Use Tools

1. Use three bowls. Fill one with cold water. Fill the second with lukewarm water. Fill the third bowl with hot water. **CAUTION:** *Make sure the hot water is not hot enough to burn you.*

2. Use a thermometer to measure the temperature of the lukewarm water.

3. Place one hand in the cold water and your other hand in the hot water. Keep them in the bowls of water for two minutes.

4. Now, put both hands into the bowl of lukewarm water. Record in your Science Journal how the temperature of the lukewarm water feels to each hand.

Science Journal

In your Science Journal, write a paragraph listing the tools you used in this experiment. Why is it important for scientists to use tools to measure information? Use your observations and data from the Explore Activity as examples.

1·1 What is science?

Science in Society

What You'll Learn

► How science is a part of your everyday life
► What skills are used in science

Vocabulary
science
technology

Why It's Important

► What and how you learn in science class can be applied to other areas of your life.

Science. When you hear this word, do you think it has little to do with what's important in your life? You go to science class. You have a science teacher. You learn science terms and facts. But, what is the connection between sitting in the class and the rest of your daily life? Science is more than just terms or facts. You and other people are curious about what is happening in the world. You may have problems to solve or questions that need answers, as illustrated in **Figure 1-1. Science** is a way or a process used to investigate what is happening around us. It provides some possible answers.

Science is not new. Throughout history, people have tried to find answers to questions about what was happening around them. Many used observations to find the answers. These observations were based on using their senses of sight, touch, smell, taste, and hearing. They made up stories based on their observations. From the Explore Activity, you know that only using your senses can't answer all questions. Seeing is not always believing. Cold may feel hot. Tools such as thermometers are needed to make mathematical measurements. Numbers can be used to describe observations. Scientists use both observations and experiments to find answers. Let's see how science can be useful to you.

Figure 1-1 Science is used every day as you make decisions.

Science as a Tool

As Luis and Midori walked into science class, they were still talking about their new history assignment. Mr. Johnson overheard them and asked what they were all excited about.

"We have a special assignment celebrating the founding of our town 200 years ago," answered Luis. "We need to do a project tying together a past event with something now going on in the community. We need to demonstrate the similarities and the differences in the two events."

Mr. Johnson put down his pencil and responded. "That sounds like a big undertaking. Have you chosen the two events yet?"

"We were looking through some old newspaper articles and came across several stories about a cholera epidemic that killed ten people and made more than 50 others ill. It happened in 1871—right after the Civil War. Midori and I think that it's like the *E. coli* outbreak going on now in our town," replied Luis.

"What do you know about outbreaks of the disease cholera and problems caused by *E. coli*, Luis?"

"Well, Mr. Johnson, cholera is a disease caused by a bacterium that is found in contaminated bodies of water," Luis replied. "People who eat seafood from this water or drink this water get really sick. They have bad cases of diarrhea and may become badly dehydrated, which can lead to death. *E. coli* is another type of bacterium that causes similar intestinal problems when polluted food and water are consumed."

"In fact," added Midori, "one of the workers at my dad's store is just getting over being sick. We hope no one else in his family gets it. Anyway, Mr. Johnson, we want to know if you can help us with the project. We want to compare how people tracked down the source of the cholera in 1871 with how they are now tracking down the source of the *E. coli*."

Figure 1-2 Newspapers, magazines, books, and the Internet are all good sources of information.

EARTH SCIENCE

INTEGRATION

Reducing Water Pollution
The U.S. Congress has helped reduce water pollution by passing several laws. The 1986 Safe Drinking Water Act is a law to ensure that drinking water in our country is safe. The 1987 Clean Water Act gives money to the states for building sewage- and wastewater-treatment facilities.

Figure 1-3 Scientists are like detectives, making conclusions based on clues. Such skills can be practiced by playing board games and solving puzzles.

A Puzzles require such skills as observing and inferring. **What other skills may be involved?**

B Board games often include skills such as communicating and sequencing. **What are some other skills involved in playing such games?**

Using Science Every Day

"I'll be glad to help," grinned Mr. Johnson. "This sounds like a great way to show how science is a part of everyone's life. In fact, you are acting like scientists right now."

Luis had a puzzled look on his face. "What do you mean? How can we be doing science? This is really a history project."

"Well, you're acting like a detective right now. You have a problem to solve. You and Midori are looking for clues that show how the two events are similar and different. As you complete the project, you will use several skills and tools to find the clues. You will then follow the clues to determine the similarities and differences. These things will help you solve your problem."

Mr. Johnson continued, "In many ways, scientists do the same thing. People in 1871 followed clues to track the source of the cholera epidemic and solve their problem. Scientists are doing the same now by finding and following clues to track the source of the *E. coli.*"

Using Prior Knowledge

Mr. Johnson continued talking as he walked over to the chalkboard. "Let's look at another way that your history project is like science. Luis, how do you know what is needed to complete the project?"

Luis thought for a minute before responding. "The report must be at least three pages long and have maps, pictures, or charts and graphs. Our teacher, Miss Hernandez, also said that we had to use several different sources for our information. These could be newspaper or magazine articles, letters, videotapes of educational programs, the Internet, or government documents. I also know that it must be handed in on time and that correct spelling and grammar count."

"Did Miss Hernandez actually talk about correct spelling and grammar?" asked Mr. Johnson.

At this point, Midori quickly responded, "No, she didn't have to. Everyone knows that Miss Hernandez counts off for incorrect spelling or grammar. I certainly learned that with my last report. I forgot to check my spelling and I got a whole point taken off."

"Ah-ha! That's where your project is like science," exclaimed Mr. Johnson. "You know from experience what will happen. Each time you don't follow her rule, your grade is lowered. You can predict, or make an educated guess, that Miss Hernandez will react the same way with future reports."

Mr. Johnson continued, "Scientists also use prior experience to predict what will happen under certain circumstances. If the results support their prediction, they continue to follow the same procedure. If the results change or don't support their prediction, they must change their predictions."

Figure 1-4 It is important to discover background information about any problem you are attempting to solve. Different sources of information can provide such information. **How would you find information on a specific topic? What sources of information would you use?**

9

Using Science Technology and Skills

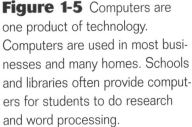

*inter*NET
CONNECTION

Visit the Glencoe
Science Web Site at
**www.glencoe.com/
sec/science** for more
information about how
to do research on the
Internet.

"Midori, you said that you want to compare the tracking of the two diseases. I said that, like scientists, you will use some skills and tools to find the similarities and differences." Mr. Johnson then pointed to Luis. "You listed a variety of resource materials that can be used to find out the information. How will you know which materials will be useful?"

"We'll go to the library and use the computer." Luis smiled as he pointed to the library book in his hand. "We can use the computer to find which books, magazines, newspapers, or videos have information we need."

"We also can use the computer to get on the Internet and find different Web pages or links that might help us," added Midori.

"Exactly," said Mr. Johnson. "And, that's another way that you are acting like scientists. The computer is one tool that modern scientists use to find and analyze data. The computer is a product of technology. Remember that **technology** is the application of science to make products or tools that people can use. In fact, I'm sure that one of the big differences you will find between the way diseases were tracked in 1871 and how they are tracked now is the result of new technology."

Figure 1-5 Computers are one product of technology. Computers are used in most businesses and many homes. Schools and libraries often provide computers for students to do research and word processing.

Figure 1-6 The **Skill Handbook** describes many skills used in science. You may refer to these pages whenever you need to refresh your memory about scientific methods.

Science Skills

"Perhaps one of the similarities between the two time periods will be some of the skills used to track the disease," continued Mr. Johnson. "Today's doctors and scientists might have new technological gadgets to use, but they still practice the same skills such as observing, classifying, and interpreting data. In fact, you might want to review the science skills we've talked about in class. That way, you'll be able to identify how they were used during the cholera outbreak and how they are still used today."

Luis and Midori had a lot to think about during the next few days as they started working on their project. They began by following Mr. Johnson's suggestion to review the science skills. The skills used by scientists are described in the **Skill Handbook,** shown in **Figure 1-6** and found at the back of this book. The more you practice these skills, the more comfortable you will become using them.

Think about the Explore Activity at the beginning of this chapter. Observing, measuring, and comparing and contrasting are three skills you used to complete the activity. Scientists probably use these skills more than any others. But, you will learn that sometimes observation alone does not provide a complete picture of what is actually happening. In addition to making careful observations, you must provide other information such as precise measurements to have the best data possible. ✔

Luis and Midori want to find the similarities and differences between the disease-tracking techniques of the late 1800s and today. They will be using the skill of comparing and contrasting. They will compare the techniques available when they look for similarities. They will contrast the techniques when they look for differences.

Reading Check ✔

List three common skills used in science.

Picture 1

Picture 2

Mini Lab

Inferring from Pictures

Procedure

1. In your Science Journal, copy the following table.

Observations and Inferences		
Picture	**Observations**	**Inferences**
1		
2		

2. Study the two pictures on this page. Write down all your observations in the table.

3. Make inferences based on your observations. Record your inferences.

4. Share your inferences with others in your class.

Analysis

1. Analyze the inferences that you made. Are there other explanations for what you observed?

2. Why must you be careful when making inferences?

3. Create your own picture and description. Have other students make inferences based on the picture and description.

Communication in Science

What do scientists do with their findings? The results of their observations, experiments, and hard work will not be of use to the rest of the world unless they are shared. Scientists use several methods to communicate their observations.

Results and conclusions of experiments are often reported in scientific journals or magazines, where other scientists can read of their work. Hundreds of scientific journals are published weekly or monthly. In fact, scientists often spend a large part of their time reading journal articles in an effort to keep up with new information being reported.

Another method of maintaining records is to keep a Science Journal or log. Descriptions of experiments with step-by-step procedures, listings of materials, and drawings of how equipment is set up may be in a log or journal, as well as specific results. The journal may include descriptions of all of their observations and mathematical measurements or formulas.

Additional questions that come up during experiments also can be recorded. Problems that occur also are noted, along with possible solutions. Data may be recorded or summarized in the form of tables, charts, or graphs, or it may just be recorded in a paragraph. Remember, it's important to use correct spelling.

You will be able to use your Science Journal to communicate your observations, questions, thoughts, and ideas as you work in science class, as illustrated in **Figure 1-7.** You will practice many of the science skills and become better at identifying problems and planning ways to solve these problems. At the same time, you will gain more scientific knowledge. In the next section, follow Luis and Midori as they continue to research their project. You will have a chance to practice some science skills as you solve problems.

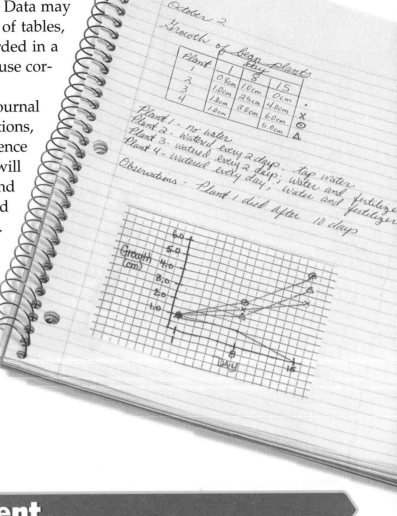

Figure 1-7 Science Journals are used to communicate scientific observations, questions, thoughts, and ideas. They may include graphs, tables, and illustrations.

Section Assessment

1. Why do scientists use tools, such as thermometers and rulers, when they make observations?

2. How are scientists like detectives?

3. What are some skills used in science?

4. **Think Critically:** What is the difference between science and technology?

5. **Skill Builder**
   Communicating In your Science Journal, draw a shape that includes angles, curves, and straight lines. Find a partner, but do not show this shape to your partner. Describe this shape and have your partner try to reproduce it. If you need help, refer to Communicating in the **Skill Handbook** on page 697.

*inter*NET
CONNECTION

Visit the Glencoe Science Web Site at **www.glencoe.com/ sec/science** for more information about disease control. In your Science Journal, report two different diseases that the Centers for Disease Control and Prevention (CDC) has tracked down and identified in the past.

1·2 Doing Science

Solving Problems

Midori and Luis spent several more minutes discussing their project with Mr. Johnson. As they talked, it became apparent that they had different ideas about how to complete the project. After listening to them, Mr. Johnson commented, "You both have some good ideas. How about a friendly suggestion before you get started. Even though you are working on a history project, I think you might find some helpful ideas written on the science poster that's hanging on the wall. Scientists know that there is more than one way to solve a problem. There are usually several scientific methods that can be used, or sometimes one method is used more than another. **Scientific methods** are approaches taken to try to solve a problem. The poster shows one method. Come back on Monday and let me know if it has helped."

Getting Organized

Midori and Luis are learning what scientists already know. The quality of a solution to a problem depends on how well the entire project is planned and carried out. They are finding out that preparation is as important as any of the other steps of the problem-solving method presented in **Figure 1-8.**

You can't solve a problem if you haven't identified the problem. Before scientists move on to the other steps of the method, they make sure that everyone working on the problem has a clear understanding of what needs to be solved. Sometimes, the problem is easy to identify. Sometimes, scientists find out that they are dealing with more than one problem. There may be several problems to be solved. For example, a scientist trying to find the source of a disease might first have to make sure of the correct identification of the disease.

What You'll Learn

► The steps scientists follow to solve problems
► How a well-designed experiment is developed

Vocabulary
scientific methods
model
hypothesis
independent variable
dependent variable
constant
control

Why It's Important

► Using step-by-step methods and carefully thought-out experiments can help you solve problems.

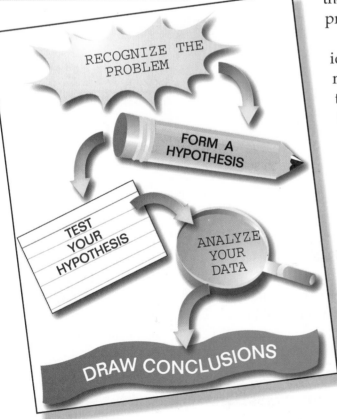

RECOGNIZE THE PROBLEM

FORM A HYPOTHESIS

TEST YOUR HYPOTHESIS

ANALYZE YOUR DATA

DRAW CONCLUSIONS

Figure 1-8 This poster shows one way to solve problems using scientific skills.

Making Plans

Once the problem is identified, a detailed plan is developed that includes possible ways to solve the problem. Part of the plan includes listing what is already known about the problem. For the doctors working on tracking the source of the 1871 cholera outbreak, part of their prior knowledge would be based on what was learned during the cholera epidemic that spread across the United States in 1866. This would include being able to identify cholera as the disease causing the deaths. They also knew that cholera is spread in unclean water. They might have known that boiling the water kills whatever causes cholera. However, they would not know the actual bacterium that caused the disease.

Another part of the plan includes carefully studying the problem. Maybe more than one problem needs to be solved. Or, maybe a large problem needs to be broken down into smaller problems. If this occurs, a decision is made on which problem should be solved first. Suppose people in your school are getting sick with an infectious disease. Identifying the disease is the first problem to solve. This may be difficult if two diseases share the same symptoms but are caused by different sources of contamination. For example, two diseases might cause high fever, a similar rash, and coughing. Bacteria released into the air might cause one. The other might be spread only by direct physical contact with the infected person. Once the disease is identified, a plan can be made to stop its spread.

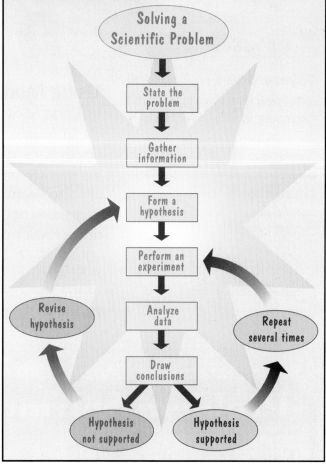

Figure 1-9 The steps in solving a problem in science are a series of procedures called scientific methods.

Carrying Out the Plan

Once a plan is made, the next step is to carry it out. Perhaps only one scientist is needed to complete the plan. However, in today's society, it is normal for several different scientists or teams to work on solving different parts of a problem, as illustrated in **Figure 1-10.** In the case of an *E. coli* outbreak, some scientists will work to identify the bacterium, and some will survey the victims affected by the disease (including age, sex, ethnic group, occupation, and where they live). Other scientists will test the many possible sources of contamination for the presence of the bacterium.

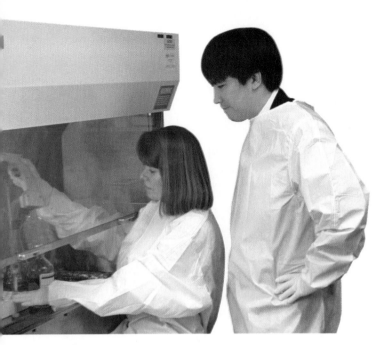

Figure 1-10 It takes many different people to solve major medical problems such as AIDS and other epidemics. The technician here is filling a container with a drug discovered by the onlooking medical student. This drug helps fight AIDS.

Using Models

A part of carrying out the plan might include making models. In science, a **model** is a mathematical equation or physical object that is used to think about things that happen too slowly, too quickly, or are too big or small to observe directly. Models are also useful in situations where observation would be too dangerous or expensive. Scientists in 1871 could make a model of the town by using a map.

In 1854, Dr. Snow made a model of the cholera outbreak that took place in London. He plotted the location of the cholera victims on a map, as illustrated in **Figure 1-11.** He knew that the most likely source of the disease would be in the area

Problem Solving

Using Flex Your Brain

All reliable problem-solving methods begin with a plan. Some plans are easy enough to be stored in your mind. More complicated plans need to be written down. *Flex Your Brain* is a process that will help you organize a plan to solve a problem. This process is shown in the chart.

Think Critically: Use the *Flex Your Brain* chart to explore information about cholera. How does *Flex Your Brain* help you organize your search?

Flex Your Brain

1. **Topic:** _____
2. ? **What do I already know?** 1. ___ 2. ___ 3. ___
3. **Q:** Ask a question 4. ___
4. **A:** Guess an answer
5. **How sure am I? (circle one)** Not sure 1 2 3 4 Very sure 5
6. ? **How can I find out?** 1. ___ 2. ___ 3. ___ 4. ___
7. **Explore**
8. **Do I think differently?** → yes no
9. ? **What do I know now?** 1. ___ 2. ___ 3. ___ 4. ___
10. **SHARE** 1. ___ 2. ___ 3. ___

Figure 1-11 Dr. Snow plotted the distribution of deaths in London on a map. He determined that an unusually high number of deaths were taking place near a water pump on Broad Street.

where the most victims were located. The source of cholera in the map he made appeared to be a contaminated water pump.

Today, many people in different careers use models to complete projects. Computers are used to make many kinds of these models. For example, computers can analyze information and predict how far and how quickly the spruce beetle will spread across an area. Scientists will then have a prediction of how many spruce trees may be killed by the beetle within the next five years. Computers can produce three-dimensional models of a microscopic bacterium or a huge asteroid. They are used to design safer airplanes and office buildings. All kinds of models save time and money by testing ideas that otherwise are too small, too large, or take too long to build. Luis and Midori know that computer modeling is an important part of modern scientists' work as they try to track diseases affecting current societies.

Planning an Experiment

Even with their increased role in science, computers cannot provide all of the answers. Experiments often are needed. Scientists continue to include experiments as part of their plans to solve problems. Luis and Midori learned that doctors in the 1800s often used trial-and-error techniques to treat patients. These treatments were not planned experiments and often led to more problems when patients did not respond well. Modern science and medicine use carefully planned experiments to provide solutions. Activities in this book give you the opportunity to design your own experiments.

Recognize the Problem

Recall how important it is for scientists to know exactly what question needs to be answered or which problem needs to be solved. Your first step in designing your experiment is to be sure about what you want to find out. Some helpful information can be found in the activity's introductory statement. Additional information might come from material presented earlier in the chapter or that you already have learned in other science classes.

Form a Hypothesis

Figure 1-12 Suspecting the Broad Street water pump (A) as the source of the cholera, Dr. Snow had the water pump handle removed and thus ended the epidemic. *Vibrio cholerae* (B) is the microorganism responsible for causing cholera in people.

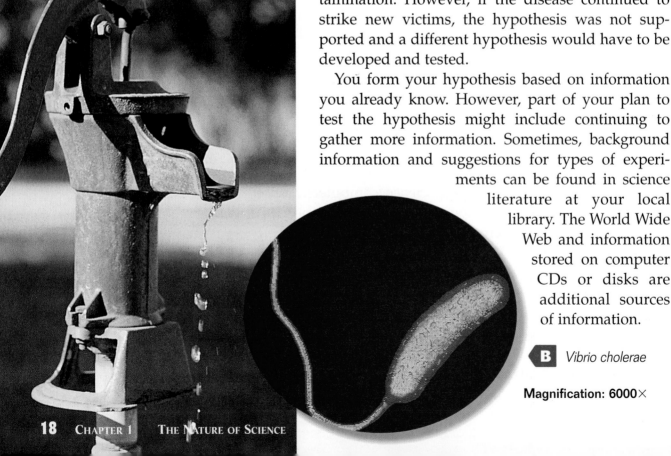

Use your prior knowledge, new information, and any previous observations to form a hypothesis (hi PAH thuh sus). A **hypothesis** is a prediction or statement that can be tested. You learned that the doctor in London used a map to plot cholera deaths. He used the information from the map to make a hypothesis, or prediction. He hypothesized that a particular water pump was the source of the cholera contamination, as illustrated in **Figure 1-12**. He then needed to test his hypothesis. To test it, he convinced the town authorities to close down the water pump by removing its handle. If no new cases of the disease appeared, then his hypothesis was supported. The water pump was the source of contamination. However, if the disease continued to strike new victims, the hypothesis was not supported and a different hypothesis would have to be developed and tested.

You form your hypothesis based on information you already know. However, part of your plan to test the hypothesis might include continuing to gather more information. Sometimes, background information and suggestions for types of experiments can be found in science literature at your local library. The World Wide Web and information stored on computer CDs or disks are additional sources of information.

B *Vibrio cholerae*

Magnification: 6000×

Plan the Experiment

It is important to design your experiment carefully. Suppose, instead of tracking the source of a disease, you want to test the effectiveness of antibiotics in killing the bacteria that cause the disease. Let's look at how each condition might influence the results.

Variables and Controls

In well-planned experiments, variables are tested. Experiments are reliable only if the variables are controlled. This means that only one factor, or variable, is changed at a time. The variable that is changed is called the **independent variable.** A **dependent variable** is the factor being measured.

To test which of two antibiotics will kill a type of bacterium, you must make sure that every variable but the type of antibiotic remains the same. The variables that stay the same are called **constants.** For example, you cannot run the experiments at two different room temperatures, with different amounts of antibiotics, with applications made at different times, or with different types of bacteria. If you are going to test two antibiotics, then everything else about your experiment must be the same. If you change any of the variables, you will not be sure if it is one of the antibiotics alone that killed the bacteria, one of the other variables, or a combination of the factors.

Your experiment will not be valid unless a control is used. A **control** is a sample that is treated exactly like the other experimental groups except that the independant variable is not applied to it. In the experiment described above, your control will be a culture of bacteria that is not treated with either antibiotic. The control shows how the bacteria grow when left untreated by one of the antibiotics. **Figure 1-13** gives another example of a well-planned experiment.

Figure 1-13 In this experiment, a student wanted to test the effect of sunlight on the growth of radish plants. The amount of sunlight received by the radish plants is the independent variable.

A At the beginning of the experiment, radish seeds received the same amount of water. One group of seeds was kept in the sunlight and another group of radish seeds were grown in a dark area.

B The photos above show the young radish plants after being grown for the same period of time. All factors were kept constant with the exception of the amount of sunlight. **Based on these photographs, what would you conclude about the effects of sunlight on radish plants?**

Mini Lab

Comparing Paper Towels

Procedure

1. Make a data table similar to the data table in **Figure 1-14.**

2. Cut a 5 cm by 5 cm square from each of three brands of paper towel. Lay each piece on a smooth, level, waterproof surface.

3. Add one drop of water to each square.

4. Continue to add drops until the piece of paper towel can no longer absorb the water.

5. Record your observations in your data table and graph your results.

Analysis

1. Did all the squares of paper towels absorb equal amounts of water?

2. If one brand of paper towel absorbs more water than the others, can you conclude that it is the towel you should buy? Explain.

3. Which scientific methods did you use to answer the question of which paper towel is more absorbent?

Number of Trials

Experiments do not always have the same results. To make sure that your results are valid, you need to conduct several trials of your experiment. Multiple trials mean that an unusual occurrence, which changes the outcome of the experiment, won't be considered the true result. For example, if another substance is accidentally spilled on one of the containers with an antibiotic, that substance might kill the bacteria. Without results from other trials to use as comparisons, you might think that the antibiotic killed the bacteria. Errors in labeling or measuring or timing can occur at any time. The more trials you do using the exact same methods, the more likely it is that your results will be reliable and repeatable.

The actual number of trials you choose to do will vary with each experiment, but the more trials completed, the more reliable the results will be. Your decision will be based on how much time you have to complete the experiment. It also will depend on the cost of running each trial, the availability of materials, or possibly the amount of space you have to set up the trials.

Selecting Your Materials

Scientists try to use the most up-to-date materials they can find. If possible, you should use balances, spring scales, microscopes, and metric measurements when performing experiments and gathering data. These tools will help to

Figure 1-14 Data tables help you organize your observations and test results.

A Most tables have a title that tells you, at a glance, what the table is about.

B A table is divided into columns and rows. The items to be compared are listed in columns—different brands of paper towels.

C The first column lists the trials or characteristics to be compared across in rows.

Paper Towel Absorbency (drops of water/sheet)			
Trial	Brand A	Brand B	Brand C
1			
2			
3			
4			

make your data more accurate. Calculators and computers can be helpful in evaluating the data or for visually displaying it. However, remember that you don't have to have the latest or most expensive materials and tools to conduct good experiments. Your experiments can be successful with materials found in your home or classroom. Paper, colored pencils, or markers work well for displaying your data. An organized presentation of data done neatly is as effective as a computer graphic.

Safety

Forming a hypothesis will be one important part of your science experiences. Once you have developed your own hypothesis, your next goal is to design an experiment that will test the hypothesis. As you design the experiment, you need to be aware of any possible safety issues that might occur as you complete your work. Some good safety habits include the following suggestions. Always check with your teacher at several times in the planning stage and while doing your experiment to make sure your actions and materials are safe. Remember to use safety goggles and always wash your hands after working with materials. **Figure 1-15** lists several safety rules. Safety symbols are listed inside the front cover of this book.

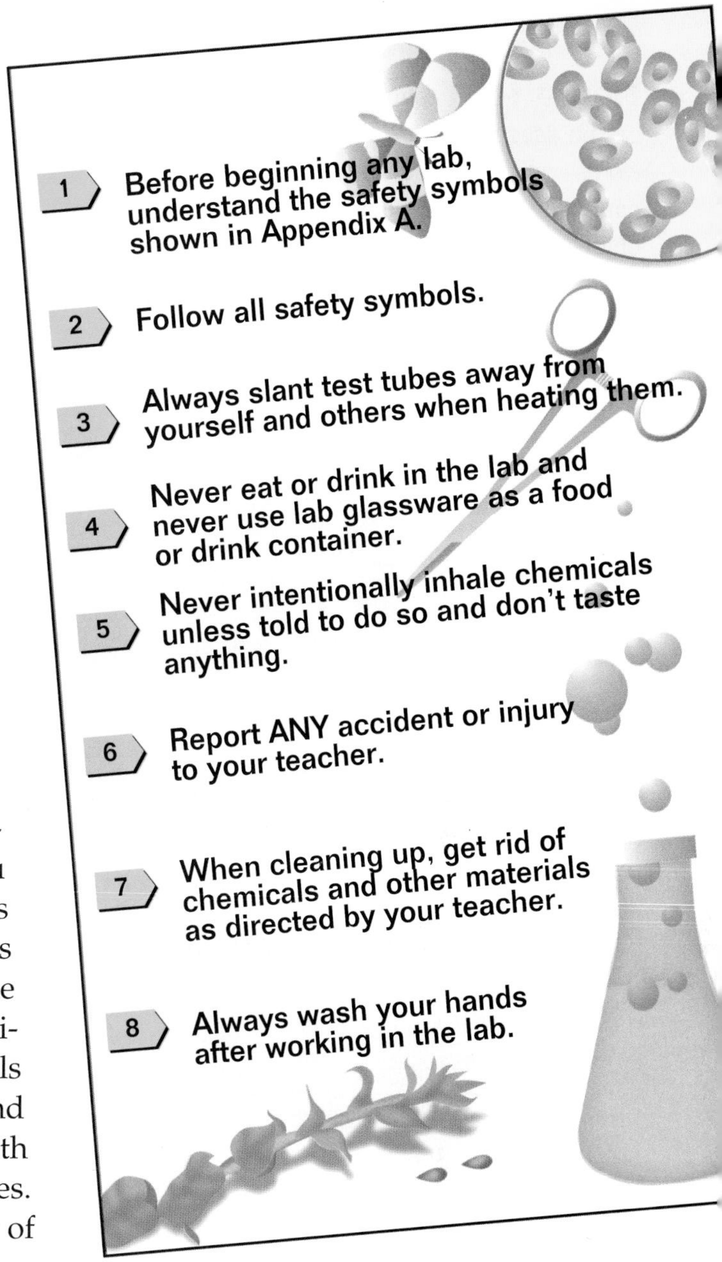

Designing Your Data Tables

A well-thought-out experiment includes a way to accurately record results and observations. Data tables are one way to organize and record your results and observations.

Most tables have a title that tells you, at a glance, what the table is about. It is divided into columns and rows. The items to be compared are listed in columns, and the first column lists the trials or characteristics to be compared across in rows.

As you complete the data table, you will know that you have the information you need to accurately analyze the results of the experiment. It is wise to make all of your data tables before beginning the experiment. That way, you will have a place for all of your data as soon as they become available. You also save time by not having to go back and organize the data or trying to decide where it goes at a later date.

1. Before beginning any lab, understand the safety symbols shown in Appendix A.

2. Follow all safety symbols.

3. Always slant test tubes away from yourself and others when heating them.

4. Never eat or drink in the lab and never use lab glassware as a food or drink container.

5. Never intentionally inhale chemicals unless told to do so and don't taste anything.

6. Report ANY accident or injury to your teacher.

7. When cleaning up, get rid of chemicals and other materials as directed by your teacher.

8. Always wash your hands after working in the lab.

Figure 1-15 Here are a few safety rules you should follow when you are doing an experiment.

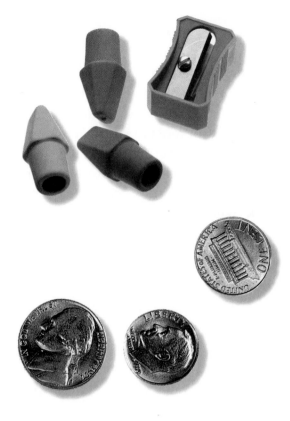

Figure 1-16 Items can be described by using words and numbers. **How could you describe these objects using both of these methods?**

Eliminating Bias

It's a Saturday afternoon. You want to see a certain movie, but your friends are not interested in seeing it. To sway them to your way of thinking, you tell them about a part of the show that you know will interest them. You slant the information you give them so they will make the choice you want. Similarly, scientists may want or simply expect that the results of experiments will come out a certain way. However, good experiments are set up to avoid bias. One way to avoid bias is to take measurements of all the results. Numerical measurements provide quantitative data. They are more precise than descriptions. Saying that a plant grew 12 cm in a day is more precise than saying the plant grew a lot. Twelve centimeters means the same for every person reading the results. The phrase "a lot" means different amounts to different people. How would you describe the objects in **Figure 1-16?**

Another type of bias may occur in surveys or groups that are chosen for experiments. Suppose you need to find out what the students want as a theme for the next school dance. You might choose to have only girls answer your questions. However, any conclusion you reach will not accurately reflect the opinions of the whole school. To get a more accurate result, you need to take a random sample. In this case, you might ask every fifth student entering the cafeteria for lunch to make a suggestion.

Do the Experiment

You have formed your hypothesis and planned your experiment. Before you actually begin the experiment, you will give a copy of it to your teacher. Your teacher must give approval to begin. He or she must know that all of your materials are safe to use and that your plans are safe to follow. This is also a good way to find out if any problems exist in how you plan to set up the experiment. Potential problems might include length of time to complete the experiment and the cost or availability of materials. You might also need to figure out how to keep an experiment running over a holiday period or where to set up a large experiment in a classroom.

Once you begin the experiment, make sure to carry it out as planned. Don't skip steps or change your plans in the middle of the process. If you skip steps or change procedures, you will have to begin the experiment again. Also, record your observations and complete your data tables in a timely manner. Incomplete observations and data reports mean that it is difficult to analyze the data. This threatens the accuracy of your conclusions.

Figure 1-17 Safety is important when doing a laboratory experiment. The safety symbols used throughout this book can be found at the front of the book. **Can you tell which safety cautions are being followed in this picture?**

Table 1-1

Common SI Measurements			
Measurement	**Unit**	**Symbol**	**Equal to**
Length	1 millimeter	mm	0.001 (1/1000) m
	1 centimeter	cm	0.01 (1/100) m
	1 meter	m	1 m
	1 kilometer	km	1000 m
Volume	1 milliliter	mL	1 cm^3
	1 liter	L	1000 mL
Mass	1 gram	g	1000 mg
	1 kilogram	kg	1000 g
	1 metric ton	t	1000 kg = 1 metric ton

International System of Units (SI)

Scientists use a system of measurements to make observations. Scientists around the world have agreed to use the International System of Units, or SI. SI is based on certain metric units. Using the same system gives scientists a common language. They can understand each other's research and compare results. Most of the units you will use in science are shown in **Table 1-1.** Because you may be used to using the English system of pounds, ounces, and inches, see Appendix B to help you convert English units to SI.

SI is based on units of ten. Multiplying or dividing by ten makes calculations easy to do. Prefixes are used with units to change them to larger or smaller units. **Figure 1-18** shows equipment used for measuring in SI.

Figure 1-18 Some of the equipment used by scientists is shown here.

A The amount of space occupied by an object is its volume. Liquid volumes are found using a graduated cylinder.

B Mass is the amount of matter in an object. Mass is measured with a balance.

D A microscope is used to observe items that cannot be seen easily.

C Scientists often use a thermometer with the Celsius scale to measure temperature. On the Celsius scale, water freezes at 0°C and boils at 100°C.

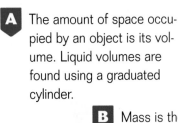

Analyze Your Data

Your experiment is over. You breathe a sigh of relief. Now, you have to figure out what your results mean. You have to analyze your data. To do this, you have to review all of the observations and measurements you recorded. You have to organize the data in an orderly fashion. Charts and graphs are excellent ways to organize data. You can draw the charts and graphs or use a computer to make them.

Draw Conclusions

Once you have organized your data, you are ready to draw a conclusion based on the data. Do the data allow you to make a conclusion that supports your hypothesis? Sometimes they will, but sometimes they won't support the hypothesis. You may be concerned if your data don't support your hypothesis. You may think that your hypothesis is wrong. But, this is not true. There are no wrong hypotheses—just results that don't support your hypothesis. Scientists know that it is important to learn if something doesn't work. In looking for an antibiotic to kill bacteria, scientists spend years finding out which antibiotics will work and which won't. Each time they find one that doesn't work, they learn some new information. They use this information to help make other antibiotics that have a better chance of working. A successful experiment is not always the one that comes out the way you originally wanted it to end.

Communicating the Results

Every experiment begins because there is a problem to solve. Analyzing data and drawing conclusions are the end of the experiment. However, they are not the end of the work a scientist does. Usually, scientists communicate their results to other scientists, government agencies, private industries, or the public. To do this, they write reports and give presentations. The reports and presentations provide details on how experiments were carried out, summaries of the data, and final conclusions. They may include recommendations on what direction further research should take. They may also include a recommendation to try a specific course of action as a way of solving the original problem. Charts, graphs, tables, posters, and models are included with both the written reports and verbal presentations as **Figure 1-19** demonstrates.

Using Math

What do domestic cats, warthogs, and grizzly bears have in common? Speed! All of these animals can reach speeds of 48 km/h. How many meters can these animals go in 1 s?

Figure 1-19 Communication is important in science. Giving talks, writing papers, and presenting information on the Internet are just a few ways of communicating science.

Just as scientists communicate their findings, you will have the chance to communicate your findings to other members of your science class. You may not give an oral presentation after each of your experiments, but you will have the chance to talk with other students or your teacher. You will share with other groups the charts, tables, and graphs that show your data. Other students will share their work with you, too. Sharing experimental data, like the students in **Figure 1-20,** is an important part of scientific experimentation. In the next section, you will learn some other ways that science is a part of your real world.

Figure 1-20 Communicating laboratory results to your class-mates is an important part of the laboratory experience. Results are shared and better conclusions are made.

Section Assessment

1. Why do scientists use models?
2. What is a hypothesis?
3. Name the three steps scientists might use when designing an experiment to solve a problem.
4. **Think Critically:** The data gathered during an experiment do not support your original hypothesis. Explain why the experiment is not a failure.
5. **Skill Builder**
   Measuring in SI Measurements are one way to communicate experimental results. Do the **Chapter 1 Skill Activity** on page 726 to discover what units are most useful for measuring various lengths.

Using Math

A town of 1000 people is divided into five areas, each with the same number of people. Use the data below to make a bar graph showing the number of people ill with cholera in each area.
Area A–50%; Area B–5%; Area C–10%; Area D–16%; Area E–35%

Using a Scale Drawing

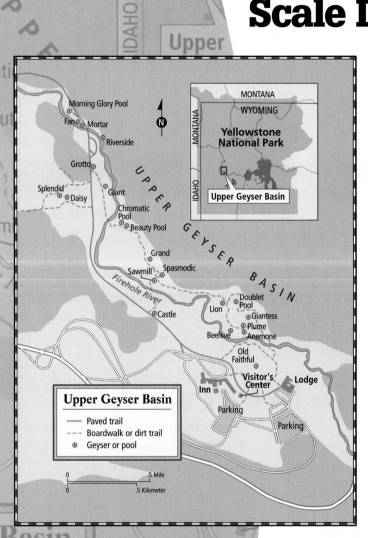

Upper Geyser Basin

Using a scale drawing of an area helps you know how far it is from one place to another. A scale drawing shows the area as it appears but makes it look smaller. The scale gives the relationship between actual distances and distances on the drawing.

Look at the map of Upper Geyser Basin in Yellowstone National Park. The scale used is 2 cm = 0.5 km. That means that 2 cm on the map represent a distance of 0.5 km on Earth. Follow these steps to find out how far it is in a straight line from Old Faithful geyser to Castle geyser.

Solution

1. With a metric ruler, measure the distance between those two places on the map.
2. Compare scale distances to actual distances and write a proportion.

Let d represent the distance from Old Faithful to Castle geyser.

Scale Distances	**Distances from Old Faithful to Castle geyser**
map distance →	2 cm = 3.1 cm ← map distance
actual distance →	0.5 km = d ← actual distance

$2 \times d = 0.5 \times 3.1$ *Find the cross products*

$2d = 1.55$ *Multiply*

$\dfrac{2d}{2} = \dfrac{1.55}{2}$ *Divide each side by 2*

$0.775 = d$

The distance from Old Faithful to Castle geyser is 0.775 km or 775 m.

Practice PROBLEMS

1. What is the actual distance between Grand geyser and Daisy geyser?

2. How far is it along the path shown from the Visitor Center to Morning Glory Pool?

Using Scientific Methods

You are to use scientific methods to determine how salt affects the growth of brine shrimp. Brine shrimp are tiny organisms that live in the ocean. How can you find out why they live where they do?

Possible Materials

- Widemouthed, 0.5-L containers (3)
  clear plastic cups (3)
- Brine shrimp eggs
- Wooden splint
- Distilled water (500 mL)
- Weak salt solution (500 mL)
- Strong salt solution (500 mL)
- Wax pencil
  labels (3)
- Hand lens
  Alternate Materials

Recognize the Problem

How can you use scientific methods to determine how salt affects the hatching and growth of brine shrimp?

Form a Hypothesis

Based on your observations, make a hypothesis about how salt affects the hatching and growth of brine shrimp.

Goals

- **Design and carry out an experiment** using scientific methods.
- **Infer** why brine shrimp live in the ocean.

Safety Precautions

Protect clothing and eyes. Be careful when working with live organisms.

Test Your Hypothesis

Plan

1. As a group, agree upon and **write out** the hypothesis statement.

2. **List** the steps that you need to take to test your hypothesis. Be specific. **Describe** exactly what you will do at each step. **List** your materials.

3. How will you know whether brine shrimp hatch and grow?

4. **Decide** what data you need to collect during the experiment. **Design** a data table in your Science Journal to **record** your observations.

5. **Identify** the steps in solving a problem that each of your actions presents. For example, what action have you taken that represents stating the problem or gathering information? Make sure you include all the steps needed to reach a conclusion.

6. **Read** over your entire experiment to make sure that all steps are in logical order.

7. **Identify** any constants, variables, and controls of the experiment.

8. Can you explain what variable you are testing?

9. **Decide** whether you need to run your tests more than once. Can your data be summarized in a graph?

Do

1. Make sure your teacher approves your plan before you proceed.

2. **Carry out** the experiment as planned.

3. While the experiment is going on, **write down** any observations that you make and complete the data table in your Science Journal.

Analyze Your Data

1. **Compare** your results with those of other groups.

2. Was your hypothesis supported by your data? **Explain** your answer.

Draw Conclusions

1. **Describe** how the physical conditions in the container in which the brine shrimp hatched and grew best are similar to those in the ocean.

2. How did you use scientific methods to solve this problem? Give examples from this activity.

Science and Technology

What You'll Learn

▶ How science and technology influence your life
▶ How modern technology has led to a globalization of science

Why It's Important

▶ Due to modern communications systems, scientific information is discovered by and shared with people all over the world.

Science in Your Daily Life

You have learned how to do science. How is this useful and meaningful to your daily life? The most obvious answer is that it helps you succeed in science class. Remember that doing science means more than just completing a science activity or reading a science chapter. Doing science is not following just one method to find answers. **Figure 1-21** illustrates some aspects of science.

Scientific Discoveries

Besides being a way of thinking, science is meaningful in your everyday life in other ways. New discoveries are constantly incorporated into products that influence your style of

Science is a process in which you . . .

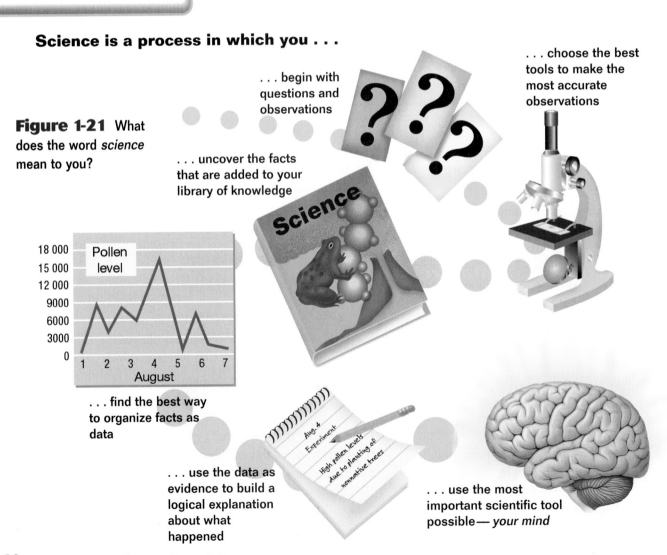

. . . begin with questions and observations

. . . choose the best tools to make the most accurate observations

Figure 1-21 What does the word *science* mean to you?

. . . uncover the facts that are added to your library of knowledge

. . . find the best way to organize facts as data

. . . use the data as evidence to build a logical explanation about what happened

. . . use the most important scientific tool possible— *your mind*

living, such as those shown in **Figure 1-22.** For example, in the last 100 years, technological advances have allowed entertainment to move from live stage shows to large movie screens. Movies that once were shown only in theaters are now seen on television sets in the home and you don't even have to get up to adjust the volume, thanks to the remote control. Videotapes allow viewers to watch shows whenever they please on their television sets. And now, DVDs allow computer users to choose a variety of options while viewing a movie on their computer monitor. Do you want to hear English dialogue with French subtitles or Spanish dialogue with English subtitles? Do you want to change the ending?

Technology also makes your life more convenient. Watches and clock faces glow in the dark for easier reading. Small calculators fit in a wallet or checkbook cover. Laptop computers can be carried in a briefcase. Foods can be prepared in minutes in the microwave, and hydraulic tools (running on compressed air) make construction work faster. Pagers make communication easier and garage-door openers save time. A satellite tracking system can even give you verbal and visual directions to a destination as you drive your car in an unfamiliar city.

New discoveries influence other areas of your daily life, including your health. A disease may be controlled because a skin patch releases a constant dose of medicine into your body. Miniature instruments allow doctors to operate on unborn children and save their lives. Bacteria is even being used to make important drugs such as insulin for people with diabetes. ☑

Figure 1-22 Technology has become part of our everyday lives.

Reading Check ☑

What scientific discovery have you used?

B Garrell A. Morgan invented an early traffic signal in 1923.

C Flossie Wong-Staal is involved in AIDS research.

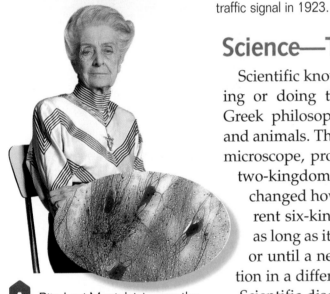

A Rita Levi-Montalciniv won the 1986 Nobel Prize in medicine for her discovery of nerve growth factors.

Figure 1-23 Science and technology are the results of many people's efforts.

*inter*NET
CONNECTION

Visit the Glencoe Science Web Site at **www.glencoe.com/ sec/science** for more information about different inventions.

Science—The Product of Many

Scientific knowledge also can mean that old ways of thinking or doing things are challenged. Aristotle, an ancient Greek philosopher, classified living organisms into plants and animals. This system worked until new tools, such as the microscope, produced new information that challenged the two-kingdom classification system. The new information changed how scientists viewed the living world. The current six-kingdom classification system will be used only as long as it continues to answer questions scientists have or until a new discovery allows them to look at information in a different way.

Scientific discoveries have never been limited to one race, sex, culture, or time period, as illustrated in **Figure 1-23**. As in the past, people all over the world are making discoveries. These people are not always professional scientists. Often, discoveries are made by people pursuing a hobby. In fact, students your age have made some important discoveries.

Advances in Technology

Information about new discoveries is not limited to pure science, either. The modern electronic communications network quickly spreads word of new discoveries throughout the world. New knowledge and technology brought about by these discoveries are shared by people in all countries.

Science can provide information that people use to make decisions. A new car can be designed. A new drug can be found. A new way to produce electricity can be developed. However, science cannot decide if the information is good or harmful, moral or immoral. People decide if the information is used to help or to harm the world and its inhabitants.

E Albert Einstein, a physicist, studied the motion of atoms, gravity, and the space-time continuum.

D Eloy Rodriguez makes substances in the lab that occur naturally in plants. Some may cure human diseases.

F Mae Jemison was a Space Shuttle astronaut on the *Endeavor* in 1992.

Looking to the Future

Midori and Luis discovered that several of these factors have changed how modern scientists track the source of a disease. New information about bacteria and modern tools, such as the electron microscope, mean they can identify specific strains of these organisms. Computers are used to model how the toxins kill healthy cells or which part of a population the bacteria will infect. Today's scientists use cellular phones and computers to communicate with each other even when they are in remote parts of the world. This information technology has led to the globalization, or worldwide distribution, of information.

Section Assessment

1. What is the most important tool scientists use?
2. What will cause scientists to change a theory they have believed in for more than 100 years?
3. **Think Critically:** Explain why modern communications systems are important to scientists.
4. **Skill Builder**
   Comparing and Contrasting
   Make a drawing showing how a modern scientist and one from the 1800s communicated their data with other scientists of their time. If you need help, refer to Comparing and Contrasting in the **Skill Handbook** on page 704.

Using Computers

Word Processing Research the life of a famous scientist. Find at least two sources for your information. Take notes on ten facts and use them to write a short biography of the scientist on a word processor. If you need help, refer to page 716.

For a **preview** of this chapter, study this Reviewing Main Ideas before you read the chapter. After you have studied this chapter, you can use the Reviewing Main Ideas to **review** the chapter.

The Glencoe MindJogger, Audiocassettes, and CD-ROM provide additional opportunities for review.

Section 1-1 WHAT IS SCIENCE?

Science is a process that can be used to solve problems or answer questions about what is happening in the world. Scientists use tools to make accurate mathematical measurements that quantify or put a numerical value on observations. Observations are clues to help solve problems. Scientists hypothesize based on prior experiences. These hypotheses will change procedures they follow if responses change. The **Skill Handbook** lists skills scientists use to solve problems. Computers are a valuable technological tool. Communication is an important part of all aspects of science. *What are some skills scientists use to solve problems?*

Section 1-2 DOING SCIENCE

No single **scientific method** is used to solve all problems. Organization and careful planning are important in solving problems. The first step is to make sure that everyone has clearly identified the problem. Models save time and money by testing ideas that are too difficult to build or do. Computers are used to make models, and experiments are needed to solve problems. The steps of a well-designed experiment include: recognize the problem, form a **hypothesis,** test the hypothesis, do the experiment, analyze the data, and draw conclusions. *What is the next step after scientists have analyzed data and drawn conclusions?*

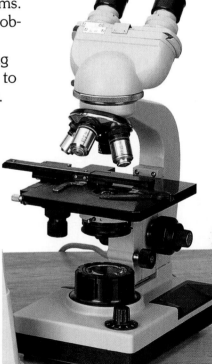

Section
1-3 SCIENCE AND TECHNOLOGY

Science is part of everyone's daily lives. New discoveries lead to new technology and products. Science continues to challenge old knowledge and ways of doing things. Old ideas are kept until new discoveries prove them wrong. People of all races, ages, sexes, cultures, and professions practice science. Modern communication assures that scientific information is spread around the world. *A new discovery is made in a South American rain forest. How can a scientist in Chicago find out about the data?*

Career
CONNECTION

Dr. Enriquetta Barrera, Geochemist

Enriquetta Barrera studies the chemistry of rocks, which hold clues to Earth's past. Enriquetta loves her job but admits that the job is not easy. Scientific research involves careful observations and analyses to formulate hypotheses. As she practices science, Enriquetta is constantly revising her ideas and learning about her field. It takes years of hard work to become established in a field of research. *Why is it important to be able to revise your ideas?*

Using Vocabulary

a. constant
b. control
c. dependent variable
d. hypothesis
e. independent variable
f. model
g. science
h. scientific methods
i. technology

Match each phrase with the correct term from the list of Vocabulary words.

1. the factor being measured in an experiment
2. a statement that can be tested
3. use of knowledge to make products
4. sample treated like other experimental groups except variable is not applied
5. way of thinking to solve a problem

Checking Concepts

Choose the word or phrase that best answers the question.

6. To make sure an experiment's results are valid, you must complete which of the following tasks?
   A) conduct multiple trials
   B) pick your hypothesis
   C) add bias
   D) communicate the results

7. In an experiment on bacteria, using different amounts of antibiotics is an example of which of the following?
   A) control   C) bias
   B) hypothesis   D) variable

8. Computers are used in science to do which of the following processes?
   A) analyze data
   B) make models
   C) communicate with other scientists
   D) all of the above

9. Which of the following skills is being used by scientists when they interpret an observation?
   A) hypothesizing
   B) inferring
   C) taking measurements
   D) making models

10. Using a computer to make a three-dimensional picture of a building is a type of which of the following?
    A) model   C) control
    B) hypothesis D) variable

11. Which of the following provides access to the Internet?
    A) variable   C) control
    B) hypothesis D) computer

12. Which of the following is the first step toward finding a solution?
    A) analyze data
    B) draw a conclusion
    C) identify the problem
    D) test the hypothesis

13. Predictions about what will happen can be based on which of the following?
    A) controls   C) technology
    B) prior knowledge D) number of trials

14. Which of the following terms describes a variable that stays the same throughout an experiment?
    A) hypothesis
    B) dependent variable
    C) constant
    D) independent variable

15. Which of the following is a prediction that can be tested?
    A) conclusion   C) observation
    B) data table   D) hypothesis

Thinking Critically

16. What is the advantage of eliminating bias in experiments?

17. Why is it important to record data as they are collected?

18. What is the difference between analyzing data and drawing conclusions?

19. How is a Science Journal a valuable tool for scientists?

20. When solving a problem, why do scientists have to make a list of what is already known?

Developing Skills

If you need help, refer to the Skill Handbook.

21. **Recognizing Cause and Effect:** If three variables were changed at one time, what would happen to the accuracy of the conclusions made for an experiment?

22. **Making and Using Graphs:** Scientists recorded the following data about victims of a disease. Prepare a bar graph of the number of people in each age group that contracted the disease.

    Which age group appears to be the most likely to get the disease? Do adults have to worry about getting the disease? Why or why not?

Disease Victims	
Age Group	**Number of People**
0-1 yr.	10
1-5 yr.	27
5-10 yr.	20
10-15 yr.	2
15-20 yr.	1
20-25 yr.	0
over 25 yr.	0

23. **Forming a Hypothesis:** Basketball practice is scheduled for two hours after school every Tuesday through Friday. Your friend goes home sick every Tuesday. Form a hypothesis about why your friend gets sick. How can the hypothesis be tested?

THE PRINCETON REVIEW

Test-Taking Tip

Words Are Easy to Learn Make a huge stack of vocabulary flash cards and study them. Use your new words in daily conversation. The great thing about learning new words is the ability to express yourself more specifically.

Test Practice

Use these questions to test your Science Proficiency.

1. In an experiment using bean plants, all the variables were kept constant except for the amount of fertilizer given to the different plants. Which of the following describes the fertilizer in this experiment?
   A) constant
   B) control
   C) independent variable
   D) dependent variable

2. In the experiment described above in question 1, the measured growth indicated how the fertilizer affects plants. Which of the following terms describes growth in this experiment?
   A) constant
   B) control
   C) independent variable
   D) dependent variable

3. Which of the following is **NOT** an example of technology?
   A) wagon
   B) copper
   C) braces on teeth
   D) bicycle

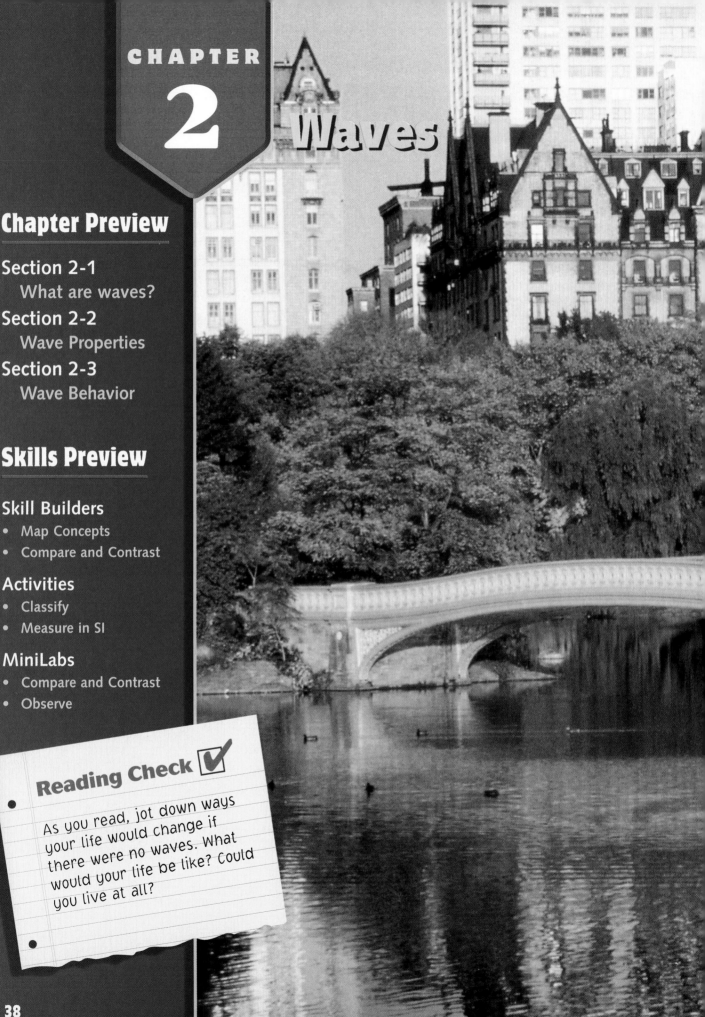

CHAPTER
2

Waves

Chapter Preview

Skills Preview

Skill Builders
- Map Concepts
- Compare and Contrast

Activities
- Classify
- Measure in SI

MiniLabs
- Compare and Contrast
- Observe

Reading Check ✔

As you read, jot down ways your life would change if there were no waves. What would your life be like? Could you live at all?

Explore Activity

Think about a beautiful autumn day. You are sitting by a lake in a park. You hear music coming from a nearby school band practicing for a big game. A fish jumps out of the water and falls back making a splash. You see a circle of waves that move away from the fish's entry point. The circular waves pass by a floating leaf that fell from a tree nearby. How does the leaf move in response to the waves?

Observe Wave Behavior

1. Set a large, clear, plastic plate (such as the ones carryout meals often come in) on your table.

2. Fill the plate with water to a depth of about 1 cm.

3. Fill a dropper with water.

4. Release a single drop of water onto the water's surface and observe what happens. Repeat as necessary.

5. Float a small cork or 1-cm piece of a soda straw on the surface of the water near the middle of the plate.

6. After the water becomes still again, release single drops at regular intervals from a height of about 10 cm and not directly above the floating object.

7. Repeat the procedure, but release the single drops from a height of about 20 cm.

In your Science Journal, record your observations and describe the movements of the floating object.

2•1 What are waves?

Waves Carry Energy

In the Explore Activity, you saw that falling drops of water can move a floating object. You know that you can make something move by giving it a push or pull. But, the drops didn't hit the floating object. How did the energy from the falling drops travel through the water and move the object? Did you also notice that the ripples that moved in circles from the drop's entry point had peaks and valleys? These peaks and valleys make up water waves.

Waves are regular disturbances that carry energy through matter or space without carrying matter, as shown in **Figure 2-1A.** You also transfer energy when you throw a basketball or baseball to a friend. But, there is an important difference between a moving ball and a moving wave. As shown in **Figure 2-1B,** throwing a ball involves the transport of matter as well as energy.

Mechanical Waves

How does a wave carry energy but not matter? Here is one example you already know about. Sound travels as one type of wave motion. The sounds from a CD player reach your ears when the speakers vibrate back and forth, and make sound waves.

What You'll Learn

► Waves carry energy, not matter
► The difference between transverse waves and compressional waves

Vocabulary
wave
mechanical wave
electromagnetic wave
transverse wave
compressional wave

Why It's Important

► You can hear music because of waves.

Figure 2-1 The wave and the ball both carry energy.

A Waves on the water's surface carry energy from place to place, but the water itself moves mostly up and down.

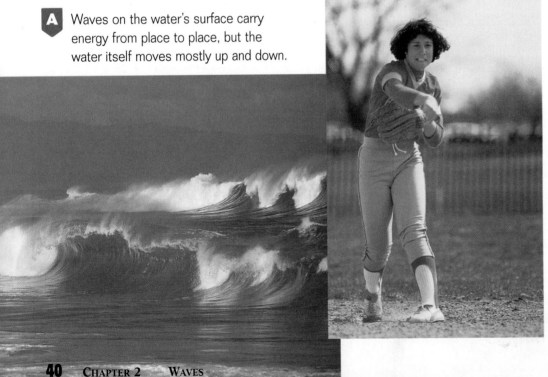

B When you throw a ball to a friend, the ball carries both energy and matter. **What is another example of a moving object carrying both energy and matter?**

The sound waves transfer energy to anything in their path. When the waves reach your ears, they make your eardrums vibrate, as in **Figure 2-2.** If you've ever felt your house shake after a clap of thunder, you know that sound waves can carry large amounts of energy.

Waves that require matter to carry energy are called **mechanical waves.** The matter through which a mechanical wave travels is called a medium. A mechanical wave travels as energy is transferred from particle to particle in the medium. For example, a sound wave travels through the air because energy is transferred from gas molecule to gas molecule. Without a medium, you would not hear sounds. For example, sound waves can't travel in outer space. Imagine that you're standing on the moon. A person standing near you is telling you what she sees. But because there is no air on the moon to carry the sound, you won't hear a word she says—even if she yells at the top of her lungs.

Figure 2-2 When you hear a sound, it's because sound waves traveling through the air make your eardrums vibrate.

Water Waves

Water waves—like the ones you made in the Explore Activity—are also mechanical waves. Each falling water drop touched water molecules when it hit the water's surface. Thus, the droplet's energy was carried from molecule to molecule through the water. Remember that the molecules of water do not move forward along with the wave. Rather, the water's surface moves up and down. In this same way, the wave transfers energy to a boat or other floating object, as shown in **Figure 2-3.** Absorbing some of the energy, the object bobs up and down and moves slowly away from the source of the wave.

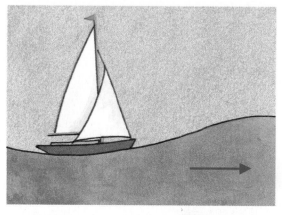

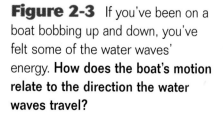

Figure 2-3 If you've been on a boat bobbing up and down, you've felt some of the water waves' energy. **How does the boat's motion relate to the direction the water waves travel?**

inter NET
C O N N E C T I O N

Visit the Glencoe Science Web Site at **www. glencoe.com/sec/ science** for more information about electromagnetic waves.

Electromagnetic Waves

When you listen to the radio, watch TV, or use a microwave oven to cook, you use a different kind of wave—one that doesn't need matter as a medium.

Waves that do not require matter to carry energy are called **electromagnetic waves.** Electromagnetic waves can travel through air. They can even travel through the solid walls of your home. These are the kind of waves that bring you radio and TV programs. Electromagnetic waves also can travel through space to carry information to and from spacecraft. The X rays a doctor uses to see if you broke a bone and the light that carries the sun's energy to Earth are also electro-magnetic waves.

Transverse Waves

In a mechanical **transverse wave,** matter moves back and forth at right angles to the direction the wave travels. All elec-tromagnetic waves are transverse waves. You can make a model of a transverse wave. Tie one end of a rope to a door-knob. Hold the other end in your hand. Now, shake the end in your hand up and down. By adjusting the way you shake the rope, you can create a wave that seems to vibrate in place.

Reading Check ☑

What are the highest points of transverse waves called?

Does the rope appear to move toward the doorknob? It doesn't really move toward the door, because if it did, you also would be pulled in that direction. What you see is energy mov-ing along the "rope" wave. You can see that the wave has peaks and valleys at regular intervals. As shown in **Figure 2-4,** the high points of transverse waves are called crests. The low points are called troughs. ☑

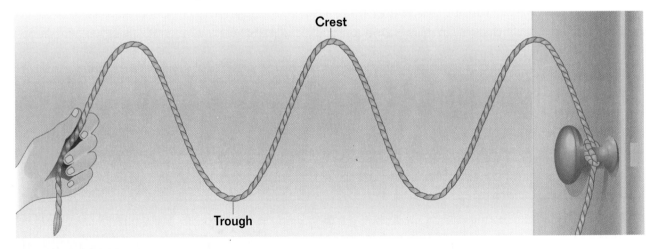

Crest

Trough

Figure 2-4 What does the vibrating rope carry from the hand to the door?

Figure 2-5 Sound waves are compressional waves.

 A This compressional wave carries energy along the spring, while the spring itself vibrates forward and backward.

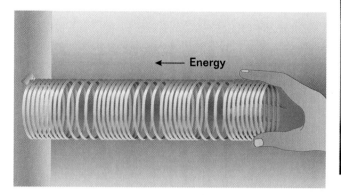

← Energy

B Vibrating strings make compressional waves that carry the harp's music to your ears. **What do you think vibrates to make compressional waves when a musician plays a trumpet?**

Compressional Waves

Mechanical waves can be either transverse or compressional. In a **compressional wave,** matter in the medium moves forward and backward in the same direction the wave travels. You can make a compressional wave by squeezing together and releasing several coils of a coiled spring toy, as shown in **Figure 2-5A.** When a compressional wave travels along a coiled spring, does the whole spring move along with the wave? If you tied a string around a single coil, you could watch that coil's movement as the wave passes. You would see that the coil moves forward and backward as the wave passes. So, like transverse waves, compressional waves carry only energy forward along the spring. The matter of the spring does not move along with the wave.

Sound Waves

Sound waves are compressional waves. How do you make sound waves when you talk or sing? If you hold your fingers against your throat while you hum, you can feel vibrations. These vibrations are actually the movements of your vocal cords. If you touch a stereo speaker while it's playing, you can feel the vibrations of the speaker, too. The sounds produced by the harp shown in **Figure 2-5** are made when the strings of the instrument are made to vibrate.

Comparing Sounds

Procedure
1. Hold a wooden ruler firmly on the edge of your desk so that most of it extends off the edge of the desk.
2. Pluck the free end of the ruler so that it vibrates up and down. Pluck it easily at first, then with more energy.
3. Repeat step 2, moving the ruler about 1 cm further onto the desk. Continue until only about 5 cm extend off the edge.

Analysis
1. Compare the loudness of the sounds produced by using little energy with those using more energy.
2. Compare the pitches produced by the longer and shorter lengths of the object.

Making Sound Waves

How do vibrating vocal cords, strings, and other objects make sound waves? To find out, look at the drumhead stretched over the open end of the drum shown in **Figure 2-6.** When the drumhead moves upward, it touches some of the invisible particles that make up the air. When everything is quiet, the air particles are spaced about the same distance apart. But when the drumhead moves up, it pushes the air particles together. These groups of particles that are squeezed together are called a compression. When the drumhead moves downward, the air particles have more room and move away from each other. A place where particles are spaced far apart is called a rarefaction (rar uh FAK shun).

Figure 2-6 A vibrating drumhead makes compressions and rarefactions in the air. **How do your vocal cords make compressions and rarefactions in air?**

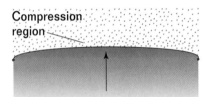
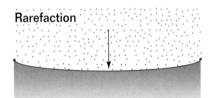

Section Assessment

1. Give one example of a transverse wave and one example of a compressional wave.

2. Why can't a sound wave travel from a satellite to Earth?

3. Is light a mechanical wave or an electromagnetic wave? A transverse wave or a compressional wave?

4. **Think Critically:** How is it possible for a sound wave to transmit energy, but not matter?

5. **Skill Builder**
Concept Mapping Create a concept map that shows the relationships between the following: *waves, mechanical waves, electromagnetic waves, compressional waves,* and *transverse waves.* If you need help, refer to Concept Mapping in the **Skill Handbook** on page 698.

Using Computers

Word Processing Use word-processing software to write short descriptions of the waves you encounter during a typical day. If you need help, refer to page 716.

Wave Properties

Amplitude

Waves have characteristics that you can see and measure. For example, you can describe a wave in a lake or ocean by how high it rises above, or falls below, the normal water level. This is called the wave's amplitude. The **amplitude** of a transverse wave is one-half the distance between a crest and a trough, as shown in **Figure 2-7A.** In a compressional wave, the amplitude is greater when the particles of the medium are squeezed closer together in each compression and spread farther apart in each rarefaction.

Amplitude and Energy

A wave's amplitude is important. It is a measure of the energy the wave carries. For example, the waves that make up bright light have greater amplitudes than the waves that make up dim light. Waves of bright light carry more energy than the waves that make up dim light. In a similar way, loud sound waves have greater amplitudes than soft sound waves. Loud sounds carry more energy than soft sounds.

If you've seen pictures of a hurricane that strikes a coastal area, you know that the waves caused by the hurricane can damage anything that stands in their path. Waves with large amplitudes carry more energy than waves with smaller amplitudes. The waves caused by the hurricane have much more energy than the small waves or ripples on a pond, as you can see in **Figure 2-7B.**

Figure 2-7 A wave's amplitude is a measure of how much energy it carries.

A The higher the crests (and the lower the troughs) of a wave, the greater the wave's amplitude is.

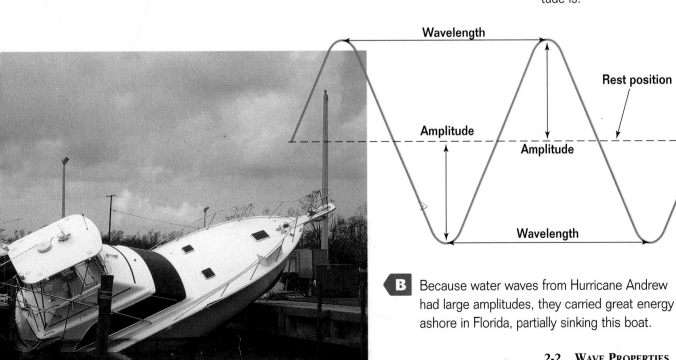

Wavelength

Rest position

Amplitude

Amplitude

Wavelength

B Because water waves from Hurricane Andrew had large amplitudes, they carried great energy ashore in Florida, partially sinking this boat.

Tsunamis are huge sea waves that are caused by under-water earthquakes or volcanic eruptions. Because of their large amplitudes, tsunamis carry tremendous amounts of energy. They cause great damage when they move ashore.

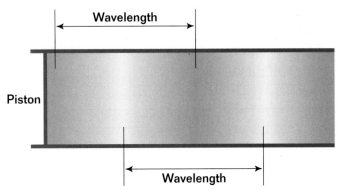

Figure 2-8 The wavelength of a compressional wave is measured from one compression or rarefaction to the next. **When the piston moves to the right, does it make a compression or a rarefaction?**

Figure 2-9 The wavelengths and frequencies of electromagnetic waves vary greatly. **Which waves have longer wavelengths, radio waves or visible light waves?**

Wavelength

Another way to describe a wave is by its wavelength. **Wavelength** is the distance between a point on one wave and an identical point on the next wave—from a crest to a crest or from a trough to a trough, as shown in **Figure 2-7A.** For a compressional wave, the wavelength is the distance between adjacent compressions or rarefactions, as shown in **Figure 2-8.**

Wavelength is an important characteristic of a wave. For example, the difference between red light and green light is that they have different wavelengths. Like all electromagnetic waves, light is a transverse wave. The wavelength of visible light determines its color. In this example, the wavelength of red light is longer than the wavelength of green light. Some electromagnetic waves, like X rays, have short wavelengths. Others, like microwaves in an oven, have longer wavelengths. The range of wavelengths of electromagnetic waves is shown in **Figure 2-9.**

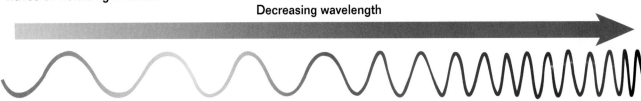

Decreasing wavelength

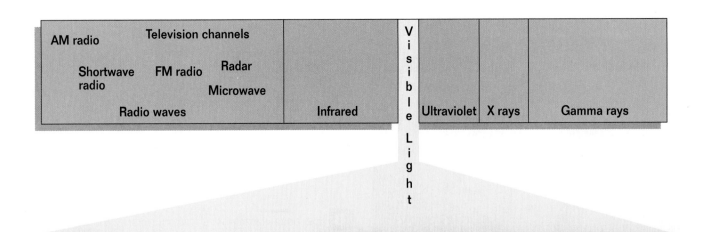

AM radio	Television channels		Visible Light			
Shortwave radio	FM radio	Radar				
		Microwave				
Radio waves			Infrared	Ultraviolet	X rays	Gamma rays

Frequency

The **frequency** of a wave is the number of waves that pass a given point in 1 s. Frequency is measured in waves per second, or hertz (Hz). For a given speed, waves with longer wavelengths have lower frequencies. Fewer long waves pass a given point in 1 s. Waves with shorter wavelengths have higher frequencies because more waves pass a given point in 1 s. Frequency is illustrated in **Figure 2-10A** and **B.**

The wavelength of an electromagnetic light wave determines the color of the light. In a sound wave, the frequency (associated with its wavelength) determines the pitch. Pitch is the highness or lowness of a sound. A flute makes musical notes with a high pitch. A tuba produces notes with a low pitch. When you sing "do re mi fa so la ti do," both the pitch and frequency increase from note to note. In other words, high-pitched sound waves have high frequencies. Low-pitched sound waves have low frequencies.

Global Positioning Systems
Maybe you've used a global positioning system (GPS) receiver to determine your location while driving, boating, or hiking. Earth-orbiting satellites send out electromagnetic radio waves that give the satellites' exact locations and times of transmission. The GPS receiver calculates the distance to each satellite and displays your location to within about 16 m.

Wave Speed

You've probably watched a distant thunderstorm approach on a hot summer day. You see a bolt of lightning flash between a dark cloud and the ground. Do the sound waves, or thunder, produced by the lightning bolt reach your ears at the same instant you see the lightning? If the thunderstorm is many kilometers away, several seconds may pass between the time you see the lightning and you hear the thunder. This happens because light travels much faster in air than sound does. Light is an electromagnetic wave that travels through air at about 300 million m/s. Sound is a mechanical wave that travels through air at about 340 m/s.

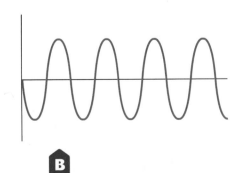

Reading Check
What determines the pitch of a sound?

Figure 2-10 Wave A has a longer wavelength and a lower frequency than wave B. **Why does a wave with a long wavelength have a low frequency?**

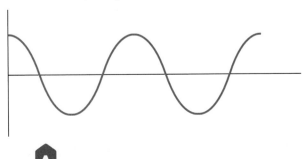

A

B

Determining Wave Speed

You can calculate the speed of a wave by multiplying its frequency by its wavelength. For example, suppose you know that a sound wave has a frequency of 266 Hz and a wavelength of 1.29 m. (Remember that 266 Hz means that 266 sound waves pass a given point in 1 s.) The wave's speed is given by the following calculation.

wave frequency × wavelength = wave speed
266 Hz × 1.29 m = 343 m/s

The speed of the wave is 343 m/s.

Light travels through different types of matter at different speeds. For example, the speed of light waves is slightly higher in empty space than in air. And, light waves travel only about 200 million m/s in glass. You can see that this is much slower than the speed light travels in air. The speed of sound waves varies, too. Have you ever heard sounds while swimming underwater? Have you ever put your ear against a wall or on the ground to hear something more clearly? If you have, you may have noticed something interesting. Sound travels faster in liquids and solids than in gases like air.

Section Assessment

1. Why is the statement "The speed of light is 300 million m/s" not always correct?

2. How does the frequency of a wave change as its wavelength changes?

3. In what part of a compressional wave are the particles spaced farthest apart?

4. Why is a sound wave with a large amplitude more likely to damage your hearing than one with a small amplitude?

5. **Think Critically:** Explain the differences between the waves that make up bright, green light and dim, red light.

6. **Skill Builder**
   Interpreting Scientific Diagrams
   Scientific diagrams can help you understand wave properties. Do the **Chapter 2 Skill Activity** on page 727 to learn about a compressional wave, its parts, and its wavelength.

Using Math

If a sound wave traveling through water has a speed of 1470 m/s and a frequency of 2340 Hz, what is its wavelength?

Waves on a Spring

Waves are rhythmic disturbances that carry energy through matter or space. Studying waves can help you understand how the sun's energy reaches Earth and sounds travel through the air.

Materials

- Long, coiled spring toy
- Meterstick
- Stopwatch
- Piece of colored yarn (5 cm)

What You'll Investigate

In this activity, you will create transverse and compressional waves on a coiled spring and investigate some of their properties.

Goals

- **Create** transverse and compressional waves on a coiled spring.
- **Investigate** wave properties such as speed and amplitude.

Procedure

1. **Prepare a data table** such as the one shown.
2. Work in pairs or groups and clear a place on an uncarpeted floor about 6 m long and 2 m wide.
3. While one team member grasps one end of the coiled spring toy with one hand, another team member should stretch it to the length suggested by the teacher. **Measure** the length of the coiled spring toy. **CAUTION:** *Coiled springs can be damaged permanently by overstretching or tangling. Be careful to follow the teacher's instructions.*
4. **Create** a wave by having one team member make a quick sideways snap of the wrist. Time several waves as they travel from one end of the coiled spring toy to the other. Record the average time in your data table.
5. Repeat step 4 using waves that have slightly larger amplitudes.
6. Use one hand to squeeze together about 20 of the coils near you. **Observe** what happens to the unsqueezed coils. Release the coils and **observe** what happens.
7. Quickly push one end of the coiled spring toward your partner, then pull it back to its original position.
8. Tie the piece of colored yarn to a coil near the middle of the coiled spring toy. Repeat step 7, **observing** what happens to the string.

Wave Data	
Length of stretched spring toy	
Average time for a wave to travel from end to end—step 4	
Average time for a wave to travel from end to end—step 5	

Conclude and Apply

1. **Classify** the wave pulses you created in steps 4 and 5 and those you created in steps 6 to 8 as compressional or transverse.
2. **Calculate** and **compare** the speeds of the waves in steps 4 and 5.
3. **Classify** the unsqueezed coils in step 6 as a compression or a rarefaction.
4. **Compare and contrast** the motion of the yarn in step 8 with the motion of the wave. Did the coil that had the yarn attached to it move along the coiled spring toy or did the wave's energy pass through that coil?

2•3 Wave Behavior

Reflection

What You'll Learn

► Waves can reflect from some surfaces
► How waves usually change direction when they move from one material into another
► Waves are able to bend around barriers

Vocabulary

reflection   diffraction
refraction   interference

Why It's Important

► Without wave reflection, you couldn't read the words on this page.

You've probably yelled to a friend across a gymnasium or down a long hallway. When you did this, you might have heard an echo of your voice. What property of sound caused the echo?

When you look in a mirror, what property of light lets you see your face? Both the echo of your voice and the face you see in the mirror are caused by wave reflection. **Reflection** occurs when a wave strikes an object or surface and bounces off. An echo is reflected sound. Sound reflects from all surfaces. Your echo bounced off the walls, floor, ceiling, furniture, and people. In old western movies, light reflected off a mirror was often used to send a message over long distances. When you see your face in a mirror, as shown in **Figure 2-11A,** reflection occurs. Light that reflects from your face hits the mirror and reflects back to your eyes.

A mirror is smooth and even. However, when light reflects from an uneven or rough surface, you can't see an image because the reflected light scatters in many different directions, as shown in **Figure 2-11B.**

Figure 2-11

A If light didn't reflect from you and the mirror, you wouldn't be able to see yourself in the mirror.

B The building at the far left has a rough surface that scatters light in different directions. Its surface is not smooth and shiny like the building on the right, which is mirrorlike. **Why should a mirror's reflective surface be made as smooth as possible?**

Refraction

You've already seen that a wave changes direction when it reflects from a surface. Can a wave change its direction at other times? Perhaps you've used a magnifying glass to examine your skin, an insect, a coin, or a stamp. An object appears larger when viewed through a magnifying glass. This happens because the light rays from the object change direction when they pass from the air into the glass. They change direction again when they pass from the glass into the air. The bending of a wave as it moves from one medium into another is called **refraction.**

Refraction and Wave Speed

The speed of a wave is different in different substances. For example, light waves move slower in water than in air. Refraction occurs when the speed of a wave changes as it passes from one substance to another. As shown in **Figure 2-12A** and **B,** a line has been drawn perpendicular to the water's surface. This line is called the normal.

Try at Home
Mini Lab

Observing How Light Refracts

Procedure

1. Fill a large, opaque drinking glass or cup nearly to the brim with water.
2. Place a white soda straw in the water at an angle, with approximately one-third of its length extending out of the water.
3. Looking directly down into the cup from above, observe the straw where it meets the water.
4. Placing yourself so that the straw angles to your left or right, slowly back away about 1 m. If necessary, lower your head until you eliminate any unwanted glare from the water's surface. Observe the straw as it appears above, at, and below the surface of the water.

Analysis

1. Describe the straw's appearance as you looked directly down on it.
2. Compare the straw's appearance above and below the water's surface when you looked at it from the side. Draw a diagram and explain the apparent effect.

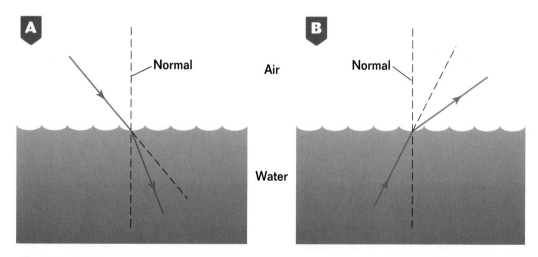

Figure 2-12 As the light ray in A passes from air into water, it refracts toward the normal. As the light ray in B passes from water into air, it refracts away from the normal.

When a light ray passes from air into water, it slows down and bends toward the normal. The more the light ray slows, the more its direction changes. When the ray passes from water into air, it speeds up and bends away from the normal.

You notice refraction when you look at an angle into a lake or pond and spot a fish near the bottom. Refraction makes the fish appear to be closer to the surface and farther away from you than it really is, as shown in **Figure 2-13.** Refraction also gives diamonds and other gems their wonderful sparkle. **Figure 2-14** illustrates how refraction and reflection produce a rainbow when light waves from the sun pass into and out of water droplets in the air. ☑

Reading Check ☑

What produces a rainbow?

Diffraction

It's time for lunch. You're walking down the hallway to the cafeteria. As you near the open door, you can hear people talking and the clink and clank of tableware. But how do the sound waves reach your ears before you get to the door? The sound waves must be able to bend around the corners of the door, as shown in **Figure 2-15A. Diffraction** is the bending of waves around a barrier.

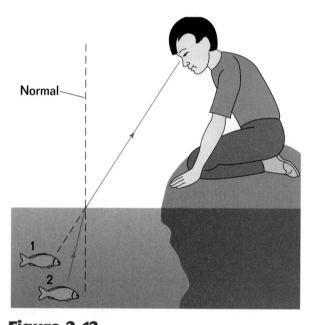

Figure 2-13
Refraction makes the fish at location 2 appear to be at location 1.

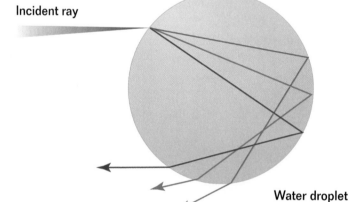

Figure 2-14 Light rays refract when they enter and leave a raindrop, and they reflect from the far side of the drop. Because different colors refract at different angles, they leave the drop separated into the colors of the spectrum. (Ray angles have been shown larger than they actually are for clarity.) **Which color of light shown on the diagram refracts most?**

Figure 2-15 Sound waves and light waves diffract differently through an open door.

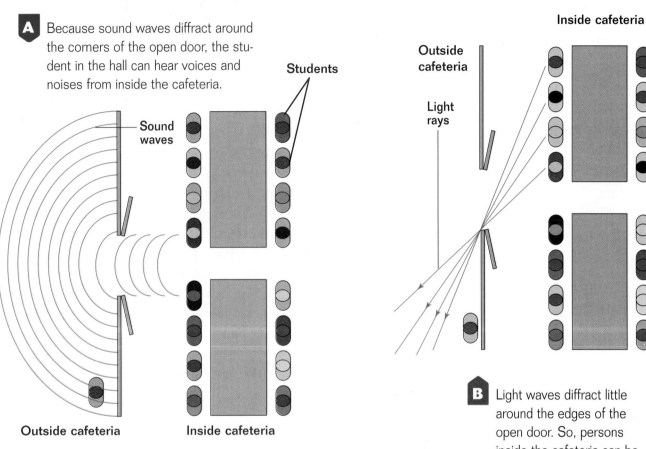

A Because sound waves diffract around the corners of the open door, the student in the hall can hear voices and noises from inside the cafeteria.

Students

Sound waves

Outside cafeteria

Inside cafeteria

Inside cafeteria

Outside cafeteria

Light rays

B Light waves diffract little around the edges of the open door. So, persons inside the cafeteria can be seen only when the student in the hall meets light rays streaming through the door. **How does diffraction explain why a boat inside a harbor rocks slightly from water waves outside the harbor?**

Diffraction of Light

Can light waves diffract, too? You can't see your friends in the cafeteria until you reach the open door, so the light waves must not diffract as much as the sound waves, as shown in **Figure 2-15.**

Are light waves able to diffract at all? As a matter of fact, light waves do bend around the edges of an open door. You can see some effects of light diffraction when you view a bright light through a small slit such as the one between two pencils held close together. However, the amount the light bends is extremely small. As a result, the diffraction of light is far too small to allow you to see around the corner into the cafeteria. The reason that light waves don't diffract much when they pass through an open door is that the wavelengths of visible light are much smaller than the width of the door. Sound waves that you can hear have much longer wavelengths. They bend more readily around the corners of an open door. A wave diffracts best when its wavelength is similar in size to the barrier or opening.

Interference

inter**NET**
C O N N E C T I O N

Visit the Glencoe Science Web Site at **www.glencoe.com/sec/science** for more information about wave interference.

Imagine a marching band that has only one of each kind of instrument. When this band performs on a football field, will it fill the stadium with sound? Having several of each instrument play the same notes at the same times produces much louder and more spectacular music. For example, the sound waves of many trumpets combine to make sound waves with larger amplitudes. The sound produced by many trumpets is therefore louder than the sound from a single trumpet. The ability of two or more waves to combine and form a new wave when they overlap is called **interference** (ihn tur FEER uns).

Constructive interference occurs when waves meet, for example, crest to crest and trough to trough. The amplitudes of these combining waves add together to make a larger wave, as shown in **Figure 2-16A, B,** and **C.** Destructive interference occurs, for example, when the crest of one wave meets the trough of another wave. In destructive interference, the amplitudes of the combining waves make a smaller wave. Sometimes, they produce no wave at all, as shown in **Figure 2-16D, E,** and **F** on the next page.

Reflected light waves sometimes produce interesting interference patterns. The colorful interference patterns that result from the microscopic pits in compact discs are one example.

Problem Solving

Scattering Light

Why is the sky blue and the sunset red? Surprisingly, both effects have the same cause. Sunlight contains all colors of the visible spectrum. When sunlight passes through Earth's atmosphere, particles in the air scatter some colors more than others. Shorter-wavelength violet and blue light waves are scattered most, green and yellow waves a little, and longer-wavelength orange and red light waves even less.

The sky appears blue during the day because the scattered blue light waves reflect to your eyes from dust particles and water droplets in the air. However, at sunrise and sunset, the sky appears red because light waves from the sun pass through more of the atmosphere before reaching Earth's surface. With so much of the blue and violet light scattered away, only the orange and red waves reach your eyes.

Think Critically: You've seen the beautiful array of colors in a rainbow on a day that has both sunshine and water droplets in the air. You've viewed the colorful light pattern from a compact disc. What do the blue color of the daytime sky, the red color of a sunset, a multicolored rainbow, and the light pattern from a compact disc have in common? How are they different?

Figure 2-16

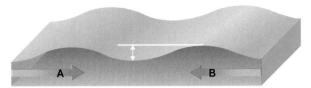

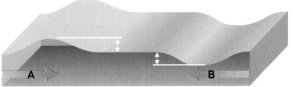

A **Constructive Wave Interference**
Crests of waves A and B approach each other from different directions. The waves have equal amplitudes.

D **Destructive Wave Interference**
A crest of wave A and trough of wave B approach each other from different directions. The amplitude of A equals the amplitude of B.

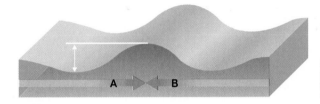

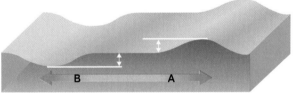

B When crests A and B meet, they briefly form a new wave, A + B, which has an amplitude equal to the sum of the amplitudes of the two waves.

E When the waves meet, they briefly form a new wave, A + B, which has an amplitude of zero for an instant.

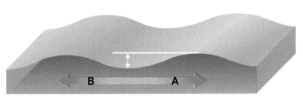

C The waves have passed through each other unchanged.

F The waves have passed through each other unchanged. **Compare and contrast constructive and destructive interference.**

Useful Interference

You may have seen someone cut grass with a power lawn mower or cut wood with a chain saw. In the past, many people who've performed these tasks have damaged their hearing because of the loud noises produced by these machines. Today, ear protectors can reflect and absorb some of the noise from lawn mowers and chain saws. The ear protectors lower the amplitudes of the harmful waves. The smaller-amplitude waves that reach the ears no longer damage eardrums.

Pilots of small planes have had an interesting problem. They couldn't shut out all the noise of the plane's motor. If they did, they wouldn't be able to hear instructions from air-traffic controllers. Engineers invented special earphones that contain electronic circuits. These circuits produce sound frequencies that destructively interfere with engine noise that might be harmful.

However, the sound frequencies produced do not interfere with human voices, allowing the pilot to hear and understand normal conversation. In these examples, destructive interference can be a benefit, as shown in **Figure 2-17**.

Figure 2-17 Some airplane pilots use ear protectors that muffle engine noise but don't block human voices. People who operate chain saws need ear protectors that greatly reduce the engine noise that could be harmful.

Section Assessment

1. White objects reflect light. Why don't you see your reflection when you look at a building made of rough, white stone?

2. If you're standing on one side of a building, how are you able to hear the siren of an ambulance on the other side of the building?

3. What behavior of light enables magnifying glasses and contact lenses to bend light rays and help people see more clearly?

4. **Think Critically:** Why don't light rays that stream through an open window into a darkened room spread evenly through the entire room?

5.  **Skill Builder**
   Comparing and Contrasting When light rays pass from water into a certain type of glass, the rays refract toward the normal. Compare and contrast the speed of light in water and in the glass. If you need help, refer to Comparing and Contrasting in the **Skill Handbook** on page 704.

Science Journal
Look and listen carefully as you travel home from school or walk down the street where you live. What examples of wave reflection and refraction do you notice? Describe each of these in your Science Journal, and explain whether it's an example of reflection or refraction.

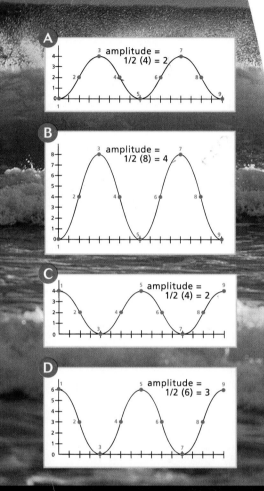

Graphing Waves

Constructive and Destructive Interference

Waves have special characteristics. The wavelength is the horizontal distance between a point on one wave and an identical point on the next wave. The amplitude is the vertical distance from the crest (or trough) of a wave to a position halfway between crest and trough.

When two waves meet in such a way that a new wave with greater amplitude is formed, it is called constructive interference. If the new wave formed has a smaller amplitude than either original wave or an amplitude of zero, it is called destructive interference.

Problem

Draw a graph for the new wave formed by combining Waves A and B.

Solution

Notice that nine points on each wave are labeled with red dots and numbers. These points will be used to graph the new wave.

To graph the new wave formed by combining Waves A and B, find nine points for the new graph by adding the "height" of Waves A and B at each labeled point.

Point 1 (new): height of Wave A point 1 + height of Wave B point 1 = 0 + 0 = 0.

Point 2 (new): height of Wave A point 2 + height of Wave B point 2 = 2 + 4 = 6.

Point 3 (new): height of Wave A point 3 + height of Wave B point 3 = 4 + 8 = 12.

Continuing the process, you'll find that the remaining points have heights 6, 0, 6, 12, 6, and 0. A graph for the new wave looks like this:

To find a wave's amplitude, count the vertical units between the lowest and highest points on the graph and divide by 2. Because the new wave has greater amplitude (6) than either Wave A (2) or B (4), this problem is an example of constructive interference.

Practice PROBLEMS

In the following problems, draw the graph and determine whether each is a case of constructive or destructive interference.

1. Draw a graph for the new wave formed by combining Waves B and D.

2. Draw a graph representing the combination of Waves C and D.

3. Draw a graph representing the combination of Waves A and C.

4. Draw graphs for two waves of your choice. Show the new wave formed by combining the two.

On The Internet

Activity 2•2

Doing the Wave

When an earthquake occurs, the waves of energy are recorded at points all over the world by instruments called seismographs. By comparing the data that they collected from their seismographs, scientists discovered that the interior of Earth must be made of layers of different materials. How did the seismographs tell them that Earth is not the same medium all the way through?

Materials

- Coiled spring toy
- Stopwatch
  *clock with a second hand
- Meterstick
- Tape

  *Alternate Materials

Recognize the Problem

Can the speed of a wave be used to identify the medium through which it travels?

Form a Hypothesis

Think about what you know about the relationship between the frequency, wavelength, and speed of a wave in a medium. **Make a hypothesis** about how you can measure the speed of a wave within a medium and use that information to identify an unknown medium.

Goals

- **Measure** the speed of a wave within a coiled spring toy.
- **Predict** whether the speed you measured will be different in other types of coiled spring toys.

Data Sources

Go to the Glencoe Science Web Site at **www.glencoe.com/sec/science** for more information, hints, and data collected by other students.

Sample Data

Wave Data						
Trial	Length spring was stretched (m)	Number of crests	Wavelength (m)	Number of vibrations timed	Number of seconds vibrations were timed (s)	Wave speed (m/s)
1						
2						
3						

Test Your Hypothesis

Plan

1. **Make a data table** in your Science Journal like the one shown.
2. **Write** a detailed description of the coiled spring toy you are going to use. Be sure to include its mass and diameter, the width of a coil, and what it is made of.

3. Decide as a group how you will **measure** the frequency and length of waves in the spring toy. What are your variables? Which variables must be controlled? What variable do you want to measure?
4. Repeat your experiment three times.

Do

1. Make sure your teacher approves your plan before you begin.
2. Carry out the experiment as you have planned.

3. While you are doing the experiment, **record** your observations and measurements in your data table.

Analyze Your Data

1. **Calculate** the frequency of the waves by dividing the number of vibrations you timed by the number of seconds you timed them. Record your results in your data table.

2. Use the following formula to **calculate** the speed of a wave in each trial.

    wavelength $\times$ wave frequency = wave speed

3. **Average** the wave speeds from your trials to determine the speed of a wave in your coiled spring toy.

Draw Conclusions

1. **Post** the description of your coiled spring toy and your results on the Glencoe Science Web Site.
2. **Compare and contrast** your results with the results of other students.
3. How does the type of coiled spring toy and the length it was stretched affect the wave speed? Was your hypothesis supported?
4. Would it make a difference if an earthquake wave were transmitted through Earth's solid mantle or the molten outer core?

For a **preview** of this chapter, study this Reviewing Main Ideas before you read the chapter. After you have studied this chapter, you can use the Reviewing Main Ideas to **review** the chapter.

 The Glencoe MindJogger, Audiocassettes, and CD-ROM provide additional opportunities for review.

2-1 WAVES CARRY ENERGY

Waves are rhythmic disturbances that carry energy but not matter. **Mechanical waves** can travel only through matter. Other waves, called **electromagnetic waves,** can travel through space. *What kind of waves carry the sun's energy to Earth? An earthquake's energy through Earth?*

TRANSVERSE AND COMPRESSIONAL WAVES

In a mechanical **transverse wave,** matter in the medium the wave travels through moves back and forth at right angles to the direction the wave travels. In a **compressional wave,** matter in the medium moves forward and backward in the same direction as the wave. *Why doesn't a sound wave travel through space?*

2-2 AMPLITUDE, FREQUENCY, AND WAVELENGTH

Waves can be described by their characteristics. The **amplitude** of a transverse wave is one half the distance between a crest and a trough. **Wavelength** is the distance between a point on one wave and an identical point on the next wave. The **frequency** of a wave is the number of waves that pass a given point in 1 s. *How is the amplitude of a wave related to the amount of energy it carries?*

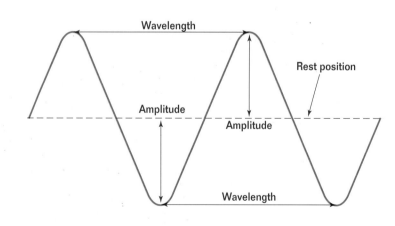

Reading Check ✔

• Construct a chart that compares and contrasts reflection, refraction, diffraction, and interference.

Section 2-3 REFLECTION

Reflection occurs when a wave strikes an object or surface and bounces off. You can see your image in a mirror because of reflection. *How does wave reflection explain echoes in a large canyon?*

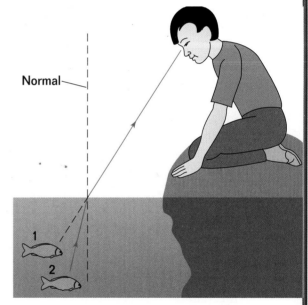

Normal

1
2

REFRACTION

The bending of a wave as it moves from one medium into another is called **refraction.** A wave changes direction, or refracts, when its speed changes. *In what situation does a wave not change its direction when it passes from one medium into another?*

DIFFRACTION AND INTERFERENCE

The bending of waves around a barrier is called **diffraction.** The ability of two or more waves to combine and form a new wave when they overlap is called **interference.** *What kind of interference produces waves with the largest amplitudes?*

Chapter 2 Assessment

Using Vocabulary

a. amplitude
b. compressional wave
c. diffraction
d. electromagnetic wave
e. frequency
f. interference
g. mechanical wave
h. reflection
i. refraction
j. transverse wave
k. wave
l. wavelength

Using the list above, replace the underlined words with the correct Vocabulary words.

1. <u>Diffraction</u> is the change in direction of a wave.
2. The type of wave that has rarefactions is a <u>transverse wave</u>.
3. The distance between two adjacent crests of a transverse wave is the <u>frequency</u>.
4. The more energy a wave carries, the greater the <u>wavelength</u> of the wave.
5. A <u>mechanical wave</u> can travel through space.

Checking Concepts

Choose the word or phrase that best answers the question.

6. What is the material through which mechanical waves travel?
   A) charged particles
   B) space
   C) a vacuum
   D) a medium

7. What is carried from particle to particle in a water wave?
   A) speed   C) energy
   B) amplitude   D) matter

8. What are the lowest points on a transverse wave called?
   A) crests   C) compressions
   B) troughs   D) rarefactions

9. What determines the pitch of a sound wave?
   A) amplitude   C) speed
   B) frequency   D) refraction

10. What is the distance between adjacent wave compressions?
    A) one wavelength C) 1 m/s
    B) 1 km   D) 1 Hz

11. What occurs when a wave strikes an object or surface and bounces off?
    A) diffraction   C) a change in speed
    B) refraction   D) reflection

12. What is the name for a change in the direction of a wave when it passes from one medium into another?
    A) refraction   C) reflection
    B) interference   D) diffraction

13. What type of wave is a sound wave?
    A) transverse
    B) electromagnetic
    C) compressional
    D) refracted

14. When two waves overlap and interfere destructively, what does the resulting wave have?
    A) a greater amplitude
    B) more energy
    C) a change in frequency
    D) a lower amplitude

15. What is the difference between blue light and green light?
    A) They have different wavelengths.
    B) One is a transverse wave and the other is not.
    C) They travel at different speeds.
    D) One is mechanical and the other is not.

Thinking Critically

16. Explain what kind of wave, transverse or compressional, is produced when an engine bumps into a string of coupled railroad cars on a track.

17. Is it possible for an electromagnetic wave to travel through a vacuum? Through matter? Explain your answers.
18. Why does the frequency of a wave decrease as the wavelength increases?
19. Why don't you see your reflected image when you look at a white, rough surface?
20. If a cannon fires at a great distance from you, why do you see the flash before you hear the sound?

Developing Skills

If you need help, refer to the **Skill Handbook.**

21. **Using Numbers:** A microwave travels at the speed of light and has a wavelength of 0.022 m. What is its frequency?
22. **Forming a Hypothesis:** Form a hypothesis that can explain this observation. Waves A and B travel away from Earth through Earth's atmosphere. Wave A continues on into space, but wave B does not.
23. **Recognizing Cause and Effect:** Explain how the object shown below causes compressions and rarefactions as it vibrates in air.

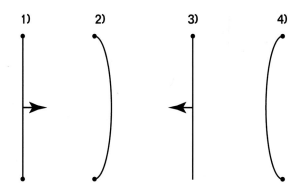

24. **Comparing and Contrasting:** AM radio waves have wavelengths between about 200 m and 600 m, while FM radio waves have wavelengths of about 3 m. Why can AM radio signals often be heard behind buildings and mountains while FM radio signals cannot?

THE PRINCETON REVIEW

Test-Taking Tip

Don't Cram If you don't know the material by the week before the test, you're less likely to do well. Set up a time line for your practice and preparation so that you're not rushed. Then, you will have time to deal with any problem areas.

Test Practice

Use these questions to test your Science Proficiency.

1. Two sounds have the same pitch, but one is louder than the other. What is different about the two sounds?
   A) their amplitudes
   B) their frequencies
   C) their wavelengths
   D) their speeds

2. What produces the colors seen when light reflects from CDs?
   A) wavelength
   B) interference
   C) refraction
   D) compression

3. The speed of a light ray increases as it passes at an angle from one medium into another. What happens to the ray?
   A) Its direction does not change.
   B) It travels along the normal.
   C) It bends toward the normal.
   D) It bends away from the normal.

4. What kind of waves requires a medium?
   A) all transverse waves
   B) only some compressional waves
   C) all electromagnetic waves
   D) all mechanical waves

Light, Mirrors, and Lenses

Chapter Preview

Skills Preview

Skill Builders
- Form a Hypothesis
- Compare and Contrast

Activities
- Observe and Infer
- Use Scientific Methods

MiniLabs
- Observe and Infer
- Form a Hypothesis

Reading Check ✔

As you read this chapter, list vocabulary terms that are also used in other subject areas, such as *medium* and *frequency*. Explain the meaning of these terms.

Explore Activity

What do you see when you look around you? Everything you see results from light waves that enter your eye. These light waves are emitted by objects like the sun or light-bulbs and are reflected by objects such as trees, books, people, and furniture. Laser beams like the ones shown here are also made of light waves. Lenses and mirrors can cause light waves to change direction and make objects seem larger or smaller. What happens to light as it passes from one material to another?

Observe Light Bending

1. Place two paper cups next to each other and put a penny in the bottom of each cup.

2. Stand so you can look straight down into both cups.

3. Fill one of the cups with water and observe what happens to the penny in that cup.

4. Slide the cup with no water away from you just until you can no longer see the penny.

5. Have your partner pour water into this cup and observe what seems to happen to the penny.

Science Journal

In your Science Journal, record your observations. Did adding water make the cup look deeper or shallower?

3•1 Properties of Light

What is light?

Have you ever dropped a rock on the smooth surface of a pond and watched the ripples spread outward, as shown in **Figure 3-1?** You produced a wave. The wave was all the ripples made by the rock striking the water. The impact of the rock added energy to the water. As the ripples spread out, they carried some of that energy.

Light also carries energy. A source of light like the sun or a lightbulb gives off light waves, just as the rock hitting the pond caused ripples to spread out from the point of impact. The ripples spread out only on the surface of the pond, but light waves spread out in all directions from the light source as shown in **Figure 3-2.**

Sometimes, it is easier to talk about just one narrow beam of light traveling in a straight line, which is called a **light ray.** You can think of a source of light as emitting light rays that are traveling away from the source in all directions.

However, light waves are different from ripples on a pond. If the pond dried up and there was no water, there could be no ripples. Waves on a pond need a material in which to travel—water. Any material in which a wave travels is called a **medium.** Light is a special type of wave called an electromagnetic wave. An **electromagnetic wave** is a wave that does not need a medium in which to travel. Electromagnetic waves can travel in a vacuum, as well as in materials such as air, water, and glass.

What You'll Learn

► The wave nature of light
► How light interacts with materials
► Why objects appear colored

Vocabulary
light ray
medium
electromagnetic wave
reflection
wavelength
frequency

Why It's Important

► Most of what you know about your surroundings comes from information carried by light waves.

Figure 3-1 Ripples on the surface of a pond are produced by an object hitting the water. As the ripples spread out from the point of impact, they carry energy.

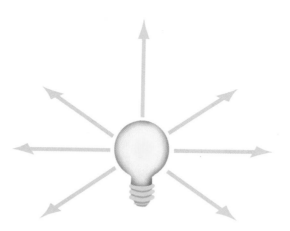

Figure 3-2 A source of light, such as a lightbulb, emits light rays in all directions. **Why does a flashlight emit only a narrow beam of light?**

Light and Matter

Have you ever been in a closed room with no windows? You can see nothing until you turn on a light or open a door and let in light from outside. Unlike a candle flame, a lightbulb, or the sun, most objects do not give off light on their own. These objects can be seen only if light waves from another source bounce off the object and into your eyes, as shown in **Figure 3-3.** The process of light striking an object and bouncing off is called **reflection.** Right now, you can see these words because light is reflecting from the page and into your eyes. ☑

Reading Check ☑

What must happen for you to see an object?

Figure 3-3 Light waves are given off by the lightbulb. Some of these light waves hit the page and are reflected. The student sees the page when some of these reflected waves enter the student's eyes.

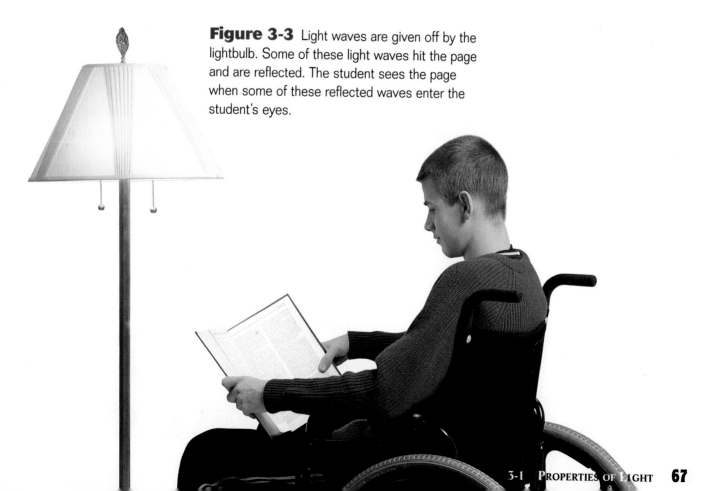

A An opaque object allows no light to pass through it.

B A translucent object allows some light to pass through it.

C A transparent object allows almost all light to pass through it.

Figure 3-4 Materials are opaque, translucent, or transparent depending on how much light passes through them.

Opaque, Translucent, and Transparent

When light waves strike an object, some of the light can be absorbed by the object, some of the light is reflected, and some of the light may pass through the object. How much light is absorbed, reflected, and passes through the object depends on what the object is made of.

Materials that let no light pass through them are *opaque* (oh PAYK). You cannot see other objects through opaque objects. Materials, such as glass, that allow nearly all the light to pass through are *transparent*. You can clearly see other objects through transparent materials. Other materials allow only some light to pass through so objects behind them cannot be seen clearly. These materials, such as waxed paper or frosted glass, are *translucent* (trans LEW sent). Examples of opaque, translucent, and transparent objects are shown in **Figure 3-4.**

Figure 3-5 Like all waves, ripples on a water surface have a wavelength.

A The wavelength is the distance between ripples.

B A cross section of the water surface is shown. The energy added by the impact of the rock causes water to pile up at each ripple.

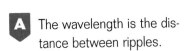

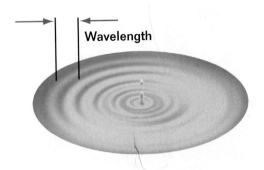

Wavelength

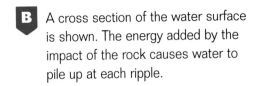

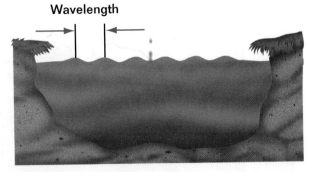

Wavelength

The Electromagnetic Spectrum

Light waves, like all waves, have a property called wavelength. Look at **Figure 3-5.** For ripples on a pond, the **wavelength** is the distance between the tops of two adjacent ripples. The number of wavelengths that pass a point in one second is the **frequency** of the wave. For waves that travel at the same speed, frequency and wavelength are related. As the wavelength decreases, the frequency increases.

The electromagnetic waves you see as light are part of the electromagnetic spectrum. **Figure 3-6** shows how electromagnetic waves are classified according to their wavelengths. All electromagnetic waves travel with a speed of about 300 million m/s in a vacuum. Electromagnetic waves also carry energy, just like the ripples in the pond. The energy carried by an electromagnetic wave increases as the wavelength decreases and the frequency increases.

Of all the electromagnetic waves, radio waves carry the least energy. They have wavelengths longer than about 1 cm. Television signals, as well as AM and FM radio signals, are types of radio waves. You can't see these waves with your eyes, nor can you sense them in any other way, but they are being absorbed, reflected, and transmitted by your body even as you read this! The highest-energy radio waves are called microwaves.

Earth's Ozone Layer
Ozone is formed high in Earth's atmosphere by sunlight striking oxygen molecules. However, chemical compounds called CFCs, which are used in air conditioners and refrigerators, can remove ozone from the ozone layer. To prevent this, the use of CFCs is being phased out. Visit the Glencoe Science Web Site at **www.glencoe.com/sec/ science** for more information about the effects of CFCs on the ozone layer.

Figure 3-6 Electromagnetic waves are classified according to their wavelengths and frequencies. Visible light is only a small section of the electromagnetic spectrum.

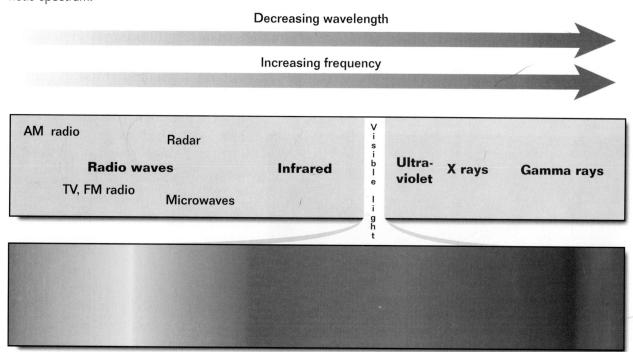

Decreasing wavelength

Increasing frequency

AM radio
Radar
Radio waves   Infrared   Visible light   Ultra-violet   X rays   Gamma rays
TV, FM radio
Microwaves

Mini Lab

Viewing Colors Through Color Filters

Procedure

1. Obtain sheets of red, green, and blue construction paper.
2. Obtain a piece of red cellophane and green cellophane.
3. Look at each sheet of paper through the red cellophane and record the color of each sheet.
4. Look at each sheet of colored paper through the green cellophane and record the color of each sheet.
5. Hold both pieces of cellophane together and look at each sheet of colored paper. Record the color of each sheet.

Analyze

Explain why the sheets of paper changed color when you looked at them through the pieces of cellophane.

Electromagnetic waves with wavelengths less than radio waves, but greater than visible light, are called infrared waves. You can't see these waves either, but they are emitted by the sun and make your skin feel warm.

The sun also emits ultraviolet waves that carry enough energy to damage living cells. Earth's atmosphere contains a layer of a compound called ozone that blocks most of the sun's ultraviolet waves from reaching Earth's surface. Still, exposure to those ultraviolet waves that do get through can cause sunburn. Exposure to these waves over a long period of time can lead to early aging of the skin and possibly skin cancer.

Visible light is the narrow range of the electromagnetic spectrum that we can detect with our eyes. What we see as different colors are electromagnetic waves of different wavelengths. Red light has the longest wavelength (lowest frequency), and blue light has the shortest wavelength (highest frequency).

Color

Why does grass look green or a rose look red? The answer has to do with the way objects absorb and reflect light. The light from the sun or a lightbulb may look white, but it is actually a mixture of light waves of all visible colors from red to blue, as shown in **Figure 3-7.** When all these colors are mixed together, the eye and the brain do not distinguish the individual colors but interpret the mixture as being white.

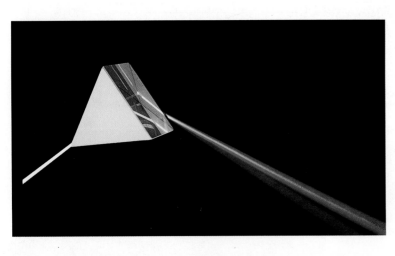

Figure 3-7 A beam of white light passing through a prism is separated into a spectrum of all the visible colors.

Figure 3-8

A Examine the pair of gym shoes and socks as seen under white light. **Why do the socks appear blue under white light?**

B The same shoes and socks were photographed through a red filter. **Why do the blue socks appear black when viewed under red light?**

When this mixture of waves strikes an object that is not transparent, the object absorbs some of the light energy. Some of the light waves that are not absorbed are reflected. If the object reflects the red waves and absorbs all the others, the object appears red. Similarly, objects that look blue reflect only the blue waves. Some objects reflect all the colors in the visible spectrum. These objects appear white, while objects that absorb all visible light appear black. **Figure 3-8** shows gym shoes and socks as seen under white light and as seen when viewed through a red filter, which allows only red light to pass through.

The Primary Colors

How many colors are there? Often, the visible spectrum is said to be made up of red, orange, yellow, green, blue, indigo, and violet light. But, this is usually done for convenience. In reality, humans can distinguish thousands of colors, including many such as brown, pink, and purple that are not found in the spectrum.

Light of almost any color can be made by mixing different amounts of red light, green light, and blue light. Red, green, and blue are called the primary colors. Look at **Figure 3-9.** White light is produced where beams of red, green, and blue light overlap. Yellow light is produced where red and green light overlap. However, even though the light looks yellow, it still consists of light waves of two different wavelengths. You see the color yellow because of the way your brain interprets the combination of the red and green light striking your eye.

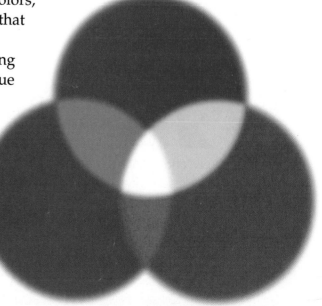

Figure 3-9 By mixing together light from the three primary colors—red, blue, and green—all the visible colors can be made.

Color Pigments

If you have ever painted a picture, you may have mixed together paints of different colors to make a new color. Materials like paint that are used to change the color of other objects, like the walls of a room or an artist's canvas, are called *pigments*. If you've ever tried mixing red and green paint together, you've probably realized that mixing piments forms colors in a different way than mixing colored lights.

Like all colored materials, pigments absorb some colors and reflect others. When you mix pigments, the colors that reach your eye are the colors that are not absorbed by the mixture. The primary pigment colors are not red, blue, and green, but instead are yellow, magenta, and cyan. You can make any colored pigment by mixing different amounts of these primary pigment colors, as shown in **Figure 3-10.**

The primary pigment colors are related to the primary light colors. A yellow pigment absorbs blue light and reflects red and green. A magenta pigment absorbs green light and reflects red and blue. A cyan pigment absorbs red light and reflects blue and green. Thus each of the primary pigment colors is white light with one of the primary light colors removed.

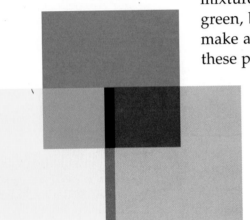

Figure 3-10 The three primary color pigments—yellow, magenta, and cyan—can form all the visible colors when mixed together in various amounts.

Section Assessment

1. Which has a higher frequency, red light or blue light?

2. What is the difference between an opaque object and a transparent object?

3. What colors are reflected by an object that appears black? Explain.

4. **Think Critically:** Why is it cooler to wear light-colored clothes on a hot day than dark clothes?

5. **Skill Builder**
   Observing and Inferring A white plastic bowl and a black plastic bowl have been sitting in sunlight. You observe that the black bowl feels warmer than the white bowl. From this information, infer which bowl absorbs and which bowl reflects more sunlight. If you need help, refer to Observing and Inferring in the **Skill Handbook** on page 704.

Science Journal Read an article about the greenhouse effect and draw a diagram in your Science Journal explaining how the greenhouse effect works.

Reflection and Mirrors

The Law of Reflection

Have you ever noticed your image in a pool or lake? If the surface of the water is smooth, you can see your image clearly. If the surface is wavy, your image seems to be distorted. The image you see is the result of light reflecting from the surface and traveling to your eye.

When a light ray strikes a surface and is reflected, the reflected ray obeys the law of reflection. **Figure 3-11** shows a light ray striking a surface and being reflected. Imagine a line drawn perpendicular to the surface where the light ray strikes the surface. This line is called the normal to the surface. The incoming ray and the normal form an angle called the angle of incidence. The reflected light ray also forms an angle with the normal called the angle of reflection. The **law of reflection** states that the angle of incidence is equal to the angle of reflection. This is true for any surface, no matter what material it is made of.

Reflection from Surfaces

Why can you see your reflection in some surfaces such as mirrors, and not see any reflection from a surface such as a piece of paper? The answer is related to difference in smoothness of the two surfaces.

What You'll Learn

► How light is reflected from rough and smooth surfaces
► How a plane mirror forms an image
► How concave and convex mirrors form an image

Vocabulary
law of reflection
focal point
focal length

Why It's Important

► Mirrors can change the direction of light waves and enable you to see images, such as your own face, that normally would not be in view.

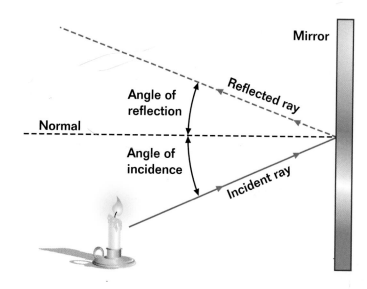

Figure 3-11 A light ray strikes a surface and is reflected. The angle of incidence is always equal to the angle of reflection. This is the law of reflection.

Figure 3-12 A highly magnified view of the surface of a paper towel shows that the surface is made of many cellulose wood fibers that make it rough and uneven.

Magnification: 35×

The surface of the paper is not as smooth as the surface of a mirror. Even though the paper may look smooth, **Figure 3-12** shows that under a microscope, its surface looks rough. The uneven surface of the paper causes light rays to be reflected in many directions as shown in **Figure 3-13.** The reflection of light waves from a rough surface is diffuse reflection. The mirrorlike reflection from a smooth surface that produces a sharp image of an object is called regular reflection. ☑

A piece of foil is smooth enough to act like a mirror and produce a regular reflection. If you crumple the foil, its surface no longer acts like one mirror. Now it acts like many tiny mirrors. Each of these tiny mirrors produces a regular reflection, but the reflections go in many different directions.

Reading Check ☑

Why does a rough surface cause a diffuse reflection?

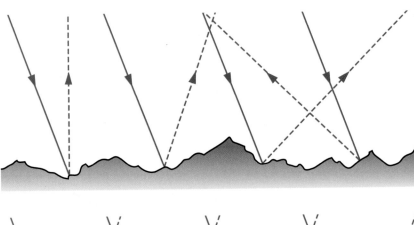

A

Figure 3-13 A rough surface (A) causes parallel light rays to be reflected in many different directions. A smooth surface (B) causes parallel light rays to be reflected in a single direction.

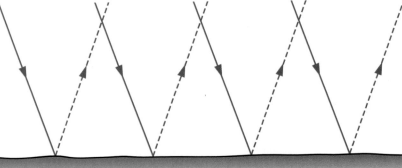

B

Reflection by Plane Mirrors

Did you glance in the mirror before leaving for school this morning? If you did, you probably saw your reflection in a plane mirror. A plane mirror is a mirror with a flat reflecting surface. The mirror produced an image of you that seemed to be coming from behind the mirror. The image in the mirror also had your left and right sides reversed. How was that image formed?

Figure 3-14A shows a person looking into a plane mirror. Light waves from the sun or a source of artificial light strike each part of the person. These light rays bounce off the person according to the law of reflection, and some of these rays strike the mirror. The rays that strike the mirror also are reflected according to the law of reflection. **Figure 3-14A** shows the path traveled by some of the rays that have bounced off the person and have been reflected by the mirror into the person's eye.

Why does the image seem to be behind the mirror? Your brain processes the light rays that enter your eyes and creates the sensation of seeing. Your brain interprets the light rays that have bounced off the mirror as having followed the path shown by the dashed lines in **Figure 3-14B.** The resulting image looks as though it is behind the mirror, even though there is nothing there. The image appears to be the same distance behind the mirror as the person is in front of the mirror.

Wave or Particle?

When a particle like a marble or a basketball bounces off a surface, it obeys the law of reflection. Because light also obeyed the law of reflection, people once thought that light must consist of streams of particles. Today, experiments have shown that light can behave as though it were both a wave and a stream of energy bundles called photons. Read an article about photons and write a description in your Science Journal.

Figure 3-14 A plane mirror forms an image by changing the direction of light rays.

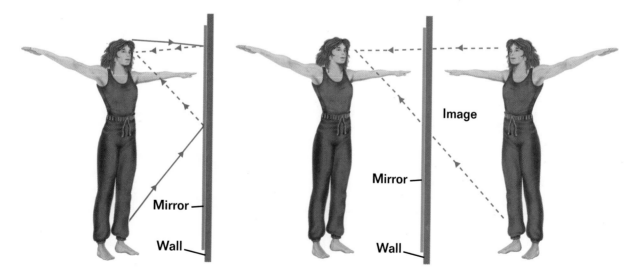

A Light rays that bounce off a person strike the mirror. Some of these light rays are reflected into the person's eye. As examples, the figure shows a light ray from the person's head and a ray from the leg.

B The light rays shown entering the person's eye in **Figure 3-14A** seem to be coming from a person behind the mirror.

Concave and Convex Mirrors

Some mirrors are not flat. A concave mirror has a surface that is curved inward, like the inside of a spoon. Unlike plane mirrors, concave mirrors cause light rays to come together, or converge. This difference causes the two types of mirrors to form different types of images.

A straight line drawn perpendicular to the center of a concave or convex mirror is called the optical axis. Look at **Figure 3-15A.** For a concave mirror, light rays that travel parallel to the optical axis and strike the mirror are reflected so that they pass through a single point on the optical axis called the **focal point.** The distance along the optical axis from the center of the mirror to the focal point is called the **focal length.**

VISUALIZING
Images Formed by Concave Mirrors

Figure 3-15 The image formed by a concave mirror depends on the location of the object.

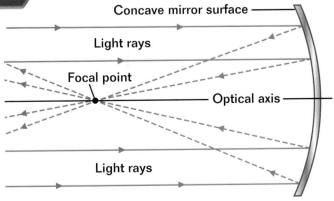

A A concave mirror reflects all light rays traveling parallel to the optical axis so that they pass through the focal point.

B If the object is farther from the mirror than the focal length, the mirror forms an image that is inverted.

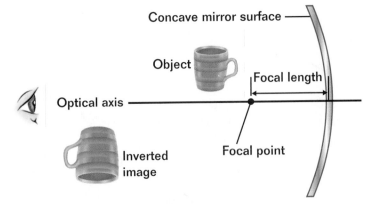

C This photograph shows the image formed by a concave mirror when the object is more than one focal length from the mirror.

The image formed by a concave mirror depends on the position of the object relative to the focal point of the mirror. **Figure 3-15B** shows how the image is formed if the object is farther from the mirror than the focal point, and **Figure 3-15C** is a photograph of such an image. The image is upside down, or inverted, and the size of the image decreases as the object is moved farther away from the mirror.

Light rays from an object placed at the focal point strike the mirror and are reflected so they travel parallel to the optical axis. If a light source is placed at the focal point, a beam of light will be produced. For example, in a flashlight the bulb is placed at the focal point of a concave reflector.

However, if the object is closer to the mirror than the focal point, **Figures 3-15D** and **3-15E** show that the image formed is upright. The image gets larger as the object moves closer to the mirror.

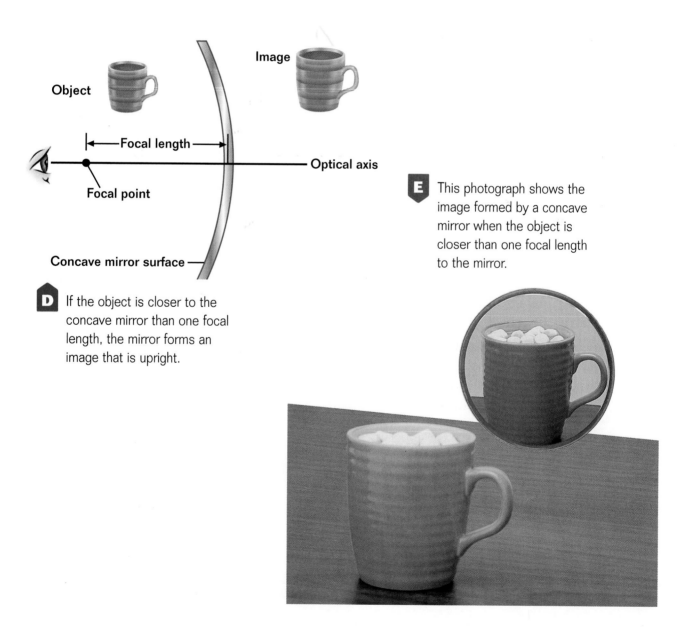

D If the object is closer to the concave mirror than one focal length, the mirror forms an image that is upright.

E This photograph shows the image formed by a concave mirror when the object is closer than one focal length to the mirror.

Figure 3-16 A convex mirror forms an image.

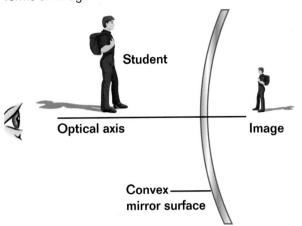

Student

Optical axis

Image

Convex mirror surface

A No matter how far the object is from a convex mirror, the image is always upright and smaller than the object.

B A convex mirror causes incoming light rays that are traveling parallel to the optical axis to spread apart after they are reflected.

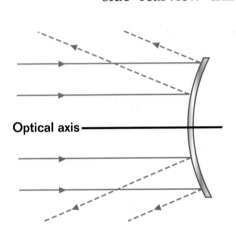

Optical axis

A convex mirror has surface that curves outward, like the outside of a spoon. **Figure 3-16A** shows how a convex mirror causes light rays to spread apart, or diverge. **Figure 3-16B** shows that the image formed by a convex mirror seems to be behind the mirror, like the image formed by a plane mirror. Like a plane mirror, the image formed by a convex mirror is always upright. But unlike a plane mirror, the image formed by a convex mirror is always smaller than the object.

Convex mirrors are used as security mirrors mounted above the aisles in stores and as outside rearview mirrors on cars and trucks. When used in this way on cars and trucks, objects seem smaller and farther away than they really are. As a result, these mirrors sometimes carry a warning that objects viewed in the mirror are closer than they seem.

Section Assessment

1. As you walk toward a large, vertical plane mirror, describe what happens to your image.

2. If the surface of a concave mirror is made more curved, what happens to its focal length?

3. **Think Critically:** The surface of a car is covered with dust and looks dull. After the car is washed and waxed, you can see your image reflected in the car's surface. Explain.

4. **Skill Builder**
   Forming a Hypothesis When you look at a window at night, you can sometimes see two images of yourself. Make a hypothesis to explain why two images are seen. If you need help, refer to Forming a Hypothesis in the **Skill Handbook** on page 706.

Using Computers

Spreadsheet Design a table using spreadsheet software to compare the images formed by plane, concave, and convex mirrors. Include in your table how the images depend on the distance of the object from the mirror. If you need help, refer to page 722.

Reflection from a Plane Mirror

Materials

- Flashlight
- Small plane mirror, at least 10 cm on a side
- Protractor
- Metric ruler
- Scissors
- Black construction paper
- Tape
- Modeling clay

A light ray strikes the surface of a plane mirror and is reflected. Is there a relationship between the direction of the incoming light ray and the direction of the reflected light ray?

What You'll Investigate

How does the angle of incidence compare with the angle of reflection for a plane mirror?

Goals

- **Measure** the angle of incidence and the angle of reflection for a light ray incident on a plane mirror.

Procedure

1. With the scissors, **cut** a slit in the construction paper and **tape** it over the flashlight lens. Make sure the slit is centered on the lens.

2. **Place** the mirror at one end of the unlined paper. Push the mirror into the lump of clay so it stands vertically, and tilt the mirror so it leans slightly toward the table.

3. **Measure** with the ruler to find the center of the bottom edge of the mirror and mark it. Then,

use the protractor and the ruler to **draw** a line on the paper perpendicular to the mirror from the mark. Label this line P.

4. Using the protractor and the ruler, **draw** lines on the paper outward from the mark at the center of the mirror at angles of 30°, 45°, and 60° to line P.

5. Turn on the flashlight and place it so the beam is along the 60° line. This is the angle of incidence. **Locate** the reflected beam on the paper, and **measure** the angle the reflected beam makes with line P. **Record** this angle in your data table. This is the angle of reflection. If you cannot see the reflected beam, slightly increase the tilt of the mirror.

6. Repeat step 5 for the 30°, 45°, and P lines.

Conclude and Apply

1. What happened to the beam of light when it was shined along line P?

2. What can you **infer** about the relationship between the angle of incidence and the angle of reflection?

Refraction and Lenses

Refraction

If you have ever looked at a glass of water that had a pencil in it, you may have noticed that the pencil appeared bent, as in **Figure 3-17.** You may have noticed in the Explore Activity that the penny under water seemed closer than the other penny. These images are due to the bending of light rays as they pass from one material to another. What causes light rays to change direction?

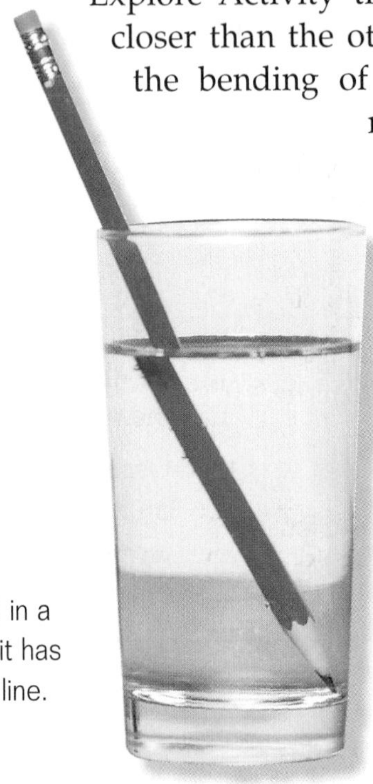

Figure 3-17 A pencil in a glass of water looks as if it has been broken at the water line.

The Speeds of Light

The speed of light in empty space is about 300 million m/s. Light passing through a medium such as air, water, or glass travels slower than the speed of light in empty space. This is because the atoms that make up the medium interact with the light wave and slow it down. **Figure 3-18** shows how slowly light moves in some materials.

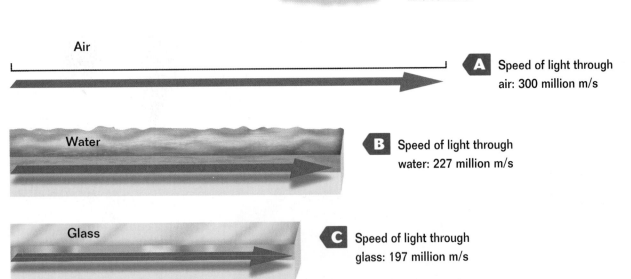

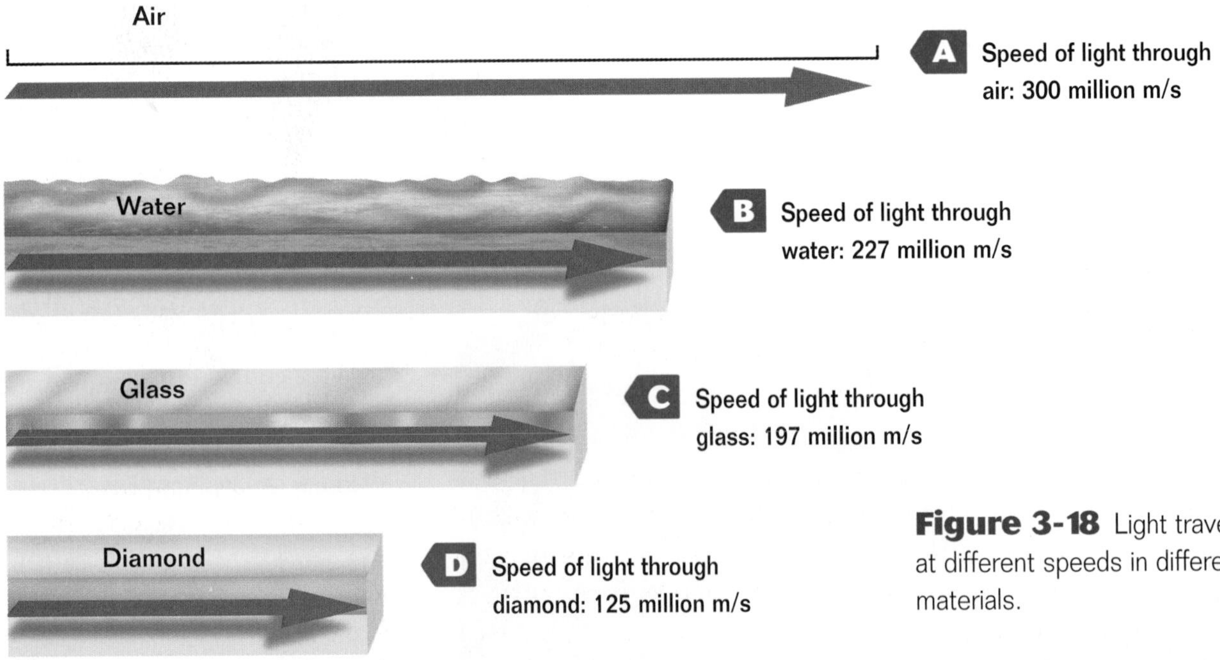

Air

A Speed of light through air: 300 million m/s

Water

B Speed of light through water: 227 million m/s

Glass

C Speed of light through glass: 197 million m/s

Diamond

D Speed of light through diamond: 125 million m/s

Figure 3-18 Light travels at different speeds in different materials.

Figure 3-19 A light ray is bent as it travels from air into glass. **In which medium does light travel more slowly?**

The Refraction of Light Waves

What happens when light waves travel from air into water where the speed of light is different? If the wave is traveling at an angle to the boundary between two materials, it changes direction. The bending of a light wave due to a change in speed when the wave moves from one medium to another is called **refraction. Figure 3-19** shows an example of refraction. The larger the change in speed, the more the light wave is refracted. ☑

Why does a change in speed cause the light wave to bend? Imagine a set of wheels on a car that travels from pavement to mud. The wheel that enters the mud first is slowed, while the other wheel continues at the original speed. This causes the wheel axle to turn as shown in **Figure 3-20,** and the wheels change direction.

Light behaves in a similar manner. Imagine again a light wave traveling from air into water. The first part of the wave to enter the water is slowed, just as the wheel that first hits the mud is slowed. Then, the rest of the wave is slowed down as it enters the water so the whole wave is turned, just like the axle.

Reading Check

What causes light to bend?

Convex and Concave Lenses

Do you like snapping pictures of your friends and family with a camera? Have you ever watched a bird through binoculars or peered at something tiny through a magnifying glass? All of these involve the use of lenses. A **lens** is a transparent object with at least one curved side that causes light to bend. The amount of bending can be controlled by making the sides more or less curved. The more curved the sides, the more a ray of light entering the lens is bent.

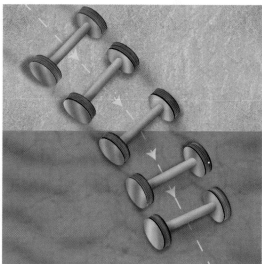

Figure 3-20 An axle turns as the wheels cross the boundary between pavement and mud. **How would the axle turn if the wheels were going from mud to pavement?**

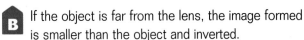

Mini Lab

Forming an Image with a Lens

Procedure

1. Fill a glass test tube with water and seal it with a stopper.
2. Write your name on a 3 × 5 card. Lay the test tube on the card and observe the appearance of your name. Record your observations.
3. Hold the test tube about 1 cm above the card and observe the appearance of your name. Record your observations.
4. Now, observe what happens to your name as you slowly move the test tube away from the card. Record your observations.

Analyze

1. Is the water-filled test tube a concave lens or a convex lens?
2. Compare the image formed when the test tube was close to the card with the image formed when the test tube was far from the card.

Convex Lenses

A lens that is thicker in the center than at the edges is a **convex lens.** Convex lenses are also called converging lenses. Light rays traveling parallel to the optical axis are bent so they meet at the focal point, as shown in **Figure 3-21A.** If the surface is highly curved, the focal point is close to the lens and the focal length is short.

The image formed by a convex lens is similar to the image formed by a concave mirror. For both, the type of image depends on how far the object is from the focal point. Look at **Figure 3-21B.** If the object is farther than two focal lengths from the lens, the image is inverted and smaller than the object.

If the object is closer to the lens than one focal length, then the rays coming from points on the object diverge after passing through the lens, as shown in **Figure 3-21C.** The image formed is right-side up and larger than the object. Have you ever used

Figure 3-21 A convex lens forms an image that depends on the distance from the object to the lens.

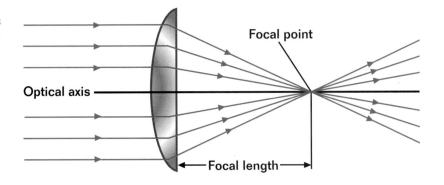

A Light rays parallel to the optical axis are bent so that they pass through the focal point.

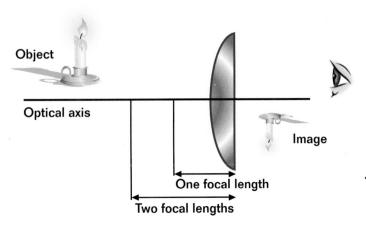

B If the object is far from the lens, the image formed is smaller than the object and inverted.

C If the object is closer to the lens than one focal length, the image formed is enlarged and upright.

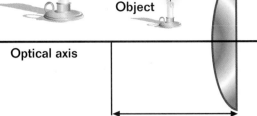

a magnifying glass? The image formed was right-side up and larger than the object. The image continues to get larger as the magnifying glass is brought closer to the object.

Concave Lens

A lens that is thicker at the edges than in the middle is a **concave lens.** A concave lens is also called a diverging lens. **Figure 3-22** shows how light rays traveling parallel to the optical axis are bent after passing through a concave lens.

A concave lens causes light rays to diverge, and the light rays are not brought to a focus. The type of image formed by a concave lens is similar to that formed by a convex mirror. The image is upright and smaller than the object. Concave lenses are used in eyeglasses to correct problems people sometimes have in seeing objects that are far away.

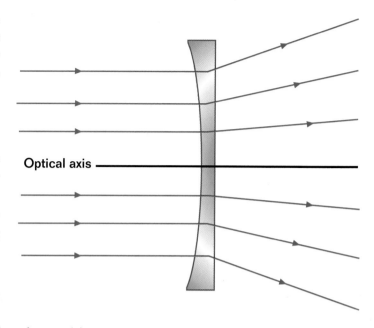

Optical axis

Figure 3-22 A concave lens causes light rays traveling parallel to the optical axis to diverge.

Section Assessment

1. How is the image formed by a concave lens similar to the image formed by a convex mirror?
2. To magnify an object, would you use a convex lens or a concave lens?
3. Describe two ways, using convex and concave lenses, to form an image that is smaller than the object.
4. **Think Critically:** A light wave is bent more as it travels from air to glass than in traveling from air to water. Is the speed of light greater in water or glass? Explain.
5. **Skill Builder**
   Predicting Air that is cool is more dense than air that is warm. Look at **Figure 3-18** and predict whether the speed of light is faster in warm air or cool air. If you need help, refer to Predicting in the **Skill Handbook** on page 714.

Using Math

Earth is about 150 000 000 km from the sun. Use the formula *distance = speed × time* to calculate how many seconds it takes a beam of light to travel from Earth to the sun. About how many minutes does it take?

Materials

* Convex lens
* Modeling clay
* Meterstick
* Flashlight
* Masking tape
* Cardboard with white surface, about 20-cm square

Image Formation by a Convex Lens

The type of image formed by a convex lens, also called a converging lens, is related to the distance of the object from the lens. This distance is called the object distance. The location of the image is also related to the distance of the object from the lens. The distance from the lens to the image is called the image distance. What happens to the position of the image as the object gets nearer or farther from the lens?

What You'll Investigate

How are the image distance and object distance related for a convex lens?

Goals

* **Measure** the image distance as the object distance changes.
* **Observe** the type of image formed as the object distance changes.

Safety Precautions

Procedure

1. **Design** a data table in which to record your data. You will need three columns in your table. One column will be for the object distance, another will be for the image distance, and the third will be for the type of image.

2. **Use** the modeling clay to make the lens stand vertically upright on the lab table.

3. **Form** the letter F on the glass surface of the flashlight with masking tape.

4. Turn on the flashlight and place it 1 m from the lens. **Position** the flashlight so the flashlight beam is shining through the lens.

5. **Record** the distance from the flashlight to the lens in the object distance column in your data table.

6. Hold the cardboard vertically upright on the other side of the lens, and move it back and forth

Convex Lens Data		
Object Distance	Image Distance	Image Type

until a sharp image of the letter F is obtained.

7. **Measure** the distance of the card from the lens using the meterstick, and **record** this distance in the image distance column in your data table.

8. **Record** in the third column of your data table whether the image is upright or inverted, and smaller or larger.

9. Repeat steps 6–9 for object distances of 50 cm and 25 cm.

Conclude and Apply

1. How did the image distance change as the object distance decreased?

2. How did the image change as the object distance decreased?

3. What would happen to the size of the image if the flashlight were much farther away than 1 m?

Microscopes, Telescopes, and Cameras

Microscopes

Lenses have been used since the early 1600s to produce images of objects too small to be seen with the eye alone. Today, a compound microscope like the one in **Figure 3-23A** uses a combination of lenses to magnify objects by as much as 2500 times.

Figure 3-23B shows how a microscope forms an image. An object, such as a drop of water from a pond, is placed close to a convex lens called the objective lens. This lens produces an enlarged image inside the microscope tube. The light rays from that image then pass through a second convex lens called the eyepiece, or ocular, lens. This lens further magnifies the image formed by the objective lens. This results in a much larger image than a single lens can produce.

Figure 3-23 A compound microscope uses lenses to magnify objects.

A A compound microscope often has more than one objective lens, each giving a different magnification. A light underneath the objective lens makes the image bright enough to see clearly.

B The objective lens in a compound microscope forms an enlarged image, which is then magnified by the eyepiece lens. **How would the image be affected if the eyepiece lens were a concave lens?**

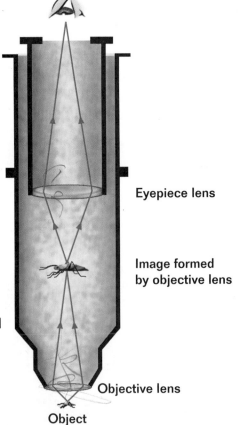

Eyepiece lens

Image formed by objective lens

Objective lens

Object

Telescopes

While microscopes are used to magnify very small objects, telescopes are used to examine objects that may be quite large but are far away. The first telescopes also were invented in the early 1600s, at about the same time as the first microscopes. Much of what we know about the distant universe has come from images and other information gathered by telescopes.

Refracting Telescopes

The simplest refracting telescopes use two convex lenses to form an image of a distant object. Just as in a compound microscope, light passes through an objective lens that forms an image. That image is then magnified by an eyepiece lens, as shown in **Figure 3-24.**

An important difference between a telescope and a microscope is the size of the objective lens. More light from a faraway object can enter a large objective lens than a small one. This makes images appear brighter and more detailed when they are magnified by the eyepiece. Increasing the size of the objective lens makes it possible to see stars and galaxies that are too far away to see with a telescope that has a small objective lens. Thus, the main purpose of a telescope is not to magnify the image, but to gather as much light as possible from distant objects. In **Figure 3-25**, the largest refracting telescope ever made is shown.

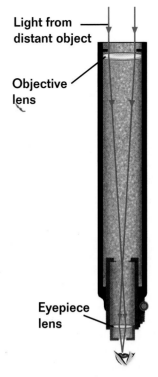

Figure 3-24 A refracting telescope is made from an objective lens and an eyepiece lens. The objective lens forms an image that is magnified by the eyepiece lens.

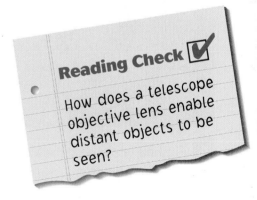

Reading Check

How does a telescope objective lens enable distant objects to be seen?

Figure 3-25 The refracting telescope at the Yerkes Observatory in Wisconsin has the largest objective lens in the world. It has a diameter of 1 m.

Reflecting Telescopes

There are limits to how big a refracting telescope can be. One problem is that its objective lens can be supported only around its edges. If the lens is extremely large, it cannot be supported enough to keep it from sagging slightly under its own weight. This causes the image it forms to become distorted.

Reflecting telescopes can be made much larger than refracting telescopes. This is because they use a concave mirror instead of an objective lens to gather light from a distant object, as shown in **Figure 3-26B.** A small plane mirror called a secondary mirror is used to reflect the image toward the side of the telescope tube, where it is magnified by an eyepiece.

Because only the one reflecting surface on the mirror needs to be carefully made, telescope mirrors are less expensive to make than lenses of a similar size. Also, mirrors can be supported more rigidly on their back side so they can be made much larger without sagging under their own weight. The Keck Telescope in Hawaii is the largest reflecting telescope in the world with a mirror 10 m in diameter. **Figure 3-26A** shows another one of the largest telescopes in the world, the reflecting telescope at Mount Palomar in southern California.

Figure 3-26 Reflecting telescopes gather light by using a concave mirror.

A The Hale telescope at the Mount Palomar observatory in southern California has a concave mirror that is 5.1 m in diameter.

B Light entering the telescope tube is reflected by a concave mirror onto the secondary mirror. An eyepiece lens is used to magnify the image formed by the concave mirror. The secondary mirror in the largest telescopes usually reflects the rays through a hole in the concave mirror, instead of the side of the tube.

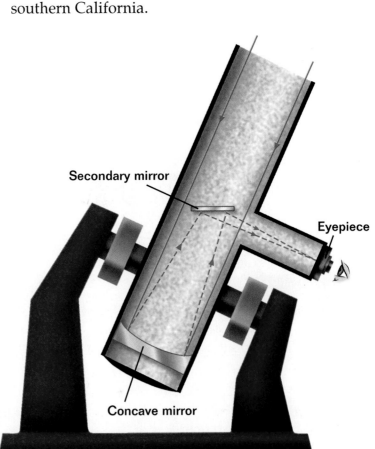

Secondary mirror

Eyepiece

Concave mirror

Cameras

You may have seen a number of photographs today in books, magazines, and newspapers. And, you may have used acamera yourself to take photographs. A typical camera hasa convex lens that forms an image on a section of film. Remember that a convex lens forms an image that is reduced and inverted if the object is more than two focal lengths away. A camera lens is a convex lens used in this way. Look at the camera shown in **Figure 3-27.** When the shutter is open, the convex lens forms an image on a piece of film that is sensitive to light. The film contains chemicals that undergo chemical reactions when struck by light. This causes light areas and dark areas in the image to be recorded. If the film is sensitive to color, the colors of the object also are recorded.

An image that is too bright may overexpose the film. If there is too little light that reaches the film, the image may be too dark. To control the amount of light reaching the film, a camera also contains a device called the diaphragm.

Figure 3-27 A camera uses a convex lens to form an image on a piece of light-sensitive film. The image formed by a camera lens is smaller than the object. The amount of light striking the film is controlled by the diaphragm.

Problem Solving

Radio Telescopes

On a clear night, you may be able to see the visible light from hundreds of stars. But, stars and galaxies emit radio waves, as well as visible light. Unlike light waves, radio waves from space are not affected by turbulence in Earth's atmosphere. These radio waves can be detected even on cloudy or stormy nights when no stars can be seen. By studying these radio waves, scientists can learn about the birth and death of stars and galaxies.

Just as reflecting and refracting telescopes collect light from distant stars and galaxies, radio telescopes collect radio waves. The photograph shows the radio telescope at Green Banks, West Virginia. The collector of a radio telescope is usually called the *dish,* and the device supported above the center of the dish is the *detector.* The detector contains electronic instruments that help to amplify and record the radio waves.

Solve the Problem

1. Examine the photograph carefully. Is a radio telescope a reflecting telescope or a refracting telescope? Explain.
2. How are the position of the detector and the focal point of the radio telescope related?

Think Critically: Do you think the information gathered by radio telescopes could be improved if a radio telescope were placed into orbit above Earth's atmosphere? Why or why not?

interNET
CONNECTION

Visit the Glencoe
Science Web Site at
**www.glencoe.com/
sec/science** for more
information about
cameras.

The diaphragm is opened to let more light onto the film and closed to reduce the amount of light striking the film.

Camera Lenses

The image on the film depends on the camera lens used. Suppose you wished to photograph a friend. The size of your friend's image on the film depends on the focal length of the lens. The shorter the focal length, the smaller the image. To focus the image sharply, the lens must be moved closer to the film as the focal length is made smaller.

If you wanted the photograph to include your friend and the surrounding scenery, you would use a wide-angle lens. This lens has a short focal length and is positioned close to the film. If, instead, you wished to photograph only your friend's face, you might use a telephoto lens. This lens has a long focal length and must be positioned far from the film.

With a zoom lens, you can control the size of your friend's image in a photograph. The focal length of a zoom lens can be adjusted by moving the lens closer or farther from the film. A zoom lens is useful because it can be used as both a telephoto and a wide-angle lens.

Section Assessment

1. How is a compound microscope different from a magnifying glass?

2. Why are reflecting telescopes the biggest telescopes and not refracting telescopes?

3. Why is the objective lens of a refracting telescope bigger than the objective lens of a microscope?

4. **Think Critically:** If you could buy only one lens for your camera, what type of lens would you buy? Why?

5. **Skill Builder**
   Communicating Scientists need to clearly explain to others the results of their experiments, as well as their hypotheses and ideas. They do this by carefully writing research papers. Do the **Chapter 3 Skill Activity** on page 728 to learn how to write a research paper.

Using Math

The size of an image is related to the magnification of an optical instrument by the following formula:

Image size = magnification × object size

A blood cell has a diameter of about 0.001 cm. How large is the image formed by a microscope with a magnification of 1000?

Scientific Notation

A microscope allows us to see extremely small organisms. A cell that measures only 0.0007 cm in diameter can be seen clearly with a powerful microscope. A telescope can be used to see far-away objects, such as the galaxy, left. By using a telescope, we can see a galaxy as far as 2.2 million light-years away.

Scientists and mathematicians have devised a short way to write extremely small or large numbers. This is known as scientific notation. In scientific notation, a number is written as a number that is at least 1 but less than 10 multiplied by a power of 10.

How to Determine Scientific Notations

1. To write 2 200 000 in scientific notation, you first need a number that is at least 1 but less than 10. The number 2.2 is related to 2 200 000 and is at least 1 but less than 10. If you divide 2 200 000 by 2.2, you get 1 000 000. So, 2 200 000 = 2.2 × 1 000 000. Numbers such as 1 000 000 can be written as a power of ten.

$$10 = 10^1$$
$$100 = 10 \times 10 = 10^2$$
$$1000 = 10 \times 10 \times 10 = 10^3$$
$$10\ 000 = 10 \times 10 \times 10 \times 10 = 10^4$$
$$100\ 000 = 10 \times 10 \times 10 \times 10 \times 10 = 10^5$$
$$1\ 000\ 000 = 10 \times 10 \times 10 \times 10 \times 10 \times 10 = 10^6$$

$2.2 \times 1\ 000\ 000$ in scientific notation is 2.2×10^6.

2. To write 0.0007 in scientific notation, you first need a number that is at least 1 but less than 10. You can see that 7 is related to 0.0007 and is at least 1 but less than 10. If you divide 0.0007 by 7, you get 0.0001. So, 0.0007 = 7 × 0.0001. Numbers such as 0.0001 can be written as a power of ten using a negative number.

$$0.1 = \frac{1}{10} = 10^{-1}$$

$$0.01 = \frac{1}{100} = 10^{-2}$$

$$0.001 = \frac{1}{1000} = 10^{-3}$$

7×0.0001 in scientific notation is 7×10^{-4}.

Practice PROBLEMS

1. One type of bacteria measures 0.000 015 cm in length. Write this number in scientific notation.
2. Pluto is 5.92 billion km from the sun. Write this number in scientific notation.
3. A light-year is the distance that light travels in one year. Light travels at about 300 million m/s. How many kilometers are in a light-year? Write your answer in scientific notation.

For a **preview** of this chapter, study this Reviewing Main Ideas before you read the chapter. After you have studied this chapter, you can use the Reviewing Main Ideas to **review** the chapter.

The Glencoe MindJogger, Audiocassettes, and CD-ROM provide additional opportunities for review.

Section 3-1 PROPERTIES OF LIGHT

Light is an **electromagnetic wave** and can travel in a vacuum. The energy carried by a light wave increases as the **frequency** gets larger. When a light wave strikes an object, some of the light wave's energy may be reflected, some may be absorbed, and some may be transmitted through the object. The color of a light wave depends on its wavelength. The color of an object depends on which wavelengths of light are reflected by the object. Light of almost any color can be made by mixing different amounts of red, green, and blue light. Mixing pigments such as paints makes colors by subtracting colors from the light that strikes the pigments. *How does the wavelength of a light wave change as its frequency increases?*

Section 3-2 REFLECTION OF LIGHT

Light reflected from the surface of an object obeys the **law of reflection:** the angle of incidence equals the angle of reflection. Diffuse reflection occurs when a surface is rough, while regular reflection occurs from very smooth surfaces and produces a clear, mirrorlike image. The image seen in a plane mirror seems to come from behind the mirror and is the same size as the object. The image formed by a concave mirror depends on the position of the object relative to the **focal point** of the mirror. Convex mirrors cause light waves to diverge and produce upright images smaller than the object. *Why doesn't diffuse reflection produce sharp, clear images?*

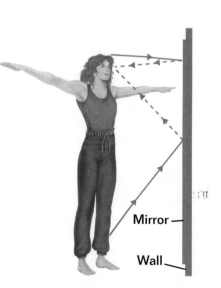

Mirror

Wall

Reading Check ✔

- Describe **Figure 3-15** so that a student in the third or fourth grade could understand the ideas shown.

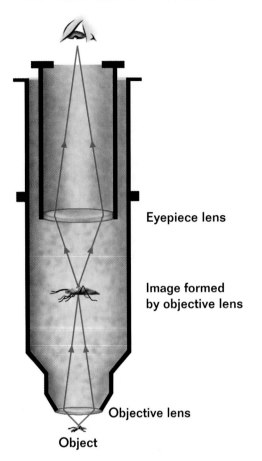

Eyepiece lens

Image formed by objective lens

Objective lens

Object

Section 3-3 REFRACTION OF LIGHT

Light waves tend to travel in straight lines, unless they change speed when they travel into another medium. Then, the waves change direction at the boundary between the two media. This change in direction is called **refraction.** A **convex lens** causes light waves to converge. The type of image formed by a convex lens depends on the location of the object relative to the focal point. A **concave lens** causes light waves to diverge. *How close must an object be to a convex lens to form an enlarged image?*

Section 3-4 MICROSCOPES, TELESCOPES, AND CAMERAS

A compound microscope is used to enlarge small objects. A convex objective lens forms an enlarged image that is further enlarged by an eyepiece lens. Most telescopes today are reflecting telescopes that use a concave mirror to form a real image that is enlarged by an eyepiece. The larger the mirror, the more light it can gather and the better the image formed by the telescope. Cameras use a lens to form an image on a light-sensitive piece of film. *Do the lenses used in microscopes, telescopes, and cameras cause light rays to converge or diverge?*

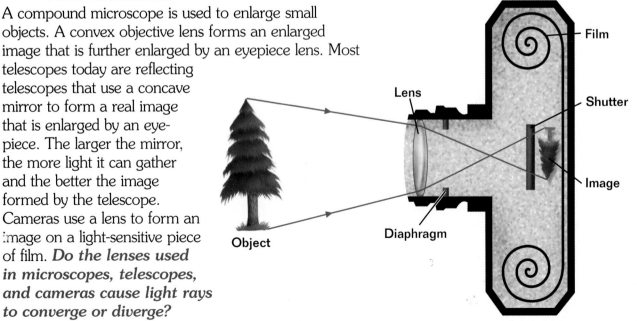

Film

Lens

Shutter

Image

Object

Diaphragm

Using Vocabulary

a. concave lens	**g.** law of reflection
b. convex lens	**h.** lens
c. electromagnetic wave	**i.** light ray
	j. medium
d. focal length	**k.** reflection
e. focal point	**l.** refraction
f. frequency	**m.** wavelength

Match each phrase with the correct term from the list of Vocabulary words.

1. the bending of light when it changes speed in passing from one material to another
2. a part of a light wave traveling in a single direction
3. the number of wavelengths that pass a point in 1 s
4. the distance of the focal point from the center of the lens or mirror
5. the material in which a light wave travels

Checking Concepts

Choose the word or phrase that completes the sentence or answers the question.

6. What type of image does a plane mirror form?
   A) upright
   B) inverted
   C) magnified
   D) all of the above

7. How are light waves different than radio waves?
   A) Light waves have a higher frequency.
   B) Light waves have a longer wavelength.
   C) Light waves have a longer focal length.
   D) Radio waves are sound waves.

8. Which of the following types of electromagnetic waves is the most energetic?
   A) visible
   B) X rays
   C) infrared
   D) ultraviolet

9. The lowest-frequency visible light waves have what color?
   A) blue
   B) red
   C) infrared
   D) ultraviolet

10. Which of the following is true about an object that looks red?
    A) It absorbs only red light.
    B) It transmits only red light.
    C) It can be seen only in red light.
    D) None of the above.

11. In reflection, how is the angle of incidence related to the angle of reflection?
    A) It is always the same.
    B) It is always greater.
    C) It is twice as large.
    D) It depends on the change in the speed of light.

12. Why does a camera have a diaphragm?
    A) to control the amount of light striking the film
    B) to move the lens closer to the film
    C) to change the focal length of the lens
    D) to close the shutter

13. Which of the following can be used to magnify objects?
    A) a concave lens
    B) a convex lens
    C) a convex mirror
    D) all of the above

14. What is an object that reflects some light and transmits some light called?
    A) colored
    B) diffuse
    C) opaque
    D) translucent

15. How do the sides of a convex lens change as its focal length decreases?
    A) They become flatter.
    B) They become concave.
    C) They become more curved.
    D) They become regular reflectors.

Thinking Critically

16. Do all light rays that strike a convex lens pass through the focal point?

17. Does a plane mirror focus light rays? Why or why not?

18. Explain why a rough surface, such as a road, is a better reflector when it is wet.

19. If the speed of light were the same in all materials, could lenses be used to magnify objects? Why or why not?

20. A singer is wearing a blue outfit. What color spotlights would make the outfit appear black? Explain.

Developing Skills

If you need help, refer to the Skill Handbook.

21. **Using Graphs:** The graph below shows how the distance of an image from a convex lens is related to the distance of the object from the lens.

    A) How does the image move as the object gets closer to the lens?
    B) The magnification of the image is given by:
    $$magnification = \frac{image\ distance}{object\ distance}$$
    How does the magnification change as the object gets closer to the lens?
    C) What is the magnification when the object is 20 cm from the lens?

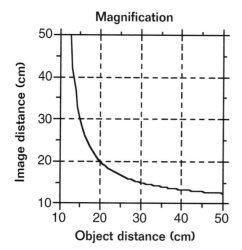

Test-Taking Tip

Practice, Practice, Practice Practice to improve *your* performance. Don't compare yourself with anyone else.

Test Practice

Use these questions to test your Science Proficiency.

1. Two vases are identical except one is glass and the other is made of black plastic. If they are side by side in a well-lit room, which vase absorbs more light energy?
   A) The black vase absorbs more.
   B) The glass vase absorbs more.
   C) They absorb the same amount.
   D) They both absorb no light energy.

2. In glass, blue light travels slightly slower than red light. If a beam of white light passes through a glass convex lens, which statement describes what happens?
   A) The blue light is brought to a focus closer to the lens than the red light.
   B) The red light is focused closer to the lens than the blue light.
   C) All colors are focused at the same point, regardless of how slowly they move in the glass lens.
   D) Not enough information has been given.

States of Matter

Skills Preview

Skill Builders
- Make and Use a Graph
- Compare and Contrast

Activities
- Observe
- Design

MiniLabs
- Predict

Reading Check ✔

Before beginning this chapter,
read the Reviewing Main Ideas
pages at the end of the chapter. They will help you focus
on the most important ideas
in each section.

Explore Activity

Arctic glaciers flow across Greenland's landscape and break off into the sea, creating icebergs. The icebergs slowly melt as they travel across Earth's oceans. As cold water mixes with warm, some of it is drawn into the air as vapor—only to fall again as rain, sleet, or snow. Sometimes the rain falls in torrents driven by furious, hurricane-force winds. What unseen and relentless forces drive this never-ending cycle of water changing from a solid to a liquid to a gas and back again?

Observe a Freezing Liquid

1. Your teacher will bring you a test tube containing an unknown, liquid substance. Place the test tube in a rack, and insert a thermometer into the substance.

2. Starting immediately, read and record the substance's temperature, appearance, and physical state every 30 s.

3. Continue making measurements and observations until your teacher tells you to stop or the substance reaches room temperature.

Science Journal

In your Science Journal, describe your experiment and what you discovered. Were you surprised by anything that happened while you were taking data? Explain why you think the mystery substance behaved as it did.

4·1 Solids

Kinetic Theory of Matter

Figure 4-1 In nature, water can exist in three physical states. **What physical states of water do you see in this photo taken near Juneau, Alaska?**

You're familiar with water in the three physical states shown in **Figure 4-1.** The **state of matter** tells you whether a material is a solid, a liquid, or a gas. You know from experience that solids, liquids, and gases behave quite differently from one another. But, do you know why? Learning about matter and the types of particles that make it up will help you understand why.

Matter is anything that takes up space and has mass. Anything you can touch, taste, or smell is matter. For example, Earth, the food you eat, the books you read, and your body are matter. Your thoughts and emotions are not matter because they don't have mass or take up space. Heat and light aren't matter, either.

Atoms

An atom is the smallest particle that makes up a given type of matter. For example, atoms of gold make up a gold ring. Atoms of helium make up the helium gas that fills balloons for a birthday party. When two or more atoms combine, they form a particle called a molecule. Two atoms of hydrogen combine with one atom of oxygen to make a water molecule. Similarly, one atom of carbon combines with two atoms of oxygen to form a carbon dioxide molecule.

Most matter is made up of atoms or molecules. But, you've probably noticed some important differences in the many types of matter that are all around you. Looking around the room, you see many things that are solids. When you wash your hands, you see and feel water, a liquid. The air you

What You'll Learn

▶ Matter is made of particles that are in constant motion
▶ How a solid forms and what happens when it melts

Vocabulary
state of matter
matter
kinetic theory of matter
melting point
heat of fusion
freezing point

Why It's Important

▶ Anything that you can see, touch, taste, or smell is matter. The particles that make up matter are in a state of constant motion.

breathe is a mixture of gases. What makes a solid a solid? A liquid a liquid? A gas a gas? The physical state of a type of matter depends mostly upon how its atoms and molecules are arranged and how they move.

Matter in Motion

While watching a shaft of sunlight stream into a room, you've probably noticed the constant, irregular motion of dust particles in the air. In 1827, a Scottish botanist named Robert Brown saw something similar while observing water samples with a microscope. He noticed that pollen grains suspended in the water moved continuously—and in random patterns. Studying dye particles in water, Brown saw that they moved in the same way. Today, scientists understand that Brown's pollen grains and dye particles moved because of their collisions with moving water molecules, as illustrated in **Figure 4-2.** In Brown's honor, the constant, random motion of tiny particles of matter is called Brownian motion. The idea that the particles of all matter are in constant, random motion is called the **kinetic theory of matter.** The energy of moving particles is called kinetic energy.

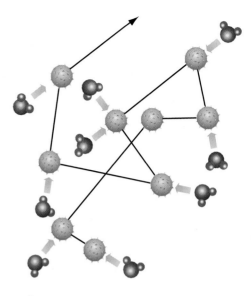

Figure 4-2 Water molecules colliding with a pollen grain in a water droplet push it first in one direction, then another. **What causes the random motion of dust particles in the air?**

Temperature and Heat

Think about the difference between hot tea and iced tea. Although both contain the same kinds of particles, the movements of the particles are different. The temperature of a material is an indirect measure of the average kinetic energy of the particles that make up the material. The higher the temperature, the faster the particles are moving. **Figure 4-3** illustrates particle movement in hot tea and iced tea.

Figure 4-3 The particles in hot tea move faster than those in iced tea. **In which container do the particles have more kinetic energy?**

Figure 4-4 It's a hot day, and this girl is playing in cool water. **How does heat transfer help her keep comfortable?**

PHYSICS
INTEGRATION

Kinetic Energy
The kinetic energy of an object is its energy of motion. Kinetic energy depends upon both the mass and the speed of the object. The unit of energy is the joule (J).

As the temperature falls, the particles slow down. Although it's impossible to completely stop particles of matter from moving, scientists have come close. The temperature at which the particles of matter would cease to move is called absolute zero. Absolute zero is –273.15°C.

When matter at a higher temperature touches matter at a lower temperature, faster-moving particles collide with slower ones. The faster particles transfer some of their energy to the slower particles. For example, suppose you walk outside on a cold winter day while wearing a short-sleeved shirt. The slower-moving molecules that make up the air hit the faster-moving molecules that make up your warm skin. The molecules that make up your skin transfer energy to those in the air. Your nervous system senses this, and your brain tells you to go indoors or put on a coat because you're losing too much heat to the cold air. Heat is energy transferred from matter at a higher temperature to matter at a lower temperature. Just as heat transfer can make you shiver on a cold day, it can keep you comfortable on a hot day, as shown in **Figure 4-4.**

Matter in the Solid State

Water molecules attract each other, and the attractions are especially strong when the molecules are close together. For example, imagine an ice cube at a temperature of –250°C. At this low temperature, the water molecules are barely moving and the attractions hold them together easily. Now, imagine slowly heating the ice cube. As the temperature rises, the molecules shake more in all directions, but each molecule remains in its original position. This is how kinetic theory describes a solid—an arrangement of shaking particles.

Crystalline Solids

In some solids, particles of matter are arranged in repeating geometric patterns. Solids that have such arrangements are crystalline solids. As more particles become part of a crystalline solid, the geometric pattern is repeated over and over.

The geometry of a crystal depends on many factors, such as the sizes and numbers of particles that make it up. In the

Figure 4-5 The particles that make up crystals of table salt shake back and forth, but they don't move out of their positions completely. **What happens to the motion of the particles if a salt crystal is heated?**

magnified view of **Figure 4-5,** you can see that crystals of table salt are shaped like cubes. Diamond, another crystalline solid, is made entirely of carbon atoms that form pyramid-shaped crystals. This shape gives a diamond its great hardness.

The large crystal shown in **Figure 4-6** is unusual. Crystals usually don't grow large. The pull of gravity, the presence of impurities, the rate of cooling, and abnormal growth patterns all limit a crystal's final size. NASA is trying to grow large crystals in space, where the effect of gravity is greatly reduced. These crystals will be used to make more reliable computer chips.

Noncrystalline Solids

Some solids form without creating crystal structures. These solids often consist of large molecules that don't arrange into repeating patterns to form crystals as they cool. The molecules get stuck in a random arrangement. These solids have no definite pattern or form. Glass and many types of plastic are examples of this type of solid.

Figure 4-6 Large crystals, such as the blue, copper sulfate crystal shown here, contain more atoms than small crystals. **What location would you choose for growing the largest crystals possible?**

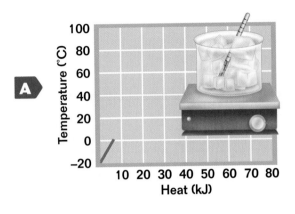

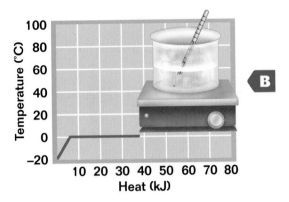

Figure 4-7 As heat is added to ice below its melting point of 0°C (A), its temperature rises. However, as heat is added at the melting point (B), the temperature remains constant until all the ice melts. **What happens to the molecules while the temperature remains constant at 0°C?**

Figure 4-8 At such high temperatures, glass flows so much that it drips off the blowing tube if not turned continually.

How does a solid become liquid?

Think again about the ice cube being heated. As its temperature continues to rise, the water molecules shake faster. But, each molecule is still held captive by the attractive forces from the molecules around it. When the temperature of the ice cube reaches 0°C, the molecules begin to break free. Their movements have become so large that the attractive forces of neighboring molecules can no longer hold them in place. The crystal structure then begins to collapse, and the solid becomes a swarm of freely flowing molecules. The molecules have entered the liquid state. The temperature at which a substance changes from a solid to a liquid is called the substance's **melting point.**

Heat of Fusion

While ice melts, its temperature remains the same, as shown in **Figure 4-7.** This means the molecules aren't moving any faster. The heat that is entering the solid is only breaking down the crystal's structure and freeing the molecules. The heat required to melt 1 kg of a solid at its melting point is called its **heat of fusion.** Water's heat of fusion is 334 kJ/kg. That's how much energy you would use taking the stairs to the top of the 110-story Sears Tower in Chicago.

Solids without crystalline structure don't melt in exactly the same way as crystalline solids. Because they don't have crystal structures to break down, these solids just get softer and softer as heat is added. For example, glass is such a solid at room temperature. As glass is heated, it begins to flow at a temperature of about 1000°C. Above 2000°C, glass is so soft that you can cut it with scissors and blow it up like a balloon. The glass blower shown in **Figure 4-8** continually turns the glass so it won't drip off the blowing tube.

Freezing

The process of melting a crystalline solid can be reversed if the liquid is cooled. As the liquid cools, its particles slow down and come closer together. Attractive forces begin to trap particles here and there, and crystals begin to form. The temperature at which this occurs, called the liquid's **freezing point,** is the same temperature as the solid's melting point. The temperature remains constant while the crystal structure forms and the heat of fusion is released. After all of the liquid has become a solid, the temperature can continue to fall. ✔

Viscosity is a material's resistance to flow. For a material such as glass, the liquid becomes more and more viscous as its temperature decreases. This means it becomes thicker and more resistant to flow, until it finally becomes brittle glass. So, glass has no definite freezing point—it just gradually hardens as it cools. The particles settle into a random arrangement rather than a crystal structure.

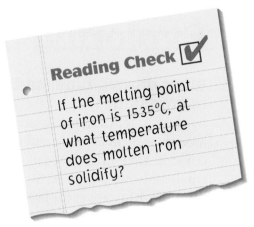

Reading Check ✔

If the melting point of iron is 1535°C, at what temperature does molten iron solidify?

Section Assessment

1. What happens to the particles of a crystalline solid as it is heated at its melting point?

2. What property must a solid have to be considered a crystalline solid?

3. Describe the motion of the particles of a solid as it cools from −250°C to −273.15°C.

4. **Think Critically:** On a cold winter day, you leave the door open when you come in from school. Someone shouts, "Close the door, you're heating the neighborhood!" Explain the meaning of this statement according to the kinetic theory of matter.

5. **Skill Builder**
   Making and Using Graphs Using the data you collected in the Explore Activity, plot a temperature-time graph. Draw a smooth curve through the data points. Describe your graph. At what temperature does the graph level off? What was the liquid doing during this time period? Compare your graph with others in the class. What do you conclude? If you need help, refer to Making and Using Graphs in the **Skill Handbook** on page 701.

Using Math

If it takes 334 kJ of energy to melt 1 kg of ice, how much energy does it take to melt 150 g of ice placed in a glass of warm tea? What is the source of the heat that melts the ice?

NATIONAL
GEOGRAPHIC

Exploring Symmetry

What do salt, gold, and diamonds have in common?*

In the sixteenth century, scientists began to look more closely at crystals and their structure. They discovered that many kinds of crystals are made up of small unit cells that have a characteristic and uniform shape. For instance, table salt is made up of unit cells that are cube shaped (see salt crystals at right). Unit cells can bond together to form larger crystals.

A cube is a three-dimensional figure with six square faces (like the dice below). A square is a four-sided figure with all sides having the same length. An important property of crystals is symmetry. When a figure can be folded in half so that the two parts are identical, the figure is said to have symmetry. A line of symmetry is the line where the fold is made.

Symmetry of a Square

Follow these steps to find how many lines of symmetry a square has:

1. On a sheet of paper, draw and cut out a square with sides that are 10 cm long.

2. Fold the square in half so that you end up with two identical parts, or halves. The paper crease between the two identical halves represents a line of symmetry. Find other ways you can fold the square to form identical halves. Make a crease for each line of symmetry.

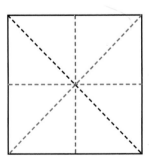

3. Count the creases that you have made on your square. Your square should have four lines of symmetry.

Practice PROBLEMS

1. Crystalline gold can occur in the shape of an octahedron. An octahedron is a three-dimensional figure with eight triangular faces. Draw and cut out a triangle having all three sides equal in length. Find the number of lines of symmetry for the triangle.

2. Diamond crystals can occur in several shapes. One shape is a dodecahedron. A dodecahedron is a three-dimensional figure with 12 faces that are pentagons. Draw and cut out a pentagon having all five sides equal in length. Find the number of lines of symmetry for the pentagon.

3. Three-dimensional figures can have a plane of symmetry. On a piece of paper, draw a cube and sketch in three planes of symmetry.

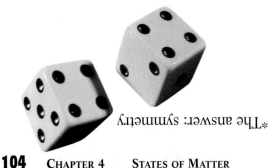

*The answer: symmetry

Liquids and Gases

Matter in the Liquid State

The kinetic theory of matter considers atoms and molecules to be like billiard balls that are constantly moving and bouncing into each other. However, unlike billiard balls, there's no friction or noise when atoms and molecules collide. Therefore, they don't lose their energy of motion. As long as the temperature of the particles remains constant, they will continue to collide with the same overall kinetic energy forever.

The particles that make up a liquid move more freely than particles in a solid, as illustrated in **Figure 4-9.** The attractive forces between particles are strong enough to keep them close together but not strong enough to hold them in fixed positions. Because the particles are free to move about, gravity makes them flow, and the liquid takes the shape of its container. For example, when you pour yourself a glass of water, attractive forces hold the molecules together as a liquid while gravity holds them at the bottom of the glass.

Figure 4-9 Particles in liquids move in a different way than particles in solids.

What You'll Learn

▶ How liquids and gases are formed
▶ The enormous amounts of energy involved in evaporation and condensation

Vocabulary
boiling point
heat of vaporization
evaporation
condensation

Why It's Important

▶ The kinetic theory explains how your body cools itself on a hot summer day and why you shiver when you get out of the shower.

Liquid

Solid

A Liquid particles have enough energy to move around each other but not enough energy to break away from each other completely.

B Solid particles can't move from place to place because they don't have enough energy to overcome their attractions for one another. **What holds liquid and solid particles in the bottom of an open container?**

Figure 4-10 Water's surface tension gives it interesting properties.

A Surface tension gives this glob of water photographed aboard the space shuttle *Columbia* a spherical shape.

B Surface tension is caused by cohesive forces between molecules, as shown in the drawing of a water droplet. Inside the droplet, molecules are pulled equally in all directions by the cohesive forces. However, at the surface of the drop, the water molecules are only pulled inward by the cohesive forces.

Cohesive forces

C This water strider uses the surface tension of water to stand on its surface. **What would happen if a water strider tried to walk on the surface of a liquid that had almost no surface tension?**

Predicting Drops of Water on a Penny

Procedure

1. Predict how many drops of water you can put on a penny before the water spills.
2. Set a penny on the counter or lab table near a sink.
3. Fill a dropper with water and carefully place a drop at the center of the penny.
4. Counting drops, carefully add more drops until the water spills off the penny.

Analysis

1. How many drops were you able to place on the penny and how does the number compare with your prediction?
2. Why were you able to put so many drops on the penny before the water spilled off the edge? Base your explanation on adhesive and cohesive forces.

Forces Between Molecules

You've probably watched astronauts play with, and then drink, floating globs of water while orbiting Earth. The attractive forces between water molecules produce the wiggly sphere of liquid shown in **Figure 4-10A.** On Earth, attractive forces make water molecules pull themselves together and form beads of water on a freshly waxed car.

If you're careful, you can float a needle on water. The water molecules at the surface pull themselves together, resulting in surface tension, as shown in **Figure 4-10B.** Water does not adhere to the metal needle, and water's surface tension is strong enough to support the needle's weight. Surface tension enables water striders to scoot around on the surface of a pond or lake, as in **Figure 4-10C.**

How does a liquid become a gas?

Have you watched a pan of water being heated on the stove? First, you'll notice small bubbles collecting on the sides and bottom of the pan. These bubbles are made of air that was dissolved in the water.

Continuing to heat the water, you start to see a swirling motion. While the warmer, less-dense water moves upward, the colder, heavier water at the surface falls to the bottom.

As the water becomes hotter still, you see trails of bubbles spiraling upward. The swirling motion becomes more active, and large bubbles of steam form at the bottom, as in **Figure 4-11.** At this temperature (100°C for water), called the **boiling point,** some of the water is entering the gaseous state. Boiling also is called vaporization.

Heat of Vaporization

The temperature remains the same at the boiling point while the added heat continues to vaporize the water, as illustrated in **Figure 4-12.** The amount of energy required to change 1 kg of a liquid to a gas is called the liquid's **heat of vaporization.** Water's heat of vaporization is 2260 kJ/kg, which is almost seven times the amount of heat needed to melt the same amount of ice.

Evaporation

You've seen large puddles on the sidewalk or roadway after a rainstorm. These puddles can quickly disappear if the sun comes out and the weather is warm. Does the water boil away? That seems impossible. Its temperature must be well below 100°C. The kinetic theory of matter can help you understand this mystery behavior.

Figure 4-11 When water is heated to boiling, large bubbles of steam form and rise to the surface. **Why does water take up more space as steam than it does as liquid water?**

Figure 4-12 Adding heat energy to liquid water causes the molecules to move faster. The graph (A) shows the steady rise in temperature after the ice melts at 0°C. Adding the heat of vaporization completely overcomes the force of attraction between molecules and changes the water to steam (B). **Why is water's heat of vaporization so much greater than its heat of fusion?**

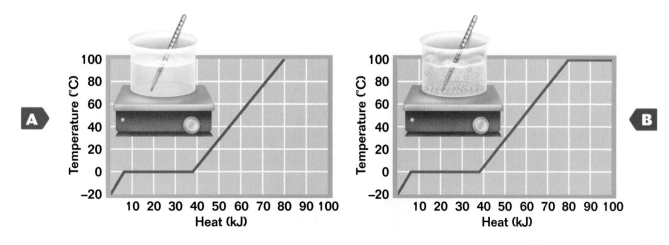

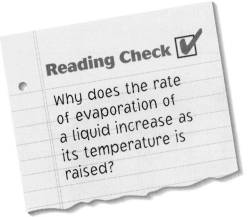

Reading Check ✔

Why does the rate of evaporation of a liquid increase as its temperature is raised?

Imagine that you could watch individual water molecules in a glass of water. You would notice that the molecules move at different speeds. Although the temperature of the water may be constant, remember that temperature is a measure of the average kinetic energy of the molecules. Some of the fastest-moving molecules actually overcome the attractive forces of other molecules and escape from the surface of the water. The process by which individual particles of a liquid escape from the surface of a liquid that is not boiling and form a gas is called **evaporation.** But, it takes more than speed for water molecules to escape. These faster molecules also must be near the surface, heading in the right direction, and avoid hitting other water molecules as they leave. ✔

Cooling by Evaporation

With the faster molecules evaporating from the surface of a liquid, the molecules that remain are the slower, cooler ones. So, evaporation cools the liquid and anything the liquid touches. You experience this cooling effect whenever perspiration evaporates from your skin. In fact, you sometimes have a chill when you climb out of a swimming pool on a hot day as your body provides the heat to evaporate even more of the water.

Using Math

If you step out of a swimming pool and 85 g of water remain on your skin, how much heat does your body lose to evaporate this much water?

Have you noticed that it sometimes cools down outside after a rain storm? The storm's water is absorbing energy from everything around as it evaporates, leaving the air a lot cooler than before the storm. With the sun shining, the air's energy is quickly replaced, sometimes leading to powerful storms, such as the ones seen in **Figure 4-13.**

Ⓐ

Ⓑ

Figure 4-13 This powerful Texas tornado (A) and hurricane Emilia (B) unleashed some of the sun's energy that had been stored in Earth's atmosphere.

Matter in the Gaseous State

When water evaporates, each molecule escapes completely from the attractions of its neighboring molecules. When water is in the gaseous state, the molecules are much farther apart than they are in the liquid state. This is why it's a lot easier to wave your arms through the air than to wave them through water. There's lots of empty space between the molecules in air.

If you pour only enough of a liquid into a glass to fill the glass halfway, the liquid stays in the bottom half of the glass. But, something different happens with a gas. A gas completely fills any container you put it in. If the container has no lid, the gas particles will keep spreading out until they meet some other barrier, such as the walls of a room.

Condensation

As a gas cools, its particles slow down. When particles move slowly enough for their attractions to bring them together, droplets of liquid form. This process is called **condensation.** As a gas condenses to a liquid, it releases the heat absorbed by the liquid when it became a gas. For this reason, steam can cause severe burns. Steam burns the skin not only because it's hot, but also because it releases even more heat as it condenses to liquid water.

*inter*NET
CONNECTION

Visit the Glencoe Science Web Site at **www.glencoe.com/ sec/science** for more information about the powerful forces that drive the melting of the polar ice caps and the development of hurricanes.

Section Assessment

1. Have you noticed water collecting on the outside of a glass containing an ice-cold drink? Where did this water come from, and why did it collect on the glass?

2. A glass of water is placed next to a puddle that contains the same amount of water. Explain why water in the glass evaporates more slowly than water in the puddle.

3. **Think Critically:** Use the kinetic theory to explain why a gas completely fills its container while a liquid or solid may not.

4.  **Skill Builder**
   Making and Using Graphs The melting point of aluminum is 660°C. Draw the heating graph for a sample of aluminum between 500°C and 800°C. If you need help, refer to Making and Using Graphs in the **Skill Handbook** on page 701.

Science Journal
In your Science Journal, explain why you can step out of the shower into a warm bathroom and begin to shiver.

Materials

- Hot plate
- Ice cubes (100 mL)
- Stirring rod
- Celsius thermometer
- Beaker (250 mL)
- Wall clock with a second hand
  - *stopwatch
  - *Alternate Materials

Visit Three States in Science Class

The cycle of the seasons is marked by major changes in the weather driven by the sun's energy. Because water covers much of Earth, changes in water's physical state greatly affect people's lives.

What You'll Investigate

What energy changes occur as water changes its temperature and physical states?

Goals

- **Measure** the temperature of water as it is heated.
- **Observe** what happens as the water changes state.
- **Graph** a heating curve.

Procedure

1. **Copy** the data table shown.
2. Put about 150 mL of water and 100 mL of ice into the beaker and place the beaker and contents on the hot plate.
3. Put the thermometer into the ice-water mixture. **Do not** stir with the thermometer or allow it to rest on the bottom of the beaker. After 30 s, **measure** and record the temperature in your data table. Be sure to stir the ice and water before making each temperature measurement. Record the physical state(s) in your data table.
4. Plug in the hot plate and turn the temperature knob to the medium setting.

5. Every 30 s, **measure** and record the temperature and **observe** and record the physical state of the ice and/or water in the beaker.
6. Continue until the water has reached boiling and boiled for three minutes.

Conclude and Apply

1. Use your data to **make a Temperature-Time graph.** Draw a smooth curve through the data points. Do not connect the data points with straight lines.
2. On the graph, what was happening to the water during the flat portions of the graph? Write down the temperatures for these portions.
3. How do the flat portions relate to water's heat of fusion and heat of vaporization?

Heating Data and Observations		
Time (min)	Temperature (°C)	Physical State
0.0		
0.5		
1.0		
1.5		
2.0		

Behavior of Liquids and Gases

Diffusion

Imagine you're walking by a bakery's open door. The wonderful aroma of baking bread fills the air. If the aroma consists of molecules in the gaseous state, how do the molecules reach your nose? According to the kinetic theory, the warm molecules are moving about rapidly, and many of them flow out the door and mix with the cool morning air. Because of their ability to flow, liquids and gases are called fluids.

Because particles of a gas are far apart and move about freely, they easily mix with particles of other gases. For example, **Figure 4-14** shows the gradual mixing of bromine gas with air as liquid bromine evaporates at the bottom of a glass container. This mixing of particles is called **diffusion.** Many times, you don't notice a gas mixing with other gases because you can't see or smell its particles. Although you can smell some of the gases emitted from automobile engines, you can't smell the deadly gas carbon monoxide. Because you can't smell carbon monoxide mixing with the air you breathe, a car with its engine running should always be parked in a well-ventilated area.

What **You'll Learn**

▶ How pressure is transmitted through fluids
▶ Why some things float while others sink

Vocabulary
diffusion
pressure
Pascal's principle
density
Archimedes' principle
buoyancy

Why **It's Important**

▶ Pressure enables you to squeeze toothpaste from a tube and to float in water.

Figure 4-14 As time passes, liquid bromine vaporizes and mixes with the gases that make up air.

Pressure

Suppose you fill a plastic drink bottle completely full of water, put the cap on tightly, and squeeze. Nothing happens because it's nearly impossible to compress solids and liquids. The force applied by your muscles is spread out over the surface area of your hand that is in contact with the bottle. This creates **pressure,** which is the amount of force applied per unit of area. Pressure (*P*), force (*F*), and area (*A*) are related by the following formula.

$$\text{Pressure} = \frac{\text{force}}{\text{area}}$$

$$P = \frac{F}{A}$$

The SI unit of pressure is the pascal (Pa). One *pascal* is the pressure produced by a force of one newton (N) applied per square meter (m^2) of surface area. What pressure is produced when 25.0 N of force are applied to an area of 10.0 m^2? ☑

$$P = \frac{F}{A}$$

$$P = \frac{25.0 \text{ N}}{10.0 \text{ m}^2} = 2.50 \ \frac{\text{N}}{\text{m}^2} = 2.50 \text{ Pa}$$

The pressure produced is 2.50 pascals.

Reading Check ☑

What pressure is created when 5.0 N of force are applied to an area of 2.0 m^2?

Problem Solving

Calculating Pressure

The circus is coming to your town. You're in charge of installing a floor that will withstand the antics of all the animals and performers. Zebras will prance on the floor. Elephants will rear up, standing on two legs. A performer shot from a cannon will land after flying 50 m through the air. Someone wearing spike heels will maneuver animals through their routines. Which is the greater threat to your floor, an elephant standing on two feet or the person wearing spike-heeled shoes? The circus's largest elephant has a weight of 9250 N. The elephant's two feet contact the ground over a surface area of 0.180 m^2. The person wearing spike-heeled shoes has a weight of 485 N and sometimes stands on the heel of one shoe, contacting the ground over an area of 0.000 200 m^2.

Think Critically: Calculate the pressures exerted on the floor by the elephant and the heel of one spike-heeled shoe. Which is greater? How is your result possible?

Figure 4-15
Pascal's principle explains many common events.

A Applying pressure to the bottom of the bottle makes water shoot out of a small hole near the top.

B Applying pressure to the tube forces toothpaste out of the opening. **Why can't the particles that make up the water and toothpaste be squeezed closer together?**

Pascal's Principle

What happens if you make a small hole near the top of a full plastic drink bottle and squeeze it near the bottom? Why does water shoot out the hole near the top, as shown in **Figure 4-15A?** When you squeeze the bottle, molecules throughout the water press against each other. In this way, the pressure applied at any point to a confined fluid is transmitted unchanged throughout the fluid. This statement is known as **Pascal's principle.** Every time you squeeze a tube of toothpaste, you see Pascal's principle in action, as in **Figure 4-15B.**

Gas Pressure

Gases are easy to compress because their particles are so far apart. When you pump up a bicycle tire or a basketball, as shown in **Figure 4-16,** you increase the pressure by forcing more particles into the same amount of space. Gases exert pressure because their particles collide with each other, the walls of the container, and anything else that gets in their way. By increasing the number of gas particles in a given space, you increase the number of collisions and the pressure.

Figure 4-16 What do you think would happen to the pressure inside the ball if you took it outside on a cold day after inflating it to the correct pressure in a warm building? Explain your answer.

VISUALIZING
Air Particles

Figure 4-17 The volume of air in these two cylinders is the same. The unheated air in the left cylinder exerts enough pressure to lift a 1-kg block. The heated air in the right cylinder exerts more pressure—enough to lift a 2-kg block. **Why does the heated air exert more pressure than the unheated air?**

Visit the Glencoe Science Web Site at **www.glencoe.com/ sec/science** for more information about pressure and temperature.

Have you ever noticed that the instructions on some tires caution you to inflate them a bit below the recommended pressure during the summer months? The tires on a car become hot after driving for a while on a hot day, and gas particles move faster at higher temperatures. The particles inside the tires collide more frequently and with greater kinetic energies, increasing the pressure. For this reason, the pressure inside tires can increase to a dangerously high level and cause them to burst on a hot day.

To better understand the relationship between temperature and pressure, examine **Figure 4-17.** A sample of gas is trapped inside a container with a fixed volume. When you heat the gas, its particles move faster and exert more pressure. When you cool the gas, its particles move slower and exert less pressure.

Atmospheric Pressure

Particles in Earth's atmosphere are constantly colliding with the surface of your body. You don't notice the collisions because they're the same on all sides of your body. These collisions exert a pressure of 101.3 kPa at sea level, which is about 100 000 N of force for every square meter. A force of 100 000 N is approximately the weight of a large truck. A pressure of 101.3 kPa is equal to 1 atmosphere (atm).

Your body is very sensitive to changes in air pressure. Why does a trip to the top of a tall building, a drive up a mountain road, or a flight on an airplane make your ears pop?

In the seventeenth century, a French physician named Blaise Pascal measured the pressure of the atmosphere at different altitudes. For one of his experiments, Pascal had his brother-in-law carry a partially filled balloon to the top of the

Puy-de-Dome mountain in France. (Pascal would have performed the experiment himself but his health was so poor that he could not make the climb.) Pascal's experiment is illustrated in **Figure 4-18.** As Pascal had predicted, the balloon expanded as it was carried up the mountain, indicating that air gets "thinner" at higher altitudes. That is, air contains fewer particles per cubic meter at higher altitudes than at lower altitudes. For this reason, you may feel the difference in air pressure when you travel to higher altitudes. Because the air pressure in your ear canals is greater than the air pressure outside your body, some of the air trapped inside your ears is released. This release of air can make your ears pop.

As the atmospheric pressure decreases, the boiling points of liquids also become lower. For example, if you boiled your vegetables in water in an open pot on Mount Everest, they would be served uncooked because water boils there at a temperature of only 76.5°C, whereas at sea level, water boils at 100°C. Boiling occurs when the pressure of the liquid's moving molecules matches the air pressure pushing down on the surface.

Density and Buoyancy

One day, the king of Syracuse asked the mathematician Archimedes (287–212 B.C.) to solve a riddle. The king had asked a jeweler to make him a crown made entirely of gold. When the king received the crown, it looked magnificent. But, when it was placed upon his head, it seemed lighter than he expected. The king told Archimedes to find out if some of the gold had been replaced with a cheaper metal. To make his task more difficult, Archimedes had to do it without damaging the crown.

Puy-de-Dome mountain

Figure 4-18 Why did the balloon become larger as it was carried up the mountain?

Try at Home

Observing Water in a Glass

Procedure

1. Fill a glass to the brim with water.
2. Cover the top of the glass with an index card.
3. Holding the card in place, turn the glass upside down over a sink, then let go of the card.
4. Put your hand back on the card before turning the glass right side up and emptying the water.

Analysis

1. What happened to the water in the glass when you turned the glass upside down?
2. Explain your observation based on the kinetic theory of matter.

Density

Archimedes loved to solve problems—and this one was a serious challenge. He could weigh the crown, but that wouldn't reveal the presence of impurities. But, if he also could measure the crown's volume, then he could divide the mass by the volume to get the crown's density. **Density** (D) equals mass (m) divided by volume (V). The equation form follows.

$$\text{Density} = \frac{\text{mass}}{\text{volume}}$$

$$D = \frac{m}{V}$$

For example, the density of a 16.4-g object that has a volume of 4.0 mL is calculated as follows.

$$D = \frac{m}{V}$$

$$D = \frac{16.4 \text{ g}}{4.0 \text{ mL}} = \frac{4.1 \text{ g}}{\text{mL}}$$

The density of the object is 4.1 g/mL.

Gold has a density of 19.3 g/mL. Knowing that any other metal that had been used in place of gold had a lower density, Archimedes put a sample of pure gold that weighed the same as the crown into a tub of water and measured how much water it pushed aside. Then, he did the same thing with the crown. When he saw that the pure gold pushed aside less water than the crown, he knew that the crown could not be pure gold.

Using Math

A woman's ring has a mass of 3.82 g and a volume of 0.294 mL. What is the ring's density? Can the ring be made of pure gold?

Figure 4-19 Why do some people find it difficult to float in a swimming pool?

A When an object is immersed in water, the water pushes upward on the object with a force called the buoyant force. The buoyant force is equal to the weight of the water displaced. Because the buoyant force opposes the force of gravity that pulls the object downward, the apparent weight of the object is less than the actual weight.

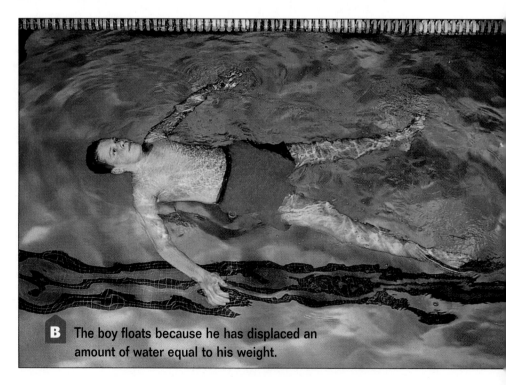

B The boy floats because he has displaced an amount of water equal to his weight.

Buoyancy

What Archimedes discovered is called Archimedes' Principle. **Archimedes' principle** states that when an object is placed in a fluid, the object weighs less by an amount equal to the weight of the displaced fluid. The net upward force caused by the displaced fluid is called the buoyant force. You experience **buoyancy,** which is the decrease in weight caused by the buoyant force, when you float in a swimming pool or lake. Archimedes' principle is illustrated and explained in **Figure 4-19.**

You can use Archimedes' principle to explain why some things sink and others float. If an object's density is less than that of a fluid, it floats in the fluid. On the other hand, if an object's density is greater than that of the fluid, it sinks. That's why a beach ball floats in water while an anchor sinks, as illustrated in **Figure 4-20.**

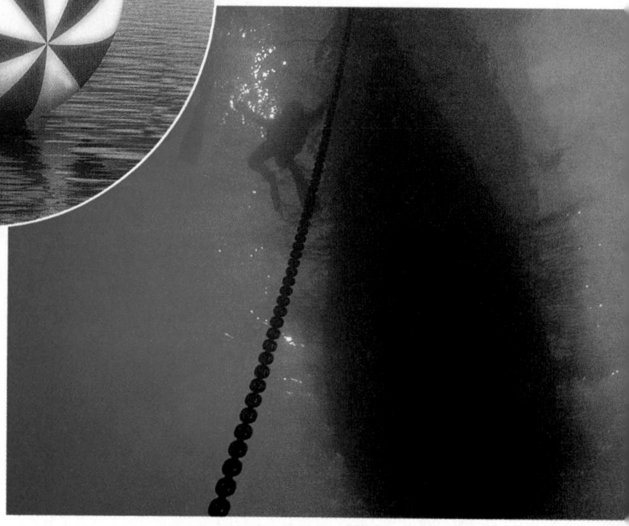

Figure 4-20 Because the anchor attached to the boat's chain is more dense than water, it sinks to the bottom and holds the boat in place.

Section Assessment

1. Use the kinetic theory to explain why a balloon bursts when overinflated.

2. Calculate the density of an object that has a mass of 3.0 g and a volume of 5.0 cm^3. Will the object float or sink when placed in water, which has a density of 1.0 g/cm^3?

3. Why is atmospheric pressure greater at sea level than at the top of a mountain 5000 m above sea level?

4. **Think Critically:** Use Archimedes' principle to explain why a helium balloon rises while a balloon filled with air falls.

5. **Skill Builder**
   Comparing and Contrasting Do the **Chapter 4 Skill Activity** on page 729 to form a hypothesis about what kinds of matter were in the cup.

Using Computers

Word Processing Use word processing software to create a report explaining how water creates the buoyant force that causes an ice cube to float. If you need help, refer to page 716.

Design Your Own Boat

Possible Materials

- Balance
- Small plastic cups (2)
- Graduated cylinder into which the cups will fit
- Metric ruler
- Scissors
- Marbles
- Sink or basin
  basin, pan, or bucket
  Alternate Materials

Have you ever wondered how a boat designer knows how much cargo a particular boat can carry? If you were given an amount of cargo and asked to design a boat that would just hold the cargo afloat, how would you decide what size to make the boat?

Recognize the Problem

How can you determine the size of boat needed to float a certain mass of cargo?

Form a Hypothesis

Think about Archimedes' principle and how it relates to buoyant force. **Form a hypothesis** about how the volume of water a boat displaces relates to the mass of cargo the boat can float.

Goals

- **Design an experiment** that uses Archimedes' Principle to determine the size of boat needed to carry a given amount of cargo.

Test Your Hypothesis

Plan

1. Your teacher will give you a set of marbles or other cargo that your boat must float. Decide how your group is going to test your hypothesis.

2. List the steps you need to take to test your hypothesis. Include in your plan how you will (a) **measure** the mass of your cargo, (b) **calculate** how much water your boat must displace in order to just float your boat and cargo, (c) **measure** the volume and mass of the displaced water, and (d) **determine** how to trim your cup to the exact size so that it will just float your cargo.

3. **Prepare a data table** in your Science Journal so that it is ready to use as your group collects data.

Do

1. Make sure your teacher approves your plan and your data table before you proceed.

2. Carry out your experiment as planned.

3. While doing the experiment, **record** your observations and **complete** the data table in your Science Journal.

Analyze Your Data

1. **Show** your calculations to determine the volume of displaced water needed to float your boat and cargo.

2. Did your boat (a) just float the cargo, (b) sink, or (c) float with excess freeboard, which is the distance between the waterline and the top of the boat?

Draw Conclusions

1. If your boat sank or had excess freeboard, how would you change your experiment or calculations to correct the problem?

2. What does the density of a ship's cargo have to do with the volume of cargo the ship can carry?

For a **preview** of this chapter, study this Reviewing Main Ideas before you read the chapter. After you have studied this chapter, you can use the Reviewing Main Ideas to **review** the chapter.

GLENCOE TECHNOLOGY The Glencoe MindJogger, Audiocassettes, and CD-ROM provide additional opportunities for review.

4-1 KINETIC THEORY OF MATTER

All **matter** is composed of incredibly small particles. The **kinetic theory of matter** describes the way these particles move about. Temperature is an indirect measure of the average kinetic energy of these particles. *When the particles that make up a material collide with each other, how much energy is lost? Explain your answer.*

SOLIDS

In the solid state, the attractive forces between particles lock them in place. A crystalline solid consists of particles in an orderly arrangement, while an noncrystalline solid consists of particles arranged in a random manner. If enough heat is added to a solid, melting occurs as the attractive forces between particles are overcome and the solid becomes a liquid. *Why does a liquid release heat as it freezes?*

4-2 LIQUIDS

Molecules in the liquid state are free to move about within the liquid. When gravity is present, a liquid takes the shape of its container. At a liquid's **boiling point,** its particles enter the gaseous state in large numbers. *How do cohesive forces explain why water beads up on a waxed surface?*

Reading Check ☑

What would cause water to change its state? What would cause it to change again?

GASES

To enter the gaseous state from the liquid state, particles must absorb the **heat of vaporization.** Particles in the gaseous state are much farther from neighboring particles than in the liquid state. Gaseous particles move about freely and completely fill their containers. *Use the kinetic theory to explain what happens to the particles of a gas when it condenses to a liquid.*

4-3 PRESSURE

Pressure is force per unit area. Pressure applied to a liquid is transmitted throughout the liquid. This is known as **Pascal's principle.** Gases exert pressure because their moving particles continually collide with each other and the walls of their container. *Why do the boiling points of liquids depend upon the atmospheric pressure?*

BUOYANCY

Archimedes' principle states that when an object is placed in a fluid, the object seems lighter by an amount equal to the weight of the displaced fluid. The displaced fluid's weight creates additional pressure throughout the fluid, resulting in **buoyancy.** *What determines whether an object floats or sinks in a fluid?*

Chapter 4 Assessment

Using Vocabulary

a. Archimedes' principle
b. boiling point
c. buoyancy
d. condensation
e. density
f. diffusion
g. evaporation
h. freezing point
i. heat of fusion
j. heat of vaporization
k. kinetic theory of matter
l. matter
m. melting point
n. Pascal's principle
o. pressure
p. state of matter

Using the list above, replace the underlined words with the correct Vocabulary words.

1. When a liquid freezes, the <u>heat of vaporization</u> is given off.
2. The particles of gas coming together to form a liquid is called <u>evaporation.</u>
3. Mass divided by volume equals <u>pressure.</u>
4. The temperature at which a solid becomes a liquid is called the <u>boiling point.</u>
5. <u>Archimedes' principle</u> states that the pressure exerted on a fluid is transmitted unchanged throughout the fluid.

Checking Concepts

Choose the word or phrase that best answers the question.

6. Which of the following is used to explain whether an object will sink or float?
   A) Archimedes' principle
   B) viscosity
   C) temperature
   D) kinetic theory of matter

7. What holds the molecules of a substance together?
   A) buoyant force   C) attractive forces
   B) pressure   D) temperature

8. What is required to melt a kilogram of a solid at the melting point?
   A) heat of fusion   C) density
   B) boiling   D) heat of vaporization

9. Which of the following is a unit of pressure?
   A) Pa   C) J/m^2
   B) J/kg D) kg/m^3

10. What is glass an example of?
    A) viscous liquid   C) noncrystalline solid
    B) crystalline solid
    D) fluid

11. Which of the following is used to explain how temperature affects matter?
    A) density   C) pressure
    B) Pascal's principle D) kinetic theory

12. Which of the following is not a state of matter?
    A) gas   C) density
    B) solid   D) liquid

13. What is greatly affected by atmospheric pressure?
    A) melting point   C) boiling point
    B) freezing point   D) heat of fusion

14. What best explains how you can smell burned toast from another room?
    A) evaporation   C) diffusion
    B) fusion   D) fire

15. What is a characteristic shared by solids and liquids?
    A) incompressibility C) fluidity
    B) low density   D) buoyancy

Thinking Critically

16. Use the kinetic theory to explain why the bathroom mirror becomes fogged after you take a shower.

17. A crown is found to have a volume of 110 cm^3 and a mass of 1800 g. The density of gold is 19.3 g/cm^3. Is the crown pure gold?

18. When you travel on an airplane, your ears pop and a pen leaks ink in your pocket. Explain why these events occur.

19. After Archimedes discovered his principle on buoyancy, it became clear that a boat could be made out of a metal like iron, even though a piece of iron sinks in water. Explain how this is possible.

20. If you have an automatic ice-cube maker in your freezer, you may have noticed that the older ice cubes at the bottom of the tray are much smaller than the newer cubes at the top. Use the kinetic theory to explain why.

Developing Skills

If you need help, refer to the **Skill Handbook**.

21. Forming Operational Definitions: Write operational definitions that explain the properties of and differences between solids, liquids, and gases.

22. Making and Using Graphs: In May of 1997, the Cuban free-diver Francesco Ferraras dove to a new record depth of 150 m without any scuba equipment. Make a Depth-Pressure graph for the pressure he felt as he descended. Estimate the water pressure at a depth of 300 m.

Deep Depth Dive	
Depth (m)	**Pressure (atm)**
0	1.0
25	3.5
50	6.0
75	8.5
100	11.0
125	13.5
150	16.0

THE PRINCETON REVIEW

Test-Taking Tip

All or None When filling in answer ovals, remember to fill in the whole oval. A computer will be scoring your answers. Don't give the right answer for a problem only to lose points on it because the computer couldn't read your oval.

Test Practice

Use these questions to test your Science Proficiency.

1. Pascal was the first to suggest that Earth's atmosphere did not extend out into space forever. Which statement **BEST** describes his reasoning for this?
A) Hot air expands and gets thinner as it rises.
B) Part of the atmosphere is water vapor, and it forms clouds that are not high off the ground.
C) If you walk up a mountain, the air pressure drops.
D) The sky is blue during the day when the sun shines on the atmosphere, but at night the sky is dark and clear, even when there is a full moon.

2. Which of the following statements explains what happens to a liquid at the freezing point?
A) The temperature falls rapidly.
B) The temperature rises.
C) For most substances, the solid that forms is much less dense than the liquid.
D) The temperature remains constant until all of the solid has formed.

Chapter Preview

Skills Preview

Skill Builders

- Classify
- Sequence

Activities

- Observe and Infer
- Measure in SI

MiniLabs

- Compare and Contrast

Reading Check ✔

Several vocabulary words in this chapter share the same base word from a Latin term that means "to loosen or solve." Write and define the words that share this base word.

Explore Activity

Have you ever gone hiking in the mountains on a warm day and come across the entrance to a cave? A nice, cool cave is a welcome sight—almost as welcome as a cold fruit drink. Once inside a cave, you may see formations called stalagmites and stalactites. These large spikes hang down from the roof of the cave and stick upward from the cave floor. You might be surprised to learn that the formations inside the cave and the cold fruit drink have something in common—they both involve solutions. To understand how, you'll need to know how stalactites and stalagmites form.

Observe Stalagmite Growth

1. Wash and dry a glass dish or jar lid.

2. Using forceps, place a few small crystals of sodium acetate on the glass dish.

3. Slowly drip the solution provided by your teacher onto the crystals and observe what happens.

Science Journal

In your Science Journal, record what happens and describe how you think stalagmites might be formed on the floor of a cave.

5·1 What is a solution?

Substances

Atoms are the basic building blocks of matter on Earth. All the atoms of an element have the same number of protons. For example, the dark gray material inside your pencil is made up mostly of atoms that contain six protons—graphite, a form of carbon (not lead, as the name "pencil lead" might make you believe), as shown in **Figure 5-1.**

A compound is a type of matter made from atoms of two or more elements that are combined chemically. The ratio of the different atoms in a compound is always the same. For example, water is composed of the elements hydrogen and oxygen, and always in the ratio of two hydrogen atoms to one oxygen atom.

Elements and compounds are called substances and can't be broken down to simpler parts by ordinary physical processes, such as squeezing, grinding, or filtering. Only a chemical process can change a substance into one or more new substances. For instance, you can't separate water into hydrogen and oxygen by ordinary means. It takes a chemical process to break water down into the two elements.

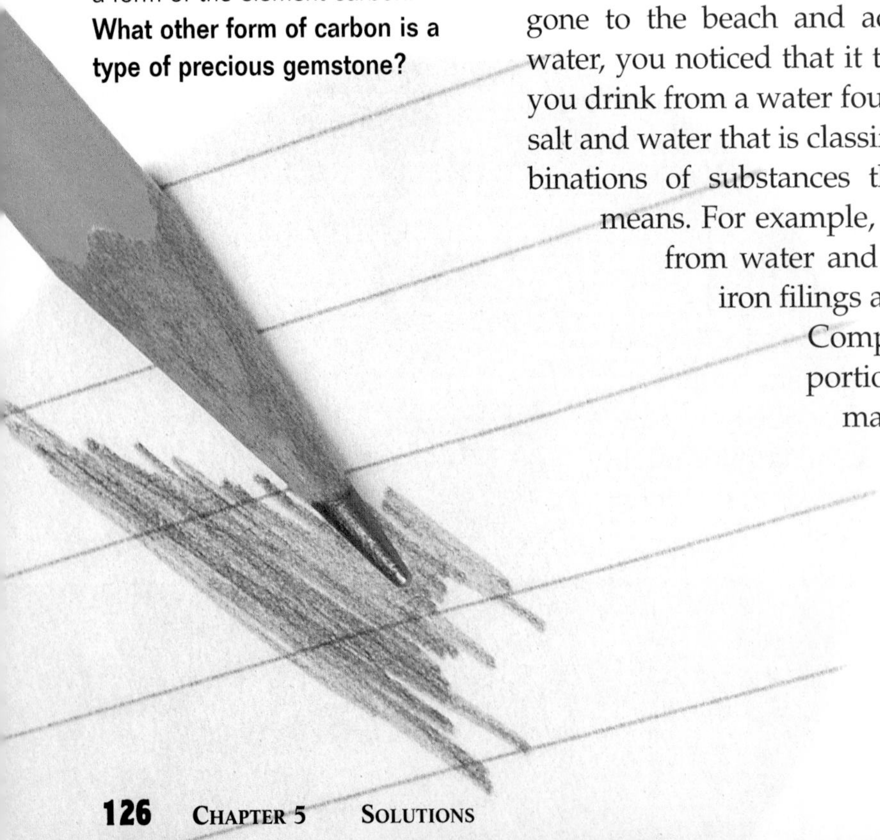

Mixtures

Lots of things around you are not pure substances. If you've gone to the beach and accidentally swallowed some ocean water, you noticed that it tasted salty—not like the freshwater you drink from a water fountain. Salt water is a combination of salt and water that is classified as a mixture. **Mixtures** are combinations of substances that can be separated by physical means. For example, you can use boiling to separate salt from water and a magnet to separate a mixture of iron filings and sand.

Compounds always contain the same proportions of the different substances that make them up, but mixtures don't. For

What You'll Learn

► The different types of solutions that can exist
► How solutions form

Vocabulary
mixture   solute
solution   solvent

Why It's Important

► The air you breathe, the water you drink, and even your own body are all solutions.

Figure 5-1 The "lead" in a wooden pencil is actually graphite, a form of the element carbon. **What other form of carbon is a type of precious gemstone?**

example, if you're wearing clothing made of permanent-press fabric, it's a mixture of two fibers—polyester and cotton. Your permanent-press fabric may contain varying amounts of polyester and cotton, a fact that you can find out by looking at a label like the one in **Figure 5-2.**

Heterogeneous Mixtures

The prefix *hetero-* means "different." The substances that make up a heterogeneous mixture are not mixed evenly, so different parts of the mixture have different compositions. The different parts of a heterogeneous mixture are usually easy to tell apart. Think about a watermelon. If you cut the watermelon open, you can tell the difference between the part you eat and the seeds.

Homogeneous Mixtures

The prefix *homo-* means "the same." Accordingly, the composition of a homogeneous mixture is the same throughout. The substances that make up a homogeneous mixture are not usually easy to tell apart. For example, when you look at the salt water that you might have tasted at the beach, you can't see the salt. Salt water can be separated by physical means, though. If you boil salt water, the water will evaporate and form steam, but the salt will be left behind, as shown in **Figure 5-3.** The steam can be collected and cooled to make pure water. Some countries that don't have much freshwater but are close to salt water use this property of mixtures to supply their fresh drinking water. Another name for a homogeneous mixture is a **solution.**

Figure 5-2 The label on this garment tells you what mixture its fabric is made of.

Figure 5-3 When salt water boils, the water leaves as a gas but the salt remains behind. **Why did the water boil away while the salt did not?**

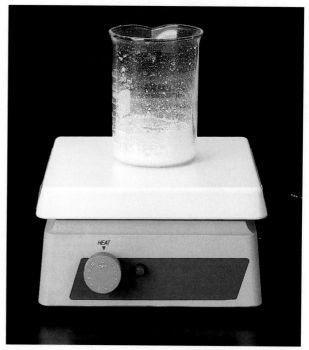

Think again about the cold fruit drink you enjoy on a warm day. What does the drink resemble most: a substance such as water? A watermelon? Salt water? It's liquid, like water, but it has a sweet flavor something like the watermelon. The fruit drink looks the same throughout, and you can't see the fruit substances in it. In fact, the molecules of water and the particles that give the drink its taste and sweetness are so small that they can't be seen, even with a microscope. The fruit drink is a solution. Use the **Field Guide to Kitchen Chemistry** at the end of this chapter to learn more about mixtures.

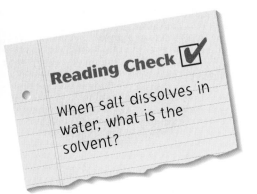

Reading Check ✔

When salt dissolves in water, what is the solvent?

How Solutions Form

The manufacturer of the fruit drink probably combined several materials to make the drink. If crystals of solid were added to water, the crystals were separated into some combination of atoms, ions, and molecules. This process, forming a solution, is called dissolution. A solution is made up of two or more substances, one or more of which seem to disappear in the other. The substance that seems to disappear, or dissolves, is called the **solute.** The solute that you saw in **Figure 5-3** is salt. The substance that dissolves the solute is called the **solvent.** The solvent in **Figure 5-3** was water. A solution usually contains more solvent than solute. A substance that readily dissolves in another is said to be soluble. Therefore, you would say that salt is soluble in water. Similarly, one that does not readily dissolve is insoluble. ✔

Some soluble substances can be made to fall out of a liquid solution. When this happens, the solid formed is called a precipitate. One way this happens is by chemical reaction, as seen in **Figure 5-4.** In fact, you need look no further than your sink or shower to see a precipitate. Minerals are dissolved in your tap water, and when you combine them with soap, the product falls out of solution. The resulting precipitate, called soap scum, forms on your sink and the walls and floor of your tub or shower.

Figure 5-4 When you mix lead (II) nitrate and potassium iodide solutions, solid lead (II) iodide forms because it's insoluble in water. **Why doesn't solid potassium nitrate form, too?**

Table 5-1

Common Solutions			
Solution	**Solvent and State**	**Solute and State**	**State of Solution**
Earth's atmosphere	nitrogen/gas	oxygen/gas carbon dioxide/gas argon/gas	gas
Ocean water	water/liquid	salt/solid oxygen/gas carbon dioxide/gas	liquid
Carbonated beverage	water/liquid	carbon dioxide/gas	liquid
Brass	copper/solid	zinc/solid	solid

Now that you know about solutions and precipitates, can you better understand how stalactites, stalagmites, and a fruit drink are related? The fruit drink is a solution formed when certain substances dissolve in water. Stalactites and stalagmites form from solutions. How does this happen? The cave formations are the result of minerals dissolving in water as it flows through the soil and rocks at the top of the cave. The resulting solutions then form precipitates as they drip from the ceiling of the cave onto its floor.

Types of Solutions

So far, you've learned about only one kind of solution—one in which a solid solute dissolves in a liquid solvent. But, many kinds of solutions can involve combinations of solids, liquids, and gases. Several examples of types of solutions are described in **Table 5-1.** Would you be surprised to know that solutions are all around you and even in you? The water you drink, the gasoline you put in a car, the air you breathe, the blood in your arteries and veins, and the ground you walk on are all solutions of one type or another.

Gaseous Solutions

Gaseous solutions are solutions in which a smaller amount of one gas is dissolved in a larger amount of another gas. This is a gas-gas solution.

The air you breathe is a gaseous solution. Nitrogen makes up about 78 percent of dry air. Other gases in air include oxygen and smaller amounts of argon, carbon dioxide, neon, helium, krypton, hydrogen, xenon, and ozone. Nitrogen is considered to be the solvent, and the other gases are solutes.

EARTH SCIENCE
INTEGRATION

Erosion by Groundwater
Erosion by groundwater can be a major problem in areas that have large amounts of rainfall. As groundwater flows through soil and rocks, these substances can dissolve in the water and be carried away from their original locations. This dissolution by groundwater can lead to the formation of underground caves or sinkholes.

VISUALIZING
Air Fractionation

Figure 5-5 The gases in air can be separated by fractionation. The liquid oxygen formed by fractionation is used for life-support systems in hospitals and at high altitudes. Liquid nitrogen is used to manufacture fertilizers.

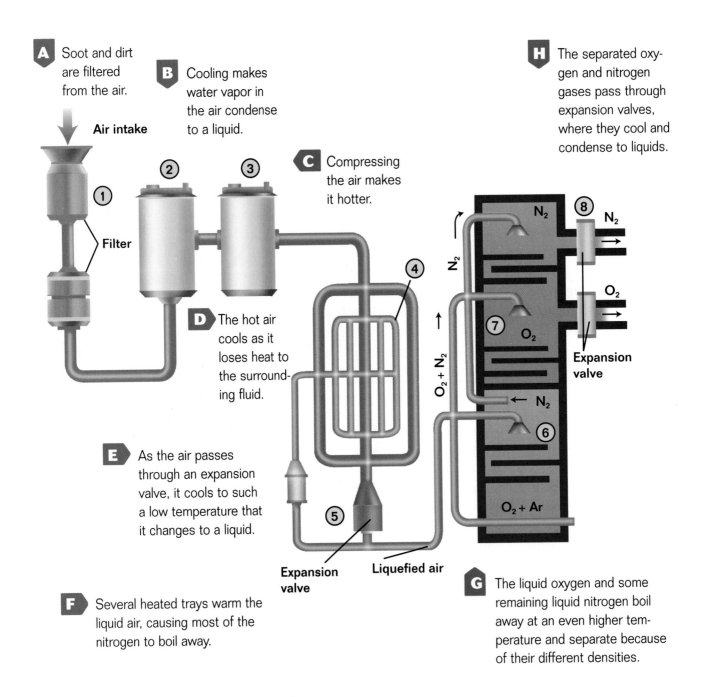

A Soot and dirt are filtered from the air.

B Cooling makes water vapor in the air condense to a liquid.

C Compressing the air makes it hotter.

D The hot air cools as it loses heat to the surrounding fluid.

E As the air passes through an expansion valve, it cools to such a low temperature that it changes to a liquid.

F Several heated trays warm the liquid air, causing most of the nitrogen to boil away.

G The liquid oxygen and some remaining liquid nitrogen boil away at an even higher temperature and separate because of their different densities.

H The separated oxygen and nitrogen gases pass through expansion valves, where they cool and condense to liquids.

Air intake

Filter

Expansion valve

Liquefied air

Expansion valve

N_2 O_2 $O_2 + N_2$ $O_2 + Ar$

Is it possible to separate the gases that make up air? If air is a solution, there should be some way to use physical means to separate the different gases that make it up. But, it's not easy or simple. For air, the separation process is called fractionation, which is described in **Figure 5-5**.

Liquid Solutions

You're probably most familiar with liquid solutions; that is, solutions in which the solvent is a liquid. The solute can be another liquid, a solid, or even a gas. Carbonated beverages are gas-liquid solutions. Carbon dioxide is the gas, and water is the liquid. The carbon dioxide gas gives the beverage its fizz and some of its tartness. Of course, the beverage normally contains other solutes too, like the compounds that give it its flavor and sweetness.

In a liquid-liquid solution, both the solvent and the solute are liquids. Vinegar, which you might put on your salad as a dressing, is a liquid-liquid solution made of 95 percent water (the solvent) and 5 percent acetic acid (the solute). In a solid-liquid solution, the solute is a solid and the solvent is a liquid. You've already learned about several solid-liquid solutions, such as a fruit drink, salt water, and the solutions that produce cave formations.

Solid Solutions

Solid solutions are solutions in which the solvent is a solid. A gas-solid solution can form when a gas-liquid solution is frozen and the gas remains in the solid that results. An example is a bottle of frozen carbonated beverage.

The most common solid solutions are solid-solid solutions—ones in which both the solvent and solute are solids. Solid-solid solutions containing two or more metals are commonly called alloys. Several alloys are shown in **Figure 5-6.**

Figure 5-6 Alloys are solid-solid solutions containing two or more metals. **Why are pots and pans that are used for cooking often made of stainless steel rather than pure iron?**

A This sterling silver pitcher is a solid-solid solution containing 92.5 percent silver and 7.5 percent copper.

B The brass that you see in musical instruments like trumpets, trombones, and tubas is made up of copper and zinc.

C To make this steel faucet more resistant to rusting, chromium and nickel are added. The resulting alloy is called stainless steel.

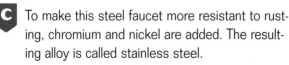

It's also possible to include elements that are not metals in alloys. Alloys containing the elements aluminum, gallium, and arsenic can give off light. The color of the light depends on the amounts of aluminum and gallium in the alloy. The blue sapphire, red ruby, and purple amethyst shown in **Figure 5-7** are solid solutions. Aluminum oxide, or silicon dioxide, contains trace amounts of other elements that give these gems their distinctive color.

Figure 5-7 Both the blue sapphire and the red ruby are gem-quality forms of the mineral corundum. The blue sapphire contains trace amounts of iron and titanium. The red ruby contains chromium. Trace amounts of iron in quartz gives the amethyst its color.

Section Assessment

1. Describe the differences between elements, compounds, and mixtures. Into which of these categories does a solution fall? Explain.

2. How is a container of hydrogen gas and oxygen gas different from a container of water in the gaseous state, known as water vapor?

3. **Think Critically:** Carbonated-beverage cans are made out of aluminum alloys with three different compositions. The body of the can is made of one alloy, the top of the can is made of a second alloy, and the tab you pull on to open the can is made of a third alloy. Which of these alloys do you think is the strongest? Which is the most flexible? Explain your answer.

4. **Skill Builder**
   Comparing and Contrasting Compare and contrast the following types of solutions: the active material in a helium-neon laser (glows like a neon light), bronze (copper-tin), cloudy ice cubes, and ginger ale. If you need help, refer to Comparing and Contrasting in the **Skill Handbook** on page 704.

Science Journal Read about ancient peoples in a world history book. Record in your Science Journal the names of some of the eras of human existence that were named after the materials and alloys people used for making tools. Discuss why each new material was an improvement over the ones used before.

Aqueous Solutions

Water—The Universal Solvent

You've learned about a number of solutions that have water as a solvent—salt water, fruit drinks, the solutions that form stalactites and stalagmites, and vinegar. These solutions and the many others in which water is the solvent are called **aqueous** (AH kwee us) solutions. Because water can dissolve so many different solutes, chemists often call it the universal solvent. What is it about water that makes it such a great solvent?

Understanding Molecular Compounds

You'll better understand water and its properties by thinking back to what you learned about atoms and bonding. Atoms are neutral because they contain equal numbers of positively charged protons and negatively charged electrons. When atoms come together to form compounds, they often share electrons.

In water, the two hydrogen atoms share electrons with the single oxygen atom. Sharing electrons, called covalent bonding, results in molecular compounds; that is, compounds made up of molecules. If the atoms that make up a molecule share electrons equally, the atoms remain electrically neutral and the resulting molecule has an even distribution of positive and negative charges. Such a molecule is said to be nonpolar, as in **Figure 5-8**. However, that's not what happens with water. Water is a compound made up of H_2O molecules. Because the hydrogen atoms don't share electrons equally with the oxygen atom, polar covalent bonds are formed. So, one region of the water molecule has a somewhat positive charge while another region has a somewhat negative charge. Such a molecule is said to be polar.

What You'll Learn

► Why water is able to dissolve many substances
► Why solvents can dissolve some solutes but not others
► How to describe the concentration of a solution
► What factors affect a solution's maximum concentration

Vocabulary
aqueous   concentration
solubility   concentrated
saturated   dilute

Why It's Important

► Solutions, including the liquids that you drink and bodily fluids like blood, allow your body to function.

Figure 5-8 Because the two oxygen atoms in an O_2 molecule share electrons equally, the molecule is nonpolar. **Why is the nitrogen molecule, N_2, nonpolar?**

Oxygen molecule

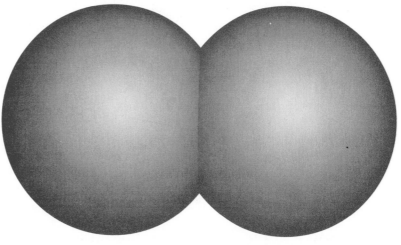

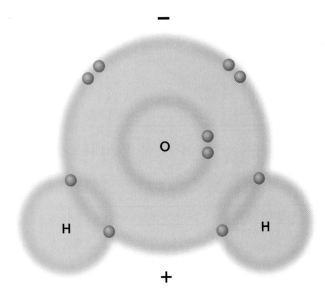

Figure 5-9 In the water molecule, the oxygen atom attracts electrons more than the hydrogen atoms, making the oxygen side of the molecule somewhat negative.

Figure 5-10 Sodium chloride dissolves in water because opposite charges attract each other. Once dissolved, water molecules surround the sodium and chloride ions. **What part of the water molecule attracts the positive calcium ions when calcium chloride dissolves in water?**

Understanding Ionic Compounds

An ionic compound is formed when one or more of the bonding atoms loses electrons and one or more of the bonding atoms gains electrons. That's what happens when sodium combines with chlorine to form table salt, which is sodium chloride. Each sodium atom loses one electron and becomes a positively charged sodium ion. Each chlorine atom gains one electron, becoming a negatively charged chloride ion. The formula NaCl tells you that sodium chloride contains equal numbers of sodium ions and chloride ions.

How Water Dissolves Things

Now, think about the properties of water and the properties of ionic compounds as you visualize how an ionic compound dissolves in water. Because water molecules are polar, as shown in **Figure 5-9**, they can attract both positive and negative ions. Water dissolves ionic compounds by literally pulling apart the ions, as shown with table salt in **Figure 5-10**. The more positive ends of water molecules are attracted to salt's negative chloride ions, while the more negative ends of water molecules are attracted to the positive sodium ions.

Water can dissolve a molecular compound such as sugar because sugar contains many polar bonds. Sugar molecules are polar, just like water molecules. Similar to the dissolving of ionic compounds, the more positive ends of water molecules are attracted to the more negative portions of sugar molecules, and the more negative ends of water molecules are attracted to the more positive portions of sugar molecules. If you've ever added sugar to your iced tea, you know the result: sugar dissolves in water.

Solubility

When you stir a spoonful of sugar into your iced tea, the sugar dissolves, but the spoon doesn't. Why are some substances soluble in a certain solvent while others are not? What determines how much solute can be dissolved in a solvent? **Solubility** is the term used to describe how much solute dissolves in a given amount of solvent.

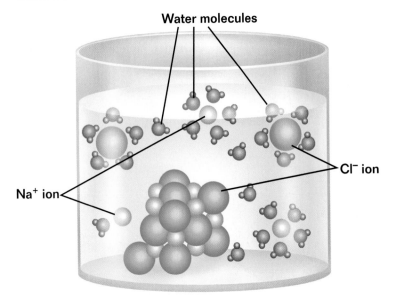

Water molecules

Cl⁻ ion

Na⁺ ion

 When a mixture of baby oil (colorless) and water (dyed blue) is shaken and then sits for a time, the oil and water separate into layers.

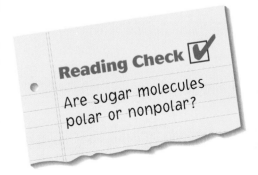 Olive oil (greenish-gold) and safflower oil (nearly colorless) mix with water and remain mixed upon sitting.

Like Dissolves Like

Water dissolves many things, but it can't dissolve everything. When trying to predict which solvents can dissolve which solutes, chemists use the rule of thumb that "like dissolves like." This statement means that dissolution of the solute occurs when the solvent and the solute are similar. In the case of sugar and water, both are made up of polar molecules, so sugar is soluble in water. In the case of salt and water, the water molecule is like a charged particle because it has excess positive charge at one end and excess negative charge at the other end. ☑

Have you ever heard the expression "they don't mix, like oil and water"? When baby oil and water are mixed, they separate rather than forming a solution, as shown in **Figure 5-11A.** Baby oil is a mixture of nonpolar molecules, so it is unlike water. You've probably noticed the same thing about the oil-and-water solutions that make up many salad dressings. Oils generally dissolve better in solvents that have nonpolar molecules. Some other oils, though, such as olive oil and safflower oil, are made up of molecules that are more polar. Because these oils are more like water, they mix with it more readily, as in **Figure 5-11B.**

Figure 5-11 Some liquids mix with each other more readily than others do. **Why doesn't gasoline mix with water?**

Reading Check ☑
Are sugar molecules polar or nonpolar?

How much will dissolve?

Solubility often is given as the amount of a substance that can dissolve in 100 g of solvent at a given temperature. Some solutes are highly soluble, meaning that a large amount of solute can be dissolved in 100 g of solvent. For example, 315 g of potassium chromate can be dissolved in 500 g of water at 25°C, **Figure 5-12.** However, some solutes are not very soluble, meaning that only a small amount of solute can be dissolved in 100 g of solvent. For example, only 0.00025 g of barium sulfate will dissolve in 100 g of water at 25°C. Barium sulfate and other compounds with extremely low solubilities are usually said to be insoluble in water.

Saturated Solutions

You would say that calcium carbonate, commonly called limestone, is insoluble in water. However, 0.0014 g of calcium carbonate dissolves in 100 g of water at 25°C. Such a solution, one that contains all of the solute that it can hold under the given conditions, is called a **saturated** solution. If any more solute is added to a saturated solution, the extra solute will not dissolve. If the solution is a solid-liquid solution, the extra solute added will settle to the bottom of the container. It's important for you to know that solubility does not tell you *how fast* a solute will dissolve. A solute dissolves faster when the solution is stirred or shaken. Increasing temperature and surface-area contact between solute and solvent also makes a solute dissolve faster.

Of course, it's possible to make solutions that have less solute than they would need to become saturated. Such solutions are called unsaturated solutions. An example of an unsaturated solution would be one containing 50 g of sugar in 100 g of water at 25°C. That's much less than the 204 g of sugar the solution would need to be saturated. If a saturated solution is cooled slowly, sometimes the excess solute remains dissolved for a period of time. Such a solution is said to be supersaturated.

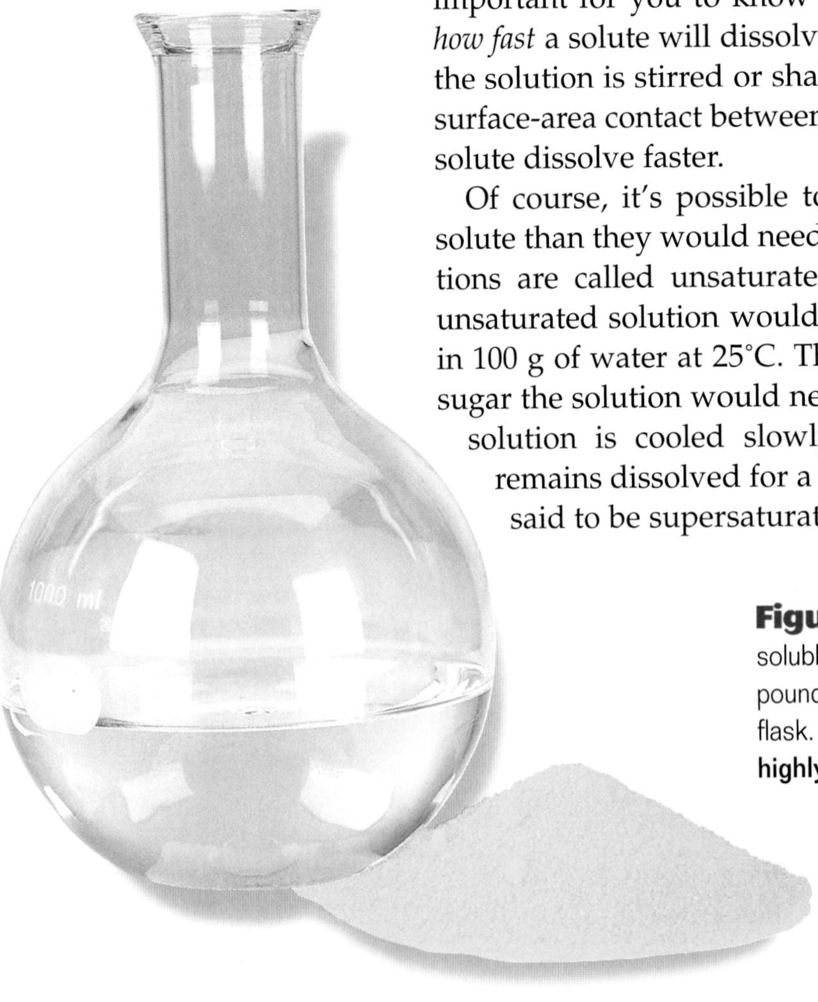

Using Math

In a laboratory, a flask of sodium chloride solution contains 60 g of sodium chloride in 1.0 L of solution. If 75 mL of this solution are poured into a beaker, how many grams of solute are contained in the beaker?

Figure 5-12 Potassium chromate is so soluble in water that the entire pile of the compound shown can dissolve in the water in the flask. **What is another compound that is highly soluble in water?**

Concentration

The **concentration** of a solution tells you *how much* solute is present compared to the amount of solvent. If you don't need to know exactly what the concentration is, you can describe the solution in relative terms as being either concentrated or dilute. A **concentrated** solution is one that contains a large amount of solute per given amount of solvent. A **dilute** solution is one that contains a small amount of solute per given amount of solvent. A comparison of concentrated and dilute solutions is shown in **Figure 5-13.**

Suppose you're in the hospital and your doctor decides to administer an intravenous (IV) solution. Would you feel safe if the doctor simply ordered a "dilute IV solution" or a "concentrated IV solution"? Absolutely not! Those terms would not be exact enough. As is true in this case and many others, it's often necessary to specify the exact concentration of a solution. One way is to state the percentage of the volume of the solution that is made up of solute and the percentage made up of solvent. A fruit-drink label may advertise that the drink is 20 percent fruit juice. This means that the remaining 80 percent is water and other substances such as sweeteners and flavorings. This drink is more concentrated than another brand that contains ten percent fruit juice, and it's more dilute than pure juice, which is 100 percent juice.

Observing Gas Solubility

Procedure

1. Obtain any size bottle of a thoroughly chilled, carbonated beverage.
2. Carefully remove the cap from the bottle with as little agitation as possible.
3. Quickly cover the opening with an uninflated balloon. Use tape to secure and seal the balloon to the top of the bottle.
4. **CAUTION:** *Be careful not to point the bottle at anyone.* Gently agitate the bottle from side to side for two minutes and observe the size of the balloon.
5. Set the bottle of soft drink in a container of hot tap water for ten minutes and observe the final size of the balloon.

Analysis

1. Compare and contrast the amounts of carbon dioxide gas released from the cold and warm soft drinks.
2. Why does the soft drink contain a different amount of carbon dioxide when warmed than it does when chilled?

Figure 5-13 The cherry drink on the left is more concentrated than the one on the right. Canned fruit is sometimes packed in light sugar syrup and sometimes in heavy sugar syrup. **Which syrup is more concentrated?**

Factors That Affect Solubility

The solubility of many solutes changes if you change the temperature of the solvent. This effect is shown in **Figure 5-14.** If you raise the temperature of water, you can add more sugar before the solution becomes saturated.

Another factor can change solubility. In gas-liquid solutions, if the pressure of the gas is increased, its solubility also is increased. You can see this in action when you open a bottle of carbonated beverage. Before you open the bottle, you don't see any bubbles in the liquid. But when you open the bottle, bubbles are suddenly visible as the liquid fizzes. When the bottle was originally filled, extra carbon dioxide gas was squeezed into the space above the liquid. This increased the pressure in the bottle and forced most of the gas into solution in the liquid. When you open the cap, the extra pressure is released into the air and the solubility of the gas in the liquid becomes less. The carbon dioxide gas comes out of solution by forming small bubbles that float to the top of the soft drink and make it fizz.

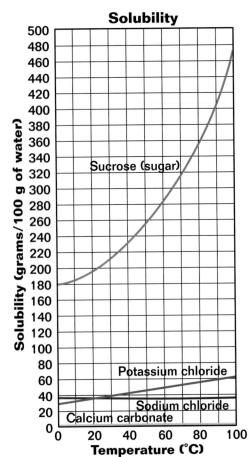

Figure 5-14 This solubility graph tells how much of four substances can dissolve in 100 g of water at various temperatures.

Section Assessment

1. Why is water called the universal solvent? Why does it have these properties?

2. The new bottles of concentrated laundry detergent are much smaller than the old bottles, but the labels claim they can clean the same amount of clothing. Explain how this might be so.

3. **Think Critically:** Why can the fluids used to dry-clean clothing remove grease from clothes even when water cannot?

4. **Skill Builder**
    Separating and Controlling Variables Scientists pay close attention to controls, dependent variables, and independent variables when they design experiments. Do the **Chapter 5 Skill Activity** on page 730 to learn how to identify controls and variables.

Using Computers

Spreadsheet Use a spreadsheet to make a graph showing the solubility of potassium nitrate on the vertical axis and temperature on the horizontal axis. What is the approximate solubility of potassium nitrate in water at 25°C? If you need help, refer to page 722.

Growing Crystals

If you create a supersaturated solution of alum and then introduce a seed crystal, the alum in solution will attach to the seed crystal and make it grow.

What You'll Investigate

How does a crystal grow in a supersaturated solution?

Goals

- **Observe** the formation of a large alum crystal from a supersaturated solution.

Safety Precautions

Procedure

1. Pour water into the 150-mL beaker to the 100-mL mark.

2. Heat the water on a hot plate to a temperature of 45°C.

3. Dissolve 25 g of alum powder in the heated water.

4. Use the heatproof mitt to remove the beaker from the hot plate and set it on your laboratory table.

5. **Measure** and record the initial size of the alum seed crystal.

6. Tie one end of a thin string or wire around the seed crystal and the other end to a support stick.

7. Place the seed crystal support stick across the top of the beaker so that the seed crystal is submerged just below the surface of the solution.

8. Allow the solution to sit overnight.

9. The following day, **measure** and record the size of your alum crystal again. If you wish, let the solution sit overnight again and then repeat the measurement.

Materials

- Heat-resistant beaker (150 mL)
- Alum powder
- Balance
- Hot plate
- Stirring rod
- Heatproof mitt
  *beaker tongs
- Alcohol thermometer
- Metric ruler

  *Alternate Materials

Conclude and Apply

1. **Compare and contrast** the size of the crystal after one day to the crystal's original size.

2. Where does the extra crystal material come from?

3. Why does the crystal grow?

Alum Crystal Data	
Day	**Size of Crystal**

5·3 Acids and Bases

Acids

What You'll Learn

► What acids and bases are
► Properties of acidic and basic solutions
► Why some acids and bases are stronger than others
► What happens when acids and bases are brought together

Vocabulary

acid   indicator
base   neutralization
pH

Why It's Important

► Many common products work because they are acids or bases.

You've probably enjoyed a glass of cold lemonade on a warm summer day. What gives lemonade its thirst-quenching, sour taste—a taste shared by many other foods, including vinegar, dill pickles, orange juice, and grapefruit? Acids cause the sour taste of the foods shown in **Figure 5-15.** **Acids** are substances that contain hydrogen and produce hydronium ions when they dissolve in water. Hydronium ions are positively charged and have the formula H_3O^+. How do acids produce hydronium ions? When acids are dissolved in water, they release positively charged hydrogen ions, H^+. The H^+ ions then combine with water molecules to form hydronium ions, as shown in **Figure 5-16.**

Properties of Acidic Solutions

Sour taste is one of the properties of acidic solutions. The taste allows you to detect the presence of acids in your food. Even though you can identify acidic solutions by their sour taste, you should NEVER use taste to test for the presence of acids. In fact, some acids can cause burns and damage body tissues.

Acidic solutions can conduct electricity because they contain ions. Acidic solutions are corrosive, which means they can eat away at certain substances. The solutions of some acids react strongly with certain metals, forming metallic compounds and hydrogen gas and leaving holes in the metal in the process.

When carbon dioxide from the air dissolves in water, carbonic acid is formed. Because carbon dioxide is dissolved in water to produce carbonated beverages, these beverages contain carbonic acid. The stalagmite and stalactite formations you saw earlier in the chapter involved carbonic acid solutions, too. Naturally formed carbonic acid in the soil begins to dissolve the calcium carbonate that makes up most of the

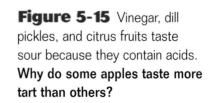

Figure 5-15 Vinegar, dill pickles, and citrus fruits taste sour because they contain acids.
Why do some apples taste more tart than others?

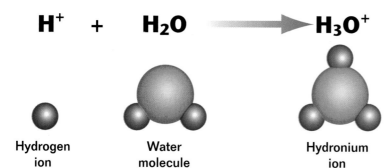

$$H^+ + H_2O \longrightarrow H_3O^+$$

Hydrogen ion   Water molecule   Hydronium ion

Figure 5-16 When hydrogen ions from acids combine with water molecules, hydronium ions are formed.

limestone rock in the cave. When drops of the resulting solution cling to the roof of the cave and evaporate, they create the hanging rock formations called stalactites. When drops of the solution fall onto the floor of the cave and evaporate, they form stalagmites, which look like upside-down stalactites. This same kind of reaction occurs when acid rain, which can form from air pollution and other sources, falls on statues and eats away at the stone, as shown in **Figure 5-17.**

Uses of Acids

You're probably familiar with many acids. Vinegar, which is used in salad dressing and in making pickles, contains acetic acid. Lemons and oranges have a sour taste because they contain citric acid. Your body needs ascorbic acid, which is vitamin C. Ants that sting inject formic acid to cause pain in their victims.

Try at Home

Mini Lab

Observing a Nail in a Carbonated Drink

Procedure

1. Observe the initial appearance of the iron nail.
2. Pour some of the carbonated soft drink into a cup or beaker, filling it about twice as deep as the nail is long.
3. Drop the nail into the soft drink and observe what happens.
4. Leave the nail in the soft drink overnight and observe it again the next day.

Analysis

1. Describe what happened when you first dropped the nail into the soft drink and the appearance of the nail the following day.
2. Based upon the fact that the soft drink was carbonated, explain why you think the drink reacted with the nail as you observed.

Figure 5-17 Acid rain has eaten away some of the stone in these columns at the Acropolis in Athens, Greece. **Why is acid rain usually more of a problem near or downwind of industrial areas?**

Acids are often used in batteries because their solutions conduct electricity and because the ions they produce can react in certain ways. Sulfuric acid is used in the production of fertilizers, steel, paints, and plastics. Because sulfuric acid is an important ingredient in automobile batteries, it is sometimes called battery acid. Hydrochloric acid, which is known commercially as muriatic acid, is used in a process called pickling. Pickling removes impurities from the surfaces of metals. Hydrochloric acid also can be used to clean mortar from brick walls. Nitric acid is used in the production of fertilizers, dyes, plastics, and explosives.

Bases

The ammonia solutions that people sometimes use to clean windows have properties that are distinctly different from those of acidic solutions. Ammonia is called a base. **Bases** are substances that produce hydroxide ions when they dissolve in water. Hydroxide ions are negatively charged and have the formula OH^-.

Properties of Basic Solutions

Most soaps are bases, and if you think about how you use soap, you can figure out some of the properties of basic solutions. Basic solutions feel slippery to the touch. While acids in water solution taste sour, bases taste bitter—as you know, if you have ever accidentally gotten soap in your mouth.

Like acids, bases are corrosive. Touch or taste tests should NEVER be used to test for bases because they can cause burns and damage tissue. Like acidic solutions, basic solutions contain ions and can conduct electricity. Unlike acidic solutions, basic solutions usually do not react with metals.

Uses of Bases

Bases give soaps and many other cleaning products, as shown in **Figure 5-18,** some of their useful properties. That's because the hydroxide ions produced by bases can interact strongly with certain substances, such as dirt and grease. Ammonia is a part of many household cleaners and also is used in the manufacture of fertilizers, fibers, and plastics.

Antacid tablets, chalk, oven cleaner, and many other familiar products and substances contain bases. Magnesium hydroxide is a base found in some

interNET CONNECTION

Visit the Glencoe Science Web Site at **www.glencoe.com/ sec/science** for more information about acids and their uses.

Figure 5-18 Bases give soaps and ammonia some of their cleaning qualities. **What ion is likely involved in the cleaning ability of soaps?**

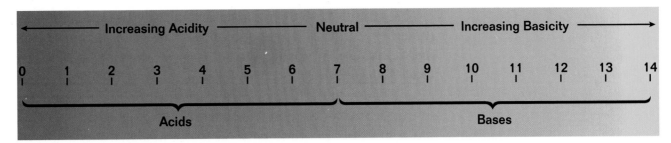

Increasing Acidity — Neutral — Increasing Basicity

0 1 2 3 4 5 6 7 8 9 10 11 12 13 14

Acids

Bases

antacids. Your blood is a basic solution. Calcium hydroxide, a base that is often called lime, is used to mark the lines on athletic fields. Calcium hydroxide is also found in chalk, mortar, plaster, and paving materials, and it can be used to treat lawns and gardens that have acidic soil. Sodium hydroxide, also known as lye, is a strong base that can cause burns and other health problems. Lye is used to make soap, clean ovens, and unclog drains.

Figure 5-19 The pH scale is a quick way to classify a solution as acidic, basic, or neutral. **Does an ammonia solution have a pH above 7 or below 7?**

pH

If you've seen someone test the water in a swimming pool, you know that the water's pH is important to the safety of swimmers. You've probably heard of pH-balanced shampoo. A solution's **pH** is a measure of how acidic or basic the solution is. The pH scale generally ranges from 0 to 14. More acidic solutions have lower pH values, and a solution with a pH of 0 is highly acidic. A solution that has a pH of 7 is neutral. More basic solutions have higher pH values, and a solution with a pH of 14 is extremely basic, as shown in **Figure 5-19.** ☑

The pH of a solution is directly related to its concentrations of hydronium ions and hydroxide ions. As shown in **Figure 5-20,** acidic solutions have more hydronium ions than hydroxide ions. Neutral solutions have equal numbers of the two ions. Basic solutions have more hydroxide ions than hydronium ions.

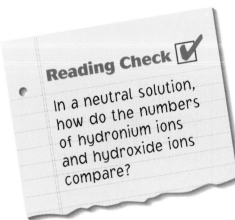

Reading Check ☑

In a neutral solution, how do the numbers of hydronium ions and hydroxide ions compare?

Figure 5-20 What makes a pH 7 solution neutral?

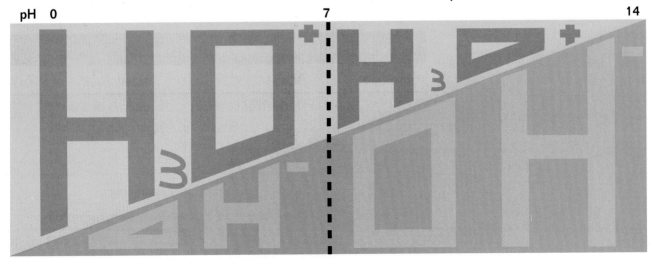

pH 0   7   14

The pH scale is not a simple linear scale like mass or volume. For example, if one book has a mass of 2 kg and a second book has a mass of 1 kg, the mass of the first book is just twice that of the second. However, a change of 1 pH unit represents a tenfold change in the acidity of the solution. For example, if one solution has a pH of 1 and a second solution has a pH of 2, the first solution is not just twice as acidic as the second. Rather, it's ten times more acidic! In a similar way, a solution with a pH of 12 is 100 times more basic than one with a pH of 10.

pH and Strengths of Acids and Bases

Sometimes, acids and bases can be confusing. On one hand, you've learned that acids give foods a sour taste. On the other hand, acids can cause burns and damage tissue. Both are properties of acids, but what's the difference between food acids and the acids that can burn you? The acids have different strengths. The acids in food are fairly weak acids, while the dangerous acids are strong acids. The strength of an acid is related to the number of hydronium ions it produces when it dissolves to form a solution. For the same concentration, a strong acid forms more hydronium ions in solution than a weak acid. More hydronium ions mean the strong-acid solution has a lower pH than the weak-acid solution. Similarly, the strength of a base is related to the number of hydroxide ions it produces when it dissolves to form a solution. The relative strengths of some common acids and bases are shown in **Table 5-2.**

Indicators are compounds that react with acidic and basic solutions to produce certain colors. For that reason, indicators can help you find out how acidic or basic a solution is. Some indicators, such as litmus, are soaked into paper strips. When litmus paper is placed in an acidic solution, it turns red. But, when placed in a basic solution, litmus paper turns blue.

Table 5-2

Strengths of Some Acids and Bases		
Strength	**Acid**	**Base**
Strong	Hydrochloric Sulfuric Nitric	Sodium hydroxide Potassium hydroxide
Weak	Acetic Carbonic Ascorbic	Ammonia Aluminum hydroxide Iron(III) hydroxide

Some indicators can change through a wide range of colors, with each different color appearing at a different pH value.

Acid rain can result from the introduction of acid-forming compounds into the air by power plants. This rain falls across the countryside and into bodies of water. Many lakes have become unfit for fish to live in because much of the lake water comes from acid rain.

Neutralization

Perhaps you've heard someone complain about heartburn or an upset stomach after eating a large meal. To feel better, the person may have taken an antacid. How do antacids work?

Heartburn or stomach discomfort is caused by excess hydrochloric acid in the stomach. Hydrochloric acid helps break down the food you eat, but too much acid can irritate your stomach or digestive tract. The antacid product, often made from the base magnesium hydroxide, neutralizes the excess acid. **Neutralization** (new truh luh ZAY shun) is the interaction that occurs between acids and bases in which the properties of each are canceled out by the other.

*inter*NET
CONNECTION

Visit the Glencoe Science Web Site at **www.glencoe.com/ sec/science** for more information about acid rain.

Problem Solving

The Statue Mystery

When members of the art museum's board of directors returned for their annual meeting, they happened to look at the old marble and metal statues in front of the museum. They noticed that the previously beautiful statues were deteriorating badly. They suspected that acid rain might be the problem.

To check their hypothesis, they designed and carried out an experiment that produced the following results. First, when marble chips are placed in a dilute sulfuric acid solution, gas bubbles form and the chips dissolve slowly. (Sulfuric acid is a component of acid rain.)

Then, when mossy zinc is placed in a dilute sulfuric acid solution, a rapid reaction occurs. (Zinc is a component of the metal in statues.) Many gas bubbles form, and the zinc dissolves quickly.

Think Critically: Infer how the damage to the statues may have occurred based on the results of the experiment. Research and explain some ways that the museum's board of directors and other segments of society, such as energy companies, might minimize the problems caused by acid rain.

How does neutralization happen? Remember that each water molecule contains two hydrogen atoms and one oxygen atom. When one hydronium ion reacts with one hydroxide ion, the product is simply two water molecules, **Figure 5-21.** This reaction occurs during acid-base neutralization, in which equal numbers of hydronium ions and hydroxide ions react to produce water. Water has a pH of 7, which means that it's neither acidic nor basic.

In the case of an antacid that contains magnesium hydroxide, the excess hydrochloric acid combines with magnesium hydroxide to form water and magnesium chloride. Water is neutral. Magnesium chloride, the other substance formed, is neither an acid nor a base. Magnesium chloride is called a salt. Salts have a number of uses in your body. Calcium salts are needed for healthy teeth and bones. Iron salts are found in your blood. Other salts are needed for muscle function and the control of fluid balance in your body's cells.

Figure 5-21 When acidic and basic solutions react, hydronium ions react with hydroxide ions to form water molecules.

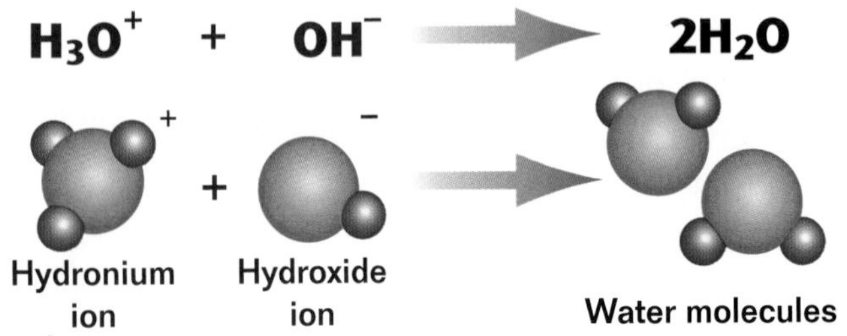

$$H_3O^+ \; + \; OH^- \longrightarrow 2H_2O$$

Hydronium ion

Hydroxide ion

Water molecules

Section Assessment

1. Why do acidic and basic solutions conduct electricity?

2. Name three acids that are important in industry. Give one use for each.

3. What is the pH of pure water at 25°C?

4. **Think Critically:** Strong acids are used in many industrial applications, but they can be hazardous to humans. How do you think a company that uses a strong acid would handle a situation in which that acid spills onto the factory floor?

5. **Skill Builder**

   Sequencing Arrange the following list of solutions in order from most basic to most acidic. If you need help, refer to Sequencing in the **Skill Handbook** on page 698.

Tomato juice, pH 5	Milk of magnesia, pH 10.5
Baking soda, pH 9	Seawater, pH 8
Lemon juice, pH 2	Drain cleaner, pH 13

Using Math

How much more acidic is a solution with a pH of 2 than one with a pH of 6? How much more basic is a solution with a pH of 13 than one with a pH of 10?

Making Paper

Paper vs. Rock

Your backpack may feel heavy, but suppose it were loaded with stone tablets instead of paper? Before the invention of paper, ancient people wrote on stone. By 3500 B.C., Egyptians were making a type of paper from the papyrus plant. Later, people created another form of paper, called parchment, from animal skins.

The Chinese (left) were using vegetable fibers to make paper by the beginning of the second century A.D. The paper made from these fibers was so valuable that the process of making it was kept secret for 500 years. Only when the Arabs in Samarkand (a city in what is now Uzbekistan) captured Chinese papermakers did the rest of the world learn how to manufacture paper. With the invention of the printing press, paper became even more important. In 1798, the invention of papermaking machines made it possible to mass-produce paper.

Perfecting Paper

Early paper had one major problem—the wood pulp used to make paper had impurities and fibers that had to be broken down. To do this, paper manufacturers began to boil the wood pulp with various chemicals. This process often made the paper acidic. Because acidic paper is fragile, examples of early paper are rare.

Today, alkalis, a mixture of soluble salts, are used to strengthen paper and to improve the way it feels. Papermaking plants (right) make most paper from wood. Cloth rags are used to make fine writing paper and artists' paper. Some papers can be recycled and used again.

Science
JOURNAL

In your Science Journal, write about how life would change if there were no paper available. Would computers be able to fill the gap?

Activity 5•2

Testing pH Using Natural Indicators

Materials

- Small test tubes (9)
- Test-tube rack
- Concentrated red cabbage juice in a dropper bottle
- Labeled bottles containing: household ammonia, baking soda solution, soap solution, hydrochloric acid solution, white vinegar, colorless carbonated soft drink, sodium hydroxide, drain cleaner solution, distilled water
- Grease pencil

You have learned that certain substances, called indicators, change color when the pH of a solution changes. Indicators can be used to determine the approximate pH of a solution and to show changes in pH. The juice from red cabbage is one of these substances.

What You'll Investigate

How can you use red cabbage juice as an indicator to determine the relative pH of solutions? Why do the solutions of some bases have higher pH values than solutions of other bases? What ion is involved in the cleaning process?

Goals

- **Determine** the relative pH values of several common solutions.
- **Compare** the strengths of several common acids and bases.

Safety Precautions

Use caution when working with acids and bases. Wear laboratory aprons and safety goggles.

Cabbage Juice Data	
Cabbage Juice Color	**Relative pH**
bright red	strong acid
red	medium acid
reddish-purple	weak acid
purple	neutral
blue-green	weak base
green	medium base
yellow	strong base

Procedure

1. **Design** a data table in which you can record the names of the solutions to be tested, the colors caused by the added cabbage juice indicator, and the relative pH values of the solutions.

2. Mark each test tube with the identity of the solution it will contain.

3. Fill each test tube about halfway with the solution to be tested. **CAUTION:** *If you spill any liquids on your skin, rinse the area immediately with water. Alert your teacher if any liquid is spilled in the work area.*

4. Add ten drops of the cabbage juice indicator to each of the solutions to be tested. Gently agitate or wiggle each test tube to mix the cabbage juice with the solution.

5. **Observe** and record the color of each solution in your data table.

Conclude and Apply

1. **Compare** your observations with the cabbage juice color table. Record the relative pH of each solution tested in your data table.

2. **Classify** which solutions were acidic and which were basic.

3. Which solution was the weakest acid? The strongest base?

4. **Predict** what ion might be involved in the cleaning process based upon your pH values for the ammonia, soap, and drain-cleaner solutions.

5. **Form a hypothesis** that explains why the sodium hydroxide solution had a much higher pH than an ammonia solution of approximately the same concentration.

FIELD GUIDE to Kitchen Chemistry

It's early morning in the kitchen, and chemistry surrounds you. Breakfast—with its wake-up sights and smells—is almost ready. Freshly squeezed orange juice, hot tea, yogurt with strawberries, butter, and syrup wait on the counter. Eggs and pancakes sizzle on the griddle. Slices of bread are toasting. Some foods are liquids. Others are solids. Most are mixtures. Some are undergoing delectable changes while you watch. Using this field guide, you can identify the different types of mixtures that you drink and eat, and the chemical and physical changes that occur as foods are prepared.

How Mixtures Are Classified

Mixtures contain two or more substances that have not combined to form a new substance. The proportions of the substances that make up a mixture can vary. Mixtures are classified as either homogeneous or heterogeneous.

- You cannot see the substances in a homogeneous mixture no matter how closely you look.
- You easily can identify the substances that are in a heterogeneous mixture.

Homogeneous Mixtures—Solutions

Much of the chemistry in your kitchen takes place in solutions. Because solutions are homogeneous mixtures, you can't see their different parts. Both tea and syrup are solutions of solids dissolved in liquids.

Acids

Many foods contain acids or acidic solutions. One noticeable property of an acidic solution is its sour taste. Of course, you should never taste a solution simply to determine if it's acidic! For example, lactic acid gives yogurt its sour taste. While fruits such as oranges, lemons, and apples contain many other substances that are not acidic, citric acid gives them their tartness or sour taste. Acidic solutions have pH values below 7.

Heterogeneous Mixtures

You can see the different parts of most heterogeneous mixtures. For example, strawberries are clearly visible in the yogurt.

How Changes Are Classified

A change to a substance can be classified as either a chemical or physical change. A chemical change is one in which one or more new substances are formed. When a physical change occurs, the identity of the substance does not change.

Chemical Changes

Chemical changes can be recognized by the following signs.
- The color changes.
- A solid forms when solutions are mixed.
- Heat or light is absorbed or released.
- An odor forms or changes.
- A gas is released.

Gas Production

The bubbles you see in pancake batter are caused by a chemical change in the batter. Baking powder is a mixture containing mostly baking soda and an acidic substance. When water is added to baking powder, the acidic solution that forms reacts with baking soda to make carbon dioxide gas.

Protein Denaturation

The proteins in a raw egg are folded into balls, sheets, and coils. Heating the egg breaks some of the bonds holding the proteins in these tight shapes. As cooking continues, the proteins unravel and begin forming weak bonds with other proteins, causing the egg to solidify.

Browning

Browning is a chemical change in which sugars and proteins in foods form new flavors and smells. Browning produces the barbecue flavors of foods cooked on a grill and the caramelized flavor of a roasted marshmallow.

Physical Changes

You can recognize a physical change when one of the following occurs.

- The substance changes shape.
- The substance changes size.
- The substance changes form. For example, a liquid changes to a solid or gas.

Melting

The pad of butter is changing from a solid to a liquid. Melting occurs because heat from the warm toast weakens and breaks bonds between the molecules in the butter.

Freezing

An ice-and-salt brine cools the liquid mixture of cream, sugar, and flavorings inside an ice-cream freezer. Most of the water in the mixture freezes into small ice crystals, and air bubbles give the solid mixture its smooth, creamy texture.

PICK UP HERE
HANDLE CAREFULLY:
CONTAINS HOT OIL AND STEAM

HEAT THIS SIDE DOWN
REMOVE PLASTIC OVERWRAP

Microwave Popcorn

Boiling

Popcorn kernels contain 11 to 14 percent water. When the kernels are heated, the liquid water changes to steam. The steam creates pressure that bursts the kernels. The hot steam also cooks the starchy interior of the corn, forming a light, crisp, and edible snack.

Chapter 5 Reviewing Main Ideas

For a **preview** of this chapter, study this Reviewing Main Ideas before you read the chapter. After you have studied this chapter, you can use the Reviewing Main Ideas to **review** the chapter.

The Glencoe MindJogger, Audiocassettes, and CD-ROM provide additional opportunities for review.

Section 5-1 SOLUTIONS

Materials can be elements, compounds, or mixtures. A **solution** is a homogeneous **mixture** in which the components cannot be distinguished easily. **Solutes** dissolve in **solvents** to form solutions. Solutions are classified as gaseous, liquid, or solid. *What is the difference between a compound and a mixture or solution?*

Water molecules

Na⁺ ion

Cl⁻ ion

Section 5-2 AQUEOUS SOLUTIONS

Water is known as the universal solvent because it can dissolve many solutes. This is possible because water molecules are polar. The **concentration** of a solution is a measure of the amount of solute in a particular volume of solvent. Solutions can be unsaturated, **saturated,** or supersaturated. *What kind of substances cannot be dissolved by the polar molecules that make up water? Explain why.*

SOLUBILITY

The maximum amount of solute that can be dissolved in a given amount of solvent at a particular temperature is called the **solubility** of the solute. Temperature and pressure can affect solubility. *How do you describe a solution that contains the maximum amount of solute possible under a given set of conditions?*

5-3 ACIDS AND BASES

Acids produce hydronium ions when dissolved in water, forming acidic solutions. **Bases** produce hydroxide ions when dissolved in water, forming basic solutions. Acidic and basic solutions have many distinctive properties. *List two properties of acidic solutions and two properties of basic solutions.*

pH

In aqueous solutions, **pH** expresses the concentrations of hydronium ions and hydroxide ions. Solutions with pH values below 7 are acidic. Solutions with a pH of 7 are neutral. Solutions with pH values above 7 are basic. *How do the acidities of two solutions with pH values of 3 and 5 compare?*

NEUTRALIZATION

In a neutralization reaction, an acid reacts with a base to form water and a salt. **Neutralization** cancels the properties of the acid and base as they are reacting and produces a neutral solution. *What salt will be formed when hydrochloric acid neutralizes aluminum hydroxide?*

$$H_3O^+ \; + \; OH^- \; \longrightarrow \; 2H_2O$$

Hydronium ion + Hydroxide ion ⟶ Water molecules

Using Vocabulary

a. acid
b. aqueous
c. base
d. concentrated
e. concentration
f. dilute
g. indicator
h. mixture
i. neutralization
j. pH
k. saturated
l. solubility
m. solute
n. solution
o. solvent

Each of the following sentences is false. Make the sentence true by replacing the italicized word with a word from the list above.

1. A *base* is substance that produces hydronium ions in solution.
2. A measure of how much solute is in a solution is its *solubility*.
3. The amount of a substance that can dissolve in 100 g of solvent is its *pH*.
4. The *solvent* is the substance that dissolves to form a solution.
5. The reaction between an acidic and a basic solution is called *concentration*.

Checking Concepts

Choose the word or phrase that best answers the question.

6. What is the solid substance that falls out of a solution?
   A) polymer   C) reactant
   B) ion   D) precipitate
7. What has a pH greater than 7?
   A) salt   C) acidic solution
   B) basic solution   D) solid
8. When chlorine is dissolved in pool water, what is the water?
   A) the alloy   C) the solution
   B) the solvent   D) the solute

9. A solid may become less soluble in a liquid when you decrease what?
   A) stirring   C) temperature
   B) pressure   D) container size
10. Which acid is used in the industrial process known as pickling?
    A) hydrochloric   C) sulfuric
    B) carbonic   D) nitric
11. At different pH values, indicators change what?
    A) odor   C) color
    B) smell   D) taste
12. What is formed by combining negative ions from an acid and positive ions from a base?
    A) a salt   C) lime
    B) lye   D) steel
13. Bile, a body fluid involved in digestion, is acidic, so its pH is what?
    A) 11   C) less than 7
    B) 7   D) greater than 7
14. Which of the following is a solution?
    A) pure oxygen in a firefighter's tank
    B) an oatmeal raisin cookie
    C) copper
    D) vinegar
15. Which of the following is potentially most dangerous to human skin?
    A) neutral solution
    B) concentrated basic solution
    C) dilute basic solution
    D) dilute acidic solution

Thinking Critically

16. Why do deposits form in the steam vents of irons in some parts of the country?
17. Is it possible for a solution to be both saturated and dilute? Explain your answer.
18. In which type of container is orange juice more likely to keep its freshly squeezed taste, a metal can or a paper carton? Explain.

19. Knowing what you do about the relative amounts of iron and carbon in regular steel, which do you think is the solvent? Which is the solute? Explain.

20. Water molecules can break apart to form H⁺ ions and OH⁻ ions. Water is known as an amphoteric substance, which is something that can act as an acid or a base. Explain how this can be so.

Developing Skills

If you need help, refer to the Skill Handbook.

21. **Making and Using Graphs:** Using the solubility graph below, estimate the solubilities of potassium chloride and sugar in grams per 100 g of water at 70°C.

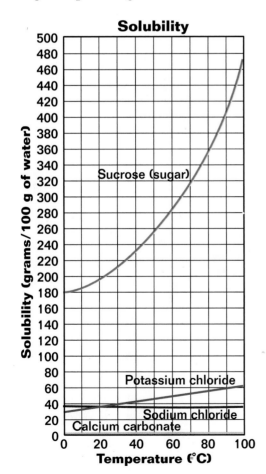

THE PRINCETON REVIEW

Test-Taking Tip

Make Yourself Comfortable When you take a test, try to make yourself as comfortable as possible. You will then be able to focus all of your attention on the test.

Test Practice

Use these questions to test your Science Proficiency.

1. Which of the following statements about acids is false?
   A) Metals can be eaten away by acids.
   B) Acids release hydroxide ions when dissolved in solution.
   C) Sour tastes can be a result of acids being present.
   D) Acids help in the digestion of food.

2. Which of the following approaches might be of use if you want to dissolve more potassium nitrate in 100 g of water?
   A) Increase the pressure.
   B) Decrease the amount of time you take to add the potassium nitrate.
   C) Increase the size of the container.
   D) Increase the temperature of the water.

3. A carbonated soft drink contains carbonic acid. Why does a carbonated soft drink have a higher pH than hydrochloric acid?
   A) The soft drink contains a sweetener.
   B) Carbonic acid is stronger than hydrochloric acid.
   C) Hydrochloric acid is stronger than carbonic acid.
   D) Carbonic acid contains more hydrogen atoms than hydrochloric acid.

2

Electricity & Magnetism

What's Happening Here?

The sun is the source of what we call daylight. But what accounts for Hong Kong's light display (left) in the night sky? The city's glow comes from streams of electrons flowing through circuits—electricity. Because electricity can be transported from place to place and easily converted into heat, light, and mechanical energy, it has transformed human life. In this unit, you will learn how electricity is created and how a force called magnetism, driven by attraction and repulsion is a main ingredient. You will also learn how Earth itself is a giant magnet. Homing pigeons (below) navigate by the sun, except on cloudy days when it is hypothesized that they use Earth's magnetic properties to find their way.

*inter*NET
CONNECTION

Explore the Glencoe Science Web Site at **www.glencoe.com/sec science** to find out more about topics found in this unit.

CHAPTER
6

Electricity

Chapter Preview

Section 6-1
Static Electricity

Section 6-2
Electric Current

Section 6-3
Electric Circuits

Skills Preview

Skill Builders

- Observe and Infer
- Form a Hypothesis

Activities

- Make a Model
- Use Scientific Methods

MiniLabs

- Observe and Infer
- Form a Hypothesis

Reading Check ✔

As you read this chapter about electricity, write down the cause-effect relationships you identify.

Explore Activity

No computers, no CD players, no video games—can you even imagine life without electricity? You depend on it every day, and not just to make life more fun. Electricity also helps to heat and cool your homes and to provide light. Electric lighting even makes cities and towns visible from space, as shown in this satellite photo. Why is electricity so useful? Electricity provides energy that can be used to do work. This energy comes from the forces that electric charges exert on each other. What is the nature of these electric forces?

Observe Electric Forces

1. Inflate a rubber balloon.

2. Put some small bits of paper on your desktop and bring the balloon close to the bits of paper. Observe what happens.

3. Charge the balloon by holding it by the knot and rubbing the balloon on your hair or on a piece of wool.

4. Bring the balloon close to the bits of paper and observe what happens.

5. Charge two balloons using the procedure in step 3 and bring them close to each other. Observe what happens.

6. Repeat step 3, then touch the balloon with your hand. Now what happens when you bring the balloon close to the bits of paper?

Science Journal

In your Science Journal, record your observations of electric forces.

What You'll Learn

▶ How objects can become electrically charged
▶ How electric charges affect other electric charges
▶ The difference between insulators and conductors
▶ How electric discharges such as lightning occur

Vocabulary

static charge
insulator
conductor
electric discharge

Why It's Important

▶ Lightning and other electric discharges can cause damage.

Electric Charge

You can't see, smell, or taste electricity, so maybe it seems mysterious. But, electricity is not so hard to understand when you start by thinking small—very small. All solids, liquids, and gases are made of tiny particles called atoms. Atoms themselves are made of even smaller particles called protons, neutrons, and electrons as shown in **Figure 6-1**. Protons and neutrons are held together tightly in the nucleus at the center of an atom, while electrons swarm around the nucleus in all directions. Protons and electrons possess electric charge, while neutrons have no electric charge.

Positive and Negative Charge

There are two types of electric charge. Protons carry a positive electric charge and electrons carry a negative charge. No one knows exactly what electric charge is, but it cannot be removed from a proton or an electron.

The amount of negative charge on an electron is exactly equal to the amount of positive charge on a proton. Atoms normally have equal numbers of protons and electrons. So, the amount of positive charge on all the protons in the nucleus of an atom is exactly balanced by the negative charge on all the electrons moving around the nucleus. Thus, atoms are electrically neutral, which means they behave as if they have no charge at all.

Sometimes, though, an atom will gain extra electrons and become negatively charged. If an atom loses electrons, it becomes positively charged.

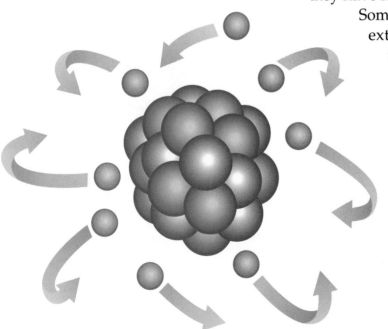

Figure 6-1 An atom is made of positively charged protons (purple), negatively charged electrons (red), and neutrons (green) with no electric charge. **Where are the protons and neutrons located?**

Electrons Move Between Objects

Electrons can move from atom to atom in a single object and also from the atoms in one object to the atoms in another object. Rubbing is one way that electrons can be transferred as shown in **Figure 6-2.** Suppose you rub a balloon on your hair as in the Explore Activity. The atoms on the balloon hold their electrons more tightly than the atoms in your hair hold their electrons. As a result, electrons are transferred from the atoms in your hair to the atoms on the surface of the balloon. Because your hair loses electrons, it becomes positively charged, while the balloon gains electrons and becomes negatively charged. The buildup of electric charges on an object is called a **static charge.**

You may wonder whether objects can be charged by transferring protons from one object to another. After all, protons have a positive charge, so moving them from one object to another should change the charge on the two objects. But, protons cannot be moved from one object to another because they are held together tightly with neutrons in the nuclei of atoms. It is always electrons that are gained or lost when an object becomes charged, and never protons.

Analyzing Electric Forces

Procedure

1. Rub a glass rod with a piece of silk.
2. Quickly separate the glass rod and the silk, and then slowly bring them close together.
3. Charge two pieces of silk by rubbing each on a glass rod.
4. Bring the two charged pieces of silk together slowly.

Analysis

Which materials have the same charge? Which have different charges? How do you know?

Reading Check How does an object become electrically charged?

Figure 6-2 Electrons can be moved from one object to another by rubbing.

A Before being rubbed together, a glass rod and a piece of silk cloth both have equal numbers of positive and negative charges.

Before rubbing

B Rubbing causes electrons to be transferred from the atoms in the glass rod to atoms in the silk. **Which object has become positively charged and which has become negatively charged?**

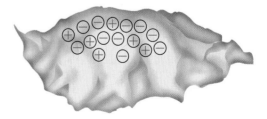

After rubbing

Opposite charges attract

Like charges repel

Figure 6-3 Two positive charges repel each other, as do two negative charges. The two like charges move away from each other, as shown by the arrows. A positive charge and a negative charge attract each other. The two unlike charges move toward each other.

Electric Forces

Charged objects exert an electric force on each other. The electric force between two charges can be attractive or repulsive as shown in **Figure 6-3.** Objects with the same type of charge repel one another, while objects with opposite charges attract one another. This rule is often stated as "like charges repel and unlike charges attract."

What keeps the nucleus of an atom from flying apart? Remember, the nucleus contains protons that have positive charges and neutrons that have no charge. You would expect the protons to repel each other. However, another force called the strong nuclear force is even stronger than the electric force. This strong nuclear force is the glue that holds protons and neutrons together in the nucleus.

Electric Fields

You may have noticed that two charged balloons repel each other even though they are not touching and that bits of paper and a charged balloon don't have to be touching for the paper to be attracted to the balloon. This behavior shows that charged objects don't have to be touching to exert an electric force on each other. The electric force acts on charged objects even though they may be some distance apart.

Electric charges exert a force on each other at a distance through an electric field, which exists around every electric charge. **Figure 6-4** shows the electric field around a positive and a negative charge. An electric field gets stronger as you get closer to a charge, just as the electric force between two charges becomes greater as the charges get closer together.

Figure 6-4 The arrows represent the electric field around electric charges. The direction of each arrow is the direction a positive charge would move if it were placed on the arrow.

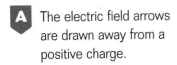 The electric field arrows are drawn away from a positive charge.

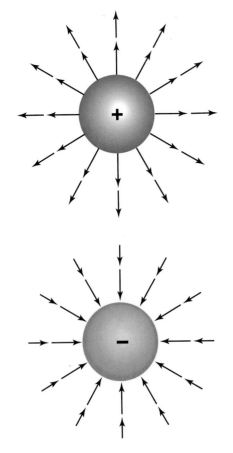

B The electric field arrows are drawn toward a negative charge. **Why are these arrows in the opposite direction of the arrows around the positive charge?**

Insulators

Rubbing a balloon on your hair transfers electrons from your hair to the balloon. But, only the part of the balloon that was rubbed on your hair becomes charged. This is because electrons cannot move easily through rubber. As a result, the electrons that were rubbed onto the balloon stayed in one place, as shown in **Figure 6-5A.** A material in which electrons cannot move easily from place to place is called an **insulator.** Examples of common materials that are insulators are plastic, wood, glass, and rubber.

Conductors

Materials that are **conductors** allow electrons to move through them more easily. Electrons placed on the surface of a conductor spread out over the entire surface, as shown in **Figure 6-5B.** The best conductors are metals such as copper, silver, and iron. An electrical wire is made from copper coated with an insulator such as plastic. Electrons move easily through the copper but do not move from the copper to the plastic insulation. This prevents electrons from escaping from the wire and causing an electric shock if someone touches the wire.

Do you think your body is an insulator or a conductor? Compared to common insulators, the human body is a conductor. You may have observed in the Explore Activity that if you touched the balloon after it had been charged, the balloon no longer attracted the bits of paper. Because electrons can move more easily along the surface of your skin than on the balloon, the excess electrons on the balloon were transferred to your hand when you touched the balloon.

Figure 6-5 Electric charges can move more easily through conductors than through insulators.

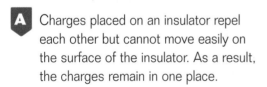

A Charges placed on an insulator repel each other but cannot move easily on the surface of the insulator. As a result, the charges remain in one place.

B Charges placed on a conductor repel each other but can move easily on the conductor's surface. Thus, they spread out as far apart as possible.

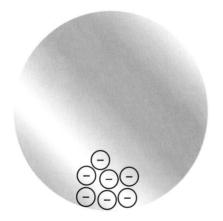

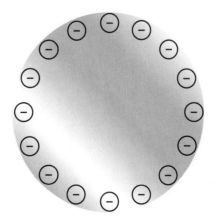

Induced Charge

Has this ever happened to you? You walk across a carpet, and as you reach for a metal doorknob, you feel an electric shock. Ouch! Maybe you even see a spark jump between your fingertip and the doorknob. To find out what happened, look at **Figure 6-6.**

As you walked, your shoes rubbed electrons off the rug, as shown in **Figure 6-6A.** The electrons then spread over the surface of your skin. As you brought your hand close to the doorknob, the electric field around the excess electrons on your hand repelled the electrons in the doorknob.

Because the doorknob was a good conductor, its electrons could move easily. The excess electrons on your hand repelled the electrons in the doorknob, as shown in **Figure 6-6B.** The part of the doorknob closest to your hand then became positively charged. This separation of positive and negative charges due to an electric field is called an induced charge.

If the electric field in the space between your hand and the knob is strong enough, electrons can be pulled across that space from your hand, as shown in **Figure 6-6C.** This rapid movement of excess electrons from one place to another is an **electric discharge.** See **Figure 6-7** for another familiar example of an electric discharge.

*inter*NET
CONNECTION

Visit the Glencoe Science Web Site at **www.glencoe.com/ sec/science** for more information about other types of lightning.

Figure 6-6 A spark that jumps between your fingers and a metal doorknob starts at your feet.

A As you walk across the floor, you rub electrons from the carpet onto the bottom of your shoes. These electrons then spread out all over your skin, including your hands.

B As you bring your hand close to the metal doorknob, electrons on the doorknob move as far away from your hand as possible. The part of the doorknob closest to your hand is left with a positive charge.

C The attractive electric force between the electrons on your hand and the induced positive charge on the doorknob may be strong enough to pull electrons from your hand to the doorknob. You may see this as a spark and feel a mild electric shock.

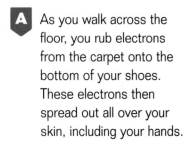

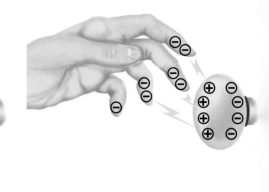

Figure 6-7

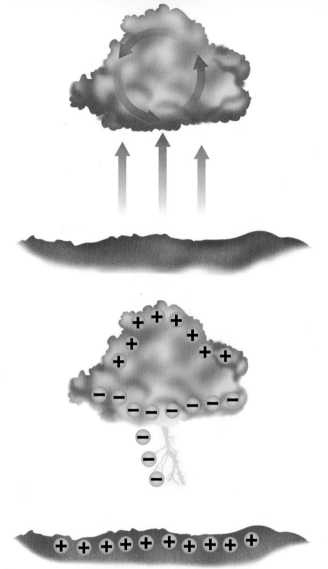

A The sun heats the air near the ground, causing it to rise. This rising air can sometimes cause a storm cloud to form. Air currents within the storm cloud carry electrons from the top of the cloud to its bottom.

B As electrons build up on the bottom of the cloud, they repel electrons in the ground beneath the cloud. This causes the ground beneath the cloud to have an induced positive charge. At some point, electrons in the cloud bottom begin to move toward the ground in a zigzag pattern.

C When the electrons get close to the ground, they attract the positively charged atoms in the ground. These positive charges move upward, forming a discharge. A tremendous surge of positive charge flows from the ground up to the cloud. This is the discharge you see as a lightning flash.

Grounding

Electric discharges such as lightning can cause damage because they can release large amounts of electrical energy. Even electric discharges that release small amounts of energy can damage delicate circuitry in devices such as computers. One way to avoid the damage caused by electric discharges is to make the charges flow harmlessly into Earth's surface. Earth is a conductor, and because it is so large, it can absorb an enormous quantity of excess charge.

The process of providing a pathway to drain excess charge into Earth is called grounding. The pathway is usually a conductor such as a wire or a pipe. You may have noticed lightning rods at the top of buildings and towers, as shown in **Figure 6-8.** These rods are made of metal and connected to metal cables that conduct electric charge into the ground if the rod is struck by lightning. Objects that have lost electrons and are positively charged also can be grounded. In this case, electrons move from Earth to the object to make it electrically neutral.

Figure 6-8 A lightning rod can protect a building from being damaged by a lightning strike. **Should a lightning rod be an insulator or a conductor?**

Section Assessment

1. What is the difference between an object that is negatively charged and one that is positively charged?

2. Two electrically charged objects repel each other. What can you say about the type of charge on each object?

3. Suppose Earth's surface were an insulator instead of a conductor. Would lightning still strike Earth's surface? Why or why not?

4. **Think Critically:** Any excess charge placed on the surface of a conductor tends to spread out over the entire surface, while excess charge placed on an insulator tends to stay where it was placed originally. Explain.

5.  **Skill Builder**
   Recognizing Cause and Effect Clothes that are dried on a clothesline outdoors don't stick to each other when they are taken out of the laundry basket. Clothes that are dried in a clothes drier do tend to stick to each other. What is the reason for this difference? If you need help, refer to Recognizing Cause and Effect in the **Skill Handbook** on page 705.

Science Journal You are sitting in a car. You slide out of the car seat, and as you start to touch the metal car door, a spark jumps from your hand to the door. In your Science Journal, describe how the spark was formed.

Electric Current

Voltage

An electric discharge such as a lightning stroke can release a huge amount of energy in an instant. However, electric lights, refrigerators, TVs, and stereos need a steady, constant source of electric energy. This source of electric energy comes from an **electric current,** which is the steady flow of electrons through a conductor. Electric current is measured in units of amperes (A).

Electrons flow continuously only if they are connected in an electric circuit. A **circuit** is a closed path through which an electric current can flow. Any device that uses electric current to operate has to be part of a circuit. Look at the diagram in **Figure 6-9.** A simple circuit consists of a source of electric energy such as a battery, and a conductor that provides the path for electrons to follow. A switch stops and starts the current flow by opening and closing the circuit.

Electric Energy in a Simple Circuit

How does an electric current provide electrical energy? In some ways, an electric current is a controlled electric discharge. However, instead of releasing a quick burst of energy, an electric current releases energy gradually in a continuous flow. In some ways, the electric current is similar to a continuous flow of water as shown in **Figure 6-10.** Just as a flow of water can be made to do work, an electric current also can do work.

What You'll Learn

► How voltage is related to the electric energy carried by an electric current
► How a battery produces an electric current
► Why materials have electric resistance

Vocabulary
electric current
circuit
voltage
resistance

Why It's Important

► The electric appliances you use every day need an electric current to operate.

Battery

Lightbulb

Switch

Figure 6-9 A simple circuit consists of a source of electric energy, such as a battery, a closed path for electrons to follow, and a switch that opens and closes the circuit.

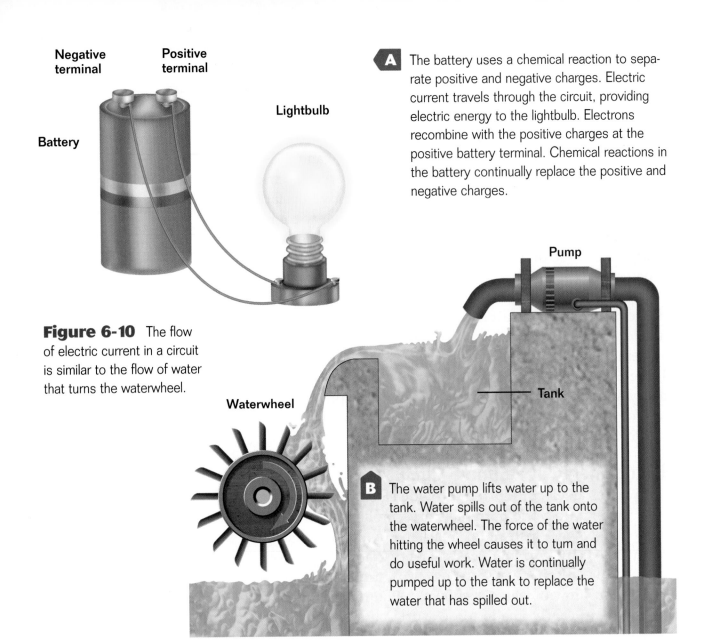

Negative terminal   Positive terminal

Battery

Lightbulb

A The battery uses a chemical reaction to separate positive and negative charges. Electric current travels through the circuit, providing electric energy to the lightbulb. Electrons recombine with the positive charges at the positive battery terminal. Chemical reactions in the battery continually replace the positive and negative charges.

Pump

Tank

Figure 6-10 The flow of electric current in a circuit is similar to the flow of water that turns the waterwheel.

Waterwheel

B The water pump lifts water up to the tank. Water spills out of the tank onto the waterwheel. The force of the water hitting the wheel causes it to turn and do useful work. Water is continually pumped up to the tank to replace the water that has spilled out.

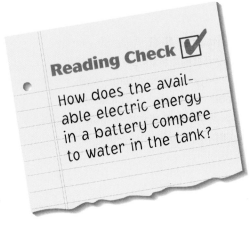

Reading Check ☑

How does the available electric energy in a battery compare to water in the tank?

In a simple circuit, the battery is like the water pump shown in **Figure 6-10.** A chemical reaction in the battery separates electrons from atoms and piles them up at the negative battery terminal. The atoms that have lost electrons and are positively charged pile up at the positive terminal. The negatively charged electrons on the negative terminal can recombine with the positively charged atoms on the positive terminal only by traveling through a circuit connecting the two terminals.

Separating positive and negative charges enables electric energy to be stored. The electrons at the negative terminal of the battery are like the water in the tank in **Figure 6-10B.** This stored electric energy is released when the electrons flow from the negative terminal to the positive terminal of the battery. The water in the tank releases its stored energy when it falls from the tank and strikes the waterwheel. ☑

The total stored electric energy in the battery is called the electric potential energy because it is energy that is potentially available to do work. The water in the tank also has potential energy because it can do work when it falls on the waterwheel.

In a battery, the electric potential energy is determined by the chemical reactions that occur inside the battery. By using different chemical reactions to separate the charges, different types of batteries have different electric potential energies. The **voltage** of the battery is a measure of the electric potential energy and is measured in units of volts (V).

The higher the voltage is, the more electric energy there is available to do work. The batteries in your portable boom box have a voltage of 1.5 V. By contrast, the voltage between the bottom of a thundercloud and the ground beneath can be 100 million volts.

Mini Lab

Lighting a Bulb with One Wire

Procedure

1. The filament in a lightbulb is a piece of wire. For the bulb to light, an electric current must flow through the filament in a complete circuit. Examine the base of the flashlight lightbulb carefully. Where are the ends of the filament connected to the base?

2. Connect a piece of wire, a battery, and a flashlight bulb to make the bulb light. (There are four possible ways to do this.)

Analysis

Draw and label a diagram showing the path followed by electrons in your circuit. Explain your diagram.

Batteries

You probably have replaced run-down batteries in a flashlight or portable radio. And, maybe you've looked under the hood of a car to see an automobile battery. How are these types of batteries different, and how does each type work? The batteries that are used to power flashlights, toys, portable radios, and CD players are examples of dry-cell batteries.

Dry Cells

Figure 6-11 shows a cutaway view of a dry cell. The dry cell consists of a carbon rod surrounded by a moist paste. The positive terminal of the battery is in contact with the carbon rod. The paste is surrounded by a container made of the metal zinc. When the two terminals of the battery are connected in a circuit, a chemical reaction occurs between several compounds in the paste and the zinc container. This chemical reaction causes positive charges to pile up on the carbon rod and electrons to pile up on the zinc. These electrons then flow through the circuit back to the carbon rod, where they recombine with the positive charges. The chemical reaction continues to produce electrons as long as the circuit remains closed.

Figure 6-11 In a dry-cell battery, a chemical reaction causes electrons to move to the zinc container. Atoms that have lost electrons move to the carbon rod. The container is the negative terminal and the carbon rod is the positive terminal.

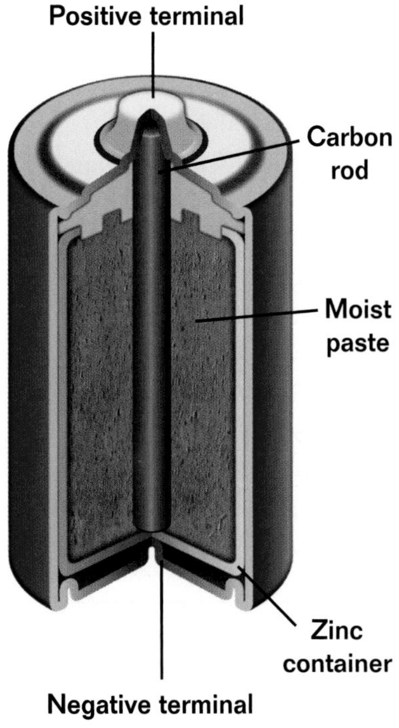

Positive terminal

Carbon rod

Moist paste

Zinc container

Negative terminal

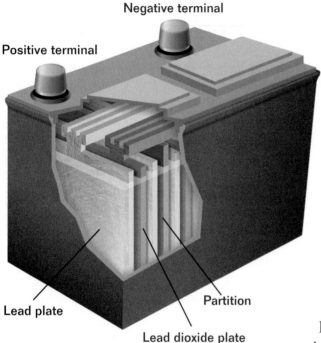

Figure 6-12 A car battery has several wet cells connected together. This type of battery can be recharged.

Negative terminal

Positive terminal

Lead plate

Partition

Lead dioxide plate

CHEMISTRY
INTEGRATION

Long-Lived Batteries
One of the chemicals in the moist paste of an ordinary dry cell is ammonium chloride. In an alkaline dry cell, this chemical is replaced by potassium hydroxide. The result is a battery with the same voltage but a longer life. Visit the Glencoe Science Web Site at **www.glencoe. com/sec/science** for information about other types of long-lived batteries and their applications.

Wet Cells

A different type of battery, the wet-cell battery, is used in cars for starting engines. Unlike a dry-cell battery, a wet-cell battery is partially filled with a liquid. The automobile battery shown in **Figure 6-12** actually contains a series of six wet cells connected together. Each wet cell produces about 2 V and consists of two plates, one made of lead and the other made of lead dioxide bathed in a solution of sulfuric acid. A chemical reaction causes electrons to move from the lead dioxide plate to the lead plate. The lead plate becomes the negative terminal and the lead dioxide plate becomes the positive terminal. The six cells together give a total voltage of 12 V for the battery.

Battery Life

Batteries can't supply power forever. You know that's true if you've ever noticed taped music getting slower and slower after a portable tape player has been playing for several hours. Or, maybe you know someone whose car wouldn't start after the lights have been left on for a long time. Why do batteries run down? It's because the voltage they produce gradually decreases as some of the compounds that are involved in the chemical reactions are used up.

Batteries are not the only devices that separate positive and negative charges and create a continuous electrical current. Electric generators also work this way. Electric power plants use generators to supply electric current to the electric wall outlets in your home and school. In the United States, this current has a voltage of 120 V.

Resistance

Electrons can move much more easily through conductors than through insulators, but even conductors interfere with the flow of electrons. The measure of how difficult it is for electrons to flow through a material is called **resistance.** The unit of resistance is the ohm. Insulators generally have much higher resistance than conductors.

As electrons flow through a circuit, they collide with the atoms in the materials that make up the circuit. These collisions cause some of the electrons' electrical energy to be converted into thermal energy and light. The amount of electrical energy converted into heat and light depends on the resistance of the materials in the circuit. The amount of electrical energy lost as heat and light increases as the resistance increases.

For example, copper is one of the best electrical conductors and has a low resistance. Copper is used in household wiring because very little electrical energy is lost as current flows through copper wires. Also, not much heat is produced, which makes fires less likely. On the other hand, tungsten wire has a higher resistance and can be made to glow with a bright light as current passes through it. That makes tungsten wire a good choice for the filaments of lightbulbs.

The length and thickness of a conductor also affects its resistance. A short, thick wire has less resistance than a long, thin wire as shown in **Figure 6-13.** Think about walking down a hallway in your school to get to your next class. If the hallway is long and narrow, making your way through a crowd of other students like that shown in **Figure 6-14** will take you a long time. You'll be more likely to get to class on time if the hallway is short and wide. The shorter, wider hallway offers less resistance to you than a longer, narrower hallway.

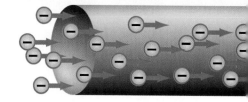

Figure 6-13 It is easier for electrons to flow through a thick wire than a thin wire.

Figure 6-14 Between classes, the hallway is filled with students. **How is a good electrical conductor similar to a hallway during classes?**

Section Assessment

1. How does increasing the voltage in a circuit affect the energy of the electrons flowing in the current?

2. What causes positive and negative charges to be separated in a battery?

3. **Think Critically:** Two identical 1.5-V batteries have the positive terminal of one battery connected to the negative terminal of the other. How does the voltage of the combination compare with the voltage of a single battery? Explain.

4. **Skill Builder**
   Observing and Inferring Observe the size of various batteries such as a camera battery, a flashlight battery, and an automobile battery. Infer whether the voltage produced by a battery is related to its physical size. If you need help, refer to Observing and Inferring in the **Skill Handbook** on page 704.

Using Computers

Spreadsheet A thundercloud and the ground beneath it are like a battery. The bottom of the cloud is like the negative terminal, and the ground beneath is like the positive terminal. Design a table using spreadsheet software to compare and contrast the thundercloud battery, dry-cell batteries, and wet-cell batteries. If you need help, refer to page 722.

A Model for Voltage and Current

Materials

- Plastic funnel
- Rubber or plastic tubing of different diameters (1 m each)
- Meterstick
- Ring stand with ring
- Stopwatch
  *clock displaying seconds
- Hose clamp
  *clothespin
- Beakers (500 mL) (2)
  *Alternate Materials

The flow of electrons in an electric circuit is something like the flow of water. By raising or lowering the height of a water tank, you can increase or decrease the potential energy of the water. In this activity, you will use a water system to investigate how the flow of water in a tube depends on the height of the water and the diameter of the tube the water flows through.

What You'll Investigate

How is the flow of water through a tube affected by changing the height of a container of water and the diameter of the tube?

Goals

- **Make a model** for the flow of current in a simple circuit.

Safety Precautions

Procedure

1. **Design** a data table in which to record your data similar to the example below.
2. **Connect** the tubing to the bottom of the funnel and

   place the funnel in the ring of the ring stand.
3. **Measure** the diameter of the rubber tubing. **Record** your data.

Flow Rate Data				
Trial number	Height (cm)	Diameter of tubing (cm)	Time (s)	Rate of flow (mL/s)
1				
2				
3				
4				

4. Place a 500-mL beaker at the bottom of the ring stand, and lower the ring so the open end of the tubing is in the beaker.

5. Use the meterstick to **measure** the height from the top of the funnel to the bottom of the ring stand. **Record** your data.

6. **Pour** water into the funnel fast enough to keep the funnel full but not overflowing. **Measure** the time needed for 100 mL of water to flow into the beaker. Use the hose clamp to start and stop the flow of water. **Record** your data.

7. **Connect** tubing with a different diameter to the funnel and repeat steps 2–6.

8. **Reconnect** the original piece of tubing and repeat steps 4–6 for several lower positions of the funnel, lowering the height by 10 cm each time.

9. **Calculate** the rate of flow for each trial by dividing 100 mL by the measured time.

Conclude and Apply

1. **Make a graph** to show how the rate of flow depends on the funnel height.

2. How does the rate of flow depend on the diameter of the tubing?

3. Which of the variables that you changed in your trials corresponds to the voltage in a circuit? Which variable corresponds to the resistance in a circuit? What part of a circuit would the hose clamp correspond to?

4. Based on your results, how would the current in a circuit depend on the voltage? How would the current depend on the resistance?

Electric Circuits

What You'll Learn

► How voltage, current, and resistance are related in an electrical circuit
► The difference between series and parallel circuits
► What determines the electrical power used in a circuit
► How to avoid dangerous electric shock

Vocabulary
Ohm's law
series circuit
parallel circuit
electrical power

Why It's Important

► Overloading electric circuits can create a fire hazard.

Voltage, Resistance, and Current (Ohm's law)

When you connect a conductor, such as a wire or a lightbulb, between the positive and negative terminals of a battery to form a circuit, an electrical current flows through the circuit. The amount of current is determined by the voltage supplied by the battery and the resistance of the conductor. To help understand this relationship, imagine a tank with a tube connected to a hole in the bottom, as shown in **Figure 6-15.** If the tank is raised higher, water will flow out of the tube faster and the water current will increase.

Think back to the waterwheel in **Figure 6-10B.** Remember that the water in the tank has potential, or stored, energy that is released when the water falls on the wheel. Raising the tank higher increases the potential energy of the water. Increasing the stored energy of the water is similar to increasing the voltage in a circuit. Just as the water current increases when the tank is raised higher, the electric current in a circuit should increase as voltage increases.

Now, imagine that the diameter of the tube in **Figure 6-15** is decreased. Then, there is more resistance to the flow of the water and the current decreases. In the same way, as the resistance in an electrical circuit increases, the current flowing in the circuit decreases.

Figure 6-15 Raising the tank higher increases the potential energy of the water in the tank. This causes the water to flow out of the tank faster.

The relationship between voltage, current, and resistance is known as **Ohm's law.** The electrical current is usually represented by I, and if V represents the voltage and R the resistance, Ohm's law can be written in equation form as follows.

$$\text{Voltage} = \text{current} \times \text{resistance}$$

$$V = IR$$

Voltage is measured in volts (V), current is measured in amperes (A), and resistance is measured in V/A, or ohms.

Series and Parallel Circuits

Circuits control the movement of electric current by providing a path for electrons to follow. Have you ever been putting up holiday lights and had a string that wouldn't light because a single bulb was missing or had burned out? Or, maybe you've noticed that some strings of lights don't go out no matter how many bulbs burn out or are removed. These strings of holiday lights are examples of the two kinds of basic circuits.

Using Math

Calculating Resistance Using Ohm's Law

Example Problem

A hair dryer uses 12.5 A of current when it is plugged into a 120-V outlet. What is the electrical resistance of the hair dryer?

Problem-Solving Steps

1. What is known?
   voltage, $V = 120$ V; current, $I = 12.5$ A
2. What is unknown? resistance, R
3. Use Ohm's law $V = IR$.
4. Rearrange Ohm's law by dividing both sides by I to give $R = \dfrac{V}{I}$.
5. **Solution:** $R = \dfrac{V}{I}$

$$R = \frac{120 \text{ V}}{12.5 \text{ A}} = 9.6 \text{ ohms}$$

The electrical resistance of the hair dryer is 9.6 ohms.

Practice Problem

A lightbulb with a resistance of 10 ohms is plugged into a 120-V outlet. What is the current through the lightbulb?
Strategy Hint: In what units will your answer be given?

Figure 6-16 This circuit is an example of a series circuit. A series circuit has only one path for electric current to follow. **What happens to the current in this circuit if any of the connecting wires are removed?**

Series Circuits

A **series circuit** is a circuit that has only one path for the electric current to follow, as shown in **Figure 6-16.** If this path is broken, the current will no longer flow and all the devices in the circuit stop working. The string of lights that wouldn't work when only one bulb burned out was wired as a series circuit. When a bulb burns out, the filament in the bulb actually breaks and current stops flowing through the bulb.

In a series circuit, electrical devices are connected together on the same current path. As a result, the current is the same through every device. However, each new device that is added to the circuit decreases the current. This is because each device has electrical resistance, and in a series circuit, the total resistance to the flow of current is found by adding the resistance of all the devices. By Ohm's law, as the resistance increases, the current decreases. ☑

Parallel Circuits

What if you wanted to watch TV and had to turn on all the lights, hair dryers, and every other electrical appliance in the house? That's what it would be like if all the electrical appliances in your house were connected in a series circuit.

Instead, houses, schools, and other buildings are wired using parallel circuits. A **parallel circuit** is a circuit that has more than one path for the electric current to follow, as shown in **Figure 6-17.** The current leaving the battery or electrical outlet branches so that electrons flow through each of the paths. If one path is broken, current continues to flow through the other paths.

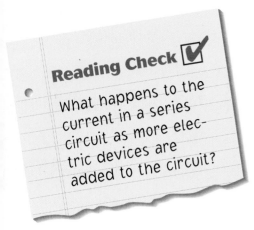

Reading Check

What happens to the current in a series circuit as more electric devices are added to the circuit?

Figure 6-17 This circuit is an example of a parallel circuit. A parallel circuit has more than one path for electric current to follow. **What happens to the current in the circuit if either of the wires connecting the two light bulbs is removed?**

Unlike a series circuit, the current through each path in a parallel circuit is different and depends on the electrical resistance in each path. The lower the resistance in a path is, the more current that flows in that path. Adding or removing additional devices in a parallel circuit does not affect the other branches, so the devices on those branches continue to work normally.

Fuses

In a parallel circuit, the current that flows out of the battery or electrical outlet increases as more devices are added to the circuit. As the current flowing through the circuit increases, the wires heat up.

To keep the heat from building up enough to cause a fire, the circuits in houses and other buildings have fuses or circuit breakers, like those shown in **Figure 6-18,** that limit the amount of current in the wiring. When the current becomes larger than 15 A or 20 A, a piece of metal in the fuse melts or a switch in the circuit breaker opens, stopping the current. The cause of the overload can then be removed, and the circuit can be used again by replacing the fuse or resetting the circuit breaker.

Figure 6-18 You have fuses or circuit breakers in your home to prevent a fire.

A In some buildings, each circuit is connected to a fuse. The fuses are usually located in a fuse box.

Wire →

B A fuse contains a piece of wire that melts and breaks when the current flowing through the fuse becomes too large.

Electric Power

Electric energy is used in many ways to do useful work. Toasters and electric ovens convert electric energy to heat, stereos convert electric energy to sound, and a rotating fan blade converts electrical energy to mechanical energy. The rate at which an appliance converts electrical energy to another form of energy is the **electrical power** used by the appliance. The unit of electrical power is the watt (W). Sometimes, it is convenient to express electrical power in kilowatts (kW). One kilowatt equals 1000 watts.

An electric current releases electrical energy as it flows in a circuit. The rate at which energy is used in the circuit is related to the amount of energy carried by the electrons, which increases as the voltage increases. The energy used also is related to the number of electrons or current flowing in the circuit. The power being used in a circuit can be determined by multiplying the voltage by the current.

$$\text{Power} = \text{current} \times \text{voltage}$$

$$P = IV$$

One watt of power is used when a current of 1 A flows through a circuit with a voltage of 1 V. For household appliances such as televisions, refrigerators, and stereos that are

Using Math

A current of 6 A flows through a refrigerator plugged into a 120-V wall outlet. Calculate the electric power used by the refrigerator using the formula $P = IV$.

Problem Solving

The Cost of Using Electricity

Has someone ever told you to turn off an electric light because it was wasting electricity? Or, do you know someone who turns off all the unused lights in your house in order to save money? How much does it really cost to use a lightbulb? If the power used by an appliance is known, you can calculate the cost of total energy used by multiplying the power (P) the appliance uses in kilowatts by the number of hours (t) the appliance is used and the cost per kilowatt-hour.

The table shows the power consumed by some common household appliances and the amount of time they are typically used in a day. If the cost is $0.09 per kilowatt-hour, calculate the monthly cost of each remaining appliance.

Think Critically: Estimate the number of lightbulbs in your home. How much energy could be saved each month if these bulbs were used only four hours per day instead of six?

Power Consumption of Common Appliances

Appliance	Power Usage (W)	Time Used (hours/day)	Monthly Cost
Hair dryer	1 000	0.25	$0.67
Microwave	700	0.5	
Stereo	110	2.5	
Refrigerator	700	10	
Television	200	4	
100-W lightbulb	100	6	

plugged into wall outlets, the voltage is always 120 V. If a current of 1 A flows through a household appliance, the power used is 1 A × 120 V = 120 W.

Cost of Electric Energy

Power is the rate at which energy is used, or the amount of energy used per second. When you use a hair dryer, the amount of electrical energy used depends on the power of the hair dryer and the amount of time you use it. If you used it for five minutes yesterday and ten minutes today, you used twice as much energy today as yesterday.

Using electrical energy costs money. The electricity in homes, schools, and businesses is supplied by electric companies, which generate electrical energy and sell it in units of kilowatt-hours. One kilowatt-hour (kWh) is an amount of electrical energy equal to using 1 kW of power continuously for one hour. This would be the amount of energy needed to light ten 100-W lightbulbs for one hour, or one 100-W lightbulb for ten hours.

An electric company usually charges its customers for the number of kilowatt-hours they use every month. The number of kilowatt-hours used in a building such as a house or a school is measured by an electric meter, which is usually attached to the outside of the building.

Electrical Safety

Have you ever had a mild electric shock? You probably felt only a mild tingling sensation, but electricity can have much more dangerous effects. In 1993, electric shocks killed an estimated 550 people in the United States.

You experience an electric shock when an electric current enters your body. In some ways, your body is like a piece of insulated wire. Inside your body, the electric resistance is low so the inside of your body is a good conductor. The electric resistance of dry skin is much higher, but not as high as insulators such as plastic and rubber. Still, skin insulates the body like the plastic insulation around an electric wire. But, in this case, the purpose of the insulation is to keep the electric current from getting inside.

For a current to enter your body, you must be part of an electric circuit. One way to do this is to touch a wire that is connected to a source of electric energy while you are in contact with the ground. Then, current will flow through you into the ground. Whether you receive a deadly shock depends on the amount of current that flows into your body.

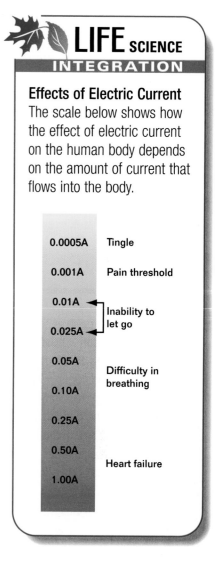

LIFE SCIENCE
INTEGRATION

Effects of Electric Current
The scale below shows how the effect of electric current on the human body depends on the amount of current that flows into the body.

Current	Effect
0.0005A	Tingle
0.001A	Pain threshold
0.01A	Inability to let go
0.025A	
0.05A	Difficulty in breathing
0.10A	
0.25A	
0.50A	Heart failure
1.00A	

Even relatively small amounts of current can be dangerous. Even a current as small as 0.001 A can cause a tingling sensation. A current of only 0.01 A passing through the chest can cause the heart muscle to start twitching uncontrollably and stop pumping blood. This amount of electric current also can cause the muscles in the hand to contract violently, so a person who has grasped a current-carrying wire cannot let go.

Surprisingly, a large current can sometimes cause the heart to start beating after it has stopped. Hospitals and emergency medical teams often use a device called a defibrillator, like the one shown in **Figure 6-19,** to apply a brief pulse of current directly to a patient's chest.

Situations to Avoid

Never touch any exposed wire connected to a wall socket. Ordinary household current at a voltage of 120 V is particularly dangerous and can cause a shock that affects the heart and the ability to breathe.

Avoid using a metal ladder in the vicinity of power lines. A person touching the ladder will be electrocuted if the metal ladder touches the power line.

Avoid touching electric power lines under any circumstances. Even if a power line has been broken by a storm or a car accident, you will form a circuit into the ground if you touch it and you will be severely shocked. You may have noticed that birds can sit on a power line without receiving a shock. This is because birds are not in contact with the ground and touch only a single wire, as shown in **Figure 6-20.**

Do not use electric appliances while standing in water or on wet ground. Standing on wet ground or in water provides a good contact with Earth, so if you were to handle an appliance that was not properly insulated, your chances of

Figure 6-19 A defibrillator can sometimes restart a heart that has stopped beating or is beating irregularly. The condition in which the heart is beating irregularly is called fibrillation. The paddles are placed on the person's chest, and a brief current pulse is sent through the paddles. This current can be as high as 6 A.

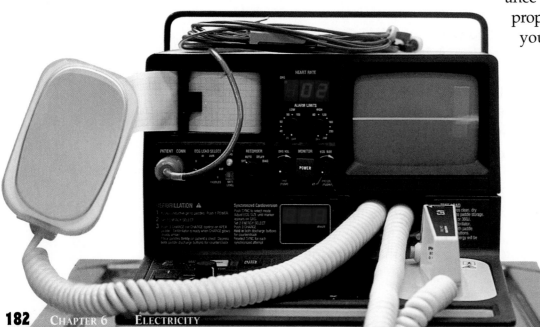

Figure 6-20 A bird can sit on one wire without being electrocuted. Touching only one wire is like being connected to only one terminal of a battery. There is no electric current through the bird. However, the bird would be in danger if it touched both power lines at the same time. Touching both power wires at the same time is like being connected to the terminals of a high-voltage battery. The current through the bird would cause a fatal shock.

receiving a dangerous shock would be increased. If the appliance such as a hair dryer or radio accidentally fell into the bathwater, you could be electrocuted.

Always respect signs warning of high voltage and dangerous electric shock, and keep a safe distance from these warning signs. The best rule is to avoid making contact with any electric current.

Section Assessment

1. As the resistance in a simple circuit increases, what happens to the current?

2. What is the difference between a series circuit and a parallel circuit?

3. Explain why you should avoid handling electrical appliances when standing on wet ground.

4. **Think Critically:** What determines whether a 100-W lightbulb costs more to use than a 1500-W hair dryer?

5. **Skill Builder**
   Sequencing A sequence is the order in which something is done or arranged. Putting your socks on before your shoes is a sequence. The alphabet is a sequence of letters. Do the **Chapter 6 Skill Activity** on page 731 to use a flow chart to help you arrange a sequence.

Using Math

A typical household uses 1000 kWh of electric energy every month. If a power company supplies electricity to 10 000 households, how much electric energy must it supply every year?

Materials

- Lightbulbs (1.5 V) (4)
- Batteries (1.5 V) (2)
- Pieces of insulated wire, each about 10 cm long (8)
- Battery holder (2)
- Minibulb sockets (4)

Current in a Parallel Circuit

In this activity, you will investigate how the current in a circuit changes when two or more lightbulbs are connected in parallel. Because the brightness of a lightbulb increases or decreases as more or less current flows through it, the brightness of the bulbs in the circuits can be used to determine which circuit has more current.

What You'll Investigate

How does connecting devices in parallel affect the electric current in a circuit?

Goals

- **Observe** how the current in a parallel circuit changes as more devices are added.

Procedure

1. **Connect** one lightbulb to the battery in a complete circuit. After you've made the bulb light, disconnect the bulb from the battery to keep the battery from running down. This circuit will be the brightness tester.

2. **Make** a parallel circuit by connecting two bulbs as shown in the diagram. **Reconnect** the bulb in the brightness tester and compare its brightness with the brightness of the two bulbs in the parallel circuit. **Record** your observations.

3. Add another bulb to the parallel circuit as shown in the figure. How does the brightness of the bulbs change? **Record** your observations.

4. **Disconnect** one bulb in the parallel circuit. What happens to the brightness of the remaining bulbs?

Conclude and Apply

1. Compared to the brightness tester, is the current in the parallel circuit more or less?

2. How does adding additional devices affect the current in a parallel circuit?

3. Are the electric circuits in your house wired in series or parallel? How do you know?

Energy Sources

Think of all the ways you used energy today. Much of this energy comes from burning fossil fuels such as coal to generate electricity. Other fossil fuels such as gasoline and natural gas power automobiles and heat homes.

However, fossil fuels are being used up at an ever-increasing rate. Fossil fuels are a nonrenewable energy resource, which means they can't be replaced once they are used up. Some scientists estimate that most of the world's fossil fuels such as oil (being drilled at left) will be nearly gone by the end of the twenty-first century.

Fuel Cells

As the world's population and the demand for energy grow, many scientists and engineers are trying to develop alternative energy sources for the future. A pioneer in this research is Dr. Meredith Gourdine, a prominent engineer and physicist, who was born in Newark, New Jersey, in 1929.

Dr. Gourdine has developed a method to improve the operation of fuel cells that produce an electric current. The chemicals most commonly used in fuel cells are hydrogen and oxygen gases, both of which can be obtained from ocean water. Unlike a battery, a fuel cell does not contain a limited amount of chemicals that gradually are used up. Instead, hydrogen and oxygen are injected into a reaction chamber in a fuel cell, and the fuel cell continues to produce electricity as long as the gases are added to the reaction chamber. Dr. Gourdine has designed a specially shaped reaction chamber that enables the gases to react with each other efficiently.

Ocean water is much more plentiful than fossil fuels and could provide a supply of oxygen and hydrogen for an extremely long time. Other renewable energy resources include solar energy, geothermal energy, and wind energy. The demand for skilled scientists and engineers to research alternative energy sources is expected to increase in the years to come.

For a **preview** of this chapter, study this Reviewing Main Ideas before you read the chapter. After you have studied this chapter, you can use the Reviewing Main Ideas to **review** the chapter.

The Glencoe MindJogger, Audiocassettes, and CD-ROM provide additional opportunities for review.

Section 6-1 ELECTRIC CHARGE

There are two types of electric charge: positive and negative. An object becomes negatively charged if it gains electrons and positively charged if it loses electrons. Electrically charged objects have an electric field surrounding them and exert electric forces on one another. Objects with like charges repel one another, while objects with unlike charges attract one another. Electrons can move easily through **conductors**, but not so easily through **insulators**. *Why are atoms usually electrically neutral?*

Section 6-2 ELECTRIC CURRENT

Electrons can do useful work by flowing in a closed, unbroken path known as a **circuit.** The energy carried by electrons in a circuit increases as the **voltage** in the circuit increases. A battery provides a source of **electric current** by using chemical reactions to separate positive and negative charges. As electrons flow in a circuit, some of their electric energy is lost due to electric **resistance** in the circuit. *In a simple circuit, why do electrons stop flowing if the circuit is broken?*

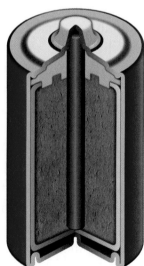

Reading Check ☑

Someone says "Electricity is dangerous!" Is this a fact or an opinion? Explain your answer.

Section

6-3 ELECTRIC CIRCUITS

In an electric circuit, the voltage, current, and resistance are related by **Ohm's law,** $V = IR$. As a result, increasing the voltage in a circuit increases the current, while increasing the resistance decreases the current. There are two basic kinds of electric circuits: **parallel circuits** and **series circuits.** A series circuit has only one path for the current to follow, while a parallel circuit has more than one path. The rate at which electrical devices use electric energy is the **electric power** used by the device. Electric companies charge customers for using electric energy in units of kilowatt-hours. *Why are parallel circuits used for the wiring in homes and schools, rather than series circuits?*

ELECTRICAL SAFETY

Electricity can damage the human body by causing the heart to stop beating properly and by interfering with the ability to breathe, which can lead to suffocation. The amount of current flowing through the body determines how much damage occurs. The current from wall outlets can be dangerous. Operating electrical appliances while standing in water or on wet ground can lead to dangerous electric shocks. *Why are high-voltage lines dangerous?*

Chapter 6 Assessment

Using Vocabulary

a. circuit
b. conductor
c. electric current
d. electric discharge
e. electrical power
f. insulator
g. Ohm's law
h. parallel circuit
i. resistance
j. series circuit
k. static charge
l. voltage

Match each phrase with the correct term from the list of Vocabulary words.

1. the flow of electrons through a conductor
2. the relationship between voltage, current, and resistance in an electric circuit
3. a material through which electrons cannot move easily
4. an unbroken path for electrons to follow
5. a buildup of electric charge in one place

Checking Concepts

Choose the word or phrase that best answers the question.

6. Why is an object positively charged?
   A) It has more neutrons than protons.
   B) It has more protons than electrons.
   C) It has more electrons than protons.
   D) It has more electrons than neutrons.

7. What is the electric force between two electrons?
   A) unbalanced   C) attractive
   B) neutral   D) repulsive

8. What happens when the voltage in a circuit increases?
   A) The energy carried by the electric current increases.
   B) The chemicals in the battery are used up.
   C) The current decreases.
   D) The positive and negative battery terminals are connected.

9. What property of a wire increases when it is made thinner?
   A) resistance   C) current
   B) voltage   D) charge

10. What property does Earth have that causes grounding to drain away static charges?
    A) It is a planet.
    B) It has a high resistance.
    C) It is a conductor.
    D) It is like a battery.

11. Why is a severe electrical shock dangerous?
    A) It can stop the heart from beating.
    B) It can cause burns.
    C) It can interfere with breathing.
    D) All of the above are true.

12. Because an air conditioner uses more electrical power than a lightbulb, what also must be true?
    A) It must have a higher resistance.
    B) It must use more energy every second.
    C) It must have its own batteries.
    D) It must be wired in series.

13. What unit of electrical energy is sold by electric companies?
    A) ampere   C) volt
    B) ohm   D) kilowatt-hour

14. What surrounds electric charges that causes them to affect each other even though they are not touching?
    A) an induced charge
    B) a static discharge
    C) a conductor
    D) an electric field

15. As more devices are added to a series circuit, what happens to the current in the circuit?
    A) It decreases.   C) It stays the same.
    B) It increases.   D) It has a higher voltage.

Thinking Critically

16. Why do materials have electrical resistance?

17. Explain why a balloon that has a static charge will stick to a wall.

18. If you have two charged objects, how could you tell if the type of charge on them was the same or different?

19. Explain why the outside cases of electrical appliances are usually made of plastic.

20. Your hand has excess electrons on it, and you bring it close to a metal doorknob. Why do the electrons in the doorknob move and not the electrons on your hand?

Developing Skills

If you need help, refer to the **Skill Handbook.**

21. **Making and Using Graphs:** The following data show the current and voltage in a circuit containing a portable CD player and in a circuit containing a portable radio.
    A) Make a graph with the horizontal axis the current and vertical axis the voltage, and plot the data for the radio and the CD player.
    B) Which line is more horizontal: the plot of the radio data or the CD player data?
    C) Use Ohm's law to determine the electrical resistance of each device.
    D) For which device is the line more horizontal: the device with the higher or lower resistance?

Portable Radio		Portable CD Player	
Voltage (V)	Current (A)	Voltage (V)	Current (A)
2.0	1.0	2.0	0.5
4.0	2.0	4.0	1.0
6.0	3.0	6.0	1.5

THE PRINCETON REVIEW

Test-Taking Tip

Read the Label No matter how many times you've taken a particular type of test or practiced for an exam, it's always a good idea first to read the instructions provided at the beginning of each section. It only takes a moment.

Test Practice

Use these questions to test your Science Proficiency.

1. If you connect lightbulbs together so that the current flowing through each lightbulb is the same, you have made which type of circuit?
   A) a series circuit
   B) a parallel circuit
   C) a combination circuit
   D) none of these

2. Earth and the moon each contain an enormous number of both protons and electrons. Which of the following statements **BEST** describes the electric force between Earth and the moon?
   A) There is a repulsive electric force because they contain the same types of electric charges.
   B) There is an attractive electric force because Earth has a negative charge that induces a positive charge on the moon.
   C) There is no electric force because Earth and the moon contain nearly equal numbers of protons and electrons and so both are electrically neutral.
   D) The electric force depends on how far apart they are.

Magnetism

Skills Preview

Skill Builders
- Communicate
- Compare and Contrast

Activities
- Observe and Infer
- Design an Experiment

MiniLabs
- Observe and Infer
- Compare and Contrast

Reading Check ✔

Use a dictionary to find the connection between *magnetism* and an ancient city in Turkey.

Explore Activity

Beautiful multicolored sheets of light sometimes appear in the sky near Earth's poles. They can appear as far south as the northern United States. The colors can appear as patches of color or moving streaks. This wonderful light show, called the aurora borealis, or northern lights, occurs when electrically charged particles from the sun are pulled towards the north pole and interact with Earth's atmosphere. A similar phenomenon over the south pole is called the aurora australis, or southern lights. The following activity will demonstrate how the Earth might pull in these particles from a distance.

Observe and Measure Force Between Magnets

1. You'll need a sheet of graph paper and two bar magnets. Place one magnet at each end of the graph paper. Mark the positions of the magnets.

2. Slide one magnet forward one square.

3. Repeat step 2 until one of the magnets moves without being touched. Measure the distance between the magnets.

4. Turn one magnet around 180°. Repeat the activity. Then, turn the other magnet and repeat again.

5. Repeat the activity with one magnet perpendicular to the other, in a T shape.

Science **Journal**

In your Science Journal, record the results of the Explore Activity. In each case, how close did the magnets have to be to affect each other? Did the magnets move together or apart? Do you think magnetism could be used to make a large object, like a train, move? Explain.

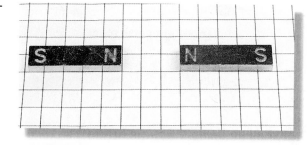

7·1 What is magnetism?

What You'll Learn

► How a magnet acts
► What a magnetic field is

Vocabulary
magnetic domain
magnetism
magnetic field
compass

Why It's Important

► Magnetism is one of the basic forces of nature.

Magnets

Have you used a magnet to attach papers to a metal surface such as a refrigerator? Have you ever wondered how magnets and metal attract? Thousands of years ago, curious people noticed that a certain mineral, now called magnetite, could attract other pieces of magnetite and small bits of iron. The Chinese discovered that when they rubbed small pieces of iron with magnetite, the iron would act like magnetite. When these pieces were free to turn, one end pointed north. These were the first compasses. The compass was an important development for navigation and exploration, especially at sea. Before compasses, sailors had to depend on the sun or the stars to know which direction they were going. But, with a compass, a traveler could know which way to go even if the sky was cloudy.

The two ends of a magnet are called poles. One end is the north pole and the other end is the south pole. If you break a bar magnet in half, each half will still have a north pole and a south pole. Even the smallest piece of a magnet has two poles. You cannot have a magnet with just one magnetic pole.

Like poles repel and opposite poles attract. As shown in **Figure 7-1,** a north magnetic pole repels other north poles and attracts south poles. A south magnetic pole repels other south poles and attracts north poles.

Figure 7-1 Two north poles (or two south poles) repel each other. North and south magnetic poles are attracted to each other.

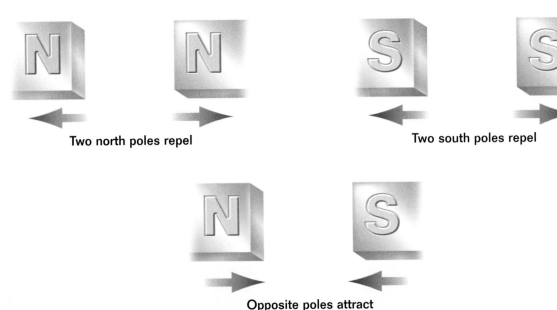

Two north poles repel

Two south poles repel

Opposite poles attract

VISUALIZING
Magnetizing

Figure 7-2 Some materials can become temporary magnets.

A Microscopic sections of iron and steel act as tiny magnets. These sections are called domains. Normally, the domains are oriented randomly and cancel each other.

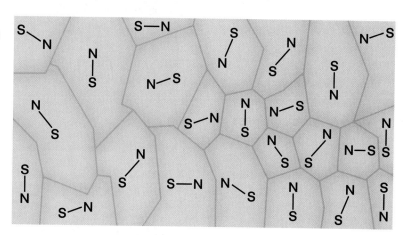

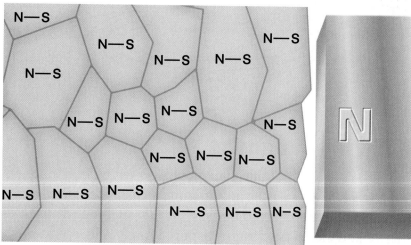

B When a strong north pole is brought near the material, the magnet attracts the south poles in each magnetic domain. The magnetic domains all add up, and the whole piece acts like a magnet.

C The bar magnet magnetizes the paper clips. The top of each paper clip is now the north pole of a magnet, and the bottom of each is a south pole.

What makes a magnet?

How do magnets attract other materials? All atoms contain negatively charged particles called electrons. The atoms that make up magnets have their electrons arranged so that each atom is like a small magnet. The fields of these atom-magnets line up so that all the north poles point in the same direction. A group of atoms with their magnetic poles pointing the same direction is called a **magnetic domain.**

A material that can become magnetized, such as iron or steel, contains many magnetic domains. When the material is not magnetized, these domains are oriented in different directions, as shown in **Figure 7-2A.** The magnetic domains cancel each other, so the material does not act like a magnet. When a strong magnet is held close to the material, each magnetic domain lines up with the magnet's field. **Figure 7-2B** illustrates this effect. As you can see in **Figure 7-2C,** you can use this method to magnetize a paper clip.

Figure 7-3 A magnetic field surrounds a magnet.

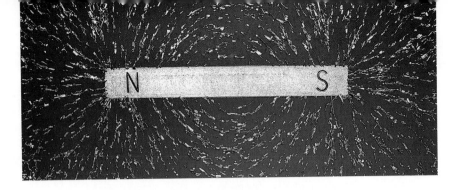

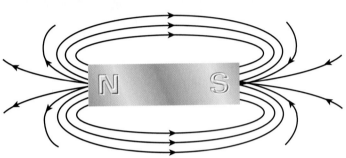

A Iron filings show the magnetic field lines around a bar magnet. Where the lines are close together, the field is strong. **Where is the field strongest?**

B When the field lines are drawn, they run from north to south. The lines run in loops that pass through the magnet.

Reading Check ✓
Explain why magnetism is a force.

What is a magnetic field?

At the beginning of the chapter, you observed that magnets can attract or repel each other from a distance. How can a magnet cause an object to move without touching it? Just like gravity and electricity, **magnetism** is a force. A force is a push or a pull and can cause an object to move. Magnetic force can either attract or repel objects. ✓

Magnetic force acts through a **magnetic field.** The field can be shown by sprinkling iron filings around a magnet. The magnetic field magnetizes the bits of iron, and they line up along the field lines.

A magnetic field extends between a magnet's north and south poles, as shown in **Figures 7-3** and **7-4.** The field lines

Problem Solving

Design a System of Magnets

Magnets occur naturally in the mineral magnetite. What applications did people find for this mineral? Records suggest that inventors in Egypt 2000 years ago used magnetite to make statues float in midair. The statue was carved out of magnetite. Pieces of magnetite in the floor, walls, and ceiling could keep the statue suspended in air.

Think Critically: Show how the north and south poles of the statue and supporting magnets could have been arranged to suspend the statue. Do you think there was a limit on the size of the statue?

Figure 7-4 Magnetic fields exist in three dimensions, all around a magnet. **Based on the photo, where is the magnetic field strongest? How can you tell?**

Mini Lab

Observing Magnetic Fields

Procedure

1. Place iron filings in a plastic petri dish. Put the cover on and tape it closed.
2. Collect several magnets. Place the magnets on the table and hold the dish over each one. Draw a diagram of what happens to the filings in each case.
3. Arrange two or more magnets under the dish. Observe the pattern of the filings.

Analysis

1. What happens to the filings close to the poles? Far from the poles?
2. Compare the fields of the individual magnets. How can you tell which magnet is strongest? Weakest?
3. What do the patterns of filings for two or more magnets show about the magnetic field?

are drawn with arrows pointing from north to south. Magnetic field lines are not real lines. They are a helpful tool for picturing the continuous field that surrounds a magnet. The field lines are close together where the field is strong and get farther apart as the field gets weaker. As you can see in the figures, the magnetic field is strongest close to the magnetic poles and grows weaker farther from the poles.

Field lines that meet show attraction. Field lines that curve away from each other show repulsion. **Figure 7-5** illustrates the magnetic field lines between a north and south pole and two north poles.

A The magnetic field lines connecting the north and south poles show attraction.

B The magnetic field lines between two like poles curve away from each other, showing that the poles repel.

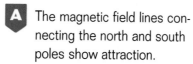
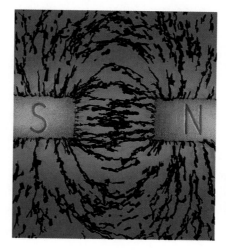

Figure 7-5 Field lines show attraction and repulsion. **What would the field between three south poles look like?**

Visit the Glencoe
Science Web Site at
**www.glencoe.com/
sec/science** for more
information about Earth's
magnetic field.

LIFE SCIENCE
INTEGRATION ➤

Earth's Magnetic Field

Magnetism isn't limited to bar magnets and iron. Earth has a magnetic field, as shown in **Figure 7-6.** This field extends into space and is called the magnetosphere. No one knows exactly how Earth's magnetic field is produced, but scientists suspect it is due to liquid metals moving in Earth's interior.

Honeybees, rainbow trout, and homing pigeons have something in common with sailors and hikers. They all take advantage of magnetism to find their way. Instead of using compasses, these animals and others have tiny pieces of magnetite in their brains. These pieces are so small that they contain a single magnetic domain. Scientists have shown that several animals use these natural magnets to detect Earth's magnetic field. They may use magnetic fields, along with other clues like the position of the sun or stars, to navigate.

If animals depend on Earth's magnetic field to help them find their way, what might happen if the magnetic field changes? It can happen. Earth's magnetic poles have reversed many times in the past. Scientists learned this by studying the magnetism of ancient rocks. When molten rock cools, magnetic domains of iron in the rock line up with Earth's magnetic field. By studying the magnetic fields of rocks of different ages, we

Figure 7-6 Earth's magnetic field surrounds Earth. The field lines are similar to those for a huge bar magnet running between the Arctic and Antarctic.

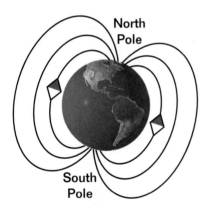

A On Earth's surface, the field lines are roughly parallel to the ground. Only near the poles do they tip down toward Earth. This is similar to the field lines around a bar magnet, which are almost parallel to the middle of the magnet and curve sharply at the poles.

B Earth's magnetosphere, extending into space, is affected by the sun. You will learn more about this in the next section.

have learned that Earth's magnetic field is not always the same. Sometimes it reverses. No one knows what causes this or exactly how long it takes. Scientists also have learned that the exact locations of Earth's magnetic poles change. Magnetic north today is slightly different than 20 years ago.

The Compass

How can humans detect and measure Earth's magnetic field? The compass is a useful tool for finding and mapping magnetic fields. A **compass** is a magnetic needle that is free to turn. The needle will align itself along the magnetic field lines of the nearest strong magnet. The field is usually Earth's. The north pole of the compass needle points toward Earth's north pole in the Arctic Circle. The south pole of the compass needle points toward Earth's south pole in Antarctica. This is how the poles of a magnet got their names.

If you put another magnet close to a compass, the magnet's field will change the direction the needle points. The compass needle will lie along the magnet's magnetic field lines, as shown in **Figure 7-7.** The north pole of the compass needle will point toward the south pole of the magnet. A compass can be used to find and map magnetic fields.

Figure 7-7 The compass needles align with the magnetic field lines around the magnet and point toward the poles. **What happens to the compass needles when the bar magnet is removed?**

Section Assessment

1. Why can't you break a magnet in half to get one north pole and one south pole?

2. A piece of iron has magnetic domains pointed in all directions. What happens to the domains when a strong magnet is placed next to the piece of iron?

3. When a piece of iron is magnetized as in question 2, why doesn't it ever repel the bar magnet?

4. **Think Critically:** A horseshoe magnet is a bar magnet bent into a letter C. When would you expect two horseshoe magnets to attract each other? Repel each other? Have little effect?

5. **Skill Builder**
   Comparing and Contrasting Compare and contrast electricity and magnetism. If you need help, refer to Comparing and Contrasting in the **Skill Handbook** on page 704.

Science Journal Pretend you are an early explorer. In your Science Journal, explain how a compass would change your work.

Make a Compass

Materials

- Petri dish
  *clear bowl
- Water
- Sewing needle
- Magnet
- Tape
- Marker
- Paper
- Plastic spoon
  *plastic fork

  *Alternate Material

You might have used a compass to find your way on a hike. It is a valuable tool, especially when you can't see the sun or stars to find your direction. Chinese inventors found a way to magnetize pieces of iron. They used this method to manufacture compasses 1000 years ago. You can use the same procedure to make a compass.

What You'll Investigate

How do you create a magnet and a compass?

Goals

- **Observe** induced magnetism.
- **Build** a compass.

Procedure

1. Reproduce the circular protractor shown. Tape it under the bottom of your dish so you can see the protractor but it won't get wet. Fill the dish halfway with water.

2. Mark one end of the needle with a marker. Magnetize a needle by placing it on the magnet aligned north and south for one minute.

3. **Make** a compass by floating the needle carefully in the dish. Use a plastic spoon or fork to lower the needle into the water. Turn the dish so the marked part of the needle is over 0°. This is a compass.

4. Bring the magnet near your compass. **Observe** what happens to the needle. **Measure** the angle the needle turns.

Conclude and Apply

1. **Explain** why the marked end of the needle always pointed the same way in step 3, even though you rotated the dish.

2. **Describe** the behavior of the compass when the magnet was brought close.

3. Does the marked end of your needle point to the north or south pole of the bar magnet? **Infer** whether the marked end of your needle is a north or south pole. How do you know?

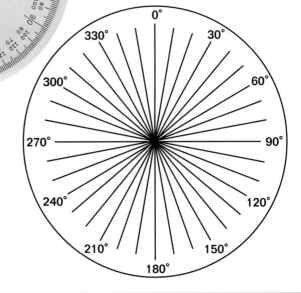

Electricity and Magnetism

Electric Current Can Create a Magnet

A bar magnet is not the only source of a magnetic field. Electricity and magnetism are two aspects of the force called **electromagnetism.** When electrons move in a wire (an electric current), there is a magnetic field around the wire, as shown in **Figure 7-8A.** When the current in the wire is turned off, the field vanishes. When you change the direction of the current, the north and south poles of this magnetic field reverse.

Examine the magnetic field lines around the coils of wire in **Figure 7-8B.** The small magnetic fields around each coil of wire add together to form a stronger magnetic field. When the coils are wrapped around an iron core, the magnetic field of the coils magnetizes the iron. The iron then becomes a magnet, which adds to the total magnetic field. A current-carrying wire wrapped around an iron core is called an **electromagnet,** shown in **Figure 7-8C.**

Figure 7-8 A current-carrying wire produces a magnetic field.

A Black iron particles show the magnetic field lines around the current-carrying wire in the center.

B The field lines make circles around the wire. When the wire is wrapped in a coil, the fields inside the coil add up. **Where is the north pole of the magnetic field inside the coil?**

Current

C An iron core inside the coils increases the magnetic field because the core is magnetized. This arrangement is called an electromagnet. Its magnetic field can be turned on and off.

Making an Electromagnet

Procedure 🤚 🤝 🥽 ⚡

1. Wrap a wire around a 16-penney steel nail ten times. Connect one end of the wire to a battery, as shown in **Figure 7–8C.** Leave the other end loose until you use the electromagnet. **CAUTION:** *When current is flowing in the wire, it can become very hot over time.*

2. Connect the wire. Observe how many paper clips you can pick up with the magnet.

3. Disconnect the wire and rewrap the nail with 20 coils. Connect the wire and observe how many paper clips you can pick up. Disconnect the wire again.

Analysis

1. How many paper clips did you pick up each time? Did more coils make the electromagnet stronger or weaker?

2. Make a graph of number of coils vs. number of paper clips attracted. Predict how many paper clips would be picked up with five coils of wire. Check your prediction.

Electromagnets at Work

The magnetic field of an electromagnet is turned on or off when the electric current is turned on or off. This has led to a number of practical uses. An electromagnet can be attached to a construction crane and used to lift objects that contain iron or steel, as shown in **Figure 7-9.** With the power to the electromagnet off, the crane moves it into position over the object. When the current is turned on, a powerful magnetic field is produced. Just as paper clips become magnetized by a bar magnet, the iron and steel are magnetized by the electromagnet. The force of the magnetic field is strong enough to lift the object. The crane then lifts the electromagnet and the attached object. The crane moves the object to the desired spot, and the current is switched off. The magnetic field vanishes, and the object then drops.

A doorbell is another familiar use of an electromagnet. When you press the button by the door, you close a switch in a circuit that includes an electromagnet. The magnet attracts an iron bar attached to a hammer. The hammer strikes the bell. When the

Figure 7-9 An electromagnet can be powerful. This one is used to lift crushed cars.

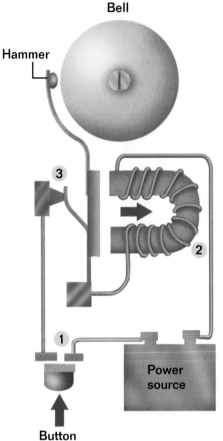

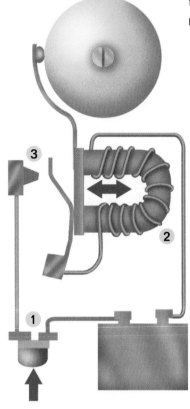

Bell

Hammer

3

2

1

Power source

Button

Figure 7-10 An electric doorbell uses an electromagnet. Each time the electromagnet is turned on, the hammer strikes the bell. **How is the electromagnet turned off?**

A When you press the button of an electric bell (1), you close a circuit. The current turns on the electromagnet (2). The magnet attracts a plate attached to a hammer, which hits the bell. When the plate reaches the magnet, the electrical connection at (3) is opened.

B When the connection is opened, the electromagnet is turned off. The plate with the hammer is pulled back by a spring, completing the circuit at (3) and starting the cycle over. This continues until you release the button.

hammer strikes the bell, the hammer has moved far enough to open the circuit again, as shown in **Figure 7-10.** The electromagnet loses its magnetic field, and a spring pulls the iron bar and hammer back in place. This movement closes the circuit, and the cycle begins again. The hammer strikes the bell several times a second.

Magnets Can Move Currents

Look around you. Are there any electric appliances that use motion, such as a fan? A magnetic field can be used to move a current-carrying wire, turning electric energy into the energy of motion.

*inter***NET**
CONNECTION

Visit the Glencoe Science Web Site at **www.glencoe.com/ sec/science** for more information about electromagnetism.

Figure 7-11 An electric motor uses the interaction between electricity and magnetism.

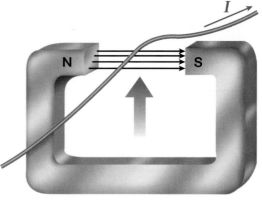

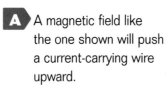

A A magnetic field like the one shown will push a current-carrying wire upward.

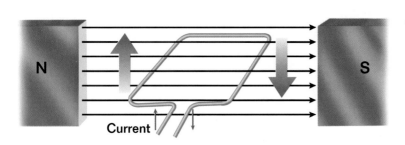

Current

B If the current runs in the opposite direction, the wire is pushed downward. The right half of the loop here is pushed downward. When the loop is straight up and down, it should stop spinning because the top of the loop is pushed upward and the bottom of the loop is pushed downward.

C To keep the loop in motion, the contact between the loop and the battery is designed to switch sides. Study the mechanism of the contacts. When the loop is straight up and down, the contacts switch and the current changes direction. The top of the loop is pushed downward and the bottom is pushed upward, so the motor keeps turning.

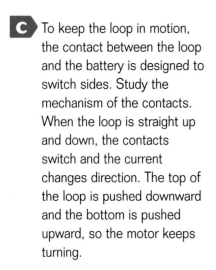

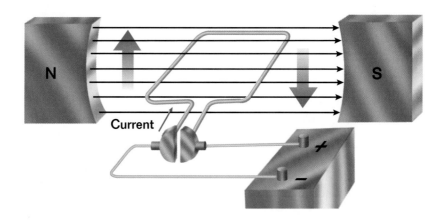

Current

Electric Motor

An **electric motor** converts electric energy into motion. The invention of the electric motor made it possible to harness electricity to do work, such as running an escalator or turning a tape in a tape deck.

How does an electric motor work? A magnetic field can move a current-carrying wire, as shown in **Figure 7-11A.** When the current is reversed, the wire is pushed in the opposite direction. **Figure 7-11B** shows how this effect can spin a loop of wire. Study **Figure 7-11C** to understand how an electric motor can keep a loop spinning.

Electromagnetism in the Magnetosphere

The opening photo in this chapter showed the northern lights. The aurora seen from Earth and from above Earth's surface is shown in **Figure 7-12.** The interaction of Earth's magnetic field and the electrically charged particles in the solar wind creates the aurora. Refer back to **Figure 7-6,** which shows Earth's magnetic field and the solar wind.

Recall that a magnetic field can move an electric current. The current does not need to be in a wire. Any moving electric charge can be moved by a magnetic field. When the charged particles in the solar wind reach Earth, they are turned aside by Earth's magnetic field. The force of Earth's magnetic field causes the particles that reach Earth to move back and forth along the magnetic field lines above Earth, rather than falling to Earth. The charged particles stay in an area around Earth's equator, called the Van Allen radiation belts. Thus, Earth's magnetic field protects the biosphere from the solar wind. ☑

When the sun emits unusually high numbers of charged particles, they move along Earth's magnetic field lines to the magnetic poles. This is why the northern and southern lights are seen near Earth's poles. At the poles, some of the charged particles enter Earth's atmosphere. The particles transfer energy to the atoms in the atmosphere. These atoms, mostly oxygen and nitrogen, emit the brilliant colors of the aurora when they release the extra energy. The colors that result depend on the atoms. Oxygen produces green and red lights. Nitrogen produces red lights and some blue and violet lights. The exact colors and shapes depend on local conditions.

Reading Check ☑

How does Earth's magnetic field protect the biosphere?

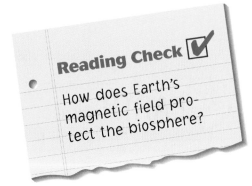

Figure 7-12 The aurora borealis is an amazing sight from Earth or from space.

Figure 7-13 When this loop is spun, an electric current flows up the left side of the loop (A) and down the right side. When (A) has moved to the right, the current flows downward. The current will switch directions twice in a full turn of the loop. **This shows the energy of motion being transformed into what?**

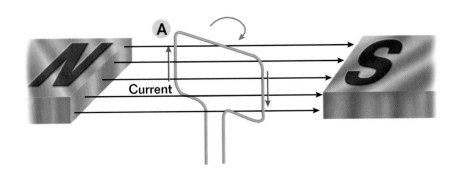

A Magnet Can Create a Current

In an electric motor, a magnetic field turns electricity into motion. You also can use a magnetic field to turn motion into electricity, as shown in **Figure 7-13.** When a wire loop moves through a magnetic field, the field can induce, or cause, a current in the loop. Moving a magnet in and out of a coil of wire also would cause an electric current. Using a changing magnetic field to cause, or induce, an electric current is called **induction.**

Electric Generator

An **electric generator** uses induction to produce electric power. In a generator, a wire coil spins in a strong magnetic field, as shown in **Figure 7-14.** An electric current is induced in the coil.

Electric generators produce electricity all over the world both in small generators that produce electricity for one household and in large generators that provide electric power for several states. Different energy sources such as gas, coal, and water are used to create the needed motion.

Figure 7-14 In this electric generator, a power source spins the loop between two magnets. This generator produces alternating current, which changes direction. Study the contacts between the loop and the circuit. If this generator had contacts like the motor in **Figure 7-11C,** it would produce direct current, like the current produced by a battery.

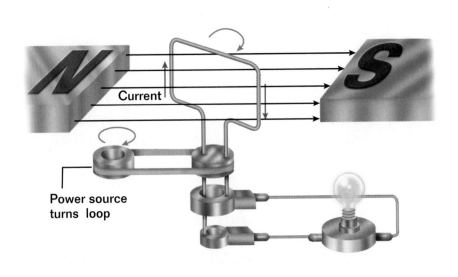

Power source turns loop

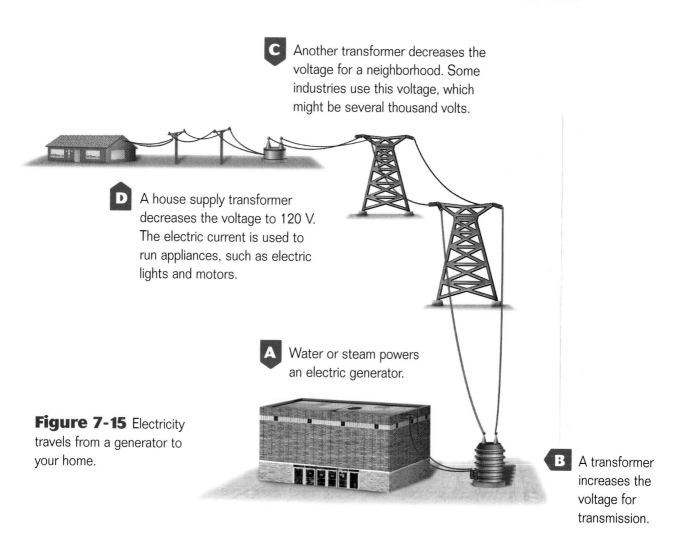

C Another transformer decreases the voltage for a neighborhood. Some industries use this voltage, which might be several thousand volts.

D A house supply transformer decreases the voltage to 120 V. The electric current is used to run appliances, such as electric lights and motors.

A Water or steam powers an electric generator.

Figure 7-15 Electricity travels from a generator to your home.

B A transformer increases the voltage for transmission.

Transformer

The electricity produced at a power plant is carried to your home in wires. The wires transmit electricity at high voltage (about 700 000 V) because at low voltage, the wires are less efficient. But, homes and businesses need low voltage—120 V for most uses and 220 V for heavy equipment such as a stove and a clothes dryer.

A generator can produce two types of current. *Direct current* (DC) is like that produced by a battery. It flows in one direction. *Alternating current* (AC) changes direction many times each second. Large generating plants produce alternating current because the voltage can be increased and decreased easily using a transformer.

A **transformer** changes the voltage of an alternating current. It is used to increase the voltage before transmitting an electric current through the power lines. It is then used to decrease the voltage to the level needed for home or industrial use. Such a power system is shown in **Figure 7-15.**

A transformer has two coils of wire wrapped around an iron core, as shown in **Figure 7-16.** One coil is connected to an alternating current source. The current creates a magnetic field in the iron core, just like in an electromagnet.

Input

Output

Figure 7-16 A transformer can increase or decrease voltage. The ratio input coils/output coils equals the ratio input voltage/output voltage. **If the input voltage here is 60 V, what is the output voltage?**

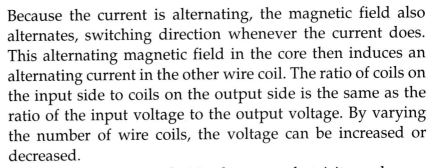

Because the current is alternating, the magnetic field also alternates, switching direction whenever the current does. This alternating magnetic field in the core then induces an alternating current in the other wire coil. The ratio of coils on the input side to coils on the output side is the same as the ratio of the input voltage to the output voltage. By varying the number of wire coils, the voltage can be increased or decreased.

There are many similarities between electricity and magnetism. Both forces depend on charged electrons. Both forces can repel or attract. In both cases, likes repel and unlikes attract. Electricity can produce magnetism, and magnetism can produce electricity. People take advantage of this connection in many areas, including the electric guitar shown in **Figure 7-17.**

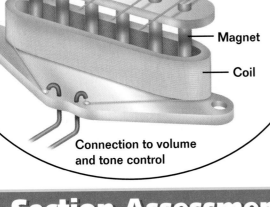

Metal strings

Magnet

Coil

Connection to volume and tone control

Figure 7-17 The magnets produce magnetic fields around the strings. When you strum the guitar, the strings vibrate. The vibrating strings change the magnetic field. The magnetic field changes and induces a changing electric current in the coil. This current goes to the tone and volume controls. **How is this similar to a transformer?**

Section Assessment

1. What is an electromagnet?
2. How does a transformer work?
3. How does a magnetic field affect a current-carrying wire?
4. **Think Critically:** Suppose the head of a nail in the core of an electromagnet attracts the south pole of a bar magnet. If the wires of the electromagnet are switched so that the current runs in the opposite direction, will the head of the nail still attract the south pole of a bar magnet? Will it still pick up paper clips? Explain.
5. **Skill Builder**
   Concept Mapping How do you evaluate science writing? Do the **Chapter 7 Skill Activity** on page 731 to learn about communicating scientific information.

Using Math

A transformer has ten turns of wire on the input side and 50 turns of wire on the output side. If the input voltage is 120 V, what will the output voltage be?

Early Women Inventors

Who invented the tools in your kitchen, the equipment in the school lab, and the programming for the computers you use? Women inventors contributed to all of these.

One of the earliest female inventors in recorded history, known only as Maria, an alchemist who worked in Egypt in the first century A.D., is credited with inventing equipment such as the double boiler.

During much of human history, a woman who wanted training beyond her own experience had to work with a male relative. Because most women could not own property, they could not receive patents for their inventions. The first American woman inventor we know by name is Sybilla Masters, who had her husband secure two patents for her for processing corn and palmetto leaves.

U.S. Women Inventors

In 1809, Mary Kies became the first woman to obtain a U.S. patent in her own name. She developed a way of making a cost-effective work bonnet for women. After this, many women received patents and credit for their work. Sarah Goode, the first African-American woman to receive a patent, designed a folding cabinet bed.

Many early inventions by women made household chores easier, such as Sarah Boone's invention of the ironing board, patented in 1892. However, inventions by women have affected every branch of science and society. In 1840, Ada Byron Lovelace (inset) outlined the basic concepts of computer programming and computer language. Hertha Ayrton, who experimented with electromagnetism, improved projector lamps for movies. Margaret Knight received some two dozen patents, an achievement that earned her the nickname "the female Edison." In 1942, actress Hedy Lamar (far left) was granted a patent for a secret communication system used during World War II.

Women continue to play an important role in science and in the search for technological solutions to problems.

Science JOURNAL

Think of an invention that you could not live without. Find out who invented it, and write a paragraph about this person and the invention in your Science Journal.

Materials

- Insulated wire (22 guage) (2 m)
- Steel knitting needle
  *steel rod
- Nails (4)
- Hammer
- Bar magnets (2)
- Insulated wire (16 guage) (60 cm)
- Masking tape
- Fine sandpaper
- Wooden board (approximately 15 cm)
- Wooden blocks (2)
- Battery (6 V)
  *batteries connected in a series (1.5 V) (4)
- Wire cutters
  *scissors

  *Alternate Materials

How does an electric motor work?

Electric motors are used in many appliances. A fan, whether used to cool a room or a computer hard drive, transforms electric energy into motion.

What You'll Investigate

How can you change electric energy into motion?

Goals

- **Make** a small electric motor.
- **Observe** how the motor works.

Safety Precautions

 Hold only the insulated part of each wire when they are attached to the battery.

Procedure

1. **Use** the wire cutters or sandpaper to strip the insulation from about 4 cm of each end of the 22-gauge wire.

2. Leaving the stripped ends free, **make** this wire into a coil of at least 30 turns. Wrap tape around the coil to hold it in place.

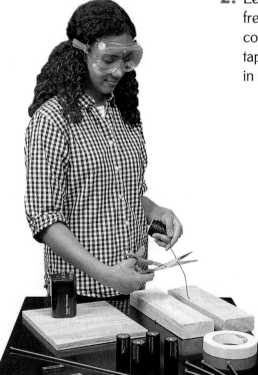

3. Insert the knitting needle through the coil. Try to have an equal number of turns on each side of the needle. Pull the wire's two ends to one end of the needle. Tape one bare wire to each side of the needle.

4. Tape a bar magnet to each block so that a north pole extends from one and a south pole from the other.

5. **Make** the motor. Tap the nails into the wood block as shown in the figure below. Try to cross the nails at the same height as the magnets so that the coil will be suspended right between the magnets. Place the needle on the nails. If the coil is not directly between the magnets, use bits of wood or folded paper to adjust the pieces until they are in line. The magnets should be as close to the coil as possible without touching it.

6. **Cut** two 30-cm lengths of 16-gauge wire. Strip both ends and attach one length to each terminal of the battery. Holding only the insulated part of each wire, place one wire against each of the bare wires taped to the needle to **close the circuit.** Observe what happens.

Conclude and Apply

1. **Describe** what happens when you close the circuit by connecting the wires.

2. **Describe** what happens when you open the circuit.

3. **Predict** what would happen if you used twice as many coils of wire.

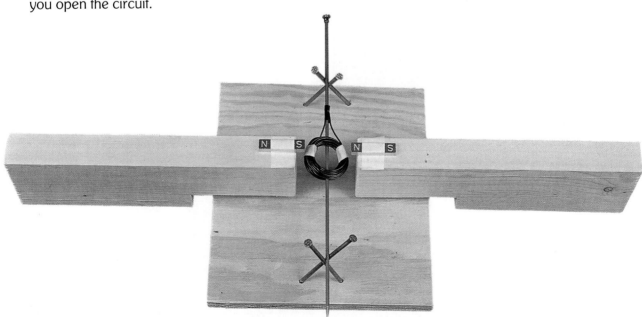

For a **preview** of this chapter, study this Reviewing Main Ideas before you read the chapter. After you have studied this chapter, you can use the Reviewing Main Ideas to **review** the chapter.

The Glencoe MindJogger, Audiocassettes, and CD-ROM provide additional opportunities for review.

Section 7-1 MAGNETS

A magnet attracts metals like iron and steel. It can attract or repel other magnets. A magnet has two poles—north and south. Like poles repel each other. Unlike poles attract. Each atom in a magnet is like a tiny magnet. The magnetic fields of the atom-magnets are aligned with each other to create the large magnet. A magnet can briefly magnetize a piece of iron or steel by aligning the fields of the **magnetic domains** in the material. *Where is the field of a bar magnet strongest? Weakest?*

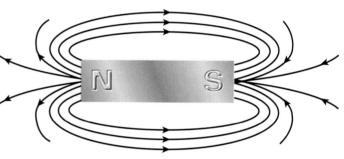

MAGNETIC FIELDS

Magnetic force acts through a **magnetic field.** You can "see" the field around a magnet with a petri dish of iron filings. The filings will lie in lines going from one pole to the other. Field lines are defined to run from north pole to south. *What does the field between two magnetic north poles look like?*

THE COMPASS

A **compass** is a magnet suspended so that it is free to turn. It aligns itself with the nearest strong magnetic field. This is usually Earth's magnetic field. *How would you use a compass to map the field around a bar magnet?*

Section
7-2   ELECTRICITY AND MAGNETISM

Electricity and magnetism are two aspects of the force **electromagnetism.** An electric current creates a magnetic field. This is used to make an **electromagnet,** a strong magnet that can be turned on and off. *How does an electromagnet differ from a bar magnet?* A magnetic field accelerates charged particles that move through it. This effect is used to make an **electric motor,** which uses a magnetic field to transform electrical energy to mechanical energy. *Name three uses for motors.* A changing magnetic field can induce an electric current in a wire loop. This is used to make a **generator,** which uses mechanical energy to produce electricity. A **transformer** uses **induction** to change the voltage of an alternating current. *What is induction?*

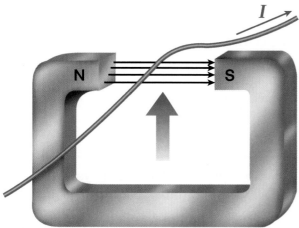

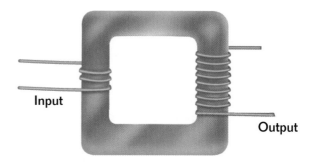

Input

Output

Chapter 7 Assessment

Using Vocabulary

a. compass
b. electric generator
c. electric motor
d. electromagnet
e. electromagnetism
f. induction
g. magnetic domain
h. magnetic field
i. magnetism
j. transformer

For each set of terms below, explain the relationship that exists.

1. magnetism, electromagnetism
2. induction, transformer
3. compass, magnetic field
4. electric motor, electromagnet
5. electric motor, electric generator

Checking Concepts

Choose the word or phrase that best answers the question.

6. What can iron filings be used to show?
   A) magnetic field lines
   B) electric field lines
   C) gravitational field lines
   D) none of these

7. Why does a compass point to magnetic north?
   A) Earth's north pole is strongest.
   B) Earth's north pole is closest.
   C) Only the north pole attracts compasses.
   D) The compass aligns itself with Earth's magnetic field.

8. What will the north poles of two bar magnets do when brought together?
   A) attract
   B) create an electric current
   C) repel
   D) not interact

9. How many poles do all magnets have?
   A) one
   B) two
   C) three
   D) an unlimited number

10. When a current-carrying wire is wrapped around an iron core, what can it create?
    A) an aurora
    B) a magnet
    C) a generator
    D) a motor

11. What does a transformer between utility wires and your house do?
    A) increases voltage
    B) decreases voltage
    C) leaves voltage the same
    D) changes DC to AC

12. Which types of energy does an electric motor convert between?
    A) electrical to mechanical
    B) electrical to magnetic
    C) magnetic to mechanical
    D) mechanical to electrical

13. What prevents charged particles from the solar wind from hitting Earth?
    A) the aurora borealis
    B) Earth's magnetic field
    C) high-altitude electric fields
    D) Earth's atmosphere

14. What do magnetic fields **NOT** interact with?
    A) magnets
    B) steel
    C) electric current
    D) paper

15. Which types of energy does an electric generator convert between?
    A) electrical to mechanical
    B) electrical to magnetic
    C) magnetic to electrical
    D) mechanical to electrical

Thinking Critically

16. A compass needle is floated on water or oil. Why don't ordinary bar magnets line themselves up with Earth's magnetic field when you set them on a table?

17. If you were given a magnet with unmarked poles, how could you determine which pole was which?

18. A nail is magnetized by holding the south pole of a magnet against the head of the nail. Is the point of the nail a north or south pole? Explain.

19. If you add more coils to an electro-magnet, does the magnet get stronger or weaker? Why?

20. Magnetism is a force. How can you demonstrate this?

Developing Skills

If you need help, refer to the **Skill Handbook.**

21. **Design an Experiment:** How could you test and compare the strength of two different magnets?

22. **Using Math:** A transformer has 30 coils on the input side and five coils on the output side. What input voltage creates an output voltage of 600 V?

23. **Making Operational Definitions:** Give an operational definition of an electro-magnet.

24. **Concept Mapping:** Explain how a door-bell uses an electromagnet by placing the following phrases in the cycle concept map: *circuit open circuit closed, electro-magnet turned on, electromagnet turned off, hammer attracted to magnet and strikes bell,* and *hammer pushed back by spring.*

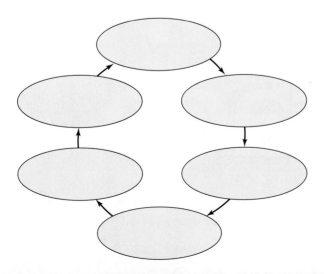

THE PRINCETON REVIEW

Test-Taking Tip

The Best Answer Is Often the Least Incorrect If none of the answer choices look right, use the process of elimination to eliminate the *worst* ones. The one you've got left is the least incorrect.

Test Practice

Use these questions to test your Science Proficiency.

1. The north pole of a magnet will strongly attract to which part of another magnet?
   A) the south pole
   B) the north pole
   C) the center
   D) any part

2. A current carrying wire is deflected upward by a magnetic field. What happens when the current is reversed?
   A) The wire is still deflected upward.
   B) The wire is deflected downward.
   C) The wire is deflected to one side.
   D) The wire is no longer deflected.

3. What does a transformer do?
   A) changes the voltage of an alternating current
   B) changes electrical energy to energy of motion
   C) changes energy of motion to electrical energy
   D) changes electrical energy to potential energy

Earth's
Changing
Surface

What's Happening Here?

Dip your hand into water, and it feels soft to the touch—yet water is also nature's most powerful sculptor. Take Arizona's Antelope Canyon (left). About 190 million years ago, sand dunes formed in this area. Over time, these dunes were turned into rock, forming sandstone. Later, a stream gradually wore a wide canyon through the dunes. Later, the climate became so dry that the canyon filled in with sand. Flash floods carved out this chasm, and water-borne grit polished the stone sides. What gives the rock its glowing red color? Iron in the rock is rusting from exposure to the water and the oxygen in the air. Other elements also shape Earth's contours. In California's Death Valley (below), the dry climate enables the wind to mound the sandy soil into dunes. In this unit, you will learn about forces and processes that rearrange the surface of Earth—sometimes slowly as with rusting, drying, and cracking, or rapidly as with floods and storms.

interNET CONNECTION

Explore the Glencoe Science Web Site at **www.glencoe. com/sec/science** to find out more about topics found in this unit.

CHAPTER 8

Weathering and Soil

Chapter Preview

Section 8-1
Weathering

Section 8-2
Soil

Skills Preview

Skill Builders
- Recognize Cause and Effect
- Map Concepts

Activities
- Hypothesize
- Interpret Data

MiniLabs
- Observe
- Compare and Contrast

Reading Check ✔

As you read, identify and define forms of the word *weather.* Then use a dictionary to find and define additional forms of this word.

Explore Activity

The rock formations shown here are in Bryce Canyon National Park. For millions of years, nature has been working on these rocks, weathering them from horizontal layers into the pinnacles seen today. Weathering pits and roughens the stone of monuments and rocks in nature.

All stone and rock weather over time. Grains of sediment fall out of rocks. Cracks develop on the surface and deep inside rocks. Weathering causes the stone of monuments to crumble away gradually. Weathering also causes rocks in nature to fracture, buckle, and crumble into soil and sediment.

Observe Weathering

1. Obtain two or three kinds of rocks.
2. Over white paper, rub one rock against a metal file.
3. Repeat this process with each kind of rock.
4. Compare the amount of particles broken from each rock.

Science Journal

In your Science Journal, record which rock breaks apart most easily. Describe each rock based upon your observations.

Weathering

Evidence of Weathering

The next time you take a walk or a drive, notice the sand and grit along the sidewalk and curb. Much of the gritty sediment you see comes from small particles that break loose from concrete curbs and from rocks exposed to the natural elements. These sediments are evidence that weathering is taking place.

Weathering is the process that breaks down rocks into smaller and smaller fragments. Conditions and processes in the environment cause the weathering of rock and concrete. Rocks break down into small pieces called sediment. These sediments also can form soil. Soil formation is dependent upon the process of weathering.

Over millions of years, the process of weathering has helped change Earth's surface. It continues today. **Figure 8-1** illustrates how weathering wears down mountains to hills. Weathering makes it difficult to read the writing on tombstones and slowly breaks down statues. Weathering also can cause potholes in streets. The two types of weathering are mechanical and chemical. They work together to break down rock.

What **You'll Learn**

▶ The difference between mechanical weathering and chemical weathering
▶ The effects of climate on weathering

Vocabulary
weathering
mechanical weathering
ice wedging
chemical weathering
oxidation
climate

Why **It's Important**

▶ Weathering causes rocks to crumble and landforms to change shape over time.

Figure 8-1 Over long periods of time, weathering helps change sharp, jagged mountains into smooth, rolling mountains and hills.

A The Grand Tetons in Wyoming (A) have not been exposed to agents of weathering as long as the mountains of Mount Washington Valley, New Hampshire, (B) have been.

Figure 8-2 Pavements such as driveways and sidewalks can be broken up by tree roots.

B As roots grow under a sidewalk, their increased size forces the concrete to crack.

A As trees grow, their roots spread throughout the soil.

C Over time, the sidewalk buckles and breaks apart.

Mechanical Weathering

Mechanical weathering breaks apart rocks without changing their chemical composition. Each fragment and particle weathered away by a mechanical process keeps the same characteristics as the original rock. Mechanical weathering can be caused by growing plants, expanding ice, mineral crystal growth, lightning, and expansion and contraction when an area heats and cools. These physical processes produce enough force to break rocks into smaller pieces. ✓

Plants

Plant roots grow into cracks of rocks where they find water and nutrients. As roots grow, they wedge rocks apart. If you've skated on a sidewalk and tripped over a crack near a tree, you have experienced the results of mechanical weathering. The sidewalk near the tree in **Figure 8-2C** shows signs of weathering. How could cracks in rocks occur in the same way? **Figure 8-3** might give you some ideas.

Reading Check
What is mechanical weathering?

Lichen plants also cause mechanical weathering. Parts of the plant expand and shrink with the amount of available water. This is similar to the process of ice wedging described below.

Ice Wedging

The mechanical weathering process known as **ice wedging** is illustrated in **Figure 8-4.** In cold areas, low temperatures freeze water. Warmer temperatures thaw the ice. Ice wedging is noticeable in the mountains. It is one factor that wears down sharp mountain peaks to rounded hills—a process pictured in **Figure 8-1.** This cycle of freezing and thawing not only breaks up rocks but also breaks up roads and highways. When water enters cracks in road pavement and freezes, it forces the pavement apart. This can cause potholes to form in roads. Weathering by both roots and ice wedging rapidly can reduce rocks to smaller pieces. Breaking up rocks through mechanical weathering exposes a greater surface area to additional weathering. As the amount of surface area increases, the rate of weathering increases.

Figure 8-3 Tree roots cause mechanical weathering of rocks as shown by this tree in Glacier National Park, Montana.

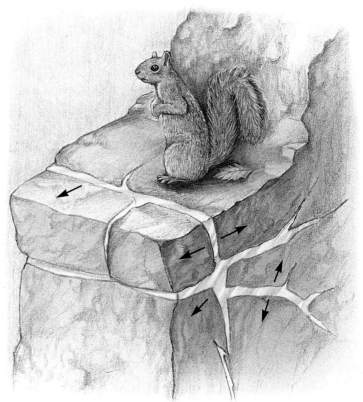

Figure 8-4 When water freezes in cracks of rocks, it expands. Pressure builds and breaks apart the rock. As the ice thaws and then the water refreezes, this process occurs again.

Chemical Weathering

The second type of weathering occurs when water, air, and other substances react with the minerals in rocks. This type of weathering is called **chemical weathering** because the chemical composition of the rock changes. Let's see how chemical weathering happens.

Water

Water is an important agent of chemical weathering. When the hydrogen and oxygen atoms in water react with the chemicals in some rocks, new substances form. These substances are much different from those of the original rock.

Acids

Naturally formed acids can weather rocks chemically. When water mixes with carbon dioxide from the air, a weak acid, called carbonic acid, forms. Carbonic acid is the same weak acid that makes soft drinks fizzy. Carbonic acid reacts with minerals such as calcite, the main mineral in limestone. The product of this reaction then dissolves and can be carried away with the acid. Over thousands of years, carbonic acid has weathered so much limestone that caves have formed, such as the one shown in **Figure 8-5.**

Chemical weathering also occurs when carbonic acid comes in contact with granite rock. Over a long time, the mineral feldspar in granite is broken down into the clay mineral kaolinite. Kaolinite clay makes up most of the material in some soils. Clay is an end product of weathering.

Some roots and decaying plants give off acids that can dissolve minerals in rock. Removing these minerals weakens the rock. Eventually, the rock will break into smaller pieces. The next time you find a moss-covered rock, peel back the moss and look at the small pits underneath. Acids from the rootlike structures of the moss caused the pits.

CHEMISTRY
◄ INTEGRATION

Figure 8-5 Lehman Cave in Great Basin National Park, Nevada, is a product of chemical weathering. **How did water help form this cave?**

CHEMISTRY
INTEGRATION

Cave Beauty
Some cave formations are made of calcite. The chemical formula for calcite, a common rock-forming mineral, is $CaCO_3$.
Use the periodic table in the back of the book to identify the elements in this formula.

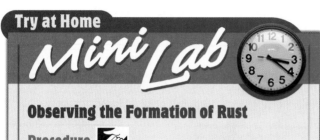

Mini Lab

Observing the Formation of Rust

Procedure

1. Place some steel wool in a glass dish with 1 cm of water.
2. Observe for several days.

Analysis

1. What changes occurred?
2. What caused the changes?
3. How are these changes related to weathering?

Oxygen

Oxygen helps cause chemical weathering. You've seen rusty swing sets and cars. Rust is caused by oxidation. **Oxidation** (ahk sih DAY shun) occurs when a material such as iron is exposed to oxygen and water. When rocks containing iron are exposed to water and the oxygen in the air, the iron in the rock rusts and turns reddish, as seen in **Figure 8-6.**

Climate and Weathering

Mechanical and chemical weathering occur everywhere. However, climate affects the rate and type of weathering. **Climate** is the pattern of weather that occurs in a particular area over many years. In cold climates, where freezing and thawing are frequent, mechanical weathering breaks down rocks rapidly through the process of ice wedging.

Chemical weathering is more rapid in warm, wet climates. Thus, chemical weathering occurs quickly in tropical areas such as the Amazon River region of South America. Lack of moisture in deserts and low temperatures in polar regions slow down chemical weathering. How weathering affects rock depends on the type of rock, as illustrated in **Figure 8-7.**

Mechanical and chemical weathering work together. For example, when rocks break apart because of mechanical weathering, more surface area is exposed, and the rate of chemical weathering increases.

Figure 8-6 These rocks in Utah have been chemically weathered. **What caused them to be a reddish color?**

Figure 8-7 These old tombstones are about the same age, but they have weathered differently. The type of rock also influences how fast a surface weathers. **Why?**

CHARLES K. TOWNSEND
DIED
Aug. 19, 1850,
Aged 50 Yrs. 5 Mo.
7 Ds.
JOHN
Died Aug. 19, 1847
Aged 1 Yr. 2 Mo. 15 Ds
JOHN KINNERSLEY
Died Aug. 19, 1850
Aged 2 Yrs. 1 Mo. 9 Ds.
ELIZABETH
Died Aug. 21, 1850
Aged 7 Yrs. 3 Mo. 19 Ds
Children of
Chas. K. & Ann
TOWNSEND.

Now you can understand how weathering affects roads, buildings, streets, cemeteries, sidewalks, rocks, caves, and mountains. When weathering breaks down rocks, it contributes to the rock cycle by making sediment that can form sedimentary rocks. Weathering also begins the process of breaking down rock into soil. These steps are discussed in the next section.

Section Assessment

1. What is the difference between mechanical and chemical weathering?

2. How is mechanical weathering affected by climate?

3. **Think Critically:** How can water be a factor in both mechanical and chemical weathering?

4. **Skill Builder**
   Observing and Inferring Do the **Chapter 8 Skill Activity** on page 733 to learn more about mechanical weathering.

Using Computers

Spreadsheet Make a spreadsheet that identifies examples of weathering that you see around your neighborhood and school and classifies each example as the result of mechanical weathering, chemical weathering, or both. If you need help, refer to page 722.

Design Your Own Experiment

Activity 8•1

Weathering Chalk

Possible Materials

- Equal-sized pieces of chalk (6)
- Small beakers or clear plastic cups (2)
- Metric ruler
- Water
- White vinegar (100 mL)
- Hot plate
- Graduated cylinder (250 mL)

Chalk is a type of limestone made of the shells of tiny organisms. When you write your name on the chalkboard or draw a picture on the driveway with a piece of chalk, what happens to the chalk? It is mechanically weathered. This experiment will help you understand how chalk can be chemically weathered.

Recognize the Problem

How can chalk be chemically weathered? What variables affect the rate of chemical weathering?

Form a Hypothesis

How do you think acidity, surface area, and temperature affect the rate of chemical weathering of chalk? What happens to chalk in water or acid (vinegar)? How will the size of the chalk pieces affect the rate of weathering? What will happen if you heat the acid? **Make hypotheses** to support your ideas.

Goals

- **Design** experiments to compare the effects of acidity, surface area, and temperature on the rate of chemical weathering of chalk.
- **Describe** factors that affect chemical weathering.

Safety Precautions

Wear safety goggles when pouring acids.

CAUTION: *If mixing liquids, always add acid to water.* Be careful when using a hot plate and heated solutions.

Test Your Hypothesis

Plan

1. **Develop** hypotheses about the effects of acidity, surface area, and temperature on the rate of chemical weathering.

2. Decide how to test your first hypothesis. **List** the steps needed to test the hypothesis.

3. Repeat step 2 for your other two hypotheses.

4. **Design** data tables in your Science Journal. Make one for acidity, one for surface area, and one for temperature.

5. **Identify** what remains constant in your experiment and what varies. Each test should have only one variable. Have you allowed for a control in each experiment?

6. **Summarize** your data in a graph. Decide from reading the **Skill Handbook** which type of graph to use.

Do

1. Make sure your teacher approves your plan before you start the experiment.

2. Carry out the three experiments as planned.

3. While the experiments are going on, **write** your observations and **complete** the data tables in your Science Journal.

Analyze Your Data

1. **Analyze** your graph to find out which substance—water or acid—weathered the chalk more quickly. Was your hypothesis supported by your data?

2. **Infer** from your data obtained in the surface-area experiment whether the amount of surface area makes a difference in the rate of chemical weathering. Explain why this occurs.

Draw Conclusions

1. **Explain** how the chalk was chemically weathered.

2. How does heat affect the rate of chemical weathering?

3. What does this imply about weathering in the tropics?

8•2 Soil

What You'll Learn

- How soil develops from rock
- How to describe soil by comparing the A, B, and C soil horizons
- How environmental conditions affect the development of soils
- Ways to reduce soil erosion

Vocabulary

soil	horizon
humus	litter
soil profile	leaching

Why It's Important

- Some regions of Earth are more fertile than others because soil forms in different ways.

Formation of Soil

How often have you been told "Take off those dirty shoes before you come into this house"? Ever since you were a child, you've had experience with what many people call dirt, which is actually soil. Soil is found in lots of places: empty lots, farm fields, gardens, and forests.

What is soil and where does it come from? The surface of Earth is covered by a layer of rock and mineral fragments produced by weathering. As you learned in Section 8-1, weathering gradually breaks rocks into smaller and smaller fragments. But, these fragments are not soil until plants and animals live in them. Plants and animals add organic matter such as leaves, twigs, and dead worms and insects to the rock fragments. Then, soil begins to develop. **Soil** is a mixture of weathered rock, organic matter, mineral fragments, water, and air. **Figure 8-8** illustrates the process of soil development. Soil is a material that supports vegetation. Climate, types of rock, slope, amount of moisture, and length of time rock has been weathering affect the formation of soil.

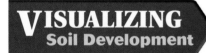

VISUALIZING Soil Development

Figure 8-8 Soil is constantly developing from rock.

A Rock at the surface begins to fracture and break down.

B As rock weathers into smaller fragments, plants begin to grow in the weathered rock.

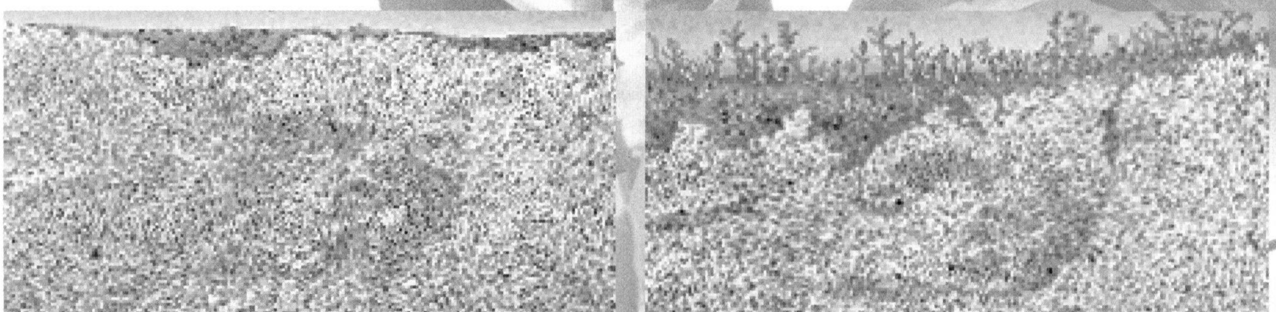

Composition of Soil

Soil may contain small rodents, insects, worms, algae, fungi, bacteria, and decaying organic matter. As soil develops, organic material, such as plants, decays until the original form of the matter has disappeared. The material turns into dark-colored matter called **humus** (HYEW mus). Humus serves as a source of nutrients for plants, providing nitrogen, phosphorus, potassium, and sulfur. Humus also promotes good soil structure and helps soil hold water. As worms, insects, and rodents burrow throughout soil, they mix the humus with the fragments of rock. In good-quality surface soil, about half of the volume is humus and half is broken-down rock. ☑

Soil can take thousands of years to form and can range in thickness from 60 m in some areas to just a few centimeters in others. A fertile soil is one that supplies nutrients for plant growth. Soils that develop near rivers often are fertile. Other soils, such as those that develop on steep slopes, may be poor in nutrients and have low fertility.

Soils have small spaces in them. These spaces fill with air or water. In swampy areas, water may fill these spaces year-round. In other areas, soil may fill up with water after rains or during floods.

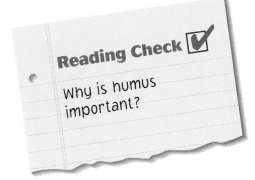

Reading Check ☑

Why is humus important?

C Worms, insects, bacteria, and fungi living among the plant roots add organic matter to the soil.

D When plants and animals in the soil die, they break down, or decay, and form dark humus.

Soil Profile

You may have seen layers of soil if you've ever dug a deep hole or driven by a steep slope such as a road cut where the soil and rock are exposed. You might have observed that plants grow in the top layer of soil. The top layer of soil is darker than the soil layers below it. These different layers of soil make up what is called a **soil profile.** Each layer in the soil profile is called a **horizon.** There are generally three horizons. They are labeled A, B, and C, as in the diagram in **Figure 8-9.**

Figure 8-9 Under this meadow is soil with a specific profile.

B The horizons in this soil profile reflect the climatic conditions under which it formed. The A horizon contains humus and small grains of rocks. The dark color reflects the organic material it contains. The B horizon contains minerals that have been dissolved and moved from the A horizon plus some clay. The C horizon consists mainly of original rock that has not been changed and that has no organic material.

A The soil profile of this meadow has three main horizons.

The photo in **Figure 8-10** shows soil horizons in an eroded hillside. You might also see soil profiles in streambeds, at construction sites, or even in your own garden.

Horizon A

The A horizon is the top layer of soil. In a forest or unplowed area, it may be covered with litter. **Litter** is composed of leaves, twigs, and other organic material that changes to humus when it is exposed to decomposing organisms. Litter helps prevent erosion and hold water. The A horizon is also known as topsoil. Topsoil has more humus and smaller rock and mineral particles than the other layers in a soil profile. A scoop of topsoil will show dark-colored soil, grains of rocks and minerals, decayed leaves, plant roots, insects, and worms. The A horizon is the key to successful plant growth and development.

Figure 8-10 Each soil horizon is unique due to the amount of minerals and organic material. **In which direction are minerals moved?**

Horizon B

The layer below the A horizon is the B horizon. It contrasts sharply with the A horizon. Because litter does not add to this horizon, it is lighter in color than the A horizon and contains less humus. The B horizon also contains elements washed down from the A horizon by the process of leaching.

Leaching is the removal of minerals that have been dissolved in water. The process of leaching resembles making coffee in a drip coffeemaker. In a coffeemaker, water drips into ground coffee. In the soil, water seeps into the A horizon. In a coffeemaker, the water absorbs the flavor and color from the coffee and flows down into a coffeepot. In the soil, the water reacts with humus to form an acid. This acid dissolves some of the elements from the minerals in the A horizon and carries them into the B horizon. Some leaching also occurs in the B horizon and moves minerals into the C horizon.

Horizon C

The C horizon is below the B horizon. It is the bottom of the soil profile and consists mostly of partially weathered parent rock. Leaching from the B horizon also may provide other minerals. What would you find if you dug all the way to the bottom of the C horizon? As you might have guessed, there would be solid rock. This is the rock that gave rise to the soil horizons above it.

In many places on Earth, the land is covered by material that was deposited by glaciers. This unsorted mass of ground-up rock, broken rock, and boulders has filled in the low spots in many places, creating, for example, the flat landscapes of the Midwest. The soils that developed on this glacial material are extremely fertile. The rich soils are an important part of the Midwest's agricultural industry. How does this soil profile differ from the one described above? If you were to dig down through the C horizon, you would find solid bedrock as before, but it would not be the rock that the soil formed from. What is the material that formed this soil profile?

Problem Solving

Interpret Crop Data

Good soil is necessary for crop production. Fertilizers and good farming practices help improve soil quality. Today's increasing world population requires that more food be produced to curb starvation. The chart below shows how world agricultural yield and population increased from 1950 to 1996.

Think Critically: Analyze the chart. Is the increase in agricultural production keeping up with human population growth? What do you think is the reason?

Food and Population Data		
Time Span	Percent increase in world agricultural production	Average percent growth rate in population
1960s	3.0	1.95
1970s	2.4	1.83
1980s	2.2	1.78
1990–1996	1.6	1.61

Types of Soil

The texture of soil depends on the amounts of sand, silt, and clay that are in it. In turn, the texture of soil affects how water runs through it. That is not all you'll discover from examining soil profiles.

If you examine a soil profile in one place, it will not look exactly like a soil profile from another location. Different locations affect the way a profile looks. Deserts are dry. Prairies are semidry. The temperate zone profile represents a soil from an area with a moderate amount of rain and moderate temperatures. Crops like the wheat in **Figure 8-11** grow well in temperate zone soils.

Soil Types Reflect Climate

The thickness of the soil horizons and the soil composition of the profiles also depend on a number of conditions, including climate. Examples of three soil profiles from different climates are shown in **Figure 8-12.**

Chemical weathering is much slower in areas where there is little rainfall, and soils in desert climates contain little organic material. The soil horizons in drier areas also are thinner than soil horizons in wetter climates. The amount of precipitation affects how much leaching of minerals occurs in the soil. Soils that have been leached are light in color. Some can be almost white.

Time also affects soil development, changing the characteristics of soil. If the weathering of the rock has been going on for a short time, the parent rock of the soil determines the soil characteristics. As the weathering continues for a longer time, the soil resembles the parent rock less and less.

*inter*NET
CONNECTION

Visit the Glencoe Science Web Site at **www. glencoe.com/sec/ science** for more information about soil and climate.

Figure 8-11 These golden stalks of wheat were grown in the fertile soils of the midwestern United States. **What do you think the A horizon is like here?**

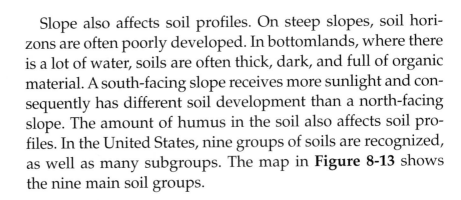

Slope also affects soil profiles. On steep slopes, soil horizons are often poorly developed. In bottomlands, where there is a lot of water, soils are often thick, dark, and full of organic material. A south-facing slope receives more sunlight and consequently has different soil development than a north-facing slope. The amount of humus in the soil also affects soil profiles. In the United States, nine groups of soils are recognized, as well as many subgroups. The map in **Figure 8-13** shows the nine main soil groups.

Soil—An Important Resource

Soil is important. Many of the things we take for granted—food, paper, and cotton—have a direct connection to the soil. Vegetables, grains, and cotton come from plants. Livestock such as cattle and pigs feed on grasses. Paper comes from

VISUALIZING Soil Profiles

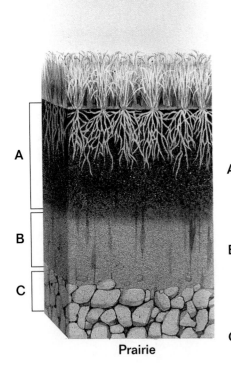

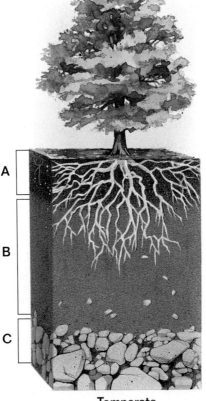

Prairie

Temperate

Desert

Figure 8-12 Prairie soils are brown and fertile with thick grass roots that fill the deep A horizon. Temperate soils are loose, brown soils with less-developed A horizons than prairie soils. Desert soils are coarse, light-colored, and contain a lot of minerals. Of the three soil types shown here, desert soils have the least-developed A horizon.

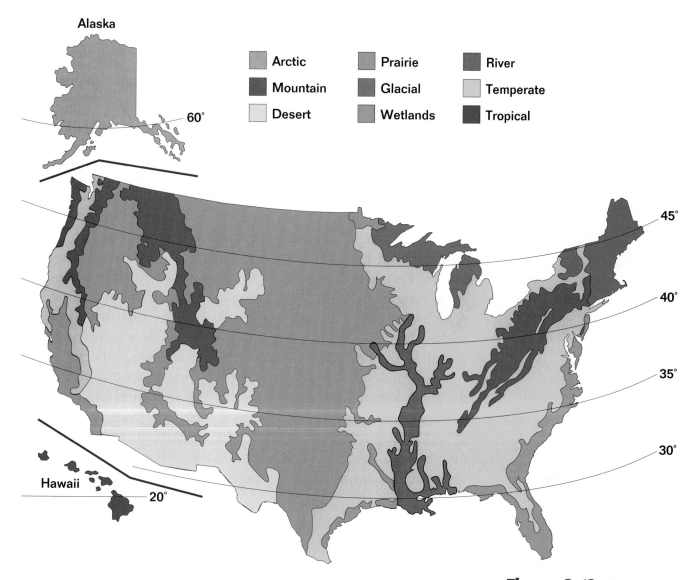

Alaska

Arctic	Prairie	River
Mountain	Glacial	Temperate
Desert	Wetlands	Tropical

60°

45°

40°

35°

30°

Hawaii 20°

Figure 8-13 The United States has nine different soil types. They vary in color, depth of horizons, soil moisture, texture, and fertility.

trees. Plants, grasses, and trees all grow in soil. Without soil, we cannot grow food, raise livestock, or produce paper or other products we need.

When vegetation is removed from soil, the soil is exposed to the direct action of rain and wind. Rain and wind can erode the topsoil and carry it away, destroying the soil's structure. Also, without plants, soil development slows and sometimes stops because humus is no longer being produced.

Plowing and Soil Loss

Every year, the population of Earth increases by nearly 95 million people. More people means a need for more food. Farmers plow more fields to raise more food for the increasing population. This increases the use of our soil resources.

It is difficult to manage soils effectively. Plowing soil mechanically turns and loosens the soil, improving it for crops. However, plowing soil removes the plant cover that

Figure 8-14 With some farming practices, soil loss can occur.

Figure 8-15 Soil in tropical rain forests weathers quickly when trees are cut down. **What type of weathering is occurring here?**

holds soil particles in place, leaving soils open to wind and water erosion. Wind is harmful when the soil is dry. Sometimes, as shown in **Figure 8-14,** the wind blows soil from a newly plowed field. Soil erosion in many places occurs at a much faster rate than the natural processes of weathering can replace it.

Soil Erosion in the Tropics

Soil loss is severe in the tropics. Tropical rains running down steep slopes quickly erode soil. Each year, thousands of square kilometers of tropical rain forest are cleared for farming and grazing. Soils in tropical rain forests appear rich in nutrients but are almost infertile below the first few centimeters. **Figure 8-15** shows what happens when the rain forest is removed. The soil is useful to farmers for only a few years before the nutrients are gone. The soil then becomes useless for farming or for grazing. Farmers clear new land, repeating the process and increasing the damage to the soil.

Near the deserts of the world, sheep and cattle eat much of the grass. When natural vegetation is removed from land that receives little rain, plants don't grow back. This leads to a loss of soil through wind erosion. Groundwater evaporates. The dry, unprotected surface can be blown away. The desert spreads. Desert formation happens on every continent.

B Harsh results of deforestation can be seen in the Tobago Rain Forest in the Caribbean.

A In the Cuyabeno Wildlife Reserve in Equador, portions of the rain forest have been cut down for use in settlements.

Farmers Work to Minimize Soil Loss

All over the world, farmers take steps to slow down soil erosion. They plant shelter belts of trees to break the force of the wind. They cover bare soils with decaying plants to hold soil particles in place. In dry areas, instead of plowing under the natural vegetation to plant crops, farmers graze animals on the vegetation. Proper grazing management can keep plants in place and reduce soil erosion.

Steep slopes, prone to erosion, can be taken out of cultivation or terraced. In the tropics, planting trees to block the force of rain falling on open ground reduces erosion. On gentle slopes, plowing along the natural contours of the land or planting crops in strips helps reduce water erosion. In strip cropping, a crop that covers the ground is alternated with a crop such as corn that leaves a considerable amount of land exposed. In recent years, many farmers have begun to practice no-till farming. Normally, farmers till or plow their fields three or more times a year. In no-till farming, seen in **Figure 8-16,** plant stalks are left in the field. At the next planting, farmers seed crops without destroying these stalks and without plowing the soil. No-till farming provides cover for the soil all year-round and reduces erosion.

Figure 8-16 In no-till farming, the soil is not plowed before planting. **How does this conserve soil?**

Section Assessment

1. How do organisms help soils develop?
2. Why do soil profiles contain layers or horizons?
3. Why does horizon B contain minerals from horizon A?
4. **Think Critically:** Why is the soil profile in a rain forest different from one in a desert?
5. **Skill Builder**
   Concept Mapping Make an events chain map that explains how soil develops. Use the following terms and phrases: *soil is formed, humus develops, rock is weathered, plants grow, worms and insects move in,* and *humus mixes with weathered rock.* If you need help, refer to Concept Mapping in the **Skill Handbook** on page 698.

Using Math

Soil texture depends on the percentages of three different types of particles: clay, silt, and sand. The best texture for growing most crops is a mixture of at least two of these. If a 400-g sand sample has 150 g of clay, 200 g of silt, and 50 g of sand, what is the percentage of each type of particle?

Materials

- Soil sample
- Cheesecloth squares
- Sand
- Graduated cylinder (100 mL)
- Gravel
- Plastic coffee-can lids (3)
- Clay
- Rubber bands (3)
- Water
- Beakers (250 mL) (3)
- Watch
- Large polystyrene or plastic cups (3)
- Pie pans
- Hand lens
- Scissors
- Thumbtack

Soil Characteristics

There are thousands of soils around the world. In your area, you've probably noticed that there are a number of different soils. Collect samples of soil to compare from around your neighborhood and from designated areas of your school grounds.

What You'll Investigate

What are the characteristics of soils?

Goals

- Analyze permeability of different soils.

Procedure

1. **Spread** your soil sample in a pie pan.

2. **Describe** the color of the soil and **examine** the soil with a hand lens. Describe the different particles.

3. **Rub** a small amount of soil between your fingers. **Describe** how it feels. Also, press the soil sample together. Does it stick together? Wet the sample and try this again. Record all your observations.

4. **Test** the soil for how water moves through it. **Label** the three cups A, B, and C. Using a thumbtack, punch ten holes in and around the bottom of each cup.

5. **Cover** the area of holes with a square of cheesecloth and **secure** with a rubber band.

6. To hold the cups over the beakers, **cut** the three coffee-can lids so that the cups will just fit inside the hole (see photo). **Place** a cup and lid over each beaker.

7. Fill cup A halfway with dry sand and cup B with clay. Fill cup C halfway with a mixture of equal parts of sand, gravel, and clay.

8. Use the graduated cylinder to pour 100 mL of water into each cup. **Record** the time when the water is first poured into each cup and when the water first drips from each cup.

9. Allow the water to drip for 25 minutes, then **measure and record** the amount of water in each beaker.

Conclude and Apply

1. How does the addition of gravel and sand affect the permeability of clay?

2. **Describe** three characteristics of soil. Which characteristics affect permeability?

3. Use your observations to **explain** which soil sample would be best for growing plants.

Compost

A composter allows you to recycle food wastes, grass clippings, and other organic materials and turn them into something useful. By composting, people can reduce the amount of garbage to be picked up, save precious landfill space, and make a soil conditioner at the same time.

THE COMPOST PROCESS

1

Composting begins when plant materials such as grass clippings, organic garbage, and weeds are piled up, usually layered with soil or manure, and allowed to decay. At left, a compost heap has been prepared.

2

55°C 131°F

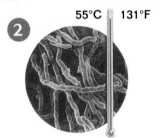

The activity of bacteria heats the interior of the compost heap. Fungi and actinomycetes (in circle), a form of bacteria, break down tough debris, enabling bacteria to decompose it more quickly.

3

Invertebrates (animals without backbones) such as insect larvae and worms eat decaying vegetation. Their droppings are added to the mix. As these organisms tunnel, they create more surface area for fungi and bacteria to work on.

4

The completed compost is a rich, crumbly, dark, soil-like substance used to fertilize soil and improve its structure. Compost also can be used as mulch on the soil surface to help retain soil moisture and prevent the growth of weeds.

Career CONNECTION

Horticulturists are people who work with plants and soil. Most horticulturists have a bachelor's degree, but this degree is not required for all horticulture-related jobs. Write a letter to your local nursery asking about the education and experience required to work there.

Think Critically

1. How does compost help plants?
2. Why does food waste decompose better in a compost pile than in a landfill?

For a **preview** of this chapter, study this Reviewing Main Ideas before you read the chapter. After you have studied this chapter, you can use the Reviewing Main Ideas to **review** the chapter.

GLENCOE TECHNOLOGY

The Glencoe MindJogger, Audiocassettes, and CD-ROM provide additional opportunities for review.

Section 8-1 MECHANICAL WEATHERING

Mechanical weathering breaks apart rocks without changing their chemical composition. Water, by expanding and contracting through freeze-and-thaw cycles, is a major agent of mechanical weathering. Plant and tree roots also weather rocks. Mechanical weathering is not limited to rocks. Roads and sidewalks also are affected by freeze-and-thaw cycles or growing roots. *Compare and contrast the different agents of mechanical weathering.*

CHEMICAL WEATHERING

Chemical weathering changes the mineral composition of rocks. Water that is acidic may dissolve rock or simply dissolve certain minerals within a rock. Exposure to oxygen causes some rocks to turn red, or rust. Some plants even cause chemical weathering by secreting acids. *Describe how water can become an agent of chemical weathering.*

A

B

C

Reading Check ☑

After reviewing the illustrations on soil development, describe the steps in your own words. Be sure to number the steps.

Section 8-2 SOIL

Soil develops when rock is weathered and organic matter is added. Soil has **horizons** that differ in their color and composition. Climate, parent rock, slope, amount of **humus,** and time affect the development of soil and give soil its characteristics. *Explain why some soils take more time to develop than others.*

Career CONNECTION

Susan Colclazer, Naturalist A naturalist is a person who studies the life sciences in the field more than in a laboratory. Many types of scientists are interested in Bryce Canyon. Naturalists, geologists, archaeologists, sociologists, and botanists have made studies there, as well. Make a list of things these types of scientists might study in the canyon, and tell how their findings would add to the overall picture of the canyon's history.

Chapter 8 Assessment

Using Vocabulary

a. chemical weathering
b. climate
c. horizon
d. humus
e. ice wedging
f. leaching
g. litter
h. mechanical weathering
i. oxidation
j. soil
k. soil profile
l. weathering

The sentences below include italicized terms that have been used incorrectly. Change the incorrect terms so that the sentence reads correctly. Underline your change.

1. When rocks break down without changing in chemical composition, *oxidation* occurs.

2. *Mechanical weathering* results in a change in a rock's composition.

3. *Desert* formation occurs when weathered rock and organic matter are mixed together.

4. *Litter* is composed of decayed organic matter.

5. The A, B, and C layers of a soil make up the soil *horizon*.

Checking Concepts

Choose the word or phrase that best answers the question.

6. What is caused when plants produce acids?
   A) desert formation
   B) overgrazing
   C) mechanical weathering
   D) chemical weathering

7. What happens to water that allows freezing and thawing to weather rocks?
   A) contracts   C) expands
   B) gets more dense D) percolates

8. What occurs when roots force rocks apart?
   A) mechanical weathering
   B) leaching
   C) ice wedging
   D) chemical weathering

9. What reacts with iron to form rust?
   A) oxygen   C) feldspar
   B) carbon dioxide   D) paint

10. What can result when poor farming practices occur in areas that receive little rain?
    A) ice wedging   C) leaching
    B) oxidation   D) desert formation

11. In what region is chemical weathering most rapid?
    A) cold, dry   C) warm, moist
    B) cold, moist   D) warm, dry

12. What is a mixture of weathered rock and organic matter called?
    A) soil   C) carbon dioxide
    B) limestone   D) clay

13. What is another term for decayed organic matter?
    A) leaching   C) soil
    B) humus   D) sediment

14. In what horizon is humus found almost exclusively?
    A) A horizon   C) C horizon
    B) B horizon   D) D horizon

15. What does no-till farming help prevent?
    A) leaching   C) overgrazing
    B) crop rotation   D) soil erosion

Thinking Critically

16. Which type of weathering, mechanical or chemical, would you expect to have more effect in a desert region? Explain.

17. Plants cause mechanical weathering. Explain how animals also can be considered agents of mechanical weathering.

18. Why is soil so important?

19. Why is it difficult to replace lost topsoil?

20. Explain how chemical weathering can form a cavern.

Developing Skills

If you need help, refer to the Skill Handbook.

21. Sequencing: Do a sequence chart of soil development.

22. Concept Mapping: Complete the events chain concept map that shows two ways in which acids can cause chemical weathering.

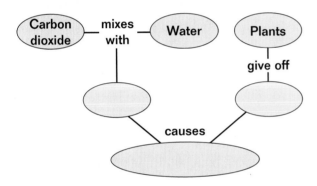

23. Using Variables, Constants, and Controls: Juan Carlos wanted to know if planting grass on a slope would prevent soil from being washed away. To find out, he put the same amount and kind of soil in two identical pans. In one of the pans, he planted grass. To create equal slopes for his test, he placed identical wooden wedges under one end of each pan. He was careful to pour the same amount of water at the same rate over the soil in the two pans. What is Juan's control? What factors in his activity are constants? What is the variable he is testing?

24. Classifying: Classify the following events as either chemical or mechanical weathering. Rocks that contain iron rust. Freezing and thawing of water cause cracks to form in the street. Acids from mosses leave small pits in rocks. Roots of trees break rocks apart. Water seeping through cracks in limestone dissolves away some of the rock.

THE PRINCETON REVIEW

Test-Taking Tip

Wear a Watch If you are taking a timed test, you should pace yourself. Do not spend too much time on any one question, but don't spend time staring at the clock. When the test begins, place your watch on the desk and check it after each section of the test.

Test Practice

Use these questions to test your Science Proficiency.

1. The curb along a street is crumbling and a big weed is growing from one of the cracks. Which of the following is an inference and not an observation?
   A) Tiny pieces of concrete are found along the base of the curb.
   B) Plant roots are located among the cracks in the curb.
   C) Mechanical and chemical weathering are causing the curb to crumble.
   D) The curb has cracks of varying lengths and widths.

2. Soils have several horizons. Which of the following **BEST** describes the B horizon?
   A) It is made of humus, small rocks, and mineral particles.
   B) It is mostly partly weathered bedrock.
   C) It is full of organisms like insects and worms.
   D) It is light in color and contains soil materials leached from the A horizon.

CHAPTER

9

Erosional Forces

Chapter Preview

Section 9-1
Gravity
Section 9-2
Glaciers
Section 9-3
Wind

Skills Preview

Skill Builders
- Compare and Contrast
- Sequence

Activities
- Design an Experiment
- Analyze Data

MiniLabs
- Observe
- Infer

Reading Check ✔

As you read this chapter, list words that have different meanings when used elsewhere, such as *slump, creep, till,* and *deposition.* Explain the other meanings of these terms.

Explore Activity

The forces of nature are strong enough to wear the jagged peaks of young mountains into the rolling, smooth tops of older mountain ranges. Weathering breaks down rocks into smaller particles. Then forces of nature move these particles and deposit them elsewhere. One of these forces, water, has eroded the canyon to the left in Grand Canyon National Park. Erosional forces constantly change the surface of Earth, making changes in our landscape.

Observe Movement of Sediments

1. Place a small pile of a sand and gravel mixture in one end of a large shoe box lid.

2. Move the pile to the other end of the lid without touching the particles with your hands.

3. Try to move the mixture in a number of different ways.

Science Journal

In your Science Journal, describe the methods you used. Explain how your methods compare with forces of nature that move sediment.

Erosion and Deposition

What You'll Learn

► The differences between erosion and deposition
► The similarities and differences of slumps, creep, rockslides, and mudflows
► Why building on steep slopes is a questionable practice

Vocabulary
erosion
deposition
mass movement
slump
creep

Why It's Important

► Landforms change because of erosion, deposition, and mass movements.

Have you ever been by a river just after a heavy rain? The water may look as muddy as the water in **Figure 9-1**. A river looks muddy when there is a lot of sediment and soil in it. Some of the soil comes from along the riverbank itself. In the upper left part of the photograph, you can see where the bank is being eroded at the curve in the river. The rest of the sediment in the photograph is carried to the river from more distant sources.

Muddy water is a product of erosion. **Erosion** is a process that wears away surface materials and moves them from one place to another. The major causes of erosion are gravity, glaciers, wind, and water. The first three will be discussed in this chapter. Another kind of erosion is shown in **Figure 9-2**.

Figure 9-1 The muddy look of some rivers comes from the load of sediment carried by water.

As you investigate the agents of erosion, you will notice that they have several things in common. Gravity, glaciers, wind, and water all wear away materials and carry them off. But, these agents erode materials only when they have enough energy of motion to do work. For example, air can't erode sediments when the air is still. But, once air begins moving and develops into wind, it carries dust, soil, and even rock along with it.

All agents of erosion deposit the sediments they are carrying when their erosion energy decreases. This dropping of sediments is called **deposition.** Deposition is the final stage of an erosional process. Sediments and rocks are deposited. The surface of Earth is changed. But, next year or a million years from now, those sediments may be eroded again.

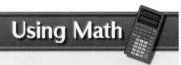

Using Math

Two rocks fall off a cliff at the same time. One rock weighs 10 N, and the other rock weighs 30 N. They both reach the ground at the same time. Explain why this happened.

Erosion and Deposition by Gravity

Gravity is the force of attraction that exists between all objects. Because Earth has great mass, other objects are attracted to Earth. This makes gravity a force of erosion and deposition. Gravity causes loose materials to move down a slope.

Figure 9-2
This hill has been eroded. **What was the agent of erosion?**

Figure 9-3 Slumps occur when material slips downslope as one large mass. **What might have caused this slump to happen?**

When gravity alone causes materials to move downslope, this type of erosion is called **mass movement.** Some mass movements are slow. You hardly notice that they're happening. Others, however, happen quickly.

Slump

A **slump** is a mass movement that happens when loose materials or rock layers slip down a slope. In a slump, strong rock or sediment lies over weaker materials. The underlying material weakens even more and can no longer support the rock and sediment above. The soil and rock slip downslope in one large mass.

Sometimes, a slump happens when water enters the upper layer on a slope but cannot flow through the lower layers. Water and mud build up. The upper layer of sediments slips along the mud and slides downslope. As shown in **Figure 9-3,** a curved scar is left where the slumped materials originally rested. Slumps happen most often after earthquakes or heavy, continuing rains.

Figure 9-4 Perhaps you can find evidence of soil creep around your home or school. Look for tilted retaining walls and fences and even sod that has stretched apart.

A Several years of creeping downslope can cause objects such as trees and fence posts to lean.

B Below the surface, as the ground freezes, expanding ice in the soil pushes up fine-grained sediment particles. Then, when the soil thaws, the sediment falls downslope, often less than 1 mm at a time.

Creep

On your next drive, look along the roadway for slopes where trees, utility poles, and fence posts lean downhill. Leaning poles show another mass movement called creep. **Creep** gets its name from the way sediments slowly inch their way down a hill. As **Figure 9-4** illustrates, creep is common in areas of freezing and thawing.

Rockslides

"Falling Rock" signs warn of another type of mass movement called a rockslide. Rockslides happen when large blocks of rock break loose from a steep slope and start tumbling. As they fall, these rocks crash into other rocks and knock them loose. More and more rocks break loose and tumble to the bottom.

Rockslides are fast and can be destructive in populated mountain areas. They commonly occur in mountainous areas or where there are steep cliffs, as shown in **Figure 9-5**. Rockslides happen most often after heavy rains or during earthquakes, but they can happen on any rocky slope at any time without warning.

The fall of a single, large rock down a steep slope can cause serious damage to structures at the bottom. During the winter, when ice freezes and thaws in the cracks of the rocks, pieces

Figure 9-5 Piles of broken rock at the bottom of a cliff, such as these rockfalls in southwestern Montana, tell you that rockslides have occurred and are likely to happen again.

Figure 9-6 In the Alps, a rock fell from the cliff above and struck this apartment building. **Why did this happen?**

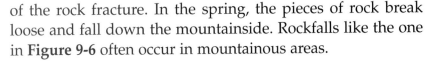

interNET CONNECTION

Visit the Glencoe Science Web Site at **www. glencoe.com/sec/ science** for more information about mudslides throughout history.

of the rock fracture. In the spring, the pieces of rock break loose and fall down the mountainside. Rockfalls like the one in **Figure 9-6** often occur in mountainous areas.

Mudflows

Imagine traveling along a mountain road during a rainstorm. Suddenly a wall of mud, the thickness of chocolate pudding, slides down a slope and threatens to cover your car. You've been caught in a mudflow, a thick mixture of sediments and water flowing down a slope. The mudflow in **Figure 9-7** caused a lot of destruction.

Mudflows usually occur in normally dry areas where there are thick layers of dry sediments. When heavy rains fall in these areas, water mixes with sediments and becomes thick and pasty. Gravity causes this mass to slide downhill. When a mudflow finally reaches the bottom of a slope, it loses its energy of motion and deposits all the sediments and other things it has been carrying. These deposits usually form a mass that spreads out in a fan shape. Why might mudflows cause more damage than flood-waters?

Mudflows, rockslides, creep, and slump are similar in some ways. They are most likely to occur on steep slopes. They all depend on gravity to make them happen. And, no matter what type of mass movement, they occur more often after a heavy rain. The water adds mass and makes the area slippery where different layers of sediment meet.

Erosion-Prone Land

Some people like to live in houses and apartments on the sides of hills and mountains. But, when you consider gravity as an agent of erosion, do you think steep slopes are safe places to live?

Building on Steep Slopes

When people build homes on steep slopes, they must constantly battle naturally occurring erosion. Sometimes, when they build, people make a slope steeper or remove vegetation. This speeds up the erosion process and creates additional problems. Some steep slopes are prone to slumps because of weak sediment layers underneath.

Making Steep Slopes Safe

People can have a beautiful view and reduce erosion on steep slopes. One of the best ways is to plant vegetation. Plant roots may not seem strong, but they do hold soil in place. Plants also absorb large amounts of water. A person living on a steep slope might also build terraces or walls to reduce erosion.

Figure 9-7 A mudflow, such as this one in Seattle, Washington, has enough energy to move almost anything in its path. **How do mudflows differ from slumps, creep, and rockslides?**

Observing Mass Movements
Procedure

1. Put a mixture of dry sand and gravel in a pan. Use these sediments to model how mass movements of sediments occur.

2. After you have modeled slumps and rockslides with dry sediment, add small amounts of water to different parts of your landforms to model mudflows, slumps, and rockslides.

Analysis

1. What factors must be present for mass movements to occur?

2. In what ways are the three mass movements similar? Different?

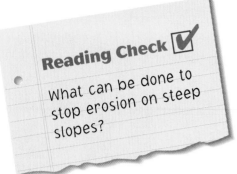

Reading Check ✓

What can be done to stop erosion on steep slopes?

*inter*NET
CONNECTION

Visit the Glencoe Science Web Site at **www. glencoe.com/sec/ science** for more information about agriculture in developing countries.

Terraces are broad, steplike cuts made into the side of a slope, as shown in **Figure 9-8.** When water flows into a terrace, it slows down and loses its energy. Terracing slows soil erosion. Walls made of concrete or railroad ties can also reduce erosion by keeping soil and rocks from sliding downhill. However, preventing mass movements on a slope is difficult because rain or earthquakes can cause the upper layers of rock to slip over the lower layers. Not even planting bushes and trees could save the houses in **Figure 9-9.** ✓

People who live in areas with erosion problems spend a lot of time and money trying to preserve their land. Sometimes, they're successful in slowing down erosion, but they can never eliminate it and the danger of mass movement. Eventually, gravity wins. Sediments move from place to place, constantly making slopes less steep and changing the shape of the land.

Figure 9-8 These terraces in Java help conserve soil so vegetables can grow. **How do terraces keep soil from eroding away?**

Figure 9-9 Heavy rains caused by El Niño resulted in this landslide in California. **What type of mass movement occurred here?**

Section Assessment

1. Define *erosion* and name the agents that cause it.

2. How does erosion change the surface of Earth?

3. What characteristics do all types of mass movements have in common?

4. If creep has occurred in an area, what evidence would you see?

5. **Think Critically:** When people build houses and roads, they often pile up dirt or cut into the sides of hills. Predict how these activities affect sediments on a slope.

6. **Skill Builder**

   Concept Mapping Learn more about erosional forces by doing the **Chapter 9 Skill Activity** on page 734.

Using Computers

Spreadsheets Pretend that you live along a beach where the water is 500 m from your front door. Each year, slumping causes about 1.5 m of your beach to cave into the water. Design a spreadsheet that will predict how much property will be left each year for ten years. Use the labels "Years" and "Meters Left." Type a formula that will compute the amount of land left the second year. If you need help, refer to page 722.

9•2 Glaciers

Continental and Valley Glaciers

Does it snow where you live? In some areas of the world, it is so cold that snow remains on the ground year-round. When snow doesn't melt, it begins piling up. As it accumulates, the weight of the snow becomes great enough to compress its bottom layers into ice. Eventually, the snow can pile so high that the pressure on the ice on the bottom causes partial melting. The ice becomes putty-like. The whole mass begins to slide on this putty-like layer, and it moves downhill. This moving mass of ice and snow is a **glacier.**

Glaciers are agents of erosion. As glaciers pass over land, they erode it, changing its features. Glaciers then carry eroded material along and deposit it somewhere else. Glacial erosion and deposition change large areas of Earth. There are two types of glaciers: continental glaciers and valley glaciers.

Continental Glaciers

Continental glaciers are huge masses of ice and snow. In the past, continental glaciers covered up to 28 percent of Earth. **Figure 9-10** shows how much of North America was covered

What You'll Learn

▶ How glaciers move
▶ Glacial erosion
▶ Similarities and differences between till and outwash

Vocabulary
glacier
plucking
till
moraine

Why It's Important

▶ Erosion and deposition by glaciers are responsible for creating many landforms on Earth.

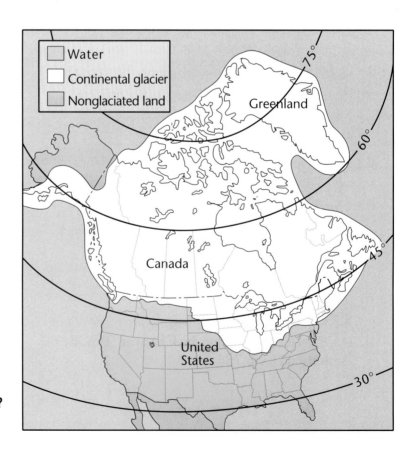

Figure 9-10 This map shows how far the continental glaciers spread in North America about 20 000 years ago. **Was your location covered? If so, what evidence of glaciers does your area show?**

A Today, a continental glacier covers Antarctica.

B Glaciers, like this one in Tibet, form between mountain peaks that lie above the snowline, where snow lasts all year.

during the last ice age. Scientists call the periods when glaciers covered much of Earth *ice ages.* The most recent ice age began over a period of 2 to 3 million years ago. During the time when much of North America was covered by ice, the average air temperature on Earth was about 5°C lower than it is today. Then, about 20 000 years ago, the ice sheets began to melt. Today, glaciers like the one in **Figure 9-11A** cover only ten percent of Earth, mostly near the poles in Antarctica and Greenland. Continental glaciers are so thick that they can almost bury mountain ranges on the land they cover. Glaciers make it impossible to see most of the land features in Antarctica.

Valley Glaciers

Valley glaciers occur even in today's warmer global climate. In the high mountains where the average temperature is low enough to prevent snow from melting during the summer, valley glaciers grow and creep along. **Figure 9-11B** shows a valley glacier in Tibet.

How is it possible that something as fragile as snow or ice can become an agent of erosion that pushes aside trees, drags along rocks, and erodes the surface of Earth?

Glacial Erosion

As they move over land, glaciers are like bulldozers, pushing loose materials they encounter. Eroded sediments pile up along its sides, as seen in **Figure 9-12A,** are pushed in front of a glacier, or are carried underneath it. Glaciers also weather and erode rock and soil that isn't loose. When glacial ice melts, water flows into cracks in rocks. Later, the water refreezes in these cracks, expands, and fractures the rock into pieces. These rock pieces are then lifted out by the glacial ice sheet. This process, called **plucking,** results in boulders, gravel, and sand being added to the bottom and sides of a glacier.

As a glacier moves forward, plucked rock fragments and sand at its base scrape the soil and bedrock, eroding even more material than ice alone could. When bedrock is gouged deeply by dragged rock fragments, marks such as those in **Figure 9-12B** are left behind. These marks, called grooves, are

Figure 9-12 The diagram and photos show landforms characteristic of glacial erosion.

Arête

Valley glaciers

Moraine

A No agent of erosion is more powerful than an advancing glacier.

B When glaciers melt, striations or grooves may be found on the rocks beneath. These glacial grooves on Kelley's Island, Ohio, are 10 m wide and 5 m deep.

deep, long, parallel scars on rocks. Less-deep marks are called striations (stri AY shuns). These marks indicate the direction the glacier moved.

Evidence of Valley Glaciers

If you visit the mountains, you can see if valley glaciers ever existed there. You might look for striations, then search for evidence of plucking. Glacial plucking often occurs near the top of a mountain where a glacier is in contact with a wall of rock. Valley glaciers erode bowl-shaped basins, called cirques (SURKS), in the sides of the mountains. A cirque is shown in **Figure 9-12C.** If two or more glaciers erode a mountain summit from several directions, a ridge, called an arête (ah RET), or sharpened peak, called a horn, forms. The photo in **Figure 9-12D** shows a mountain horn.

Mountain horn

U-shaped valley

Cirque

C This cirque, a bowl-shaped basin, was formed by erosion at the start of a valley glacier.

D A horn is a sharpened peak formed by glacial action in three or more cirques.

Valley glaciers flow down mountain slopes and along valleys, eroding as they go. Valleys that have been eroded by glaciers have a different shape from those eroded by streams. Stream-eroded valleys are normally V-shaped. Glacially eroded valleys are U-shaped because a glacier plucks and scrapes soil and rock from the sides as well as from the bottom. A U-shaped valley is illustrated in **Figure 9-12.**

Glacial Deposition

When glaciers begin to melt, they no longer have enough energy to carry much sediment. The sediment drops, or is deposited, on the land.

Figure 9-13 Till has been deposited by the Tasman Glacier in New Zealand.

Till

When the glacier slows down, a jumble of boulders, sand, clay, and silt drops from its base. This mixture of different-sized sediments is called **till. Figure 9-13** shows the unlayered appearance of till. Till deposits can cover huge areas of land. During the last ice age, continental glaciers in the northern United States dropped enough till to completely fill valleys and make these areas appear flat. Till areas include the wide swath of wheat land running northwestward from Iowa to northern Montana; some farmland in parts of Ohio, Indiana, and Illinois; and the rocky pastures of New England.

Till is also deposited in front of a glacier when it stops moving forward. Unlike the till that drops from a glacier's base, this second type of deposit doesn't cover a wide area. Because it's made of the rocks and soil that the glacier has been pushing along, it looks like a big ridge of material left behind by a bulldozer. Such a ridge is called a **moraine. Figure 9-14** shows moraines that were deposited at the end and along the sides of the glacier. A moraine that was deposited at the end of a glacier is shown in **Figure 9-15** and is called a terminal moraine.

Reading Check

What is till?

Outwash

When more snow melts than is accumulated, the glacier starts to melt and retreat. Material deposited by the meltwater from a glacier is called outwash. Outwash is shown in **Figure 9-15**. The meltwater carries sediments and deposits them in layers much as a river does. Heavier sediments drop first so the bigger pieces of rock are deposited closer to the glacier. The outwash from a glacier can also form into a fan-shaped deposit when the stream of meltwater drops sand and gravel in front of the glacier.

Another type of outwash deposit looks like a long, winding ridge. This deposit forms beneath a melting glacier when meltwater forms a river within the ice. This river carries sand and gravel and deposits them within its channel. When the glacier melts, a winding ridge of sand and gravel, called an esker (ES kur), is left behind. An esker is shown in **Figure 9-15**. Meltwater also forms outwash plains of deposited materials in front of a retreating glacier.

Figure 9-14 The Athabaska Glacier in Jasper National Park in Alberta, Canada, is surrounded by many glacial features. **Which ones do you see?**

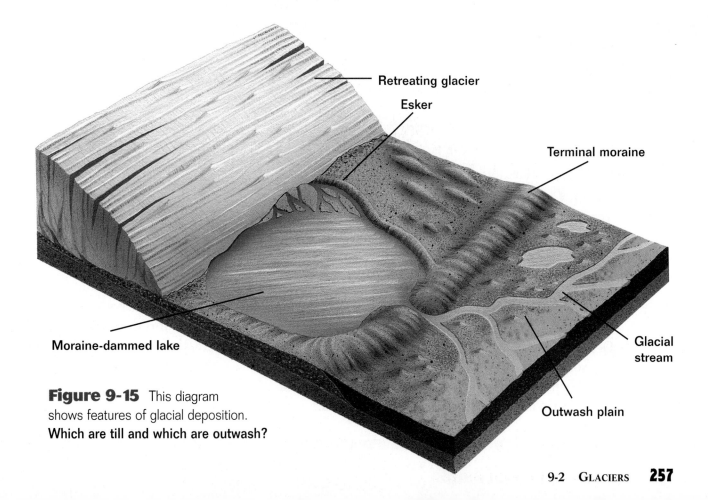

Retreating glacier

Esker

Terminal moraine

Moraine-dammed lake

Glacial stream

Outwash plain

Figure 9-15 This diagram shows features of glacial deposition. **Which are till and which are outwash?**

B This V-shaped valley, cut by the Yellowstone River in what is now Yellowstone National Park, looks different from the U-shaped valley.

Figure 9-16

A This U-shaped valley in Gates of the Arctic National Park in Alaska was carved by a glacier.

Glaciers from the last ice age changed the surface of Earth. Glaciers eroded mountaintops and dug out valleys like the U-shaped one in **Figure 9-16A.** Water erosion forms V-shaped valleys like the one in **Figure 9-16B.** Glaciers also deposited sediments over vast areas of North America and Europe. Today, glaciers in the polar regions and in mountains continue to change the surface features of Earth.

Section Assessment

1. How does a glacier cause erosion?
2. Explain how till and outwash are different.
3. How do moraines form?
4. **Think Critically:** Rivers and lakes that receive water from glacial meltwater often appear milky blue in color. Explain why this occurs.

5. **Skill Builder**
   Recognizing Cause and Effect Since 1900, the Alps have lost 50 percent of their ice caps, and New Zealand's glaciers have shrunk by 26 percent. Describe what you think is causing glaciers to melt around the world. Describe what you think the effects of melting have been. If you need help, refer to Recognizing Cause and Effect in the **Skill Handbook** on page 705.

Science Journal

An erratic is a rock fragment deposited by a glacier. Erratic comes from the Latin word *errare* meaning "to wander." Research how glaciers erode and deposit erratics. In your Science Journal, write a poem about the "life" of an erratic.

Glacial Grooving

Throughout the world's mountainous regions, there are 200 000 valley glaciers moving in response to local freezing and thawing conditions, as well as gravity.

What You'll Investigate

What happens when a valley glacier moves? How is the land affected?

Goals

- **Observe** glacial deposits.
- **Compare** stream and glacial valleys.

Procedure

1. Set up the large tray as shown. Place the books under one end of the tray to give it a slope.

2. Cut a narrow channel, like a river, through the sand. **Measure** and **record** its width and depth. **Draw** a sketch that includes these measurements.

3. Position the overhead light source to shine on the channel as shown.

4. Force the ice block into the river channel at the upper end of the stream table.

Materials

- Sand
- Large plastic or metal tray
  *stream table
- Ice block containing sand, clay, and gravel
- Books (2–3)
  *wood block
- Metric ruler
- Overhead light source with reflector

  *Alternate Materials

5. Gently push the "glacier" along the river channel until it's halfway between the top and bottom of the stream table and is positioned directly under the light.

6. Turn on the light and allow the ice to melt. **Record** what happens. Does the meltwater change the original channel?

7. **Record** the width and depth of the glacial channel. **Draw** a sketch of the channel and include these measurements.

Conclude and Apply

1. **Explain** how you can determine the direction a glacier traveled from the location of deposits.

2. **Explain** how you can determine the direction of glacial movement from sediments deposited by meltwater.

3. How do valley glaciers affect the surface over which they move?

Glacier Data			
Sample Data	Width	Depth	Observations
Original channel	6 cm	3 cm	stream channel looked V-shaped
Glacier channel			
Meltwater channel			

Music of the Dust Bowl

Blowing in the Wind

In the 1930s, a severe drought struck Texas, Oklahoma, Colorado, Kansas, and New Mexico. Years of overgrazing and overfarming had stripped vast expanses of the land of protective grass. With nothing to hold the parched soil, it blew away, forming towering clouds of dust (right) that traveled hundreds of miles. This dry region of the United States became known as the Dust Bowl.

Songs for the People

Woody Guthrie (inset) wrote and sang folk songs about the hardships faced by the people of the Dust Bowl. His song "The Great Dust Storm" describes a region where, according to Guthrie, "the dust flows and the farmer owes."

The storm took place at sundown
It lasted through the night.
When we looked out next morning
We saw a terrible sight.
We saw outside our window
Where wheat fields they had grown,
Was now a rippling ocean
Of dust the wind had blown.
It covered up our fences,
It covered up our barns,
It covered up our tractors
In this wild and dusty storm. ©

Guthrie's songs also tell of courage and humor. His lyrics in "Dust Pneumonia Blues" describe a girl so unused to water that she faints in the rain. Her boyfriend throws a bucket of dirt on her to revive her.

Science
JOURNAL

Research details of Woody Guthrie's life. In your Science Journal, compare his life with the lyrics of his songs. How did his experiences influence his lyrics? Write a song or poem that reflects an event that you or someone you know has experienced.

Wind

Wind Erosion

When air moves, it can pick up loose material and transport it to other places. Air differs from other erosional forces because it usually cannot pick up heavy sediments. But, unlike rivers and glaciers that move in channels and through valleys, wind can carry and deposit sediments over large areas. Sometimes wind carries dust from fields or volcanoes high into the atmosphere and deposits it far away.

Deflation and Abrasion

Wind erodes Earth's surface by deflation and abrasion. When wind erodes by **deflation,** it blows across loose sediment, removing small particles such as clay, silt, and sand. The heavier, coarser material is left behind. **Figure 9-17** illustrates deflation. When these windblown sediments strike rock, the surface gets scraped and worn away. This type of erosion is called **abrasion.** Both deflation and abrasion happen to all land surfaces but occur mostly in deserts, beaches, and plowed fields. In these areas, there are fewer plants to hold the sediments. When winds blow over them, there is nothing to hold them down.

What You'll Learn

▶ How wind causes deflation and abrasion
▶ How loess and dunes form

Vocabulary
deflation
abrasion
loess

Why It's Important

▶ Wind erosion and deposition help change the landscape.

Figure 9-17 Deflation produces airborne sediments and leaves behind what is called desert pavement.

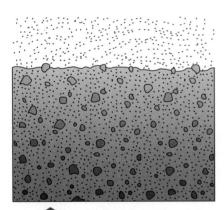

A As deflation begins, wind blows away silt and sand.

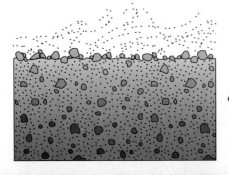

B Deflation continues to remove finer particles. Deflation lowers the surface.

C After finer particles are blown away, the larger pebbles and rocks left behind form a pavement that prevents further deflation.

Figure 9-18 Wind erosion can be just like sandblasting.

A When modern archaeologists discovered the Sphinx, it was buried up to its neck in sand. The head shows how abrasive Egypt's desert winds can be.

B This worker is using abrasion to clean and smooth a limestone waterfall.

Abrasion works similar to sandblasting that a crew of restoration workers might do. These workers use machines that spray a mixture of sand and water against a building. The blast of sand wears away dirt from stone, concrete, or brick walls. It also polishes the building walls by breaking away small pieces and leaving an even, smooth finish.

Wind acts like a sandblasting machine rolling and blowing sand grains along. These sand grains strike rocks and break off small fragments. The rocks become pitted or worn down. **Figure 9-18** shows how machine and wind abrasion are similar.

Reading Check ✔

How is wind erosion similar to sandblasting?

Sandstorms

Even when the wind blows strongly, it seldom bounces sand grains higher than one-half meter from the ground. Sand grains are too heavy for wind to lift high in the air. However, sandstorms do occur. When the wind blows forcefully in the sandy parts of deserts, sand grains bounce along and hit other sand grains, causing more and more grains to rise into the air. These wind-blown sand grains form a low cloud, just above the ground. Most sandstorms occur in deserts and sometimes on beaches and in dry riverbeds.

Dust Storms

When soil is moist, it stays packed on the ground. But, when the soil dries out, it can be eroded by wind. Because soil particles weigh less than sand, wind can pick them up and blow them high into the atmosphere. But, because silt and clay particles are small and closely packed, a faster wind is needed to lift these fine particles of soil than is needed to lift grains of sand. Once the wind does lift them, it can hold these particles and carry them long distances. In the 1930s, silt and dust picked up in Kansas fell in New England and in the North Atlantic Ocean. Today, dust blown from the Sahara can be traced as far as the West Indies.

Dust storms play an important part in soil erosion. Where the land is dry, dust storms can cover hundreds of miles. The storms blow topsoil from open fields, overgrazed areas, and places where vegetation has disappeared. A dust storm is shown in **Figure 9-19.**

Figure 9-19 During the 1930s, the southern part of the Great Plains of the United States was known as the Dust Bowl because dust storms swept away the soil. Dust storms still occur around the world in places such as Mongolia, in western India, in northern Africa, and in the United States.

Problem Solving

Deserts

Precipitation, like rainfall and snowfall, and temperature help determine whether or not a region is a desert. Some deserts have such low amounts of precipitation that evaporation from the soil and plants is actually greater than the amount of precipitation. When this happens, plants must get their moisture from underground sources near their deep roots. Deserts also receive a varying amount of precipitation from year to year.

The temperature of deserts can vary a great deal, also. All deserts are not hot. Some deserts in mountain valleys can be quite cold. Because deserts absorb and give up their heat quickly, they can be much warmer during the day than at night.

The graph on the right shows how the amount of precipitation and temperature compare for different kinds of ecological communities (biomes). Study the graph to answer the questions.

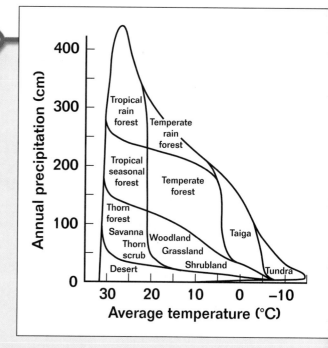

Think Critically: Of all the ecological communities shown in the graph, which shows the greatest range of average temperature? What is the greatest annual precipitation an ecological community can receive and still be classified as a desert? In which ecological community do you live?

Figure 9-20 This marram grass was planted to limit the erosion of sand dunes in Cornwall, England. **How does grass slow erosion?**

Reducing Wind Erosion

As you've learned, wind erosion is most common where plants do not exist to protect the soil. One of the best ways to slow or stop wind erosion is to plant vegetation.

Windbreaks

People in many countries plant vegetation to reduce wind erosion. For centuries, farmers have planted trees along their fields that act as windbreaks and prevent soil erosion. As the wind hits the trees, its energy of motion is reduced and no longer has the energy to lift particles.

In one study, a thin belt of cottonwood trees reduced the effect of a 25 km/h wind to about 66 percent of its normal speed. Tree belts also trap snow and hold it on land, adding to the moisture of the soil, which helps prevent further erosion.

Roots

Along many steep slopes, seacoasts, and deserts, vegetation is planted to help reduce erosion. Plants with fibrous root systems, such as grasses, are the best to stop wind erosion. Grass roots are shallow and slender. They also have many fibers. They twist and turn between particles in the soil and hold the soil in place.

Try at Home

Observing How Soil Is Held in Place

Procedure

1. Obtain a piece of sod (a chunk of soil about 5 cm thick with grass growing from it).
2. Carefully remove the soil from the sod roots by hand. Examine the roots with a magnifying glass or hand lens.

Analysis

1. Draw several of these roots in your Science Journal.
2. What characteristics of grass roots help hold soil in place and thus help reduce erosion?

Planting vegetation is a good way to reduce the effects of deflation and abrasion. But, if the wind is strong and the soil is dry, nothing can stop it completely. **Figure 9-20** shows a project to stop wind erosion.

Deposition by Wind

Sediments blown away by wind are eventually deposited. These windblown deposits develop into several types of landforms.

Loess

Some large deposits of wind-blown sediments are found near the Mississippi River. These wind deposits of fine-grained sediments are known as **loess** (LUSS). Strong winds that blew across glacial outwash areas carried the sediments and deposited them. The sediments settled on hilltops and in valleys. Once there, the particles were packed together, creating a thick, unlayered yellow-brown–colored deposit.

Loess is as fine as talcum powder. Many farmlands of the midwestern United States are on the fertile soils that have developed from loess deposits. The loess pictured in **Figure 9-21** was deposited by winds that blew across the outwash plains of retreating glaciers.

Dunes

What happens when wind blows sediments against an obstacle such as a rock or a clump of vegetation? The sediments settle behind the obstacle. More and more sediments build up, and eventually a dune is formed. A dune is a mound of sand drifted by the wind.

Sand dunes move as wind erodes them and deposits the sand downwind of the dune. On Cape Cod, Massachusetts, and along the Gulf of California, the coast of Oregon, and the eastern shore of Lake Michigan, you can see beach sand dunes. Sand dunes build up where there is sand and prevailing winds or sea breezes that blow daily.

To understand how a dune forms, think of the sand at the back of a beach. That sand is dry because the ocean and lake waves do not reach these areas. The wind blows this dry sand farther inland until something such as a rock or a fence slows the wind. The wind sweeps around or over the rock. Like a river, air drops sediment when its energy decreases.

Figure 9-21 Scott's Bluff, near Scott's Bluff, Nebraska, is composed partially of windblown loess.

LIFE SCIENCE

INTEGRATION

Plant Roots
Red clover has a taproot system consisting of one main root that grows directly downward. Sea oats have a fibrous root system that branches out in all directions. Infer which type of plant would be better to plant along coastal sand dunes to prevent wind erosion. Explain your answer.

Figure 9-22 Dunes are the most common wind deposits. Sand dunes form in deserts and beaches where sand is abundant. They are constantly changing and moving as wind erodes them. **What is the wind direction in this photo?**

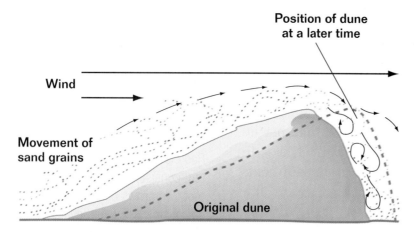

Figure 9-23 As wind blows the sand, the grains jump, roll, and slide up the gentler slope of the dune, accumulate at the top, then slide down the steeper slope on the side away from the wind.

Sand starts to build up behind the rock. As the sand continues to build up, the mound of sand becomes an obstacle itself and traps even more sand. If the wind blows long enough, the mound of sand will become a sand dune, as shown in **Figure 9-22.**

Sand will continue to build up and form a dune until the sand runs out or the obstruction is removed. Some sand dunes may grow to 50 m to 180 m high, but most are much lower.

Dune Movement

A sand dune has two sides. The side facing the wind has a gentler slope. The side away from the wind is steeper. Examining the shape of a dune tells you the direction from which the wind usually blows.

Unless sand dunes are planted with grasses, most dunes don't stay still. They move away or migrate from the direction of the wind. This process is shown in **Figure 9-23.** Some dunes are known as traveling dunes because they move across desert areas as they lose sand on one side and build it up on the other.

Dune Shape

The shape of a dune can also tell you the wind direction. The most commonly known dune shape is a crescent-shaped dune. The open end of a crescent-shaped dune points downwind. When viewed from above, the points are directed downwind. This type of dune forms on hard surfaces where the sand supply is limited. They often occur as single dunes. **Figure 9-24** shows several dune shapes.

When dunes and loess form, the landscape is changed. Wind, like gravity, running water, and glaciers, shapes the land as it erodes sediments. But, the new landforms created by these agents of erosion are themselves being eroded. Erosion and deposition are part of a cycle of change that constantly shapes and reshapes the land.

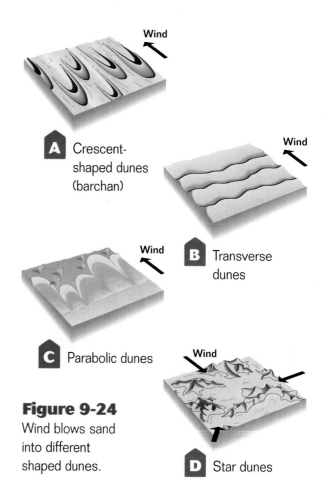

A Crescent-shaped dunes (barchan)

B Transverse dunes

C Parabolic dunes

D Star dunes

Figure 9-24
Wind blows sand into different shaped dunes.

Section Assessment

1. Compare and contrast abrasion and deflation. How do they affect the surface of Earth?

2. Explain the differences between dust storms and sand-storms. Describe how the energy of motion affects the deposition of sand and dust by these storms.

3. **Think Critically:** You notice that snow is piling up behind a fence outside your apartment building. Why?

4. **Skill Builder**
   Sequencing Sequence the following events that describe how a sand dune forms. If you need help, refer to Sequencing in the **Skill Handbook** on page 698.

   a. Grains collect to form a mound.

   b. Wind blows sand grains until they hit an obstacle.

   c. Wind blows over an area and causes deflation.

   d. Vegetation grows on the dune.

Using Math

Between 1972 and 1992, the Sahara Desert in northern Africa increased by nearly 700 km^2 in Mali and the Sudan. Calculate the average number of square kilometers the desert increased each year between 1972 and 1992. At this rate, predict how much additional desert that area will have by 2002.

Design Your Own Experiment

Blowing in the Wind

Possible Materials

- Flat pans (4)
- Fine sand (400 mL)
- Gravel (400 mL)
- Hair dryer
- Sprinkling can
- Water
- Cardboard sheets (28 cm × 35 cm) (4)
- Tape
- Mixing bowl
- Metric ruler

Have you ever played a sport outside and suddenly had the wind blow dust into your eyes? What did you do? Turn your back? Cover your eyes? How does wind pick up sediment? Why does wind pick up some sediments and leave others on the ground?

Recognize the Problem

What factors affect wind erosion? Do both sediment moisture and speed of wind affect the rate of wind erosion?

Form a Hypothesis

How does the amount of moisture in the sediment affect the ability of wind to erode the sediments? Does the speed of the wind limit the size of sediments it can transport? Form a hypothesis about how sediment moisture affects wind erosion. Form another hypothesis about how wind speed affects the size of the sediment the wind can transport.

Goals

- **Observe** the effects of soil moisture and wind speed on wind erosion.
- **Design** and carry out experiments that test the effects of soil moisture and wind speed on wind erosion.

Safety Precautions

Wear your safety goggles at all times when using the hair dryer on sediments.

Test Your Hypothesis

Plan

1. As a group, agree upon and write out your hypothesis statements.

2. List the steps needed to test your first hypothesis. Plan specific steps and vary only one factor at a time. Then, list the steps needed to test your second hypothesis. Test only one factor at a time.

3. Mix the sediments in the pans. Plan how you will fold cardboard sheets and attach them to the pans to keep sediments contained.

4. Design data tables in your Science Journal. Use them as your group collects data.

Do

1. Make sure your teacher approves your plan before you proceed.

2. Carry out the experiments as planned.

3. During the experiments, record observations that you make and complete the data tables in your Science Journal.

Analyze Your Data

1. **Compare** your results with those of other groups.

2. **Graph** the relationship that exists between the speed of the wind and the size of the sediments it transports.

Draw Conclusions

1. How does the energy of motion explain the results of your experiment?

2. **Explain** the relationship between the sediment moisture and the amount of sediment eroded.

3. Based on your graph, **explain** the relationship between wind speed and sediment size.

For a **preview** of this chapter, study this Reviewing Main Ideas before you read the chapter. After you have studied this chapter, you can use the Reviewing Main Ideas to **review** the chapter.

The Glencoe MindJogger, Audiocassettes, and CD-ROM provide additional opportunities for review.

GLENCOE TECHNOLOGY

Section 9-1 GRAVITY

Erosion is the process that wears down and transports sediments. **Deposition** occurs when an agent of erosion loses its energy of motion and can no longer carry its load. **Slump, creep,** rockslides, and mudflows are all mass movements related to gravity. *What characteristics do slump and creep have in common?*

EROSION-PRONE LAND

Vegetation, terraces, and retaining walls can reduce erosion on slopes. Removing vegetation from and building on steep slopes increases erosion. The roots that help hold the soil together and the plants that block wind and rain on the surface are no longer there to do their job. *What do you think happened in this picture?*

Reading Check ☑

Choose a section of this chapter and rewrite the main headings as questions. Then, answer each question.

Section 9-2 GLACIERS

Glaciers are powerful agents of erosion. **Plucking** adds rock and soil to a glacier's sides and bottom as water freezes and thaws and breaks off pieces of surrounding rocks. Glaciers deposit two kinds of material, **till** (sediments dropped directly from glacial ice and snow) and outwash (debris deposited by its meltwater). *Which of these two sediments is a jumbled pile of rocks?*

Section 9-3 WIND

Deflation occurs when wind erodes only fine-grained sediments, leaving coarse sediments behind. The pitting and polishing of rocks and sediments by windblown sediments is called **abrasion.** Wind deposits include loess and dunes. **Loess** consists of fine-grained particles that are tightly packed. Dunes form when windblown sediments pile up behind an obstacle. *What determines how far dust and sand are blown by the wind?*

Chapter 9 Assessment

Using Vocabulary

a. abrasion
b. creep
c. deflation
d. deposition
e. erosion
f. glacier
g. loess
h. mass movement
i. moraine
j. plucking
k. slump
l. till

Explain the difference in the terms given below. Then, explain how the terms are related.

1. abrasion, plucking
2. creep, mass movement
3. deflation, loess
4. erosion, slump
5. glacier, till

Checking Concepts

Choose the word or phrase that best answers the question.

6. Which of the following is the slowest type of mass movement?
   A) abrasion   C) slump
   B) creep   D) mudflow

7. The best vegetation to plant to reduce erosion has what kind of root system?
   A) taproot system
   B) striated root system
   C) fibrous root system
   D) sheet root system

8. What does a valley glacier create at the point where it starts?
   A) esker   C) till
   B) moraine   D) cirque

9. What happens when glacial erosion occurs?
   A) Eskers form.
   B) Landforms such as arêtes and grooves are formed.
   C) Moraines are deposited.
   D) The climate gets warmer.

10. What term describes a mass of snow and ice in motion?
    A) loess deposit   C) outwash
    B) glacier   D) abrasion

11. What shape do glacier-created valleys have?
    A) V shaped   C) U shaped
    B) L shaped   D) S shaped

12. Which term is an example of a structure created by deposition?
    A) cirque   C) striation
    B) abrasion   D) dune

13. Which characteristic is common to all agents of erosion?
    A) They carry sediments when they have enough energy of motion.
    B) They are most likely to erode when sediments are moist.
    C) They create deposits called dunes.
    D) They erode large sediments before they erode small ones.

14. What type of wind erosion leaves pebbles and boulders behind?
    A) deflation   C) abrasion
    B) loess   D) sandblasting

15. What is a ridge formed by deposition of till called?
    A) striation   C) cirque
    B) esker   D) moraine

Thinking Critically

16. How can striations give information about the direction a glacier moved?

17. How effective would a retaining wall made of fine wire mesh be against erosion?

18. Sand dunes often migrate. What can be done to prevent the migration of beach dunes?

19. Scientists have found evidence of movement of ice within a glacier. Explain how this could occur. (HINT: Recall

how putty-like ice forms at the base of a glacier.)

20. The front end of a valley glacier is at a lower elevation than the tail end. How does this explain melting at its front end while snow is still accumulating at its tail end?

Developing Skills

If you need help, refer to the **Skill Handbook.**

21. **Making Tables:** Make a table to contrast continental and valley glaciers.

22. **Designing an Experiment:** Explain how to test the effect of glacial thickness on a glacier's ability to erode.

23. **Sequencing:** Copy and complete the events chain to show how a sand dune forms. Use the terms *sand rolls, migrating, wind blows, sand accumulates, dune, dry sand, obstruction traps,* and *stabilized.*

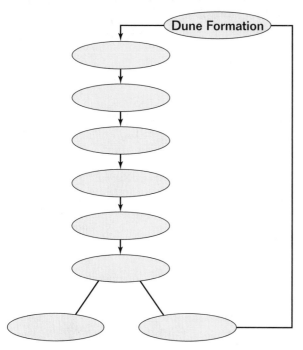

24. **Hypothesizing:** Hypothesize why the materials of loess deposits were transported farther than those of sand dune deposits.

THE
PRINCETON
REVIEW

Test-Taking Tip

Ignore Everyone While you take a test, pay no attention to anyone else in the room. Don't worry if your friends finish a test before you do. If someone tries to talk to you during a test, don't answer. You run the risk of the teacher thinking you were cheating—even if you weren't.

Test Practice

1. A glacier doesn't develop overnight. Several things must happen before a glacier forms. Of the choices below, which occurs first?
   A) Snow falls in an area. It doesn't melt but instead begins piling up.
   B) The mass of snow and ice moves downhill.
   C) The bottom of the snow layer is compressed into layers of ice.
   D) The bottom of the snow layer partially melts and becomes putty-like.

2. All of the following can be classified as erosional features of a glacier except one. Which one doesn't fit?
   A) striations   C) cirque
   B) U-shaped valley   D) till

3. Wind can be a strong erosional force. What determines the amount of erosion that wind can cause in a particular region?
   A) the size of the sediments
   B) the amount of cloud cover
   C) the number of sand dunes
   D) the amount of loess

Water Erosion and Deposition

Skills Preview

Skill Builders
- Compare and Contrast
- Map Concepts

Activities
- Hypothesize
- Classify

MiniLabs
- Make a Model
- Record Observations

Reading Check ✓

Before you read the chapter, it helps to read the Reviewing Main Ideas pages at the end of the chapter. This helps you to know what the most important ideas are.

Explore Activity

Do you know what caused the patterns in this landscape in Canyonlands National Park in Utah? Water! The Green River wears away and moves tons of sediment. Water is the major cause of erosion. It's easy to see why—moving water has great energy. Sometimes, rainwater just soaks into sediments. Other times, it moves down the slope because of gravity's pull. What determines whether rain soaks into the ground or runs off and erodes the surface?

Observe Erosion

1. Place an aluminum pie pan on your desktop.

2. Make a pile of dry soil in the pan.

3. Slowly drip water from a dropper onto the pile and observe what happens.

4. Drip the water more quickly and continue to observe what happens.

5. Repeat steps 1–4, but this time change the slope of the hill. Start again with dry soil.

Science Journal

In your Science Journal, record what effect your rainwater had on the different slopes.

Runoff

Water that doesn't soak into the ground or evaporate but instead flows across Earth's surface is called **runoff.** If you've ever spilled milk while pouring it, you've experienced something similar to runoff. You can picture it in your mind. You start pouring a glass of milk, but it overflows, spilling all over the table. Then, before you can grab a towel to clean up the mess, the milk runs off the table and onto the floor. This is similar to what happens to rainwater that doesn't soak into the ground or evaporate. It runs along the ground and eventually enters streams, lakes, or the ocean.

Factors Affecting Runoff

What factors determine whether rain soaks into the ground or runs off? The amount of rain and the length of time it falls are two factors that affect the amount of runoff. Light rain

Figure 10-1 In areas with gentle slopes and much vegetation, such as the Emerald Hills in New Zealand (A), there is little runoff and erosion. Lack of vegetation has led to severe soil erosion in some areas (B).

Figure 10-2 During floods, the high volume of fast-moving water erodes large amounts of soil.

falling over several hours will probably have time to soak into the ground. Heavy rain falling in less than an hour or so will run off because it doesn't have time to soak in.

Another factor that affects the amount of runoff is the slope of the land. Gentle slopes and flat areas hold water in place, giving it a chance to evaporate or sink into the ground. On steep slopes, however, gravity causes water to run off before either of these things can happen.

As you can see in **Figure 10-1,** the amount of vegetation, such as grass, also affects the amount of runoff. Just like milk running off the table, water will run off smooth surfaces that have little or no vegetation. Plants and their roots act like sponges to soak up and hold water. By slowing down runoff, plants and roots help prevent the erosion of soil. In areas where plants have been cleared, large amounts of soil erosion may occur.

The Effects of Gravity

Gravity is the attracting force all objects have for one another. The greater the amount of matter or mass of an object, the greater its force of gravity. Because Earth has a much greater mass than any of the objects on it, Earth's gravitational force pulls objects toward its center. Water falling down a slope is evidence of gravity. As objects drop to Earth's surface, they pick up speed. Thus, when water falls down a slope, it too picks up speed. Its energy of motion is much greater, and, as shown in **Figure 10-2,** it erodes more quickly than slower-moving water.

Water Erosion

Suppose you and several friends walk the same way to school each day through a field or an empty lot. You always walk in the same footsteps as you did the day before. After a few weeks, you've worn a path through the field. Water also wears a path as it travels down a slope time after time.

Figure 10-3 Heavy rains can remove large amounts of soil and sediment, forming a deep gully in the side of a slope.

Figure 10-4 The runoff that causes sheet erosion eventually loses its energy of motion. Note how the running water appears to stop at the bottom center of the photo. The sediments left behind cover the soil like a sheet.

PHYSICS
INTEGRATION

Gravity
Erosion is the result of forces that act on rocks and soil to change their shape. One force that drives most types of erosion is gravity. Gravity gives water its potential, or stored, energy. When this energy is changed into kinetic energy, or energy of motion, water becomes a powerful force strong enough to move mountains. Visit the Glencoe Science Web Site at www.glencoe.com/sec/science for more information on gravity.

Rill and Gully Erosion

You may have seen a scar or small channel on the side of a slope that was left behind by running water. This is evidence of rill erosion. **Rill erosion** begins when a small stream forms during a heavy rain. As this stream flows along, it has enough energy to carry away plants and soil. There's a scar left on the slope where the water eroded the plants and soil. If a stream frequently flows in the same path, rill erosion may change over time into gully erosion.

In **gully erosion,** a rill channel becomes broader and deeper. Large amounts of soil are removed to form a gully as shown in **Figure 10-3.**

Sheet Erosion

Water often erodes without being in a stream channel. For example, when it rains over a fairly flat area, the rainwater builds until it eventually begins moving down a gentle slope. **Sheet erosion** happens when rainwater flows into lower elevations, carrying sediments with it, as shown in **Figure 10-4.** At these lower elevations, the water loses some of its energy, and it drains into the soil or slowly evaporates.

Stream Erosion

Sometimes, water continues to flow along a low place it has formed. It then becomes a stream like the one shown in **Figure 10-5.** As the water in a stream moves along, it continues to pick up sediments from the bottom and sides of its channel. Water picks up and carries some of the lightweight sediments, while large, heavy particles just roll along the bottom of the stream channel. All of these different-sized materials scrape against the bottom and sides of the channel, where they continue to knock loose more sediments. Because of this, a stream continually cuts a deeper and wider channel.

River System Development

Is there a stream in your neighborhood or town? Maybe you've been fishing in that stream. Each day, thousands of liters of water flow through your neighborhood or town in that stream. Where does all the water come from?

Figure 10-5 This is a cross section of a typical stream channel. **How will the shape of this channel change over time?**

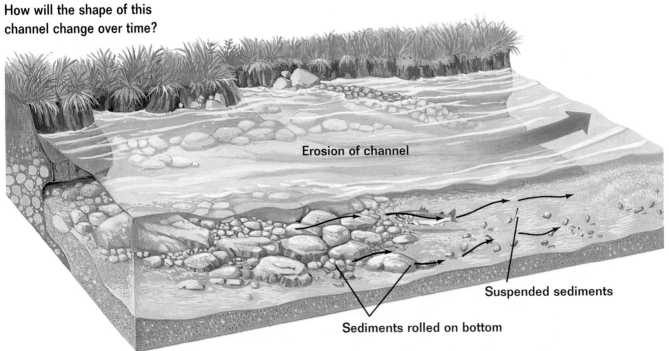

Erosion of channel

Suspended sediments

Sediments rolled on bottom

Figure 10-6 River systems can be compared with the structure of a tree.

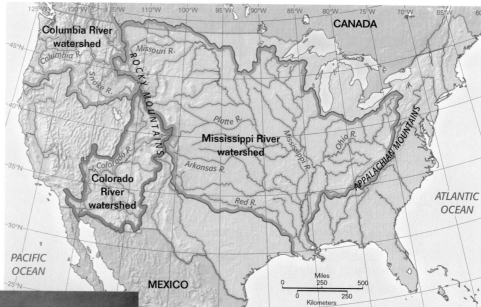

A A large portion of the streams and rivers in the United States are part of the Mississippi River drainage basin or watershed. **What river represents the "trunk" of the river system?**

B The system of twigs, branches, and the trunk that make up a tree is similar to the system of streams and rivers that make up a river system.

River Systems

The stream in your neighborhood is really a part of a river system. The water in the stream came from rills, gullies, and smaller streams located upstream. Just as the tree in **Figure 10-6** is a system containing twigs, branches, and a trunk, a river system also has many parts. Water runs off of the ground and enters small streams. Where small streams join, a larger stream forms. Finally, these larger streams join together, forming a larger body of water called a *river*.

Drainage Basins

The land area from which a stream gets its water is called a **drainage basin.** A drainage basin can be compared to a bathtub. Water that collects in a bathtub flows toward one location—the drain. Likewise, all of the water in a river system eventually flows to one location—the main river. The largest drainage basin in the United States is the Mississippi River drainage basin as shown in **Figure 10-6A.**

*inter*NET
CONNECTION

Visit the Glencoe Science Web Site at **www. glencoe.com/sec/ science** for more information on rivers.

VISUALIZING
Stream Development

Figure 10-7 Streams at all stages of development can be found in most major river systems.

A Young streams are found in mountainous or hilly regions and flow down steep slopes. **Would you expect to see the water moving rapidly or slowly in a young stream?**

Waterfall

Rapids

Meander

B A curving stream that flows down a gradual slope is a mature stream. **Why wouldn't you expect to see many large rapids or waterfalls along a mature stream?**

Stages of Stream Development

There are many different types of streams. Some are narrow and swift moving, and others are wide and slow moving. Streams differ because they are in different stages of development. These stages depend on the slope of the ground over which the stream flows. Streams are classified as young, mature, or old. **Figure 10-7,** on these two pages, describes how each of the stages come together to form a drainage basin.

The stages of development aren't always related to the age of a river. The New River in West Virginia, for example, is one of the oldest rivers in North America. However, it has a steep valley, and flows swiftly through rapids and, as a result, is classified as a *young stream.*

Young Streams

A stream that flows swiftly through a steep valley and has steep sides is a young stream. A young stream may have whitewater rapids and waterfalls. Because the water is flowing rapidly downhill, it has a high level of energy and erodes the stream bottom more than its sides.

Mature Streams

The next stage in the development of a stream is the mature stage. A mature stream flows less swiftly through its valley. Most of the rocks in the streambed that cause waterfalls and rapids have been eroded away.

Floodplain

C Old streams flow slowly through flat, broad floodplains. **What happens to the area surrounding an old-stage stream during floods?**

Levee

Figure 10-8 Flooding causes problems for people who live along major rivers. Floodwater broke through a levee during the Mississippi River flooding in 1993 (A). Kansas City, Missouri, experienced severe flooding during this 1993 flood (B).

Reading Check

What is a meander?

The ability of a mature stream to erode is no longer concentrated on its bottom. Now, the stream starts to erode more along its sides. Curves develop. These curves form because the speed of the water changes throughout the width of the channel.

Water in shallow areas of a stream is slowed down by the friction caused by the bottom of the river. In deep areas, less of the water comes in contact with the bottom. This means that deep water has less friction with the bottom of the stream and therefore flows faster. This faster-moving water erodes the side of the stream where the current is strongest, forming curves. A curve that forms in this way is called a **meander** (mee AN dur). **Figure 10-7C** shows what a meandering stream looks like from the air.

The broad, flat valley floor carved by a meandering stream is called a **floodplain.** When a stream floods, it will often cover a part of or the whole floodplain.

Old Streams

The last stage in the development of a stream is the old stage. An old stream flows slowly through a broad, flat floodplain that it has carved. Below St. Louis, Missouri, the lower Mississippi River is in the old stage.

Major river systems usually contain streams in all stages of development. At the outer edges of a river system, you find whitewater streams moving swiftly down mountains and hills. At the bottom of mountains and hills, you find streams that are starting to meander and are in the mature stage of development. These streams meet at the trunk of the drainage basin to form a major river.

Too Much Water

What happens when a river system has too much water in it? The water needs to go somewhere, and out and over the banks is the only choice. A river that overflows its banks can bring disaster. To prevent this type of flooding, dams and levees are built. A dam is built to control the water flow downstream. It may be built of soil or sand, or steel and concrete.

*inter*NET
CONNECTION

Visit the Glencoe Science Web Site at **www. glencoe.com/sec/ science** for more information on floods.

Problem Solving

Predicting Floods

Each year, floods claim more than 100 lives, drive about 300 000 Americans from their homes, and cause more than $3 billion in property damage. That's why flood prediction is so important. To accurately predict floods, a lot must be known about the drainage basin of a particular stream. One important piece of information is how fast water drains from the basin.

When it rains, it takes a while for runoff to drain a basin and reach the stream channel. Imagine that it rains on a parking lot with a drain near one end. All of the water does not reach the drain at the same time because it takes longer for the water at the far end of

the parking lot to travel to the drain. Also, the parking lot is probably not level, so some areas drain more quickly than others. This is similar to runoff from a drainage basin flowing into a stream channel.

The graphs below show runoff of two drainage basins after a 3-cm rainfall. The graphs show the speed of the flow over time. Study the two graphs and interpret the data to explain the differences.

Think Critically: Which of these two drainage basins will most likely flood? What might be different about the two drainage basins that would explain the differences in their flow rates?

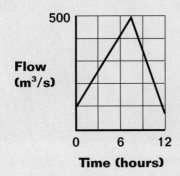

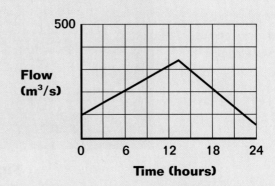

In either case, its function is still the same. Levees are mounds of earth that are built along the sides of a river. They prevent rivers from overflowing their banks. Unfortunately, dams and levees cannot stop the water when flooding is great. This was the case in 1993 when the Mississippi River flooded parts of nine midwestern states. **Figure 10-8** shows some of the damage that resulted from this flood.

Deposition by Surface Water

As water moves throughout a river system, what do you suppose happens as it loses some of its energy of motion? The water can no longer carry some of its sediments, and they are deposited.

Some stream sediments aren't carried far at all before they are deposited. In fact, many sediments are deposited within the stream channel itself. Other stream sediments travel great distances before they are deposited. Sediments picked up when rill and gully erosion occur are examples. Water usually has a lot of energy as it moves down a steep slope. When the water begins flowing on a level surface, it slows down, loses energy, and drops its sediments.

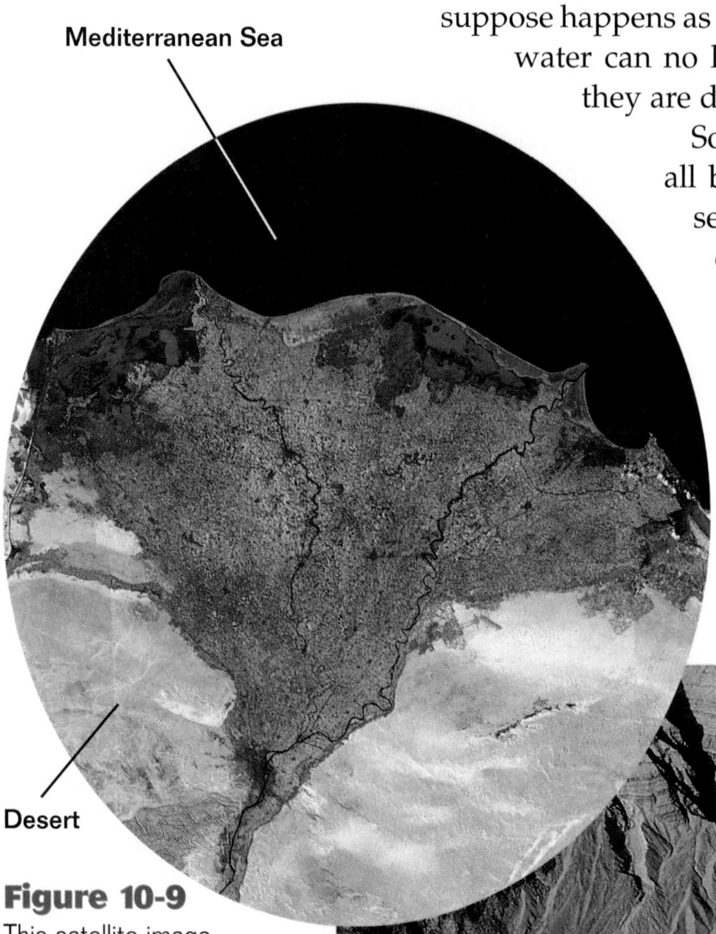

Mediterranean Sea

Desert

Figure 10-9
This satellite image of the Nile River Delta in Egypt shows the typical triangular shape. The green color shows areas of vegetation.

Figure 10-10 Alluvial fans commonly occur at the base of steep mountain slopes. They form on land. **How might the amount and type of vegetation affect the alluvial fan?**

Sediments that are deposited as the water empties into an ocean, gulf, or lake form a triangular or fan-shaped deposit called a **delta,** as shown in **Figure 10-9.** When the river waters empty from a mountain valley out onto a flat open plain, the deposit is called an **alluvial** (uh LEW vee ul) **fan,** as shown in **Figure 10-10.**

The Mississippi River provides a real-life example of the topics presented in this section. Runoff causes rill and gully erosion as it picks up sediments and carries them into the larger streams that flow into the Mississippi River. The Mississippi is large and has a lot of energy. It can erode a great deal of sediment. As it flows, it cuts into its banks and picks up more sediments. In other places, where the land is flat, the river deposits some of its sediments in its own channel.

Eventually, the Mississippi River reaches the Gulf of Mexico. There it flows into the gulf, loses most of its energy of motion, and dumps its sediments in a large deposit on the Louisiana coast. This deposit, shown in **Figure 10-11,** is the Mississippi Delta.

Figure 10-11 This satellite image of the Mississippi Delta shows how sediments accumulate where the Mississippi River empties into the Gulf of Mexico.

Section Assessment

1. How does the slope of an area affect its runoff?
2. Describe the three stages of stream development.
3. What is a delta?
4. **Think Critically:** How is a stream's rate of flow related to the amount of erosion it causes and the size of the sediments it deposits?

5. **Skill Builder**
   Interpreting Scientific Illustrations Do the **Chapter 10 Skill Activity** on page 735 to interpret a scientific illustration on drainage basins.

Using Computers

Spreadsheet Design a table using spreadsheet software to compare and contrast sheet, rill, gully, and stream erosion. For help with spreadsheets see page 722.

Stream Speed

Possible Materials

- Paint pan
- Sand
- Cups (2)
  *beakers
- Rubber tubing
- Meterstick
- Small cork
- Water
- Stopwatch
- Funnel
- Clothespin
  *hose clamp

  *Alternate Materials

Have you ever wondered what it would be like to make a raft and use it to float on a river? Do you think that guiding a raft would be easy? Probably not. You'd be at the mercy of the current. The greater the speed of the river, the stronger the current.

Recognize the Problem

What factors affect a stream's speed? How does the speed of a stream affect the water's ability to erode?

Form a Hypothesis

Think about streams, then consider various factors that may affect how fast a stream flows. Based on your observations, the goals of this experiment, and the possible materials, make a hypothesis about how the speed of a stream affects erosion.

Goals

- **Design** an experiment to show the relationship between the speed of a stream and a stream's ability to erode.

- **Observe** the effects of slope of a stream on speed of the stream.
- **Observe** the effects of speed of a stream on erosion.

Safety Precautions

Wash your hands after you handle the sand.

Test Your Hypothesis

Plan

1. Decide how your group will test its hypothesis.

2. List the steps that you need to take to test your hypothesis. Include in your plan how you will (a) make your stream channel, (b) adjust the height of the slope, (c) **measure** the length of the stream channel, (d) use tubing and one of the cups to begin the water flowing down the stream, (e) catch the overflow water at the other end of the pan with your other cup, (f) **determine** the time it takes the cork to flow down the stream channel, and

(g) **observe** the amount of erosion that takes place. Make a complete materials list.

3. **Prepare** a data table in your Science Journal so that it is ready to use as your group collects data. Will the data be summarized in graphs? Decide which type of graph to use.

4. **Identify** any constants and the variables of the experiment. Have you allowed for a control in your experiment? Do you have to run any tests more than one time?

Do

1. Make sure your teacher approves your plan and your data table before you proceed.

2. Carry out the experiment as planned.

3. While doing the experiment, record your observations and complete the data table in your Science Journal.

Analyze Your Data

1. **Calculate** the speed of your streams by dividing the distance by the time (speed = distance/time).

2. Were sediments carried along with the water to the end of your stream channels?

3. Did the slope affect the speed of the streams in your experiment?

Draw Conclusions

1. Did the streams with the greatest or least slopes erode the most sediments? Explain.

2. How would your results change if a stronger flow of water was used? How does this compare to flooding?

10·2 Groundwater

Groundwater System Development

What would have happened if the spilled milk in Section 10-1 had run off the table onto a carpeted floor? It would have quickly soaked into the carpet. Water that falls on Earth can also soak into the ground.

What happens to the water then? Water that soaks into the ground becomes a part of a system, just as water that stays above ground becomes a part of a river system. Soil is made up of many small rock fragments. Weathered rock lies beneath the soil. Between these fragments and pieces of weathered rock are spaces called pores, as shown in **Figure 10-12.** Water that soaks into the ground collects in these pores and becomes part of what is called **groundwater.**

What You'll Learn

▶ The importance of groundwater
▶ The effect that soil and rock permeability have on groundwater movement
▶ Ways that groundwater erodes and deposits sediments

Vocabulary

groundwater   water table
permeable   spring
impermeable   geyser
aquifer   cave

Why It's Important

▶ The groundwater system is one of our important sources of drinking water.

Figure 10-12 Some soils and rocks have connected pores through which water can move.

Pore space

Soil or rock fragment

Permeability

A groundwater system is similar to a river system. However, instead of having channels that connect different parts of the drainage basin, the groundwater system has connecting pores. Soil and rock are **permeable** (PUR mee uh bul) if the pore spaces are connected and water can pass through them. Sandstone is an example of a permeable rock.

Soil or rock that has many large, connected pores is highly permeable. Water can pass through it easily. Soil or rock is less permeable if the connected pore spaces are fewer in number or if the pores themselves are fewer or smaller. Some material, such as clay, has small pore spaces or no pores at all. This material is **impermeable,** which means that water cannot pass through it.

Groundwater Movement

How deep into Earth's crust do you suppose groundwater can go? Groundwater will keep going deeper into Earth until it reaches a layer of impermeable rock. When this happens, the water can't move down any deeper. As a result, water begins filling up the pores in the rocks above the impermeable layer. A layer of permeable rock that lets water move freely is an **aquifer** (AK wuh fur). The area where all of the pores in the rock are filled with water is the zone of saturation. The upper surface of this zone is the **water table,** as seen in **Figure 10-13.**

Using Math

In an experiment, you find that 100 mL of gravel can hold 31 mL of water. Calculate the percentage of pore space.

Figure 10-13 If you want to know where the water table is in a particular area, find a stream. A stream's surface level is the water table. Below that is the zone of saturation.

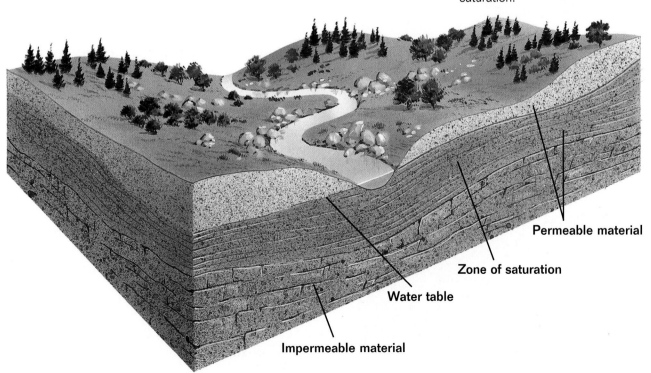

Permeable material

Zone of saturation

Water table

Impermeable material

Figure 10-14 The years on the pole show how much the ground level dropped in the San Joaquin Valley, California, between 1925 and 1977.

Water Table

What's so important about the zone of saturation and the water table? Think about how much water you use each day. An average person in the United States uses about 397 L every day. That's enough to fill 1138 soft-drink cans. If your water supply comes from a seemingly endless source, such as a large lake, you may never think about limiting your usage. But many people get drinking water from groundwater through wells that have been drilled into the zone of saturation.

Wells

A good well extends deep into the zone of saturation, past the top of the water table. Groundwater flows into the well, and a pump brings it to the surface. Because the water table sometimes drops during dry seasons, even a good well can go dry. Time is needed then for the water table to rise, either by rainfall or from an increase in the amount of groundwater.

In a city or town where groundwater is the main source of drinking water, the number of wells becomes important. Imagine that a large factory is built in such a town. Now the demand on the groundwater supply is even greater. Even in times of normal rainfall, the wells could go dry. This is because more water is taken out of the ground than can be replaced by rain.

If too much water is pumped out, the land level could sink from the weight of the sediments above the now-empty pore spaces. **Figure 10-14** shows what happens when too much groundwater was removed in California.

One type of well doesn't need a pump to bring water to the surface. An artesian well is a well in which water rises to the surface under pressure. Artesian wells are less common than other wells because of the special conditions they require, as shown in **Figure 10-15.**

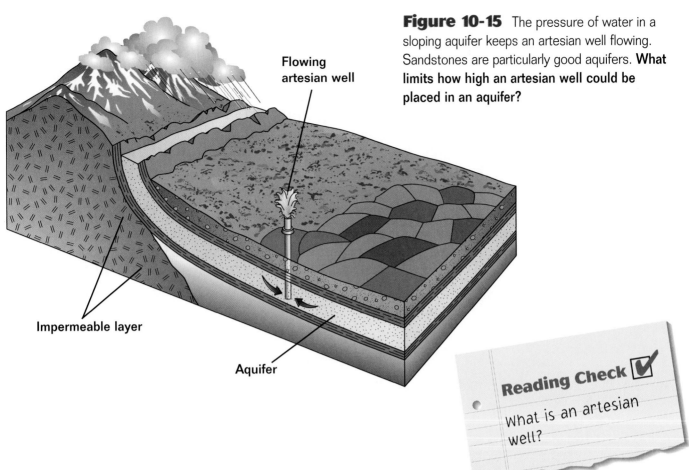

Figure 10-15 The pressure of water in a sloping aquifer keeps an artesian well flowing. Sandstones are particularly good aquifers. **What limits how high an artesian well could be placed in an aquifer?**

Flowing artesian well

Impermeable layer

Aquifer

Reading Check

What is an artesian well?

An artesian well needs a sloping aquifer located between two impermeable layers. Water will enter at the high part of the sloping aquifer. Water in the higher part of the aquifer puts pressure on the water in the lower part. If a well is drilled into the lower part of the aquifer, the pressurized water will flow to the surface. Sometimes, the pressure is great enough to force the water into the air, forming a fountain.

Springs

In some places, the water table meets Earth's surface. When this happens, water flows out and forms a **spring.** Springs are found on hillsides or in any other place where the water table is exposed at the surface. Springs can often be used as a source of freshwater, as shown in **Figure 10-16.**

The water from most springs is cold. But, in some places, groundwater is heated and comes to the surface as a hot spring. The groundwater is heated by rocks that come in contact with molten material beneath Earth's surface.

Figure 10-16 This natural spring in the Grand Canyon is called Vasey's Paradise.

Geysers

One of the places where groundwater is heated is in Yellowstone National Park in Wyoming. Yellowstone has hot springs and geysers. A **geyser,** like the one in **Figure 10-17A,** is a hot spring that erupts periodically, shooting water and steam into the air. Groundwater is heated to high temperatures, causing it to expand underground. This expansion forces some of the water out of the ground, taking the pressure off of the remaining water. The remaining water boils quickly, with much of it turning to steam. The steam shoots out of the opening like steam out of a teakettle, forcing the remaining water out with it. Yellowstone's famous geyser, Old Faithful, pictured in **Figure 10-17B,** shoots between 14 000 and 32 000 L of water and steam into the air on average once every 80 minutes.

Groundwater Erosion and Deposition

Just as water is the most powerful agent of erosion on Earth's surface, it can also have a great effect underground. When water mixes with carbon dioxide in the air, it forms a weak acid. One type of rock that is easily dissolved by this acid is limestone. As acidic groundwater moves through natural cracks in limestone, it dissolves the rock. Gradually, the cracks in the limestone are enlarged until an underground opening called a **cave** is formed.

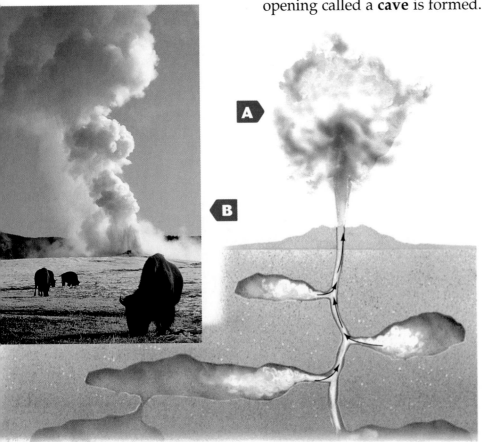

Figure 10-17 After a geyser erupts (A), water runs back into underground openings where it is heated and erupts again. Yellowstone's famous geyser, Old Faithful (B), used to erupt about once each 76 minutes. An earthquake on January 9, 1998, slowed Old Faithful's "clock" down four minutes to an average of one eruption about every 80 minutes. The average height of the geyser's water is 40.5 m.

Cave Formation

You've probably seen a picture of the inside of a cave, or perhaps you've visited one. Groundwater not only dissolves limestone to make caves, but it also can make deposits on the insides of caves, as shown in **Figure 10-18.**

Water often drips slowly from cracks in the cave walls and ceilings. This water contains calcium ions dissolved from the limestone. If this water evaporates while hanging from the ceiling of a cave, a deposit of calcite is left behind. Stalactites form when this happens over and over. Where drops of water fall to the floor of the cave, a stalagmite forms.

Sinkholes

If underground rock is dissolved near the surface, a sinkhole may form. A sinkhole is a depression that forms when the roof of a cave collapses.

In summary, when rain falls and becomes groundwater, it might dissolve a cave, erupt from a geyser, or be pumped from a well to be used at your house.

Figure 10-18 Water containing dissolved calcium ions forms interesting features in caves. Look at the features in the cave shown above. **How do you think these features formed?**

Section Assessment

1. How does water enter the groundwater system?
2. How does the permeability of soil and rocks affect the flow of groundwater?
3. Explain how caves form.
4. **Think Critically:** Would you expect water in wells, geysers, and hot springs to contain eroded materials? Why or why not?
5. **Skill Builder**
   Comparing and Contrasting Compare and contrast wells, geysers, and hot springs. If you need help, refer to Comparing and Contrasting in the **Skill Handbook** on page 704.

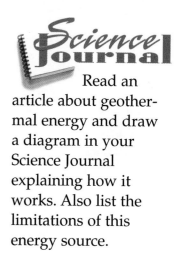

Science Journal

Read an article about geothermal energy and draw a diagram in your Science Journal explaining how it works. Also list the limitations of this energy source.

10·3 Ocean Shoreline

The Shore

Picture yourself sitting on a beautiful, white-sand beach. Palm trees sway in the breeze above your head, and small children play in the quiet waves lapping at the water's edge. It's hard to imagine a place more peaceful than this shore. Now, picture yourself sitting along another shore. You're on a high cliff, overlooking waves crashing onto huge boulders below. Both of these places are shorelines. A shoreline is where land meets the ocean.

The two shorelines just described are very different. Why are they so different? Both experience surface waves, tides, and currents. These cause both shorelines to change constantly. Sometimes, you can see these changes from hour to hour. We'll look at why these shorelines are different, but first, let's learn about the forces that carve shores.

Shoreline Forces

Along all shorelines, like the one in **Figure 10-19A,** surface waves continue to move sediments back and forth. Waves shape shorelines by eroding and redepositing sediments. The

What You'll Learn

► The forces that cause shoreline erosion
► How different types of shorelines compare
► Some origins of sand

Vocabulary
longshore current
beach
barrier island

Why It's Important

► Shorelines look the way they do because forces shape them.

Figure 10-19

A Waves, tides, and currents cause shorelines to change constantly.

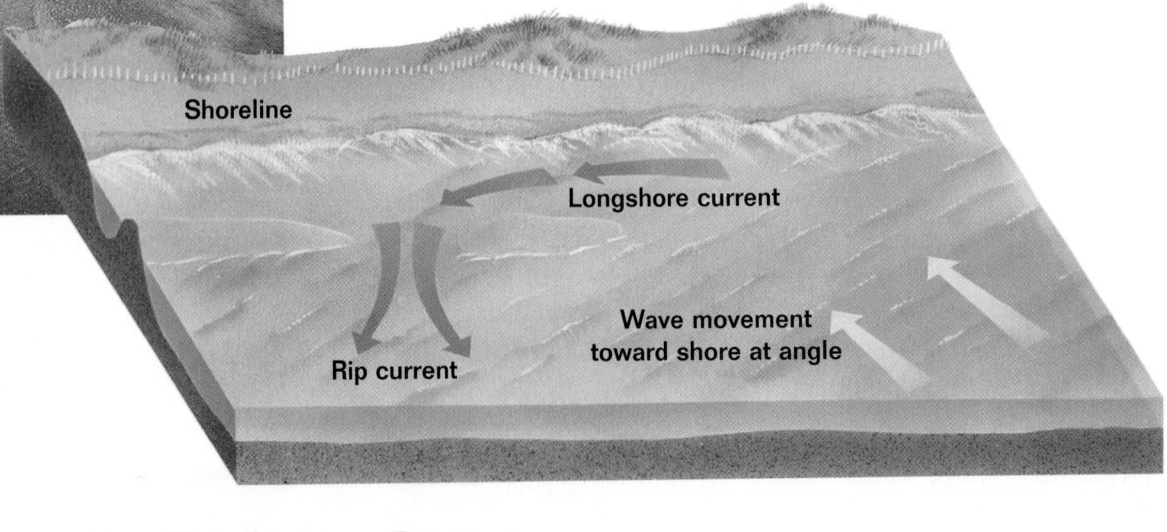

B Waves approaching the shoreline at an angle create a longshore current. When the water built up by waves returns to sea, a rip current forms. **Why is it wise to avoid rip currents when swimming at a beach?**

Shoreline

Longshore current

Rip current

Wave movement toward shore at angle

Figure 10-20 Along a rocky shoreline, the force of pounding waves breaks rock fragments loose and grinds them into smaller and smaller sediments.

tides also shape shorelines. Every day, tides raise and lower the place on the shoreline where surface waves erode and deposit sediments.

Waves usually collide with a shore at slight angles. This creates a **longshore current** of water that runs along the shore, as shown in **Figure 10-19B.** Longshore currents carry many metric tons of loose sediments and act like rivers of sand in the ocean. What do you suppose happens if a longshore current isn't carrying all of the sand it has the energy to carry? It will use this extra energy to erode more shoreline sediments. ✓

You've seen the forces that affect all shorelines. Now, we'll look at the differences that make one shore a flat, sandy beach and another shore a steep, rocky cliff.

Reading Check ✓

What is a longshore current?

Rocky Shorelines

Along rocky shorelines like the one in **Figure 10-20,** rocks and cliffs are the most common features. Waves wear away the rocks to form hollows. Over time, these enlarge and become caves. When too much erosion occurs, the overhanging rock may fall off into the ocean. Rock fragments broken from the cliffs are ground up by the endless motion of waves. They are transported as sediment by the longshore current. These fragments act like the sand on sandpaper.

Softer rocks are eroded away before harder rocks, leaving islands of harder rocks. This takes many years, but remember that the ocean never stops. In a single day, about 14 000 waves will crash onto any shore.

The rock fragments produced by eroding waves are sediments. When rocky shorelines are being eroded, where do you think the sediments go? Waves carry them away and deposit them where water is quieter. If you want to relax on a nice wide, sandy beach, you shouldn't go to a rocky shoreline.

Sandy Beaches

Smooth, gently sloping shorelines are different from steep, rocky shorelines. Beaches are the main feature here.

Beaches are deposits of sediment that run parallel to the shore. They stretch inland as far as the tides and waves are able to deposit sediment.

Beaches are made of different materials like the sand shown in **Figure 10-21.** Some are made of rock fragments from the shoreline, and others are made of seashell fragments. These fragments range from pebbles large enough to fill your hand to fine sand. Sand grains are 0.07 mm to 2 mm in diameter. Why do many beaches have this size particles? This is because waves break rocks and seashells down to sand-sized particles. The constant wave motion bumps sand grains together and, in the process, rounds their corners.

Figure 10-21 Sand varies in size, color, and composition. This sand contains shell fragments and tiny grains of quartz.

What kinds of materials do you think make up most beach sands? Most are made of resistant minerals such as quartz. However, sand in some places is made of other things. For example, Hawaii's black sands are made of basalt, and green sands are made of the mineral olivine. Jamaica's white sands are made of coral and shell fragments.

Baymouth bar

Spit

Figure 10-22 Longshore currents move sediment along shorelines, changing beaches and creating baymouth bars and spits, like those in this aerial photograph of Martha's Vineyard, Massachusetts.

Sand Erosion and Deposition

Sand is carried down beaches by longshore currents to form features such as those seen in **Figure 10-22.** Sand is also moved by storms and the wind. Thus, beaches are fragile, short-term land features that are easily damaged by storms and human activities such as construction.

Barrier Islands

Barrier islands are sand deposits that parallel the shore but are separated from the mainland, as shown in **Figure 10-23.** These islands start as underwater sand ridges formed by breaking waves. Hurricanes and storms add sediment to them, raising some to sea level. Once a barrier island is exposed, the wind blows the loose sand into dunes, keeping the island above sea level. As with all seashore features, barrier islands are short-term, lasting from a few years to a few centuries.

Figure 10-23 Many barrier islands have formed along North America's Atlantic Coast and the Gulf of Mexico. The size and shape of these islands constantly change due to wave action.

Section Assessment

1. What causes shoreline erosion?
2. Contrast the features you'd find along a steep, rocky shoreline with the features you'd find along a gently sloping shoreline.
3. **Think Critically:** Why is there no sand on many of the world's shorelines?
4. **Skill Builder**
   Concept Mapping Make a cycle concept map that discusses how the sand from a barrier island that is currently in place can become a new barrier island 100 years from now. Use these terms: *barrier island, breaking waves, wind, longshore currents*, and *new barrier island.* If you need help, refer to Concept Mapping in the **Skill Handbook** on page 698.

Using Math

If in a single day, about 14 000 waves crash onto a shore, how many waves crash onto a shore in one year? Calculate how many have crashed onto a shore since you were born. Explain how you found your answer.

What's so special about sand?

Materials

- Samples of different sands (3)
- Hand lens
- Magnet
  *stereomicroscope

  *Alternate Materials

You know that sand is made of many different kinds of grains, but did you realize that the slope of a beach is actually related to the size of its grains? The coarser the grain size, the steeper the beach. Did you know that many sands are mined because they have economic value?

What You'll Investigate

What characteristics can be used to classify beach sands?

Goals

- **Observe** differences in sand.
- **Classify** characteristics of beach sand.

Procedure

1. **Design** a data table in which to record your data when you **compare** the three sand samples. You will need five columns in your table. One column will be for the samples and the others for the characteristics you will be examining. If you need help in designing your table, refer to the **Skill Handbook.**

2. Use the diagram below to determine the average roundness of each sample.

| Angular | Sub-Angular | Sub-Rounded | Rounded |

3. **Identify** the grain size of your samples by using the sand gauge on this page. To determine the grain size, place sand grains in the middle of the circle of the sand gauge. Use the upper half of the circle for dark-colored particles and the bottom half of the circle for light-colored particles.

4. Decide on two other characteristics to examine that will help you **classify** your samples.

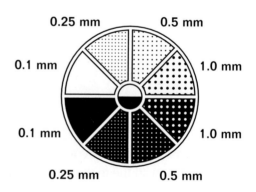

Sand Gauge

Conclude and Apply

1. **Compare and contrast** some characteristics of beach sand.

2. Why are there differences in the characteristics of different sand samples?

Water Wars

Mono Lake

The algae, brine shrimp, alkali flies, and birds of Mono Lake (left) don't know it, but they are living in an 800 000-year-old habitat. Mono Lake, located at the base of the Sierra Nevada mountain range in California, is fed by mountain streams and groundwater. Its drainage basin averages eight inches of rainfall each year. Under natural conditions, the only way that water leaves the lake is through evaporation.

Freshwater springs containing the chemical calcium rise up through the carbon dioxide–rich lake water. This forms calcium carbonate. This solid then forms around the mouth of the springs. Algae grow around these springs and give off additional calcium deposits, which become stiff and thick. These structures, called tufa (inset), can be more than three meters tall and can be 900 years old.

Human Impact

Human activities have been harmful to the lake. Since 1941, water has been pumped from some of the streams that flow into Mono Lake. Without freshwater to refill the lake, in 50 years its level dropped 14 m, its volume decreased by half, and the amount of salt in the lake (salinity) has doubled. Dusts that contained salt, blowing from the area once covered by the lake, caused air pollution. The duck population dropped from millions to just a few thousand by 1995. Some scientists who study the brine shrimp believe that the increase in salinity has caused the reproductive rate of the shrimp to decrease. As the lake level dropped, ghostly tufa structures were exposed and subjected to weathering and erosion.

The Public Takes a Stand

As a result of pressure from people worried about the future of Mono Lake, authorities decided to limit the amount of water pumped from the mountain streams that feed it. This allowed the lake to rise. The required lake level is now about halfway between the 1941 and the 1995 lake levels.

interNET CONNECTION

Visit the Glencoe Science Web Site at **www.glencoe.com/sec/science** for more information about solutions to the water shortage problems in the southwestern United States.

For a **preview** of this chapter, study this Reviewing Main Ideas before you read the chapter. After you have studied this chapter, you can use the Reviewing Main Ideas to **review** the chapter.

The Glencoe MindJogger, Audiocassettes, and CD-ROM provide additional opportunities for review.

Section

10-1 SURFACE WATER

When rain falls on a slope, gravity pulls it down the slope. This water is called **runoff.** As the runoff flows along, it carries sediment with it. If enough rain falls and the slope is steep enough, large amounts of sediment can be transported with the runoff. The steeper the slope, the faster the water flows, and the more sediment the runoff can carry. **Rill, gully,** and **sheet erosion** are all types of surface water erosion caused by runoff. Gentle slopes or vegetation enable water to soak into the ground or be taken up by the plants. *How does water change the landforms that make up Earth's surface? How has it affected the land near you?*

RIVER SYSTEMS

Runoff generally flows into streams that merge with larger and larger rivers until it reaches a lake or ocean. Major river systems usually contain different types of streams. In the mountains, a young stream flows through a steep valley and has rapids and waterfalls. These streams flow down steep hills, and therefore flow quickly and have lots of energy. Mature streams flow through gentler terrain and have less energy. Curves start to develop as the river **meanders** across a broad, flat valley floor. Old streams, which flow slowly, are often wide and snake back and forth across their floodplains. *Describe how a mountain stream changes over time. How does the speed at which the water flows affect how much sediment it can carry?*

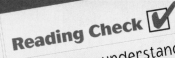

Reading Check ✓

To help you understand the main ideas of this chapter, make a list of the vocabulary words and review their meanings.

10-2 GROUNDWATER

When water soaks into the ground, it becomes part of a vast water system called **groundwater.** Although rock may seem solid, many types are filled with a network of connected spaces called pores. When water fills these spaces, a layer of saturated rock forms, the top of which is called the **water table.** This layer is often the source of water for many homes. As water slowly flows underground, it can carry dissolved minerals away, leaving behind large underground **caves.** *Why is a spring considered part of the groundwater system? How can groundwater erosion result in the formation of a sinkhole?*

10-3 OCEAN SHORELINE

Ocean shorelines are active systems. Sand is deposited by rivers and moved along the coast by waves and currents. Waves and currents give tremendous amounts of energy to water. Pounding waves break up rocks into tiny fragments called sediment. Over time, the waves and currents move this sediment and redeposit it, constantly changing **beaches,** sandbars, and spits. *How could a severe storm such as a hurricane change the shape of a beach?*

Chapter 10 Assessment

Using Vocabulary

a. alluvial fan	**k.** gully erosion
b. aquifer	**l.** impermeable
c. barrier island	**m.** longshore current
d. beach	**n.** meander
e. cave	**o.** permeable
f. delta	**p.** rill erosion
g. drainage basin	**q.** runoff
h. floodplain	**r.** sheet erosion
i. geyser	**s.** spring
j. groundwater	**t.** water table

Each phrase below describes a science term from the list. Write the term that matches the phrase describing it.

1. water that flows over Earth's surface

2. water that flows parallel to the shore

3. a curve in a stream channel

4. a triangular deposit that forms when a river enters a gulf or lake

5. water that soaks into the ground

Checking Concepts

Choose the word or phrase that best answers the question.

6. What is an example of a structure created by deposition?
   A) beach
   B) rill
   C) cave
   D) geyser

7. What is a deposit that forms when a mountain river runs out onto a plain called?
   A) subsidence
   B) an alluvial fan
   C) infiltration
   D) water diversion

8. What is a layer of rock that water flows through?
   A) an aquifer
   B) a pore
   C) a water table
   D) impermeable

9. What is the network formed by a river and all the smaller streams that contribute to it?
   A) groundwater system
   B) zone of saturation
   C) river system
   D) water table

10. Which term describes soils through which fluids can easily flow?
    A) impermeable
    B) meanders
    C) saturated
    D) permeable

11. Which stage of development are mountain streams in?
    A) young
    B) mature
    C) old
    D) meandering

12. What forms when the water table is exposed at the surface?
    A) meander
    B) spring
    C) aquifer
    D) stalactite

13. What contains heated groundwater that reaches Earth's surface?
    A) water table
    B) cave
    C) aquifer
    D) hot spring

14. Where are beaches most common?
    A) rocky shorelines
    B) flat shorelines
    C) aquifers
    D) young streams

15. Why does water rise in an artesian well?
    A) a pump
    B) erosion
    C) heat
    D) pressure

Thinking Critically

16. Explain why the Mississippi River has meanders.

17. What determines whether a stream, erodes its bottom or its sides?

18. Why would you be concerned if developers of a new housing project started drilling wells near your well?

19. A stack is an island of rock along certain shorelines. Along what kind of shoreline would you find stacks? Explain.

20. Explain why beach sands collected from different locations will differ in composition, color, and texture.

Developing Skills

If you need help, refer to the **Skill Handbook.**

21. **Concept Mapping:** Complete the concept map below using the following terms: *developed meanders, gentle curves, gentle gradient, old, rapids, steep gradient, wide floodplain, young.*

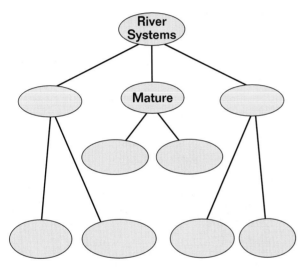

22. **Interpreting Data:** If the Brahmaputra River in India flows at a rate of 19 800 m³/s and the La Plata River in South America flows at 79 300 m³/s, infer which river erodes more sediments.

23. **Hypothesizing:** Hypothesize why most of the silt in the Mississippi Delta is found farther out to sea than the sand-sized particles.

24. **Outlining:** Make an outline that explains the three stages of stream development.

25. **Using Variables, Constants, and Controls:** Explain how you could test the effect of slope on the amount of runoff produced.

THE PRINCETON REVIEW

Test-Taking Tip

Use the Buddy System Study in a group. A small group of people works well because together the group can share each others' knowledge and skills. Keep it small and keep on target.

Test Practice

Use these questions to test your Science Proficiency.

1. If you wanted to have an exciting white-water raft ride, where would you go?
   A) to a meandering river
   B) to a delta
   C) to a place where there is sheet erosion
   D) to a young stream

2. It is believed that our planet is getting warmer. Which statement best supports this theory?
   A) Most sand is made of quartz.
   B) Ice caps are melting and shoreline erosion is increasing.
   C) Deltas are forming at the mouths of rivers.
   D) Old streams are developing meanders.

3. Read the table below and determine which river will likely cause more erosion.

River	Length of River (km)	Average Width of River (m)	Flow Rate (km/hr)
Bowman	400	75	4
Canadys	400	75	3.5
St. George	400	75	4.65
Snyder	400	75	5

A) Bowman   C) St. George
B) Canadys   D) Snyder

Oceans

What's Happening Here?

The Indian Ocean carved these pillars (left) along Australia's southeastern coast. Earth's seas are powerful and always in motion. Tides rise and fall. Waves build and crash. Swift currents carry sediments and living things from one place to another. Beneath the surface, forms of life carry on their own rhythms. A forest of kelp provides habitat for many sea creatures, which attract predators such as these sea lions (below). What causes Earth's vast bodies of water to stay in motion? How deep are these waters, and what lives within their depths? These are some of the questions explored in this unit.

interNET CONNECTION

Explore the Glencoe Science Web Site at **www.glencoe.com/sec/science** to find out more about topics found in this unit.

Chapter Preview

Skills Preview

Skill Builders
- Predict
- Compare and Contrast

Activities
- Recognize Cause and Effect
- Measure in SI

MiniLabs
- Make a Model
- Observe and Infer

Reading Check ✔

Use a dictionary to figure out the relationship between an ocean *current* and *currency,* the coins and dollars we use to buy things.

Explore Activity

The ocean is constantly in motion. Waves, such as the one on the left, break against the shore with great energy. Wind causes most waves in the ocean, ranging in size from small ripples to the giant waves of hurricanes. Some reach more than 30 m high. Winds also cause general movements of ocean water in currents around the world. In this chapter, you will learn more about the interaction between the atmosphere and the oceans, as well as how waves, currents, and tides work.

Observe Currents

1. In a bowl, melt some ice to make ice water.

2. Add three drops of food coloring to the ice water.

3. Fill a 250-mL beaker with warm water.

4. Use a dropper to place three to four drops of the ice water on the surface of the warm water.

5. Repeat the experiment, but this time, *slowly* insert the full dropper until the tip is 1 cm from the bottom of the beaker. Squeeze out the dropper and *slowly* pull it back out.

Science Journal

In your Science Journal, record which procedure produced a current. Describe what the current looked like. Look up the word *convection* in the dictionary. Infer why the current created is called a convection current.

11·1 Ocean Water

Oceans and You

WhatYou'll Learn

► The origin of the water in Earth's oceans
► Why the ocean is salty
► The composition of seawater

Vocabulary
basin
salinity

WhyIt's Important

► Oceans affect weather and provide food, oxygen, and natural resources.

Oceans affect your life, and your life affects oceans. No matter where you live, the ocean influences you. When it rains, most of the water that falls comes from oceans. If the day is sunny, it is partly due to weather systems that develop over oceans. Oceans are a source of food and resources. **Figure 11-1A** shows a rig drilling oil from beneath the ocean floor. Fish taken from the sea are shown in **Figure 11-1B**.

Oceans also act as barriers between continents. The price of clothing, cars, and gasoline may include the cost of shipping these materials across oceans. To go from the United States to Europe, a traveler must fly or take a ship across the ocean. In the past, humans have migrated across oceans to new lands. Oceans also provide a means of transportation for plants and animals. Animals migrate with ocean currents. Plant seeds are washed from one coast to another by oceans.

Figure 11-1 We depend on the oceans. Some of our oil comes from wells drilled through rock layers under the oceans (A). Some food comes from the oceans (B).

A

B

Human activity also affects the oceans. If you live near a stream that is polluted, that pollution can travel to an ocean. Cities near oceans regularly dump sewage sludge into the ocean. Oil spills destroy beaches and marshes along the ocean.

Origin of Oceans

In the first billion years after Earth formed, its surface was much more volcanically active than it is today, as illustrated in **Figure 11-2.** When volcanoes erupt, they spew lava and ash, and they also give off water vapor, carbon dioxide, and other gases. Scientists hypothesize that about 4 billion years ago, this water vapor began to be stored in Earth's early atmosphere. Over millions of years, it cooled enough to condense into storm clouds. Torrential rains began to fall. Oceans were formed as this water filled low areas on Earth called **basins.**

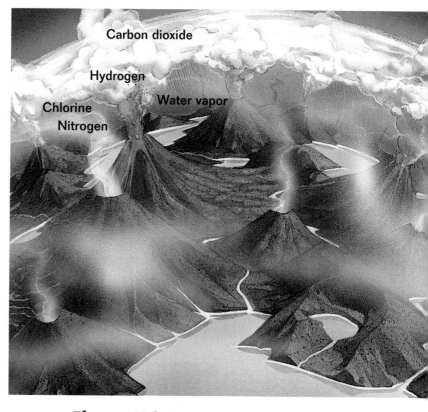

Figure 11-2 Earth's oceans may have formed from water vapor. This water vapor was released into the atmosphere by volcanoes that also gave off chlorine, carbon dioxide, nitrogen, and hydrogen.

Composition of Oceans

Humans use a lot of water each day. In some areas, freshwater is limited. When water demand in these areas increases, too much water may be pumped from aquifers. This can cause a decrease in the freshwater supply.

Seventy percent of Earth's surface is covered by ocean water. If we could use ocean water to meet our water needs, the demand on the freshwater supply would be decreased. But, water from an ocean is different from drinking water. It tastes salty because the ocean contains many dissolved salts. In the water, these salts are separated into chloride, sodium, sulfur, magnesium, calcium, and potassium.

These salts come from rivers and groundwater that slowly dissolve elements such as calcium, magnesium, and sodium from rocks and minerals. Rivers carry these elements to the oceans. Erupting volcanoes add elements, such as sulfur and chlorine, to the atmosphere and oceans.

Using Math

Make a circle graph to show the percentage of Earth's surface that is ocean. Explain the steps you took to complete your graph. Compare your procedures and graph with those of other students.

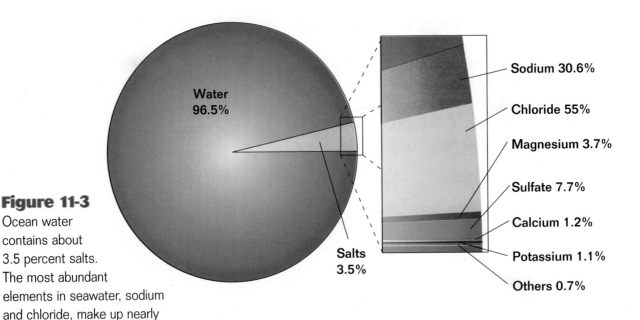

Figure 11-3

Ocean water contains about 3.5 percent salts. The most abundant elements in seawater, sodium and chloride, make up nearly 86 percent of the substances in seawater.

Reading Check ☑

How do sodium and chloride get into seawater?

LIFE SCIENCE
INTEGRATION ➤

Salinity

The most abundant elements in seawater are sodium and chlorine. As rivers flow to the ocean, they dissolve sodium along the way. Volcanoes add chlorine gas. These elements also make up most of the salt in seawater. If seawater evaporates, the sodium and chlorine combine to form a salt called halite. Halite is the salt you use to season food. It is this salt and similar ones that give ocean water its salty taste. ☑

Salinity (say LIH nuh tee) is a measure of the amount of salts dissolved in seawater. It is usually measured in grams of salt per kilogram of water. One kilogram of ocean water contains about 35 g of dissolved salts, or about 3.5 percent dissolved salts. The graph in **Figure 11-3** lists the most abundant salts in ocean water. The proportion and amount of dissolved salts in seawater remain nearly constant and have stayed about the same for hundreds of millions of years. This tells us that the composition of the oceans is in balance. Oceans are not growing saltier.

Element Removal

Although rivers, volcanoes, and the atmosphere constantly add substances to the ocean, the oceans are considered to be in a steady state. As new substances are added to the oceans, elements are being removed. They are removed by becoming sediment and by biological processes. Sea animals and algae use dissolved substances. Some marine animals use calcium to form bones. Other animals, such as oysters and clams, use calcium to form shells. Some algae, called diatoms, have silica shells. Because many organisms use calcium and silica, these substances are removed more quickly from seawater than substances such as chloride or sodium.

Desalination

Salt also can be removed from ocean water. The process that removes salt from ocean water is called desalination. If you have ever gone swimming in the ocean, you know what happens when your skin dries. The white, sticky substance on your skin is salt. As seawater evaporates, the salt is left behind. As the demand for freshwater increases throughout the world, scientists are developing technology to remove salt from seawater and make it drinkable. A desalination plant is shown in **Figure 11-4.** Some methods include evaporating the seawater and collecting the freshwater as it condenses on a glass roof. An electric current can be passed through the water to collect the salt. Also, frozen seawater can be separated into salt crystals and freshwater ice crystals.

The oceans originally formed from water vapor that condensed and fell as rain, then collected in basins. Volcanoes, groundwater, and rivers added salts and other elements to seawater, giving the oceans their compositions.

Figure 11-4 This desalination plant is in Saudi Arabia. **Which body of water do you think Saudi Arabia uses to make freshwater from salt water?** (Hint: Locate Saudi Arabia on a map.)

Section Assessment

1. According to scientific theory, how were Earth's oceans formed?

2. Why does ocean water taste salty?

3. How have ocean currents affected the distribution of plants and animals on Earth?

4. **Think Critically:** Why does the salinity of Earth's oceans remain constant?

5.  **Skill Builder**
   Concept Mapping Make a concept map that shows how halite becomes dissolved in the oceans. Use the terms *rivers, volcanoes, halite, source of, sodium, chlorine,* and *combine to form.* If you need help, refer to Concept Mapping in the **Skill Handbook** on page 698.

Science Journal What is happening in this excerpt from "The Rime of the Ancient Mariner" by S. T. Coleridge?

As idle as a painted ship
Upon a painted ocean.
Water, water, everywhere,
And all the boards did shrink;
Water, water, everywhere,
Nor any drop to drink.

Water, Water, Everywhere

Materials

- Pan balance
- Table salt
- Water (500 mL)
- Flask (1000 mL)
- Beaker (600 mL)
- Plastic spoon
- Hot plate
- Scissors
- Ice
- 1-hole rubber stopper with curved or bent plastic tubing
- Rubber tubing (60 cm)
- Cardboard sheet (12 cm^2)
- Metal washers (4–5)
- Shallow pan
- Watch glasses (2)

Imagine being stranded on an island. You're thirsty, but you can't find any freshwater. There's plenty of salt water. How can you remove the salts from the water so that you can drink it?

What You'll Investigate

How can you make freshwater from salt water?

Goals

- **Make a model** to demonstrate desalination.
- **Observe** and **infer** how desalination works.

Procedure

1. **Dissolve** 18 g of table salt in a beaker containing 500 mL of water. Use the spoon to thoroughly mix the saltwater solution.

2. **Pour** the solution into the flask. **Insert** the stopper into the flask. Make sure the plastic tubing is above the surface of the solution. Place the flask on the hot plate. Do not turn on the hot plate.

3. Use the scissors to cut a small hole in the piece of cardboard. **Insert** the free end of the rubber tubing through the hole. Be sure to keep the tubing away from the hot plate.

4. **Place** the cardboard over a clean beaker. Add several washers to the cardboard to hold it in place.

5. Set the beaker in a shallow pan filled with ice.

6. Turn on the hot plate. Bring the solution to a boil. **Observe** what happens in the flask and in the beaker.

7. Continue boiling until the solution is almost, but not quite, boiled away. Turn off the hot plate and let the water in the beaker cool.

8. **Measure** the volume of water in the beaker and the volume of salt water remaining in the flask.

9. **Pour** a small sample of water from the beaker into one watch glass and water from the flask into the other watch glass. **Evaporate** the water samples on the hot plate. **Observe** each sample.

Conclude and Apply

1. **Compare** the combined volumes of water in the beaker and flask with the volume of the salt water at the beginning. Are they the same? Explain.

2. **Explain** your results by drawing a diagram of the experiment. **Label** the processes involved.

Ocean Currents

Surface Currents

The ocean is always moving. A mass movement or flow of ocean water is called a current. When you stir chocolate flavoring into milk or stir a pot of soup, you make currents with the spoon. The currents are what mix the liquid. An ocean current is like a river within the ocean. It moves masses of water from place to place.

Ocean currents carry water in various directions. **Surface currents** move water horizontally—parallel to Earth's surface. Surface currents are powered by wind. The wind and the currents force the ocean to move in huge circular patterns all around the world. **Figure 11-5** shows these major surface currents. Surface currents in the ocean also are related to the general circulation of wind on Earth.

What You'll Learn

► How winds, the Coriolis effect, and continents influence surface currents
► The temperatures of coastal waters
► Density currents

Vocabulary
surface current
upwelling
density current

Why It's Important

► Ocean currents and atmosphere transfer heat to create the climate you live in.

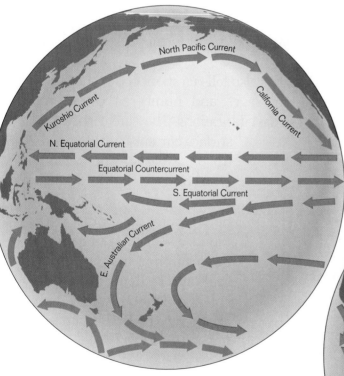

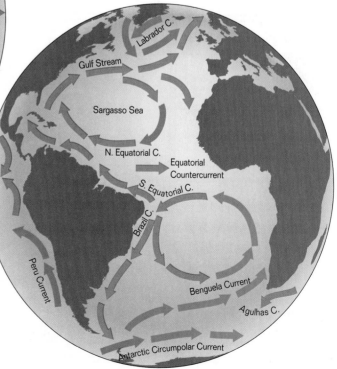

Figure 11-5 These are the major surface currents of Earth's oceans. Red arrows indicate a warm current. Blue arrows indicate a cold current.

Surface currents move only the upper few hundred meters of seawater. Seeds and plants are carried between continents by surface currents. Sailors use these currents along with winds to sail more efficiently from place to place. The Antarctic Circumpolar current is the strongest current in the ocean.

The Gulf Stream

Although satellites provide new information about ocean movements, much of what we know about surface currents comes from records that were kept by sailors in the nineteenth century. Sailors always have used surface currents to help them travel quickly. Sailing ships depend on one surface current to carry them west and another to carry them east. During the American colonial era, ships floated on the 100-km-wide Gulf Stream current to go quickly from North America to England. On the map in **Figure 11-5,** find the Gulf Stream current in the Atlantic Ocean.

In the late 1600s, the British explorer William Dampier first wrote about the Gulf Stream in his *Discoveries on the Trade Winds.* A century later, Benjamin Franklin published a map of the Gulf Stream that his cousin Captain Timothy Folger, a Massachusetts whaler, had drawn. This map is shown in **Figure 11-6.**

What washes up on beaches also tells us about ocean currents. Drift bottles containing messages and numbered cards are released from a variety of coastal locations. They are carried by surface currents and may end up on a beach. The person who finds a bottle writes down the date and the location where the bottle was found. Then, it is sent back to the institution that launched the bottle. By doing this, valuable information is provided about the current that carried the bottle.

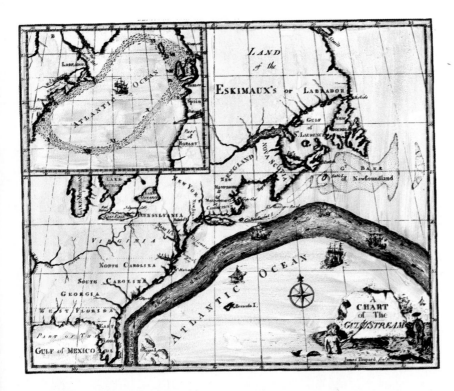

Figure 11-6 Captain Timothy Folger drew this map of the Gulf Stream around 1770.

Other Factors That Influence Surface Currents

Surface ocean currents and surface winds are affected by the Coriolis effect. The Coriolis effect is caused by the rotation of Earth. Imagine that you throw a ball straight up into the air. If it could stay up long enough and come straight back down, the ball would not return to you. Why? Because Earth has rotated while the ball was in flight. And, because you are standing on Earth, you have moved also. The same thing happens to wind. Although the wind may be blowing in a straight line, Earth's rotation causes the wind to be turned. It is turned clockwise in the northern hemisphere and counterclockwise in the southern hemisphere. Surface currents are produced by surface winds. As the surface winds are turned, so are the surface currents. The Coriolis effect turns currents north of the equator, such as the Gulf Stream, clockwise. Currents south of the equator are turned counterclockwise. Look again at the map of surface currents in **Figure 11-5.**

The continents also influence ocean currents. Notice that currents moving toward the west in the Pacific Ocean are turned north and south by Asia and Australia. Then, currents affected by the Coriolis effect move eastward until North and South America turn them. According to the map in **Figure 11-5,** what other surface currents are turned by continents?

Why are surface currents important?

Currents on the west coast of continents are usually cold, but currents on eastern coasts are warm. West coast currents begin near the poles where the waters are colder. East coast currents originate near the equator where the water is warmer. **Figure 11-7** shows the warm waters of the Gulf Stream. How do warm and cold surface currents affect the east and west coasts of the United States?

Surface currents distribute heat from equatorial regions to other areas of Earth. As warm waters flow away from the equator, heat is released to the atmosphere. The atmosphere is warmed. This transfer of heat influences climate.

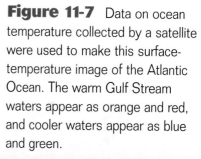

*inter*NET
CONNECTION

Visit the Glencoe Science Web Site at **www. glencoe.com/sec/ science** for more information about ocean currents.

Figure 11-7 Data on ocean temperature collected by a satellite were used to make this surface-temperature image of the Atlantic Ocean. The warm Gulf Stream waters appear as orange and red, and cooler waters appear as blue and green.

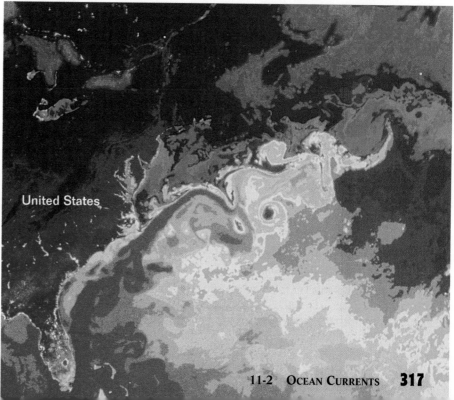

United States

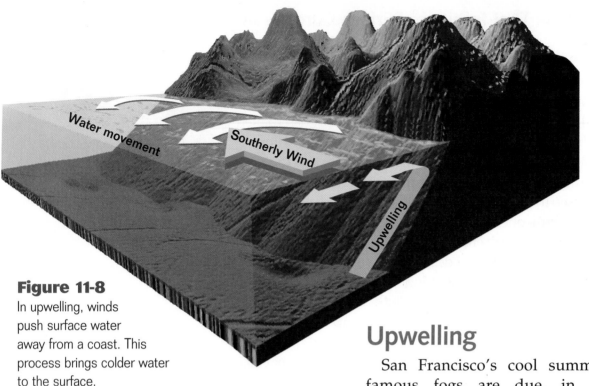

Figure 11-8
In upwelling, winds push surface water away from a coast. This process brings colder water to the surface.

Upwelling

San Francisco's cool summers and famous fogs are due, in part, to upwelling. **Upwelling** is a circulation in the ocean that brings deep, cold water to the ocean surface. Wind blowing offshore or parallel to the coast carries water away from the land as shown in **Figure 11-8.** Cold, deep ocean water rises to the surface and replaces the water that has been blown away. This water contains high concentrations of nutrients from organisms that died, sank to the bottom, and decayed. These nutrients bring fish to areas of upwelling along the coasts of Oregon, Washington, and Peru, which are known as good fishing areas. Upwelling also affects the climate of nearby coastal areas.

Density Currents

Wind-driven surface currents affect only the upper layers of Earth's oceans. Deep in the ocean, waters circulate not because of wind but because of density differences.

A **density current** forms when more dense seawater sinks under less dense seawater. This movement pushes surface ocean water deeper into the ocean.

Try at Home

Mini Lab

Modeling a Density Current

Procedure

1. Fill a clear, plastic storage box (shoe box size) with room-temperature water.

2. Mix several teaspoons of table salt into an 8-ounce glass of water at room temperature.

3. Add a few drops of food coloring to the salt-water solution. Pour the solution slowly into the freshwater in the large container.

Analyze

1. Describe what happened when you added salt water to freshwater. Explain.

2. How does this lab relate to density currents?

You made a density current in the Explore Activity at the beginning of this chapter. The cold water was more dense than the warm water in the beaker. The cold water sank to the bottom. This created a density current that moved the food coloring.

The density of seawater can be increased by an increase in salinity or by a decrease in temperature. Changes in temperature, salinity, and pressure work together to create density currents. Density currents circulate ocean water slowly. ✔

An important density current occurs in Antarctica where the most dense ocean water forms during the winter. As ice forms, seawater freezes, but the salt is left behind in the unfrozen water. This extra salt increases the density of the ocean water until it is very dense. This dense water sinks and slowly spreads along the ocean bottom toward the equator, forming a density current. In the Pacific Ocean, this water may take 1000 years to reach the surface at the equator. In the Atlantic Ocean, dense surface waters that sink circulate more quickly. In the Atlantic, a density current may take 275 years to bring water from the bottom to the surface.

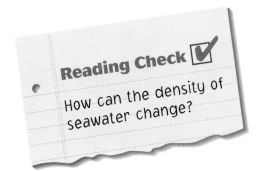

Reading Check ✔

How can the density of seawater change?

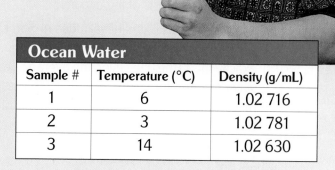

Problem Solving

Interpreting Ocean Temperatures

Imagine that your job is to analyze the data shown in the chart below. The data were collected from three different water masses in the North Atlantic Ocean. You know that one sample came from near the surface, one came from a depth of 750 m, and a third came from the ocean floor. The samples are not labeled and became mixed up in shipment.

Solve the Problem

1. Which sample came from near the surface? How do you know?

2. Which sample of water came from the bottom? How do you know?

3. Hypothesize how less dense seawater can be colder than denser seawater.

Ocean Water		
Sample #	Temperature (°C)	Density (g/mL)
1	6	1.02 716
2	3	1.02 781
3	14	1.02 630

Think Critically: During El Niño, the surface winds blow toward South America. How do you think the usual upwelling near Peru is affected?

Figure 11-9 Surface currents in the ocean carry objects from long distances. In May 1991, thousands of sneakers washed up on Oregon beaches. The North Pacific drift and California current had carried 80 000 new shoes from the site of a shipping accident a year earlier in the mid-Pacific and deposited them on the western edge of the United States.

A density current also occurs in the Mediterranean, a nearly enclosed sea. Warm temperatures evaporate water from the surface, increasing the salinity and the density of the water. This dense water from the Mediterranean flows into the less dense water of the Atlantic Ocean. When it reaches the Atlantic, it flows deeper in a density current.

Our knowledge has come a long way since early investigations of the Gulf Stream. Today, we can track ocean currents by objects that wash up on shore as shown in **Figure 11-9** and by satellite. This information helps ships navigate, fishing fleets locate upwellings, and us to understand climate and track hurricanes.

Section Assessment

1. How does the energy from wind affect surface currents?

2. How do density currents affect the circulation of water in deep parts of the oceans?

3. **Think Critically:** The latitudes of San Diego, California, and Charleston, South Carolina, are exactly the same. However, the average yearly water temperature in the ocean off Charleston is much higher than the water temperature off San Diego. Why?

4. **Skill Builder**
   Predicting A river flows into the ocean. Predict what will happen to this layer of freshwater. Explain your prediction. If you need help, refer to Predicting in the **Skill Handbook** on page 714.

Using Computers

Spreadsheet Make a spreadsheet that compares surface and density currents. Focus on characteristics such as wind, horizontal and vertical movement, temperature, and density. If you need help, refer to page 722.

Ocean Waves and Tides

Waves

If you've been to the seashore or seen a beach on TV, you've watched waves roll in. Waves in water are caused by winds, earthquakes, and the gravitational force of the moon and sun. You have probably heard about ocean waves or tsunamis that are caused by earthquakes. But, what is an ocean wave? A **wave** is a rhythmic movement that carries energy through matter or space. In the ocean, waves move through seawater.

Several terms are used to describe waves. **Figure 11-10** shows that the **crest** is the highest point of a wave. The **trough** (TROF) is the lowest point. Wave height is the vertical distance between crest and trough. Wavelength is the horizontal distance between the crests or troughs of two waves.

Wave Movement

When you watch an ocean wave, it looks as though the water is moving forward. But, unless the wave is breaking onto shore, the water itself does not move forward. Each molecule of water stays in about the same place as the wave passes. **Figure 11-11** shows this. To see another example of a wave carrying energy, tie a rope to a tree. Shake the rope up and down until a wave starts across it. Notice that as the

What You'll Learn

▶ Wave formation
▶ How water particles move in a wave and how wave energy moves
▶ How ocean tides form

Vocabulary

wave	breaker
crest	tide
trough	tidal range

Why It's Important

▶ Waves and tides influence how we use oceans and affect life in coastal areas.

Figure 11-10 The crest, trough, wavelength, and wave height are parts of a wave. **What other types of waves have you learned about?**

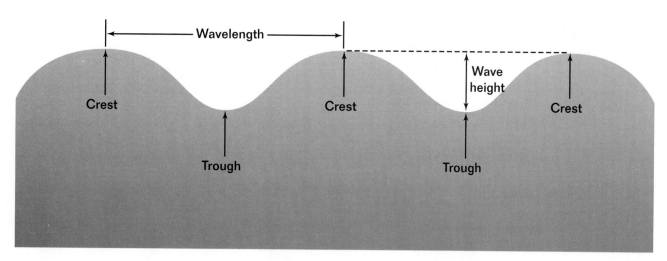

energy passes along the rope, the rope moves. But, each piece of rope is still the same distance from the tree.

In the same way, an object floating on water will rise and fall as a wave passes, but the object will not move forward. Only the energy moves forward, while the water particles remain in the same place.

A wave changes shape in the shallow area near shore. Friction with the ocean bottom slows water at the bottom of the wave. As the wave slows, its crest and trough come closer together. The wave height increases. The top of a wave, not slowed by friction, moves faster than the bottom. Eventually, the top of the wave outruns the bottom and collapses. The wave crest falls, and water tumbles over on itself. The wave breaks onto the shore. **Figure 11-12** illustrates this process. This collapsing wave is a **breaker.** It is the collapse of this wave that propels a surfer and surfboard onto shore. After a wave breaks onto shore, gravity pulls the water back into the sea. ☑

Reading Check
What causes an ocean wave to slow down?

VISUALIZING Waves

Figure 11-11 In a wave, individual particles of water move in circles as the energy passes through.

Direction of wave

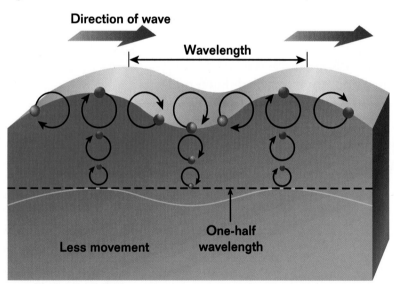

Wavelength

One-half wavelength

Less movement

Little water movement occurs below a depth equal to one-half wavelength.

A Particles of water in a wave move around in circles. The farther below the surface, the smaller the circles are. Below a depth equal to about half the wavelength, particle movement stops.

B Wave energy moves forward somewhat like the motion of falling dominoes. Like water particles, individual dominoes remain near where they were standing as they fall, transferring energy to the next domino.

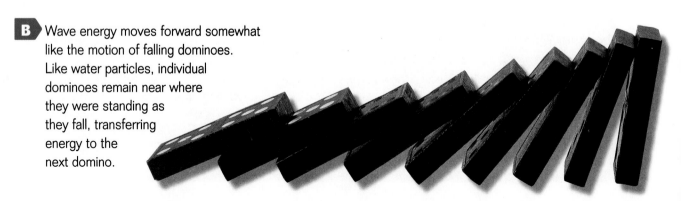

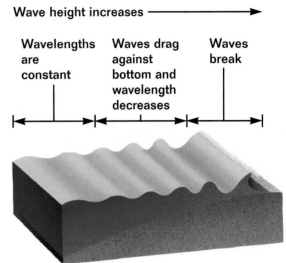

Wave height increases ⟶

| Wavelengths are constant | Waves drag against bottom and wavelength decreases | Waves break |

Figure 11-12 Wavelength decreases and wave height increases as waves approach the shore. This causes breakers to form.

There are two different types of ocean waves—the common sea waves caused by wind and the long waves of the tides.

Waves Caused by Wind

When wind blows across a body of water, friction causes the water to move along with the wind. If the wind speed is great enough, the water begins to pile up, forming a wave. As the wind continues to blow, the wave increases in height. The height of waves depends on the speed of the wind, the distance over which the wind blows, and the length of time the wind blows. When the wind stops blowing, waves stop forming. But, once set in motion, waves continue moving for long distances even if the wind stops. Waves at a seashore may have originated halfway around the world.

Modeling Water Movement in a Wave

Procedure

1. Put a piece of tape on the outside bottom of a clear, rectangular, plastic storage box. Fill the box with water.
2. Float a cork in the container above the piece of tape.
3. Use a spoon to make gentle waves in the container.
4. Observe the movement of the waves and the cork.

Analysis

1. Describe the movement of the waves and the motion of the cork.
2. Compare the movement of the cork with the movement of water particles in a wave.

Tides

Have you ever been to the beach and noticed the level of the sea rise and fall during the day? This rise and fall in sea level is called a **tide.** A tide is caused by a giant wave. This wave is only 1 m or 2 m high but thousands of kilometers long. As the crest of this wave approaches the shore, sea level appears to rise. This is called high tide. A few hours later, as the trough of the wave approaches, sea level appears to drop. This is referred to as low tide.

One low-tide–high-tide cycle takes 12 hours and 25 minutes. A daily cycle of two high and two low tides occurs in most places and takes 24 hours and 50 minutes—slightly more than a day. The **tidal range** is the difference between the level of the ocean at high tide and low tide. Notice the tidal range in the photos of **Figure 11-13.**

The Gravitational Effect of the Moon

For the most part, these tides are caused by the interaction of gravity in the Earth-moon system. The moon's gravity exerts a strong pull on Earth. The water in the oceans responds to this pull. The water is pulled outward as Earth and the moon revolve around a common center of mass between them. These events are explained in **Figure 11-14.**

Two bulges of water form, one at the point closest to the moon and one on the exact opposite side of Earth. As Earth spins, these bulges follow the moon. To the earthbound observer, these bulges appear as waves traveling across the oceans. The crests of the waves are the high tides.

As Earth rotates, different locations on Earth's surface pass through high and low tide. The change between high and low tide is different across the world. Near the equator, where the water is spread out over a large area, the difference in high and low tide is hardly noticeable. But, as seen in **Figure 11-13,** water in a smaller area experiences a much larger tidal range.

The Gravitational Effect of the Sun

The sun also affects tides. The sun can strengthen or weaken the moon's effects. When the moon, Earth, and sun are lined up together, they cause spring tides. During spring tides, high tides are higher and low tides are lower than normal. When the sun, Earth, and moon form a right angle, high tides are lower and low tides are higher than normal. These are called neap tides.

Figure 11-13 The large difference between high and low tide is seen at Mt. Saint Michel off the northwestern coast of France on a summer day.

A High tide at 6 A.M.

B Low tide at 6:25 P.M.

Figure 11-14 (A) The moon doesn't really revolve around Earth. They both revolve around a common center of mass. The action of the moon and Earth around the common center causes the bulge of water on the side of Earth opposite the moon. The bulge of water on the side of Earth nearest the moon is caused by the moon's gravity exerting a force on Earth. (B) When the sun, moon, and Earth are aligned, spring tides occur. (C) When the sun, moon, and Earth form a right angle, neap tides occur.

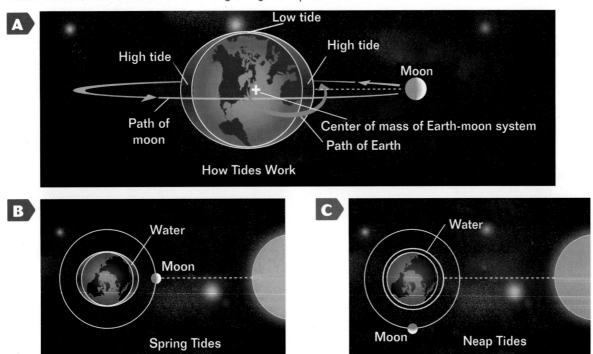

In this section, you've learned how the energy of the wind causes the formation of surface waves. You've also learned how gravity affects the motion of the ocean, with help from Earth, the moon, and sun on the longest waves—tides.

Section Assessment

1. Describe the parts of an ocean wave.
2. What causes high tides?
3. **Think Critically:** At the ocean, you spot a wave about 200 m from shore. A few seconds later, the wave breaks on the beach. Explain why the water in the breaker is not the same water that was in the wave 200 m away.
4. **Skill Builder**
   Comparing and Contrasting To learn more about tides, do the **Chapter 11 Skill Activity** on page 736.

Using Math

The crest of a wave is 35 m above the ocean floor. The trough of a wave is 28 m above the ocean floor. Calculate the wave height.

Making Waves

Wind helps generate some waves. The energy of motion is transferred from the wind to the surface water of the ocean. The force of the wind affects the waves that are created. What other factors influence the generation of waves?

What You'll Investigate

How does the speed of the wind and the length of time it blows affect the height of a wave?

Materials

- White paper (11" × 14")
- Electric fan (three-speed)
- Light source
- Clock or watch
- Rectangular, clear-plastic storage box
- Ring stand with clamp
- Water
- Metric ruler

Goals

- **Observe** how wind speed and duration affect wave height.

Procedure

1. **Position** the box on white paper beside the ring stand.

2. **Clamp** a light source on the ring stand or use a gooseneck lamp. Direct the light onto the box. Fill the plastic box with water to within 3 cm of the top. **CAUTION:** *Do not allow any part of the light or cord to come in contact with the water.*

3. **Place** the fan at one end of the box to create waves. Start on slow. Keep the fan on during measuring. **CAUTION:** *Do not allow any part of the fan or cord to come in contact with the water.*

4. After three minutes, **measure** the height of the waves caused by the fan. **Record** your observations in a table similar to the one shown. Through the plastic box, **observe** the shadows of the waves on the white paper.

5. After five minutes, **measure** the wave height and **record** your observations.

6. Repeat steps 3 to 5 with the fan on medium, then on high.

7. Turn off the fan. Observe what happens.

Conclude and Apply

1. **Analyze** your data to determine whether the wave height is affected by the length of time that the wind blows. Explain.

2. **Analyze** your data to determine whether the height of the waves is affected by the speed of the wind. Explain.

3. **Infer** how wave energy could be used to reduce Earth's dependence on its decreasing supply of fossil fuels.

Wave Data			
Fan speed	Time	Wave height	Observations
Low			
Medium			
High			

Tidal Power

Are you looking for an energy supply that just won't quit? Try harnessing tides. Tides are the movement of Earth's oceans primarily in response to the gravitational pull of the moon. At high tide, the water is pulled toward shore. At low tide, it is pulled away. Tidal range is a measure of the difference in water level at low tide and at high tide. The Bay of Fundy in eastern Canada boasts the greatest tidal range on Earth—16 m. This immense range makes the Bay of Fundy a perfect place to tap the energy of the tides. In the early 1980s, the Canadian government built a pilot power-generating plant there (left).

Tidal Dams

Tidal power is harnessed by tidal dams. At high tide, the gates of the dam open to let water enter. Then, the gates close, storing the water behind the dam. As the tide goes out, the dammed-up water is passed over turbines in the dam. The turbines contain blades similar to those of a fan. When the water pushes against the blades, the turbines spin and generate electricity.

Electric power-generating plants that use tidal power also have been built in Russia, China, and France. The largest tidal power plant constructed so far is located on the Rance River in France. It provides enough power for the region of Brittany and surrounding areas (about the size of the state of Kentucky).

Generating electric power using tides has many advantages. Tidal energy does not run out. There are no expenses for fuel, pollution control, or waste disposal. The cost of the power to customers is relatively low.

Possible Problems

Building a tidal dam is expensive, and tidal dams don't always produce electricity at times of peak demand because the electricity can't be stored. Tidal dams can cause environmental problems such as loss of habitat for shorebirds and fish. Also, boating can be affected if water becomes too shallow due to dam operation.

*inter*NET CONNECTION

Visit the Glencoe Science Web Site at **www.glencoe.com/sec/science** to research the latest development in the Bay of Fundy project. Has a larger plant been built? How much power is the current one generating? Have there been environmental consequences?

For a **preview** of this chapter, study this Reviewing Main Ideas before you read the chapter. After you have studied this chapter, you can use the Reviewing Main Ideas to **review** the chapter.

The Glencoe MindJogger, Audiocassettes, and CD-ROM provide additional opportunities for review.

Section 11-1 ORIGIN OF OCEANS

The oceans are an important feature of Earth; they provide habitat for many organisms, and food and transportation for humans. The oceans are a mix of water and dissolved salts in constant motion. Water that fills Earth's oceans may have started as water vapor released from volcanoes. Over millions of years, the water vapor condensed and rain fell, forming the oceans. *How does early Earth's volcanic activity compare to today's activity?*

OCEAN SALTS

Ocean water is salty because groundwater and rivers dissolve elements from rocks on land and release them into the water. Once in the oceans, these elements combine chemically with the elements released from underwater volcanoes. *What kind of salt makes up nearly 90 percent of the salt in the ocean?*

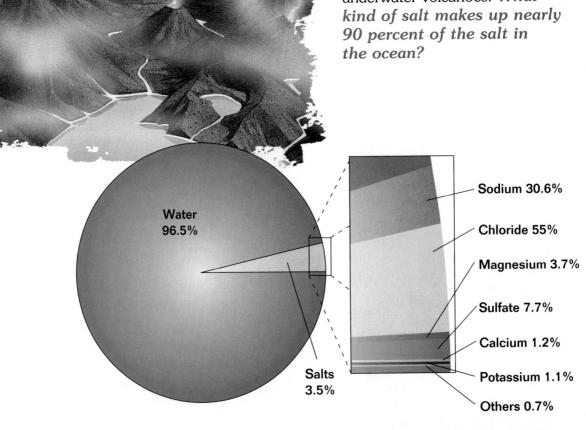

Water 96.5%

Salts 3.5%

Sodium 30.6%

Chloride 55%

Magnesium 3.7%

Sulfate 7.7%

Calcium 1.2%

Potassium 1.1%

Others 0.7%

North Pacific Current
Kuroshio Current
California Current
N. Equatorial Current
Equatorial Countercurrent
S. Equatorial Current
E. Australian Current

Labrador C.
Gulf Stream
Sargasso Sea
N. Equatorial C.
Equatorial Countercurrent
S. Equatorial C.
Brazil C.
Peru Current
Benguela Current
Agulhas C.
Antarctic Circumpolar Current

Reading Check ✓

Write three generalizations about the ocean. Exchange them with a partner and discuss whether each other's generalizations are accurate.

Section
11-2 SURFACE CURRENTS

Friction between air and the ocean's surface causes **surface currents.** Surface currents are affected by the Coriolis effect. Currents are also deflected by landmasses. Surface currents can greatly affect climate and economic activity, such as fishing. Ocean transportation is also affected by surface currents. *Why are some currents cold, while others are warm?*

DEEP-WATER CURRENTS

Differences in temperatures and densities between water masses in the oceans set up circulation patterns called **density currents.** *How do density currents originate in the Mediterranean Sea?*

Section
11-3 WAVES

A **wave** is a rhythmic movement that carries energy. The **crest** is the highest point of the wave. The **trough** is the lowest point. Energy moves forward while water particles move in place. Wind causes most water waves, but **tides** are not caused by wind. *What causes tides?*

Chapter 11 Assessment

Using Vocabulary

a. basin
b. breaker
c. crest
d. density current
e. salinity
f. surface current
g. tidal range
h. tide
i. trough
j. upwelling
k. wave

Answer the following questions using complete sentences.

1. Explain the difference between a surface current and a density current.
2. How are breakers and crests related?
3. How is a tide like a wave?
4. Describe the relationship between rivers and a basin.
5. What does *salinity* mean?

Checking Concepts

Choose the word or phrase that best answers the question.

6. Where might ocean water have originated?
   A) salt marshes
   B) volcanoes
   C) basins
   D) surface currents

7. What causes chlorine gas to enter the oceans?
   A) volcanoes   C) density currents
   B) rivers   D) groundwater

8. What is the most common ocean element?
   A) chloride   C) boron
   B) calcium   D) sulfate

9. What causes most surface currents?
   A) density differences
   B) the Gulf Stream
   C) salinity
   D) wind

10. What is the highest point on a wave called?
    A) wave height   C) crest
    B) trough   D) wavelength

11. In the ocean, what are movements in which water alternately rises and falls called?
    A) currents   C) crests
    B) waves   D) upwellings

12. How long is the cycle of one low tide and one high tide?
    A) 12 hours
    B) 24 hours
    C) 12 hours, 25 minutes
    D) 24 hours, 50 minutes

13. The Coriolis effect causes currents in the northern hemisphere to turn in which direction?
    A) eastward   C) counterclockwise
    B) southward   D) clockwise

14. Tides are affected by the positions of which celestial bodies?
    A) Earth and the moon
    B) Earth, the moon, and the sun
    C) Venus, Earth, and Mars
    D) the sun, Earth, and Mars

15. What affects surface currents?
    A) crests   C) the Coriolis effect
    B) upwellings   D) calcium

Thinking Critically

16. Describe the position of the moon and sun when a low tide is higher than normal.

17. Halite makes up nearly 90 percent of the salt in ocean water. How much halite is found in 1000 kg of ocean water?

18. Why do silica and calcium remain in seawater for a shorter time than sodium?

19. Describe the Antarctic density current.

20. How might the use of fertilizers on farm crops affect the composition of the oceans?

Developing Skills

If you need help, refer to the **Skill Handbook.**

21. **Recognizing Cause and Effect:** What causes upwelling? What effect does it have? When upwelling disappears from an area, what effect can this have?

22. **Comparing and Contrasting:** Compare and contrast ocean waves and ocean currents.

23. **Interpreting Data:** Refer to the graph below. On what day(s) is the high tide highest? Lowest? On what day(s) is the low tide lowest? Highest? On which day would Earth, the moon, and the sun be lined up? On which day would the moon, Earth, and the sun form a right angle?

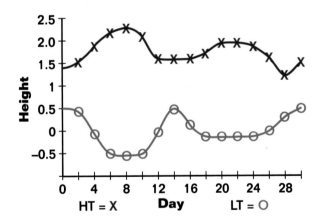

HT = X   **Day**   LT = O

24. **Recognizing Cause and Effect:** In the Mediterranean Sea, a density current forms because of the high rate of evaporation of water from the surface. Explain how evaporation can lead to the formation of a density current.

THE PRINCETON REVIEW

Test-Taking Tip

Take Five and Stay Sharp Wanting to perform well on your exam is good. But, if you take it too seriously, you'll actually end up hurting your chances for a good score. Remember to take frequent, short breaks in your studies to keep your mind fresh.

Test Practice

Use these questions to test your Science Proficiency.

1. When a wave enters shallow water, what happens?

   A) Its crest and trough come closer together, and the wave height increases.

   B) Its crest and trough get farther apart, and the wave height increases.

   C) Its wavelength gets longer, and the wave height increases.

   D) Its wavelength gets shorter, and the wave height decreases.

2. The table below shows the high and low tides on four different beaches on the same day. Which beach experienced the greatest tidal range on this day?

Beach	High tide in meters	Low tide in meters
Glomar	2.3	1.4
Travelers	1.8	−0.4
Station	5.2	4.1
State	3.0	−0.6

   A) Glomar   C) Station

   B) Travelers   D) State

12 Oceanography

Chapter Preview

Skills Preview

Skill Builders
- Use Variables
- Identify Constants and Controls

Activities
- Make and Use a Graph
- Interpret Data

MiniLabs
- Make Inferences
- Observe

Reading Check ✔

When you come to a word you don't know, it's best to not skip over it. Look it up in a dictionary. Then reread the sentence it was in to fully understand its meaning.

Explore Activity

Deep under the oceans' waters lies another sort of landscape called the ocean floor. Numerous and different communities of organisms live deep in the ocean. Scientists were not aware of some communities of organisms until Alvin, a submersible, began exploring the ocean bottom in 1963. How do submersibles like Nautile, shown here, dive and surface in the oceans?

Model a Submersible

1. Fill a 2-L plastic soda bottle three-quarters full of water.

2. Draw water into a dropper. Leave some air in the dropper and place it in the plastic bottle, bulb end up. The top of the dropper should barely float.

3. Put a cap on the bottle, then gently squeeze the sides of the bottle.

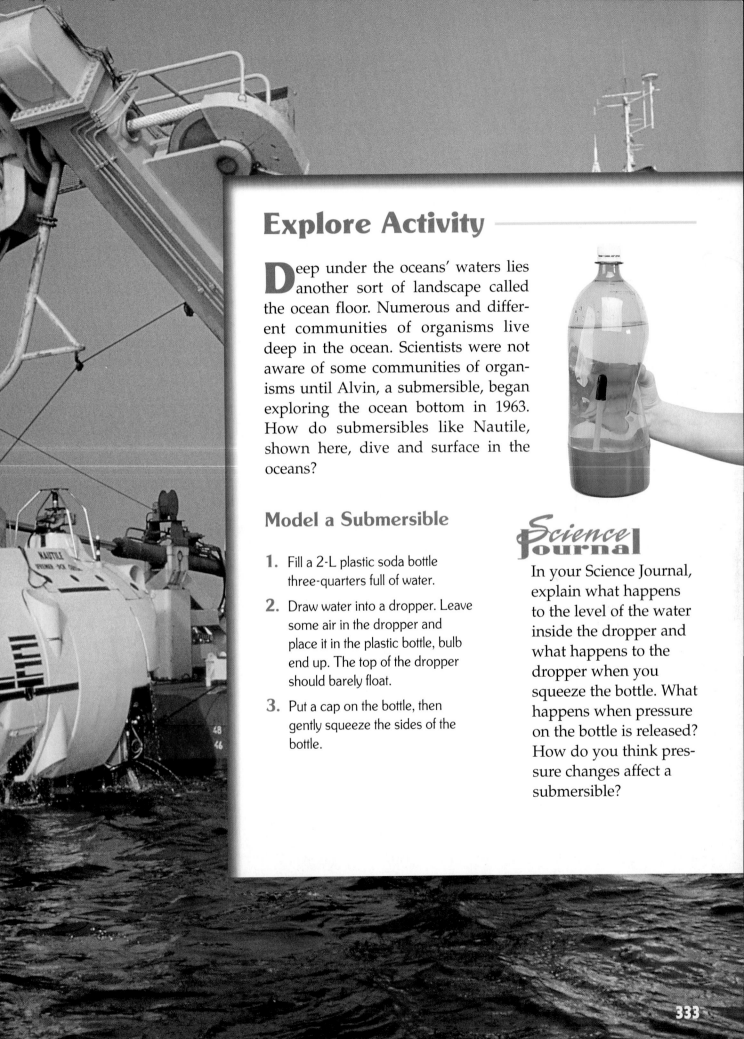

Science Journal

In your Science Journal, explain what happens to the level of the water inside the dropper and what happens to the dropper when you squeeze the bottle. What happens when pressure on the bottle is released? How do you think pressure changes affect a submersible?

Ocean Basin Features

You can find the biggest mountains, the deepest valleys, and the flattest plains on Earth not on land but at the bottom of the oceans. In this chapter, you'll learn how the mountains, valleys, and plains on the oceans' bottoms differ from those on the continents. **Figure 12-1** shows major features of the ocean basins.

Beyond the ocean shoreline is the continental shelf. The **continental shelf** is a gradually sloping end of a continent that extends out under the ocean. Along some coasts, the continental shelf extends a long distance. For instance, on North America's Atlantic and Gulf coasts, it extends 100 km

Figure 12-1 This map shows the features of the ocean basins: the continental shelf, mountain ranges, trenches, valleys, and plains. **Locate a trench and locate the Mid-Atlantic Ridge.**

to 350 km into the sea. But, on the Pacific Coast, where mountains are close to the shore, the shelf is only 10 to 30 km wide. The ocean covering the shelf varies from a few centimeters to about 150 m deep. As you will see, the continental shelf resembles a flat shelf.

At the end of the continental shelf is the continental slope. The **continental slope** is the end of the continent extending from the outer edge of the continental shelf down to the ocean floor. The continental slope is steeper than the continental shelf. Beyond the continental slope lie the trenches, valleys, plains, and ridges of the ocean basin.

In the ocean, currents flow along the continental shelves and down the slopes, depositing sediment on the seafloor. These deposits fill in valleys and create flat, seafloor areas called **abyssal** (uh BIHS ul) **plains.** Abyssal plains are from 4000 km to 6000 km below the ocean surface. Abyssal plains can be seen in several places on the map below.

PHYSICS INTEGRATION

Buoyancy
Buoyant force is the upward force of fluid on an object within the fluid. If an object is sinking in the ocean, infer which is greater: the buoyant force being exerted on it or the force of gravity upon it.

*inter*NET CONNECTION

Visit the Glencoe Science Web Site at **www.glencoe.com/ sec/science** to learn more about the ocean basin.

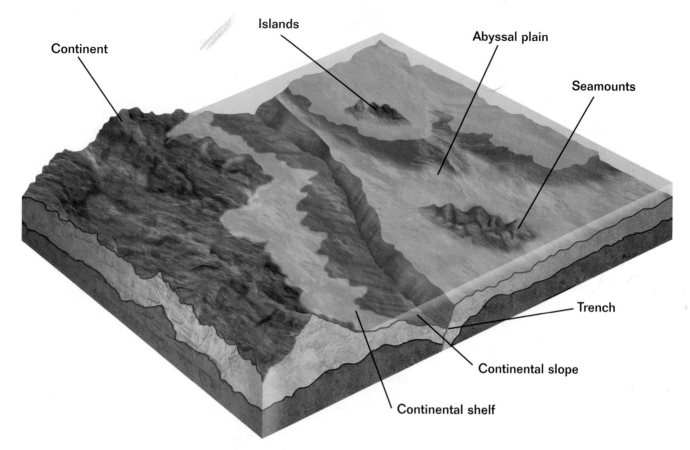

Continent

Islands

Abyssal plain

Seamounts

Trench

Continental slope

Continental shelf

Figure 12-2 Ocean basin features are continuous from shore to shore. (Features in this diagram are not to scale.) **Interpret where the continental shelf ends and the continental slope begins. Where would the mid-ocean ridge be located?**

Reading Check ✔

What are seamounts?

Plate Boundary Structures

The ocean floor map in **Figure 12-1** shows structures related to plate movements occurring on the seafloor. Some crustal plates under the ocean are separating. Where these plates separate, new crust forms. Some plates on the ocean floor are converging, which means coming together. At convergent boundaries, old ocean crust slides beneath other crust and is destroyed.

The location where new ocean floor forms is called a **mid-ocean ridge.** A mid-ocean ridge is a chain of underwater mountains. New crust forms along the mid-ocean ridge as a result of volcanic eruptions. In addition, molten lava moves up through cracks called rifts. Magma from Earth's interior oozes from these rifts. When the lava hits the water, it cools quickly into solid rock and forms new seafloor.

Seamounts, shown in **Figure 12-2,** are volcanic cones found on the ocean floor. Some scientists hypothesize that these old volcanoes erupted on mid-ocean ridges where new crust formed. As the new crust moved further from the ridge, the seamounts moved with it. After millions of years, the volcanoes became inactive. Seamounts that extend up out of the ocean are volcanic islands. ✔

On the ocean floor, crustal plates converge at trenches. A **trench** is a long, narrow, steep-sided depression in the ocean floor where one crustal plate is forced beneath another. Most trenches are found in the Pacific Basin. Oceanic trenches are usually longer and deeper than any valley on any continent. The Marianas Trench, the deepest place in the Pacific, is 11 km deep. The Grand Canyon is only 1.6 km deep. A comparison of the height of Mt. Everest and the depth of the Marianas Trench is shown in **Figure 12-3.**

Not only are trenches the deepest places on Earth, they are also the most geologically active. Earthquakes and chains of volcanoes often occur along trenches.

Height of Mt. Everest

11 000 m

8848 m

Depth of Trench

Figure 12-3 If Earth's tallest mountain, Mt. Everest, were set in the bottom of the Marianas Trench of the Pacific Basin, it would be covered with more than 2000 m of water.

Mining the Seafloor

People have always collected salt from ocean water. About one third of all table salt used to season food comes from the sea. Now, we also obtain oil and gas from under the sea.

Continental Shelf Deposits

Many petroleum and natural gas deposits are in continental shelf sediments. To pump these substances to the surface, drills are attached to floating vessels and fixed platforms. Approximately 20 percent of the world's oil comes from under the seabed.

Sometimes even the energy of ocean waves is not strong enough to carry the heavier mineral grains that have been brought in by rivers. When this occurs, the grains sink to the ocean floor. These deposits, called placer deposits, can occur in coastal regions where rivers entering the ocean suddenly slow down. Sand, metals, and even diamonds are mined from placer deposits in some coastal regions.

Try at Home

Mini Lab

Interpreting Ocean Basin Maps

Procedure
1. Use **Figure 12-1.**
2. Trace a mid-ocean ridge with your finger.
3. Observe the width of the continental shelves at various locations around the world.

Analysis
1. Locate a trench and give its approximate longitude and latitude. (Hint: Look at a world map.)
2. Describe the continental shelves of Australia and Alaska.

Deep-Water Deposits

As molten substances and hot water are forced into cool ocean water through holes and cracks along ridges, chimneys of mineral deposits sometimes form. Today, no one is trying to mine these minerals from the depths because it would be too expensive. But, in the future, these deposits may become important.

In addition to these deposits, minerals that are dissolved in ocean water precipitate out and form solids on the ocean floor. Manganese nodules are small, black lumps scattered across 20 to 50 percent of the Pacific Basin. **Figure 12-4** shows examples of these nodules. Manganese nodules form around nuclei such as discarded sharks' teeth. They grow slowly, perhaps as little as 1 mm to 10 mm per million years. These nodules are rich in manganese, nickel, and cobalt, all of which are used to manufacture steel, paint, and batteries. Most of the nodules lie thousands of meters deep in the ocean and are not currently being mined by industry, although suction devices similar to huge vacuum cleaners have been tested to collect them.

In this section, you've learned about the features of ocean basins and how they relate to seafloor spreading and seafloor disappearance. You've also been introduced to the idea of seafloor mining. In the next section, you'll learn about organisms that live in the oceans.

Figure 12-4 These manganese nodules were collected from the floor of the Pacific Ocean.

Section Assessment

1. Compare and contrast ocean ridges and trenches.
2. How do placer deposits form? What are some examples of placer deposits that are mined?
3. What types of geologic activity occur at mid-ocean ridges?
4. **Think Critically:** If sea level rises significantly because of global warming, how will continental shelf regions be affected?
5. **Skill Builder**
   Interpreting Data To learn how oceanographers determine the depth of the ocean, complete the **Chapter 12 Skill Activity** on page 737.

Using Math

After doing Activity 12-1 on the next page, use the data to calculate the average depth of the Atlantic Ocean floor along the 39°N latitude line. Does this mean that most of the ocean floor is at this average depth? Explain.

Activity 12·1

The Ups and Downs of the Ocean Floor

Materials

• Graph paper
• Pencil

Data on depth of the oceans have been collected using sonar. In this activity, you will use these data to profile the floor of the Atlantic Ocean at 39° N latitude. You'll begin at the New Jersey coast and move eastward.

What You'll Investigate

What does the ocean floor look like?

Goals

• **Graph** a profile of the ocean floor.
• **Identify** ocean-floor structures from their profiles.

Procedure

1. **Draw** a graph as shown below.

2. **Plot** the data listed in the table. Connect the points with a smooth line.

3. **Color** the ocean bottom brown and the water blue.

Conclude and Apply

1. What ocean-floor structures occur between 160 km and 1050 km east of New Jersey? Between 2000 km and 4500 km? Between 5300 km and 5600 km?

2. When a profile of a feature is drawn to scale, both the horizontal and vertical scales must be the same. Does your profile give an accurate picture of the ocean floor? **Explain.**

Ocean Depth Data		
Station Number	Distance from New Jersey (km)	Depth to Ocean Floor (m)
1	0	0
2	160	165
3	200	1800
4	500	3500
5	800	4600
6	1050	5450
7	1450	5100
8	1800	5300
9	2000	5600
10	2300	4750
11	2400	3500
12	2600	3100
13	3000	4300
14	3200	3900
15	3450	3400
16	3550	2100
17	3600	1330
18	3700	1275
19	3950	1000
20	4000	0
21	4100	1800
22	4350	3650
23	4500	5100
24	5000	5000
25	5300	4200
26	5450	1800
27	5500	920
28	5600	180
29	5650	0

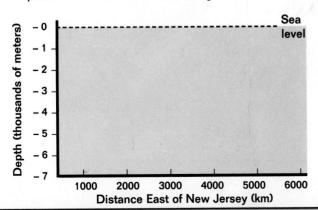

12·2 Life in the Ocean

Life Processes in the Ocean

You live on land. Your basic needs for water, energy, and food are met in your environment. This is also true of organisms that live in the ocean. A saltwater environment provides the vital necessities of life for marine organisms, such as the lionfish shown in **Figure 12-5.**

Water

All life on Earth is water based. Life began in the oceans. Organisms need water for processes that take place in cells. Water is used for all the basic processes of living things, such as digestion and cellular respiration.

Energy Relationships

Nearly all the energy used by organisms in the ocean ultimately comes from the sun. Radiant energy from the sun penetrates seawater and is trapped by chlorophyll-containing organisms in the ocean. Like chlorophyll-containing land plants, these organisms capture the sun's energy and make food using light energy, carbon dioxide, and water. This process of food making is called **photosynthesis.** Organisms that undergo photosynthesis are called producers. Organisms that feed on producers are called consumers.

Figure 12-5 A lionfish swims through the warm waters above a Pacific Ocean reef. **How does the appearance of this fish help it to survive?**

Throughout the ocean, energy from the sun is transferred through food chains. Although the organisms of the ocean capture only a small part of the sun's energy, this energy is passed from producer to consumer to other consumers. In **Figure 12-6,** notice that in one food chain, a large blue whale consumes small organisms, such as krill, as its basic food. In the other chain, phytoplankton (tiny plants) are eaten by copepods (tiny crustaceans) that are, in turn, eaten by a herring. Cod eat the herring, seals eat the cod, and eventually killer whales eat the seals. At each stage in the food chain, energy obtained from one organism is used by other organisms to move, to grow, to repair cells, to reproduce, and to eliminate waste. Energy not used in these life processes is transferred along the food chain as organisms feed on other organisms.

A food chain is a model of energy transfer. In an ecosystem, many complex feeding relationships exist because most organisms depend on more than one species for food. For example, herring eat more than copepods, and in turn are eaten by animals other than cod. Food chains are interconnected to form highly complex systems called food webs. ☑

LIFE SCIENCE
◀ **INTEGRATION**

Reading Check ☑

What gets transferred at each stage in a food chain?

Figure 12-6 Numerous food chains exist in the ocean. Some food chains are simple (B) and some are complex (A).

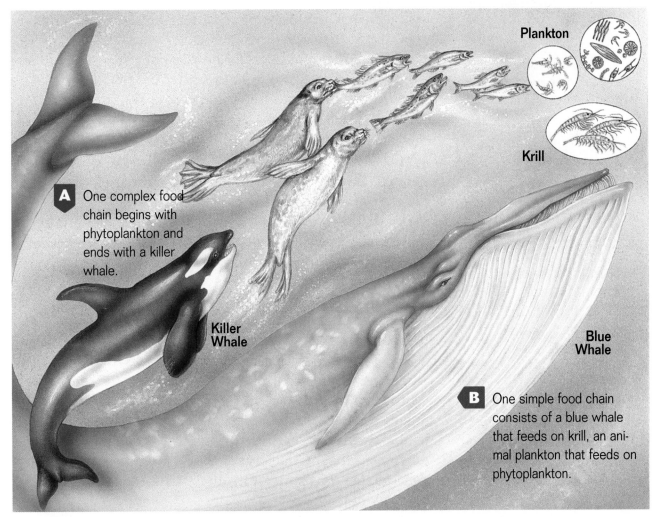

A One complex food chain begins with phytoplankton and ends with a killer whale.

Killer Whale

Plankton

Krill

Blue Whale

B One simple food chain consists of a blue whale that feeds on krill, an animal plankton that feeds on phytoplankton.

Figure 12-7 Sulfur compounds (A), escaping from a "black smoker" deep-sea vent, provide the energy for chemosynthesis. Tube worms (B) feed on bacteria at these deep-sea vents.
Why don't these bacteria perform photosynthesis?

Using Math

Blue whales can consume more than 8 metric tons of krill a day. Adults average 26 m in length and have a mass of 137 metric tons. How many grams of krill can a blue whale consume in one day? How many centimeters long is an average blue whale? What is the mass in kilograms of an average adult blue whale?

Chemosynthesis

Other types of food webs do not depend on photosynthesis. These food webs depend on bacteria that perform **chemosynthesis.** The bacteria produce food by breaking down compounds that contain elements such as sulfur, iron, or nitrogen, instead of carbon and oxygen. Bacteria that perform chemosynthesis using sulfur compounds live along portions of the mid-ocean ridges, where superheated water either seeps or blasts from the crust, as shown in **Figure 12-7.**

Other Life Processes

Another vital life process is reproduction. Ocean water provides an easy way for organisms to reproduce. Many ocean organisms release reproductive cells into the water, where they unite to form more organisms of the same type.

Seawater also provides a thermally stable environment for organisms. Because the ocean has a large volume of water, its temperature changes slowly. This slow change of temperature means that marine organisms do not experience the sudden changes in temperature that some organisms on land must adapt to.

Ocean Life

Many varieties of plants, animals, and algae live in the ocean. Most exist in the sunlight zone of the ocean. Sufficient sunlight for photosynthesis to occur can penetrate about 200 m down into ocean water. As a result, marine organisms live on the continental shelf where the greatest source of food is located.

Most organisms in the ocean are adapted to obtain food in one of three ways: they make food by photosynthesis, they move through the water to obtain food, or they filter water to obtain nutrients.

Plankton

Plankton are tiny marine algae and animals that drift with currents. Most algae plankton are one-celled organisms that float in the upper layers of the ocean where light needed for photosynthesis is found. To see most plankton, you need a microscope. A one-celled, golden alga, called a diatom, is a tiny but abundant form of plankton. Diatoms are shown in **Figure 12-8.** They are the most important source of food for animal plankton, the next step in the food chain of the oceans. Examples of animal plankton include eggs, young fish, jellyfish and crabs, and tiny adults of some organisms. Most animal plankton depend on surface currents to move them, but some can swim short distances.

Mini Lab

Observing Plankton

Procedure

1. Place one or two drops of pond, lake, or ocean water onto a microscope slide. Look for microscopic life such as plankton.
2. With light coming through the sample from beneath, use a microscope to observe your sample.
3. Find at least three different types of plankton.

Analysis

1. Draw detailed pictures of three types of plankton.
2. Classify the plankton as algae or animal.

Figure 12-8 These diatoms are tiny algae that live in both freshwater and ocean water.

A

Magnification: 60×

B Diatoms are used in many household items. Your toothpaste may contain crushed diatoms. **Why are diatoms used in toothpaste?**

Figure 12-9 Swimming animals, such as this angler fish (A) and this turtle (B), are nekton.

Nekton

In the ocean, animals that actively swim, rather than drift with the currents, are **nekton.** Nekton include all swimming forms of fish and other animals, from tiny herring to huge whales. Shrimps, squid, and seals are also nekton. In **Figure 12-9,** the swimming turtle and angler fish are nekton. Nekton move from one depth to another easily. This ability to swim reduces the effects of surface currents on them. For nekton, buoyancy is important. In the water, organisms less dense than water float. By changing how buoyant they are, that is, how easily they float, organisms can change their depth in the ocean. Changing their depth allows animals to search more areas for food. Some nekton live in cold water. Others exist in warm regions. Some, like whales, roam the entire ocean. Many nekton come to the surface at night to feed on plankton, while others remain in deeper parts of the ocean where sunlight does not reach.

Some of these deep-dwelling organisms have special light-generating organs for attracting live food in the dark depths. The angler fish, shown in **Figure 12-9,** dangles a luminous lure over its forehead. When small animals bite at the lure, the angler fish swallows them. The viper fish has luminous organs in its mouth. It swims with its mouth open, and small organisms swim right into its mouth.

Bottom-Dwellers

Plants, algae, and animals also live on the seafloor. These plants and animals living in the lowest levels of the ocean are the **benthos.** Some benthos live on the bottoms of the continental shelf in fairly shallow water. Others live on the ocean bottom hundreds of meters deep. Some are attached to the bottom like the coral shown in **Figure 12-10,** others burrow into the bottom sediments, and others walk or swim over the bottom.

Forests of kelp grow on the continental shelf, anchored to the bottom in cool water near shore. Kelp is the fastest-growing organism in the world. It can grow up to 60 cm each

Figure 12-10 Many organisms live on this coral reef in the South Pacific. **Why do you think nekton would choose to live within a reef?**

day and reach lengths of 65 m. Gas-filled bladders keep the plant upright in the water.

Other benthic organisms include crabs, corals, snails, clams, sea urchins, and bottom-dwelling fish. How do you suppose these animals get food? Many of them eat the partially decomposed matter that sinks to the ocean bottom. Some prey on other benthos. Those that are permanently attached to the bottom, such as sponges, filter food particles from water currents. Sponges are part of a group of benthic organisms that are helping scientists develop new drugs for medical treatments.

Drugs from the Sea

Did you know that half of all drugs that are developed come from living organisms? Scientists are currently looking at organisms in the oceans as sources of drugs to treat asthma, arthritis, cancers, and AIDS. Scientists are especially interested in studying soft-bodied organisms that live in the sea. This includes sponges, shown in **Figure 12-11,** slugs, soft corals, and sea worms. They seem defenseless, yet predators do not eat them. Why? Because they use chemical defense systems to stop or even kill their predators. Scientists suspect that we could develop drugs from these ocean chemicals.

Figure 12-11 These sponges and others like them may help to provide a cure for diseases such as herpes, cancer, or AIDS.

Problem Solving

Recognizing Pollution Sources

A chemical plant and a nuclear power plant are both located along Barney Beach. The chemical plant produces paint. The nuclear power plant generates power using nuclear fission, a process that produces vast amounts of energy. The chemical plant is located about 20 km north of Barney Beach. The nuclear power plant is about 10 km south of Barney Beach. Recently, many of the fish along Barney Beach died and washed ashore. Was the fish kill caused by pollution from one of these plants?

Think Critically: How could the chemical plant pollute Barney Beach? How could the nuclear power plant pollute Barney Beach? What questions would you want to ask about the Barney Beach fish kill that would help you determine the source of the pollution?

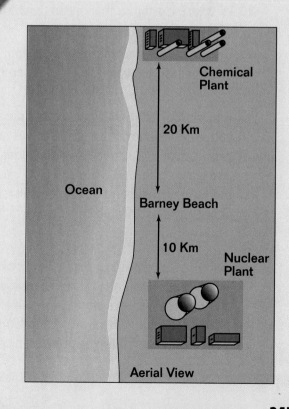

Chemical Plant

20 Km

Ocean

Barney Beach

10 Km

Nuclear Plant

Aerial View

Figure 12-12 Imagine yourself swimming above this coral reef. **What kinds of interactions among organisms would you see?**

Once a chemical is isolated from an organism and found to be an effective drug, scientists synthesize the chemical in the laboratory instead of harvesting the organisms. Why do you think this is done? As an example, the drug acyclovir fights herpes infections. It has been in use since 1982 and is derived from a Caribbean sponge.

Corals

Corals are organisms that live attached to the seafloor. Corals obtain food by stinging their prey. They need clear, warm water and a lot of light. This means that they generally form no farther than 50 m from the surface in the warm waters near the equator.

Each coral polyp builds a hard capsule around its body from the calcium it removes from seawater. Each capsule is cemented to others to form a large colony called a reef. A **reef,** as shown in **Figure 12-2,** is a rigid, wave-resistant structure built from skeletal materials and calcium carbonate.

Fish, crabs, sea urchins, and many other sea creatures congregate in reefs. Nutrients, food, and energy are cycled among these organisms in complex food webs. Plankton, nekton, and benthos all depend on each other for survival, not only in coral reefs but throughout the entire ocean.

Section Assessment

1. What are five things that oceans provide for organisms?

2. List the key characteristics of plankton, nekton, and benthos. How do they depend on one another?

3. **Think Critically:** When whales die and their carcasses sink to the bottom, sulfides sometimes are produced. Bacteria use the sulfides for food, and giant clams and worms eat the bacteria. Does this food web depend on photosynthesis or chemosynthesis? Explain.

4. **Skill Builder**
   Separating and Controlling Variables Describe how you could test the effects of salinity on marine organisms. If you need help, refer to Separating and Controlling Variables in the **Skill Handbook** on page 708.

Using Computers

Graphics Design a poster that illustrates the relationship between photosynthesis and energy in a food chain. Be creative. Try using clip art, scanned photographs, or original computer graphics. If you need help, please refer to page 718.

How it Works

Jason Jr.— The Titanic Explorer

Jason Jr. was a robotic underwater vehicle that helped scientists explore the *Titanic*, a luxury passenger ship that sank in the North Atlantic in 1912. Guided by a crew on the *Alvin* (a small submersible), *Jason Jr.* helped scientists locate parts of the sunken ship that had never been explored because the robot is small and can move easily. At far left, *Jason Jr.* trains its floodlights on *Titanic*'s anchor.

About the size of a lawn-mower, *Jason Jr.* could dive as deep as 4000 meters.

LIGHTS, CAMERA, ACTION

1. Special lights that could withstand underwater pressure illuminated the depths.

2. A video camera (A) and a 35-mm still camera (B) recorded underwater scenes. *Jason Jr.* gave the world its first views of the interior of the *Titanic*.

3. A 91-meter cord attached *Jason Jr.* to *Alvin* at this point. The cord carried fiber optic cable and power lines.

4. Thrusters powered its movement through the water.

Jason Jr. was lost in 1991 off the Galapagos Islands at a depth of 9000 feet. Its replacement is called *Jason*.

Think Critically

1. Why must scientists use remotely operated vehicles such as *Jason Jr.* to explore the deep sea—including the *Titanic*—rather than diving themselves using scuba gear?

2. Do you think that artifacts from the *Titanic* should remain under the ocean or be preserved and placed in museums? Explain your answer.

Career CONNECTION

Oceanographers usually have a college degree in one or more of the following subjects: biology, physics, geology, chemistry, mathematics, or engineering. Choose one of these subjects and write a daily schedule of activities that might take place aboard an ocean research vessel.

For more information
National Oceanic and Atmospheric Administration (NOAA)
1315 East-West Highway,
12th Floor
Silver Spring, MD 20910-3282

Resources from the Oceans

The oceans cover most of Earth's surface. We get many things from the oceans—fish, shrimp, clams, and other seafood. We also use the oceans for recreation and to transport material from place to place. But, what else do we get from the oceans? You probably use many products every day that are made from organisms that live in the oceans. Many of the ingredients in our food, in toothpaste, and in medicines come from ocean organisms.

Recognize the Problem

What products do we use that come from the oceans?

Form a Hypothesis

Think about the plants and animals that live in the oceans. **Form a hypothesis** as to what products are manufactured from organisms that live in the oceans.

Goals

- **Research and identify** organisms that are used to make useful products.
- **Explain** why it is important to keep the oceans clean.

Data Sources

Go to the Glencoe Science Web Site at **www.glencoe.com/ sec/science** to obtain information, hints, and data from other students.

Test Your Hypothesis

Plan

1. Use the web sites listed on the Glencoe Science Web Site to describe products made from organisms from the oceans.

2. **Investigate** where the organisms live and how they are harvested. Use the data table on the next page as a guide.

3. **Choose** a specific product and research how it is manufactured.

Do

1. Make sure your teacher approves your plan and your resource list before you proceed.

2. **Find** at least three ocean organisms that are used to make products you use every day.

3. **Research** where each organism is found and how it is collected or harvested.

4. **Post your list** on the Glencoe Science Web Site.

Analyze Your Data

1. **Post the locations** on the web site map found on the Glencoe Science Web Site where the organisms on your list are commonly found.

2. Are there any substitutes or alternatives in the products for the substances made from the ocean organisms?

Draw Conclusions

1. **Describe** the ways in which ocean organisms are useful to humans.

2. How might the activities of humans interfere with the ocean organism you researched?

3. Are there any substitutes for the ocean organisms in the prod-

ucts? Are the substitutes more or less expensive?

4. Can you tell if the ocean-made product is better than the substitute product? **Explain**.

5. Why is it important to conserve ocean resources and keep the oceans clean?

Ocean Resources Data			
Organism	Location Where Collected or Harvested	Product (name and use)	Alternatives

For a **preview** of this chapter, study this Reviewing Main Ideas before you read the chapter. After you have studied this chapter, you can use the Reviewing Main Ideas to **review** the chapter.

The Glencoe MindJogger, Audiocassettes, and CD-ROM provide additional opportunities for review.

Section 12-1 THE SEAFLOOR

The topography of the ocean floor is rugged, and the bottom structures reflect the way they formed. Some marine organisms live on the bottom, while others swim or float in the ocean currents. Marine organisms are dependent on the water for many life functions.

The **continental shelf** is a gently sloping part of the continent that extends out into the oceans. Beyond the shelf, the steeper **continental slope** drops down to the ocean floor. The **abyssal plain** is a flat area of the ocean floor. New seafloor crust forms along the middle of the **mid-ocean ridges**. *How do trenches form?*

Section 12-2 LIFE PROCESSES IN THE OCEAN

A water habitat provides water, nutrients, waste disposal, constant temperatures, and a means of reproduction for marine organisms. **Photosynthesis** is the basis of food chains in the ocean. **Chemosynthesis** is a special process of food making near thermal vents. *Why does most marine life live within the upper 140 m of the ocean?*

OCEAN LIFE

Tiny plants and animals that drift with ocean currents are **plankton.** Organisms that are able to swim throughout the ocean are **nekton.** They range from small to the size of a whale. Plants and animals that live at or near the bottom are the **benthos.** They may be mobile or permanently attached. *What adaptation allows nekton animals to be found at all ocean depths?*

Reading Check ✔

Are chemosynthesis and photosynthesis antonyms? Compare and contrast these terms to explain your answer.

Tania Zenteno-Savin, Marine Biologist

Tania Zenteno-Savin is a marine biologist at the University of Fairbanks, Alaska. She studies Weddell seals in Antarctica and northern elephant seals in California. Tania first became interested in seals in elementary school. She was fascinated with how long they could hold their breath. Now, Tania studies hormones in seals, trying to figure out if hormones are involved in controlling the heart rate of breath-holding seals. *How might studying the physiology of other mammals benefit humans?*

Using Vocabulary

a. abyssal plain
b. benthos
c. chemosynthesis
d. continental shelf
e. continental slope
f. mid-ocean ridge
g. nekton
h. photosynthesis
i. plankton
j. reef
k. trench

Each phrase below describes a science term from the list. Write the term that matches the phrase describing it.

1. sharp drop-off beyond the continental shelf
2. mountains formed where seafloor is spreading apart
3. drifting marine plants, algae, and animals
4. animals, algae, and plants that live on and near the ocean floor
5. production of food and oxygen using sulfur, nitrogen, or iron compounds

Checking Concepts

Choose the word or phrase that answers the question.

6. What is the flattest feature of the ocean floor?
   A) rift valley
   B) continental slope
   C) seamount
   D) abyssal plain

7. What may be found where rivers enter oceans?
   A) rift valleys
   B) manganese nodules
   C) abyssal plains
   D) placer deposits

8. What are formed along plates moving apart?
   A) mid-ocean ridges
   B) trenches
   C) continental slopes
   D) density currents

9. What do organisms do to produce food?
   A) photosynthesize
   B) excrete wastes
   C) benthos
   D) respire

10. What are ocean organisms that drift in ocean currents called?
    A) nekton
    B) fish
    C) benthos
    D) plankton

11. Where is the seafloor spreading apart?
    A) trenches
    B) mid-ocean ridges
    C) abyssal plains
    D) continental shelves

12. How do some deep-water bacteria in the ocean make food?
    A) photosynthesis
    B) chemosynthesis
    C) respiration
    D) rifting

13. Which of the following are ocean swimmers?
    A) benthos
    B) nekton
    C) kelp
    D) coral

14. What do seamounts originate as?
    A) extinct volcanoes
    B) small mountain chains
    C) active volcanoes
    D) mid-ocean ridges

15. How deep is the sunlight zone?
    A) 10 m
    B) 40 m
    C) 140 m
    D) 400 m

Thinking Critically

16. Half of all drugs that are developed come from living organisms. Some areas of the oceans are so polluted that organisms are dying. Some species are becoming extinct. What effect does pollution have on our ability to discover new drugs?

17. Animal plankton are disappearing in waters off the coast of California. How will this disappearance affect the food web in that area?

18. To widen their beaches, some cities pump offshore sediments onto beaches. How does this affect organisms that live in coastal waters?

19. Would you expect to find coral reefs growing around the bases of volcanoes off the coast of Alaska? Explain your answer.

20. Some oil leaks in the ocean are natural. Where does the oil come from?

Developing Skills

If you need help, refer to the Skill Handbook.

21. **Using Scientific Illustrations:** Use **Figure 12-6** to determine which organisms would starve to death if phytoplankton became extinct.

22. **Classifying:** Classify each of the following sea creatures as plankton, nekton, or benthos: *shrimp, dolphins, starfish, krill, coral,* and *algae.*

23. **Observing and Inferring:** At point A the echo took 2 s to reach the ship. It took 2.4 s at point B. Infer at which point the ocean is deeper.

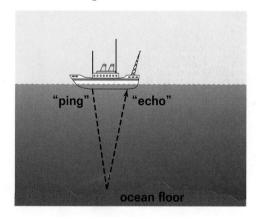

24. **Measuring in SI:** If kelp grows at a steady rate of 30 cm a day, how long would it take to reach a length of 25 m?

THE PRINCETON REVIEW

Test-Taking Tip

If It Looks Too Good to Be True...
Beware of answer choices that seem obvious. Remember that only one answer choice of the several that you're offered for each question is correct. Check each answer choice carefully before finally selecting it.

Test Practice

Use these questions to test your Science Proficiency.

1. Interpret from the drawing below where the youngest seafloor sediments are. Are the youngest sediments at locations A, B, C, or D?

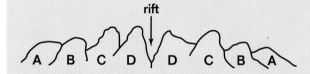

Mid–Ocean Ridge

2. What will be the effect if sea level rises?
   A) Abyssal hills will get higher.
   B) Seamounts will erode quickly.
   C) Islands will submerge.
   D) Trenches will stop developing.

3. Use the terms below to classify a larval starfish. It floats with other microscopic organisms on the ocean's surface.
   A) benthos
   B) nekton
   C) plankton
   D) photosynthetic

5

You&the
Environment

What's Happening Here?

The ocean is Earth's last frontier. Only recently have explorers searched its remotest depths to reveal some of its special secrets. In places, the water is so deep that if Mount Everest were to rise from the ocean floor, its peak would still be 2000 meters from the surface. With so much water can't the ocean wash away whatever is dumped into it? Not any longer. Each year in the United States, thousands of oil spills are reported. When the tanker *Megaborg* exploded in the Gulf of Mexico in 1990 (left), it dumped 4.6 million gallons and threatened wetlands bordering Galveston Bay. Some environmental problems are not accidental—people discarding trash in the wrong place, for instance. The rings of a six-pack holder will cut short the life of this young Western Gull (below). As the human population grows, the wear and tear on our planet is showing. How serious are the consequences, and how can we help? These are some of the questions addressed in this unit.

interNET CONNECTION

Explore the Glencoe Science Web Site at **www.glencoe.com/sec/science** to find out more about topics found in this unit.

Our Impact on Land

Chapter Preview

Skills Preview

Skill Builders
- Use a Graph
- Communicate

Activities
- Design an Experiment
- Make a Model

MiniLabs
- Classify
- Make a Model

Reading Check ✓

As you read this chapter, choose two illustrations and explain the purpose of each. Describe other types of illustrations that could replace the two that you choose.

Explore Activity

Have you ever considered the impact that each of us has on the land? Each person on Earth competes for space and resources. Each one generates trash; consumes products made in factories; uses natural resources such as water, soil, and energy; and creates pollution. Do you think our impact on land is significant?

Draw a Population Growth Model

1. Use a piece of paper and a pencil to draw a square that is 10 cm on each side. This represents 1 km^2 of Earth's land surface.

2. In 1965, the average number of people for every square kilometer of land was 21. Draw 21 small circles inside your square to represent this.

3. In 1990, the average was 35. Add 14 circles to illustrate this increase.

4. In 2025, there will be an estimated 52 people per km^2. Add circles to represent the average number of people per square kilometer of land in 2025.

5. Prepare a bar graph that shows population density for each year discussed above.

Science Journal

In your Science Journal, explain whether or not human population is increasing more rapidly as time goes on. How do you think population growth affects the environment?

13•1 Population Impact on the Environment

What You'll Learn

▶ How to interpret data from a graph that shows human population growth
▶ Reasons for Earth's rapid increase in human population
▶ Several ways each person in an industrialized nation affects the environment

Vocabulary

carrying capacity
population
population explosion

Why It's Important

▶ Humans directly impact the environment. The more humans there are, the greater the impact.

The Human Population Explosion

At one time, people thought of Earth as a world with unlimited resources. They thought the planet could provide them with whatever materials they needed. Earth seemed to have an endless supply of metals, fossil fuels, and rich soils. Today, we know this isn't true. Earth has a carrying capacity. The **carrying capacity** is the maximum number of individuals of a particular species that the planet will support. Thus, Earth's resources are limited. Unless we treat those resources with care, they will disappear.

Many years ago, few people lived on Earth. Fewer resources were used and less waste was produced than today. But, in the last 200 years, the number of people on Earth has increased at an extremely rapid rate. The increase in the world population has changed the way we must view our world and how we care for it for future generations, like the babies in **Figure 13-1.**

Figure 13-1 The human population is growing at an increasingly rapid rate. **Why does Earth have a carrying capacity?**

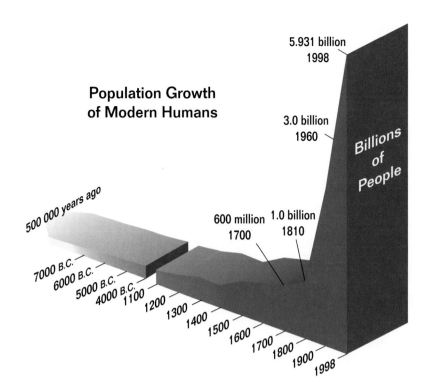

Population Growth
of Modern Humans

500 000 years ago

5.931 billion
1998

3.0 billion
1960

Billions
of
People

600 million
1700

1.0 billion
1810

7000 B.C.
6000 B.C.
5000 B.C.
4000 B.C.
1100
1200
1300
1400
1500
1600
1700
1800
1900
1998

Figure 13-2 The human species, *Homo sapiens*, may have appeared about 500 000 years ago. Our population numbers remained relatively steady until about 200 years ago. **Why have we experienced such a sharp increase in growth rate since about 1800?**

Human Population

A **population** is the total number of individuals of a particular species in a particular area. The area can be small or large. For example, we can talk about the human population of one particular community, such as Los Angeles, or about the human population of the entire planet.

Have you ever wondered how many people live on Earth? The global population in 1998 was 5.9 billion. Each day, the number of humans increases by approximately 215 000. Earth is now experiencing a **population explosion.** The word *explosion* is used because the rate at which the population is growing has increased rapidly in recent history. ☑

Our Increasing Population

Look at **Figure 13-2.** You can see that it took hundreds of thousands of years for Earth's population to reach 1 billion people. After that, the population increased much faster. Population has increased so rapidly in recent years because the death rate has been slowed by modern medicine, and we have better sanitation and better nutrition. This means that more people are living longer. Also, the number of births has increased because more people survive to the age at which they can have children.

The population explosion has seriously affected the environment. Scientists predict even greater changes as more people use Earth's limited resources. The population is predicted to be about 11 billion by 2100—nearly twice what it is now.

Reading Check ☑

Why is the increasing number of humans on Earth called a population explosion?

LIFE SCIENCE
INTEGRATION

Carrying Capacity
One of the things that affects carrying capacity is food. When a region does not have enough food, animals either migrate or starve. Infer what other factors determine the carrying capacity of a particular region for a species.

Using Math

The population density of a region is the average number of people per unit of area. Find the population density of Pennsylvania, which has a population of about 12 million people and an area of about 117 000 km².

We need to be aware of the effect such a large human population will have on our environment. We need to ask ourselves whether we have enough natural resources to support such a large population.

How People Affect the Environment

By the time you're 75 years old, you will have produced enough garbage to equal the mass of six African elephants (43 000 kg). You will have consumed enough water to fill 100 000 bathtubs (26 million L). If you live in the United States, you will have used five times as much energy as an average person living elsewhere in the world.

Our Daily Activities

In your daily activities, you use electricity, some of which is generated by the burning of fuels. The environment changes when fuels are mined and again, later, when they are burned. The water that you use must be made as clean as possible before being returned to the environment. You eat food, which takes land to grow. Much of the food you eat is grown using chemical substances, such as pesticides and herbicides, to kill insects and weeds. These chemicals can get into water supplies and threaten the health of living things if they become too concentrated. How else do you and other people affect the environment?

Many of the products you buy are packaged in plastic and paper. Plastic is made from oil. The process of refining oil produces pollutants. Producing paper requires cutting down trees, using gasoline to transport them to a paper mill, and producing pollutants in the process of transforming the trees into paper. **Figure 13-3** shows some items that may require these activities to produce them.

We change the land when we remove resources from it, and we further impact the environment when we shape those resources into usable products. Then, once we've produced and consumed products, we must dispose of them. Look at **Figure 13-4.** Unnecessary packaging is only one of the problems associated with waste disposal.

Figure 13-3 Every day, you use many of Earth's resources. **What resources were consumed to produce the items shown in this photograph?**

The Future

As the population continues to grow, more demands will be made on the environment. Traffic-choked highways, overflowing garbage dumps, shrinking forests, and vanishing wildlife are common. What can we do? People are the problem, but we also are the solution. As you learn more about how we affect the environment, you'll discover what you can do to help make the future world one that everyone can live in and enjoy. An important step that we can take is to think carefully about our use of natural resources. If everyone learns to conserve resources, we can make a positive impact on the environment.

Figure 13-4 This toy car is overpackaged. Because of consumer demands, many products now come in environmentally friendly packages.

Section Assessment

1. Using **Figure 13-2,** estimate how many years it took for the *Homo sapiens* population to reach 1 billion. How long did it take to triple to 3 billion?

2. Why is human population increasing so rapidly?

3. **Think Critically:** In nonindustrial nations, individuals have less negative impact on the environment than citizens in industrialized nations. In your Science Journal, explain why you think this is so.

4. 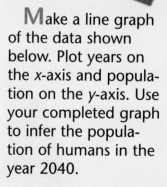 **Skill Builder**
   Making and Using Graphs Use **Figure 13-2** to answer the questions below. If you need help, refer to Making and Using Graphs in the **Skill Handbook** on page 701.

   a. Early humanlike ancestors existed more than 4 million years ago. Why does the graph indicate that it should extend back only 500 000 years?

   b. How would the slope of the graph change if, in the near future, the growth rate were cut in half?

Using Math

Make a line graph of the data shown below. Plot years on the *x*-axis and population on the *y*-axis. Use your completed graph to infer the population of humans in the year 2040.

Human Population in Billions

1998	2010	2025
5.931	6.849	7.923

Materials

- Many small objects, such as dried beans, popcorn, or paper clips
- Beaker (250 mL)
- Clock or watch

A Crowded Encounter

Think about the effects of our rapidly increasing human population. One of these is overcrowding. Every second, five people are born, and two people die. The result is a net increase of three people every second, or 180 people every minute.

What You'll Investigate

Goals

- **Make a model** of human population growth over a ten-minute time period.
- **Observe** the effects of a population increase on a limited space.
- Record, graph, and interpret population data.

Safety Precautions

Never eat or taste anything from a lab, even if you are confident that you know what it is.

Procedure

1. Use the empty beaker to represent the space left on Earth that is unoccupied by humans at the moment you begin.

2. Let each of your small objects represent five people.

3. **Design** a table with two columns. One column will show the time (1 to 10 minutes), and the other column will show the population at the designated time.

4. **Begin timing** your first minute. At the end of one minute, place the appropriate number of small items in your beaker. **Record** the data in your table. Continue for each minute of time.

5. After completing your table, **make a graph** that shows the time in minutes on the horizontal axis and the population on the vertical axis.

Conclude and Apply

1. At the end of ten minutes, what is the net increase in human population?

2. **Compare and contrast** the graph you just made with the graph shown in **Figure 13-2.** How do you account for the differences?

3. Today, approximately 5.9 billion people inhabit Earth. That number will double in about 40 years. Assuming the rate remains unchanged, **predict** what the population will be 80 years from now.

4. Suggest ways in which the net increase in human population affects Earth's limited resources.

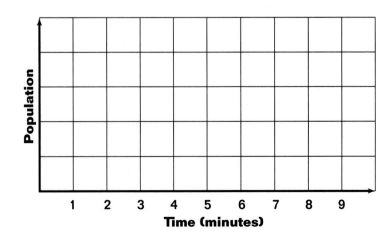

13·2 Using Land

Land Usage

You may not think of land as a natural resource. Yet, it is as important to people as oil, clean air, and clean water. Through agriculture, logging, garbage disposal, and urban development, we use land—and sometimes abuse it.

Farming

Earth's total land area is 149 million km². We use about 16 million km² as farmland. Even so, about 20 percent of the people living in the world are hungry. Millions starve and die each year. To fight this problem, some farmers work to increase the productivity of croplands by using higher-yield seeds and chemical fertilizers. Herbicides and pesticides also are used to reduce weeds, insects, and other pests that can damage crops.

Other farmers rely on organic farming techniques to lessen the environmental impact of chemicals on the land and to increase yield. **Figure 13-5** shows an organic farm in China that has been farmed for many centuries.

What You'll Learn

▶ Ways that we use land
▶ Environmental problems created because of land use
▶ Things you can do to help protect the environment

Vocabulary
landfill
hazardous waste
conservation
composting

Why It's Important

▶ Land is a resource that we need to use responsibly.

Figure 13-5 Organic farming techniques can rebuild topsoil rather than deplete it. Organic farmers use natural fertilizers, crop rotation, and biological pest controls to help their crops thrive.

Figure 13-6 Farmers reduce erosion with contour plowing, as shown on this farm in Washington State. Erosion is reduced because the path of plowing follows the shape of the land. **How can contour plowing control the direction that water flows in a farm field?**

Whenever vegetation is removed from an area, such as on construction sites, mining sites, or tilled farmland, the soil can erode easily. With plants gone, nothing prevents the soil from being carried away by running water and wind. Several centimeters of topsoil may be lost in one year. In some places, it can take more than 1000 years for new topsoil to develop and replace eroded topsoil. Some farmers practice no-till farming, which reduces erosion because land is not loosened by plowing. **Figure 13-6** shows another way farmers work to reduce erosion.

Grazing Livestock

Land also is used for grazing livestock. Animals such as cattle eat vegetation and then often are used as food for humans. In the United States, the majority of land used for grazing is unsuitable for crops. However, about 20 percent of the total cropland in our country is used to grow feed for livestock, such as the corn shown in **Figure 13-7.**

A square kilometer of vegetable crops can feed many more people than a square kilometer used to raise livestock. Some people argue that a more efficient use of the land would be to grow crops directly for human consumption, rather than for livestock. For many, however, meat and dairy products are an important part of their diet. They also argue that livestock have ecological benefits that justify livestock production.

Figure 13-7 Corn, as shown on this farm in Lancaster, Pennsylvania, is used for human food, for livestock feed, and for industrial products such as ceramics, textiles, ethanol, and paint. About half the corn grain raised in the United States is fed to livestock.

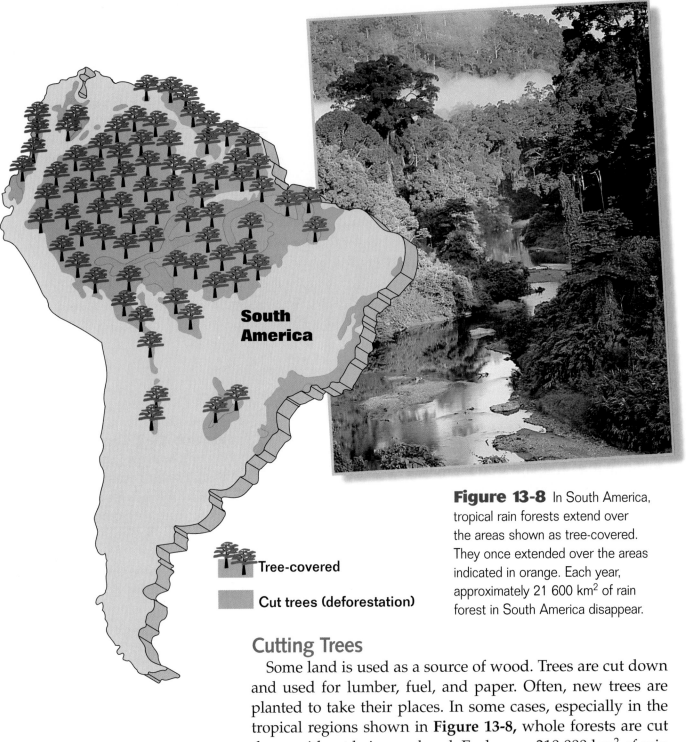

Figure 13-8 In South America, tropical rain forests extend over the areas shown as tree-covered. They once extended over the areas indicated in orange. Each year, approximately 21 600 km² of rain forest in South America disappear.

Tree-covered

Cut trees (deforestation)

Cutting Trees

Some land is used as a source of wood. Trees are cut down and used for lumber, fuel, and paper. Often, new trees are planted to take their places. In some cases, especially in the tropical regions shown in **Figure 13-8,** whole forests are cut down without being replaced. Each year, 310 000 km² of rain forest disappear worldwide. It is difficult to estimate, but evidence suggests that up to 50 000 species worldwide may become extinct each year due to loss of habitat.

Organisms living outside of the tropics also suffer because of the lost vegetation. Plants remove carbon dioxide from the air when they photosynthesize. The process of photosynthesis also produces oxygen that organisms need to breathe. Therefore, reduced vegetation may result in higher levels of carbon dioxide in the atmosphere. Carbon dioxide is a gas that may contribute to a rise in temperatures on Earth. ✓

Reading Check ✓

How do plants remove carbon dioxide from the air?

Landfills

Land also is used when we dispose of the products we consume. About 60 percent of our garbage goes into landfills. A **landfill** is an area where waste is deposited. In a *sanitary landfill*, such as the one illustrated in **Figure 13-9**, each day's deposit is covered with dirt. The dirt prevents the deposit from blowing away and reduces the odor produced by the decaying waste. Sanitary landfills also are designed to prevent liquid wastes from draining into the soil and groundwater below. A sanitary landfill is lined with plastic, concrete, or clay-rich soils that trap the liquid waste.

Sanitary landfills greatly reduce the chance that pollutants will leak into the surrounding soil and groundwater. However, some may still find their way into the environment.

Another problem is that we're filling up our landfills and running out of acceptable areas to build new ones. Many materials placed into landfills decompose slowly.

Hazardous Wastes

Some of the wastes we put into landfills are dangerous to organisms. Poisonous, cancer-causing, or radioactive wastes are called **hazardous wastes.** Hazardous wastes are put into landfills by everyone—industries and individuals alike. We contribute to this problem when we throw away insect sprays, batteries, drain cleaners, bleaches, medicines, and paints.

It may seem that when we throw something in the garbage can, even if it's hazardous, it's gone and we don't need to be concerned with it anymore. Unfortunately, our garbage does not disappear. It can remain in a landfill for hundreds of years. In the case of radioactive waste, it

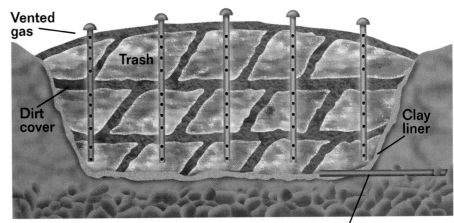

Figure 13-9 The vast majority of our garbage is deposited in landfills.
What are some problems associated with landfill disposal?

Try at Home

Mini Lab

Classifying Your Trash for One Day

Procedure

1. Prepare a table for yourself with the following column headings: *Paper, Plastic, Glass, Metal, Food Waste.*
2. During the day, record everything you throw out in the appropriate column.
3. At the end of the day, determine the number of trash items in each column.

Analysis

1. Rank each column by number from the least trash items (number 5) to the most trash items (number 1).
2. Compare your rankings with those of others in your household.
3. Compare your daily activities with others to account for differences in the tables.
4. What activities can you change to decrease the amount of trash you produce?

may remain harmful for thousands of years, creating problems for many future generations. Fortunately, industries and individuals are becoming more aware of the problems associated with landfills and are disposing of their wastes in a more responsible manner. You can help by disposing of hazardous wastes you generate at home at special hazardous waste-collection sites. Contact your local government to find out about dates, times, and locations of collections in your area. You can learn more about disposing wastes in the **Field Guide to Waste Management** at the end of this chapter.

Phytoremediation

Earlier, you learned that hazardous substances sometimes contaminate soil. These contaminants may come from nearby industries, residential areas, or landfills. Water contaminated from such a source can filter into the ground and leave behind the toxic substances within soil. Did you know that plants are sometimes used to help fix this problem? Methods of phytoremediation (*phyto* means "plant"; *remediation* means "to fix, or remedy a problem") are being studied to help decontaminate soil.

Extracting Metals

Certain varieties of plants can help remove metals from soil. When soil becomes too concentrated with metallic elements, human health may be at risk. Plant roots can absorb certain metals such as copper, nickel, and zinc. **Figure 13-10** shows how metals are absorbed from the soil and taken into plant tissue. Plants that become concentrated with metals from soil must eventually be harvested and either composted to obtain and recycle the metals or incinerated. If incineration is used to dispose of the plants, the ash residue must be handled carefully and disposed of at a hazardous waste site.

Figure 13-10 Metals such as copper can be removed from soil and incorporated into the tissues of plants. **How does this process illustrate the law of conservation of matter?**

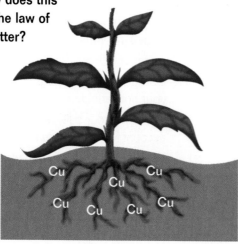
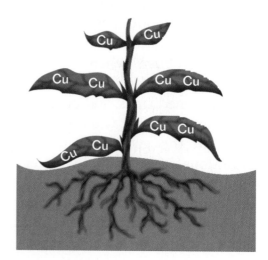

Breaking Down Organic Contaminants

Organic contaminants are hazardous wastes that contain carbon, hydrogen, and other elements such as oxygen, nitrogen, or chlorine. Some common examples of hazardous wastes are gasoline, oil, and solvents. Enzymes are chemical substances that can speed chemical reactions. Some enzymes that can break down organic pollutants are found in plant tissue. Similar to metals extraction, this type of cleanup occurs at the root of the plant. The enzyme is released by the root and causes the organic pollutant in the soil to break down into harmless substances, some of which are useful to the plant and promote its growth.

CHEMISTRY
◄ INTEGRATION

Human-Built Structures

Concrete and asphalt are quickly replacing grass and woodlands in our communities. The impact on the environment, particularly in urban and suburban areas, is easy to observe. Asphalt and concrete absorb solar radiation. The atmosphere is then heated by conduction and convection, which causes the air temperature to rise. You may have observed this if you've ever traveled from a rural area to the city and noticed a rise in temperature.

Problem Solving

The Effects of Trash Disposal

In the early days of the United States, the population was sparse and few people considered the impact of their actions on the environment. They threw their trash into rivers, buried it, or burned it. Today, we must consider the consequences of our methods of trash disposal. The graph at right shows how we deposit our waste.

Think Critically: More than half of the states in our country are running out of landfill space. New landfills will have to be made, but most people have a NIMBY attitude. NIMBY means "Not In My BackYard." People don't want to live near a landfill. What percent of our trash presently goes into landfills? If we reduce the amount of trash in landfills, what alternatives do we have for disposal? How could these

alternatives influence the environment? List the pros and cons for each alternative you think of in your Science Journal.

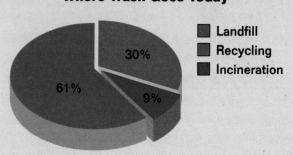

Where Trash Goes Today

- Landfill
- Recycling
- Incineration

30%

61%

9%

Figure 13-11 Some cities are working to preserve green space within city limits, such as this area in Portland, Oregon. **How does more green space in the city improve the environment?**

Mini Lab

Modeling Runoff

Procedure

1. Divide into groups of four or five.
2. Obtain two buckets of water for each group from your teacher.
3. With your teacher present, carefully take your buckets outside.
4. Find a paved area and a grassy area on your school grounds.
5. Pour one bucket of water on the paved area and observe how the water flows on the pavement.
6. Repeat step 5 for the grassy area.

Analysis

1. Describe how the water flowed over each area.
2. Infer what properties of the pavement and the grassy area control how the water flows over each.

Paving over the land prevents water from easily soaking into the soil. Instead, it runs off into sewers or streams. During heavy rainstorms in paved areas, sewer pipes can overflow or become clogged with debris. This causes increased runoff of rainwater directly into streams, and increases the risk of flooding in urban and suburban areas.

A stream's discharge increases when more water enters its channel. Stream discharge is the volume of water flowing past a point per unit of time. For example, the Mississippi River discharges an average of about 19 000 m³ of water into the Gulf of Mexico every second. This is a large volume of moving water, but the Mississippi is a major river. Many thousands more cubic meters flow per second when the Mississippi is flooding. If discharge increases too rapidly, as happens in urban areas from time to time, a stream can flow over its banks and flood a populated area. This happened to the Mississippi and Missouri Rivers and their tributaries during the summer of 1993.

Increased runoff also influences groundwater. Some of the water that does not soak into the soil evaporates. This reduces the amount of water in groundwater aquifers. Many communities rely on groundwater for drinking water. But covering more and more land with roads, sidewalks, and parking lots prevents the water from reaching aquifers.

Some cities are actively preserving more space that cannot be paved over. This type of activity, shown in **Figure 13-11,** beautifies the urban environment, increases the area into which water can soak, and provides more space for recreation.

Natural Preserves

Not all land on Earth is being utilized to produce usable materials or for storing waste. Look at **Figure 13-12.** Some land remains mostly uninhabited by people. National forest lands, grasslands, and parks in the United States are protected from many of the problems that you've read about in this section. In many countries throughout the world, land is set aside as natural preserves. As the world population continues to rise, the strain on our environment is likely to increase. Preserving some land in its natural state should continue to benefit future generations.

Conserving Resources

In the United States and other industrialized countries, people have a throwaway lifestyle. When we are done with something, we throw it away. This means more products must be produced to replace what we've thrown away, more land is used, and landfills overflow. You can help by conserving resources. **Conservation** is the careful use of resources to reduce damage to the environment.

Reduce, Reuse, Recycle

The United States makes up only five percent of the world's human population, yet it consumes 25 percent of the world's natural resources. Each of us can reduce our consumption of materials in simple ways, such as using both sides of notebook paper or carrying lunch to school in a non-disposable container. Ways to conserve resources include reducing our use of materials and reusing and recycling materials. Reusing an item means finding another use for it instead of throwing it away. You can reuse old clothes by giving them to someone else or by cutting them into rags. The rags can be used in place of paper towels for cleaning jobs around your home.

Figure 13-12 Many countries set aside land as natural preserves. **How do these natural preserves benefit humans and other living things?**

Using Math

Assume 17 fewer trees are cut down when 1000 kg of paper are recycled. Calculate the number of trees conserved per year if 150 000 kg of paper are recycled each month.

Reusing plastic and paper bags is another way to reduce waste. Some grocery stores even pay a few cents when you return and reuse paper grocery bags.

Outdoors, there are things you can do, too. If you cut grass or rake leaves, you can compost these items instead of putting them into the trash. **Composting** means piling yard wastes where they can gradually decompose. The decomposed matter can be used as fertilizer in gardens or flower beds. Some cities no longer pick up yard waste to take to landfills. In these places, composting is common. If everyone in the United States composted, it would reduce the trash put into landfills by 20 percent.

The Population Outlook

The human population explosion already has had devastating effects on the environment and the organisms that inhabit Earth. It's unlikely that the population will begin to decline in the near future. To compensate, we must use our resources wisely. Conserving resources by reducing, reusing, and recycling is an important way that you can make a difference.

Section Assessment

1. In your Science Journal, list six ways that people use land.

2. Discuss environmental problems that are sometimes created by agriculture, mining, and trash disposal.

3. How can phytoremediation positively impact the environment?

4. **Think Critically:** Choose one of the following items, and list three ways it can be reused: an empty milk carton, vegetable scraps, used notebook paper, or an old automobile tire. Be sure your uses are environmentally friendly.

5. **Skill Builder**
   Communicating Do the **Chapter 13 Skill Activity** on page 738 to find out ways in which an environmental problem can be communicated.

Using Computers

Word Processing
Suppose that a new landfill is needed in your community. Where do you think it should be located? Now, suppose that you want to convince people that you've selected the best place for the landfill. Use your word-processing skills to write a letter to the editor of the local newspaper, listing reasons in favor of your choice. If you need help, refer to page 716.

Recycling

Recyclable Objects

Did you know that any object is **recyclable** if it can be processed and then used again? Look at **Figure 13-13**. Glass and aluminum are two of the many things that can be recycled.

Paper makes up about 40 percent of the mass of our trash. If it is recycled, landfill space and trees are conserved. Also, the production of recycled paper takes 58 percent less water and generates 74 percent fewer air pollutants than the production of brand-new paper made from trees.

How much energy do you think is saved when you recycle one aluminum can? Answer: enough energy to keep a TV running for about three hours. Twenty aluminum cans can be recycled with the energy that is needed to produce a single brand-new can from aluminum ore.

What You'll Learn

▶ The advantages of recycling
▶ The advantages and disadvantages of required recycling

Vocabulary
recyclable

Why It's Important

▶ Recycling helps conserve resources and reduces solid waste.

VISUALIZING
Recycling

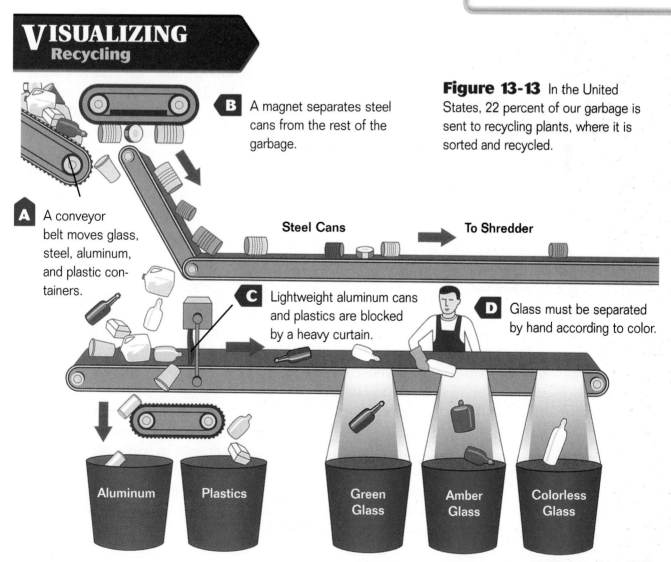

B A magnet separates steel cans from the rest of the garbage.

Figure 13-13 In the United States, 22 percent of our garbage is sent to recycling plants, where it is sorted and recycled.

A A conveyor belt moves glass, steel, aluminum, and plastic containers.

Steel Cans → To Shredder

C Lightweight aluminum cans and plastics are blocked by a heavy curtain.

D Glass must be separated by hand according to color.

Aluminum · Plastics · Green Glass · Amber Glass · Colorless Glass

Figure 13-14 Recycling saves landfill space, energy, and natural resources. Many community volunteers adopt sections of a highway. They pick up trash and recycle the salvageable part.

Everyone agrees that recycling is good for the environment. It saves landfill space, energy, and natural resources. Recycling also helps reduce the damage caused by mining, cutting trees, and manufacturing. Did you know that if you recycle, you will reduce the trash you generate in your lifetime by 60 percent? If you don't recycle, you'll generate trash equal to at least 600 times your mass. No one argues that recycling is not a good thing. The question is should recycling be required?

Required Recycling

Many things are thrown away because some people aren't in the habit of recycling. In the United States, much less garbage is recycled than in countries with mandatory recycling, such as Japan and Germany. Mandatory recycling means that people are required to recycle. This creates new jobs in reuse industries, such as the production of items from recycled plastics.

Many states already have some form of recycling laws. People in these states comply with the laws because they benefit directly in some way. For example, in some places people who recycle pay lower trash-collection fees. In other places, garbage is not collected if it contains items that should have been recycled. **Figure 13-14** shows typical containers used to help people organize their recyclable objects.

In some states, a refundable deposit is made on all beverage containers. This means paying extra money at the store for a drink. You get your money back if you return the container to the store for recycling. Some people suggest that if we had a national container law, we could save enough energy to light up a large city for four years. ☑

Reading Check ☑

In what ways have states encouraged people to participate in recycling?

Voluntary Recycling

Today, many people already recycle voluntarily because their cities provide curbside collection or convenient drop-off facilities. In this case, people have the freedom to decide whether or not to recycle, without government intervention.

Some people argue that the cost of recycling outweighs the benefits. Recycling requires money to pay for workers, trucks, and buildings. Also, some workers, such as miners and manufacturers who make brand-new containers, might lose their jobs.

Another problem is what to do with all of the recyclable items. Recycling businesses must make a profit, or they can't exist. The only way to make a profit in recycling is to sell the recycled material, so there must be a market for the material. Whether voluntary or mandatory, recycling conserves resources. In addition to saving landfill space, recycling also protects our environment by minimizing our need to extract raw materials from Earth.

*inter*NET
CONNECTION

Visit the Glencoe Science Web Site at **www.glencoe.com/ sec/science** to learn more about conservation. Make a list of conservation tips for individuals.

Section Assessment

1. List at least four advantages of recycling.
2. What are the advantages and disadvantages of mandatory recycling?
3. **Think Critically:** Spend a day at home keeping track of what you throw away and what you recycle. Record these items in your Science Journal. Did you throw away anything that could have been recycled?
4.  **Skill Builder**
   Making and Using Tables As you will see in the **Field Guide to Waste Management** at the end of this chapter, plastics must be carefully sorted before they can be reprocessed into new usable items. Do the Activity in the field guide to find out how to organize your recyclable plastic items. If you need help, refer to Making and Using Tables in the **Skill Handbook** on page 700.

Science Journal In your Science Journal, write a letter to your local chamber of commerce suggesting ways to encourage businesses to recycle.

A Model Landfill

Materials

- Bottles (2L) (2)
- Soil
- Thermometer
- Plastic wrap
- Graph paper
- Rubber band
- Trash (including fruit and vegetable scraps, a plastic item, a metal item, a foam cup, and notebook paper or newsprint)

When garbage is put into landfills, it is covered under other trash and soil and isn't exposed to sunlight and other things that help decomposition. When examined by a researcher, one landfill was found to contain grass clippings that were still green and bread that had not molded.

What You'll Investigate

At what rates do different materials decompose in a landfill?

Goals

- **Make a model** of a sanitary landfill.
- **Compare and contrast** the decomposition of different materials in a landfill.

Safety Precautions

CAUTION: *Be especially careful not to expose your skin or eyes to garbage items.*

Procedure

1. **Cut** off the tops of two 2-L bottles.
2. **Add** soil to each bottle until it is half filled.
3. On graph paper, **trace** the outline of all the garbage items that you will place into each bottle. **Label** each outline and keep the tracings.
4. **Place** the items, one at a time, in each bottle. Completely **cover** each item with soil.
5. **Add** water to your landfill until the soil is slightly moist. **Place** a thermometer in each bottle and seal the bottle with the plastic wrap

and a rubber band. **Store** one bottle in a cold place and put the other on a shelf.

6. **Check** the temperature of your landfill on the shelf each day for two weeks. **Record** the temperatures in a data table that you design.

7. After two weeks, **remove** all of the items from the soil in both bottles. Trace the outlines of each on a new sheet of graph paper. **Compare** the sizes of the items with their original sizes.

8. **Wash** your hands thoroughly after cleaning up your lab space. Be sure to dispose of each item properly as instructed by your teacher.

Conclude and Apply

1. Most decomposition in a landfill is due to the activity of microorganisms. The organisms can live only under certain temperature and moisture conditions. **Explain** how the decomposition rates would have differed if the soil had been completely dry.

2. **Compare** your results with the results from the bottle that was stored at a cold temperature. **Explain** the differences you observe.

3. Why do some items decompose more rapidly than others?

4. What problems are created in landfills by plastics?

Using Plants to Reduce Pollution

Pollution-Absorbing Plants

Plants are helping clean up hazardous chemicals in soil and water. By taking in pollutants through their roots, some plants can make hazardous substances less harmful to humans and other organisms. These helpful plants include poplar trees, mustard (left), and fescue grass (below).

Fescue to the Rescue

High concentrations of the metal selenium (suh LEE nee uhm) are harmful to the environment. In central California, soil became contaminated when irrigation water containing selenium flowed through fields. Farmers in the area planted fescue grass and Indian mustard to absorb selenium from the contaminated irrigation water. Researchers have found that mustard and fescue are able to convert selenium metal into a gas that is eventually given off by the plants. Scientists suggest that the gas is many times less harmful to the environment than concentrated levels of selenium in soils.

Advantages of Using Plants

Using plants to control or eliminate certain types of pollution is becoming increasingly popular. Cost is one reason. It is often less expensive to use plants than other methods of reducing pollutants. Plants clean up contaminated soil or water on the site, so there is no expense of digging up soil or removing water. Plants also can make an area more attractive. Finally, few, if any, people object to using plants to reverse the negative effects of pollution.

interNET CONNECTION

To find information about the Environmental Protection Agency's Citizen's Guide to Phytoremediation, visit the Glencoe Science Web Site at **www.glencoe.com/sec/science**.

FIELD GUIDE *to Waste Management*

FIELD *ACTIVITY*

The type of plastic contained in a recyclable item is indicated by a coded number placed on the item. Arrange collection centers at your school for plastic to be recycled. Name your collection activity and advertise it with posters. Operate the collection of recyclable plastics for one week. Use the Plastics Code System Table in this field guide to organize the plastic products by code number so they can be recycled. Arrange to have your plastics taken to a recycling center. Make a bar graph that shows how many pieces of each type of plastic you collected. In your Science Journal, list examples of products that can be made from the collected plastics.

Managing waste properly can reduce the use of resources and prevent pollution. People can do three things to cut down on waste production and reduce harm to the environment. They can follow the three Rs of waste management: reduce, reuse, and recycle. For example, a 450-g family-size box of cereal uses a lot less cardboard than 18 single-serving boxes that each contain 25 g of cereal. Finding another function for used items such as wrapping gifts with old magazines or newspapers greatly reduces waste. And, you can use many products every day that are recyclable. You can also help complete the cycle by purchasing items that are made from recycled materials.

Household Hazardous Wastes

- Household Hazardous Wastes (HHWs) are products containing chemicals that can cause injury or are harmful if used, stored, or disposed of improperly. Some of these products include household and car batteries, bleach and household cleaners, paint, paint thinner, old motor oil, old gasoline, herbicides and pesticides.
- These chemicals pose a threat to people (especially children, firefighters, and refuse workers) and to our environment.

- HHWs have caution words, skull and crossbones, or special handling directions.
- Some communities provide information to help people dispose of HHWs properly.
- Follow these steps to reduce HHWs:
  1. Whenever possible, buy nontoxic alternatives to hazardous products.
  2. If you buy a hazardous product, buy only what you need to do the job.
  3. Before you put leftover products on the shelf, try to find someone who can use them.

Plastics

- Plastics are among the most difficult products to recycle. Most plastics are composed of complex molecules that tend not to break down easily.
- Many different types of plastics exist, and they often cannot be recycled together.
- **Table 13-1** below lists the codes used to identify specific types of plastics used in products. This helps people sort common plastic items for proper recycling.
- Plastic beverage containers are recycled into insulation, carpet yarn, strapping, and packing material.

Table 13-1

The Plastics Code System			
Code	Material	% of Containers	Reclaimed For
1 PET	Polyethylene terephthalate	7	Carpet, food packaging, fiberfill, fibers, and auto parts
2 HDPE	High-density polyethylene	31	Drainage pipes, drums, traffic cones, plastic lumber, and combs
3 V	Vinyl chloride	5	Pipes, hoses, mud flaps, and tile
4 LDPE	Low-density polyethylene	33	Mixed with HDPE to produce cases, recycling bins, and garbage bags
5 PP	Polypropylene	9	Household and janitorial products
6 PS	Polystyrene	11	Insulation and food trays
7 Other	All others and mixed	4	Storage containers, lumber, and animal-pen floors

Glass

- Glass is often separated by color into green, brown, or colorless types before recycling.
- Most glass bottles are recyclable, but some glassware is not because it is too thin. For example, broken or burned-out lightbulbs cannot be recycled.
- New products made from recycled glass include beverage containers.

Metals

- A variety of metals are recyclable, such as aluminum beverage cans and steel used in a variety of canned goods.
- Aluminum is processed to make lawn chairs, siding, cookware, or new beverage cans.
- Even precious metals such as silver, gold, and platinum used in laboratories or in jewelry, for example, are recyclable.

Paper

- Plain white paper, newspaper, magazines, and telephone books are common paper goods that can be recycled. New products made from these items include newsprint, cardboard, egg cartons, and building materials.
- Not all glossy and colored papers are recyclable at all recycling centers.

- As for any recycled material, you should check with your neighborhood recycling center for specific instructions about properly sorting your paper goods.

Yard Waste

- Grass clippings, leaves, sticks, and other yard wastes can be placed in bags and taken to your local recycling center. Some communities provide for the collection of yard wastes from your home after you gather them together.
- Another approach is to practice your own mulching. Rake your leaves and then place them on a garden plot to compost over the winter. This will enrich the soil in your garden when you're ready to plant in the spring.
- Some communities shred sticks and leaves to make mulch. Whatever the approach, recycling yard waste reduces the amount of material we send to landfills.

For a **preview** of this chapter, study this Reviewing Main Ideas before you read the chapter. After you have studied this chapter, you can use the Reviewing Main Ideas to **review** the chapter.

The Glencoe MindJogger, Audiocassettes, and CD-ROM provide additional opportunities for review.

13-1 POPULATION IMPACT ON THE ENVIRONMENT

The rapid increase in human **population** in recent years is due to an increase in the birthrate, advances in medicine, better sanitation, and better nutrition. *How does an increase in the number of humans affect Earth's carrying capacity for other organisms?*

5.931 billion
1998

3.0 billion
1960

Billions of People

600 million
1700

1.0 billion
1810

500 000 years ago

7000 B.C.
6000 B.C.
5000 B.C.
4000 B.C.
1100
1200
1300
1400
1500
1600
1700
1800
1900
1998

Reading Check ☑

List at least two facts and two opinions related to population growth or related to recycling.

Section
13-2 USING LAND

Land is used for farming, grazing livestock, lumber, and mining coal and mineral ores. We also build structures and **landfills** on land. Land becomes polluted by **hazardous wastes** thrown away by industries and individuals. Fertilizers and pesticides pollute groundwater and soil. *What happens to soil quality and atmospheric carbon dioxide when trees are cut down?*

Section
13-3 RECYCLING

Recycling, reducing, and reusing materials are important ways we can conserve natural resources. Recycling saves energy and much-needed space in landfills. Some parts of the world have mandatory recycling, while other parts have voluntary programs. *Why do some people oppose having mandatory recycling programs?*

Using Vocabulary

a. carrying capacity
b. composting
c. conservation
d. hazardous waste
e. landfill
f. population
g. population explosion
h. recyclable

Which vocabulary word describes the phrase or process given below?

1. total number of individuals of a particular species in an area
2. careful use of resources
3. area lined with plastic, concrete, or clay where garbage is dumped
4. items that can be processed and used again
5. maximum number of individuals of a particular type that the planet will support

Checking Concepts

Choose the word or phrase that best answers the question.

6. Where is most of the trash in the United States disposed of?
   A) recycling centers
   B) landfills
   C) hazardous waste sites
   D) old mine shafts

7. Between 1960 and 1998, world population increased by how many billions of people?
   A) 5.9   C) 1.0
   B) 3.2   D) 2.9

8. What percent of Earth's resources does the United States use?
   A) 5   C) 25
   B) 10   D) 50

9. About what percent of U.S. cropland is used to grow feed for livestock?
   A) 100   C) 50
   B) 1   D) 20

10. What do we call an object that can be processed in some way so that it can be used again?
    A) trash   C) disposable
    B) recyclable   D) hazardous

11. What is about 40 percent of the mass of our trash made up of?
    A) glass   C) yard waste
    B) aluminum   D) paper

12. In which type of facility do humans cover trash with soil?
    A) recycling center C) sanitary landfill
    B) surface mine   D) coal mine

13. By what order of magnitude are people starving each year?
    A) the hundreds   C) the millions
    B) the thousands D) the billions

14. Organisms living outside the tropics suffer when rain forests are cut down. This is because fewer trees are available to produce which?
    A) carbon dioxide C) water
    B) methane   D) oxygen

15. Which of the following is an example of a hazardous waste?
    A) piece of glass C) steel can
    B) plastic jug   D) can of paint

Thinking Critically

16. How would reducing the packaging of consumer products impact our disposal of solid wastes?

17. Renewable resources are those resources that can be replenished by nature in the foreseeable future. Nonrenewable resources cannot be replenished. Which kind of resource is oxygen? Explain.

18. Although land is farmable in many developing countries, hunger is a major problem in many of these places. Give some reasons why this might be so.

19. Forests in Germany are dying due to acid rain. What effects might this loss of trees have on the environment?

20. Describe how you could encourage your neighbors to recycle their aluminum cans.

Developing Skills

If you need help, refer to the Skill Handbook.

21. **Making and Using Graphs**: In a population of snails, each snail produces two offspring each month. Each offspring also produces two offspring. Using the graph below, determine how many new snails would be produced during the fifth month if the initial population was only two snails.

22. **Interpreting Scientific Illustrations:** Why does the curve of the line graph below change its slope over time? Suppose half of the snails died after six months. Draw a new graph to illustrate the effect.

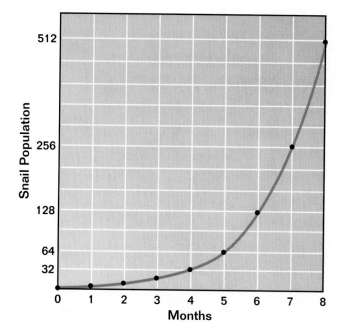

Test-Taking Tip

Don't Be Afraid to Ask for Help Ask for advice on things you don't understand. If you're practicing for a test and find yourself stuck, unable to understand why you got a question wrong, or unable to do it in the first place, ask for help.

Test Practice

Use these questions to test your Science Proficiency.

1. In some areas of the world, when rain forests are destroyed for lumber, a few fast-growing species of trees are planted in their place. Why is this a problem?
   A) The trees won't grow as quickly as the original rain forest trees.
   B) The tree farm won't produce oxygen.
   C) The roots of the new trees won't hold the soil.
   D) The biodiversity is decreased.

2. In 1946, there were 2.4 billion people on Earth. In 1998, there were 5.9 billion people. By how much did world population increase in 52 years?
   A) 226 percent
   B) 41 percent
   C) 146 percent
   D) 69 percent

3. Which of the following must be true for a recycling center to be profitable?
   A) The center must recycle glass.
   B) Mandatory recycling is enforced.
   C) Glossy and colored paper are recycled.
   D) There is a market for the recycled items.

Our Impact on Air and Water

Chapter Preview

Skills Preview

Skill Builders

- Map Concepts
- Interpret Scientific Illustrations

Activities

- Collect and Analyze Data
- Make and Use a Data Table

MiniLabs

- Experiment
- Observe and Infer

Reading Check ✔

As you read this chapter, create a timeline of the federal laws that have been enacted to help control our impact on air and water.

Explore Activity

Did you know that many sources of drinking water are polluted? The water has to be treated with chemicals or filters before it's safe to use. Air pollution is another problem. Refineries such as the one shown here release harmful chemicals into the air. We can help solve these problems by learning to reduce our input of pollutants into air and water. We also need to determine what pollutants are present now. Let's start with air. How is the air quality in your community?

Observe Your Air

1. Find a high shelf or the top of a tall cabinet in your classroom —someplace that hasn't been cleaned for a while.

2. Run a cloth over this area and observe the dirt under a microscope or magnifying lens.

Science Journal

In your Science Journal, describe and sketch what you see. Where did these particles come from? Explain what you think happens when you breathe in these particles.

387

14·1 Air Pollution

What causes air pollution?

Have you ever noticed that the air looks hazy on some days? Do you know what causes this haziness? Some industries generate dust and chemicals. Other human activities add pollutants to the air, too. Look at **Figure 14-1.** Cars, buses, trucks, trains, and planes all burn fossil fuels for energy. Their exhaust—the waste products from burning the fossil fuels—adds polluting chemicals to the air. Other sources include smoke from burning trash and dust from plowed fields, construction sites, and mines.

Natural sources also add pollutants to the air. Volcanic eruptions, forest fires, and grass fires all emit dust and chemicals into the air. Volcanic eruptions even cause temporary changes in climate by blocking out sunlight when ash erupts.

Smog

Figure 14-2 shows the major sources of air pollution. Around cities, polluted air is called *smog*, a word made by combining the words *smoke* and *fog*. Two types of smog are common—photochemical smog and sulfurous smog.

Photochemical Smog

In areas such as Los Angeles, Denver, and New York City, a hazy, brown blanket of smog is created when sunlight reacts with pollutants in the air. This brown smog is called **photochemical smog** because it forms with the aid of light. The pollutants get into the air when fossil fuels are burned. Coal, natural gas, and gasoline are burned by factories, airplanes, and cars. Burning fossil fuels causes nitrogen and oxygen to combine chemically to form nitrogen compounds. These compounds react in the presence of sunlight and produce other substances. One of the substances produced is ozone. Ozone in the stratosphere protects us

What You'll Learn

► The different sources of air pollutants
► How air pollution affects people and the environment
► How air pollution can be reduced

Vocabulary
photochemical smog
sulfurous smog
acid rain
pH scale
acid
base
Clean Air Act
scrubber

Why It's Important

► Air pollution can affect your health and the health of others.

Figure 14-1 Cars, like these in New York City, are one of the main sources of air pollution in the United States. **Describe other sources of air pollution where you live.**

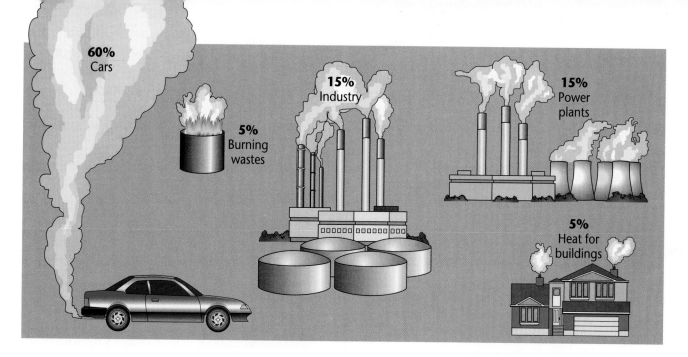

60%
Cars

5%
Burning
wastes

15%
Industry

15%
Power
plants

5%
Heat for
buildings

from the sun's ultraviolet radiation. But ozone that forms in smog near Earth's surface causes health problems.

Sulfurous Smog

A second type of smog is called **sulfurous smog.** It's created when coal is burned in electrical power plants and home furnaces. The burning releases sulfur compounds, dust, and smoke particles into the air. Sulfurous smog forms when these substances collect in an area where there's little or no wind. A blanket of gray smog may hang over a city for several days and be hazardous to breathe.

Nature and Smog

Nature plays an important role in creating smog. Sunlight helps form photochemical smog. Sulfurous smog forms when weather systems are calm and the air is not being moved around. Normally, warmer air is near Earth's surface. But, sometimes warm air overlies cool air, trapping cool air mixed with pollutants near the ground. Eventually, the weather changes and cleaner air is blown in, dispersing the pollutants in the air.

Landforms also enhance smog development. For example, air with smog can be blocked by surrounding mountains. This prevents smog from being dispersed by winds. Dense, dirty air tends to collect in valleys in this way.

Smog isn't the only air pollution problem we have. Chlorofluorocarbons (CFCs) from air conditioners and refrigerators are thought to be destroying the ozone layer in the stratosphere. Some scientists suggest that carbon dioxide released from burning coal, oil, natural gas, and forests could contribute to increasing temperatures on Earth.

Figure 14-2 There are five major sources of human-created smog. **Which three sources combined produce 90 percent of human-created smog?**

*inter*NET
CONNECTION

Visit the Glencoe Science Web Site at **www.glencoe.com/ sec/science** for more information about smog.

Mini Lab

Identifying Acid Rain

Procedure

1. The next time it rains or snows, use a glass or plastic container to collect a sample of the precipitation.

2. Use pH paper to determine the acidity level of your sample. If you have collected snow, melt it before measuring its pH.

3. Record the indicated pH of your sample and compare it with the results of other classmates who have followed the same procedure.

Analysis

1. What is the average pH of the samples obtained from this precipitation?

2. Compare and contrast the pH of your samples with those of the substances shown on the pH scale in **Figure 14-4.**

Figure 14-3 These trees are dying because acids in the soil have lowered the trees' resistance to diseases, insects, and bad weather. Acid rain also increases the acidity of streams, rivers, and lakes, killing fish. Acid rain even damages the surfaces of buildings and cars.

Acid Rain

Another major pollution problem is acid rain. Acid rain is created when sulfur dioxide from coal-burning power plants combines with moisture in the air to form sulfuric acid. It also is created when nitrogen oxides from car exhausts combine with moisture in the air to form nitric acid. The acidic moisture falls to Earth as rain or snow. We call this **acid rain.** Acid rain can poison organisms, as shown by the dying trees in **Figure 14-3.**

To understand what is meant by an acid, we use the **pH scale,** shown in **Figure 14-4.** Substances with a pH lower than seven are **acids.** The lower the number, the greater the acidity. Substances with a pH above seven are **bases.** Acid rain is sometimes as acidic as lemon juice.

Figure 14-4 The natural pH of rainwater is about 5.6. Acid rain is precipitation with a pH below 5.6.

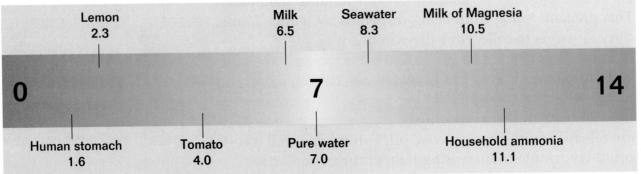

Lemon 2.3   Milk 6.5   Seawater 8.3   Milk of Magnesia 10.5

0   7   14

Human stomach 1.6   Tomato 4.0   Pure water 7.0   Household ammonia 11.1

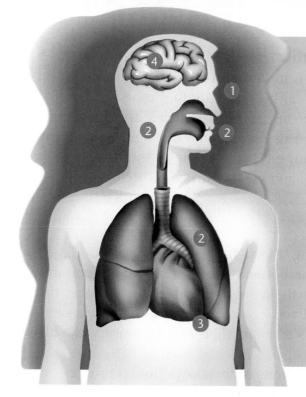

Effects of Air Pollution on the Body

1 Eyes
Compounds found in smog cause the eyes to water and sting. If conditions are bad enough, vision may be blurred.

2 Nose, throat, and lungs
Ozone irritates the nose and throat, causing burning. It reduces the ability of the lungs to fight infections.

3 Heart
Inhaled carbon monoxide is absorbed by red blood cells, rendering them incapable of transporting oxygen throughout the body. Chest pains result because of low oxygen levels.

4 Brain
Motor functions and coordination are impaired because oxygen levels in the brain are reduced when carbon monoxide is inhaled.

Figure 14-5 Air pollution is a health hazard. Compounds in the air can affect your body.

How Air Pollution Affects Your Health

Suppose you're an athlete in a large city and you're training for a big, upcoming competition. You have to get up at 4:30 A.M. to exercise. Later in the day, the smog levels will be so high that it won't be safe for you to do strenuous exercise. In southern California, in Denver, and in other areas, athletes adjust their training schedules to avoid exposure to ozone and other smog. Schools schedule football games for Saturday afternoons when smog levels are low. Parents are warned to keep their children indoors when smog exceeds certain levels. **Figure 14-5** shows how breathing dirty air, especially taking deep breaths of it, can cause health problems.

Health Disorders

How hazardous is dirty air? Approximately 250 000 people in the United States suffer from pollution-related breathing disorders. About 60 000 deaths each year in the United States are blamed on air pollution. Ozone damages lung tissue, making people more susceptible to diseases such as pneumonia and asthma. Less severe symptoms of breathing ozone include burning eyes, dry throat, and headache. ☑

Carbon monoxide also contributes to air pollution. A colorless, odorless gas, carbon monoxide makes people ill, even in small concentrations.

What do you suppose happens when you inhale the humid air from acid rain? Acid is deposited deep inside your lungs. This causes irritation, reduces your ability to fight respiratory infections, interferes with oxygen absorption, and puts stress on your heart.

Using Math

The pH scale is a logarithmic scale. This means that there is a tenfold difference for each pH unit. For example, pH 4 is ten times more acidic than pH 5 and 100 times more acidic than pH 6. Calculate how much more acidic pH 1 is than pH 4.

Reading Check ☑

How is ozone harmful to human health?

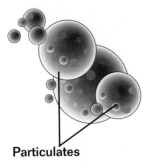

Figure 14-6 Particulate pollution is caused by solids in the air that are produced, in part, by burning fossil fuels. **Why is particulate pollution difficult to control?**

Particulates

Particulate Pollution

Particulates shown in **Figure 14-6,** can also harm people. Particulates are fine airborne solids that range in size from large visible grains to microscopic particles. The fine particles are especially dangerous because they disrupt normal breathing and can cause lung disease. Some of these particles are produced when coal and oil are burned.

Reducing Air Pollution

Pollutants moving through the atmosphere don't stop when they reach the borders between states and countries. They float wherever the wind carries them. This makes them difficult to control. Even if one state or country reduces its air pollution, pollutants from another state or country can blow across the border.

When states and nations cooperate, pollution problems can be reduced. Diplomats from around the world have met on several occasions since 1990 to try to eliminate some kinds of air pollution. Of particular concern are chlorofluorocarbons and carbon dioxide.

Air Pollution in the United States

The Congress of the United States has passed several laws to protect the air. The 1990 **Clean Air Act** attacked the problems of smog, chlorofluorocarbons, particulates, and acid rain by regulating car manufacturers, coal technologies, and other industries. In **Table 14-1,** you can read about some of these regulations.

Table 14-1

Clean Air Regulations

Urban Air Pollution	Acid Rain	Airborne Toxins	Ozone-Depleting Chemicals
By 1996, all new cars had to have their nitrogen oxide emissions reduced by 60 percent and hydrocarbons reduced by 35 percent from 1990 levels.	In 1990, nitrogen oxide emissions had to be reduced by several million tons immediately. Sulfur dioxide emissions must be reduced by 14 million tons from 1990 levels by the year 2000.	Beginning in 1995, industries had to limit the emission of 200 compounds that cause cancer and birth defects.	In 1990, industries were required to immediately phase out ozone-depleting chemicals.

The good news is that since the passage of the Clean Air Act, the quality of the air in some regions of the United States has improved. The bad news is that one of four U.S. citizens still breathes unhealthy air.

It is the role of the federal Environmental Protection Agency to monitor progress toward the goals of the Clean Air Act. However, consumers must pay increased prices and taxes and change their habits in order to really help protect the environment. The Clean Air Act can work only if we all cooperate. You can conserve energy and reduce trash in several ways. When you do these things, you also are reducing air pollution. We all must do our share to clean up the air.

Reducing Emissions

The main source of the nitric acid in acid rain is car exhaust. Better emission-control devices on cars will help reduce acid rain. So will car pooling and public transportation because they reduce the number of trips and, therefore, the amount of fuel used.

Coal-burning power plants can help reduce air pollutants, too. Some coal has a lot of sulfur in it. When the coal is burned, the sulfur combines with moisture in the air to form sulfuric acid. Power plants can wash coal to remove some sulfur before the coal is burned. Burning cleaner coal produces less sulfur in the smoke. Power plants also can run the smoke through a scrubber. A **scrubber** lets the gases in the smoke dissolve in water, as they would in nature, until the smoke's pH increases to a safe level. **Figure 14-7** illustrates how an electrostatic separator removes particulates.

Figure 14-7

Smokestack scrubbers and electrostatic separators remove the pollutants from industrial smoke.

D The smoke, now stripped of its pollutants, is released through the smokestack.

C The smoke with its positively charged particles of pollution moves past negatively charged plates. The positively charged particles are attracted by and held to the negatively charged plates.

B The plates give the particles of pollution a positive electric charge.

A A fan blows the polluted smoke past electrically charged plates.

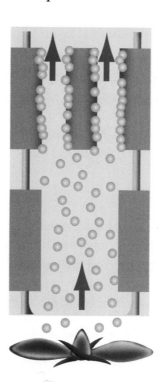

Figure 14-8 This geyser in Yellowstone Geyser Basin, Wyoming, indicates that a magma chamber, a potential source of geothermal power, exists in this area.

interNET
CONNECTION

Visit the Glencoe Science Web Site at **www.glencoe.com/sec/science** for more information about solar cars and solar cookers. How does a solar car work? How do solar cookers concentrate solar energy?

Alternative Sources of Power

Another thing humans could do to reduce air pollution is to switch to other power sources such as solar, wind, nuclear, and geothermal power. **Figure 14-8** shows a geyser that indicates a possible source of geothermal power. However, these alternative sources have disadvantages, too. And, even if everyone agreed to make changes, it would take years for some areas to change. This is because many people, especially in the midwestern states, depend on coal-burning power plants for home heating and electricity. Changing the kind of power used would be costly.

The 1990 Clean Air Act requires great reductions in auto exhaust and sulfur dioxide emissions. This will cost billions of dollars. Thousands of people have lost jobs in mining, factories, and in coal-burning power plants. However, new jobs are created as humans discover alternative sources of power.

Section Assessment

1. In what ways does air pollution affect the health of people?

2. How can changes in human activities reduce air pollution?

3. **Think Critically:** The Clean Air Act of 1970 required that coal-burning power plants use tall smokestacks so that air pollutants would be ejected high into the sky, where high-altitude winds would disperse them. Power plants in the midwestern states complied with that law, and people in eastern Canada began complaining about acid rain. Explain the connection.

4. 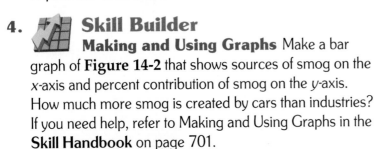 **Skill Builder**
   Making and Using Graphs Make a bar graph of **Figure 14-2** that shows sources of smog on the x-axis and percent contribution of smog on the y-axis. How much more smog is created by cars than industries? If you need help, refer to Making and Using Graphs in the **Skill Handbook** on page 701.

Science Journal In your Science Journal, create a crossword puzzle using at least 12 important terms found in this section.

Bee Probes

Honeybee colonies have been used for centuries to provide honey and pollinate flowers, fruit trees, and other crops. But now, scientists have found a new use for the busy insect. Honeybee colonies are used globally to indicate the presence of hazardous materials in the environment. Millions of established colonies provide constant monitoring. Because honeybees can live under many different environmental conditions, small colonies can be introduced almost anywhere hazardous substances are suspected.

Scientists at the University of Montana have designed electronic beehives (left) that provide useful information about the environment. Electronic hives record the behavior of every bee, including how often it flies, the pollen it gathers, and how the bees control the environment in the hives. Pollutants brought into the hives by the bees are detected using electronic instruments attached to the hives.

1. Bees leave the hives and pick up water, nectar, pollen, and airborne water particles.

2. When bees return to the hives, they fan their wings to control the air temperature in the hives.

3. Pollutants in the environment that were picked up by the bees are released into the air of the hives as the bees fan their wings.

4. Pollutants released by the bees are measured using chemical probes attached to the hives.

5. The chemical data are analyzed to determine what pollutants were brought into the hives from the local environment.

Think Critically

1. Why are bees useful animals for detecting pollution?
2. What are common causes of pollution in your area?
3. Research how a miner's canary was used to warn about hazardous substances. How is this similar to how honeybee colonies are being used?
4. Think about other environmentally sensitive organisms. In your Science Journal, write how you think other organisms could be used to protect the environment.

Career
CONNECTION

Behavioral biologists usually have a bachelor's degree in biology or zoology. They enjoy observing animals for long periods of time. Write a letter to a local zoo or animal park. Ask biologists who work there to send you information about their careers and their education.

What's in the air?

Possible Materials

- Small box of plain gelatin
- Hot plate
- Pan or pot
- Water
- Marker
- Refrigerator
- Plastic lids (4)
- Microscope
  *Hand lens

*Alternate materials

Have you ever gotten a particle of dust in your eye? Before it got there, it was one of the many pieces of particulate matter in the air. Whenever you dust off items in your household, you are cleaning up dust particles that settled out of the air. How often do you have to dust to keep your furniture clean? Just imagine how many pieces of particulate matter the air must hold.

Recognize the Problem

What kinds of particulate matter are in your environment? Are some areas of your environment more polluted with particulates than others?

Form a Hypothesis

Based on your knowledge of your neighborhood, hypothesize what kinds of particulate matter you will find in your environment. Will all areas in your community contain the same types and amounts of particulate matter?

Goals

- **Design an experiment** to collect and analyze particulate matter in the air in your community.

- **Use** gelatin to collect particulate matter present in the air.

- **Observe** and describe the particulate matter you collect.

Safety Precautions

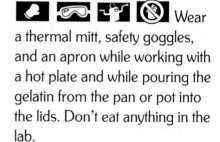 Wear a thermal mitt, safety goggles, and an apron while working with a hot plate and while pouring the gelatin from the pan or pot into the lids. Don't eat anything in the lab.

Test Your Hypothesis

Plan

1. As a group, agree upon and **write** out your hypothesis.

2. As a group, **list** the steps you need to take to test your hypothesis. Be specific, describing exactly what you will do at each step.

3. **List** your materials.

4. **Design** a data table in your Science Journal so that it is ready to use as your group collects data.

5. **Mix** the gelatin according to the directions on the box. Carefully pour a thin layer of gelatin into each lid. Use this to collect air particulate matter.

6. **Decide** where you will place each plastic lid in order to collect particulate matter in the air.

7. **Read** over your entire experiment to make sure that all steps are in a logical order.

8. **Identify** any constants, variables, and controls of the experiment.

Do

1. Make sure your teacher approves your plan before you proceed.

2. Carry out the experiment as planned.

3. While the experiment is going on, write down any observations that you make and complete the data table in your Science Journal.

Analyze Your Data

1. **Describe** the types of materials you collected in each lid.

2. **Graph** your results using a bar graph. Place the number of particulates on the *y*-axis and the test-site location on the *x*-axis.

Draw Conclusions

1. Which test-site location yielded the most particulates? **Infer** why this is so.

2. Which of the particulates can you relate directly to the activities of humans?

14•2 Water Pollution

Causes and Effects of Water Pollution

What You'll Learn

▶ Types of water pollutants and their sources

▶ Ways that international agreements and U.S. laws are designed to reduce water pollution

▶ Ways that you can help reduce water pollution

Vocabulary
Safe Drinking Water Act
Clean Water Act

Why It's Important

▶ Many human activities cause water pollution. There are ways you can help reduce the problem.

Suppose you were hiking along a stream or lake and became thirsty. Do you think it would be safe to drink the water? In most cases, it wouldn't. Many streams and lakes in the United States are polluted, such as the one shown in **Figure 14-9.** Even streams that look clear and sparkling may not be safe for drinking.

Pollutants from humans or other organisms can get into the oceans, streams, groundwater, and lakes. Sometimes pollutants travel from one source of water to another, such as when a contaminated stream flows into a lake. There is strong reason to believe that some of these pollutants cause birth defects and health problems such as cancer, dysentery, and liver damage in humans and other animals.

Pollution Sources

How do you think pollutants get into the water? Bacteria and viruses get into the water because some cities illegally dump untreated sewage directly into the water supply. Underground septic tanks can leak, too. Radioactive materials can get into the water from leaks at nuclear power plants and radioactive waste disposal sites.

Pesticides, herbicides, and fertilizers from farms and lawns are picked up by rainwater and carried into streams. Some people dump motor oil into sewers after

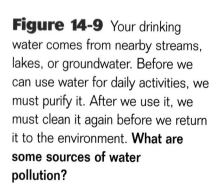

Figure 14-9 Your drinking water comes from nearby streams, lakes, or groundwater. Before we can use water for daily activities, we must purify it. After we use it, we must clean it again before we return it to the environment. **What are some sources of water pollution?**

Figure 14-10 The water hyacinth plant removes many pollutants from water. Water hyacinths can be used at wastewater-treatment facilities (shown at left) to clean water before it flows back into streams and aquifers.

they've changed the oil in their cars. Water running through mines also carries pollutants to streams and underground aquifers. Some factories illegally dump industrial chemicals directly into water. Waste from landfills and hazardous waste facilities leaks into the surrounding soil and groundwater.

Most water pollution is caused by legal, everyday activities. If left untreated, water would remain polluted after we flush our toilets, wash our hands, brush our teeth, and water our lawns. Nitrogen and phosphorus from household detergents, soaps, and other cleaning agents must be removed before water is returned to a source, such as a stream or reservoir. Water also is polluted when oil and gasoline run off of pavement, down storm sewers, and into streams. These pollutants must be removed at water-treatment facilities like those in **Figures 14-10** and **14-11**.

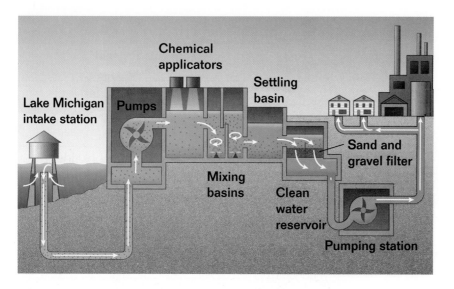

Figure 14-11 This water-purification plant in Chicago provides drinking water for millions of people. Water taken from Lake Michigan is pumped into a tank where alum, chlorine, lime, and other compounds are added to kill microorganisms. The water is thoroughly mixed, and the large particles of matter settle out. Some smaller particles are filtered by sand and gravel. Clean water is then pumped to consumers.

Reducing Water Pollution

Several countries have worked together to reduce water pollution. Let's look at one example. Lake Erie is on the border between the United States and Canada. In the 1960s, Lake Erie was so polluted by phosphorus from sewage, soaps, and fertilizers that it was turning into a green, soupy mess. Large areas of the lake bottom no longer had oxygen and, therefore, no life.

International Cooperation

In the 1970s, the United States and Canada made two water quality agreements. The two countries spent $15 billion to stop the sewage problem. Today, the green slime is gone and the fish are back. However, more than 300 human-made chemicals can still be found in Lake Erie, and some of them are hazardous. The United States and Canada are studying ways to get them out of the lake. ✔

Reading Check ✔

Which countries worked together to control water pollution in Lake Erie?

Problem Solving

Interpreting Pollution Sources

Water pollution comes in a variety of forms: heavy metals like lead and manganese from mines, bacteria from septic tanks, herbicides and pesticides from agriculture, thermal pollution from factories, acids from power plants and automobiles, sediments from construction sites, and so on.

In analyzing a possible source of water pollution in a river, chemists look for two types: point source and nonpoint source. Point sources occur where factories and cities pipe their untreated wastes directly into lakes and rivers. Nonpoint sources are runoff from farms, cities, mines, and construction sites. Analyze the map below and the chart of pollution test results to answer the Think Critically questions below.

Think Critically: What is the likely source of the nitrates and bacteria found at sites c and d that weren't present at sites a and b? Is there enough information to tell if this is a case of point-source or nonpoint-source pollution? Explain.

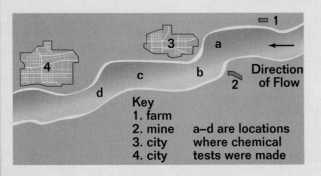

Key
1. farm
2. mine   a–d are locations
3. city   where chemical
4. city   tests were made

Pollution Test Results	
Test Site	**Chemicals Present in Water**
a	nitrates commonly found in fertilizers
b	lead and nitrates commonly found in fertilizers
c	nitrates and bacteria commonly found in sewage, lead, nitrates commonly found in fertilizers
d	nitrates and bacteria commonly found in sewage, lead, nitrates commonly found in fertilizers

The U.S. Congress also has reduced water pollution by passing several laws, including the 1996 Safe Drinking Water Act amendments and the 1987 Clean Water Act.

The 1996 **Safe Drinking Water Act** amendments aim to strengthen health standards for drinking water and to protect rivers, lakes, and streams that are sources of drinking water. These amendments also provide the public with a right to know about contaminants that could be in their tap water.

Clean Water Act

The 1987 **Clean Water Act** gives money to states for building sewage and wastewater-treatment facilities. The money is also for controlling runoff from streets, mines, and farms. Runoff caused up to half of the water pollution in the United States before 1987. This act also requires states to develop quality standards for all their streams.

The U.S. Environmental Protection Agency (EPA) makes sure that cities comply with both the Safe Drinking Water Act and the Clean Water Act. Most cities and states are working hard to clean up their water. Look at **Figure 14-12**. Many streams that once were heavily polluted by sewage and industrial wastes are now safe for recreation.

However, much remains to be done. For example, the EPA recently discovered that 30 percent of the nation's rivers, 42 percent of its lakes, and 32 percent of its estuaries are still polluted from farm runoff and municipal sewage overflows from cities. An estimated 40 percent of the country's freshwater supply is still not usable because of pollution. Since 1972, the U.S. government has spent more than 260 billion dollars on sewage system improvements. However, more than 1000 cities still have substandard water-treatment facilities.

Figure 14-12 Sewage, industrial wastes, and solid wastes pollute many rivers and lakes. However, these sources of pollution can be controlled and the water made safe for recreational purposes. **How does the 1987 Clean Water Act encourage communities to clean up their water?**

LIFE SCIENCE

INTEGRATION

Amphibian Decline
All over the world, the amphibian population is declining. Scientists do not know for sure what is causing the decline, but some suspect it is caused by pollution. What are amphibians? What types of pollution might affect amphibians?

Bioremediation

Bioremediation (*bio* = "life"; *remediation* = "the act of remedying, or fixing a problem") uses organisms to consume or make a hazardous substance harmless. Examples of resources cleaned by bioremediation include soil, sediment, groundwater, and surface water. Some hazardous substances that are removed by bioremediation include oil, gasoline, and other organic pollutants.

Microorganisms

Did you know that bacteria are organisms that are helpful in cleaning up the environment? Although these organisms are so small you would need a microscope to see them, they often are able to consume or make some toxic wastes harmless. Bacteria already may be present in a contaminated site or may be brought in from the outside. For these microorganisms to be successful, they must be kept healthy enough to consume waste in a reasonable amount of time.

One way that water is treated to remove pollutants like oil and gasoline is to inject it with oxygen. The oxygen creates a healthy environment for some types of bacteria. Nutrients such as nitrogen and phosphorus also are necessary for the bacteria. These nutrients may be in the contaminated site already or pumped in if the site does not contain enough of them. Contaminated groundwater is first pumped to the surface using extraction wells, then pretreated with concentrated bacteria to remove some of the waste. The groundwater is then injected back underground and oxygenated. The oxygen

Figure 14-13 Bioremediation can help clean water right at the location of a contaminated site.

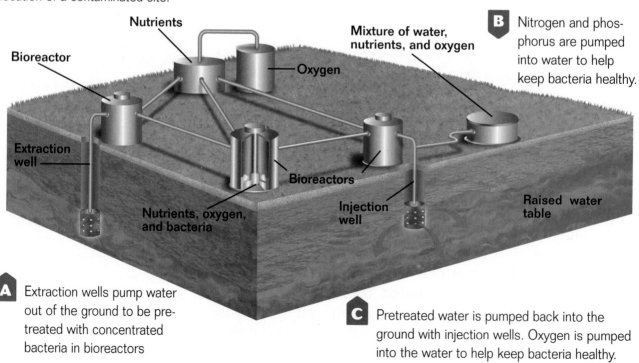

Nutrients

Bioreactor

Oxygen

Mixture of water, nutrients, and oxygen

B Nitrogen and phosphorus are pumped into water to help keep bacteria healthy.

Extraction well

Nutrients, oxygen, and bacteria

Bioreactors

Injection well

Raised water table

A Extraction wells pump water out of the ground to be pretreated with concentrated bacteria in bioreactors

C Pretreated water is pumped back into the ground with injection wells. Oxygen is pumped into the water to help keep bacteria healthy.

stimulates bacteria to consume or break down the remaining waste. **Figure 14-13** shows the basic components of *in situ* bioremediation, which means that the decontamination can take place right at the field site.

How can you help?

As you have discovered in this chapter, humans often are the cause of our environmental problems. But, we also are the solution. What can you do to help?

Dispose of Wastes Safely

When you dispose of household chemicals such as paint and motor oil, don't pour them down the drain or onto the ground. Also, don't put them out to be picked up with your other trash.

Hazardous wastes poured directly onto the ground move through the soil and eventually reach the groundwater below. When you pour them down the drain, they flow through the sewer, through the wastewater-treatment plant, and into wherever the wastewater is drained, usually a stream. This is how rivers become polluted. If you put hazardous wastes out with the trash, they end up in landfills, where they may leak out.

What should you do with these wastes? First, read the label on the container for instructions on disposal. Don't throw the container into the trash if the label specifies a different method of disposal. Recycle if you can. Many cities have recycling facilities for metal, glass, and plastic containers. Store chemical wastes so that they can't leak. If you live in a city, call the sewage office, water office, or garbage disposal service and ask them how to safely dispose of these wastes in your area.

We all must do our part to help conserve water and reduce water pollution. Consider some changes you can make in your life that will make a difference.

Figure 14-14 The industries that produce the products you use each day consume nearly half of the fresh water used in the United States.

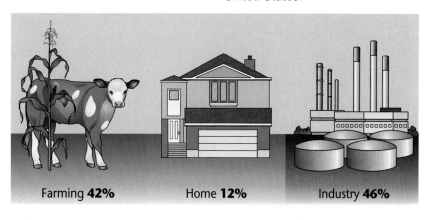

Farming **42%**   Home **12%**   Industry **46%**

Conserve Energy and Water

Another way you can reduce water pollution is to conserve energy. Decreasing the use of fuels reduces the amount of acid rain that will fall into forests and streams. Decreasing your power usage will help reduce the input of hazardous materials into the environment.

Another way you can help is to conserve water. Look at **Figure 14-14.** How much water do you use every day? You use water every time you flush a toilet, take a bath, clean your clothes, wash dishes, wash a car, or use a hose or lawn sprinkler. Typical U.S. citizens, like the one shown in **Figure 14-15,** use from 380 L to 950 L of water every day.

All of this water must be purified before it reaches your home. It takes a lot of energy to treat water and pump it to your home. Remember, when you use energy, you add to the pollution problem.

Section Assessment

1. What are three things you can do to help reduce water pollution?

2. What is the difference between point-source and nonpoint-source pollution?

3. What hazardous substances can be removed from water using bioremediation?

4. **Think Critically:** Southern Florida is home to millions of people, dairy farms, and sugarcane fields. It is also the location of Everglades National Park—a shallow river system with highly polluted waters. What kinds of pollutants do you think are in the Everglades? How do you think they got there?

5. **Skill Builder**
   Interpreting Data Have you ever wondered how scientists determine the sources of water pollution in a lake or a river? Do the **Chapter 14 Skill Activity** on page 739 to see an example of how this is done.

Using Computers

Word Processing Design a pamphlet to inform people how they can reduce the amount of water they use. Be creative and include graphics in your pamphlet. Use word-processing utilities to check your spelling and grammar. If you need help, refer to page 716.

Water Use

How much water goes down the drain at your house? Did you know that up to 75 percent of the water used in homes is used in the bathroom? Flushing the toilet accounts for 50 percent of that water. The rest is for bathing, showering, washing hands, and brushing teeth. By learning to read a water meter, you can find out how much water your family uses.

Materials

• Home water meter

What You'll Investigate

How much water does your family use?

Goals

• **Calculate** your family's water usage.
• **Infer** how your family can conserve water.

Background

There are several different types of water meters. Meter A has six dials. As water moves through the meter, the pointers on the dials rotate. To read a meter like A, find the dial in A with the lowest denomination, which in this case is 10. Record the last number that the pointer on that dial has passed. Continue this process for each dial in the meter. Meter A therefore shows 28 853 gallons. Meter B is read like a digital watch. It indicates 1959.9 cubic feet. Meter C is similar to meter B but indicates water use in cubic meters. If you have a meter that is different from these, contact your area's water department for help on reading your meter.

A

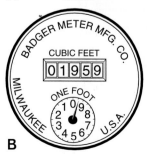

B

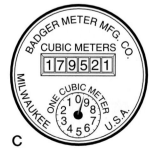

C

Procedure

1. **Design** a data table and **record** your home water meter reading at the same time of the day for eight days.

2. **Subtract** the previous day's reading to determine the amount of water used each day.

3. **Record** how much water is used in your home each day. Also, record the activities in your home that use water each day.

4. **Plot your data** on a graph like the one shown below. Label the vertical axis with the units used by your meter.

Conclude and Apply

1. **Calculate** the average amount of water each person in your family used during the week by dividing the total amount of water used by the number of persons.

2. **Infer** how the time of year might affect the rate at which your family uses water.

3. What are some things your family could do to conserve water?

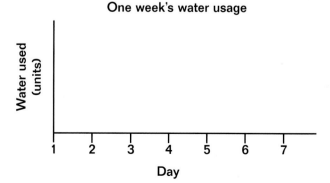

One week's water usage

Water used (units)

Day

For a **preview** of this chapter, study this Reviewing Main Ideas before you read the chapter. After you have studied this chapter, you can use the Reviewing Main Ideas to **review** the chapter.

The Glencoe MindJogger, Audiocassettes, and CD-ROM provide additional opportunities for review.

Section

14-1 CAUSES OF AIR POLLUTION

Many human activities impact our air and water. **Smog, acid rain,** and water pollution are consequences of our activities. When fossil fuels are burned, polluting chemicals are added to the air. Construction dusts and smoke from burning fuels pollute the air. Nature also contributes to air pollution. Air pollutants don't have boundaries. They float between states and countries. National and international cooperation is necessary to reduce the problem. The purpose of the **Clean Air Act** is to reduce problem chemicals in the air. *Which national agency has the job of monitoring progress toward the goals of the Clean Air Act?*

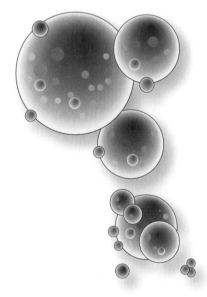

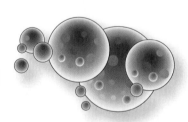

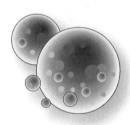

Reading Check ✔

Explain how the topics of air and water pollution might be approached differently in a health textbook than in a science book.

14-2 WATER POLLUTION

Water pollution has many sources. A few of these sources include underground septic tanks that leak; runoff of pesticides, herbicides, and fertilizers from lawns and farms; and even water flushed down toilets. National and international cooperation is necessary if water pollution is to be reduced. In the United States, the **Safe Drinking Water Act** and the **Clean Water Act** set up standards for sewage and wastewater-treatment facilities and for runoff from roadways and farms. Most water-ways are cleaner now than before these acts were voted on by Congress. But, many of the nation's streams, rivers, and lakes are still polluted. *How can oil dripping from a car eventually pollute a stream?*

Career CONNECTION

Craig Cox, Hydrogeologist

As a hydrogeologist, Craig Cox works with companies to help prevent groundwater contamination. Unused chemicals can soak into the ground, just like water can, contaminating the water table. Craig examines how industries dispose of dangerous materials to ensure they don't drain into the water table, contaminating drinking water. *What would a hydrogeologist look for to determine the danger of groundwater being contaminated by a chemical spill?*

Chapter 14 Assessment

Using Vocabulary

a. acid
b. acid rain
c. base
d. Clean Air Act
e. Clean Water Act
f. pH scale
g. photochemical smog
h. Safe Drinking Water Act
i. scrubber
j. sulfurous smog

Using the list above, replace the underlined words with the correct Vocabulary words.

1. <u>Smog that forms with the aid of light</u> contains ozone near Earth's surface.
2. <u>Acidic rain, snow, sleet, or hail</u> is created when sulfur dioxide combines with moisture in the air.
3. <u>A law passed to protect air in the United States</u> regulates car manufacturers.
4. <u>A device that lowers sulfur emissions from coal-burning power plants</u> increases the pH of smoke.
5. <u>A substance with a low pH number</u> can be toxic to organisms.

Checking Concepts

Choose the word or phrase that best answers the question.

6. What causes more smog pollution than any other source?
A) power plants
B) burning wastes
C) industries
D) cars

7. What forms when chemicals react with sunlight?
A) pH
B) photochemical smog
C) sulfurous smog
D) acid rain

8. What are substances with a low pH known as?
A) neutral
B) acidic
C) dense
D) basic

9. What combines with moisture in the air to form acid rain?
A) ozone
B) sulfur dioxide
C) lead
D) oxygen

10. The industries that produce the products you use each day consume how much of the freshwater used in the United States?
A) one-tenth
B) one-half
C) one-third
D) two-thirds

11. Which law was enacted to reduce the level of car emissions?
A) Clean Water Act
B) Clean Air Act
C) Safe Drinking Water Act
D) Hazardous Waste Act

12. What is the pH of acid rain?
A) less than 5.6
B) between 5.6 and 7.0
C) greater than 7.0
D) greater than 9.5

13. What kind of pollution are airborne solids that range in size from large grains to microscopic?
A) pH
B) ozone
C) particulate
D) photo

14. What causes most water pollution?
A) illegal dumping
B) industrial chemicals
C) everyday water use in the home
D) wastewater-treatment facilities

15. Which act gives money to local governments to treat wastewater?
A) Clean Water Act
B) Clean Air Act
C) Safe Drinking Water Act
D) Hazardous Waste Act

Thinking Critically

16. How might cities with smog problems lessen the dangers to people who live and work in the cities?

17. How are industries both helpful and harmful to humans?

18. How do plants help reduce water pollution?

19. Thermal pollution occurs when heated water is dumped into a nearby body of water. What effects does this type of pollution have on organisms living in the water?

20. What steps might a community in a desert area take to cope with water-supply problems?

Developing Skills

If you need help, refer to the **Skill Handbook.**

21. **Hypothesizing:** Earth's surface is nearly 75 percent water. Yet, much of this water is not available for many uses. Explain.

22. **Recognizing Cause and Effect:** What effect will an increase in the human population have on the need for freshwater?

23. **Concept Mapping:** Complete a concept map of the water cycle. Indicate how humans interrupt the cycle. Use the following phrases: *evaporation occurs, purified, drinking water, atmospheric water, wastewater, precipitation falls,* and *groundwater or surface water.*

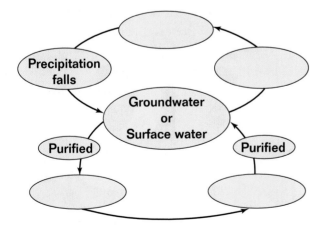

THE PRINCETON REVIEW

Test-Taking Tip

Use as Much Time as You Can You will not get extra points for finishing early. Work slowly and carefully on any test and make sure you don't make careless errors because you are hurrying to finish.

Test Practice

Use these questions to test your Science Proficiency.

1. Both acid rain and photochemical smog can be reduced by limiting emissions of a certain chemical from the exhaust of cars. Which chemical is it?
   A) sulfur   C) carbon
   B) ozone   D) nitrogen oxide

2. Determine approximately how much more acidic lemon juice is than milk. Use **Figure 14-4** and the information in Using Math in section 14-1 to help you answer this question.
   A) 100   C) 1000
   B) 10 000   D) 100 000

3. All of the following events happen when you inhale acid rain. Which event is the **LAST** in the series of events?
   A) Stress is put on your heart.
   B) Acid is deposited deep inside your lungs.
   C) Your lungs become irritated.
   D) Oxygen absorption by the lungs is difficult.

Interactions
in the
Living
World

What's Happening Here?

The world within the living cell can be filled with deception, intrigue, and deadly conflict. These jumbled rods (left, magnified 34 000 times) are particles of a tobacco mosaic virus that has taken over a cell of a tobacco plant. So, instead of following its own genetic code, the plant cell has been tricked into helping the virus multiply. Eventually the plant will weaken or die. Trickery in the living world can also be beneficial. Without asking some plants get help to spread their seeds. How? The seeds of the strawberry plant dot the surface of its delicious, juicy fruit (below). Animals eat the strawberries and deposit the seeds in new places. In this unit, you will explore the dynamic world within the cell and the processes by which cells multiply and change into various parts of complete living things. You will also learn some of the ways plants populate Earth.

inter NET CONNECTION

Explore the Glencoe Science Web Site at **www.glencoe.com/ sec/science** to find out more about topics found in this unit

Chapter Preview

Skills Preview

Skill Builders
- Use Numbers
- Map Concepts

Activities
- Measure in SI
- Conclude

MiniLabs
- Infer
- Observe

Reading Check ✔

As you read this chapter about cell processes, compare the use of the word *compound* to its use in other subject areas. What are the similarities and differences?

Explore Activity

Have you ever forgotten to water a plant and remembered when the plant began to wilt? After you watered the plant, it probably straightened up and looked healthier. What caused the plant to straighten? How long does it take for a wilted plant to return to normal? Why does this happen? In the following activity, find out about water entering and leaving plant cells.

Observe Cell Processes

1. Label a small bowl "salt water." Pour 250 mL of water into the bowl. Then, add 15 g of salt to the water and stir.

2. Pour 250 mL of water into another small bowl.

3. Place two carrot sticks into each of the small bowls. Also, place two carrot sticks on the lab table.

4. After 30 minutes, remove the carrot sticks from the bowls and examine all six carrot sticks. In your Science Journal, describe the six carrot sticks.

Science Journal

What do you think would happen if you moved the carrot sticks from the plain water to the lab table, the ones from the salt water into the plain water, and the ones from the lab table into the salt water? Enter your predictions in your Science Journal.

Chemistry of Living Things

The Nature of Matter

Do you know what makes up Earth? If you ask someone, he or she may answer "matter and energy." Matter is anything that has mass and takes up space. How many things can you think of that fit that category?

Atoms

Everything in your environment, including you, is made of matter. Matter is made of atoms. **Figure 15-1** shows a model of an oxygen atom. At the center of an atom is a nucleus. A nucleus contains protons and neutrons. A proton has a positive charge, a neutron has no charge, and they have nearly equal masses. Outside the nucleus are electrons. An electron has a negative charge. About 1837 electrons equal the mass of one proton.

But, what about energy in your environment? Sunlight and electricity are forms of energy. Energy holds the parts of an atom together. One form of energy, called chemical energy, bonds groups of atoms together. To release or transfer this energy, a chemical reaction must occur. In a chemical reaction, chemical bonds break, new bonds form, and atoms are rearranged. The substances produced are different from those that began the chemical reaction. As shown in **Figure 15-2,** chemical reactions take place in living organisms.

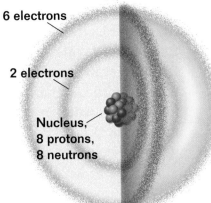

Oxygen atom

6 electrons

2 electrons

Nucleus, 8 protons, 8 neutrons

Figure 15-1 An oxygen atom model shows the placement of electrons, protons, and neutrons.

Figure 15-2 When fireflies blink and shine in the dark, energy is released in the form of light as chemical bonds are broken and new ones are formed.

Table 15-1

Elements That Make Up the Human Body

Symbol	Element	Percent
O	Oxygen	65.0
C	Carbon	18.5
H	Hydrogen	9.5
N	Nitrogen	3.3
Ca	Calcium	1.5
P	Phosphorus	1.0
K	Potassium	0.4
S	Sulfur	0.3
Na	Sodium	0.2
Cl	Chlorine	0.2
Mg	Magnesium	0.1

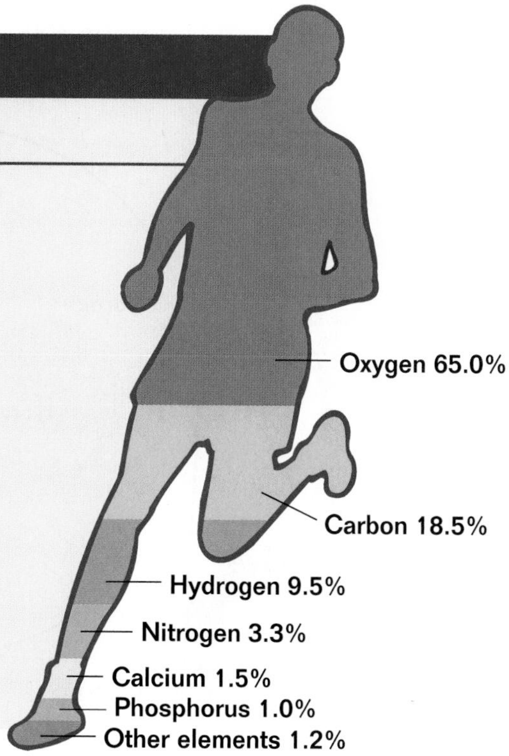

Oxygen 65.0%
Carbon 18.5%
Hydrogen 9.5%
Nitrogen 3.3%
Calcium 1.5%
Phosphorus 1.0%
Other elements 1.2%

Elements

When something is made up of only one kind of atom, it is called an element. An element can't be broken down into a simpler form by ordinary chemical reactions. The element oxygen is made up of only oxygen atoms, and hydrogen is made up of only hydrogen atoms. Each element has its own symbol. Ninety elements occur naturally on Earth. Everything, including you, is made of one, or a combination of, these elements. **Table 15-1** lists elements as they occur in the human body. What two elements make up most of your body?

How Atoms Combine

Suppose you've just eaten an apple, such as the one in **Figure 15-3.** Did you know that the apple contains a sugar made of the elements carbon, oxygen, and hydrogen? The water in the apple contains both oxygen and hydrogen. Notice that the apple and water both contain oxygen. Yet, in one case, oxygen is part of a colorless, tasteless liquid—water. Oxygen is also part of a colorful solid—the apple. How can one element be part of two materials that are so different? The atoms of elements combine chemically to form new substances called compounds.

CHEMISTRY INTEGRATION

Periodic Table of Elements
All elements are arranged in a chart known as the periodic table of elements. What information does it provide for each element?

Hydrogen 1 **H** 1.008	Carbon 6 **C** 12.011	Nitrogen 7 **N** 14.007	Oxygen 8 **O** 15.999

Figure 15-3
An apple is made up of mostly carbon, oxygen, and hydrogen.

Figure 15-4 The chemical formula for a water molecule is H_2O.

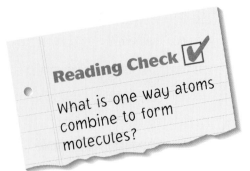

Glucose, an energy-storing sugar in plant cells, is a compound. It is made of the elements carbon, hydrogen, and oxygen and has the chemical formula $C_6H_{12}O_6$. When elements form a compound, the properties of the individual elements change. How does this happen?

One way that atoms combine is by sharing their outermost electrons. The combined atoms form a molecule. For example, two atoms of hydrogen can share electrons with one atom of oxygen to form one molecule of water as illustrated in **Figure 15-4.** Water is a compound composed of molecules. The properties of hydrogen and oxygen are changed when they combine to form water. Under normal conditions on Earth, oxygen and hydrogen are gases. Yet, water can be a liquid, a solid, or a gas. When hydrogen and oxygen combine, changes occur and a new substance forms. ☑

Ions

Some atoms combine by sharing electrons. But, atoms also combine because they've become positively or negatively charged.

Atoms are usually neutral. They have no overall electric charge. Under certain conditions, however, atoms can lose or gain electrons. When an atom loses electrons, it has more protons than electrons so the atom is positively charged. When an atom gains electrons, it has more electrons than protons so the atom is negatively charged. Electrically charged atoms—positive or negative—are called ions.

Ions are attracted to one another when they have opposite charges. Oppositely charged ions join to form electrically neutral compounds. Table salt is made of sodium (Na) and chlorine (Cl) ions. As shown in **Figure 15-5,** a chlorine atom captures an electron of a sodium atom. The chlorine becomes a negatively charged ion, and the sodium a positively charged ion. These oppositely charged ions are attracted to each other and form the compound sodium chloride, NaCl.

Reading Check ☑

What is one way atoms combine to form molecules?

Mixtures

Many times, two substances can be mixed together without combining chemically. A **mixture** is a combination of substances in which individual substances retain their own properties. For example, if you mix sugar and salt together, neither substance changes, nor do they combine chemically. Mixtures can be solids, liquids, gases, or any combination of them.

Solutions and Suspensions

Why are molecules important? In living organisms, cell membranes, cytoplasm, and other substances are all in the form of molecules. During its lifetime, a cell will make and break apart many molecules for growth, repair, and energy. Many of these molecules are found dissolved in the cytoplasm, forming a solution. A solution is a mixture in which two or more substances are mixed evenly.

Air is a mixture of many things. Weather forecasts often include information about *air quality.* Visit the Glencoe Science Web Site at **www.glencoe. com/sec/science** for more information about air quality.

VISUALIZING
Ions

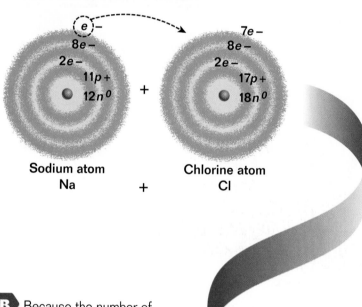

Sodium atom
Na
+

Chlorine atom
Cl

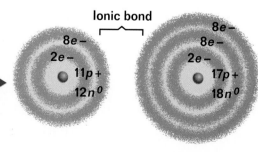

Ionic bond

Sodium ion
(+)
+
NaCl
Chloride ion
(−)

Figure 15-5 When sodium and chlorine react to form table salt, ions are formed.

A Sodium has just one electron in its outer energy level. Chlorine has seven electrons in its outer energy level. When sodium and chlorine combine, sodium loses its electron to chlorine, giving both atoms stable outer energy levels of eight electrons.

B Because the number of protons in sodium's nucleus is one more than the total number of electrons remaining around the nucleus, sodium has a 1+ charge. By gaining an electron, the total number of electrons around chlorine's nucleus is one more than than the number of protons in its nucleus, so chlorine has a 1− charge.

When you dissolve salt in water, you get a salt solution. You've probably noticed the taste of salt when you perspire. That's because your cells are surrounded by a salt solution. Living organisms also contain suspensions. A suspension is a mixture in which substances are evenly spread through a liquid or gas. Unlike solutions, the particles in a suspension eventually sink to the bottom. Blood, shown in **Figure 15-6,** is an example of a suspension. If a test tube of blood is left undisturbed, the red blood cells and white blood cells will gradually sink to the bottom. Because your blood is constantly moved by the pumping action of your heart, the cells remain suspended.

Figure 15-6 When a test tube of whole blood (right test tube) is left standing, the blood cells and the plasma separate, (left test tube).

Organic Compounds

Compounds in living organisms may be classified as either organic or inorganic. Most compounds containing carbon are **organic compounds. Table 15-2** compares the four groups of organic compounds that make up all living things—carbohydrates, lipids, proteins, and nucleic acids.

Problem Solving

Examining the Properties of Ice

Have you ever noticed that as water freezes, ice forms on the surface first, not at the bottom? When you place ice cubes in a glass of water, they float. This difference between water and ice is important in nature.

Think Critically

1. When a lake or pond freezes over, what happens to the living organisms in it?

2. Predict what would happen to the living organisms in a lake or pond if freezing occurred from the bottom up.

3. Does ice provide living organisms protection from cold temperatures? Explain.

Table 15-2

Organic Compounds That Make Up Life

	Carbohydrate	Lipid	Protein	Nucleic Acid
Elements	carbon, hydrogen, and oxygen	carbon, hydrogen, and oxygen	carbon, hydrogen, oxygen, nitrogen, and sulfur	carbon, hydrogen, oxygen, nitrogen, and phosphorus
Unit	simple sugar	fatty acid	amino acid	nucleotide
Examples	sugars, starch, and cellulose	fats, oils, and waxes	enzymes, skin, hair	DNA, RNA
Function	supply energy for cell processes; form plant structures	store large amounts of energy long term	regulate cell processes and build cell structures	carry hereditary information
Location	cell membranes, cytoplasm, and plant cell walls	cell membranes and plant cell walls	throughout cells and cell membranes	nucleus, mitochondria, ribosomes, and chloroplasts

Carbohydrates are organic compounds made up of carbon, hydrogen, and oxygen. Carbohydrates supply energy for cell processes. Lipids, commonly called fats and oils, are organic compounds that store and release even larger amounts of energy than carbohydrates.

Proteins are the building blocks of many structural components of organisms. They are scattered throughout cell membranes and are made up of smaller molecules called amino acids. Certain proteins called **enzymes** regulate nearly all chemical reactions in cells without being changed.

Nucleic acids are large organic molecules that store important coded information in cells. One nucleic acid, DNA, is found in the nucleus, in chromosomes, in mitochondria, and in chloroplasts. It carries information that directs each cell's activities. Another nucleic acid, RNA, carries the information required to make proteins and enzymes.

Mini Lab

Determining How Enzymes Work
Procedure

1. Make a mark on one of two clean test tubes. Place them in a test-tube rack then fill each halfway with milk.
2. Place a tablet of rennin, an enzyme, in a small plastic bowl. Crush the tablet using the back of a metal spoon. Add the crushed tablet to the marked test tube.
3. Let both test tubes stand undisturbed during your class period.
4. Observe what happens to the milk.

Analysis
1. What effect did the rennin have on the milk?
2. Predict what would eventually happen to the milk without rennin.
3. Infer how rennin's effect on milk might be useful to the dairy industry.

Figure 15-7 All organisms depend on water for life.

Inorganic Compounds

Most **inorganic compounds** are made from elements other than carbon. Water, an inorganic compound shown in **Figure 15-7,** makes up a large part of living matter. It is one of the most important compounds in living things. Substances used in cells must be dissolved in water. Nutrients and waste materials are carried throughout your body in solution form.

Section Assessment

1. How are atoms different from molecules?
2. What is the difference between organic and inorganic compounds?
3. What are the four groups of organic compounds that make up all living things?
4. **Think Critically:** If you mix salt, sand, and sugar with water in a small jar, will the result be a suspension, a solution, or both?
5. **Skill Builder**
   Using Numbers Chemical equations consist of letters and numbers. The letters represent elements, and the numbers are used to represent atoms and molecules. Do the **Chapter 15 Skill Activity** on page 740 to learn how numbers are used in chemical equations.

Using Computers

Spreadsheet Find the percentage of elements that make up Earth's crust. Make a spreadsheet that includes this information and the information in **Table 15-1.** Create a circle graph for each set of percentages. What five elements have the total highest percentages? If you need help, refer to page 722.

Cell Transport

Control of Materials by Cells

Cells obtain food, oxygen, and other substances from their environment. They also release waste materials into their environment. If a cell has a membrane around it, how do these things move into and out of the cell? How does the cell control what enters and leaves?

Do you enjoy opening a window to allow fresh air into a room? How do you prevent unwanted things like insects, birds, or leaves from coming through the window? As seen in **Figure 15-8,** a window screen provides the protection needed to keep unwanted things outside. It also allows some things to pass from the room to the outside like air, unpleasant odors, or smoke. A cell membrane performs in a similar way for the cell. It allows some things to enter or leave the cell while keeping other things outside or inside the cell. When membranes function this way, they are called selectively permeable. The window screen is selectively permeable based on the size of the wire grid.

Diffusion

Molecules in solids, liquids, and gases constantly and randomly move. When molecules move from areas where there are more of them, into areas where there are fewer of them, it is called **diffusion.**

What **You'll Learn**

► The function of a selectively permeable membrane
► The processes of diffusion and osmosis
► The differences between passive transport and active transport

Vocabulary

diffusion
equilibrium
osmosis
passive
  transport

active
  transport
endocytosis
exocytosis

Why **It's Important**

► Substances move in your body by entering and leaving cells.

Figure 15-8 A cell membrane, like a screen, will let some things through more easily than others. Air gets through, but insects are kept out.

Figure 15-9 Diffusion happens because molecules are in constant motion.

A Blue crystals were added to a beaker of water. In a few minutes, the blue-colored ions of the dissolving compound have partially diffused throughout the water.

B After two days, diffusion is greater.

C Complete diffusion can take months or even years if the water is left undisturbed and covered.

Mini Lab

Observing the Rate of Diffusion

Procedure

1. Use two beakers of equal size. Label one "hot," then fill it halfway with hot water. Label the other "cold," then fill it halfway with cold water. **CAUTION:** *Do not spill hot water on your skin.*

2. Add one drop of food coloring to each beaker. Carefully release the drop just above the water's surface to avoid splashing and disturbing the water.

3. Observe the beakers and record your observations. Repeat your observations after 10 minutes and record them again.

Analysis

1. Describe what happens when food coloring is added to each beaker.

2. How does temperature affect the rate of diffusion?

The random movement of molecules or particles is why diffusion happens.

Particles diffuse in liquids and in gases. **Figure 15-9** illustrates the diffusion of a blue compound in a beaker of water. You experience the effects of diffusion when someone opens a bottle of perfume in a closed room.

Drop a sugar cube into a glass of water and taste the water. Then, taste it again in three or four hours. At first, the sugar molecules are concentrated near the sugar cube in the bottom of the glass. Then, slowly, the sugar molecules diffuse throughout the water until they are more evenly distributed. When the molecules of one substance are spread evenly throughout another substance, a state of **equilibrium** occurs. Molecules don't stop moving when equilibrium is reached. They continue to move and maintain equilibrium.

Osmosis—The Diffusion of Water

You may remember that water makes up a large part of living matter. The diffusion of water through a cell membrane is called **osmosis**. Osmosis is important to cells because they contain water molecules and most cells are surrounded by water molecules. If cells aren't surrounded by relatively pure water, water will diffuse out of them. This is why water left the carrot cells in the Explore Activity at the beginning of the chapter. Because there were relatively fewer water molecules in the salt solution around the carrot cells than in the carrot cells, water moved out of the cells into the salt solution. Losing water from inside a plant cell causes the cell to shrink, pulling the cell membrane away from the cell wall, as seen in **Figure 15-10A.** This reduces the pressure against the cell wall and the plant cell becomes limp. If the carrot sticks were taken out of the salt water and put in pure water, the water around the cells would move into the cells. The cells would expand, pressing their cell membranes against their cell walls, as in **Figure 15-10B.** Pressure would increase and the plant cells would become firm. That is why the carrot sticks would be crisp again. ☑

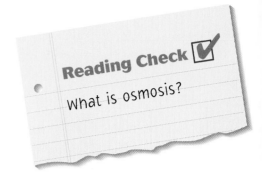

Reading Check ☑

What is osmosis?

Figure 15-10 Cells respond differently depending on whether the concentration of water inside the cell is equal to, greater than, or less than the water concentrations in the environment.

B Equilibrium occurs when water leaves and enters the cells at the same rate.

A Wilting occurs when more water leaves the cells than enters them.

Types of Transport

Cells take in many substances. Some substances pass easily through the cell membrane by diffusion. Other substances, such as glucose molecules, are so large that they enter the cell only with the help of transport protein molecules in the cell membrane. This process is known as *facilitated diffusion.* Transport proteins allow needed substances or wastes to move through the cell membrane. Diffusion and facilitated diffusion are types of passive transport. **Passive transport** is the movement of substances through the cell membrane without the use of cellular energy.

Active Transport

Sometimes, a substance is needed in a cell even though the amount of that substance inside the cell is already greater than the amount outside the cell. For example, root cells require minerals from the soil. The roots may already may contain more of those minerals than the surrounding soil. In this case, the minerals cannot move into the root cells by diffusion or facilitated diffusion. In order for the minerals to enter the root cells, cellular energy must be used. When energy is required to move materials through a cell membrane, **active transport** takes place in the cell membrane.

Active transport involves transport proteins. In active transport, a transport protein binds with the needed particle and uses cellular energy to move it through the cell membrane, as illustrated in **Figure 15-11.** When the particle is released, the transport protein is ready to move another needed particle.

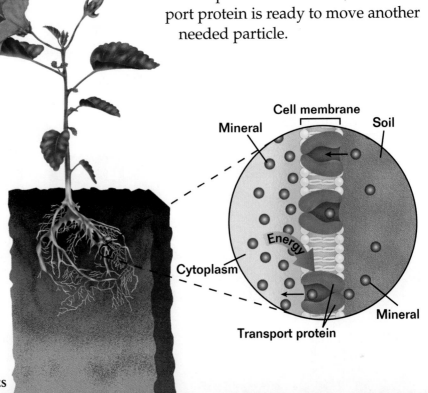

Figure 15-11 Plant root cells use active transport to take in minerals from the surrounding soil.

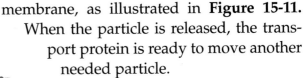

Endocytosis and Exocytosis

Large protein molecules and bacteria may enter a cell when they are surrounded by the cell membrane. The cell membrane folds in on itself, enclosing the item in a sphere. The sphere pinches off, and the resulting vacuole enters the cytoplasm. This process is called **endocytosis** (en duh sy TOH sus). Some one-celled organisms, such as amoebas, take in food this way.

Vesicles and vacuoles are transport and storage structures in a cell's cytoplasm. They release their contents outside the cell by a process called **exocytosis** (ek soh sy TOH sus). Exocytosis happens in the opposite way that endocytosis happens. The membrane of the vesicle or vacuole fuses with the cell's membrane, and the vesicle's or vacuole's contents are released. Endocytosis and exocytosis are illustrated in **Figure 15-12.**

Figure 15-12 Substances that are too large to pass through cell membranes by passive or active transport enter and leave cells by endocytosis and exocytosis.

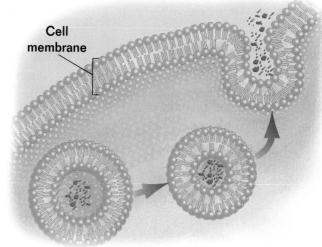

Cell membrane

A A white blood cell uses endocytosis to engulf a bacterial cell.

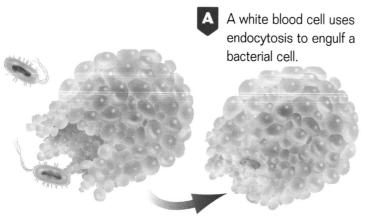

B In exocytosis, substances in vacuoles or vesicles are released at the cell membrane.

Section Assessment

1. In what way are cell membranes selectively permeable?
2. Compare and contrast osmosis and diffusion.
3. Identify the molecules that help substances move through the cell membrane.
4. **Think Critically:** Why are fresh fruits and vegetables sprinkled with water in produce markets?
5. **Skill Builder**
   Concept Mapping Make a network tree concept map to use as a study guide to help you tell the difference between passive transport and active transport. Begin with the phrase *Transport through membranes.* If you need help, refer to Concept Mapping in the **Skill Handbook** on page 698.

Science Journal Seawater has a higher concentration of salts than plain water. In your Science Journal, explain why drinking large amounts of seawater would be dangerous to humans.

Observing Osmosis

Materials

- Egg
- containers (500 mL) with covers (2)
- White vinegar (250 mL)
- Light corn syrup (250 mL)
- Graduated cylinder (100 mL)
- Labels (A and B)
- Small bowl
- Spoon

It is difficult to see osmosis occurring in cells because most cells are so small. However, a few cells can be seen without the aid of a microscope. Try this activity to see how osmosis occurs in a large cell.

What You'll Investigate

How does osmosis occur in an egg cell?

Goals

- **Observe** osmosis in an egg cell.
- **Determine** what affects osmosis.

Procedure 🥽 🧤 🚫

1. **Copy** the tables below and use them to record your data and observations.

2. **Place** label A on one of the 500-mL containers and label B on the other. **Pour** the vinegar into container A and the syrup into container B. **Record** these data on the table. **Cover** container B.

Volume Data		
	Beginning volume	**Ending volume**
Vinegar		
Syrup		

Egg Observations	
After 30 minutes	
After 2 days	
After 3 days	

3. **Place** the egg in container A and **cover** the container.

4. **Observe** the egg after 30 minutes, then again in two days. After each observation, **record** the egg's appearance on the table.

5. After the second observation, **remove** container A's cover. Carefully **remove** the egg from the liquid with a spoon and gently **rinse** the egg in a slow stream of cool tap water.

6. **Remove** the cover from container B. Carefully **place** the egg in the syrup and replace the cover.

7. **Measure** the volume of liquid in container A and **record** on the table.

8. **Observe** the egg the next day and **record** its appearance on the table.

9. **Remove** container B's cover. Gently remove the egg and allow the syrup to drain back into container B. Then, place the egg in the small bowl. **Measure** the volume of syrup and **record** on the table.

Conclude and Apply

1. What caused the change in volume of container A and container B?

2. Calculate the amount of water that moved into and out of the egg.

3. **Infer** what part of the egg controlled what moved into and out of the cell.

Energy in Cells

Trapping Energy for Life

Think of all the energy players use in a basketball game. Where does that energy come from? The simplest answer is "from the food they eat." Cells take chemical energy stored in food and change it into forms needed to perform all the activities necessary for life. In every cell, these activities begin as chemical reactions. The total of all chemical reactions in an organism is called **metabolism.**

Living things are divided into two groups—producers and consumers—based on how they obtain their food energy. Organisms that make their own food, such as plants, are called **producers.** Organisms that can't make their own food are **consumers.**

Photosynthesis

Most producers use photosynthesis to produce food that has energy stored in its chemical bonds. The energy in sunlight triggers the chemical reactions of photosynthesis. Water and carbon dioxide (CO_2) are combined, producing sugar and giving off oxygen as a by-product. The chemical bonds, which hold the sugar molecules together, store energy. In plants and other photosynthetic producers, pigments capture sunlight's energy. Chlorophyll, a green pigment, is found in the chloroplasts where photosynthesis occurs. During photosynthesis, more sugar is made than the plant needs for survival. Excess sugar is changed and stored as starches and other carbohydrates. **Figure 15-13** illustrates the products of photosynthesis such as trees, grass, and apples.

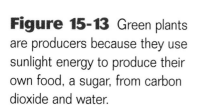

What **You'll Learn**

- ► The differences between producers and consumers
- ► The processes of photosynthesis and respiration
- ► How cells get energy from glucose through fermentation

Vocabulary

metabolism   consumer
producer   fermentation

Why **It's Important**

- ► Because of photosynthesis and respiration, energy gets from the sun to you.

Figure 15-13 Green plants are producers because they use sunlight energy to produce their own food, a sugar, from carbon dioxide and water.

Do you eat vegetables? Have you ever watched sheep graze or a bird catch a worm? People, sheep, and birds are examples of consumers. Consumers take in energy by eating producers or other consumers. These relationships form food chains. Producers are the first link in any food chain.

Releasing Energy for Life

To release and use the energy stored in food molecules, all organisms, both producers and consumers, must break down food molecules. For most cells, glucose is the food that is broken down. To break down glucose, many processes must happen. The final breakdown and energy release is called cellular respiration. This process usually requires the presence of oxygen. For some cells, it takes place in the mitochondria.

What happens in respiration?

Before respiration begins, glucose molecules in the cytoplasm are broken down into simpler substances. These substances enter the mitochondria where their stored energy is released in a series of chemical reactions called respiration. The final products of respiration are carbon dioxide, water vapor, and energy. Some of the energy released by respiration is used to produce high-energy molecules, and some is lost as heat.

Photosynthesis

$6CO_2 + 6H_2O$ + light energy $\longrightarrow$ $C_6H_{12}O_6 + 6O_2$
carbon water $\qquad$ chlorophyll $\qquad$ sugar oxygen
dioxide

Respiration

$C_6H_{12}O_6 + 6O_2$ $\longrightarrow$ $6CO_2 + 6H_2O$ + energy
sugar oxygen $\qquad\qquad$ carbon water
$\qquad\qquad\qquad\qquad$ dioxide

CHEMISTRY
INTEGRATION ➤

Fermentation

During periods of vigorous activity, your muscles need more and more energy. You begin to breathe harder to supply the oxygen needed for respiration and the release of energy. If you are unable to supply enough oxygen, your muscles can use a process called fermentation to release energy. **Fermentation** is a form of respiration that releases energy from glucose when oxygen is not available. But, fermentation releases a smaller amount of energy than respiration that uses oxygen. In muscle cells, lactic acid is produced during fermentation. The presence of lactic acid is why your muscles may become stiff and sore after you use them too much.

Fermentation takes place in the cytoplasm of cells, not in the mitochondria. Similar to respiration with oxygen, molecules of glucose are changed to simpler substances before fermentation begins. Prokaryotic organisms, one-celled organisms without a nucleus or other membrane-surrounded structures in the cytoplasm, may use fermentation to release energy from food molecules. Yeast and some bacteria use a form of fermentation, alcohol fermentation, to release energy and carbon dioxide (CO_2). **Figure 15-14** discusses the role of yeast in making the types of bread shown in the photograph. ☑

Photosynthesis and respiration are alike because both involve complex sets of reactions. Both occur in specific organelles, involve energy, and require enzymes. In many ways, photosynthesis is the opposite of respiration. The end products of respiration are the starting materials of photosynthesis. In summary, producers capture the sun's energy and store it in the form of food. Consumers eat producers. Cells use the glucose made by producers for energy. **Figure 15-15** shows the relationship between photosynthesis and respiration.

Figure 15-14 Yeast is an organism that breaks down the glucose in bread dough to produce carbon dioxide and alcohol. The bubbles of carbon dioxide cause the dough to rise. Baking the bread evaporates the alcohol.

Reading Check ☑

Where in a cell does fermentation take place?

Figure 15-15 Photosynthesis and respiration are related because the products of one may become the starting materials for the other.

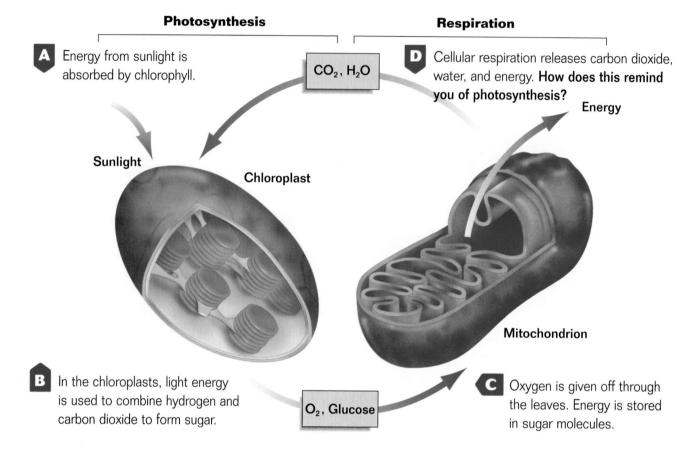

Photosynthesis

A Energy from sunlight is absorbed by chlorophyll.

CO_2, H_2O

Sunlight

Chloroplast

B In the chloroplasts, light energy is used to combine hydrogen and carbon dioxide to form sugar.

O_2, Glucose

Respiration

D Cellular respiration releases carbon dioxide, water, and energy. **How does this remind you of photosynthesis?**

Energy

Mitochondrion

C Oxygen is given off through the leaves. Energy is stored in sugar molecules.

Section Assessment

1. Explain the difference between producers and consumers.

2. Explain how the energy used by all living things on Earth can be traced back to sunlight.

3. Compare the amount of energy released by respiration, which uses oxygen, to the amount of energy released by fermentation.

4. **Think Critically:** How can indoor plants help purify the air in a room?

5. **Skill Builder**
   Comparing and Contrasting Make a table that compares and contrasts respiration and fermentation. If you need help, refer to Comparing and Contrasting in the **Skill Handbook** on page 704.

Using Math

Refer to the chemical equation for respiration. Calculate the number of carbon, hydrogen, and oxygen atoms before and after respiration. How do they compare?

Bioreactors—
Harvesting Cell By-Products

Microscopic Workforce

Q: "What's that microorganism doing in the bread dough?"
A: "Its job!"

For centuries, people unknowingly used microorganisms to make bread rise and to ferment wine and beer. Microorganisms and their by-products and processes remained a mystery until the middle of the nineteenth century. Since that time, scientists have learned a lot about the structure, processes, and uses of microorganisms. They have developed new technologies for growing microorganisms and harvesting their by-products to use in a wide variety of products.

Bioreactors

The cultivation of large quantities of microorganisms and their by-products is done in bioreactors—giant, sterile, stainless-steel vats that hold 945 000 L or more (see inset). If growing conditions are right, less than 30 g of bacteria may become a mass of nearly 3 metric tons in just one day. Growing conditions inside the vats are carefully controlled and electronically monitored. Under different growing conditions, microorganisms produce different substances. For example, when the nitrogen in its environment is below a certain level, the mold *Penicillium* (seen at far left) makes the antibiotic penicillin.

Cellular By-Products

Today, microorganisms and their by-products are cultivated in bioreactors to make medicines, vitamins, alcohol, food thickeners, and other substances. Often, the microorganism itself is the desired product. For instance, the bacterium *Bacillus thuringensis* is grown for use as a natural pesticide to kill caterpillars that damage vegetable crops.

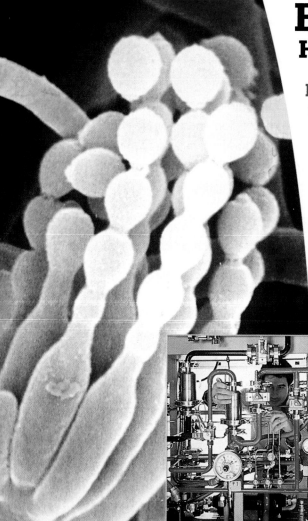

interNET CONNECTION

Visit the Glencoe Science Web Site at **www.glencoe.com/sec/science** to learn more about microorganisms. In your Science Journal, list six products that are made using this technology.

Materials

- Test tubes,
  16 mm × 150 mm
  with stoppers (4)
  *small, clear-glass baby
  food jars with lids (4)*
- Test-tube rack
- Stirring rod
- Balance scale
- Scissors
- Carbonated water
- Bromothymol blue solution in dropping bottle
- Aged tap water
  distilled water
- Pieces of *Elodea* (2)
  other water plants

  Alternate Materials

Photosynthesis and Respiration

Every living cell carries on many chemical processes. Two important chemical processes are respiration and photosynthesis. Every cell, including the ones in your body, carries on respiration. But, some plant cells, unlike your cells, carry on both. In this experiment, you will investigate when these processes occur in plant cells.

What You'll Investigate

When do plants carry on photosynthesis and respiration?

Goals

- **Observe** green water plants in the light and dark.
- **Determine** whether green plants carry on both photosynthesis and respiration.

Safety Precautions

Protect clothing and eyes and be careful using chemicals.
CAUTION: *Do not get chemicals on your skin.*

Procedure

1. **Label** each test tube using the numbers 1, 2, 3, and 4. **Pour** 5 mL aged tap water into each test tube.

2. **Add** 10 drops of carbonated water to test tubes 1 and 2.

3. **Add** 10 drops of bromothyol blue to each test tube. Bromothyol blue turns green to yellow in the presence of an acid.

4. **Cut** two 10-cm pieces of *Elodea*. **Place** one piece of *Elodea* in the liquid in test tube 1 and one piece in the liquid in test tube 3. Stopper all test tubes.

5. Copy the Test Tube Data Table in your Science Journal. **Record** the color of the solution in each of the four test tubes.

6. **Place** test tubes 1 and 2 in bright light. Place tubes 3 and 4 in the dark. Observe the test tubes for 30 minutes or until there is a color change. Record the colors.

Conclude and Apply

1. What is indicated by the color of the water in all four test tubes at the start of the activity?

2. Infer what happened in the test tube or tubes that changed color after 30 minutes.

3. What can you conclude about the test tube or tubes that didn't change color after 30 minutes?

4. Describe the purpose of test tubes 2 and 4.

5. Does this experiment show that both photosynthesis and respiration occur in plants? Explain.

Test Tube Data Table		
Test tube	Color at start	Color after 30 minutes
1		
2		
3		
4		

For a **preview** of this chapter, study this Reviewing Main Ideas before you read the chapter. After you have studied this chapter, you can use the Reviewing Main Ideas to **review** the chapter.

The Glencoe MindJogger, Audiocassettes, and CD-ROM provide additional opportunities for review.

Section

15-1 CHEMISTRY OF LIVING THINGS

Matter is anything that has mass and takes up space. Atoms are the basic building blocks of matter. Energy in matter is in the chemical bonds that hold atoms together. Matter made of only one kind of atom is an element. Elements combine chemically to form compounds. The properties of the compound are different from those of the elements that made it. In a **mixture,** another form of matter, each substance retains its own properties. All **organic compounds** contain the element carbon. The organic compounds in living things are carbohydrates, lipids, proteins, and nucleic acids. Most **inorganic compounds,** such as water, do not contain carbon. Both organic and inorganic compounds are important to living things. *What is the relationship between matter and energy?*

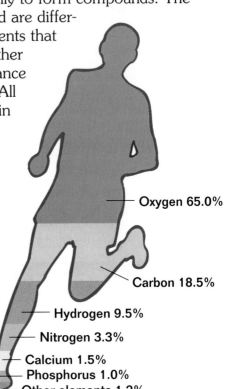

Oxygen 65.0%

Carbon 18.5%

Hydrogen 9.5%

Nitrogen 3.3%

Calcium 1.5%
Phosphorus 1.0%
Other elements 1.2%

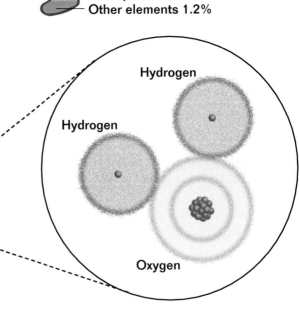

Hydrogen

Hydrogen

Oxygen

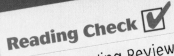

Reading Check ✓

Without reading Review Main Ideas, write a three to five sentence summary for one section of this chapter. Reread the section if necessary.

15-2 CELL TRANSPORT

Particles of matter are in constant, random motion. **Diffusion** is the movement of particles from areas where they are more numerous to areas where they are less numerous. **Osmosis** is the diffusion of water through a membrane. The cell membrane controls what enters and leaves a cell. Diffusion and osmosis are forms of **passive transport,** which is the movement of particles across a cell membrane that requires no cellular energy. When a transport protein in the cell membrane uses energy to move particles across the cell membrane, it is called **active transport.** Large particles may enter a cell by **endocytosis** and leave by **exocytosis.** *Using the concept of osmosis, explain why people with sore throats often gargle with salt water.*

15-3 ENERGY IN CELLS

Photosynthesis is the process by which some **producers** change light energy into chemical energy. Chlorophyll, in the chloroplasts of a green plant's cells, traps light energy for photosynthesis. Plants use some of the sugars they make as energy for other cellular functions. Excess sugar is stored as starch or other carbohydrates. Cells release stored energy from food molecules by respiration. Respiration that uses oxygen releases all of the energy in the food molecules and gives off carbon dioxide and water vapor as by-products. Respiration without oxygen is called **fermentation.** Fermentation releases only part of the energy in food molecules. *How are photosynthesis and respiration important to living things?*

Chapter 15 Assessment

Using Vocabulary

a. active transport
b. consumer
c. diffusion
d. endocytosis
e. enzyme
f. equilibrium
g. exocytosis
h. fermentation
i. inorganic compound
j. metabolism
k. mixture
l. organic compound
m. osmosis
n. passive transport
o. producer

Using the list of Vocabulary words, give two examples for each statement.

1. categories for the movement of materials through the cell membrane
2. classifications for substances in living organisms
3. organisms in a food chain
4. how large food particles enter and large waste particles leave an amoeba
5. types of passive transport

Checking Concepts

Choose the word or phrase that answers the question.

6. What is it called when energy is used to move molecules?
   A) diffusion
   B) osmosis
   C) active transport
   D) passive transport

7. How may bacteria be taken into cells?
   A) osmosis
   B) endocytosis
   C) exocytosis
   D) diffusion

8. What occurs when molecules are evenly distributed through a solid, liquid, or gas?
   A) equilibrium
   B) metabolism
   C) fermentation
   D) cellular respiration

9. Which of the following is an example of a carbohydrate?
   A) enzymes
   B) sugars
   C) waxes
   D) proteins

10. What are chromosomes made of?
    A) carbohydrates
    B) water molecules
    C) lipids
    D) nucleic acids

11. What organic molecule releases the greatest amount of energy?
    A) carbohydrate
    B) water
    C) lipid
    D) nucleic acid

12. What kind of molecule is water?
    A) organic
    B) lipid
    C) carbohydrate
    D) inorganic

13. Which of these is an example of an organic compound?
    A) $C_6H_{12}O_6$
    B) NO_2
    C) H_2O
    D) O_2

14. What are organisms that can't make their own food called?
    A) biodegradables
    B) producers
    C) consumers
    D) enzymes

15. What process requires chlorophyll?
    A) fermentation
    B) endocytosis
    C) diffusion
    D) photosynthesis

Thinking Critically

16. If you could place one red blood cell in distilled water, what would you see happen to the cell? Explain.

17. In snowy places, salt is used to melt ice on the roads. Explain what may happen to many roadside plants as a result.

18. Why does sugar dissolve faster in hot tea than in iced tea?

19. What would happen to the consumers in a lake if all the producers died?

20. Meat tenderizers contain protein enzymes. How do these enzymes affect meat?

Developing Skills

If you need help, refer to the **Skill Handbook.**

21. **Interpreting Data:** Water plants were placed at different distances from a light source. Bubbles coming from the plants were counted to measure the rate of photosynthesis. What can you say about how light affected the rate?

Photosynthesis in Water Plants

Beaker number	Distance from light	Bubbles per minute
1	10 cm	45
2	30 cm	30
3	50 cm	19
4	70 cm	6
5	100 cm	1

22. **Making and Using Graphs:** Using the data from question 21, make a line graph that shows the relationship between the rate of photosynthesis and the distance from light.

23. **Concept Mapping:** Complete the events chain concept map to sequence the parts of matter from smallest to largest: *element, atom,* and *compound.*

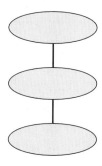

24. **Hypothesizing:** Make a hypothesis about what will happen to wilted celery when placed into a glass of plain water.

THE PRINCETON REVIEW

Test-Taking Tip

If It Looks Too Good to Be True . . . Beware of answer choices that seem obvious. Remember that only one answer choice is correct of the several that you're offered for each question. Check each answer choice carefully before selecting one.

Test Practice

Use these questions to test your Science Proficiency.

$$6CO_2 + 6H_2O + \text{light energy} \xrightarrow{\text{chlorophyll}} C_6H_{12}O_6 + 6O_2\uparrow$$

1. The equation above is a summary of photosynthesis. According to the equation, what is one product of photosynthesis?
   A) water
   B) chlorophyll
   C) carbon dioxide
   D) oxygen

2. What type of molecule are enzymes?
   A) carbohydrate
   B) lipid
   C) protein
   D) nucleic acid

3. What process keeps some raw vegetables crisp in cool water?
   A) endocytosis   C) exocytosis
   B) diffusion   D) transpiration

4. Which of these statements is **NOT** true for respiration with oxygen?
   A) It is simple chemical reaction.
   B) Energy is released.
   C) It happens in mitochondria.
   D) Water and carbon dioxide are by-products.

Chapter Preview

Skills Preview

Skill Builders
- Sequence Events
- Map Concepts

Activities
- Observe and Infer
- Compare and Contrast

MiniLabs
- Make a Model

Reading Check ✔

As you read about cell reproduction, outline meiosis I and meiosis II. Then, write a description of meiosis in your own words.

Explore Activity

Would you believe that the image to the left is part of a complicated set of coded messages found in every cell? The messages called DNA contain the instructions and information needed for the cell and the organism it is part of to survive. In the following activity, see what information is in the cells of seeds.

Observe Seeds

1. Carefully split open a bean seed that has soaked in water overnight.

2. Observe both halves of the seed. Record your observations.

3. Place four other bean seeds in a moist paper towel in a self-sealing, plastic bag.

4. Make observations for a few days.

Science Journal

In your Science Journal, describe what happened to the seeds. From your observations, hypothesize about the messages in the seed's cells.

Cell Growth and Division

What You'll Learn

▶ Why mitosis is important
▶ How mitosis compares in plant and animal cells
▶ Two examples of asexual reproduction

Vocabulary
mitosis
chromosome
asexual reproduction

Why It's Important

▶ Many cells in your body grow and divide every day.

Why do cells divide?

It's likely that each time you go to the doctor, someone measures your height and weight. Similar data collected from thousands of people over the years, shows how people grow. The main reason you grow is because the number of cells in your body increases.

Constant Change

You are constantly changing. You aren't the same now as you were a year ago or even a few hours ago. At this very moment, as you read this page, groups of cells throughout your body are growing, dividing, and dying. Worn-out cells on the palms of your hands are being replaced. Cuts and bruises are healing. Red blood cells are being produced in your bones at a rate of 10 to 15 million per second to replace those that wear out. Muscle cells that you exercise are getting larger. Other organisms undergo similar processes. New organisms are created, like the protist in **Figure 16-1A.** Other organisms, like the plant in **Figure 16-1B,** can grow because new cells are formed. How do cells increase in number?

Figure 16-1 Cell division occurs in all organisms.

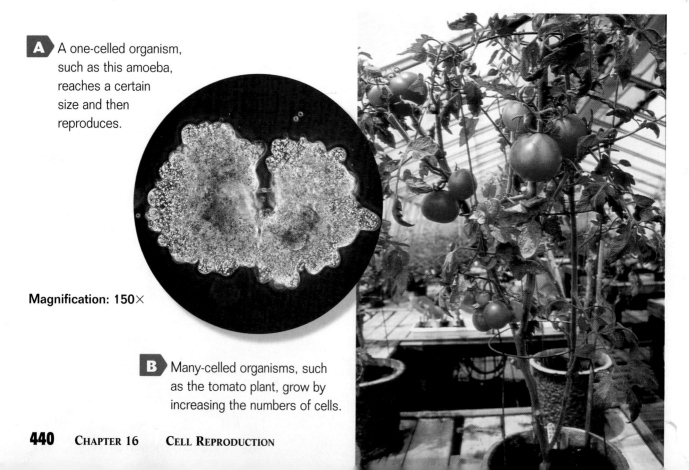

A A one-celled organism, such as this amoeba, reaches a certain size and then reproduces.

Magnification: 150×

B Many-celled organisms, such as the tomato plant, grow by increasing the numbers of cells.

Figure 16-2 An organism undergoes many changes as it develops. Below are a few stages of an oak tree's development.

The Cell Cycle

A living organism, such as the oak in **Figure 16-2,** has a life cycle. A life cycle begins with the organism's formation, is followed by growth and development, and finally, ends in death. Right now, you are in a stage of your life cycle called adolescence, a period of active growth and development. A cell also has a life cycle. Most of the life of any eukaryotic cell, a cell with a nucleus, is spent in a period of growth and development called *interphase.* During interphase, a cell grows, makes a copy of its hereditary material, and prepares for cell division. In cell division, the nucleus divides, and then the cytoplasm separates to form two new cells. Cell division is a continuous process. The cell cycle, as shown in **Figure 16-3,** is a series of events that takes place in a cell from one division to the next. The cycle is constantly repeated by cells, like skin and bone cells, that are needed for repair, growth, or replacement. Cells in your body that no longer divide, such as nerve and muscle cells, are always in interphase.

Figure 16-3 Cell division is a continuous process. **When do chromosomes duplicate?**

Cell grows and functions, organelles duplicate

DNA replicates, chromosomes duplicate

Interphase

Cell grows and prepares for mitosis

Cytoplasm divides

Mitosis

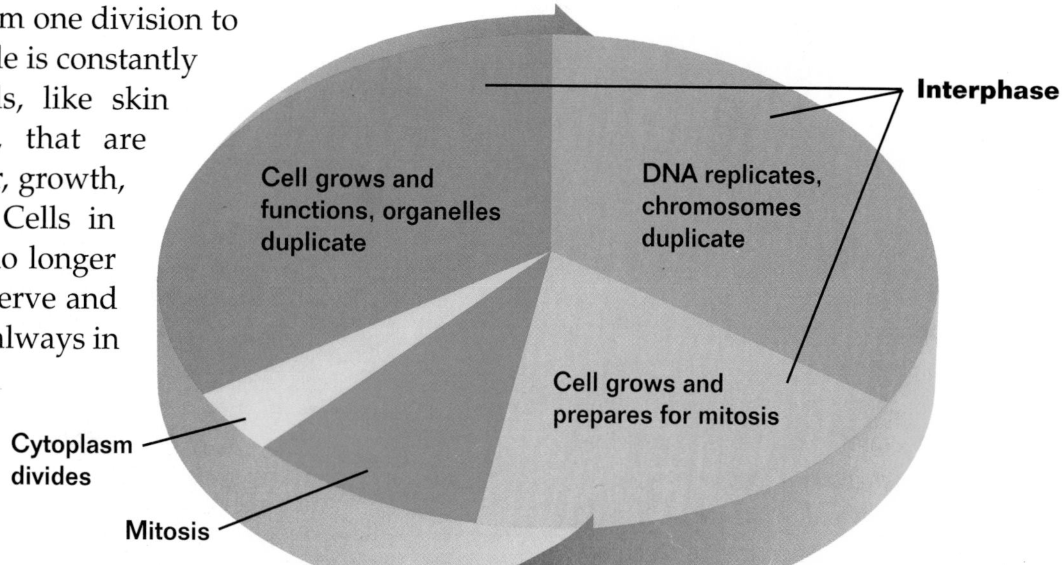

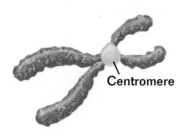

Centromere

Figure 16-4 A duplicated chromosome is two identical DNA molecules that are held together at a region called the centromere.

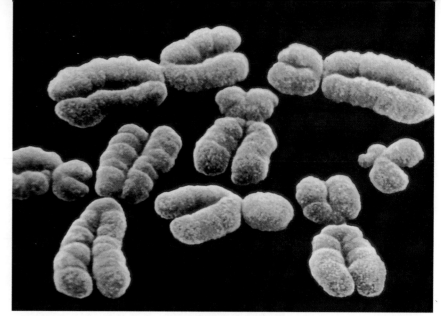

Magnification: 18 000×

Mitosis

Cells divide in two steps. First, the nucleus of the cell divides, and then the cytoplasm divides. **Mitosis** (mi TOH sus) is the process in which the nucleus divides to form two identical nuclei. Each new nucleus is also identical to the original nucleus. Mitosis is described as a series of phases or steps. The steps are named prophase, metaphase, anaphase, and telophase.

VISUALIZING
Mitosis

Figure 16-5 The steps of mitosis for an animal cell are shown here. Each micrograph shown in this figure is magnified 600 times.

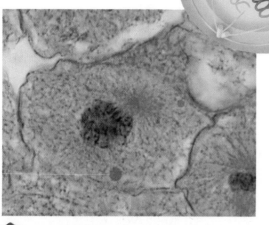

A **Prophase** During prophase, duplicated chromosomes become fully visible. The nucleolus and the nuclear membrane disintegrate. Two small structures called centrioles move to opposite ends of the cell. Between the centrioles, threadlike spindle fibers begin to stretch across the cell.

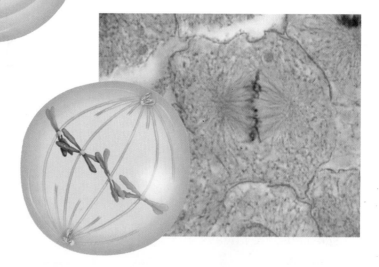

B **Metaphase** In metaphase, the duplicated chromosomes line up across the center of the cell. Each centromere becomes attached to two spindle fibers.

Animal Cell Mitosis

When a cell divides, the chromosomes in the nucleus play an important part. **Chromosomes** are structures in the nucleus that contain hereditary material. During *interphase*, you can't see chromosomes, but they are actively duplicating themselves. When the cell is ready to divide, each duplicated chromosome becomes visible because it coils tightly into two thick strands, as in **Figure 16-4**. Follow the steps of mitosis in the illustrations in **Figure 16-5** on these pages.

For most cells, after the nucleus has divided, the cytoplasm also separates, and two whole, new cells are formed. In animal cells, the cytoplasm pinches in to form the new cells. The new cells then begin the period of growth, or interphase, again. They will take in water and other nutrients that they need to carry out cell processes.

Plant Cell Mitosis

Plant cell mitosis is similar to animal cell mitosis, but there are differences. Plant cells form spindle fibers during mitosis but do not have centrioles.

Using Math

If a single cell undergoes mitosis every five minutes, how many cells will result from this single cell after one hour? Calculate the answer and record it in your Science Journal.

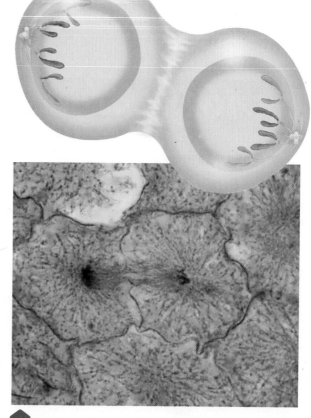

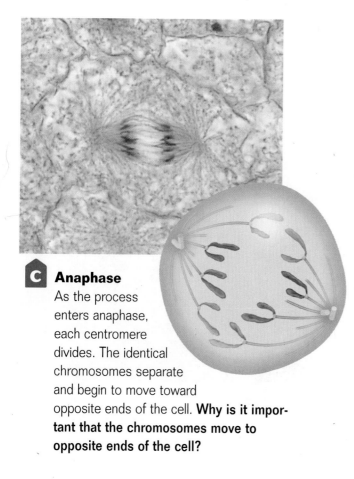

C **Anaphase**
As the process enters anaphase, each centromere divides. The identical chromosomes separate and begin to move toward opposite ends of the cell. **Why is it important that the chromosomes move to opposite ends of the cell?**

D **Telophase** In the final step, telophase, spindle fibers start to disappear. The chromosomes uncoil and are harder to see. A nuclear membrane forms around each mass of chromosomes, and a new nucleolus forms in each new nucleus.

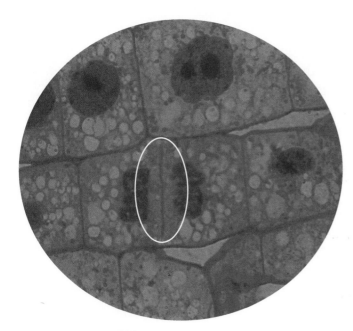

Magnification: 1230×

Figure 16-6 A cell plate (circled) forms during plant cell mitosis.

Another difference is the rigid cell wall and how the cell membrane forms. In plants, a structure called a cell plate, shown in **Figure 16-6,** forms between the two new nuclei. New cell walls form along the cell plate. Then, new cell membranes develop inside the cell walls.

Results of Mitosis

There are two important things to remember about mitosis. First, it is the division of a nucleus. Second, mitosis produces two new nuclei that are identical to each other and the original nucleus. Each cell in your body, except sex cells, has a nucleus with 46 chromosomes, because you began as one cell with 46 chromosomes in its nucleus. **Figure 16-7** shows the 46 human chromosomes. Skin cells produced to replace or repair your skin have the same 46 chromosomes as the single cell you came from. Each cell in a fruit fly has eight chromosomes, so each new cell produced by mitosis has a copy of those eight chromosomes.

Mini Lab

Modeling Mitosis

Procedure

1. Make models of cell division using materials supplied by your teacher.
2. Use four chromosomes in your model.
3. When finished, arrange the models in the order in which mitosis occurs.

Analysis

1. In which steps is the nucleus visible?
2. How many cells does a dividing cell form?

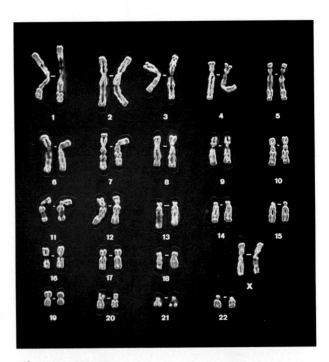

Figure 16-7 In the nucleus of most cells, there are pairs of chromosomes. Humans have 23 pairs of chromosomes including a pair of chromosomes that determine sex such as pair X above.

Asexual Reproduction

Reproduction is the process by which an organism produces others of the same kind. Among living organisms, there are two types of reproduction—asexual and sexual. Sexual reproduction is explained later in this chapter. In **asexual reproduction**, a new organism (sometimes more than one) is produced that has hereditary material identical to the hereditary material of the parent organism. Asexual reproduction of organisms with eukaryotic cells is done by mitosis. Bacteria reproduce asexually by fission. Fission is when a prokaryotic organism divides into two identical organisms.

If you've ever grown a sweet potato in a jar of water, you've seen asexual reproduction take place. All the stems, leaves, and roots that grow from the sweet potato have been produced by mitosis and have the same hereditary material. New strawberry plants can be asexually reproduced from horizontal stems called runners. In **Figure 16-8,** new cattail plants are reproduced asexually.

*inter*NET
CONNECTION

Visit the Glencoe Science Web Site at **www.glencoe. com/sec/science** for more information about other ways plants reproduce asexually.

Magnification: 8× **A**

B

Figure 16-8 Many organisms reproduce asexually. Hydra, a freshwater animal (A), and cattails (B) are examples. **How does the genetic material in the small cattail plants compare to the genetic material in the large cattail plant?**

Budding and Regeneration

Budding is a type of asexual reproduction in which a new organism grows from the body of the parent organism. **Figure 16-8** illustrates an organism called a hydra reproducing by budding. When the bud on the adult becomes large enough, it breaks away to live on its own.

Another type of asexual reproduction possible for some organisms like sponges, planaria, and sea stars is regeneration. Regeneration is when a whole organism grows from a piece of an organism or regrows damaged or lost body parts. For some organisms, injury brings about the regeneration of two organisms, as in **Figure 16-9.** If a sponge is cut into small pieces, a new sponge may develop from each piece. How do you think sponge farmers increase their crop? ☑

Fission, budding, and regeneration are types of asexual reproduction. Through cell division, organisms grow, replace worn-out or damaged cells, or produce whole new organisms.

Reading Check ☑

What is regeneration?

Figure 16-9 Some animals produce new body parts by regeneration. A planarian is a worm that can regenerate a head or a tail when cut in two.

Magnification: 8×

Section Assessment

1. What is mitosis and how does it differ in plants and animals?

2. Give two examples of asexual reproduction.

3. What happens to chromosomes before mitosis begins?

4. **Think Critically:** Why is it important for the nuclear membrane to disintegrate in mitosis?

5. **Skill Builder**
   Designing an Experiment to Test a Hypothesis Do you know if a leaf can be used to grow a new plant? A piece of stem? A root section? Do the **Chapter 16 Skill Activity** on page 741 to design and experiment to test your hypothesis.

Using Math

Find out how much you weighed at birth. Subtract that weight from what you weigh now. Divide that number by your age to find the average weight you gained each year. Predict what you will weigh five years from now.

Mitosis in Plant and Animal Cells

Reproduction of cells in plants and animals is accomplished by mitosis. In this activity, you will study prepared slides of onion root-tip cells and whitefish embryo cells. These slides are used because they show cells in the various stages of mitosis.

What You'll Investigate

How mitosis in a plant cell is different from mitosis in an animal cell.

Goals

- **Compare** the sizes of the whitefish embryo cells and the onion root-tip cells.
- **Observe** the chromosomes of the whitefish embryo and onion root tip.

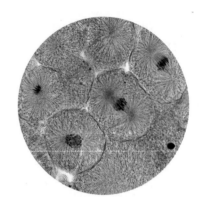

Onion root-tip cells
Magnification: 330×

Whitefish embryo cells
Magnification: 320×

Procedure

1. **Obtain** prepared slides of onion root-tip cells and whitefish embryo cells.

2. Set your microscope on low power and **examine** the onion root tip. Move the slide until you can see the area just behind the root tip. Turn the nosepiece to high power.

3. Use **Figure 16-5** to help you find a cell in prophase. **Draw** and **label** the parts of the cell you observe.

4. Repeat step 3 for metaphase, anaphase, and telophase.

5. Turn the microscope back to low power. Remove the onion root tip slide.

6. Place the whitefish embryo slide on the microscope stage under low power. Focus and find a region of dividing cells. Switch to high power.

7. Repeat steps 3 and 4 using the whitefish embryo slide.

8. Return the nosepiece to low power. Remove the whitefish embryo slide from the microscope stage.

Conclude and Apply

1. **Compare** the cells in the region behind the onion root tip to those in the root tip.

2. **Describe** the shapes of the cells in the onion root tip and the whitefish embryo.

3. **Infer** why embryo cells and root-tip cells are used to study mitosis.

4. Copy the following statements in your Science Journal then fill in each blank with the name of the correct phase of mitosis.

_____ Nuclear membrane re-forms.

_____ Chromosomes move to the center of the cell.

_____ Spindle fibers appear.

_____ Chromosomes move in opposite directions.

Sexual Reproduction and Meiosis

Sexual Reproduction

Sexual reproduction is another way that a new organism can be created. It happens when two sex cells, an egg and a sperm, come together. The joining of an egg and a sperm is called **fertilization.** Generally, the egg and the sperm come from two different organisms. Following fertilization, mitosis begins. A new organism develops that has its own unique identity.

Formation of Sex Cells

Your body forms two types of cells—body cells and sex cells. By far, your body has more body cells than sex cells. Your brain, skin, bones, and other tissues and organs are formed from body cells. Sex cells are formed from cells in reproductive organs. The **sperm** is formed in the reproductive organs of the male. A sperm has a whiplike tail and a head that is almost all nucleus. The **egg** is formed in the reproductive organs of the female and contains many food molecules along with the other cell parts. As seen in **Figure 16-10,** an egg is much larger than a sperm.

A human body cell has 46 chromosomes. Each chromosome has a similar mate, so human body cells have 23 pairs of chromosomes. Sex cells have half the number of chromosomes of a body cell. Human sex cells have only 23 chromosomes, one from each of the 23 pairs. Sex cells are produced by a process called **meiosis** (mi OH sus). Meiosis happens in the reproductive organs of plants and animals.

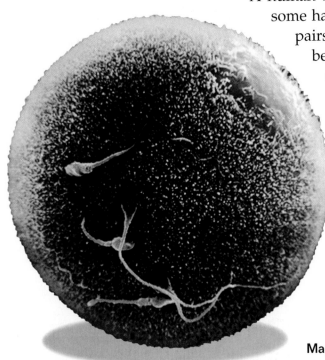

Figure 16-10 The large cell is a human egg cell, or ovum. The smaller cells on the egg are human sperm. **What is the chromosome number of each sex cell?**

Magnification: 400×

The Importance of Sex Cells

When a cell has pairs of chromosomes, it is said to be *diploid* (DIHP loyd). Human body cells are diploid cells. Because sex cells do not have pairs of chromosomes, they are said to be *haploid* (HAP loyd). Haploid means "single form." The diploid number for humans is 46, and the haploid number is 23. For corn, the diploid number is 20, and the haploid number is 10. For most organisms, the haploid number is found only in sex cells.

Fertilization

Why are sex cells so important? Sexual reproduction starts with the formation of sex cells and ends with fertilization. The new cell that forms is called a **zygote.** If an egg with 23 chromosomes joins a sperm that has 23 chromosomes, a zygote forms that has 46 chromosomes, the diploid chromosome number for that organism. The zygote undergoes mitosis, and an organism develops. This process is illustrated in **Figure 16-11.**

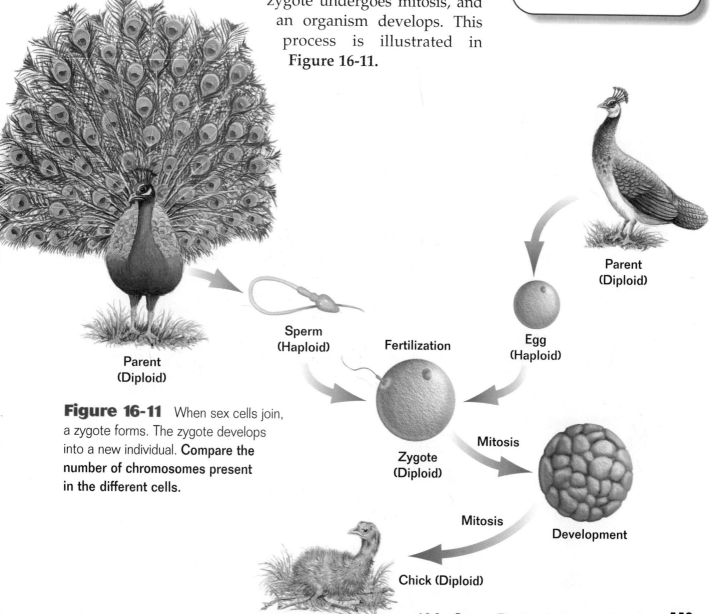

Figure 16-11 When sex cells join, a zygote forms. The zygote develops into a new individual. **Compare the number of chromosomes present in the different cells.**

Parent (Diploid)

Sperm (Haploid)

Fertilization

Egg (Haploid)

Parent (Diploid)

Zygote (Diploid)

Mitosis

Development

Mitosis

Chick (Diploid)

Meiosis

What would happen in sexual reproduction if the two cells that were formed through mitosis combined? The offspring would have twice as many chromosomes as its parent. Meiosis insures that this does not happen. During meiosis, two divisions of the nucleus occur, *meiosis I* and *meiosis II*. The different steps of each division have names like those in mitosis. Follow the steps of meiosis I and meiosis II in **Figure 16-12.**

Meiosis I

Before meiosis begins, each chromosome is duplicated, just as in mitosis. When the cell is ready for meiosis, each duplicated chromosome is visible because it coils tightly into two thick strands joined by a centromere. In *prophase I,* the spindle fibers form, and the nuclear membrane and the nucleolus disintegrate. Unlike mitosis, the duplicated chromosomes stay together as pairs. ☑

In *metaphase I,* the pairs of duplicated chromosomes line up in the center of the cell. Each centromere becomes attached to one spindle fiber. In *anaphase I,* the pair of duplicated

Reading Check ☑

What happens to the chromosomes before meiosis and mitosis?

Problem Solving

Predicting Chromosome Numbers

A horse and a donkey can mate to produce a mule. The mule is almost always sterile. Horses have a diploid chromosome number of 66. Donkeys have a diploid number of 60.

Solve the Problem

1. How many chromosomes would the mule receive from each parent?

2. What is the diploid number of the mule?

3. What would happen when meiosis occurs in the mule's reproductive organs?

Think Critically: Why might a mule be sterile?

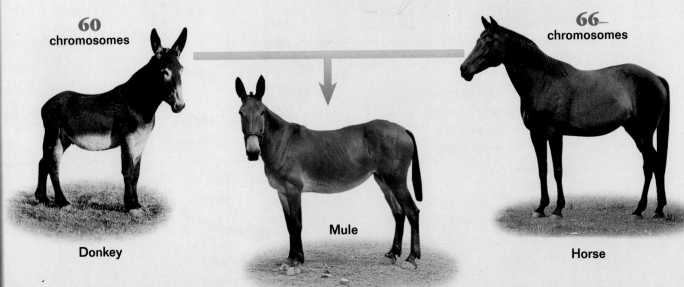

60 chromosomes

Donkey

Mule

66 chromosomes

Horse

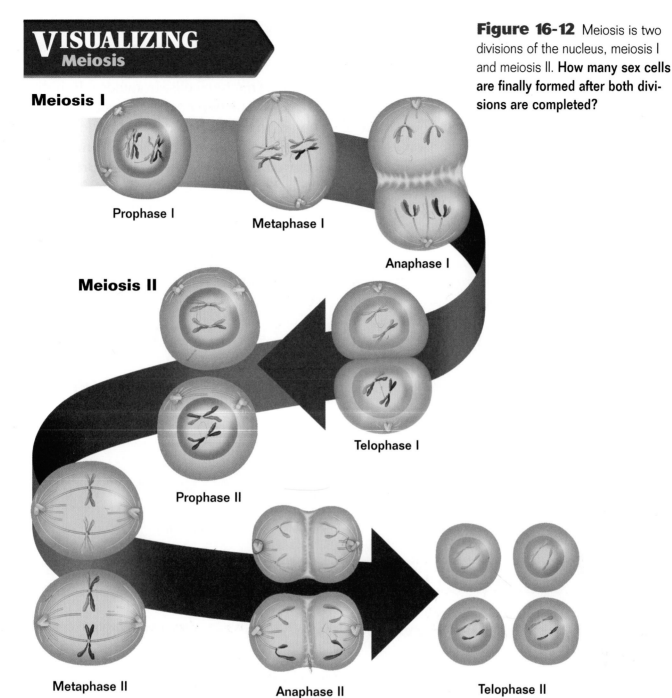

VISUALIZING
Meiosis

Figure 16-12 Meiosis is two divisions of the nucleus, meiosis I and meiosis II. **How many sex cells are finally formed after both divisions are completed?**

Meiosis I

Prophase I

Metaphase I

Anaphase I

Meiosis II

Telophase I

Prophase II

Metaphase II

Anaphase II

Telophase II

chromosomes separate. The duplicated chromosomes of each pair are pulled to opposite ends of the cell. Then, in *telophase I*, the cytoplasm divides, and two cells form.

Meiosis II

Meiosis II, the second division of the nucleus, then begins. In *prophase II*, the duplicated chromosomes and spindle fibers reappear in each new cell. In *metaphase II*, the duplicated chromosomes move to the center of the cell. There, each centromere attaches to two spindle fibers. During *anaphase II*, the centromere divides, and the identical molecules of each duplicated chromosome separate and move to opposite ends of the cell. As *telophase II* begins, the spindle fibers disappear, and a nuclear membrane forms around the chromosomes at each end of the cell. When meiosis II is finished, the cytoplasm divides. Meiosis I forms two cells. In meiosis II, both of these cells form two cells. The two nuclear divisions result in four sex cells, each having only half the number of chromosomes in their nuclei that were in the original nucleus. From a cell with 46 paired chromosomes, meiosis produces four sex cells each with 23 unpaired chromosomes. Meiosis happens many, many times in reproductive organs. Rare mistakes, such as the one in **Figure 16-13,** do occur.

Figure 16-13 Sometimes, a mistake is made. This diploid cell has four chromosomes. During Anaphase I, one pair of duplicated chromosomes did not separate. **How many chromosomes should each sex cell have?**

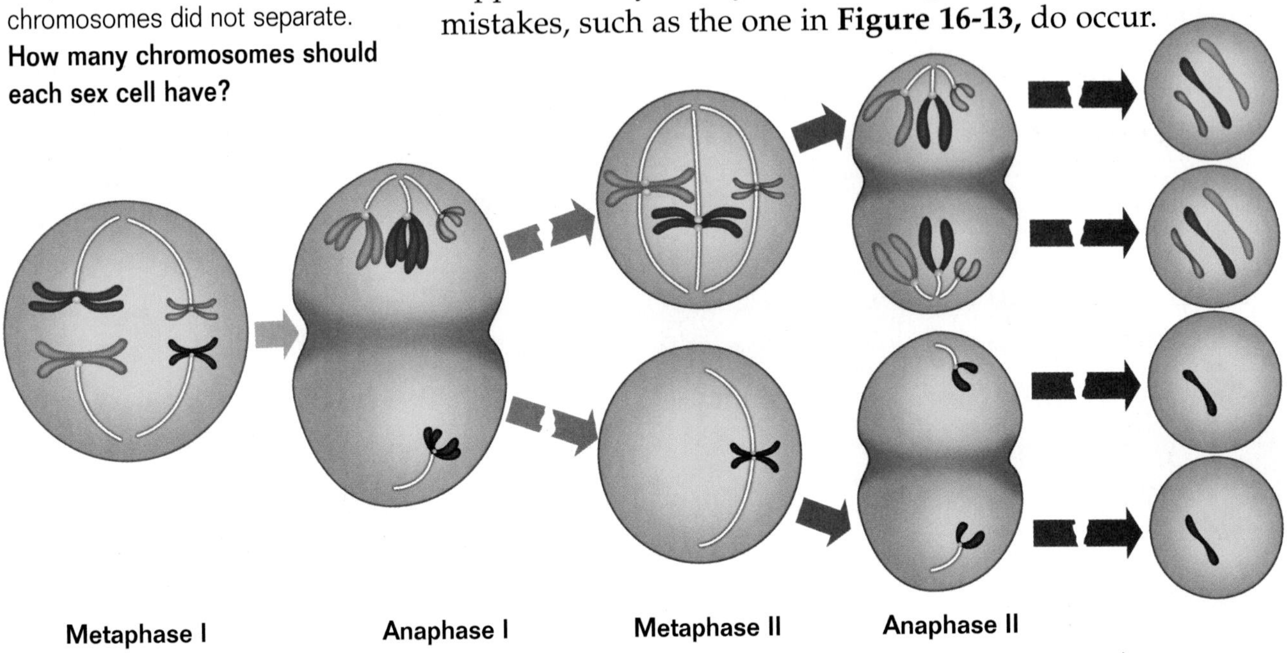

Metaphase I   Anaphase I   Metaphase II   Anaphase II

Section Assessment

1. Compare sexual and asexual reproduction.

2. What is a zygote, and how is it formed?

3. **Think Critically:** Plants grown from runners and leaf cuttings have exactly the same traits as the parent plant. Plants grown from seeds may vary from the parents in many ways. Suggest an explanation for this.

4. **Skill Builder**
   Making and Using Tables Make a table to compare mitosis and meiosis in humans. Vertical headings should include: *What type of cell* (Body or Sex), *Beginning cell* (Haploid or Diploid), *Number of cells produced, End-product cell* (Haploid or Diploid), and *Number of chromosomes in cells produced.* If you need help, refer to Making and Using Tables in the **Skill Handbook** on page 700.

Science Journal Write a poem, song, or another memory device to help you remember the steps and outcome of meiosis.

Animal Cloning

What is an animal clone?

To scientists, a clone is an animal that is genetically identical to one of its parents. For many years, genetically identical organisms have been produced in the laboratory. Fertilized eggs are grown to two-, four-, or eight-cell embryos and then separated. These separated embryo cells behave like the original fertilized egg cell and grow into genetically identical siblings. However, these are not clones because their DNA is a combination of both parents' DNA.

Hello, Dolly!

In February 1997, researchers announced that they had cloned a sheep named Dolly. In the laboratory, they removed the nucleus of an egg cell taken from a female sheep. They replaced that nucleus with the nucleus from a cell of a second breed of sheep. The egg divided and formed an embryo. This embryo was implanted into the uterus of a female sheep of a third breed. Three breeds of sheep were used to show that Dolly received her genes from the transplanted nucleus of the second sheep—not the egg cell donor (the first sheep) or birth mother (the third sheep).

Beyond Dolly

Since Dolly was born, other scientists also have successfully cloned organisms. The next decades may bring enormous changes because of cloning. It may become possible to correct disorders and eliminate diseases by making genetic changes in embryos. Of particular interest are transgenic clones, organisms carrying genes from another species. Transgenic animals may be used for researching human diseases and their treatment, which would not be possible with human subjects. It may become common to clone transgenic animals, like the calves at left, that produce human antibiotics or other valuable protein products.

inter**NET**
CONNECTION

After reading this article, you may be wondering about the possibility of human cloning. Visit the Glencoe Science Web Site at www.glencoe.com/sec/science to find the latest information about human cloning. Summarize this information in your Science Journal.

16·3 DNA

What is DNA?

Have you ever sent a message to someone using a code? To read your message, that person had to understand the meaning of the symbols you used in your code. The chromosomes in the nucleus of a cell contain a code. This code is in the form of a chemical called deoxyribonucleic (dee AHK sih ri boh noo klay ihk) acid, or DNA. **DNA** is an organism's information code. When a cell divides, the DNA code in the nucleus is copied and passed to the new cells. In this way, new cells receive the same coded information that was in the original cell. DNA controls all the activities of cells with this coded information. Every cell that has ever been formed in your body or in any other organism contains DNA.

History of DNA

Since the mid-1800s, scientists have known that the nuclei of cells contain chemicals called nucleic acids. What does DNA look like? Scientist Rosalind Franklin discovered that the DNA molecule was two strands of molecules in a spiral form.

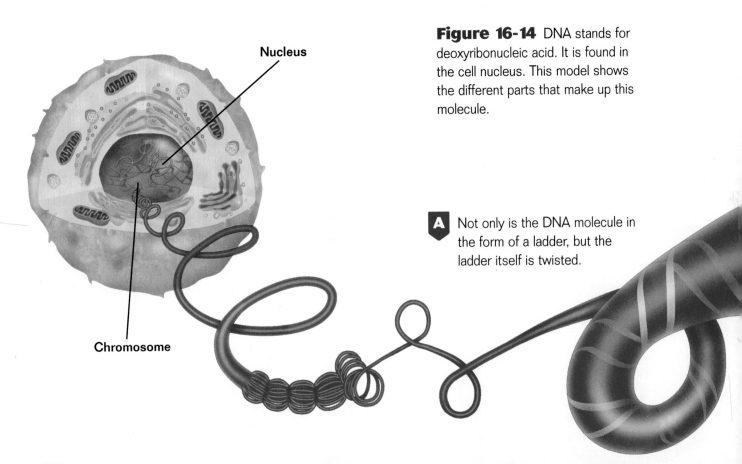

Nucleus

Chromosome

Figure 16-14 DNA stands for deoxyribonucleic acid. It is found in the cell nucleus. This model shows the different parts that make up this molecule.

A Not only is the DNA molecule in the form of a ladder, but the ladder itself is twisted.

By using an X-ray technique, Dr. Franklin showed that the spiral was so large that it was probably made up of two spirals. As it turned out, the structure of DNA is similar to a twisted ladder. In 1953, using the work of Franklin and others, scientists James Watson and Francis Crick made an accurate model of a DNA molecule.

A DNA Model

According to the Watson and Crick DNA model, each side of the ladder is made up of sugar-phosphate molecules. Each molecule consists of the sugar called deoxyribose and a phosphate group. The rungs of the ladder are made up of other molecules called nitrogen bases. There are four kinds of nitrogen bases in DNA. These are adenine, guanine, cytosine, and thymine. In **Figure 16-14C,** the bases are represented by the letters *A, G, C,* and *T.* The amount of cytosine in cells always equals the amount of guanine, and the amount of adenine always equals the amount of thymine. This led to the hypothesis that these bases occur as pairs in the DNA molecule. The Watson and Crick model shows that adenine always pairs with thymine, and guanine always pairs with cytosine. Like interlocking pieces of a puzzle, each base bonds only with its correct partner. ☑

Reading Check ☑

What are the nitrogen base pairs in a DNA molecule?

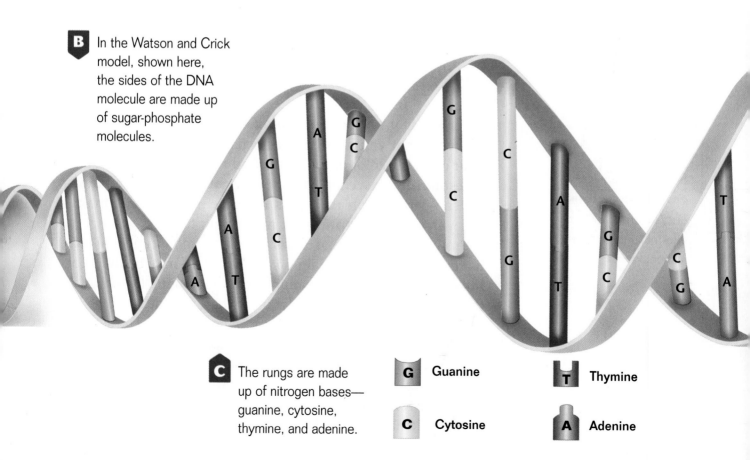

B In the Watson and Crick model, shown here, the sides of the DNA molecule are made up of sugar-phosphate molecules.

C The rungs are made up of nitrogen bases—guanine, cytosine, thymine, and adenine.

G Guanine

C Cytosine

T Thymine

A Adenine

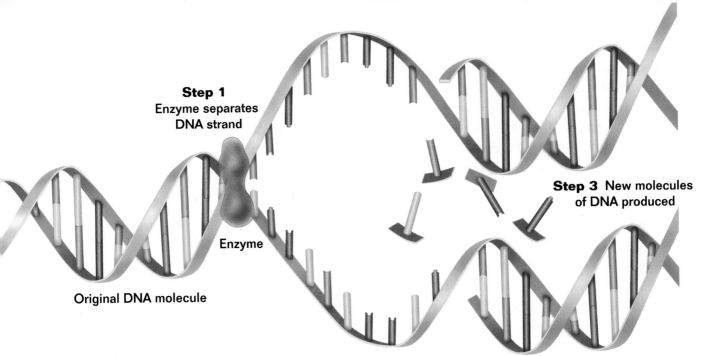

Step 1
Enzyme separates
DNA strand

Enzyme

Original DNA molecule

Step 3 New molecules
of DNA produced

Step 2 New bases in cytoplasm pair
with original bases of DNA

Figure 16-15 DNA uses itself as a pattern when it is copied.

inter**NET**
C O N N E C T I O N

DNA fingerprinting uses the process of DNA duplication. Visit the Glencoe Science Web Site at **www.glencoe.com/ sec/science** for more information about this technology.

Copies of DNA

When chromosomes are duplicated before mitosis, the amount of DNA in the nucleus is doubled. How does DNA copy itself? The Watson and Crick model shows how this takes place. The two strands of the DNA molecule unwind and separate. Each strand then becomes a pattern on which a new molecule is formed. **Figure 16-15** follows a DNA molecule as it produces two new DNA molecules identical to the original DNA molecule.

Genes

Why is DNA important? All of your characteristics are in the DNA that you have in your cells. It controls the color of your eyes, the color of your hair, and whether or not you can digest milk. These characteristics are called traits. How traits appear depends on the kinds of proteins your cells make. DNA stores the blueprints for making proteins.

Proteins are made of units called amino acids that are linked together in a certain order. A protein may be made of hundreds or thousands of amino acids. Changing the order of the amino acids changes the protein that is made.

How does a cell know which proteins to make? The section of DNA on a chromosome that directs the making of a specific protein is called a **gene.** Genes control proteins that either build cells and tissues or work as enzymes. The gene gives the directions for the order in which amino acids will be arranged for a particular protein. Think about what might happen if an important protein couldn't be made in your cells.

RNA

Proteins are made on ribosomes in cytoplasm. How does the code in the nucleus reach the ribosomes in the cytoplasm? The codes for making proteins are carried from the nucleus to the ribosomes by another type of nucleic acid called ribonucleic acid, or **RNA.** RNA is different from DNA. It is made up of only one strand, the nitrogen base uracil (U). It replaces thymine and contains the sugar ribose. RNA is made in the nucleus on a DNA pattern.

The three main kinds of RNA made from DNA in the nucleus of a cell are messenger RNA (mRNA), ribosomal RNA (rRNA), and transfer RNA (tRNA). The production of a protein begins when mRNA moves through the nuclear membrane into the cytoplasm. There, ribosomes, made of rRNA, attach to it. Transfer RNA molecules, in the cytoplasm, bring amino acids to these ribosomes. Inside the ribosomes, three nitrogen bases on the tRNA temporarily match with three nitrogen bases on the mRNA. The same thing happens for another tRNA molecule and mRNA, as shown in **Figure 16-16.** The amino acids attached to the two tRNA molecules bond. This is the beginning of a protein.

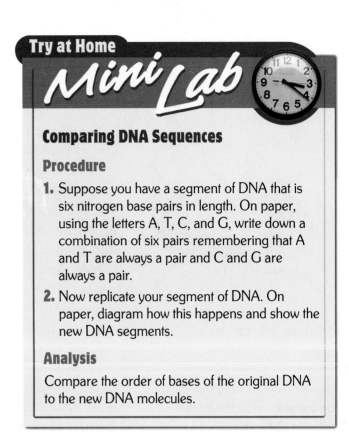

Try at Home

Mini Lab

Comparing DNA Sequences

Procedure

1. Suppose you have a segment of DNA that is six nitrogen base pairs in length. On paper, using the letters A, T, C, and G, write down a combination of six pairs remembering that A and T are always a pair and C and G are always a pair.

2. Now replicate your segment of DNA. On paper, diagram how this happens and show the new DNA segments.

Analysis

Compare the order of bases of the original DNA to the new DNA molecules.

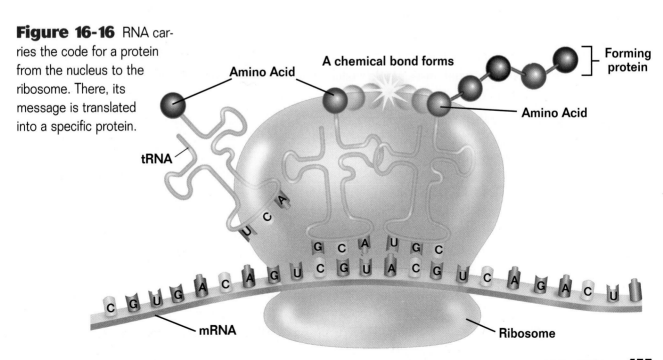

Figure 16-16 RNA carries the code for a protein from the nucleus to the ribosome. There, its message is translated into a specific protein.

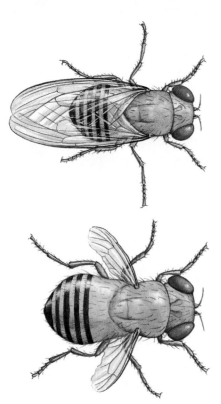

The code carried on mRNA directs the order of amino acid bonding. Once a tRNA molecule has lost its amino acid, it can move about the cytoplasm and pick up another one just like it. The ribosome moves along the mRNA. New tRNA molecules with amino acids match up and add amino acids to the protein molecule.

Mutations

Genes control the traits you inherit. Without correctly coded proteins, an organism can't grow, repair, or maintain itself. A change in a gene or chromosome, changes the traits of an organism, as illustrated in **Figure 16-17.** Sometimes an error is made during replication. Occasionally, a cell receives an entire extra chromosome. Outside factors such as X rays and chemicals have been known to cause changes in chromosomes. Any permanent change in a gene or chromosome of a cell is called a **mutation.** If the mutation occurs in a body cell, it may or may not be life threatening to the organism. If, however, a mutation occurs in a sex cell, then all the cells that are formed from that sex cell will have that mutation. Mutations add variety to a species when the organism reproduces. Many mutations are harmful to organisms, often causing their death. Some mutations do not appear to have any effect on the organism, and some may be beneficial.

Figure 16-17 Because of a defect on chromosome 2, the mutant fruit fly has short wings and cannot fly. **Could this defect be transferred to the mutant's offspring? Explain.**

Section Assessment

1. How does DNA make a copy of itself?
2. How are the codes for proteins carried from the nucleus to the ribosomes?
3. A single strand of DNA has the bases AGTAAC. Using letters, show what bases would match up to form a matching DNA strand from this pattern.
4. **Think Critically:** You begin as one cell. Compare the DNA in one of your brain cells to the DNA in one of your heart cells.
5. **Skill Builder**
   Concept Mapping Using a network tree concept map, show how DNA and RNA are alike and how they are different. If you need help, refer to Concept Mapping in the **Skill Handbook** on page 698.

Using Computers

Word Processing Make an outline of the events that led up to the discovery of DNA. Use library resources to find this information. If you need help, refer to page 716.

Modeling of DNA

Bits of metal, pieces of wire, and cardboard cutouts are not usually considered scientific equipment. But, that's what Nobel prize winners James Watson and Francis Crick used to construct their model of DNA. In this lab, you will use colored construction paper to make a model of DNA.

What You'll Investigate

You will examine the structure of a DNA molecule.

Goals

- **Design and construct** a model of DNA that is four base pairs long.

Safety Precautions

Use scissors carefully.

Procedure

1. **Plan** your DNA molecule. Write down the four base pairs and enter them in your Science Journal.

2. **Assign** one color of paper to represent each of the following: phosphate groups, sugar molecules, guanines, adenines, thymines, and cytosines.

3. Using the circle pattern for each phosphate group and the pentagon pattern for each sugar molecule, **trace** and **cut out** enough figures to make the sugar-phosphate sides of your DNA molecule.

4. **Tape** a circle to each pentagon, as seen in illustration A.

5. Use the pentagon pattern to make the nitrogen bases. For each adenine and each guanine, **trace** and **cut out** two pentagons of the same color and tape them together, as seen in illustration B. Trace and cut out just one pentagon for each thymine and each cytosine.

6. **Tape** a nitrogen base to each sugar-phosphate unit.

Materials

- 6 colors of construction paper ($8\frac{1}{2} \times 11$) (2 of each color)
- Scissors
- 2 cardboard patterns, a circle and pentagon
- Tape

7. **Construct** the DNA molecule that you planned in step 1 by taping the correct nitrogen bases together.

Conclude and Apply

1. **Compare** your models with those of other groups. Were the molecules your group created the same as those of other groups?

2. Compile a list of all the DNA sequences made and enter them in your Science Journal.

3. Based on your observations of the DNA molecule model, **infer** why a DNA molecule seldom copies itself incorrectly.

4. **Explain** why models are useful to scientists.

A.

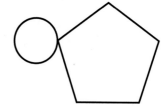

B.

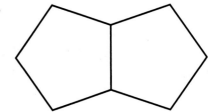

For a **preview** of this chapter, study this Reviewing Main Ideas before you read the chapter. After you have studied this chapter, you can use the Reviewing Main Ideas to **review** the chapter.

The Glencoe MindJogger, Audiocassettes, and CD-ROM provide additional opportunities for review.

Section 16-1 CELL GROWTH AND DIVISION

The life cycle of a cell has two parts: growth and development, and cell division. Cell division includes mitosis and the division of the cytoplasm. In **mitosis,** the nucleus divides to form two identical nuclei. Mitosis happens in four continuous steps, or phases: prophase, metaphase, anaphase, and telophase. Cell division in animal cells and plant cells is similar, but plant cells do not have centrioles and animal cells do not form cell walls.

Asexual reproduction produces organisms with DNA identical to the parent's DNA. Fission, budding, and regeneration are types of asexual reproduction. *What are the two parts of cell division?*

Section 16-2 SEXUAL REPRODUCTION AND MEIOSIS

Sexual reproduction results when a male sex cell, the **sperm,** enters the female sex cell, the **egg.** This event is called **fertilization,** and the cell that forms is the zygote. Before fertilization, **meiosis** happens in the reproductive organs, producing four haploid sex cells from one diploid cell. This insures that offspring produced by fertilization have the same number of chromosomes as their parents. *How do body cells differ from sex cells?*

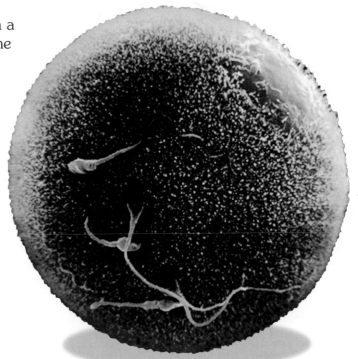

Reading Check ☑

Write out in words what DNA and RNA stand for. Think about why these letters instead of others in the words were chosen for the abbreviations.

Section

16-3 DNA

DNA, the genetic material of all organisms, is a large molecule made up of two twisted strands of sugar-phosphate molecules and nitrogen bases. The sugar in DNA is deoxyribose, and the bases are adenine, thymine, cytosine, and guanine. They are always found as the pairs adenine-thymine and cytosine-guanine. DNA directs all of the activities of a cell. The section of DNA on a chromosome that directs the making of a specific protein is a **gene.** DNA can copy itself and is the pattern from which RNA is made. **RNA** is single stranded and contains the sugar ribose instead of deoxyribose and the nitrogen base uracil in place of thymine. Messenger RNA carries the codes for making proteins from the nucleus to the ribosomes. Transfer RNA and ribosomal RNA are also made from patterns on DNA. Sometimes, changes in DNA occur. Permanent changes in DNA are called **mutations.** *What are the similarities and differences between DNA and RNA?*

Career CONNECTION

Dr. Khristine Lindo, Surgeon
Khristine Lindo became interested in science in seventh grade when she read a book *The Making of a Woman Surgeon* by Elizabeth Morgan. The book inspired her to become a surgeon. In high school Dr. Lindo took *every* science class she could—biology, chemistry, and physics. She was especially interested in biochemistry, the chemistry of living cells. Now as a surgeon, Dr. Lindo uses science to save lives. *Why is an understanding of the nature of science important to being a surgeon?*

Using Vocabulary

a. asexual
   reproduction
b. chromosome
c. DNA
d. egg
e. fertilization
f. gene
g. meiosis

h. mitosis
i. mutation
j. RNA
k. sexual
   reproduction
l. sperm
m. zygote

In statements 1–5, replace each underlined word with the correct Vocabulary word.

1. <u>Muscle</u> and <u>skin</u> cells are sex cells.
2. <u>Digestion</u> produces two identical cells, and <u>respiration</u> produces four sex cells.
3. Two examples of nucleic acids are <u>sugar</u> and <u>starch</u>.
4. A <u>cell</u> is found on a <u>tissue</u> and is the code for a protein.
5. A diploid <u>sperm</u> is formed when <u>mutation</u> happens.

Checking Concepts

Choose the word or phrase that best answers the question.

6. Which of the following is a double spiral molecule with pairs of nitrogen bases?
   A) RNA
   B) An amino acid
   C) A protein
   D) DNA

7. What does RNA contain that DNA does **NOT**?
   A) thymine
   B) thyroid
   C) adenine
   D) uracil

8. If a diploid tomato cell has 24 chromosomes, how many chromosomes will the tomato's sex cells have?
   A) 6
   B) 12
   C) 24
   D) 48

9. During a cell's life cycle, when do chromosomes duplicate?
   A) anaphase
   B) metaphase
   C) interphase
   D) telophase

10. When during mitosis do duplicated chromosomes separate?
    A) anaphase
    B) prophase
    C) metaphase
    D) telophase

11. How many chromosomes are in the original cell compared to those in the new cells formed by mitosis?
    A) the same amount
    B) half as many
    C) twice as many
    D) four times as many

12. What are budding, fission, and regeneration forms of?
    A) mutations
    B) sexual reproduction
    C) cell cycles
    D) asexual reproduction

13. What is any permanent change in a gene or a chromosome?
    A) fission
    B) reproduction
    C) replication
    D) mutation

14. What does meiosis produce?
    A) cells with the diploid chromosome number
    B) cells with identical chromosomes
    C) sex cells
    D) a zygote

15. In what phase of the cell cycle is most of the life of any cell spent ?
    A) metaphase
    B) interphase
    C) anaphase
    D) telophase

Thinking Critically

16. If the sequence of bases on one strand of DNA is ATCCGTC, what is the sequence on its other strand?

17. A strand of RNA made from the DNA strand ATCCGTC would have what base sequence?

18. Will a mutation in a human skin cell be passed on to the person's offspring? Explain your answer.

19. What happens in mitosis that gives the new cells identical DNA?

20. How could a zygote end up with an extra chromosome?

Developing Skills

If you need help, refer to the Skill Handbook.

21. **Comparing and Contrasting:** Make a table about mitosis and meiosis. Include the number of divisions, cells produced, and chromosomes in parent cells and in sex cells.

22. **Hypothesizing:** Make a hypothesis about the effect of an incorrect mitotic division on the new cells produced.

23. **Concept Mapping:** Complete the events chain concept map of DNA synthesis.

24. **Making and Using Tables:** Copy and complete this table about DNA and RNA.

DNA and RNA		
Nucleic acid	**DNA**	**RNA**
Number of strands		
Type of sugar		
Letter names of bases		
Where found?		

25. **Sequencing:** Sequence the events that occur from interphase in the parent cell to the formation of the zygote. Tell whether the chromosome's number at each stage is haploid or diploid.

THE PRINCETON REVIEW

Test-Taking Tip

Don't Dwell On It Many test questions look more complicated than they really are. If you find yourself having to do a great deal of work to answer a question, look again and try to find a simpler way to find the answer.

Test Practice

Use these questions to test your Science Proficiency.

1. In sex cells, chromosomes duplicate, and the nucleus divides twice, producing four nuclei each with half the number of chromosomes of the original nucleus. What is this process called?
   A) differentiation   B) meiosis
   C) mitosis   D) respiration

2. What are all the activities of a cell directed by?
   A) proteins   B) lipids
   C) DNA   D) carbohydrates

3. How is RNA different from DNA?
   A) It is single stranded and has the base uracil.
   B) It is a double spiral of lipids.
   C) It is found only in the nucleus.
   D) It is copied from other RNA.

4. Which of the following sequences is correct for the formation of a protein?
   A) tRNA–ribosome–DNA–mRNA–protein
   B) mRNA–DNA–ribosome–tRNA–protein
   C) DNA–mRNA–ribosome–tRNA–protein
   D) ribosome–DNA–tRNA–mRNA–protein

Chapter Preview

Skills Preview

Skill Builders
- Make and Use a Graph
- Map Concepts

Activities
- Predict
- Hypothesize

MiniLabs
- Collect and Analyze Data

Reading Check ☑

Choose an unfamiliar word from a section vocabulary list. Use its root, affixes, or section illustrations to predict its meaning. As you read, check the accuracy of your prediction.

Explore Activity

Pronghorn antelope like the ones in this photograph are the fastest mammals in the Western Hemisphere. They can run up to 86 km/hr and leap up to 6.1 m. Montana is home to many pronghorns. Like many other organisms, pronghorn antelope inherit traits from both of their parents. If you look closely, you will find small differences among individuals, though they have many traits in common.

Most traits found in organisms have at least two different forms. In humans, there is a noticeable difference between a straight hairline and a hairline with a widow's peak. In the following activity, observe this genetic difference. In this chapter, you will learn how you and your classmates received the genetic traits you have.

Observe Differences in Human Hairlines

1. Notice the two different kinds of hairlines in the photo above. The girl on the right has a straight hairline. The girl on the left has a pointed hairline, also called a widow's peak.

2. Record the name of each of your classmates and the kind of hairline he or she has.

Science Journal

Do most of your classmates have the same kind of hairline as you? Record the percentage of each type of hairline in your Science Journal.

What is genetics?

What You'll Learn

► How traits are inherited
► Mendel's role in the history of genetics
► How to use a Punnett square to predict the results of crosses
► The difference between genotype and phenotype

Vocabulary

heredity	Punnett square
alleles	genotype
genetics	homozygous
dominant	heterozygous
recessive	phenotype

Why It's Important

► Heredity and genetics help explain why people are different.

What have you inherited?

People have always been interested in why one generation looks like another. A new baby may look much like one of its parents. It may have eyes the same color as its father or a nose like its mother. Eye color, nose shape, and many other physical features are types of traits that you inherited from your parents. Every organism is a collection of traits, all inherited from its parents. **Heredity** (huh RED ut ee) is the passing of traits from parent to offspring. What controls these traits? As you will learn, traits are controlled by genes.

How Traits Are Inherited

Genes are made up of DNA and are located on chromosomes. To a large degree, genes control the traits that show up in an organism. The different forms a gene may have for a trait are its **alleles** (uh LEELZ). When pairs of chromosomes separate into sex cells during meiosis, pairs of genes also separate from one another. As a result, each sex cell winds up with one allele for each trait that an organism shows, as demonstrated in **Figure 17-1.** The allele in one sex cell may

Figure 17-1 An allele is one form of a gene. Alleles separate during meiosis. In this example, the alleles that control the trait for hairlines include *H*, the widow's peak hairline allele, and *h*, the straight hairline allele.

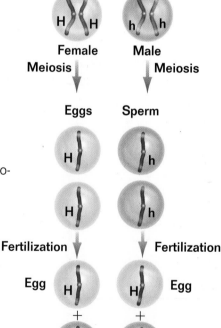

A In a pair of like chromosomes, the alleles that control a trait are located in the same position on each chromosome.

B During meiosis, like chromosomes separate. Each chromosome now contains just one allele for the hairline trait, either *H* or *h*.

C During fertilization, each parent donates one chromosome. This results in new pairs of chromosomes with two alleles for the hairline trait.

control one form of the trait, such as a widow's peak. The allele in the other sex cell may control an alternate form of the trait, such as a straight hairline. The study of how traits are inherited through the actions of alleles is the science of **genetics** (juh NET ihks).

The Father of Genetics

The first recorded scientific study of how traits pass from one generation to the next was done by Gregor Mendel, an Austrian monk born in 1822. He learned how to grow plants as a child working on his family's farm. Mendel studied science and math and eventually became a priest and teacher. While teaching, Mendel took over a garden plot at his monastery. In 1856, he began experimenting with garden peas like the ones shown in **Figure 17-2.** His observations of his father's orchard made him think that it was possible to predict the kinds of flowers and fruit a plant would produce. But, something had to be known about the parents of the plant before such a prediction could be made. Mendel made careful use of scientific methods in his research. After eight years of working with pea plants, Mendel presented a paper detailing the results of his research to the Natural History Society of Brünn, Austria. This paper was published by the Society in 1866 under the title "Experiments with Plant Hybrids."

In 1900, three other scientists working in botany rediscovered Mendel's work. These other scientists had come to the same conclusions that Mendel had reached. Since that time, Mendel has been known as the father of genetics.

Figure 17-2 Mendel's work with garden peas such as these led to the science of genetics. **Why is Mendel called the father of genetics?**

Comparing Common Traits

Procedure

1. Always obtain the permission of any person included in an experiment on human traits.
2. Survey ten students in your class or school for the presence of freckles, dimples, cleft or smooth chins, and attached or detached earlobes.
3. Make a data table that lists each of the traits.
4. Fill in the table.

Analysis

1. Compare the number of people who have one form of a trait with those who have the other form. How do those two groups compare?
2. What can you conclude about the number of variations you noticed?

Reading Check ✔

What is a purebred?

In Mendel's Garden

Mendel chose ordinary garden peas, such as the ones you eat for dinner, for his experiments. Peas are easy to breed for pure traits. An organism that always produces the same traits generation to generation is called a purebred. Tall plants that always produce tall plants are purebred for the trait of tallness. Short plants that always have short offspring are purebred for the trait of shortness. In addition to height, Mendel studied six other traits of garden peas, shown in **Table 17-1.** ✔

Dominant and Recessive Factors

In nature, insects such as the bee shown in **Figure 17-3** pollinate randomly as they move from flower to flower. In his experiments, Mendel took pollen from the male reproductive structures of flowers from purebred tall plants. He then placed the pollen on the female reproductive structures of flowers from pure short plants. This process is called cross-pollination. The results of his cross are shown in **Figure 17-4.** Notice that tall plants crossed with short plants produced all tall plants. It seemed as if whatever had caused the plants to be short had disappeared.

Mendel called the tall-height form that appeared the **dominant** (DAHM uh nunt) factor because it dominated, or covered up, the short-height form. He called the form that seemed to disappear the **recessive** (rih SES ihv) factor. But, what had happened to the recessive form?

Mendel allowed the new tall plants to self-pollinate. Self-pollination occurs when pollen is transferred from the male to the female reproductive structure in the same plant. Then, he collected the seeds from these tall plants and planted

Figure 17-3 Bees and other animals often visit only one species of flower at a time. **Why is this important to plant species pollinated by animals?**

Table 17-1

Traits Compared by Mendel							
Traits	Shape of seeds	Color of seeds	Color of pods	Shape of pods	Plant height	Position of flowers	Flower color
Dominant Trait	Round	Yellow	Green	Full	Tall	At leaf junctions	Purple
Recessive Trait	Wrinkled	Green	Yellow	Flat or constricted	Short	At tips of branches	White

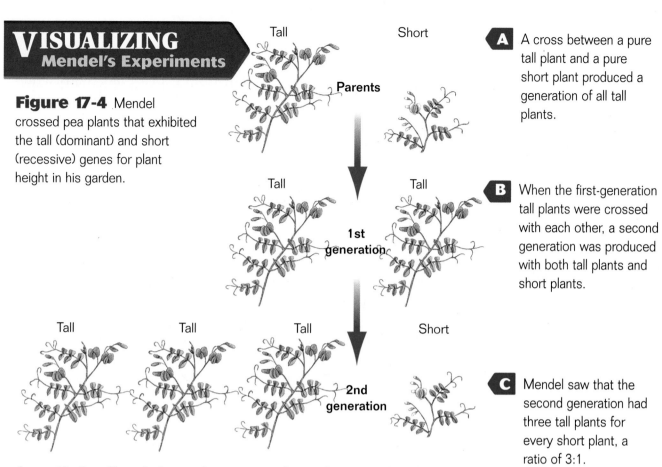

VISUALIZING
Mendel's Experiments

Figure 17-4 Mendel crossed pea plants that exhibited the tall (dominant) and short (recessive) genes for plant height in his garden.

Parents

A A cross between a pure tall plant and a pure short plant produced a generation of all tall plants.

Tall   Tall

1st generation

B When the first-generation tall plants were crossed with each other, a second generation was produced with both tall plants and short plants.

Tall   Tall   Tall   Short

2nd generation

C Mendel saw that the second generation had three tall plants for every short plant, a ratio of 3:1.

them. Both tall and short plants grew from these seeds. The recessive form had reappeared. Mendel saw that for every three tall plants, there was one short plant, or a 3:1 ratio. He saw this 3:1 ratio often enough that he knew he could predict his results when he started a test. He knew that the probability was great that he would get that same outcome each time.

Predictions Using Probability

Probability is a branch of mathematics that helps you predict the chance that something will happen. Suppose you and a friend want to go to different movies. You toss a coin to decide which movie you will see. Your friend chooses tails as the coin is in the air. What is the probability that the coin will land with the tail side of the coin facing up? Because there are two sides to a coin, you know there is one chance out of two possible outcomes that tails will land face up. The probability of one side of a coin showing is one out of two, or 50 percent. When you flip a coin, you are dealing with probabilities.

Mendel also dealt with probabilities. One of the things that made his predictions accurate was that he worked with large numbers. He counted every plant and thousands of seeds. In fact, Mendel raised and studied almost 30 000 pea plants over a period of eight years. By doing so, Mendel increased his chances of seeing a repeatable pattern. Valid scientific conclusions need to be based on repeatable results.

Using Math

Suppose Mendel had 100 second-generation pea plants. How many would he expect to be tall? How many would he expect to be short? Review **Figure 17-4** to help you determine the probability of each event.

Using a Punnett Square

Suppose you wanted to know what kinds of pea plants you would get if you used pollen from a pea plant with white flowers to pollinate a pea plant with purple flowers. How could you predict what the offspring would look like without actually making the cross? A handy tool used to predict results in Mendelian genetics is the **Punnett square** as seen in **Figure 17-6.** In a Punnett square, dominant and recessive alleles are represented by letters. A capital letter *(T)* stands for a dominant allele. A lowercase letter *(t)* stands for a recessive allele. The letters are a form of shorthand. They show the **genotype** (JEE nuh tipe), or genetic makeup, of an organism. Once you understand what the letters mean, you can tell a lot about the inheritance of a trait in an organism.

Alleles Determine Traits

Most cells in your body have two alleles for every trait. An organism with two alleles that are exactly the same is called **homozygous** (hoh muh ZI gus). This would be written as *TT* or *tt*. An organism that has two different alleles for a trait is called **heterozygous** (het uh roh ZI gus). This condition would be written *Tt*. The purebred pea plants that Mendel used were homozygous for tall, *TT*, and homozygous for short, *tt*. The hybrid plants he produced were all heterozygous, *Tt*.

The physical expression of a particular genotype is its **phenotype** (FEE nuh tipe). Red is the phenotype for red flowering plants such as the one in **Figure 17-5.** Short is the phenotype for short plants. If you have brown hair, then the phenotype for your hair color is brown.

Determining Genotypes and Phenotypes

In a Punnett square, the letters representing the two alleles from one parent are written along the top of the square. Those of the second parent are placed along the side of the square. Each section of the square is filled in like a multiplication problem, with one allele donated by each parent. The letters that you use to fill in each of the squares represent the genotypes of offspring that the parents could produce.

The Punnett square in **Figure 17-6** represents the first type of experiment by Mendel. You can see that each homozygous parent plant has two alleles for height. One parent is homozygous for tall *(TT).* The other parent is homozygous for short *(tt).* The alleles inside the squares are the genotypes of the

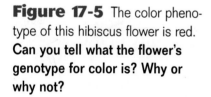

Figure 17-5 The color phenotype of this hibiscus flower is red. **Can you tell what the flower's genotype for color is? Why or why not?**

possible offspring. All of them have the genotype *Tt*. They all have tall as a phenotype because *T* represents tall, the dominant trait. Notice that you can't always figure out a genotype just by looking at the phenotype. The combinations of *TT* or *Tt* both produce tall plants when *T* is dominant to *t*. The examples below will help you understand further.

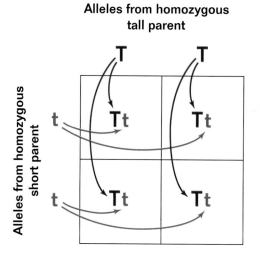

Alleles from homozygous tall parent

Alleles from homozygous short parent

Figure 17-6 A Punnett square shows you all the ways in which alleles can combine. A Punnett square does not tell you how many offspring will be produced. By observing this Punnett square, you can see why all the plants in Mendel's first cross showed the dominant form of the trait in their phenotypes.

Using Punnett Squares

Example 1: Color in Peas

In peas, the color yellow is dominant to the color green. A homozygous yellow pea plant is crossed with a homozygous green pea plant. What will the genotypes and the phenotypes of all the possible offspring be?

Outcome

Genotypes of all possible offspring: All **Yy**

Phenotypes of offspring: All yellow

Example 2: Wing Length in Fruit Flies

In fruit flies, long wings **(L)** are dominant to short wings **(l)**. Two heterozygous long-winged fruit flies (both **Ll**) are crossed. What are the possible genotypes of their offspring? What are the phenotypes?

Outcome

Genotypes of all possible offspring: **LL, Ll,** and **ll**

Phenotypes of all possible offspring:

    LL and **Ll** = long wings

    ll = short wings

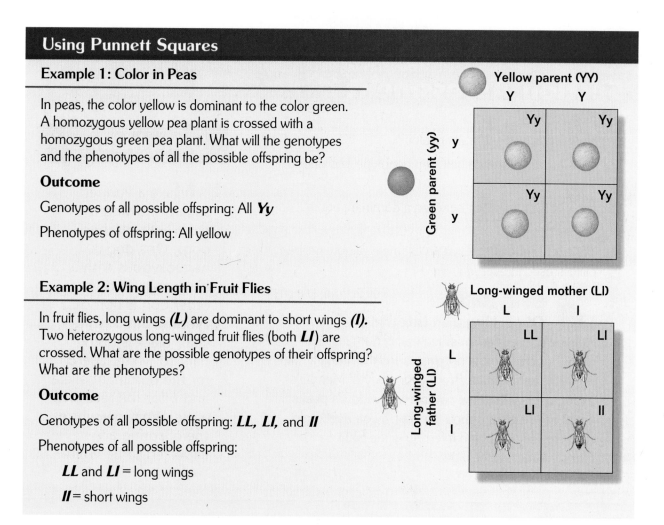

Table 17-2

Mendelian Inheritance

1. Traits are controlled by alleles on chromosomes.

2. An allele may be dominant or recessive in form.

3. When a pair of chromosomes separates during meiosis, the different alleles for a trait move into separate sex cells.

Mendel's Success

Gregor Mendel succeeded in describing how inherited traits are transmitted from parents to offspring. However, he didn't know anything about DNA, genes, or chromosomes. He did figure out that factors in the plants caused certain traits to appear. He also figured out that these factors separated when the plant reproduced. Mendel arrived at his conclusions by patient observation, careful analysis, and repeated experimentation. His work is summed up in **Table 17-2.**

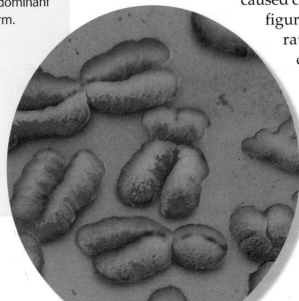

Chromosomes
Magnification: 12 000×

Section Assessment

1. How are alleles and traits related?
2. Explain the difference between genotype and phenotype.
3. What is the difference between a dominant and a recessive allele?
4. **Think Critically:** Give an example of how probability is used in everyday life.
5. **Skill Builder**
   Observing and Inferring
   Hairline shape is an inherited trait in humans. The widow's peak allele is dominant, and the straight hairline allele is recessive. From your study of Mendel's experiments, infer how parents with widow's peaks could have a child without the trait. If you need help, refer to Observing and Inferring in the **Skill Handbook** on page 704.

Using Math

Make a Punnett square showing a cross between two dogs. One dog is heterozygous with a black coat, and the other dog is homozygous with a white coat. Black is dominant to white. Use **B** for the dominant allele and **b** for the recessive allele. What percent of the offspring are expected to be white?

Activity 17•1

Expected and Observed Results

Could you predict how many white flowers would result from crossing two heterozygous red flowers if you knew that white color was a recessive trait? Try this experiment to find out.

What You'll Investigate

How does chance affect combinations of genes?

Goals

- **Model** chance events in heredity.
- **Compare and contrast** predicted and actual results.

Safety Precautions

CAUTION: Do not taste, eat, or drink any materials used in lab.

Procedure

1. Place 50 red beans and 50 white beans into a paper bag. Place 50 red beans and 50 white beans into a second bag. Each bean represents an allele for flower color.

2. **Label** one of the bags "female" for the female parent. **Label** the other bag "male" for the male parent.

3. Without looking, remove one bean from each bag. The two beans represent the alleles that combine when sperm and egg join.

4. Use a Punnett square to **predict** how many red/red, red/white, and white/white combinations are possible.

5. **Use** a data table to **record** the combination of the beans each time you remove two beans. Your table will need to accommodate 100 picks. After recording, return the beans to their original bags.

6. **Count and record** the total numbers of combinations in your data table.

7. **Compile and record** the class totals.

Conclude and Apply

1. Which combination occurred most often?

2. **Calculate** the ratio of red/red to red/white to white/white.

3. **Compare** your predicted (expected) results with your observed (actual) results.

4. Does chance affect allele combination? Explain.

5. How do the results of a small sample compare with the results of a large sample?

6. **Hypothesize** how you could get predicted results to be closer to actual results.

Gene Combinations			
Beans	Red/Red	Red/White	White/White
Your total			
Class total			

17·2 Genetics Since Mendel

What You'll Learn

► How traits are inherited by incomplete dominance
► What multiple alleles and polygenic inheritance are, and examples of each

Vocabulary
incomplete dominance
multiple alleles
polygenic inheritance

Why It's Important

► Most genetic traits are inherited in a more complicated way than Mendel originally discovered. These patterns provide additional insights into heredity.

Incomplete Dominance

When Mendel's work was rediscovered, scientists repeated his experiments. For some plants, such as peas, Mendel's results proved true again and again. However, when different plants were crossed, the results sometimes varied from Mendel's predictions. One scientist crossed pure red four o'clock plants with pure white four o'clocks. He expected to get all red flowers. To his surprise, all the flowers were pink. Neither allele for flower color seemed dominant. Had the colors become blended like paint colors? He crossed the pink-flowered plants with each other and red, pink, and white flowers were produced. These results are shown in **Figure 17-7**. The red and white alleles had not become "blended." Instead, the allele for white flowers and the allele for red flowers had resulted in an intermediate phenotype, a pink flower. **Incomplete dominance** is the production of a phenotype that is intermediate to those of the two homozygous parents. Flower color in four o'clock plants is inherited by incomplete dominance.

Multiple Alleles

Mendel studied traits in peas that were controlled by just two alleles. However, many traits are controlled by more than two alleles. A trait that is controlled by more than two alleles is considered to be controlled by **multiple alleles.** One example of a trait controlled by multiple alleles is blood type in humans.

Figure 17-7 The diagrams show how color in four o'clock flowers is inherited by incomplete dominance.

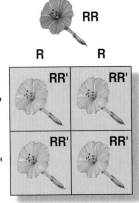

Red × White

Genotypes: All RR'
Phenotypes: All pink

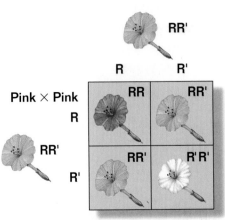

Genotypes: RR, RR', R'R'
Phenotypes: Red, pink, and white

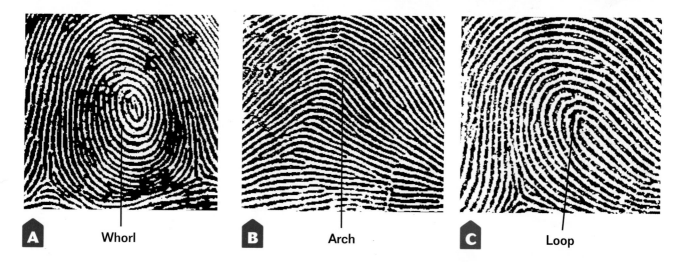

A   Whorl   B   Arch   C   Loop

Figure 17-8 Fingerprints are an example of a trait inherited through the action of a group of gene pairs. The fingerprints in your class will probably show varieties of the whorl (A), arch (B), and loop (C) patterns. These patterns have many variations. **Why are everyone's fingerprints unique?**

In 1900, one scientist found three alleles for blood types in the human population. He called them A, B, and O. A and B alleles are both dominant. When a person inherits one A and one B allele for blood type, both are expressed. Thus, a person with AB blood type shows both alleles in his or her phenotype. Both A and B alleles are dominant to the O allele, which is recessive.

A person with phenotype A blood inherited either the genotype AA or AO. A person with phenotype B blood inherited either genotype BB or BO. For a person to have type AB blood, an A allele must be inherited from one parent and a B allele must be inherited from the other parent. Finally, a person with phenotype O blood has inherited an O allele from each parent and has the genotype OO.

Polygenic Inheritance

Eye color is an example of a single trait that is produced by a combination of many genes. **Polygenic** (pahl ih JEHN ihk) **inheritance** occurs when a group of gene pairs acts together to produce a single trait. The effect of each allele may be small, but the combination produces a wide variety. For this reason, it may be hard to classify all the different shades of blue or brown eyes in your class. Fingerprints, such as those shown in **Figure 17-8**, are inherited through a combination of gene pairs.

Try at Home

Mini Lab

Interpreting Fingerprints

Procedure

1. Look at **Figure 17-8** to see some of the differences shown by fingerprints.
2. With a pencil lead, rub a spot large enough for your finger onto a piece of paper.
3. Rub your finger in the pencil markings.
4. Stick clear tape to your finger.
5. Remove the tape and stick it on the paper.
   CAUTION: Wash hands after taking fingerprints.
6. Using a magnifying lens, observe your fingerprints to see if you can find a whorl, arch, or loop pattern.

Analysis

1. What patterns did you find?
2. Are fingerprints inherited as a simple Mendelian pattern or as a more complex pattern?

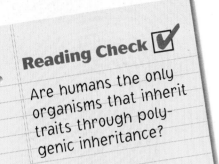

Reading Check

Are humans the only organisms that inherit traits through polygenic inheritance?

Many human traits are controlled by polygenic inheritance, as shown in **Figure 17-9.** Height; weight; body build; and shape of eyes, lips, and ears are examples of some of these traits. It is estimated that skin color is controlled by three to six genes. Even more gene pairs may control the color of your hair and eyes. It is important to note that environment also plays an important role in the expression of traits controlled by polygenic inheritance.

Polygenic inheritance is, of course, not limited to human traits. Grain color in wheat, milk production in cows, and egg production in chickens are also polygenic traits. ☑

The study of genes is no longer a simple look at a single trait controlled by one pair of alleles. Do you think Mendel would be amazed if he could see the amount of progress in genetics that began with his work?

Figure 17-9 Hair color, skin color, and eye color in humans are the results of the expression of more than one pair of genes.

Section Assessment

1. Compare inheritance by multiple alleles and polygenic inheritance.

2. Explain why a trait inherited by incomplete dominance is not a blend of two alleles.

3. Give an example of a trait that is inherited by polygenic inheritance, one controlled by multiple alleles, and one that exhibits incomplete dominance.

4. **Think Critically:** A chicken that is purebred for black feathers is crossed with one that is purebred for white feathers. All the offspring produced have gray feathers. How is the trait inherited? Explain your answer.

5. **Skill Builder**
   Making and Using Graphs
   Many genetic traits are produced by a combination of genes. Do the **Chapter 17 Skill Activity** on page 742. Make and use a graph that shows the effect of polygenic inheritance.

Science Journal

In your Science Journal, write an essay that explains why the offspring of two parents may or may not show much resemblance to either parent.

DNA Fingerprinting

DNA (deoxyribonucleic acid) is the molecule in each cell that contains information directing the cell's growth and development (see double helix, left background). DNA fingerprinting identifies you by distinguishing your DNA from the DNA of everyone else. DNA fingerprinting is based on the uniqueness of everyone's DNA, just as hand fingerprints are unique. Scientists extract cells from different areas of a person's body and process the DNA so that it appears as a pattern of dark bands. The bands show the composition of that person's DNA and form the DNA fingerprint.

HOW DNA FINGERPRINTS ARE MADE

1 Scientists use material from a person's cells to obtain DNA.

2 DNA is cut into pieces of varying sizes.

3 The pieces of DNA are placed in a gel. Then an electrical charge causes the DNA fragments to separate, with smaller pieces collecting toward the bottom of the gel.

4 The DNA sample is exposed to X-ray film or a stain so that a pattern of black bars can be seen.

5 Scientists "read" the pattern, which is unique to the person from whom the DNA was taken.

Forensic scientists (those who apply scientific knowledge to legal problems) use DNA fingerprints to identify a crime suspect or to prove someone innocent.

Medical scientists also use DNA fingerprinting to detect the presence of genetic diseases and to predict the chances of a successful transplant. Because a DNA fingerprint provides a genetic profile, scientists can predict the success of a transplant by comparing the profile of the donor with that of the recipient.

Think Critically

1. Cells from which parts of your body can be used to determine your DNA fingerprint?

2. In addition to the applications mentioned here, how else might DNA fingerprinting be used?

inter**NET** CONNECTION

Visit the Glencoe Science Web Site at **www.glencoe.com/sec/science** to learn more about forensics and the process of DNA fingerprinting.

Materials

- Meter stick
- Graph paper
- Pencil

Determining Polygenic Inheritance

When several genes at different locations on chromosomes act together to produce a single trait, a wide range of phenotypes for the trait can result. By measuring the range of phenotypes and graphing them, you can determine if a trait is produced by polygenic inheritance. How would graphs differ if traits were inherited in a simple dominant or recessive pattern?

What You'll Investigate

How can the effect of polygenic inheritance be determined?

Goals

- **Measure** the heights of students to the nearest centimeter.
- **Create** a bar graph of phenotypes for a polygenic trait.

Safety Precautions

Always obtain the permission of any person included in an experiment on human traits.

Procedure

1. **Form a hypothesis** about what a bar graph that shows the heights of students in your class will look like.

2. **Measure** and record the height of every student to the nearest centimeter.

3. **Design** a table on your paper like the one shown. Count the number of students for each interval and complete the table.

4. **Plot** the results from the table on a bar graph. The height should be graphed on the horizontal axis and the number of students of each height along the vertical axis. If you need help, refer to Making and Using Graphs in the **Skill Handbook** on page 701.

5. The *range* of a set of data is the difference between the greatest measurement and the smallest measurement. The *median* is the middle number when the data are placed in order. The *mean* is the sum of all the data divided by the sample size. The *mode* is the number that appears most often in the measurements. Calculate each of these numbers and record them in your Science Journal.

Conclude and Apply

1. How does this bar graph differ from one produced for a trait controlled by a single gene?

2. How can you tell if a trait is controlled by more than one gene?

3. Can you **infer** from your data that height is controlled by more than two genes? Explain why or why not.

Student Height	
Height in cm	**Number of Students**
A 101–110	
B 111–120	
C 121–130	
D 131–140	
E 141–150	
F 151–160	
G 161–170	
H 171–180	

Human Genetics

17·3

Genes and Health

Sometimes, a gene undergoes a mutation that results in an unwanted trait. Not all mutations are harmful, but some have resulted in genetic disorders among humans. Sickle-cell anemia and cystic fibrosis are two disorders that result from changes in DNA.

Recessive Genetic Disorders

Sickle-cell anemia is a homozygous recessive disorder in which red blood cells are sickle shaped instead of disc shaped, as shown in **Figure 17-10.** Sickle-shaped cells can't deliver enough oxygen to the cells in the body. In addition, the misshapen cells don't move through blood vessels easily. As a result, body tissues may be damaged due to insufficient oxygen. Sickle-cell anemia is most commonly found in tropical areas and in a small percentage of African Americans. Many people with sickle-cell anemia die as children, but some live longer. Sickle-cell anemia patients can be treated with drugs to increase the amount of oxygen carried by red blood cells or by transfusions of blood containing normal cells. Because sickle-cell anemia is homozygous recessive, it is possible to carry the sickle-cell allele and not have the disease. In fact, those heterozygous for sickle-cell anemia have been shown to be more resistant to malaria than those not carrying the sickle-cell trait.

What You'll Learn

- Two human genetic disorders and how they are inherited
- How sex-linked traits are inherited
- The importance of genetic engineering

Vocabulary

sex-linked gene
pedigree
genetic engineering

Why It's Important

- Human genetics and heredity explain why you look the way you do.

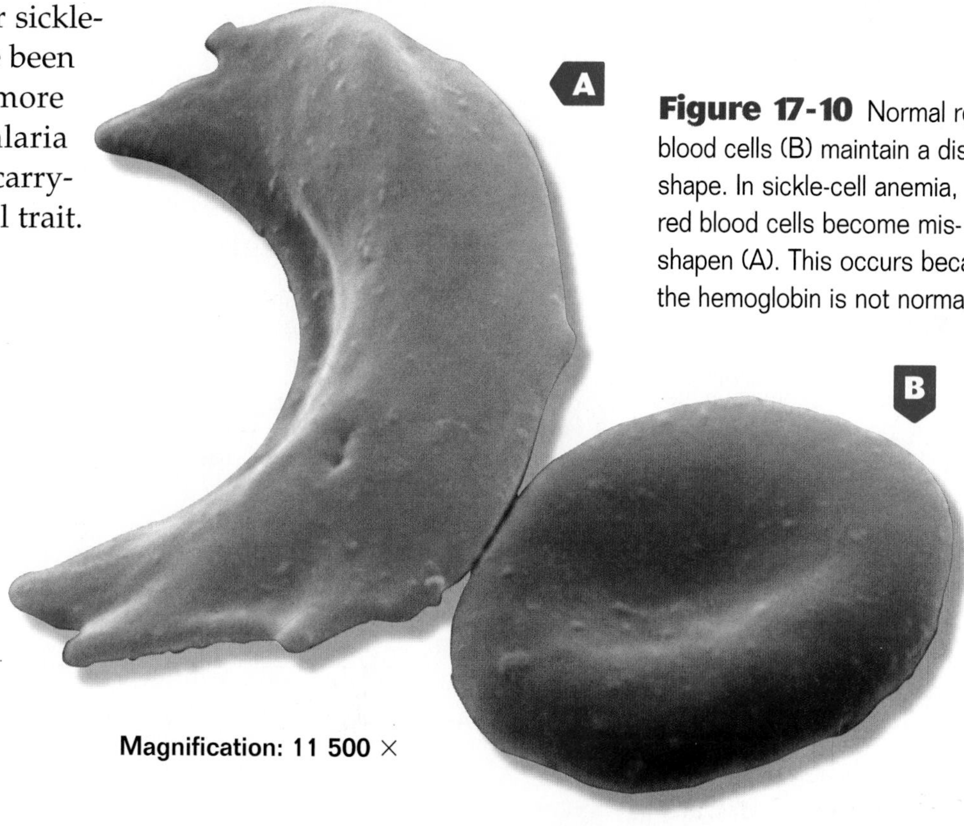
A
B
Magnification: 11 500 ×

Figure 17-10 Normal red blood cells (B) maintain a disc shape. In sickle-cell anemia, red blood cells become misshapen (A). This occurs because the hemoglobin is not normal.

Cystic fibrosis is another homozygous recessive disorder. In most people, a thin fluid is produced by the body to lubricate the lungs and intestinal tract. Instead of a thin fluid, people with cystic fibrosis have thick mucus in these areas which builds up in the lungs and digestive system. Mucus in the lungs makes it hard to breathe and is often the site of bacterial infection. Mucus in the digestive tract reduces or prevents the flow of digestive enzymes to food in the intestine. These enzymes are needed to break down food so that it can be absorbed by your body.

Cystic fibrosis is the most commonly inherited genetic disorder among Caucasians. Nearly one Caucasian in 25 carries a recessive allele for this disorder. In the United States, four Caucasian babies are born with this disorder every day. Patients with cystic fibrosis are often helped with antibiotics, special diets, and physical therapy to break up the thick mucus in their lungs and help them cough it out.

Sex Determination

What determines the sex of an individual? Information on sex inheritance in many organisms, including humans, came from a study of fruit flies. Fruit flies have eight chromosomes. Among these chromosomes are either two X chromosomes,

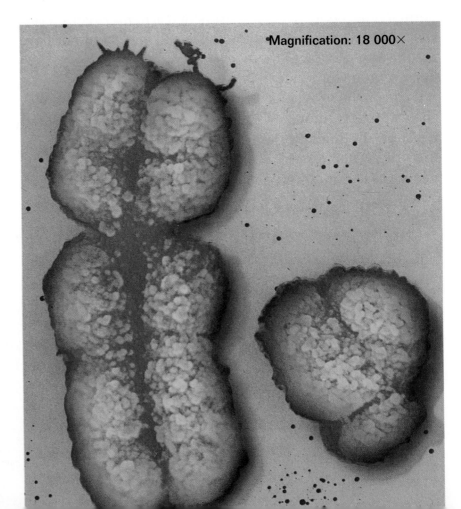

Figure 17-11 Sex in many organisms is determined by X (left) and Y (right) chromosomes. In the photograph, you can see how X and Y chromosomes differ from one another in shape and size.

Magnification: 18 000×

or an X chromosome and a Y chromosome. Scientists have concluded that the X and Y chromosomes contain genes that determine the sex of an individual. Females have two X chromosomes in their cells. Males have an X chromosome and a Y chromosome. You can see an X and a Y chromosome in **Figure 17-11.** Is this individual male or female?

Females produce eggs that have only an X chromosome. Males produce both X-containing sperm and Y-containing sperm. When an egg from a female is fertilized by an X sperm, the offspring is XX, a female. When an egg from a female is fertilized by a Y sperm, the zygote produced is XY, and the offspring is a male. Sometimes chromosomes fail to separate properly during meiosis. When this occurs, an individual may inherit an abnormal number of sex chromosomes, as in **Figure 17-12.** What pair of sex chromosomes is in each of your cells?

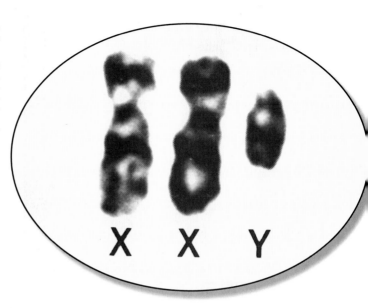

Figure 17-12 The chromosomes above are from an individual with Klinefelter syndrome. This syndrome, in which a male inherits an extra X chromosome, occurs once in every 2000 live births.

Problem Solving

Predicting a Baby's Gender

Probability refers to the chance that an event will occur. For example, if you flip a coin, it will land in only one of two ways—heads or tails. The probability of the coin landing heads or tails is one out of two, or 50 percent. If you were to toss two coins at the same time, each coin still has only a one-half probability of landing with heads or tails up.

What is the probability that any single pregnancy will result in the birth of a girl?

Rosalinda's mother is going to have a baby.

Rosalinda already has a brother, so she really hopes this baby is a girl. How would you determine the chance that this baby will be a girl?

Solve the Problem: How can the outcome of each pregnancy be predicted?

Think Critically: Does the fact that Rosalinda's mother already has one boy and one girl affect the probability of the next child being a girl? Why or why not?

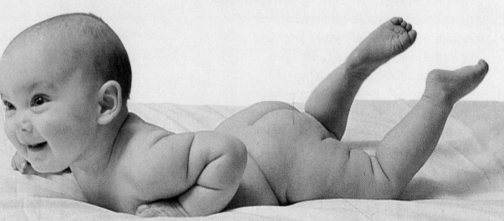

Figure 17-13 What number
do you see in this pattern?

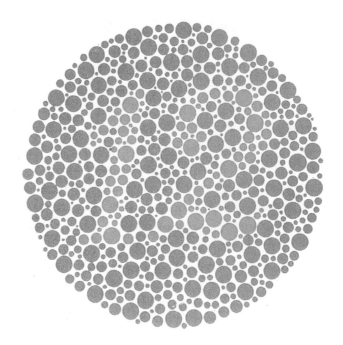

inter**NET**
C O N N E C T I O N

Visit the Glencoe
Science Web Site at
**www.glencoe.com/
sec/science** for more
information about
recent developments in
genetics.

Sex-Linked Disorders

Some inherited conditions are closely linked with the X
and Y chromosomes that determine the sex of an individual.
A story is told about a young boy who appeared to have normal intelligence but couldn't be taught to pick ripe cherries
on the family farm. His parents took him to a doctor. After
observing him, the doctor concluded that the boy couldn't
tell the difference between the colors red and green.
Individuals who are red-green color blind have inherited an
allele on the X chromosome that prevents them from seeing
these colors. Find out if you are color blind by looking at
Figure 17-13.

An allele inherited on a sex chromosome is called a **sex-
linked gene.** More males are color blind than females. Can
you figure out why? If a male inherits an X chromosome with

Figure 17-14 Color blindness is a
recessive sex-linked trait. Females who are
heterozygous see colors normally, but their
sons may be color blind. When a woman
with normal vision who carries one allele for
color blindness (XX^C) marries a man with
normal vision (XY), their children may have
normal vision (XX, XY), be carriers (XX^C), or
be color blind (X^{C}Y). **Why aren't the daugh-
ters of this marriage color blind?**

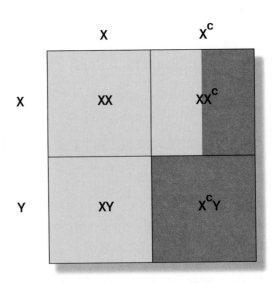

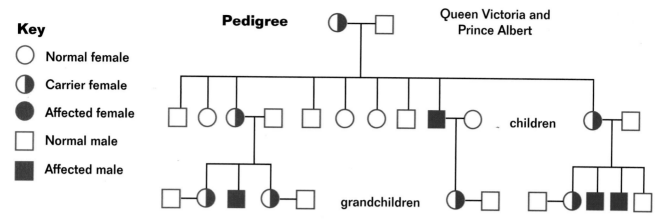

Key
- ◯ Normal female
- ◑ Carrier female
- ● Affected female
- ☐ Normal male
- ■ Affected male

Pedigree

Queen Victoria and Prince Albert

children

grandchildren

the color-blind allele from his mother, he will be color blind. Color-blind females are rare. **Figure 17-14** shows how males and females inherit the genes that result in color blindness.

Another sex-linked disorder is hemophilia. For people with this disorder, even a scrape can be life threatening because blood does not clot properly. Like color blindness, males who inherit the X chromosome with the hemophilia allele will have the disorder. For a female to be a hemophiliac, she must inherit the defective allele on both X chromosomes. Hemophilia occurs in fewer than 1 in 7000 males. Females are usually carriers, having just one allele for hemophilia.

Pedigrees Trace Traits

How can you trace a trait through a family? A **pedigree** is a tool for tracing the occurrence of a trait in a family. Males are represented by squares and females by circles. A circle or square that is completely filled in shows that the person has the condition. Half-colored circles or squares indicate carriers. A carrier has an allele for a trait but does not express the trait. People represented by empty circles or squares are neither carriers nor affected by the trait. You can see how the trait for hemophilia was inherited in Queen Victoria of England's family in the pedigree in **Figure 17-15.** ☑

Why is genetics important?

If Mendel were to pick up a daily newspaper in any country today, he probably would be surprised. News articles about developments in genetic research appear almost daily. The term *gene* has become a household word. In this chapter, you have learned that nearly every trait you have inherited is the result of genes expressing themselves. The same laws that govern the inheritance of traits in humans govern the inheritance of traits in wheat and in mice.

Figure 17-15 Pedigrees show the occurrence of a trait in a family. The icons in the key mean the same thing on all pedigree charts. Queen Victoria was a carrier of the recessive allele for hemophilia. **How many of her grandchildren on this chart are hemophiliacs? How many are carriers?**

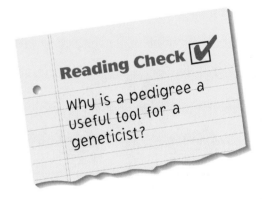

Reading Check ☑

Why is a pedigree a useful tool for a geneticist?

PKU

Information on genetic disorders has reached soft-drink cans. People with PKU, a recessive disorder, are missing the enzyme needed to break down a substance found in some artificially sweetened drinks. Cans must be labeled to ensure that individuals with this disorder do not unknowingly consume the harmful substance. Explain how a person could be born with PKU if neither parent has the disorder.

In this section, you've seen that there are inherited disorders that affect the human population. You may even know someone with one of these disorders. Many genetic disorders are controlled by diet and preventive measures. Genetics is no longer something that you read about only in textbooks.

Knowing how genes are inherited causes some people to seek the advice of a genetic counselor before having children. Couples who discover genetic traits that could lead to disorders in their children sometimes elect to adopt healthy children instead.

Genetic Engineering

Through **genetic engineering,** scientists are experimenting with biological and chemical methods to change the DNA sequence that makes up a gene. Genetic engineering is already used to help produce large quantities of medicine, such as insulin, to meet the needs of people with a disease called diabetes. Genes also can be inserted into cells to change how those cells perform their normal functions, as shown in **Figure 17-16.** Genetic engineering research also is being used to find new ways to improve crop production and quality, including the development of plants that are resistant to disease.

A **B**

Magnification: 4290×

Figure 17-16 Genetically engineered bacteria (A) have been developed to clean up environmental problems such as this oil spill in Wales (B). Such bacteria have alleles inserted into them that allow them to break down oil more efficiently than normal bacteria found in the environment.

New Plants from Old

One type of genetic engineering involves identifying genes that are responsible for desirable traits in one plant, then inserting these genes into other plants. In barley, for example, a single gene has been identified that controls several traits—including time of maturity, strength, height, and resistance to drought. Researchers plan to insert this gene into plants such as wheat, rice, and soybeans to create shorter, stronger, drought-resistant plants. Why are these traits of interest to scientists? Wheat, rice, and soybeans are subject to lodging, a condition in which plants fall over because of their own height and weight. If a new gene from the barley plant could result in shorter wheat or rice plants, fewer plants would be lost and crop yields would increase. This gene could even be used to develop lawn grass that stays a certain height and doesn't need to be watered as often. Already, corn and cotton have undergone genetic engineering to enable them to better withstand pests. Research on genetic engineering in plants is done at centers such as the one shown in **Figure 17-17.**

Figure 17-17 Researchers at the International Rice Research Institute in the Philippines are using genetic engineering techniques to develop new strains of rice.

Section Assessment

1. Describe two genetic disorders.
2. Explain why males are affected more often than females by sex-linked genetic disorders.
3. Describe the importance of genetic engineering.
4. **Think Critically:** Use a Punnett square to explain how a woman who is a carrier for color blindness can have a daughter who is color blind.
5.  **Skill Builder**
   Concept Mapping
   Use a network tree concept map to show how X and Y sex cells can combine to form fertilized eggs. Begin with female sex cells, each containing an X chromosome. Use two male sex cells. Indicate one with an X chromosome and one with a Y chromosome. If you need help, refer to Concept Mapping in the **Skill Handbook** on page 698.

Science Journal
Hugo de Vries, Walter Sutton, Barbara McClintock, and Thomas Hunt Morgan each made discoveries in the field of genetics. Research these scientists and summarize their work in your Science Journal, discussing the importance of their contributions.

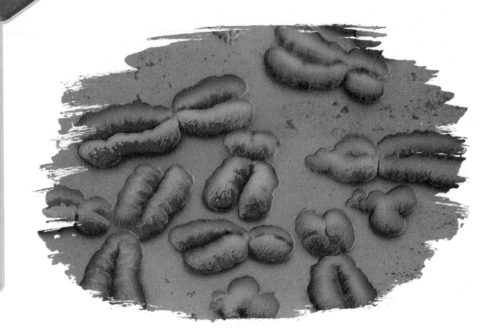

For a **preview** of this chapter, study this Reviewing Main Ideas before you read the chapter. After you have studied this chapter, you can use the Reviewing Main Ideas to **review** the chapter.

  The Glencoe MindJogger, Audiocassettes, and CD-ROM provide additional opportunities for review.

Section 17-1 GENETICS

Genetics is the study of how traits are inherited through the actions of **alleles.** Gregor Mendel determined the basic laws of genetics.

1. Traits are controlled by alleles on chromosomes.
2. An allele may be dominant or recessive in form.
3. When a pair of chromosomes separates during meiosis, the different alleles for a trait move into separate sex cells.

He found that traits followed the laws of probability and that he could predict the outcome of genetic crosses. *How can a Punnett square help to predict inheritance of traits?*

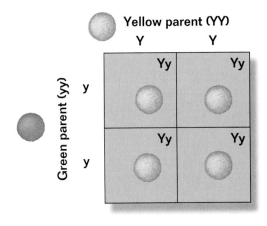

Yellow parent (YY)

	Y	Y
y	Yy	Yy
y	Yy	Yy

Green parent (yy)

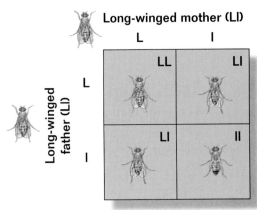

Long-winged mother (Ll)

	L	l
L	LL	Ll
l	Ll	ll

Long-winged father (Ll)

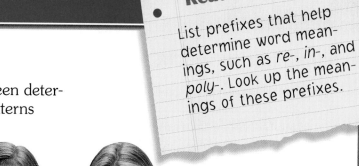

Reading Check ☑

List prefixes that help determine word meanings, such as *re-*, *in-*, and *poly-*. Look up the meanings of these prefixes.

Section

17-2 GENETICS SINCE MENDEL

Some inheritance patterns have been determined that Mendel did not see. Some patterns studied since Mendel include **incomplete dominance, multiple alleles,** and **polygenic inheritance**. These inheritance patterns allow a greater variety of phenotypes to be produced than would result from simple Mendelian inheritance. *Define incomplete dominance, multiple alleles, and polygenic inheritance, and give an example of each.*

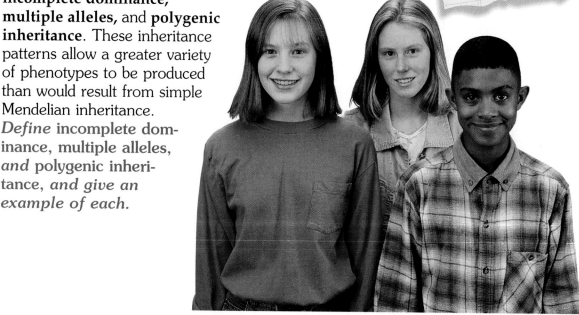

Section

17-3 HUMAN GENETICS

Some disorders are the results of inheritance and can be harmful, even deadly, to those affected. **Pedigrees** may help to reveal patterns of inheritance of a trait in a family. Pedigrees show that males express **sex-linked** traits more often than females. Breakthroughs in the field of genetic engineering are allowing scientists to do many things, including producing plants that are resistant to disease. *How may genetic engineering result in solutions to problems caused by human genetic disorders?*

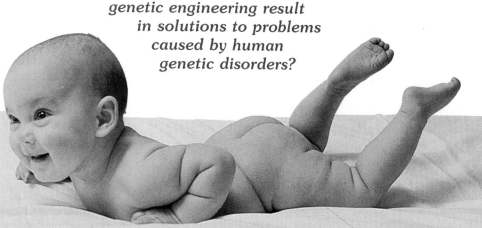

Chapter 17 Assessment

Using Vocabulary

a. alleles
b. dominant
c. genetic engineering
d. genetics
e. genotype
f. heredity
g. heterozygous
h. homozygous
i. incomplete dominance
j. multiple alleles
k. pedigree
l. phenotype
m. polygenic inheritance
n. Punnett square
o. recessive
p. sex-linked gene

Each phrase below describes a vocabulary term from the list. Write the term that matches the phrase describing it.

1. gene located on the X chromosome
2. different form of the same gene
3. a tool for predicting possible offspring
4. the study of heredity
5. shows the pattern of gene inheritance in a family

Checking Concepts

Choose the word or phrase that best answers the question.

6. Which of the following are located on chromosomes?
   A) genes
   B) pedigrees
   C) carbohydrates
   D) zygotes

7. Which of the following describes the allele that causes color blindness?
   A) dominant
   B) carried on the Y chromosome
   C) carried on the X chromosome
   D) present only in females

8. What is it called when two different alleles combine to form an intermediate phenotype?
   A) incomplete dominance
   B) polygenic inheritance
   C) multiple alleles
   D) sex-linked genes

9. What separates during meiosis?
   A) proteins
   B) phenotypes
   C) alleles
   D) pedigrees

10. What do genes control?
    A) chromosomes
    B) traits
    C) cell membranes
    D) mitosis

11. How is blood type inherited?
    A) polygenic inheritance
    B) multiple alleles
    C) incomplete dominance
    D) recessive genes

12. How is sickle-cell anemia inherited?
    A) polygenic inheritance
    B) multiple alleles
    C) incomplete dominance
    D) recessive genes

13. How is eye shape inherited?
    A) polygenic inheritance
    B) multiple alleles
    C) incomplete dominance
    D) recessive genes

14. For a normal female to be produced, what must the father contribute?
    A) an X chromosome
    B) XX chromosomes
    C) a Y chromosome
    D) XY chromosomes

15. Which of the following is a Punnett square used for?
    A) to dominate the outcome of a cross
    B) to predict the outcome of a cross
    C) to assure the outcome of a cross
    D) to number the outcome of a cross

Thinking Critically

16. Explain the relationship among DNA, genes, alleles, and chromosomes.

17. How can advances in genetic engineering help in places that are subject to food shortages caused by drought?

18. Explain how an organism with a genotype *Gg* and an organism with the genotype *GG* could have the same phenotype.

Developing Skills

If you need help, refer to the Skill Handbook.

19. **Designing an Experiment:** Design an experiment to determine if a trait is transmitted by a dominant or recessive gene.

20. **Concept Mapping:** On a separate sheet of paper, use the following terms to complete the network tree concept map below: *phenotypes, recessive, genes,* and *dominant.*

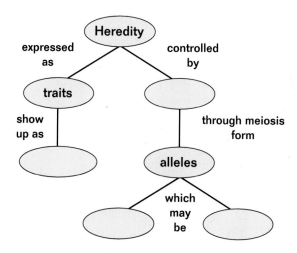

Test-Taking Tip

Don't Cram If you don't know the material by the week before the test, you're less likely to do well. Set up a time line for your practice and preparation so that you're not rushed. Then you will have time to deal with any problem areas.

Test Practice

Use these questions to test your Science Proficiency.

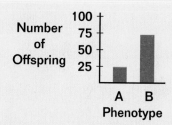

1. From the graph above, what is the inheritance pattern?
   A) dominant recessive
   B) incomplete dominance
   C) multiple alleles
   D) polygenic inheritance

2. Which of the following is true about inheritance of sex-linked traits?
   A) Sex-linked traits occur only in females.
   B) Sex-linked traits are inherited most frequently by males.
   C) Sex-linked traits require many genes to be inherited.
   D) Sex-linked traits occur equally often in males and females.

7

The Human Body

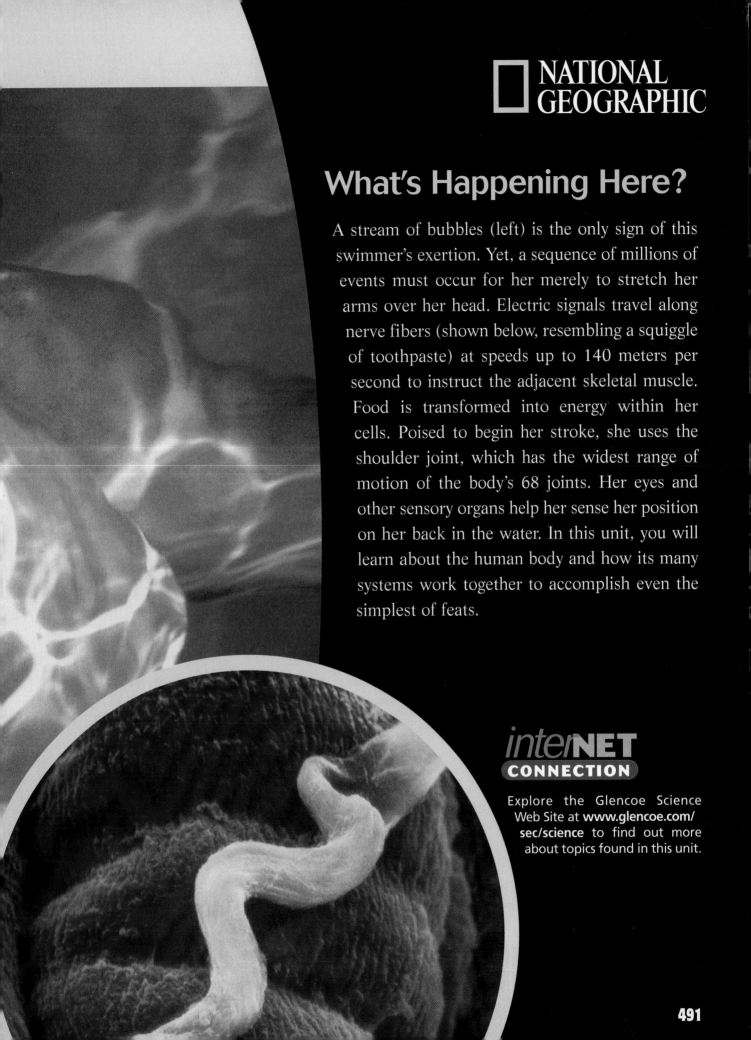

NATIONAL GEOGRAPHIC

What's Happening Here?

A stream of bubbles (left) is the only sign of this swimmer's exertion. Yet, a sequence of millions of events must occur for her merely to stretch her arms over her head. Electric signals travel along nerve fibers (shown below, resembling a squiggle of toothpaste) at speeds up to 140 meters per second to instruct the adjacent skeletal muscle. Food is transformed into energy within her cells. Poised to begin her stroke, she uses the shoulder joint, which has the widest range of motion of the body's 68 joints. Her eyes and other sensory organs help her sense her position on her back in the water. In this unit, you will learn about the human body and how its many systems work together to accomplish even the simplest of feats.

interNET CONNECTION

Explore the Glencoe Science Web Site at **www.glencoe.com/ sec/science** to find out more about topics found in this unit.

CHAPTER

18

Bones, Muscles, and Skin

Chapter Preview

Section 18-1
The Skeletal System

Section 18-2
The Muscular System

Section 18-3
Skin

Skills Preview

Skill Builders
- Outline
- Map Concepts

Activities
- Observe and Collect Data

MiniLabs
- Observe and Experiment

Reading Check ✓

Before reading this chapter, find out what these prefixes mean: *osteo-, peri-, im-,* and *epi-.* Identify and define several words that begin with each of these prefixes.

Explore Activity

Like this athlete on the left, you might have experienced tired muscles after completing some strenuous physical activity. You round the bend one last time at the school track, proud to have finished an unusually long run in good time. Your muscles feel as though they couldn't carry you another meter. You have improved your time, and you know your muscles are clenched. Try the following activity to measure muscles in different states.

Observe Muscle Size

1. Hang your straightened arm to your side in a relaxed position. Use a measuring tape to determine the size (circumference) of your upper arm when it is relaxed.

2. Flex your arm by bending it and making a fist. Measure your upper arm again.

3. How did the size of your upper arm change when you flexed your arm?

4. What happened to the muscle to cause this change? Did the muscle become larger? Or, did it shorten and bunch up?

Write a paragraph about what you think is happening to the muscles as you straighten and flex your arm.

18·1 The Skeletal System

What You'll Learn

▶ The five major functions of the skeletal system
▶ How to compare and contrast movable and immovable joints

Vocabulary
skeletal system
marrow
periosteum
cartilage
joint
ligament
immovable joint
movable joint

Why It's Important

▶ You'll gain an understanding of the motion of each of your body parts and what allows you to move these body parts.

A Living Framework

The skull and crossbones flag flying on a pirate ship has long been a symbol of death. You might think that bones are dead structures made of rocklike material. It's true that a skeleton's bones are no longer living, but the bones in your body are very much alive. Each bone is a living organ made of several different tissues. Cells in these bones take in nutrients and expend energy. They have the same requirements as your other cells.

Major Functions of Your Skeletal System

All the bones in your body make up your **skeletal system,** which is the framework of your body. The human skeletal system has five major functions. First, it gives shape and support to your body, like the framework of the building in **Figure 18-1.** Second, bones protect your internal organs: ribs surround the heart and lungs, and a skull encloses the brain. Third, major muscles are attached to bone. Muscles move bones. Fourth, blood cells are formed in the red marrow of some bones. Bone **marrow** is a soft tissue in the center of many bones. Finally, the skeleton is where major quantities of calcium and phosphorous compounds are stored for later use. Calcium and phosphorus make bone hard.

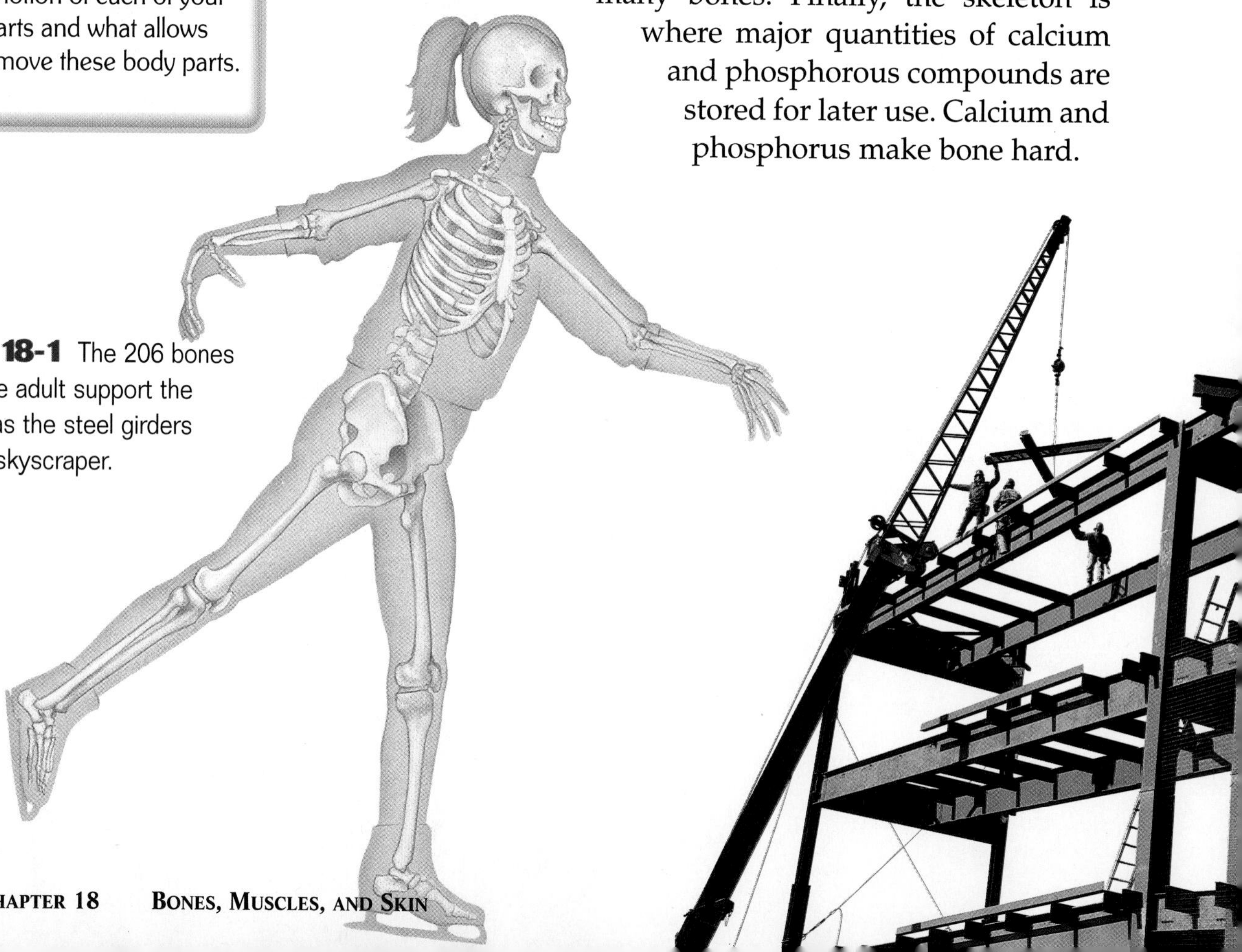

Figure 18-1 The 206 bones of a mature adult support the body just as the steel girders support a skyscraper.

Looking at Bone

As you study bones, you'll notice several characteristics. The differences in sizes and shapes are probably most obvious. Bones are frequently classified according to shape. Bone shapes, shown in **Figure 18-2,** are genetically controlled and also are modified by the work of muscles that are attached to them.

Bone Structure

Upon close examination, you'll find that a bone isn't all smooth. Bones have bumps, edges, round ends, rough spots, and many pits and holes. Muscles and ligaments attach to some of the bumps and pits. Blood vessels and nerves enter and leave through the holes. Many internal and external characteristics of bone are seen in the picture of the humerus shown in **Figure 18-3.**

As you can see in **Figure 18-3,** the surface of the bone is covered with a tough, tight-fitting membrane called the **periosteum** (per ee AHS tee um). Small blood vessels in the periosteum carry nutrients into the bone. Cells involved in the growth and repair of bone also are found here. Under the periosteum is compact bone, which is a hard, strong layer of bone. Compact bone contains bone cells, blood vessels, and a

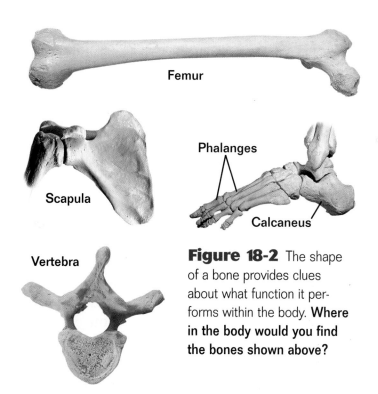

Figure 18-2 The shape of a bone provides clues about what function it performs within the body. **Where in the body would you find the bones shown above?**

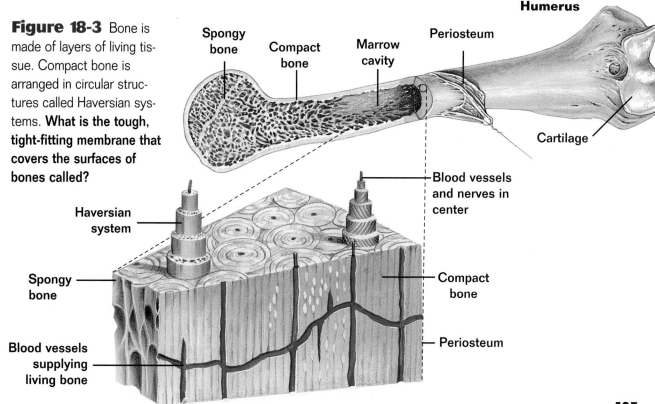

Figure 18-3 Bone is made of layers of living tissue. Compact bone is arranged in circular structures called Haversian systems. **What is the tough, tight-fitting membrane that covers the surfaces of bones called?**

protein base or scaffolding with deposits of calcium and phosphorus. The flexible protein base keeps bone from being too rigid and brittle or easily broken.

Spongy bone is found toward the ends of long bones like the humerus, as seen in **Figure 18-3.** Spongy bone is much less compact and has many small, open spaces that make bone lightweight. If all your bones were completely solid, you'd have a much greater mass. Long bones have large openings, or cavities. The cavities in the center of long bones and the spaces in spongy bone are filled with marrow. Marrow produces red blood cells at an incredible rate of more than 2 million cells per second. White blood cells also are produced in bone marrow, but in lesser amounts. ✓

Cartilage

Notice in **Figure 18-3** that the ends of the bone are covered with a thick, slippery, smooth layer of tissue called **cartilage.** Cartilage does not contain blood vessels or minerals. It is flexible and is important at joints, where it absorbs shock and makes movement easier by reducing friction. In some athletes and in older people, cartilage sometimes wears away, resulting in a condition called arthritis. People with arthritis feel pain when they move.

Reading Check ✓

What are some characteristics of bone?

Figure 18-4 Bone formation starts with cartilage. Starting in the middle of the bone, the cartilage is replaced by hard bone. The solid tissue grows outward until the entire bone has hardened. **What type of bone cell builds up bone?**

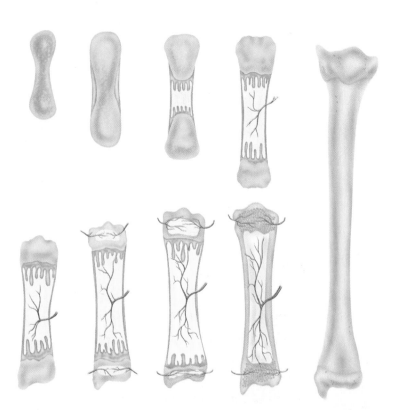

Bone Development

Months before you were born, your skeleton was first made of cartilage. Gradually, the cartilage was broken down and replaced by bone-forming cells called osteoblasts (AHS tee oh blasts). These cells deposit calcium and phosphorus that make bone tissue hard. At birth, your skeleton was made up of more than 300 bones. As you developed, some bones fused, or grew together, so that now you have only 206 bones.

Healthy bone tissue is dynamic. **Figure 18-4** shows that it is always being formed and re-formed. Osteoblasts are bone cells that build up bone. A second type of bone cell, called an osteoclast, breaks down bone tissue in other areas. This is a normal process in a healthy person.

When osteoclasts break down bone, they release calcium and phosphorus into the bloodstream. This process keeps the calcium and phosphorus in your blood at about the same levels.

Where Bones Meet

Think of the different actions you performed this morning. You opened your mouth to yawn, chewed your breakfast, reached for a toothbrush, and stretched out your arm to turn the doorknob as you walked out the door. All these motions were possible because your skeleton has joints.

Any place where two or more bones meet is a **joint.** A joint keeps the bones far enough apart that they do not rub against each other as they move. At the same time, a joint holds the bones in place. A **ligament** is a tough band of tissue that holds bones together at joints. Many joints, such as your knee, are held together by more than one ligament.

*inter*NET
CONNECTION

Visit the Glencoe Science Web Site at **www.glencoe.com/ sec/science** for more information about bone development.

Problem Solving

Shape Affects Strength

When designing a building, architects know that certain shapes provide more support. Look closely at the shapes of the Haversian systems found in the cross section of a bone. Does this system's design add to the overall strength of a bone? To find out, build two different support structures and see which is stronger.

Solve the Problem

1. Determine what geometric design is formed by Haversian systems.

2. Use two flat disks of modeling clay, plastic drinking straws, and two wooden boards to build the two different support structures.

3. Insert the straws, in random order, in one clay disk. Lay a board on top. Put pressure on the board until the structure collapses.

4. Repeat step 3, but arrange the straws in the same design as the Haversian systems.

Think Critically

1. Which structure withstood more pressure? How does this relate to the strength of your bones?

2. What geometric shape provides strength for your bones?

3. Compact bone is made of a series of Haversian systems. What impact do several of these structures have on the strength of the whole bone?

4. Suppose paper were wrapped around the straws in the second structure. What impact would this have on the strength of the structure? What part of an actual bone does the paper represent?

Types of Joints

Joints are classified as immovable or movable. Refer to **Figure 18-5** as you learn about different types of joints. An **immovable joint** allows little or no movement. The joints of the bones in your skull and pelvis are classified as immovable. A **movable joint** allows the body to make a wide range of movements. Gymnastics and working the controls of a video game require movable joints. There are several types of movable joints: pivot, ball-and-socket, hinge, and gliding. In a pivot joint, one bone rotates in a ring of another stationary bone. Turning your head is an example of a pivot movement. In a ball-and-socket joint, one bone has a rounded end that fits into a cuplike cavity on another bone. This provides a wider range of movement. Thus, your hips and shoulders can swing in almost any direction.

A third type of joint is a hinge joint. This joint has a back-and-forth movement like hinges on a door. Elbows, knees, and fingers have hinge joints. While hinge joints are less flexible than the ball-and-socket, they are more stable. They are not as easily dislocated, or put out of joint, as a ball-and-socket joint. A fourth type of joint is a gliding joint, where one part of a bone slides over another bone. Gliding joints move in a back-and-forth motion and are found in your

Figure 18-5 When a soccer player kicks a ball, several types of joints are in action. **Which type of joint permits the widest range of movement?**

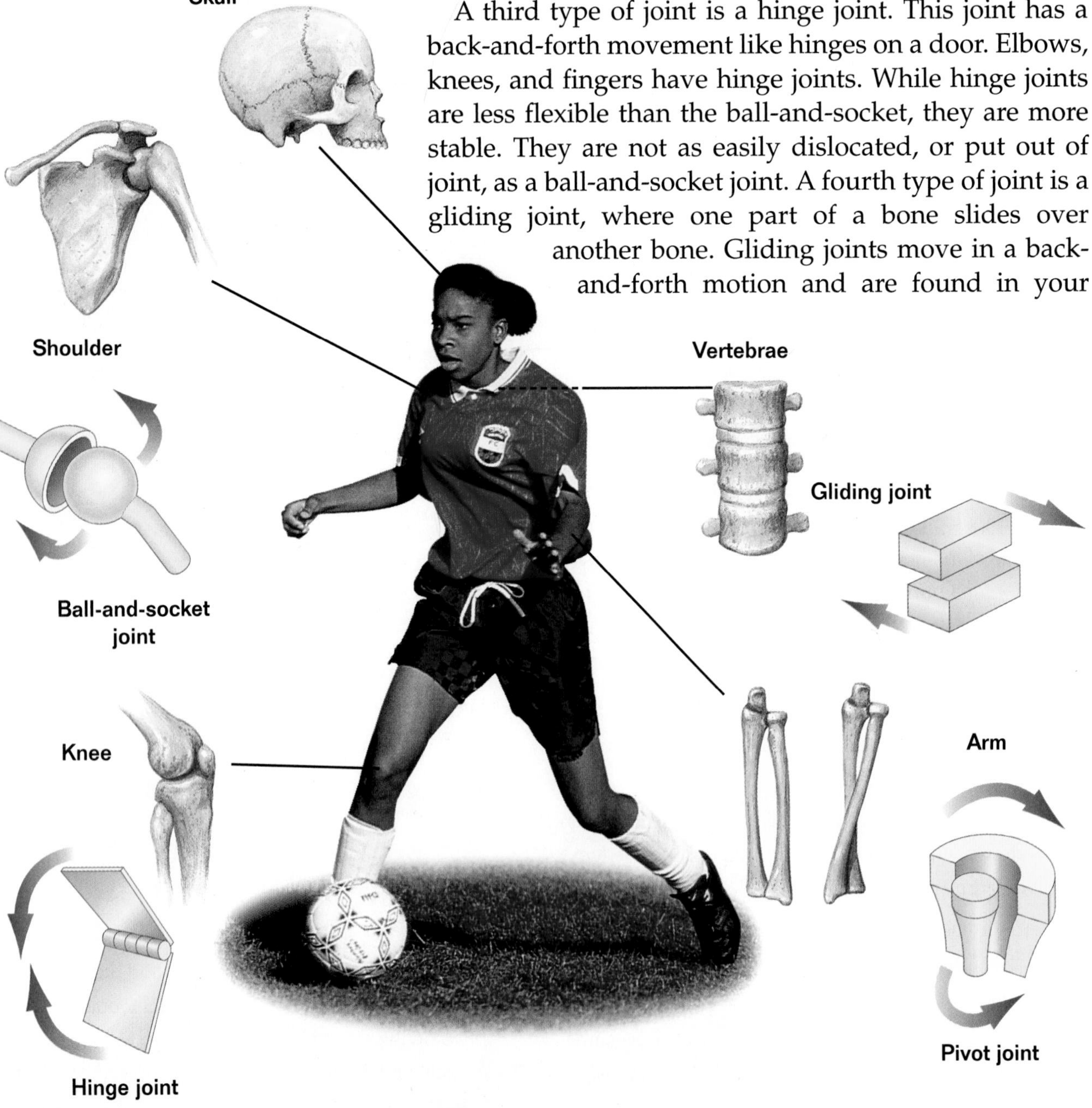

Skull

Shoulder

Ball-and-socket joint

Knee

Hinge joint

Vertebrae

Gliding joint

Arm

Pivot joint

wrists and ankles and between vertebrae. Gliding joints are the most frequently used joints in your body. You can't write a word, pick up a sock, or take a step without using a gliding joint.

Making a Smooth Move

Think about what happens when you rub two pieces of chalk together. Their surfaces begin to wear away. Without protection, your bones also wear away at the joints. Recall that cartilage is found at the ends of bones. Cartilage helps make joint movements easier. It reduces friction and allows the bones to slide over each other more easily. The joint also is lubricated by a fluid that comes from nearby capillaries. Pads of cartilage called disks are found between the vertebrae. Here, cartilage acts as a cushion and prevents injury to your spinal cord. **Figure 18-6** shows how a damaged hip joint can be replaced.

Your skeleton is a living framework in the form of bones. Bones not only support the body but also supply it with minerals and blood cells. Joints are places between bones that enable the framework to be flexible and to be more than just a storehouse for minerals.

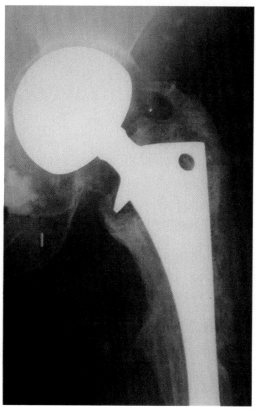

Figure 18-6 Some joints damaged by arthritis can be replaced with artificial joints. **How would this kind of surgery help a person stay active?**

Section Assessment

1. What are the five major functions of a skeleton?
2. Name and give an example of a movable joint and an immovable joint.
3. What are the functions of cartilage?
4. **Think Critically:** A thick band of bone forms around a healing broken bone. In time, the thickened band disappears. Explain how this extra bone can disappear.
5. **Skill Builder**
   Interpreting Scientific Illustrations You can learn a lot about bones when you see their internal structure. Do the **Chapter 18 Skill Activity** on page 743 to interpret sectional views of bones.

Using Computers

Database Use different references to find the names and shapes of the major bones in the human body. Classify the bones as long, short, flat, and irregular. Use your computer to make a database. Then, graph the different classifications of bones. If you need help, refer to page 717.

Observing Bones

Materials

- Beef bones (cut in half lengthwise)
- Chicken leg bone (cut in half lengthwise)
- Hand lens
- Paper towels

To move, animals must overcome the force of gravity. A skeleton aids in this movement. Land animals need skeletons that provide support against gravity. A flying animal needs a skeleton that provides support yet also allows it to overcome the pull of gravity and fly. Bones are adapted to the functions they perform. Find out if there is a difference between the bones of a land animal and those of a flying animal.

What You'll Investigate

What are the differences in the bone structures of land animals and flying animals?

Goals

- **Learn** the parts of a bone.
- **Observe** the differences between the bones of land animals and those of flying animals.

Procedure

1. Copy the data table and use it to **record** your observations.
2. **Obtain** a beef bone and a chicken leg bone that have been cut in half along the length from your teacher.
3. **Observe** the bones with a hand lens.
4. **Identify** the periosteum, compact bone, spongy bone, and the remains of any marrow that may be present.
5. In your Science Journal, **draw** a diagram of the bones and label their parts.

6. In the data table, **write** down any observations that you make.
7. Try to bend the bones to determine their flexibility.

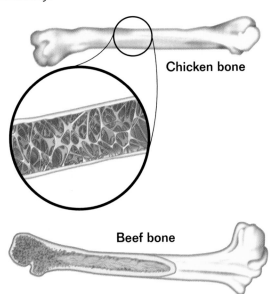
Chicken bone

Beef bone

Bone Features

Part	Description of Beef Bone	Description of Chicken Bone
Periosteum		
Compact bone		
Spongy bone		
Marrow		

Conclude and Apply

1. Do your data indicate any adaptations for flight in the bones?
2. **Infer** which type of bone would require more force to move? Explain why.
3. How do the structures of the two types of bone tissue aid in their function?
4. Which type of bone tissue is more flexible?

The Muscular System

Moving the Human Body

A driver uses a road map to find out what highway connects two cities within a state. You can use the picture in **Figure 18-7** to find out which muscles connect some of the bones in your body. A **muscle** is an organ that can relax and contract to allow movement. This contraction, or pull, within the muscle provides the force to move your body parts. In the process, energy is used and work is done. Imagine how much energy is used by the more than 600 muscles in your body each day. No matter how still you might try to be, some muscles are always moving in your body.

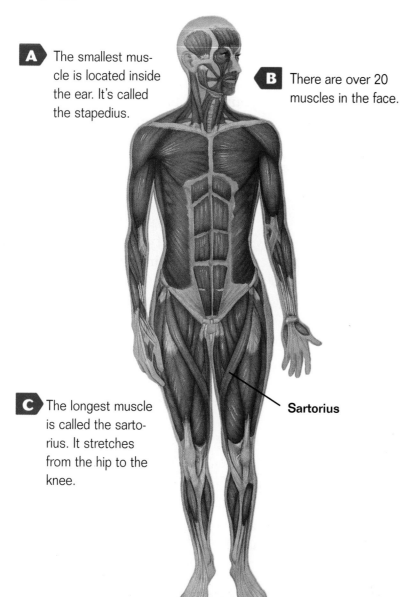

A The smallest muscle is located inside the ear. It's called the stapedius.

B There are over 20 muscles in the face.

C The longest muscle is called the sartorius. It stretches from the hip to the knee.

Sartorius

Reading Check

What is a muscle?

Figure 18-7 Your muscles come in many shapes and sizes. Even simple movements require the coordinated use of several muscles. **Do you think most of your muscles are voluntary or involuntary? Why?**

Muscle Control

Muscles that you are able to control are called **voluntary muscles.** Your arm and leg muscles are voluntary. So are the muscles of your hands and face. You can choose to move them or not to move them. In contrast, **involuntary muscles** are muscles you can't consciously control. You don't have to decide to make these muscles work. They just go on working all day long, all your life. Blood gets pumped through blood vessels, and food is moved through your digestive system by the action of involuntary muscles. You can sleep at night without having to think about how to keep these muscles working.

PHYSICS
INTEGRATION ➤

Levers—Your Body's Simple Machines

Your skeletal system and muscular system work together to move your body like machine parts move. A machine is a device that makes work easier. A simple machine does work with only one movement. The action of muscles on bones and joints often works like one type of simple machine called a lever. A lever is defined as a rigid bar that moves on a fixed point, called a fulcrum. **Figure 18-8** shows a common lever being used to cut a piece of paper. In your body, bones are the bar, a joint is the fulcrum, and contraction and relaxation of muscles provide the effort force to move the body part.

Levers are classified into three types. Examples of the three types of levers are shown in **Figure 18-9.**

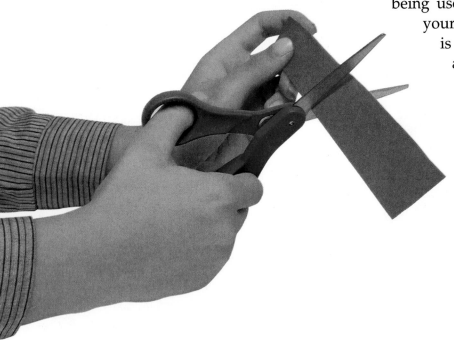

Figure 18-8 Scissors are used as a lever to cut paper. Your fingers push down on the handle of the scissors, providing the force. The blades of the scissors cut the paper. **What is the fulcrum in this lever?**

VISUALIZING
Human Body Levers

Figure 18-9 Your body uses all three types of levers for various movements.

- **E** Effort force
- **L** Load
- **F** Fulcrum

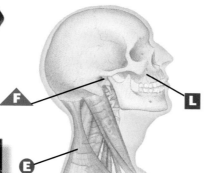

A First-Class Lever

A first-class lever has the fulcrum between the load and the effort force. In your body, the skull pivots on the top vertebra as neck muscles raise your head up and down.

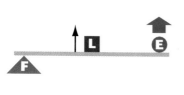

B Second-Class Lever

A second-class lever has the load between the fulcrum and the effort force. Raising the body up on your toes occurs when the leg muscles pull on the leg and foot.

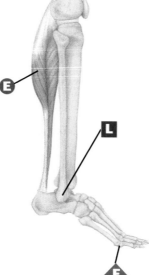

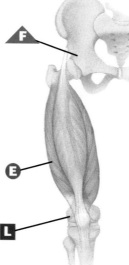

C Third-Class Lever

A third-class lever has the effort force between the fulcrum and the load. Your leg works like a lever when you move. The contracting muscle is the force that moves the bones of your leg at the knee.

Types of Muscle Tissue

Three types of muscle tissue are found in your body: skeletal, smooth, and cardiac. **Skeletal muscles** are the muscles that move bones. They are attached to bones by thick bands of tissue called **tendons.** Skeletal muscles are the most numerous muscles in the body. When viewed under a microscope, skeletal muscle cells look striped, or striated (STRI ayt ud). You can see the striations in **Figure 18-10A.** Skeletal muscles are voluntary muscles, which means you can control their use. You choose when to walk or not to walk. Skeletal muscles tend to contract quickly and tire easily.

The remaining two types of muscles, shown in **Figure 18-10B** and **C,** are involuntary. **Smooth muscles** are nonstriated, involuntary muscles that move many of your internal organs. Your intestines, bladder, and blood vessels are made of one or more layers of smooth muscles. These muscles contract and relax slowly.

Figure 18-10 There are three types of muscle tissue—skeletal muscle, cardiac muscle, and smooth muscle.

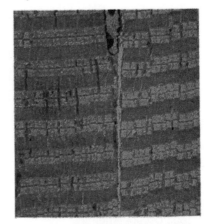

A Skeletal muscles move bones. The muscle tissue appears striped, or striated.

Magnification: 400×

B Cardiac muscle is found only in the heart. The muscle tissue has striations.

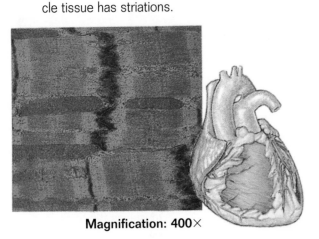

Magnification: 400×

C Smooth muscle is found in many of your internal organs, such as the intestines. The muscle tissue is nonstriated.

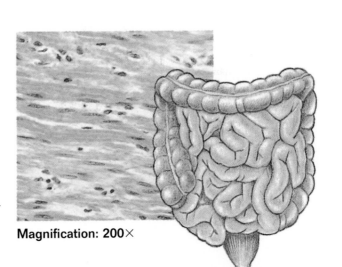

Magnification: 200×

Cardiac muscle is found only in the heart. Like smooth muscle, cardiac muscle also is involuntary. As you can see from **Figure 18-10B,** cardiac muscle has striations like skeletal muscle. Cardiac muscle contracts about 70 times per minute every day of your life.

Muscles at Work

Skeletal muscle movements are the result of pairs of muscles working together. When one muscle of a pair contracts, the other muscle relaxes, or returns to its original length. For example, when the muscles on the back of your upper leg contract, they pull your lower leg back and up. Muscles always pull. They never push. When you straighten your leg, the back muscles relax and the muscles on the front of your upper leg contract. Compare how the muscles of your legs work with how the muscles of your arms work, as shown in **Figure 18-11.**

Muscle Action and Energy

When you straightened your leg, your muscles used energy. Muscles use chemical energy in glucose. As the bonds in glucose break, chemical energy changes to mechanical energy and the muscle contracts.

Try at Home

Mini Lab

Observing Muscle Pairs at Work

Procedure

1. Find out which muscles are used to move your arm.
2. Stretch your arm out straight. Bring your hand to your shoulder, then down again.
3. Use the muscles shown in **Figure 18-11** to determine which skeletal muscles in your upper arm enable you to perform this action.

Analysis

1. How many muscles were involved in this action?
2. Which muscle contracted to bring the forearm closer to the shoulder?

Figure 18-11 When the biceps of the upper arm contract, the lower arm moves upward. When the triceps muscles on the back of the upper arm contract, the lower arm moves down. **What class of lever is shown here?**

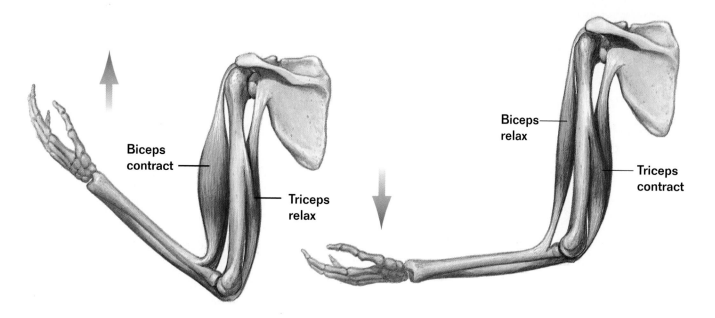

Biceps contract — Triceps relax

Biceps relax — Triceps contract

Muscle Protein

Muscle cells contain a protein called myoglobin that is similar to hemoglobin in red blood cells. Hemoglobin is a red pigment that carries oxygen. From this information, what can you infer about myoglobin?

When the supply of glucose in a muscle is used up, the muscle becomes tired and needs to rest. During the resting period, the muscle is resupplied with glucose via the bloodstream. Muscles also produce thermal energy when they contract. The heat produced by muscle contraction helps to keep your body temperature constant.

Over a period of time, muscles can become larger or smaller, depending on whether or not they are used. You can see in **Figure 18-12** that skeletal muscles that do a lot of work, such as those in your writing hand or in the arms of a physically challenged person, become large and strong. In contrast, if you watch TV all day, your muscles will become soft and flabby and will lack strength. Muscles that aren't exercised become smaller in size.

Figure 18-12 The number of muscles in an adult does not increase with exercise and body building. The cells simply get larger.

Section Assessment

1. What is the function of the muscular system?
2. Compare and contrast the three types of muscle.
3. What type of muscle tissue is found in your heart?
4. Describe how a muscle attaches to a bone.
5. **Think Critically:** What happens to your upper arm muscles when you bend your arm at the elbow?

6. **Skill Builder**

   Sequencing Sequence the activities that take place when you bend your leg at the knee. If you need help, refer to Sequencing in the **Skill Handbook** on page 698.

Write a paragraph in your Science Journal identifying the three forms of energy involved in a muscle contraction. Describe what relationship this has to being a warm-blooded animal.

Observing Muscle

Muscles can be identified by their appearance. In this activity, you will make observations to distinguish among the three types of muscle tissue.

What You'll Investigate

You will learn how to distinguish among the three types of muscle tissue. What do different types of muscles look like?

Goals
- **Examine** three types of muscle tissue.
- **Examine** muscle fibers.

Procedure

1. **Copy** the data table and use it to **record** your observations.

2. Using the microscope, first on low power and then on high power, **observe** prepared slides of three different types of muscle.

3. In the data table, **draw** each type of muscle that you **observe.**

4. **Obtain** a piece of cooked turkey leg from your teacher. Muscle tissue is made up of groups of cells held together in fibers, usually by a transparent covering called connective tissue.

5. **Place** the turkey leg in the dissecting pan. Use the forceps to remove the skin. **Locate** and **tease apart** the muscle fibers.

6. **Use** a hand lens to examine the muscle fibers and any connective tissue you see in the turkey leg.

7. **Draw** and **measure** five turkey leg fibers and describe the shape of these muscle fibers.

Materials
- Prepared slides of smooth, skeletal, and cardiac muscles
  - *detailed posters of the three types of muscle*
- Microscope
- Cooked turkey leg or chicken leg
- Dissecting pan or cutting board
- Dissecting probes (2)
- Hand lens
  - *Alternate Materials*

Muscle Types			
Types of Muscle	**Diagram of Muscle**	**Length of Fibers**	**Description of Fibers**
Skeletal			
Cardiac			
Smooth			

Conclude and Apply

1. How are muscle fibers arranged in the prepared slides?

2. **Predict** how the shape of a muscle fiber relates to its function.

3. Can you **conclude** that striations have anything to do with whether a muscle is voluntary or involuntary? **Explain.**

Frankenstein
by Mary Shelley

In this chapter, you've studied the structure of the bones and muscles of your own body. Many authors have written about the beauty and complexity of the human form. In the classic book *Frankenstein*, author Mary Shelley (inset) pays tribute to the science of anatomy in the story about a scientist, Dr. Frankenstein, who creates life from lifeless body parts. The 1931 movie, based on the book, portrayed the Frankenstein "monster" as seen in the photo, right. In the following excerpt from the book, Shelley details how Dr. Frankenstein slowly pieces together his creation.

As the minuteness of the parts formed a great hindrance to my speed, I resolved, contrary to my first intention, to make a being of a gigantic stature, that is to say, about eight feet in height, and proportionately large. After having formed this determination and having spent some months in successfully collecting and arranging my materials, I began....

His limbs were in proportion, and I had selected his features as beautiful. Beautiful!...His yellow skin scarcely covered the work of muscles and arteries beneath; his hair was of a lustrous black, and flowing; his teeth of a pearly whiteness; but these luxuriances only formed a more horrid contrast with his watery eyes that seemed almost of the same colour as the dun white sockets in which they were set, [with] his shriveled complexion and straight black lips.

Many people agree that the human body is a sort of living machine. The creation of the monster's face is like the story of a technician piecing together a complex machine. Mary Shelley's vivid descriptions have been compared to scientific writing. Which parts of this excerpt do you think would be similar to the writing of someone detailing the structure of the human body?

Science JOURNAL ▶

Choose a living organism. Imagine you are a scientist trying to describe your organism to other scientists. Try to paint a vivid picture of the organism by describing its features in detail in your Science Journal.

Skin

The Body's Largest Organ

Your skin is the largest organ of your body. Much of the information you receive about your environment comes through your skin. You can think of your skin as your largest sense organ.

Skin Structures

Skin is made up of two layers of tissue, the epidermis and the dermis. You can see in **Figure 18-13** that the **epidermis** is the surface layer of your skin. The cells on the top of the epidermis are dead. Thousands of these cells rub off every time you take a shower, shake hands, blow your nose, or scratch your elbow. New cells are constantly produced at the bottom of the epidermis. These new cells are moved up and eventually replace the ones that are rubbed off. Cells in the epidermis produce the chemical melanin. **Melanin** (MEL uh nun) is a pigment that gives your skin color. The more melanin, the darker the color of the skin. Melanin increases when your skin is exposed to the ultraviolet rays of the sun. If someone has few melanin-producing cells, little color gets deposited. These people have less protection from the sun. They burn more easily and may develop skin cancer more easily. ☑

What You'll Learn

► The differences between the epidermis and dermis of the skin
► The functions of the skin
► How skin protects the body from disease and how it heals itself

Vocabulary
epidermis
melanin
dermis

Why It's Important

► Skin plays a vital role in protecting your body against injury and disease.

Reading Check ☑

What is melanin?

Figure 18-13 Hair, nails, and sweat and oil glands are all part of your body's largest organ.
What two layers of tissue make up your skin?

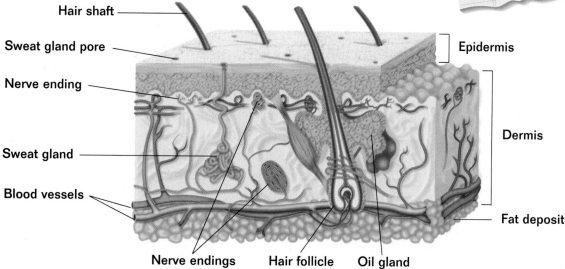

Hair shaft

Sweat gland pore

Nerve ending

Sweat gland

Blood vessels

Epidermis

Dermis

Fat deposit

Nerve endings   Hair follicle   Oil gland

Mini Lab

Recognizing Why You Sweat

Procedure

1. Examine the epidermis and the pores of your skin using a hand lens.
2. Place a small, clear plastic, sandwich-size bag on your hand. Use tape to keep the bag closed.
3. Quietly study your text for 10 minutes, then look at your hand.
4. Observe what happened to your hand while it was in the bag.

Analysis

1. Identify what formed inside the bag. Where did this substance come from?
2. Why is it necessary for this substance to form, even when you are inactive?

Figure 18-14 All animals must be able to control body temperature. Insulation of an animal's body occurs when the fur is raised. **What happens to fur when the animal's body temperature is high?**

The **dermis** is the layer of tissue under the epidermis. This layer is thicker than the epidermis and contains many blood vessels, nerves, and oil and sweat glands. Notice in **Figure 18-13** that fat cells are located under the dermis. This fatty tissue insulates the body. When a person gains too much weight, this is where much of the extra fat is deposited.

Functions of the Skin

Your skin is not only the largest organ of your body, it also carries out several major functions, including protection, sensory response, formation of vitamin D, regulation of body temperature, and the excretion of wastes. Of these functions, the most important is that skin forms a protective covering over the body. As a covering, it prevents both physical and chemical injury, as well as disease. Glands in the skin secrete fluids that damage or destroy some bacteria. Skin also prevents excess water loss from body tissues.

The skin also serves as a sensory organ. Specialized nerve cells in the skin detect and relay information about temperature, pressure, and pain. Some of the sensors are shown in **Figure 18-13.** Because of these sensors, you are able to detect the softness of a cat, the sharp point of a pin, or the heat of a frying pan.

A third vital function of skin is the formation of vitamin D. Vitamin D is essential for your good health because it helps your body to absorb calcium from the food you eat. Small amounts of this vitamin are produced in the epidermis in the presence of ultraviolet light from the sun.

Heat and Waste Exchange

Your skin plays an important role in helping to regulate your body temperature. Humans, unlike the fur-bearing animal in **Figure 18-14,** have very little hair to help them regulate body temperature. Hair is an adaptation that usually helps control body temperature. In humans, blood vessels in the skin can help release or hold heat. If the blood vessels expand or dilate, blood flow increases and heat is released. Less heat is released when the blood vessels constrict.

The dermis has about 3 million sweat glands. These glands also help regulate the body's temperature.

When the blood vessels dilate, pores leading to the sweat glands in the skin open. Perspiration, or sweat, moves out onto the skin. Heat moves from inside the body to the sweat on the body's surface. The body then cools as the sweat evaporates. This system balances heat that has been produced by muscle contractions.

The fifth function of the skin is to excrete wastes. Sweat glands release water, salt, and a protein product called urea. If too much water and salt are released during periods of extreme heat or physical exertion, you might faint.

Injury to the Skin

Despite its daily dose of scratching, burning, ripping and exposure to harsh conditions, the skin still continues to produce new cells in its outer layer, the epidermis, and repair tears in its inner layer, the dermis. When an injury occurs in the skin, as shown in **Figure 18-15,** disease-causing organisms can enter the body rapidly. An infection may result.

However, if there is injury to large areas of the skin, such as burning or rubbing away of the epidermis, there are no longer any cells left that can divide to replace this lost layer. In severe cases of skin loss or damage, nerve endings and blood vessels in the dermis are exposed. Water is lost rapidly from the dermis and muscle tissues. Body tissues are exposed to bacteria and to potential infection, shock, and death.

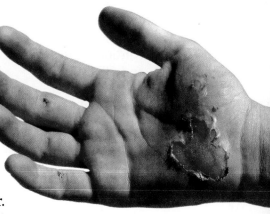

Figure 18-15 Injuries to your skin make it easier for bacteria and viruses to infect the body.

Section Assessment

1. Compare and contrast the epidermis and dermis.
2. List the five functions of skin.
3. How does skin help prevent disease in the body?
4. **Think Critically:** Why is a person who has been severely burned in danger of dying from loss of water?
5. **Skill Builder**
   Concept Mapping Make an events chain concept map to show how skin helps keep body temperature constant. If you need help, refer to Concept Mapping in the **Skill Handbook** on page 698.

Using Computers

Database Use references to research common skin lesions. Include warts, psoriasis, burns, acne, scrape wounds, insect bites, freckles, athlete's foot, and other lesions. Use your computer to make a database. Classify the lesions as flat, depressed, or elevated. If you need help, refer to page 717.

For a **preview** of this chapter, study this Reviewing Main Ideas before you read the chapter. After you have studied this chapter, you can use the Reviewing Main Ideas to **review** the chapter.

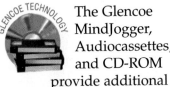

The Glencoe MindJogger, Audiocassettes, and CD-ROM provide additional opportunities for review.

Section
18-1 BONES AND MUSCLES

Bodies have a great range of movement, from picking up a feather to kicking a soccer ball, because of coordinated activities of the bones and muscles. In addition, these organs give shape to bodies, which are wrapped with a remarkable membrane, the skin. *What two systems work together to allow body movement?*

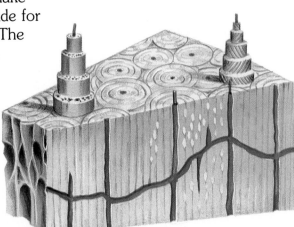

SKELETAL SYSTEM

Bones are complex, living structures that have a variety of functions. They protect other organs, give support, make blood cells, store minerals, and provide for muscle attachment that allows movement. The places where bones meet are called **joints.** Some joints are **immovable,** other joints can move slightly, and others can move a lot. Consider the difference between the movement of the toes and the movement of the wrist. *How do the shapes of bones often relate to their function?*

Reading Check ☑

Review the levers in **Figure 18-4.** Then, identify another example that could have been used to illustrate each class of lever.

Section
18-2 MUSCLES

Muscles can only contract and relax to produce movement of bones and body parts. Muscles do not stretch. **Skeletal muscle** movements are voluntary and move bones. **Smooth muscle** movements are involuntary and control internal organs. **Cardiac muscles** control the involuntary contractions of the heart. *How are skeletal muscles attached to the bones they move?*

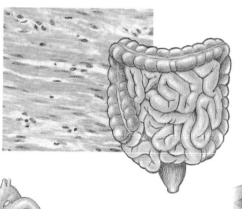

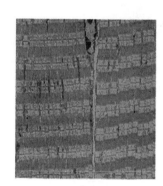

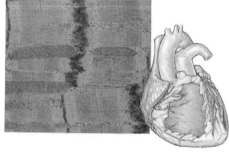

Section
18-3 SKIN

The skin is the largest organ of the body and is in direct contact with the environment. This body covering gives protection, helps retain moisture, aids in the formation of vitamin D, and assists in regulating the body's temperature. *How do sweat glands and blood vessels in the skin help the body maintain an even temperature?*

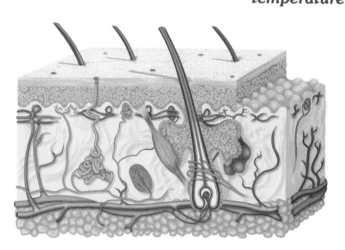

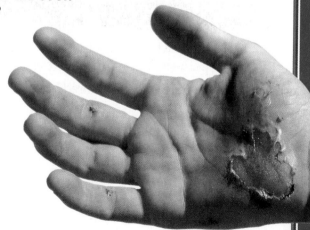

Using Vocabulary

a. cardiac muscle
b. cartilage
c. dermis
d. epidermis
e. immovable joint
f. involuntary muscle
g. joint
h. ligament
i. marrow
j. melanin
k. movable joint
l. muscle
m. periosteum
n. skeletal muscle
o. skeletal system
p. smooth muscle
q. tendon
r. voluntary muscle

Each phrase below describes a science term from the list. Write the term that matches the phrase describing it.

1. tough outer covering of bone
2. internal body framework
3. outer layer of skin
4. skin pigment
5. attaches muscle to bone

Checking Concepts

Choose the word or phrase that best answers the question.

6. Which of the following is the most solid form of bone?
   A) compact
   B) periosteum
   C) spongy
   D) marrow

7. Where are blood cells made?
   A) compact bone
   B) periosteum
   C) cartilage
   D) marrow

8. Where are minerals stored?
   A) bone
   B) skin
   C) muscle
   D) blood

9. What are the ends of bones covered with?
   A) cartilage
   B) tendons
   C) ligaments
   D) muscle

10. Where are immovable joints found?
    A) at the elbow
    B) at the neck
    C) in the wrist
    D) in the skull

11. What kind of joints are the knees and fingers?
    A) pivot
    B) hinge
    C) gliding
    D) ball-and-socket

12. Which vitamin is made in the skin?
    A) A
    B) B
    C) D
    D) K

13. Where are dead cells found?
    A) dermis
    B) marrow
    C) epidermis
    D) periosteum

14. What is a nutrient found in bone?
    A) iron
    B) calcium
    C) vitamin D
    D) vitamin K

15. What helps retain fluids in the body?
    A) bone
    B) muscle
    C) skin
    D) a joint

Thinking Critically

16. When might skin not be able to produce enough vitamin D?

17. What effects do sunblocks have on melanin?

18. What would lack of calcium do to bones?

19. Using a microscope, how could you distinguish among the three muscle types?

20. What function of skin in your lower lip changes when a dentist gives you novocaine for a filling in your bottom teeth? Why?

Developing Skills

If you need help, refer to the Skill Handbook.

21. **Observing and Inferring:** The joints in the skull of a newborn baby are flexible, whereas those of a 17 year old have grown together tightly. Infer why the infant's skull joints are flexible.

22. **Designing an Experiment:** Design an experiment to compare the heartbeat rates of athletes and nonathletes in your class.

23. **Hypothesizing:** Make a hypothesis about the distribution of sweat glands throughout the body. Are they evenly distributed?

24. **Concept Mapping:** Construct an events chain concept map to describe how a bone heals.

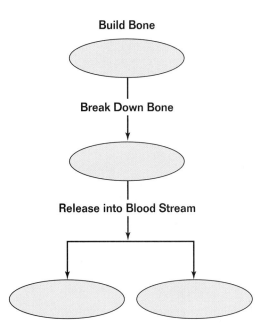

Build Bone

Break Down Bone

Release into Blood Stream

25. **Hypothesizing:** When exposed to direct sunlight, dark-colored hair absorbs more energy than light-colored hair. Given this information, make a hypothesis as to the most adaptive colors for desert animals.

THE PRINCETON REVIEW

Test-Taking Tip

Work Weak Muscles, Maintain Strong Ones It's sometimes difficult to focus on all the concepts needed for a test. So, ask yourself "What's my strongest area?" "What's my weakest area?" Focus most of your energy on your weak areas. But, also put in some upkeep time in your best areas.

Test Practice

Use these questions to test your Science Proficiency.

1. The skin has specialized sensory cells that detect and pass on information from the external environment to the body. To which group of stimuli can the skin respond?
   A) touch, temperature, time
   B) pressure, pain, sound
   C) pressure, temperature, pain
   D) hunger, odor, temperature

2. Cartilage is a specialized tissue that covers the ends of some bones. Which group of characteristics is correctly associated with this tissue?
   A) nerves and blood vessels
   B) muscles and tendons
   C) fat cells and blood vessels
   D) none of the above

3. The skeletal and muscular systems work together to move body parts like one of the simple machines called a lever. Which body movement is an example of a first-class lever?
   A) picking up an object with your hand
   B) raising the body up on your toes
   C) waving your hand up and down
   D) moving your head up and down

Nutrients and Digestion

Skills Preview

Skill Builders
- Compare and Contrast
- Observe and Infer

Activities
- Experiment
- Collect Data

MiniLabs
- Measure in SI
- Make a Model

Reading Check ✔

As you skim this chapter, choose five illustrations. Without reading the captions, write what they tell you about nutrients or digestion.

Explore Activity

What does a paper fan have in common with your stomach? Both the fan and the wall of your stomach, as shown in the photograph, are made of folds. Because of the folds and its elastic wall, the stomach can expand to hold about 2 L of food or liquid. In the stomach, one part of the process that releases energy from food occurs. How long do you think it takes for the food to go through this process?

Model the Digestive Tract

1. Use index cards to make labels for all of the organs listed below. Each card should include the name of the structure, its length, and the time it takes for food to pass through that structure. Mouth (8 cm, 5–30 s), Pharynx and Esophagus (26 cm, 10 s), Stomach (16 cm, 2–3 h), Small Intestine (4.75 m, 3 h), and Large Intestine (1.25 m, 2 days).

2. Working with a partner, place a piece of masking tape 6.5 m long on the classroom floor.

3. Beginning at one end of the tape, measure off and mark the lengths for each section of the digestive tract. Place each label next to its proper section.

Science Journal

In your Science Journal, record what factors might alter the amount of time digestion takes. Suggest reasons why there is such variation in the time food spends in each of the structures.

19•1 Nutrition

Why do you eat?

What to have for breakfast? You may base your decision on taste and amount of time available. A better factor might be the nutritional value of the food you choose. A chocolate-iced donut might be tasty and quick to eat, but it provides few of the nutrients your body needs to carry out your morning activities. **Nutrients** (NEW tree unts) are substances in foods that provide energy and materials for cell development, growth, and repair, as shown in **Figure 19-1**.

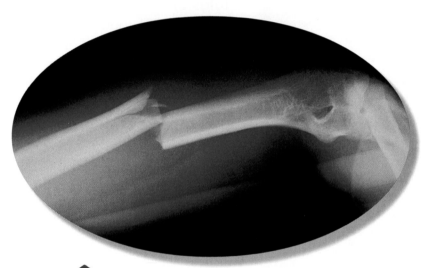

Figure 19-1 Just as a race car runs best with high-grade fuel, your body can best grow, maintain, and heal when you provide it with proper nutrients.

A To repair an injury, your body requires certain nutrients. **What nutrients do you think are needed to repair a broken bone?**

B Your body gets the nutrients it needs to grow from the food you eat.

Classes of Nutrients

Six kinds of nutrients are available in food: carbohydrates, proteins, fats, vitamins, minerals, and water. Carbohydrates, proteins, vitamins, and fats all contain carbon. Nutrients that contain carbon are called organic nutrients. In contrast, minerals and water are inorganic. These nutrients do not contain carbon. Foods containing carbohydrates, fats, and proteins are usually too complex to be absorbed right away by your body. These substances need to be broken down into simpler molecules before the body can use them. In contrast, minerals and water can be absorbed directly into your bloodstream. They don't require digestion or need to be broken down.

Carbohydrates

Study the panels on several boxes of cereal. You'll notice that the number of grams of carbohydrates found in a typical serving is usually higher than the amounts of the other nutrients. That means that the major nutrient in the cereal is in the form of carbohydrates. **Carbohydrates** (kar boh HI drayts) are the main sources of energy for your body. They contain carbon, hydrogen, and oxygen atoms. During cellular respiration, energy is released when molecules of carbohydrates break down in your cells.

Types of Carbohydrates

The three types of carbohydrates—sugar, starch, and cellulose—are shown in **Figure 19-2.** Sugars are simple carbohydrates. There are many types of sugars. You're probably most familiar with one called table sugar. Fruits, honey, and milk also are sources of sugar. Your cells use sugar in the form of glucose. Starch and cellulose are complex carbohydrates. Starch is in foods such as potatoes and those made from grains such as pasta. Cellulose occurs in plant cell walls.

Figure 19-2 Carbohydrates are found in three forms: sugar, starch, and cellulose. While all three are made of carbon, hydrogen, and oxygen, their molecules have different kinds of chemical bonds and structures.

Glucose Molecule

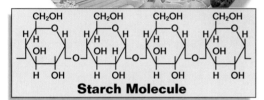

A A simple sugar called glucose is the basic fuel that provides the energy to carry out life's processes.

B Starch is stored in plant cells. During the digestive process, your body breaks down the complex starch molecules into the simple sugar glucose.

Starch Molecule

Cellulose Molecule

C Cellulose is a complex carbohydrate that is a major part of the strong cell walls in a plant. While your body cannot break down cellulose, its fiber is important in maintaining a smooth-running digestive system. Sources of cellulose include fresh fruits, vegetables, and grains.

Proteins

Your body uses proteins for growth. As enzymes, they affect the rate of chemical reactions in your body. They also are involved in the replacement and repair of body cells. **Proteins** are large molecules that contain carbon, hydrogen, oxygen, and nitrogen. A molecule of protein is made up of a large number of subunits, or building blocks, called **amino acids.** Some sources of proteins are shown in **Figure 19-3.**

Essential Amino Acids

Proteins are made according to directions supplied by genes that you inherit. Your body needs 20 different amino acids to be able to construct the proteins needed in your cells.

Twelve of these amino acids can be made in your cells. The eight remaining amino acids are called essential amino acids. Your body doesn't have genetic instructions to construct these. They must be supplied through the food you eat. Eggs, milk, and cheese contain all the essential amino acids. Beef, pork, fish, and chicken supply most of them. You might be surprised to know that whole grains such as wheat, rice, and soybeans supply many needed amino acids in addition to supplying carbohydrates. In order to get their full complement of amino acids, vegetarians need to eat a wide variety of vegetables that are good sources of protein.

Figure 19-3 Meats, poultry, eggs, fish, peas, beans, and nuts are all rich in protein. **Which of these protein-rich foods do you think a vegetarian would choose?**

Problem Solving

Analyzing a Menu

Blanca is a long-distance runner. She plans to run in the Boston Marathon on Patriot's Day. This world-famous race is more than 42 km long. Like most runners, Blanca is conscious about eating food that will provide the nutrients needed for endurance. The night before the marathon, Blanca must choose what to eat for dinner. She wants a meal with lots of carbohydrates.

Study the menu. Then, select a suitable dinner for Blanca. Keep in mind that Blanca will run in a marathon the next morning and needs foods rich in carbohydrates.

Think Critically

1. List all the foods on this menu that contain carbohydrates.

Menu

APPETIZER
Potato Skins..................$4
Caesar Salad.................$3
Sizzling Rice Soup............$2
Vegetable Salad..............$3

ENTREE
Baked Chicken...............$6
Shrimp with Lobster Sauce....$8
Grilled Pork Chop.............$7
Grilled Steak................$9

VEGETABLES
Mashed Potatoes.............$2
Baked Potato................$2
Boiled Rice.................$2
Green Beans.................$2

DESSERT
Fresh Fruit.................$3
Ice Cream..................$2
Chocolate Cake..............$3

DRINKS
Milk......................$1
Water.....................$1
Orange Juice...............$1

2. Why does Blanca want to eat carbohydrates before the marathon?

3. What foods on this menu are rich in complex carbohydrates?

Fats

You may not think of fat as being a necessary part of your diet. In today's health-conscious society, the term *fat* has a negative meaning. However, **fats** are necessary because they provide energy and help your body absorb some vitamins. Fats are stored in your body in the form of fat tissue as shown in **Figure 19-4.** This tissue cushions your internal organs. You learned that carbohydrates are the main source of energy for your body. This is because people eat a large amount of carbohydrates. However, a gram of fat can release twice as much energy as a gram of carbohydrate. During this process, fat breaks down into smaller molecules called fatty acids and glycerol. Because fat is such a good storage unit for energy, any excess energy we eat is converted to fat until the body needs it. ☑

Reading Check ☑

Why are fats a necessary part of your diet?

Types of Fat

Fats are classified as unsaturated and saturated. Unsaturated fats, which come from plants, are usually liquid at room temperature. Corn, sunflower, and soybean oils are all unsaturated fats. Some unsaturated fats also are found in poultry, fish, and nuts. Saturated fats are found in red meats and are usually solid at room temperature. Saturated fats have been associated with high levels of blood cholesterol. Cholesterol occurs normally in all your cell membranes. However, too much of it in your diet causes excess fat deposits to form on the inside walls of blood vessels. The deposits cut off the blood supply to organs and increase blood pressure. Heart disease and strokes may result if blood is cut off to the heart and brain.

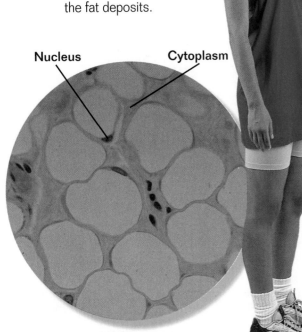

Figure 19-4 Fat is stored in certain cells in your body.

A The cytoplasm and nucleus are pushed to the edge of the cell by the fat deposits.

Nucleus   Cytoplasm

Magnification: 400×

B The first source of energy for your body comes from the sugars in carbohydrates. When the supply of sugars runs low, your body begins to use the reservoir of energy stored in body fat.

Vitamins

Those essential, organic nutrients needed in small quantities to help your body use other nutrients are called **vitamins.** For instance, bone cells need vitamin D to use calcium. In general, vitamins promote growth and regulate body functions.

Most foods, like those in **Figure 19-5,** supply some vitamins, but no one food has them all. Although some people feel that taking extra vitamins is helpful, eating a well-balanced diet is usually good enough to give your body all the vitamins it needs.

Vitamins are placed into the two groups. Some vitamins dissolve easily in water and are called water-soluble vitamins. Others dissolve only in fat and are called fat-soluble vitamins. While you get most vitamins from outside sources, your body makes vitamin D when your skin is exposed to sunlight. Some vitamin K is made with the help of bacteria that live in your large intestine. **Table 19-1** lists some major vitamins, their effects on your health, and some of the foods that provide them.

Figure 19-5 Fruits and vegetables are especially good sources of vitamins. However, to get all of the vitamins that your body needs, you must eat a balanced diet that includes a variety of foods.

Table 19-1

Vitamins		
Vitamin	**Body Function**	**Food Sources**
Water Soluble		
B (thiamine, riboflavin, niacin, B_6, B_{12})	growth, healthy nervous system, use of carbohydrates, red blood cell production	meat, eggs, milk, cereal grains, green vegetables
C	growth, healthy bones and teeth, wound recovery	citrus fruits, tomatoes, green leafy vegetables
Fat Soluble		
A	growth, good eyesight, healthy skin	green/yellow vegetables, liver and fish, liver oils, milk, yellow fruit
D	absorption of calcium and phosphorus by bones and teeth	milk, eggs, fish
E	formation of cell membranes	vegetable oils, eggs, grains
K	blood clotting, wound recovery	green leafy vegetables, egg yolks, tomatoes

Figure 19-6 Calcium and phosphorus are used in the formation and maintenance of your bones. In this x-ray, you can see that the lack of these minerals has caused the bones in this woman's spine to become less dense and, as a result, to bend.

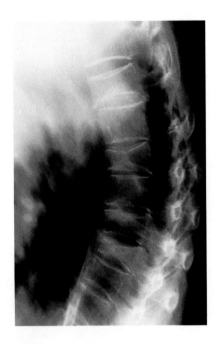

Minerals

Inorganic nutrients that regulate many chemical reactions in your body are **minerals**. They are chemical elements such as phosphorus. About 14 minerals are used by your body to build cells, take part in chemical reactions in cells, send nerve impulses throughout your body, and carry oxygen to body cells. Minerals used in the largest amounts in your body are presented in **Table 19-2**. Of the 14 minerals, calcium and phosphorus are used in the largest amounts for

Table 19-2

Minerals		
Mineral	**Health Effect**	**Food Sources**
Calcium	strong bones and teeth, blood clotting, muscle and nerve activity	milk, eggs, green leafy vegetables
Phosphorus	strong bones and teeth, muscle contraction, stores energy	cheese, meat, cereal
Potassium	balance of water in cells, nerve impulse conduction	bananas, potatoes, nuts, meat
Sodium	fluid balance in tissues, nerve impulse conduction	meat, milk, cheese, salt, beets, carrots
Iron	oxygen is transported in hemoglobin by red blood cells	raisins, beans, spinach, eggs
Iodine (trace)	thyroid activity, metabolic stimulation	seafood, iodized salt

a variety of body functions. One of these functions is the formation and maintenance of bone, as shown in **Figure 19-6**. Some minerals, called trace minerals, are required in only small amounts. Copper and iodine are usually listed as trace minerals.

Water

You don't have to be lost in a desert to know how important water is for your body. Next to oxygen, water is the most vital factor for survival. You could live a few weeks without food, but only a few days without water. Most of the nutrients you have studied in this chapter can't be used by your body unless they are carried in a solution. This means that they have to be dissolved in water. Water enables chemical reactions to take place in cells.

Water in Your Body

As shown in **Figure 19-7,** different organisms require different amounts of water to survive. The human body is about 60 percent water by weight. This water is found in and around cells and in plasma and lymph. Water removes waste products from cells. Wastes dissolved in water leave your body as urine or perspiration. To balance water lost each day, you need to drink about 2 L of liquids. But, don't think that you have to drink just water to

Figure 19-7 Humans have to consume water every couple of days, while animals like the camel have adaptations that allow them to conserve their water intake for weeks.

Table 19-3

Water Loss	
Through	**Amount (mL/day)**
Exhaled air	350
Feces	150
Skin (mostly as sweat)	500
Urine	1800

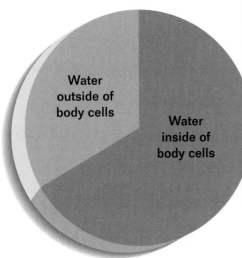

Figure 19-8 About two-thirds of your body water is located within your body cells. Water helps maintain the cells' shapes and sizes. During exercise, the water that is lost through perspiration and respiration must be replaced.

Measuring the Water Content of Food

Procedure

1. Use a pan balance to find the mass of an empty 250-mL beaker.
2. Fill the beaker with sliced celery and find the mass of the filled beaker.
3. Estimate the amount of water you think is in the celery.
4. Put the celery on a flat tray. Leave the celery out to dry for one to two days.
5. Determine the mass of the celery.

Analysis

1. How much water was in the fresh celery?
2. Infer how much water might be in other fresh fruits and vegetables.

keep your cells supplied. Most foods have more water in them than you realize. An apple is about 80 percent water, and many meats are as much as 90 percent water.

Your body also loses about 2 L of water every day through excretion, perspiration, and respiration. **Table 19-3** shows how water is lost from the body. The body is equipped to maintain its fluid content, however. When your body needs water, it sends messages to your brain, and you feel thirsty. Drinking a glass of water usually restores the body's homeostasis (hoh mee oh STAY sus). Homeostasis is the regulation and maintenance of an organism's internal environment. Once homeostasis is restored, the signal to the brain stops.

Food Groups

Because no one food has every nutrient, you need to eat a variety of foods. Nutritionists have developed a simple system to help people plan meals that include all the nutrients required for good health.

Foods that contain the same nutrients belong to a **food group.** The food pyramid in **Figure 19-9** presents the basic food groups and serving suggestions. Eating a certain amount from each food group each day will supply your body with the nutrients it needs for energy and growth. Of course, most people eat foods in combined forms. Combinations of food contain ingredients from more than one food group and supply the same nutrients as the foods they contain. Chili and macaroni and cheese are both food group combinations.

Figure 19-9 The pyramid shape reminds you that you should consume more servings from the bread and cereal group than from the meat and milk group. **Where should the least number of servings come from?**

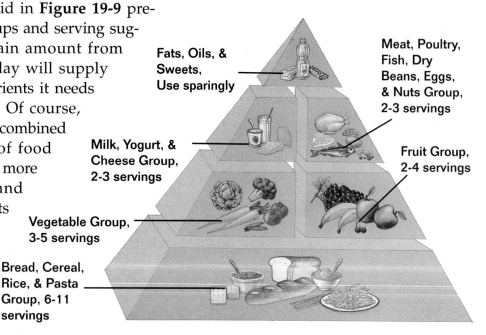

Fats, Oils, & Sweets, Use sparingly

Meat, Poultry, Fish, Dry Beans, Eggs, & Nuts Group, 2-3 servings

Milk, Yogurt, & Cheese Group, 2-3 servings

Fruit Group, 2-4 servings

Vegetable Group, 3-5 servings

Bread, Cereal, Rice, & Pasta Group, 6-11 servings

Section Assessment

1. List six classes of nutrients and give one example of a food source for each.
2. Describe a major function of each class of nutrient.
3. Discuss the relationship between your diet and your health.
4. Explain the importance of water in the body.
5. **Think Critically:** What foods from each food group would provide a balanced breakfast? Explain why.
6. **Skill Builder**
   Interpreting Data Nutritional information can be found on the labels of most foods. Do the **Chapter 19 Skill Activity** on page 744 to interpret the information found on different food-product labels.

Using Computers

Spreadsheet Use the format of **Table 19-2** and prepare a spreadsheet for a data table of the minerals. Use reference books to gather information about the following minerals and add them to the table: sulfur, magnesium, copper, manganese, cobalt, and zinc. If you need help, refer to page 722.

Identifying Vitamin C Content

Materials

- Indophenol solution
- Graduated cylinder (10 mL)
  *graduated container
- Glass-marking pencil
  *tape
- Test tubes (10)
  *paper cups
- Test-tube rack
- Dropper
- Dropping bottles (10)
- Test substances: water, orange juice, pineapple juice, apple juice, lemon juice, tomato juice, cranberry juice, carrot juice, lime juice, mixed vegetable juice
  *Alternate Materials

Vitamin C is found in a variety of fruits and vegetables. In some plants, the concentration is high; in others, it is low. Try this activity to test various juices and find out which contains the most vitamin C.

What You'll Investigate

Which juices contain vitamin C?

Goals

- **Observe** differences in the vitamin C content of juices.

Test Results for Vitamin C

Test Tube	Juice	Prediction (yes or no)	Number of drops
1	water		
2	orange		
3	pineapple		
4	apple		
5	lemon		
6	tomato		
7	cranberry		
8	carrot		
9	lime		
10	vegetable		

Procedure

1. **Make** a data table like the example shown to record your observations.

2. **Label** the test tubes 1 through 10.

3. **Predict** which juices contain vitamin C. **Record** your predictions in your table.

4. **Measure** 5 mL of indophenol into each of the ten test tubes. **CAUTION:** *Wear your goggles and apron. Do not taste any of the juices.* Indophenol is a blue liquid that turns colorless when vitamin C is present. The more vitamin C in a juice, the less juice it takes to turn indophenol colorless.

5. **Add** 20 drops of water to test tube 1. **Record** your observations.

6. Begin adding orange juice, one drop at a time, to test tube 2.

7. **Record** the number of drops needed to turn indophenol colorless.

8. **Repeat** steps 6 and 7 to test the other juices.

Conclude and Apply

1. What is the purpose of testing water for the presence of vitamin C?

2. Does the amount of vitamin C vary in fruit juices?

3. Which juice did not contain vitamin C?

Antioxidants

In the 1990s, food scientists learned that certain nutrients help lower the risk of getting various diseases. Animal studies show that some cancers may be prevented—possibly cured—by chemicals in certain nutrients. Many of these cancer-combating chemicals are being tested to find out how they enhance cellular defenses against disease.

Fighting Cancer

Scientists are closely studying one group of chemicals called antioxidants. Antioxidants are substances that prevent other chemicals from reacting with oxygen. Chemicals that enter the body from smoking or from pollutants in the air may cause cancer when combined with oxygen. By preventing this reaction, antioxidants help fight cancer. Antioxidants also can prevent cancer cells from repairing their damaged DNA. Carotenoids—the yellow-orange pigments in carrots (far left), squashes, and other produce—are antioxidants. Vitamin C (see crystals in inset) is also an antioxidant, as is vitamin D. Two unusually good sources of antioxidants are tomato sauce and green tea.

Taking antioxidants along with anticancer drugs used to fight cancer seems to make these drugs more effective. Some doctors are prescribing antioxidants for their patients, either to try to prevent cancer or to help fight an existing cancer condition. However, researchers have cautioned that the use of antioxidants may not successfully eliminate all the cancer cells in a person's body. Furthermore, some antioxidants can have harmful side effects, may disrupt certain bodily functions, and may interfere with the effectiveness of radiation treatments. But, if laboratory tests show conclusively that antioxidants are successful fighters of some diseases, you may one day hear, "Eat your antioxidants. They're good for you!"

inter**NET** CONNECTION

Visit the Glencoe Science Web Site at **www.glencoe.com/ sec/science** for more information about antioxidants. Look for the most recent information on how antioxidants are used to prevent disease.

19·2 Your Digestive System

What You'll Learn

▶ How to distinguish between mechanical and chemical digestion

▶ The organs of the digestive system and what takes place in each

▶ How homeostasis is maintained in digestion

Vocabulary
digestion
enzyme
mechanical digestion
chemical digestion
saliva
peristalsis
chyme
villi

Why It's Important

▶ Through the processes of the digestive system, the food you eat is made available to your cells.

Processing Food

Like other animals, you are a consumer. The energy you need for life comes from food sources outside yourself. To keep the cells in your body alive, you take in food every day. Food is processed in your body in four phases: ingestion, digestion, absorption, and elimination. Whether it is a fast-food burger or a home-cooked meal, all the food you eat is treated to the same processes in your body. As soon as it enters your mouth, or is ingested, food begins to be broken down. **Digestion** is the process that breaks down food into small molecules so they can move into the blood. From the

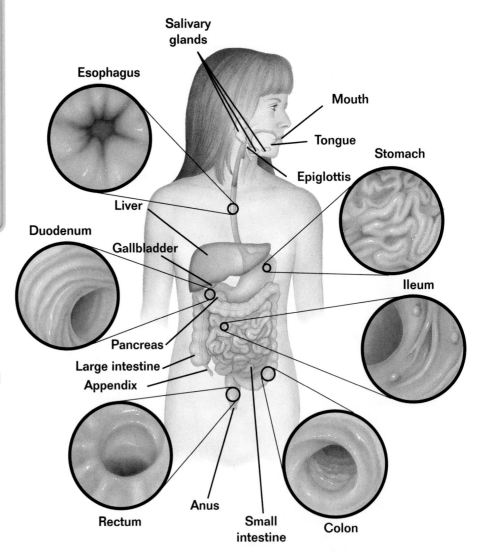

Figure 19-10 The human digestive system can be described as a tube divided into several specialized sections. If stretched out, an adult's digestive system is 6 m to 9 m long. **Where in the digestive tract does digestion begin?**

Salivary glands
Esophagus
Mouth
Tongue
Stomach
Epiglottis
Liver
Duodenum
Gallbladder
Ileum
Pancreas
Large intestine
Appendix
Rectum
Anus
Small intestine
Colon

blood, food molecules are transported across the cell membrane to be used by the cell. Molecules that aren't absorbed are eliminated and pass out of your body as wastes.

The major organs of your digestive tract—mouth, esophagus (ih SAH fuh guhs), stomach, small intestine, large intestine, rectum, and anus—are shown in **Figure 19-10.** Food passes through all of these organs. However, food doesn't pass through your liver, pancreas, or gallbladder. These three organs produce or store enzymes and chemicals that help break down food as it passes through the digestive tract.

Enzymes

Chemical digestion is possible only because of the actions of certain kinds of proteins. These proteins are called enzymes. **Enzymes** (EN zimez) are molecules that speed up the rate of chemical reactions in your body. You can see in **Figure 19-11** that they speed up reactions without themselves being changed or used up. One way enzymes speed up reactions is by reducing the amount of energy necessary for a chemical reaction to begin. ✔

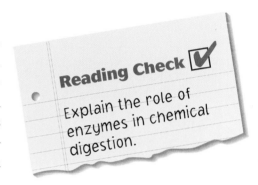

Reading Check
Explain the role of enzymes in chemical digestion.

Enzymes in Digestion

A variety of enzymes are involved with the digestion of carbohydrates, proteins, and fats. Amylase (AM uh lays) is an enzyme produced by the salivary glands in the mouth. This enzyme begins the process of breaking down the complex carbohydrate into simpler sugars. In the stomach, the enzyme pepsin causes complex proteins to break down into less complex proteins. In the small intestine, a number of other enzymes continue the process by breaking down the proteins into amino acids. The pancreas, an organ on the back side of

Figure 19-11 Enzymes speed up the rate of certain body reactions. During these reactions, the enzymes are not used up or changed in any way. **What happens to the enzyme after it is released?**

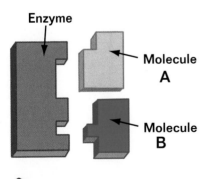

Temporary
complex forms

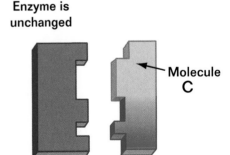

A The surface shape of an enzyme fits the shape of specific molecules that need to be broken down.

B The enzyme and the molecules join and the reaction occurs.

C Following the reaction, the enzyme and the molecule separate. The enzyme is not changed by the reaction. The resulting new molecule has a new chemical structure.

the stomach, secretes several enzymes through a tube into the small intestine. Some continue the process of starch breakdown that started in the mouth. The resulting sugars are turned into glucose and used by the body's cells. Other enzymes are involved in the breakdown of fats.

Other Enzyme Actions

Enzyme reactions are not only involved in the digestive process. Enzymes also are responsible for building your body. They are involved in the energy production activities of muscle and nerve cells. They also are involved in the blood-clotting process. Without enzymes, the chemical reactions of your body would not happen. You would not exist.

Where and How Digestion Occurs

Digestion is both mechanical and chemical. **Mechanical digestion** takes place when food is chewed and mixed in the mouth and churned in your stomach. **Chemical digestion** breaks down large molecules of food into different, smaller molecules that can be absorbed by cells. Chemical digestion takes place in your mouth, stomach, and small intestine. Some digestive processes are both physical and chemical such as when bile acts on food.

Figure 19-12 About 1.5 L of saliva are produced each day by salivary glands in your mouth. **What happens in your mouth when you think about a food you like?**

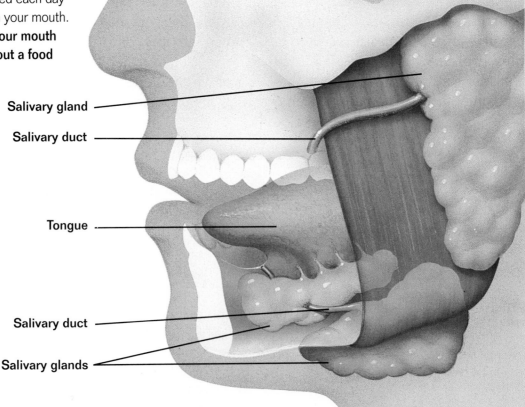

Salivary gland

Salivary duct

Tongue

Salivary duct

Salivary glands

In Your Mouth

Mechanical digestion begins in your mouth. There, your tongue and teeth break food up into small pieces. Humans are adapted with several kinds of teeth for cutting, grinding, tearing, and crushing.

Some chemical digestion also starts in your mouth. As you chew, your tongue moves food around and mixes it with a watery substance called saliva. Saliva is produced by three sets of glands near your mouth that are shown in **Figure 19-12. Saliva** (suh LI vuh) is made up mostly of water, but it also contains mucus and the enzyme salivary amylase. You learned that salivary amylase starts the breakdown of starch to sugar. Food that is mixed with saliva becomes a soft mass. The food mass is moved to the back of your tongue where it is swallowed and passes into your esophagus. Now the process of ingestion is complete, and the process of digestion has begun.

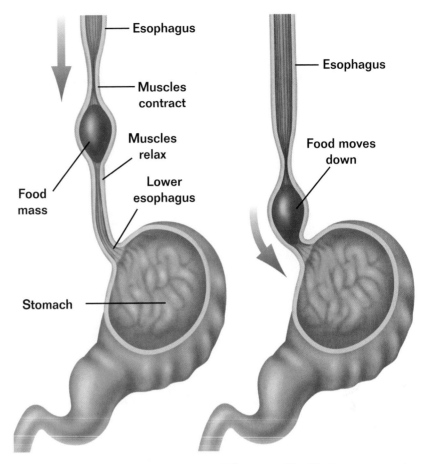

Figure 19-13 During peristalsis, muscles behind the food contract and push the food forward. Muscles in front of the food relax.

Passing Through the Esophagus

Your esophagus is a muscular tube about 25 cm long. Through it, food passes to your stomach in about 4 s to 10 s. No digestion takes place in the esophagus. Smooth muscles in the walls of the esophagus move food downward by a squeezing action. These waves, or contractions, called **peristalsis** (per uh STAHL sus), move food along throughout the digestive system. **Figure 19-13** shows how peristalsis works.

In Your Stomach

The stomach, shown in **Figure 19-13,** is a muscular bag. When empty, it is somewhat sausage shaped, with folds on the inside. As food enters from the esophagus, the stomach expands, and the folds smooth out. Both mechanical and chemical digestion take place in the stomach. Mechanically, food is mixed by the muscular walls of the stomach and by peristalsis. Food also is mixed with strong digestive juices,

PHYSICS
INTEGRATION

Surface Area
Besides mixing food and saliva, chewing food breaks it up into smaller pieces. This gives the food a larger surface area, exposing it to more digestive enzymes. Compare the surface area of two toy blocks when they are separate and when they are put together.

Figure 19-14 The stomach is a muscular, baglike organ with a band of muscle at each end. **How is food mechanically digested in the stomach?**

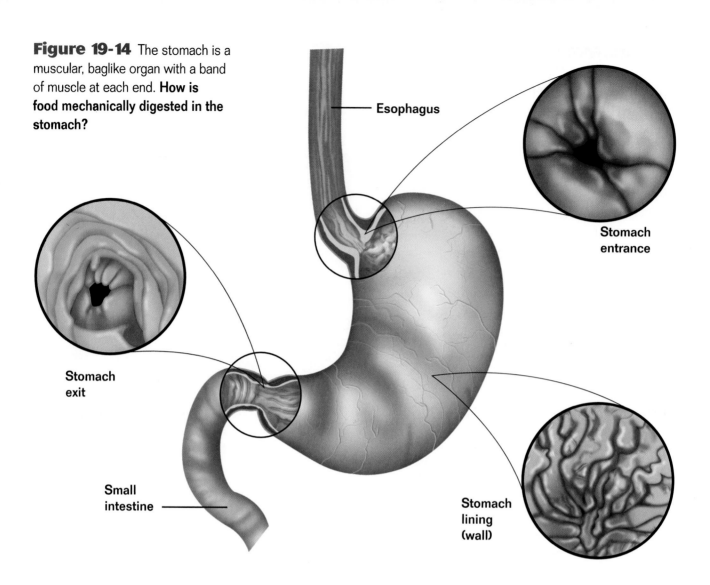

Esophagus

Stomach entrance

Stomach exit

Small intestine

Stomach lining (wall)

which include hydrochloric acid and enzymes. The acid is made by cells in the walls of the stomach. The stomach, shown in **Figure 19-14,** also produces a mucus that lubricates the food, making it more slick. The mucus protects the stomach from the strong digestive juices. Food moves through your stomach in about four hours. At the end of this time, the food has been changed to a thin, watery liquid called **chyme** (KIME). Little by little, chyme moves out of your stomach and into your small intestine.

In Your Small Intestine

Your small intestine may be small in diameter, but it is 4 m to 7 m in length. As chyme leaves your stomach, it enters the first part of your small intestine, called the duodenum (doo AUD un um). The major portion of all digestion takes place in your duodenum. Digestive juices from the liver and pancreas are added to the mixture. Your liver, shown in **Figure 19-15,** produces a greenish fluid called bile. Bile is stored in a small sac called the gallbladder. The acid from the stomach makes large fat particles float to the top of the liquid. Bile physically breaks up these particles into smaller pieces, the way detergent acts on grease on dishes. This process is called emulsification (ih mul suh fuh KAY shun). Although the bile physically breaks apart the fat into smaller droplets, the fat molecules are not changed chemically. Chemical digestion of carbohydrates, proteins, and fats occurs when the digestive juices from the pancreas are added. ☑

You learned that the pancreas produces enzymes that help break down carbohydrates, fats, and proteins. Your pancreas also makes insulin. Insulin is a hormone that allows glucose to pass from the bloodstream into your body's cells. Without a supply of glucose, your body's cells must use proteins and fats for energy.

In addition to insulin, the pancreas produces another solution. This solution contains bicarbonate. Bicarbonate helps neutralize the stomach acid that is mixed with chyme.

Mini Lab

Determining How Fats Are Emulsified

Procedure

1. Fill two glasses with warm water. Add a large spoonful of cooking oil to each glass.
2. Add a small spoonful of liquid dish-washing detergent to one glass. Stir both glasses.

Analysis

1. Compare what happens to the oil in each glass.
2. How does emulsification change the surface area of the oil drops?
3. How does emulsification speed up digestion?
4. Where in the digestive system does emulsification take place?
5. What is the emulsifier in the digestive system?

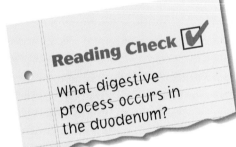

Reading Check ☑

What digestive process occurs in the duodenum?

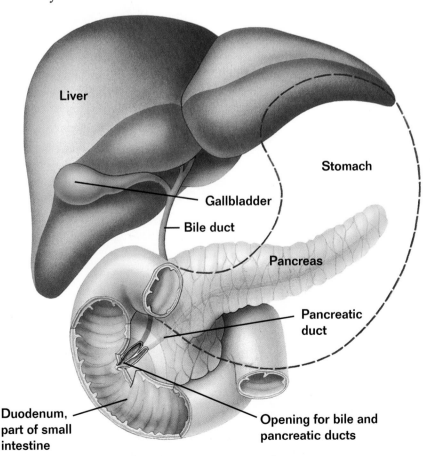

Liver

Gallbladder

Bile duct

Stomach

Pancreas

Pancreatic duct

Duodenum, part of small intestine

Opening for bile and pancreatic ducts

Figure 19-15 The liver, gallbladder, and pancreas are at the beginning of the small intestine. **If your gallbladder had to be removed, what nutrient would your doctor advise you to eat less of?**

Surface Area of the Small Intestine

Look at the wall of the small intestine in **Figure 19-16.** The walls of your small intestine are not smooth like the inside of a garden hose. Rather, they have many ridges and folds. These folds are covered with tiny, fingerlike projections called **villi.** Villi make the surface of the small intestine greater so that food has more places to be absorbed.

Food Absorption

After the chyme leaves the duodenum, it has become a soup of molecules that is ready to be absorbed through the cells on the surface of the villi. Peristalsis continues to move and mix the chyme. In addition, the villi themselves move and are bathed in the soupy liquid. Molecules of nutrients pass by diffusion, osmosis, or active transport into blood vessels in each villus. From there, blood transports the nutrients to all the cells of the body. Peristalsis continues to force the remaining materials that have not been digested or absorbed slowly into the large intestine.

Figure 19-16 Hundreds of thousands of densely packed villi give the impression of a velvet cloth surface. If the surface area of your villi could be stretched out, it would cover an area the size of a baseball diamond. **What would happen to a person's weight if the number of villi were drastically reduced? Why?**

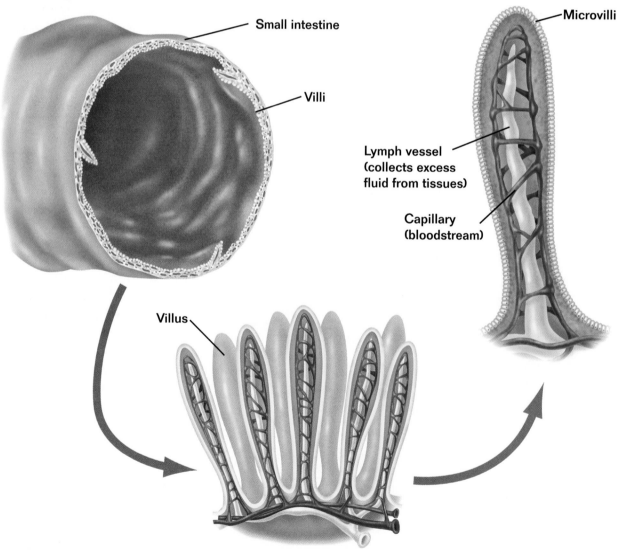

Small intestine

Villi

Villus

Microvilli

Lymph vessel (collects excess fluid from tissues)

Capillary (bloodstream)

In Your Large Intestine

As chyme enters the large intestine, it is still a thin, watery mixture. The main job of the large intestine, shown in **Figure 19-17,** is to absorb this water from the undigested mass. In doing so, large amounts of water are returned to the body, and homeostasis is maintained. Peristalsis slows down somewhat in the large intestine. As a result, chyme may stay in the large intestine for as long as three days. After the excess water is absorbed, the remaining undigested materials become more solid.

The Role of Bacteria

Bacteria that live in your large intestine feed on undigested materials like cellulose. This is a symbiotic relationship. The bacteria feed on cellulose, and in return they produce several vitamins that you need. Muscles in the rectum and anus control the release of solidified wastes from the body in the form of feces.

Food is processed in your digestive system for the purpose of supplying your body with raw materials for metabolism. These raw materials are in the form of nutrients. What is not digested is eliminated.

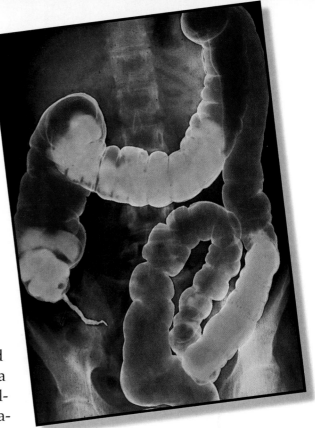

Figure 19-17 The large, twisting tube in this X ray is the large intestine. **What do you think the thinner tube connected to the left end of the intestine is?**

Section Assessment

1. Compare mechanical and chemical digestion.
2. Name, in order, the organs through which food passes as it moves through the digestive system.
3. How do activities in the large intestine help maintain homeostasis?
4. **Think Critically:** Crackers contain starch. Explain why a cracker held in your mouth for five minutes begins to taste sweet.
5. **Skill Builder**
   Observing and Inferring What would happen to food if the pancreas did not secrete its juices into the small intestine? If you need help, refer to Observing and Inferring in the **Skill Handbook** on page 704.

Science Journal
Write a paragraph in your Science Journal explaining what would happen to the mechanical and chemical digestion process of foods if a person had a major portion of the stomach removed due to a disease.

Design Your Own Experiment

Activity 19·2

Protein Digestion

Possible Materials

- Test tubes with gelled, unflavored gelatin (3)
- Dropper
- Test-tube rack
- Pepsin powder
- Glass-marking pen
- Cold water
- Dilute hydrochloric acid
- Beaker
- Watch or clock

You learned that proteins are large, complex, organic compounds necessary for living things to carry out their life processes. To be useful for cell functions, proteins must be broken down into their individual amino acids. The process of chemically breaking apart protein molecules involves several different factors, one of which is the presence of the enzyme pepsin in your stomach.

Recognize the Problem

Under what conditions will the enzyme pepsin begin the digestion of protein?

Form a Hypothesis

Formulate a hypothesis about what conditions are necessary for protein digestion to occur. When making your hypothesis, consider the various contents of the digestive juices that are found in your stomach.

Goals

- **Design** an experiment that tests the effect of a variable, such as the presence or absence of acid, on the activity of the enzyme pepsin.
- **Observe** the effects of pepsin on gelatin.

Safety Precautions

Always use care when working with acid and wear goggles and an apron. Avoid contact with skin and eyes. Wash your hands thoroughly after pouring the acid.

Test Your Hypothesis

Plan

1. **Decide** how your group will test your hypothesis.

2. Your teacher will supply you with three test tubes containing gelled, unflavored gelatin. Pepsin powder will liquefy the gelatin if the enzyme is active.

3. As a group, list the steps you will need to take to test your hypothesis. Consider the following factors as you plan your experiment. Based on information provided by your teacher, how will you use the pepsin and the acid? How often will you make observations?

Be specific, describing exactly what you will do at each step.

4. **List** your materials.

5. **Prepare** a data table and **record** it in your Science Journal so that it is ready to use as your group collects data.

6. **Read** over your entire experiment to make sure that all steps are in logical order.

7. **Identify** any constants, variables, and controls of the experiment.

Do

1. Make sure your teacher approves your plan before you proceed.

2. **Carry** out the experiment as planned.

3. While the experiment is going on, **write** down any observations that you make and complete the data table in your Science Journal.

Analyze Your Data

1. **Compare** your results with those of other groups.

2. Did you **observe** a difference in the test tubes?

3. **Identify** the constants in this experiment.

Draw Conclusions

1. Did the acid have any effect on the activity of the pepsin? How does this relate to the activity of this enzyme in the stomach?

2. **Predict** the effects of the pepsin on the gelatin if you increased or

decreased the concentration of the acid.

3. Is time a factor in the effectiveness of the pepsin on the gelatin? **Explain.**

For a **preview** of this chapter, study this Reviewing Main Ideas before you read the chapter. After you have studied this chapter, you can use the Reviewing Main Ideas to **review** the chapter.

The Glencoe MindJogger, Audiocassettes, and CD-ROM provide additional opportunities for review.

Section

19-1 NUTRIENTS

All foods can be grouped into six kinds of **nutrients: carbohydrates, fats, proteins, minerals, vitamins,** and water. Nutrients are the parts of food your body can use. Each kind of nutrient has a function in maintaining the health of the body. *How can your diet affect your health?*

FUNCTIONS OF NUTRIENTS

Carbohydrates provide energy. **Proteins** are needed for growth and repair. **Fats** store energy and cushion organs. **Vitamins** and **minerals** regulate body functions. Water is used for a variety of homeostatic functions. To keep your body strong and healthy, you must eat a balanced diet. A balanced diet contains food from the five **food groups.** *How can an apple provide energy?*

19-2 THE DIGESTIVE SYSTEM

The digestive system breaks down food mechanically by chewing and churning, and chemically with the help of enzymes. Food passes into the mouth and then through the esophagus. A wavelike motion called **peristalsis** pushes the food downward toward the stomach. In the stomach, gastric juices and **enzymes** break down some of the food. As food enters the small intestine, the digestive process continues. Bile produced by the liver helps emulsify fat. The pancreas also produces enzymes that help digest the food in the small intestine. The large intestine absorbs water, and waste is eliminated through the anus. *Where does mechanical digestion occur?*

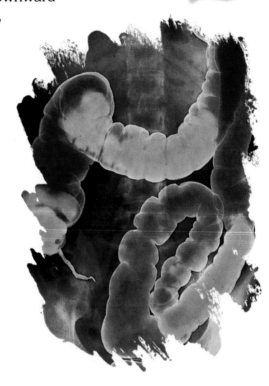

ABSORPTION OF FOOD

Nutrients are absorbed through the **villi** into the bloodstream in the small intestine. Water is absorbed in the large intestine. Bacteria that live in your large intestine produce several vitamins that are absorbed into the bloodstream at this stage. Undigested food or feces is eliminated from the body through the anus. *How do the useful substances from the nutrients reach the cells?*

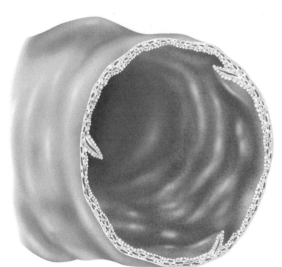

Using Vocabulary

a. amino acid
b. carbohydrate
c. chemical digestion
d. chyme
e. digestion
f. enzyme
g. fat
h. food group

i. mechanical digestion
j. mineral
k. nutrient
l. peristalsis
m. protein
n. saliva
o. villi
p. vitamin

Each phrase below describes a science term from the list. Write the term that matches the phrase describing it.

1. muscular contractions that move food
2. enzyme-containing fluid in the mouth
3. fingerlike projections in small intestine
4. subunit of protein
5. liquid product that is the result of digestion

Checking Concepts

Choose the word or phrase that best answers the question.

6. Where does most digestion occur?
   A) duodenum
   B) stomach
   C) liver
   D) large intestine

7. Which organ makes bile?
   A) gallbladder
   B) liver
   C) stomach
   D) small intestine

8. In which organ is water absorbed?
   A) liver
   B) small intestine
   C) esophagus
   D) large intestine

9. Which organ does food **NOT** pass through?
   A) mouth
   B) stomach
   C) small intestine
   D) liver

10. What is produced by bacteria in the large intestine?
    A) fats
    B) minerals
    C) vitamins
    D) proteins

11. Which vitamin is not used for growth?
    A) A
    B) B
    C) C
    D) K

12. Where is hydrochloric acid added to the food mass?
    A) mouth
    B) stomach
    C) small intestine
    D) large intestine

13. Which organ produces enzymes that digest proteins, fats, and carbohydrates?
    A) mouth
    B) pancreas
    C) large intestine
    D) gallbladder

14. Which food group contains yogurt and cheese?
    A) dairy
    B) grain
    C) meat
    D) fruit

15. From which food group are carbohydrates **BEST** obtained?
    A) milk
    B) grains
    C) meat
    D) eggs

16. From which food group should the largest number of servings in your diet come?
    A) fruit
    B) milk, yogurt, and cheese
    C) vegetable
    D) bread, cereal, rice, and pasta

Thinking Critically

17. Food does not really enter your body until it is absorbed into the blood. Explain why.

18. In what part of the digestive system do antacids work? Explain your choice.

19. Bile's action is similar to soap. Use this information to explain bile working on fats.

20. Vitamins are in two groups: water soluble and fat soluble. Which of these might your body retain? Explain your answer.

21. Based on your knowledge of food groups and nutrients, discuss the meaning of the familiar statement: "You are what you eat."

Developing Skills

If you need help, refer to the **Skill Handbook.**

22. Making and Using Graphs:
Recommended Dietary Allowances (RDA) are made for the amounts of nutrients people should take in to maintain health. Prepare a bar graph of the percent of RDA of each nutrient from the product information listed below.

Recommended Dietary Allowances

Nutrient	Percent U.S. RDA
Protein	2
Vitamin A	20
Vitamin C	25
Vitamin D	15
Calcium (Ca)	less than 2
Iron (Fe)	25
Zinc (Zn)	15
Total Fat 3.0 g	5
Saturated Fat 0.5 g	3
Cholesterol 0 mg	0
Sodium 60 mg	3

Which nutrients are given the greatest percent of the Recommended Dietary Allowance? Could a person on a fat-restricted diet eat this product? Explain.

23. Sequencing: In a table, sequence the order of organs through which food passes in the digestive system. Indicate whether ingestion, digestion, absorption, or elimination takes place in the individual organs.

24. Comparing and Contrasting: Compare and contrast the location, size, and functions of the esophagus, stomach, small intestine, and large intestine.

25. Concept Mapping: Make a concept map showing the process of fat digestion.

THE PRINCETON REVIEW

Test-Taking Tip

Don't Use Outside Knowledge When answering questions for a reading passage, do not use anything you already know about the subject of the passage, or any opinions you have about it. Always return to the passage to reread and get the details from there.

Test Practice

Use these questions to test your Science Proficiency.

1. The villi are tiny, fingerlike projections that cover the wall of the small intestine. Which statement **BEST** relates their structure with their function?
   A) They are able to contract and expand more rapidly.
   B) They offer the best protection against stomach acid.
   C) They greatly increase the surface area for digestion.
   D) They strain food passing through the intestine.

2. Certain nutrients are needed for growth and repair. Which menu is the **BEST** source of foods for this function?
   A) milk, ham, eggs, whole wheat bread
   B) cereal, milk, orange juice, donut
   C) waffles, honey, margarine, milk
   D) toast, jelly, butter, apple juice

3. Everyone depends on water to survive. Which statement **BEST** emphasizes that need?
   A) We wash our bodies with water.
   B) Many foods contain lots of water.
   C) We add water to many foods that we eat.
   D) Body nutrients are in solution.

Chapter Preview

Skills Preview

Skill Builders
- Make and Use a Table
- Compare and Contrast

Activities
- Observe
- Experiment

MiniLabs
- Compare
- Interpret Data

Reading Check ☑

Find out how a different culture views the heart. Do people in this culture draw the heart in a valentine shape? Do they think of the heart as the center of people's emotions?

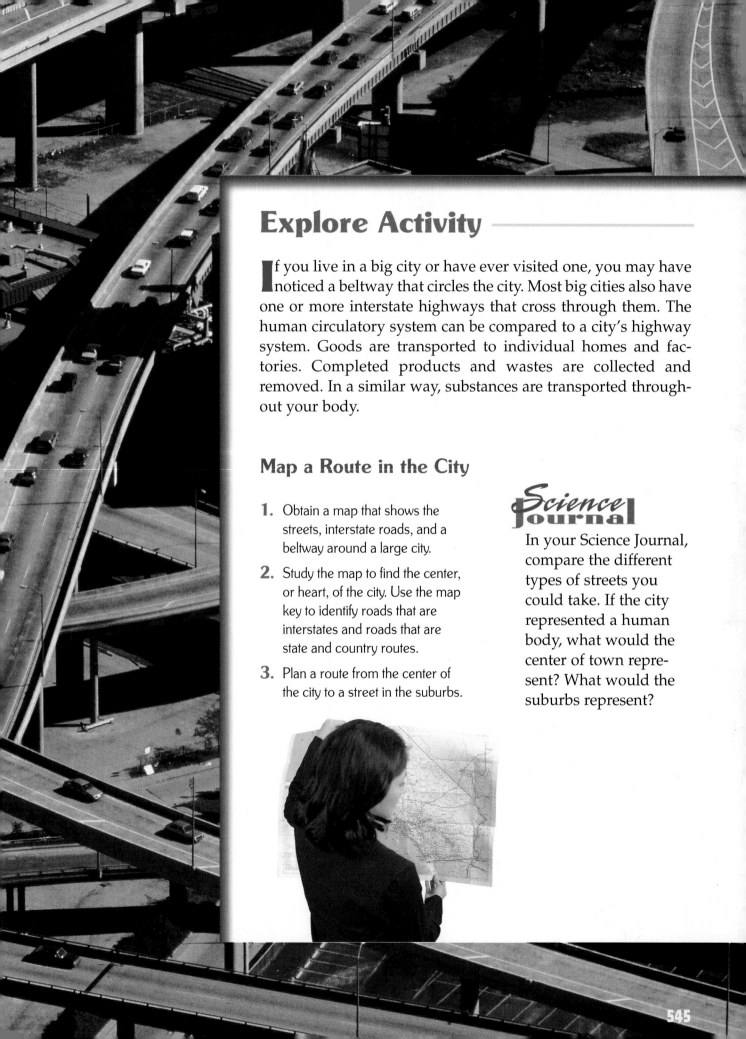

Explore Activity

If you live in a big city or have ever visited one, you may have noticed a beltway that circles the city. Most big cities also have one or more interstate highways that cross through them. The human circulatory system can be compared to a city's highway system. Goods are transported to individual homes and factories. Completed products and wastes are collected and removed. In a similar way, substances are transported throughout your body.

Map a Route in the City

1. Obtain a map that shows the streets, interstate roads, and a beltway around a large city.

2. Study the map to find the center, or heart, of the city. Use the map key to identify roads that are interstates and roads that are state and country routes.

3. Plan a route from the center of the city to a street in the suburbs.

Science Journal

In your Science Journal, compare the different types of streets you could take. If the city represented a human body, what would the center of town represent? What would the suburbs represent?

20·1 Circulation

Your Cardiovascular System

With a body made up of trillions of cells, you may seem quite different from a one-celled amoeba living in a puddle of water. But, are you really that different? Even though your body is larger and made up of complex systems, the cells in your body have the same needs as a single-celled organism, the amoeba. You both need a continuous supply of oxygen and nutrients and a way to remove cell wastes.

An amoeba takes oxygen directly from its watery environment. Nutrients are distributed throughout its single cell by moving through the cytoplasm. In your body, a cardiovascular system distributes materials. Your cardiovascular system includes your heart, blood, and kilometers of vessels that carry blood to every part of your body and then back to the heart as shown in **Figure 20-1A.** It is a closed system

What You'll Learn

▶ How to compare arteries, veins, and capillaries
▶ The pathway of blood through the chambers of the heart
▶ The pulmonary and systemic circulation systems

Vocabulary
atria
ventricle
pulmonary circulation
systemic circulation
coronary circulation
artery
vein
capillary
blood pressure
atherosclerosis
hypertension

Why It's Important

▶ Blood plays a vital role as the transport system of the body.

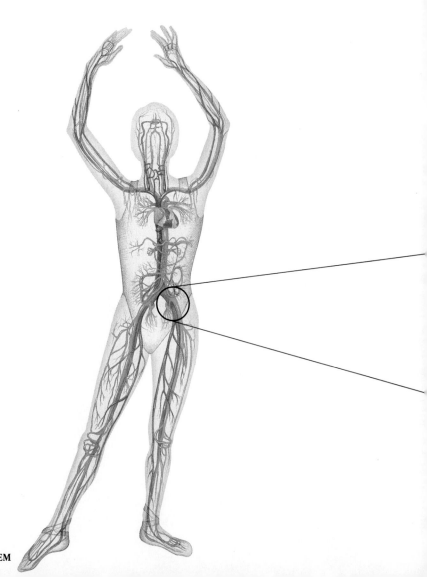

Figure 20-1 Humans have a closed circulatory system.

A The blood is pumped by a heart to all the cells of the body and back to the heart through a closed network of blood vessels.

because blood moves within vessels. The system moves oxygen and nutrients to cells and removes carbon dioxide and other wastes from the cells. Movement of materials into and out of your cells happens by diffusion. Diffusion, shown in **Figure 20-1B,** is when a material moves from an area of high concentration to an area of lower concentration.

Your Heart

Your heart is an organ made of cardiac muscle. It is located behind your sternum, which is the breastbone, and between your lungs. Your heart has four cavities called chambers. The two upper chambers are the right and left **atria** (AY tree uh). The two lower chambers are the right and left **ventricles** (VEN trih kulz). During a single heartbeat, both atria contract at the same time. Then, both ventricles contract at the same time. A valve separates each atrium from the ventricle below it so that blood flows only from an atrium to a ventricle. A wall prevents blood from flowing between the two atria or the two ventricles. It is important to separate blood rich in oxygen from blood low in oxygen to ensure that all cells get an oxygen supply.

Try at Home

Mini Lab

Inferring How Hard the Heart Works

Procedure

1. Take a racquetball and hold it in your outstretched arm.
2. Squeeze the racquetball again and again for one minute.

Analysis

1. How many times did you squeeze the racquetball in one minute? A resting heart beats at approximately 70 beats per minute.
2. What can you do when the muscles of your arm get tired? Explain why cardiac muscle in your heart cannot do the same.

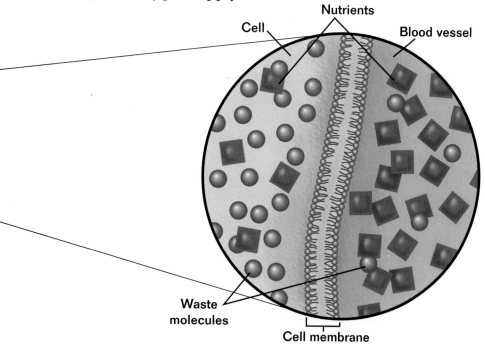

B In a closed circulatory system, blood remains in blood vessels. Nutrients move from the blood into cells by diffusion or active transport. Waste products produced by the cell move out into the circulatory system to be carried away.

Figure 20-2 Pulmonary circulation moves blood between the heart and lungs.

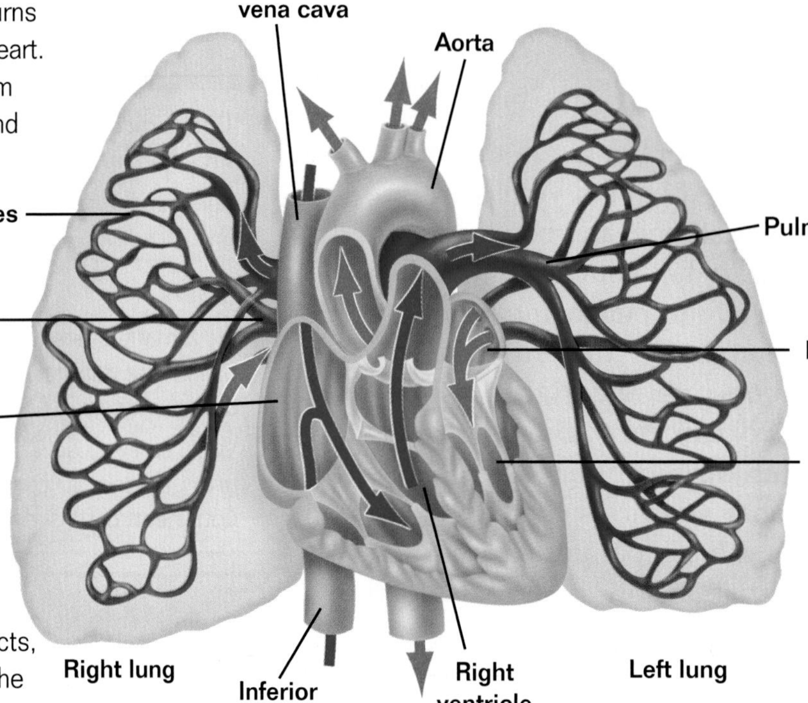

A Blood, high in carbon dioxide and low in oxygen, returns from the body to the heart. It enters the right atrium through the superior and inferior vena cavae.

C Oxygen-rich blood travels through the pulmonary vein and into the left atrium. The pulmonary veins are the only veins that carry oxygen-rich blood.

Superior vena cava

Aorta

Capillaries

Pulmonary artery

Pulmonary vein

Left atrium

Right atrium

Left ventricle

Right lung

Inferior vena cava

Right ventricle

Left lung

B The right atrium contracts, forcing the blood into the right ventricle. When the right ventricle contracts, the blood leaves the heart and goes through the pulmonary artery to the lungs, where it picks up oxygen.

D The left atrium contracts and forces the blood into the left ventricle. The left ventricle contracts, forcing the blood out of the heart and into the aorta.

Pulmonary Circulation

Blood moves continuously throughout your body in a closed circulatory system. Scientists have divided the system into three sections. The beating of your heart controls blood flow through these sections. **Figure 20-2** shows pulmonary circulation. **Pulmonary** (PUL muh ner ee) **circulation** is the flow of blood through the heart, to the lungs where it picks up oxygen, and back to the heart. Use **Figure 20-2** to trace the path blood takes through this part of the circulatory system.

Systemic Circulation

The final step of pulmonary circulation occurs when blood is forced from the left ventricle into the aorta (ay ORT uh). The aorta is the largest artery of your body. It carries blood away from the heart. **Systemic circulation** moves oxygen-rich blood to all of your organs and body tissues except for the heart and lungs. It is the most extensive of the three sections of your circulatory system. **Figure 20-3** shows the major arteries and veins involved in systemic circulation. Once nutrients and oxygen are delivered by blood to your body cells and exchanged for carbon dioxide and wastes, the blood returns to the heart in veins. From the head and neck areas, blood returns through the superior vena cava. From your abdomen and the lower parts of your body, blood returns through the inferior vena cava. More information about arteries and veins will be presented later in this chapter.

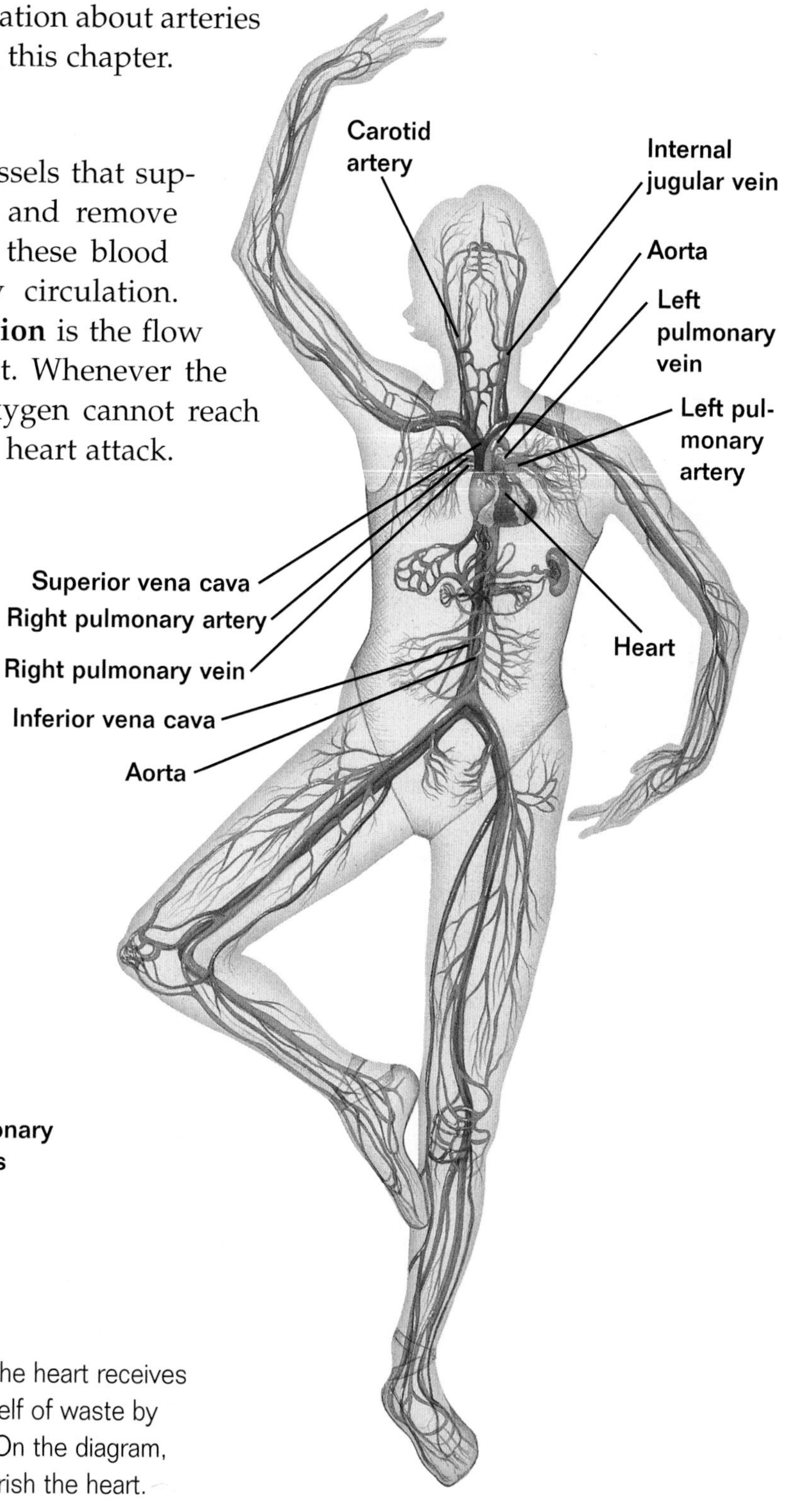

Coronary Circulation

Your heart has its own blood vessels that supply it with nutrients and oxygen and remove wastes. As shown in **Figure 20-4,** these blood vessels are involved in coronary circulation. **Coronary** (KOR uh ner ee) **circulation** is the flow of blood to the tissues of the heart. Whenever the coronary circulation is blocked, oxygen cannot reach the cells of the heart. The result is a heart attack.

Figure 20-3 The rate at which blood flows through the systemic system depends on how quickly the left ventricle contracts. **How does the rate change when a person has completed a race?**

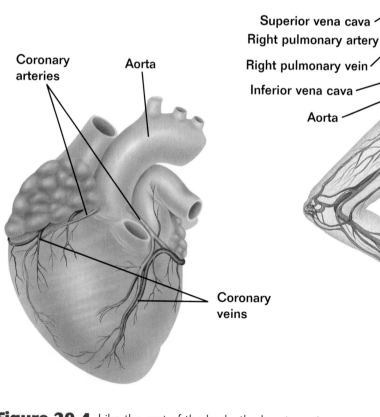

Figure 20-4 Like the rest of the body, the heart receives the oxygen and nutrients it needs and rids itself of waste by way of blood flowing through blood vessels. On the diagram, you can see the coronary arteries, which nourish the heart.

Blood Vessels

It wasn't until the middle 1600s that scientists confirmed that blood circulates only in one direction and that it is moved by the pumping action of the heart. They found that blood flows from arteries to veins. What they couldn't figure out is *how* blood gets from the arteries to the veins. With the invention of the microscope, capillaries were seen.

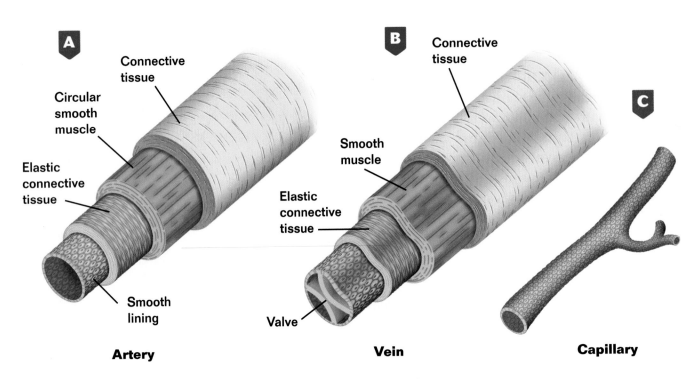

A
Connective tissue
Circular smooth muscle
Elastic connective tissue
Smooth lining

Artery

B
Connective tissue
Smooth muscle
Elastic connective tissue
Valve

Vein

C

Capillary

Figure 20-5 The structures of arteries (A), veins (B), and capillaries (C) are different. Valves in veins help blood flow back toward the heart. Capillaries are much smaller and only one cell thick.

Reading Check ✓

Compare and contrast arteries and veins.

Types of Blood Vessels

As blood moves out of the heart, it begins a journey through arteries, capillaries, and veins. **Arteries** are blood vessels that move blood away from the heart. Arteries, shown in **Figure 20-5,** have thick elastic walls made of smooth muscle. Each ventricle of the heart is connected to an artery. With each contraction of the heart, blood is moved from the heart into arteries.

Veins are blood vessels that move blood to the heart. Veins have valves to keep blood moving toward the heart. If blood flows backward, the pressure of the blood closes the valves. Veins that are near skeletal muscles are squeezed when these muscles contract. This action helps blood move toward the heart. Blood in veins carries waste materials, such as carbon dioxide, from cells and is therefore low in oxygen. ✓

Capillaries are microscopic blood vessels that connect arteries and veins. The walls of capillaries are only one cell thick. You can see the capillaries when you have a bloodshot eye. They are the tiny red lines visible in the white area of the eye. Nutrients and oxygen diffuse to body cells through thin capillary walls. Waste materials and carbon dioxide move from body cells into the capillaries to be carried back to the heart.

Blood Pressure

When you pump up a bicycle tire, you can feel the pressure of the air on the walls of the tire. In the same way, when the heart pumps blood through the cardiovascular system, blood exerts a force called **blood pressure** on the walls of the vessels. This pressure is highest in arteries. Blood pressure is lower in capillaries and even lower in veins. As the wave of pressure rises and falls in your arteries, it is felt as your pulse. Normal pulse rates are between 65 and 80 beats per minute.

Blood pressure is measured in large arteries and is expressed by two numbers, such as 120 over 80. The first number is a measure of the pressure caused when the ventricles contract and blood is pushed out of the heart. Then, blood pressure suddenly drops as the ventricles relax. The lower number is a measure of the pressure when the ventricles are filling up, just before they contract again. **Figure 20-6** shows the instruments used to measure blood pressure.

Figure 20-6 Blood pressure is measured in large arteries using a blood-pressure cuff and stethoscope.

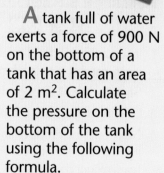

Using Math

A tank full of water exerts a force of 900 N on the bottom of a tank that has an area of 2 m². Calculate the pressure on the bottom of the tank using the following formula.

$$P = \frac{F}{A}$$

How does calculating pressure in a water tank relate to blood pressure in humans?

Figure 20-7 When pressure is exerted on a fluid in a closed container, the pressure is transmitted through the liquid in all directions. A balloon filled with water has the same amount of pressure pushing on all the inner surfaces of the balloon. Your circulatory system is like a closed container.

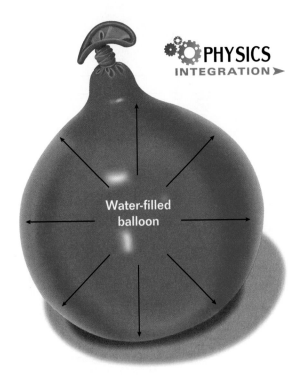

PHYSICS
INTEGRATION➤

Water-filled balloon

Mini Lab

Modeling a Blocked Artery

Procedure

1. Insert a dropperful of mineral oil into a piece of clear, narrow, plastic tubing.
2. Squeeze the oil through the tube.
3. Observe how much oil comes out the tube.
4. Next, refill the dropper and squeeze mineral oil through a piece of clear plastic tubing that has been clogged with cotton.

Analysis

1. How much oil comes out of the clogged tube?
2. Explain how the addition of the cotton to the tube changed the way the oil flowed through the tube.
3. How does this activity demonstrate what takes place when arteries become clogged?

The Big Push

You learned that a force is exerted on the inner walls of your blood vessels. The force is the result of blood being pumped through your body by the heart. Blood pressure is a measure of this force.

The total amount of force exerted by a fluid, such as blood or the gases in the atmosphere, depends on the area on which it acts. This is called pressure. In other words, as shown in **Figure 20-7**, pressure is the amount of force exerted per unit of area. This is written with the following formula.

$$\text{Pressure} = \frac{\text{Force}}{\text{Area}}$$

For example, a force of 400 N (F = 400 N) on a container with an area of 50 m² (A = 50 m²) would result in a pressure of 8 N/m².

$$P = \frac{F}{A} = \frac{400 \text{ N}}{50 \text{ m}^2} = 8 \text{ N/m}^2$$

Pressure Measurement

Scientists measure atmospheric pressure with a mercury barometer. At sea level, normal atmospheric pressure is 760 mm mercury. This means that the force of the atmosphere will raise a column of mercury (Hg) 760 mm in the barometer. Compare this to a normal blood pressure reading of 120 over 80 for a young adult. The first number is the systolic pressure (the pressure produced when the ventricles force blood from the heart). In this reading, the systolic pressure would raise a column of mercury 120 mm in a barometer. The second number is the diastolic pressure (the pressure at the end of the cardiac cycle). This pressure would raise a column of mercury 80 mm in a barometer.

Magnification: 10×

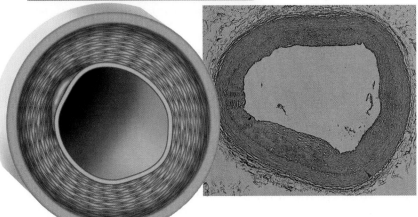

Figure 20-8 Atherosclerosis interferes with blood flow by blocking blood vessels with fatty substances. Each of these photos is paired with an illustration showing the build up of fatty deposits. **What happens if an artery in the heart is blocked?**

A This cross section of a healthy coronary artery shows a clear, wide-open pathway through which blood easily flows.

B Here, the blood-flow pathway has been narrowed by a buildup of fatty deposits. Blood flow is slowed. The heart muscle does not get enough oxygen and nutrients to do its work. The muscle begins to die.

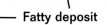 — **Fatty deposit**

Magnification: 10×

Magnification: 10×

C If the deposit continues to build, blood flow through the artery becomes limited and may stop. The person will suffer a heart attack.

Control of Blood Pressure

Special nerve cells in the walls of some arteries sense changes in blood pressure. Messages are sent to the brain, and the amount of blood pumped by the heart is regulated. This provides for a regular, normal pressure within the arteries.

*inter*NET
CONNECTION

Visit the Glencoe Science Web Site at **www.glencoe.com/ sec/science** for more information about cardiovascular disease.

Cardiovascular Disease

Any disease or disorder that affects the cardio-vascular system can seriously affect your health. Heart disease is the major cause of death in the United States. One leading cause of heart disease is **atherosclerosis** (ah thur oh skluh ROH sus), a condition, shown in **Figure 20-8,** of fatty deposits on arterial walls. Eating foods high in cholesterol and saturated fats may cause these deposits to form. The fat builds up and forms a hard mass that clogs the inside of the vessel. As a result, less blood flows through the artery. If the artery is clogged completely, blood is not able to flow through.

Another disorder is high blood pressure, or **hypertension.** Atherosclerosis can cause hypertension. A clogged artery can cause the pressure within the vessel to increase. This causes the walls to lose their ability to contract and dilate. Extra strain is placed on the heart as it works harder to keep blood flowing. Being overweight as well as eating foods with too much salt and fat may contribute to hypertension. Smoking and stress also can increase blood pressure. Regular checkups, as shown in **Figure 20-9,** a careful diet, and exercise are important to the health of your cardiovascular system.

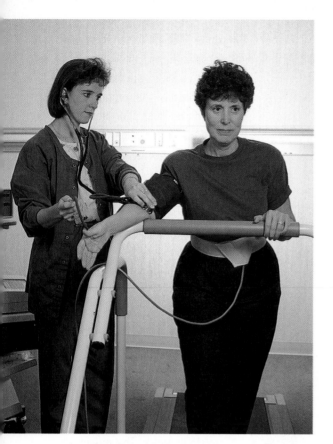

Figure 20-9 A stress test is used to determine the amount of strain placed on the heart.

Section Assessment

1. Compare and contrast the three types of blood vessels.
2. Explain the pathway of blood through the heart.
3. Contrast pulmonary and systemic circulations.
4. **Think Critically:** What waste product builds up in blood and cells when the heart is unable to pump blood efficiently?
5. **Skill Builder**
   Concept Mapping Make an events chain concept map to show pulmonary circulation beginning at the right atrium and ending at the aorta. If you need help, refer to Concept Mapping in the **Skill Handbook** on page 698.

Using Computers

Database Use different references to research diseases and disorders of the circulatory system. Make a database showing what part of the circulatory system is affected by each disease or disorder. Categories should include the organs, vessels, and cells of the circulatory system. If you need help, refer to page 717.

Activity
20•1

The Heart as a Pump

Materials
- Stopwatch, watch, or a clock with a second hand

The heart is a pumping organ. Blood is forced through the arteries and causes the muscles of the walls to contract and then relax. This creates a series of waves as the blood flows through the arteries. We call this the pulse. Try this activity to learn about the pulse and the pumping of the heart.

What You'll Investigate

How can you measure heartbeat rate?

Goals

- **Observe** pulse rate.

Procedure

1. **Make** a table like the one shown. Use it to **record** your data.
2. Your partner should sit down and take his or her pulse. You will serve as the recorder.
3. **Find** the pulse rate by placing the middle and index fingers over one of the carotid arteries in the neck as shown in the photo. **CAUTION:** *Do not press too hard.*

4. **Calculate** the resulting heart rate. Your partner should count each beat of the carotid pulse rate silently for 15 s. Multiply the number of beats by four and **record** the number in the data table.
5. Your partner should then jog in place for one minute and take his or her pulse again.
6. **Calculate** this new pulse rate and **record** it in the data table.
7. Reverse roles with your partner. You are now the pulse taker.
8. **Collect and record** the new data.

Conclude and Apply

1. How does the pulse rate change?
2. What causes the pulse rate to change?
3. What can you **infer** about the heart as a pumping organ?

Pulse Rate		
Pulse Rate	**Partner's**	**Yours**
At rest		
After jogging		

20•2 Blood

Functions of Blood

What You'll Learn

▶ The characteristics and functions of the blood
▶ The importance of checking blood types before a transfusion
▶ Diseases and disorders of blood

Vocabulary
plasma
hemoglobin
platelet

Why It's Important

▶ Blood has many important functions and plays a part in every major activity of your body.

Blood is a tissue consisting of cells, cell fragments, and liquid. Blood has many important functions. It plays a part in every major activity of your body. First, blood carries oxygen from your lungs to all body cells. It also removes carbon dioxide from your body cells and carries it to the lungs to be exhaled. Second, it carries waste products of cell activity to your kidneys to be removed. Third, blood transports nutrients from the digestive system to body cells. Fourth, materials in blood fight infections and help heal wounds. Anything that disrupts or changes any of these functions affects all the tissues of the body.

Blood makes up about eight percent of your body's total mass. If you weigh 45 kg, you have about 3.6 kg of blood moving through your body. The amount of blood in an adult would fill five 1-L bottles. If this volume falls, the body goes into shock because blood pressure falls rapidly.

Parts of Blood

If you've ever taken a ride on a water slide at an amusement park, you have some idea of the twists and turns a blood cell travels inside a blood vessel. On the ride, surrounded by water, you travel rapidly through a narrow, watery passageway, much like a red blood cell moves in the liquid part of blood, as shown in Figure 20-10.

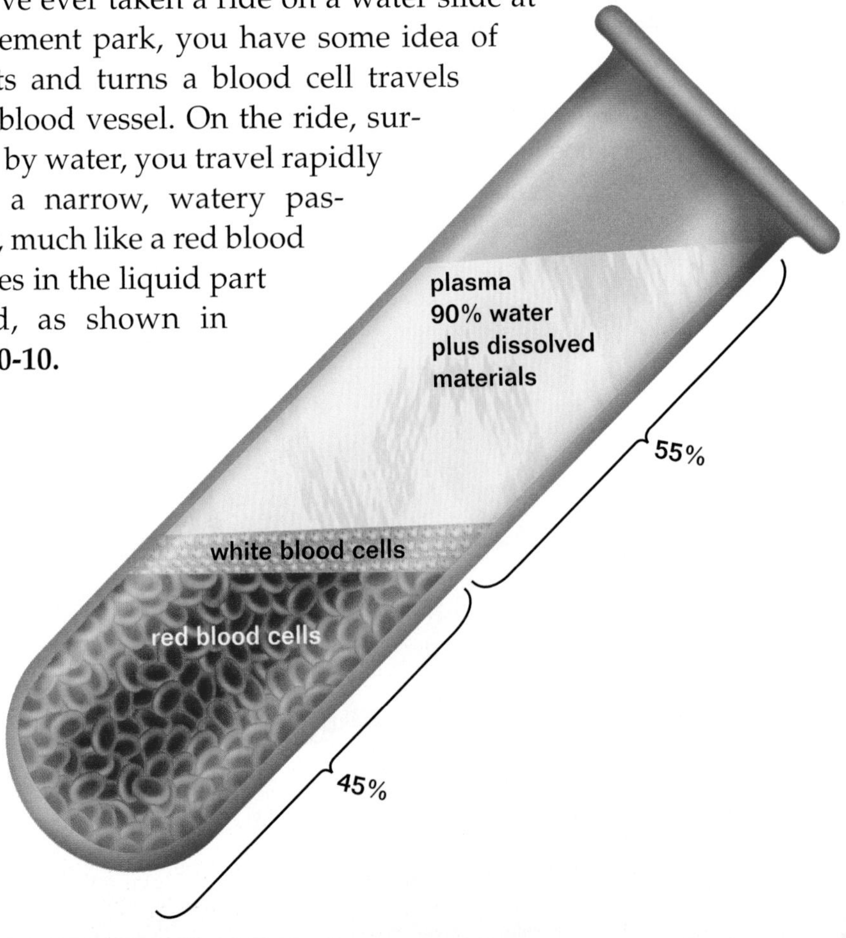

Figure 20-10 The blood in this test tube has been separated into its parts. Each part plays a key role in body functions. **What part of blood is the most dense?**

plasma
90% water
plus dissolved
materials

55%

white blood cells

red blood cells

45%

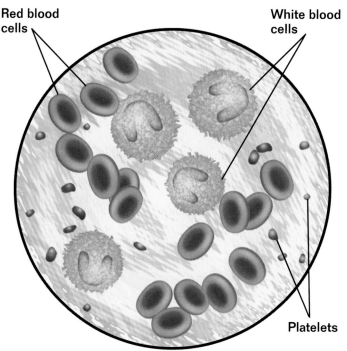

Red blood cells

White blood cells

Platelets

Blood smear

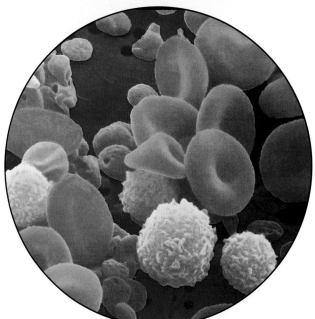

Magnification: 1000×

Figure 20-11 Blood consists of a liquid portion called plasma and a solid portion that includes red blood cells, white blood cells, and platelets. **What type of cells are most numerous in the human circulatory system?**

Plasma

If you examine blood closely, as in **Figure 20-11,** you see that it is not just a red-colored liquid. Blood is a tissue made of red and white blood cells, platelets, and plasma. **Plasma** is the liquid part of blood and consists mostly of water. It makes up more than half the volume of blood. Nutrients, minerals, and oxygen are dissolved in plasma.

Blood Cells

A cubic millimeter of blood has more than 5 million red blood cells. In these disk-shaped blood cells is **hemoglobin,** a chemical that can carry oxygen and carbon dioxide. Hemoglobin carries oxygen from your lungs to your body cells. Red blood cells also carry carbon dioxide from body

CHEMISTRY
INTEGRATION

Artificial Blood
Artificial blood substances have been developed to use in blood transfusions. They can carry oxygen and carbon dioxide. Predict what other properties they must have to be safe.

Magnification: 2000×

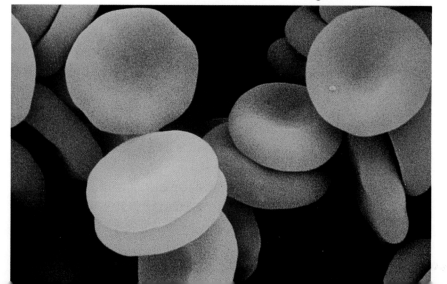

Figure 20-12 Red blood cells carry oxygen and carbon dioxide and are disk shaped.

Figure 20-13 While red blood cells supply your body with oxygen, white blood cells and platelets have more protective roles.

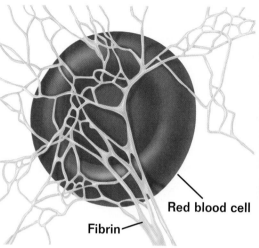

A Platelets help stop bleeding. Platelets not only plug holes in small vessels, but they also release chemicals that help form filaments of fibrin.

B Several types, sizes, and shapes of white blood cells exist. These cells destroy bacteria, viruses, and foreign substances.

Red blood cell

Fibrin

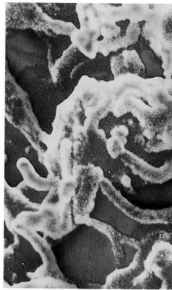

Platelets

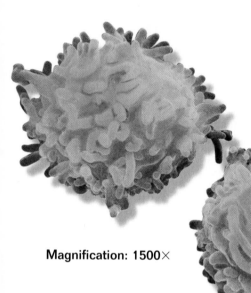

Magnification: 1500×

*inter*NET
CONNECTION

Visit the Glencoe Science Web Site at **www.glencoe.com/ sec/science** for more information about blood clotting.

cells to your lungs. Red blood cells have a life span of about 120 days. They are formed in the marrow of long bones such as the femur and humerus at a rate of 2 to 3 million per second and contain no nuclei. About an equal number of old ones wear out and are destroyed in the same time period.

In contrast to red blood cells, there are only about 5000 to 10 000 white blood cells in a cubic millimeter of blood. White blood cells fight bacteria, viruses, and other foreign substances that constantly try to invade your body. Your body reacts to infection by increasing its number of white blood cells. White blood cells slip between the cells of capillary walls and out around the tissues that have been invaded. Here, they absorb foreign substances and dead cells. The life span of white blood cells varies from a few days to many months.

Circulating with the red and white blood cells are platelets. **Platelets** are irregularly shaped cell fragments that help clot blood. A cubic millimeter of blood may contain as many as 400 000 platelets. Platelets have a life span of five to nine days. **Figure 20-13** summarizes the solid parts of blood and their functions.

Blood Clotting

Everyone has had a cut, scrape, or other minor wound at some time. The initial bleeding is usually stopped quickly, and the wounded area begins to heal. Most people will not bleed to death from a minor wound. The bleeding stops because platelets in your blood make a blood clot that helps prevent blood loss. A blood clot is somewhat like a bandage. When you cut yourself, a series of chemical reactions causes threadlike fibers called fibrin to form a sticky net that traps escaping blood cells and plasma. This forms a clot and helps prevent further loss of blood. **Figure 20-14** shows the blood-clotting process that occurs after a cut. Some people have the genetic disease hemophilia. Their blood lacks one of the clotting factors that begins the clotting process.

Figure 20-14 A sticky blood clot seals the leaking blood vessel. Eventually, a scab forms, protecting the wound from further damage and allowing it to heal.

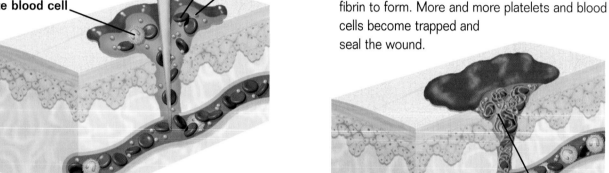

A Blood flows out of a damaged blood vessel.

White blood cell

Red blood cell

Platelets

B Platelets stick to the area of the wound and release chemicals. The chemicals make other nearby platelets sticky and cause threads of fibrin to form. More and more platelets and blood cells become trapped and seal the wound.

Fibrin

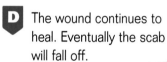

C The clot becomes harder. White blood cells destroy invading bacteria. Skin cells begin the repair process.

Scab

D The wound continues to heal. Eventually the scab will fall off.

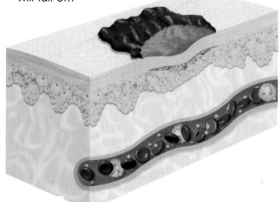

Blood Types

Sometimes, a person loses a lot of blood. This person may receive blood through a blood transfusion. During a blood transfusion, a person receives blood or parts of blood. Doctors must be sure that the right type of blood is given.

Table 20-1

Blood Types		
Blood Type	**Antigen**	**Antibody**
A	Red blood cell	A	Anti-B
B		B	Anti-A
AB		A — B	None
O		None	Anti-A Anti-B

If it is the wrong type, the red blood cells of the person clump together. Clots form in the blood vessels, and the person dies.

The ABO Identification System

Doctors know that humans can have one of four types of blood: A, B, AB, and O. Each type has a chemical identification tag called an antigen on its red blood cells. As shown in **Table 20-1,** type A blood has A antigens. Type B blood has B antigens. Type AB blood has both A and B antigens on each blood cell. Type O blood has no A or B antigens.

Each blood type also has specific antibodies in its plasma. Antibodies are proteins that destroy or neutralize foreign substances, such as pathogens, in your body. Antibodies prevent certain blood types from mixing. Type A blood has antibodies against type B blood. If you mix type A blood with type B blood, type A red blood cells react to type B blood as if it were a foreign substance. The antibodies in type A blood respond by clumping the type B blood. Type B blood has antibodies against type A blood. Type AB blood has no antibodies, so it can receive blood from A, B, AB, and O types. Type O blood has both A and B antibodies. **Table 20-2** lists the four blood types, what they can receive, and what blood types they can donate to. ☑

The Rh Factor

Just as antigens are one chemical identification tag for blood, the Rh marker is another. Rh blood type also is inherited. If the Rh marker is present, the person has Rh-positive (Rh+) blood. If it is not present, the person is said to be

Reading Check ☑

People with type O blood are said to be universal donors. Why do you think this is an appropriate term?

Table 20-2

Blood Transfusion Possibilities		
Type	Can receive	Can donate to
A	O, A	A, AB
B	O, B	B, AB
AB	all	AB
O	O	all

Rh-negative (Rh−). Any Rh− person receiving blood from an Rh+ person will produce antibodies against the Rh+ factor.

A problem also occurs when an Rh− mother carries an Rh+ baby. Close to the time when the baby is about to be born, antibodies from the mother can pass from her blood vessels into the baby's blood vessels and destroy the baby's red blood cells. If this happens, the baby must receive a blood transfusion before or right after birth. At 28 weeks of pregnancy and immediately after the birth, the mother can receive an injection that prevents the production of antibodies to the Rh factor. To prevent deadly consequences, blood groups and Rh factor are checked before transfusions and during pregnancies.

Problem Solving

The Baby Exchange

Two mothers took their new babies home from the hospital on the same day. On the first day home, when mother number one was removing the hospital name tag from her baby, she discovered that the other mother's name was on the tag. The other mother was

Blood Test Results	
Person	**Blood Type**
Mother #1	O
Father #1	O
Baby taken home by parents #1	B
Mother #2	O
Father #2	AB
Baby taken home by parents #2	O

contacted, but she was sure that she had the right baby. She did not want to give up the baby she had brought home from the hospital. Because the identity of the babies was disputed, the issue had to be decided in court. Analyze the data provided in the table and apply the laws of inheritance to solve the problem.

Think Critically: What is the only blood type the baby from family one could have? Should the babies be exchanged? Because A and B blood types are always dominant to blood type O, what other blood type could babies from family two have?

Diseases and Disorders of Blood

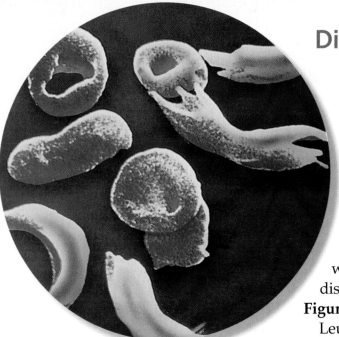

Figure 20-15 Persons with sickle-cell anemia have deformed red blood cells. The sickle-shaped cells clog the capillaries of the person with this disease. Oxygen cannot reach tissues served by the capillaries, and wastes cannot be removed. **How does this damage the affected tissues?**

Blood, like other body tissues, is subject to disease. Because blood circulates to all parts of the body and performs so many vital functions, any disease of this tissue is cause for concern. Anemia is a disorder in which there are too few red blood cells or there is too little hemoglobin in the red blood cells. Because of this, body tissues can't get enough oxygen. They are unable to carry on their usual activities. Sometimes, the loss of great amounts of blood or improper diet will cause anemia. Anemia also can result from disease or as a side effect of treatment for a disease. **Figure 20-15** illustrates another blood disease.

Leukemia (lew KEE mee uh) is a disease in which one or more types of white blood cells are produced in increased numbers. However, these cells are immature and do not effectively fight infections. Blood transfusions and bone marrow transplants are used to treat this disease, but they are not always successful, and death can occur.

Blood transports oxygen and nutrients to body cells and takes wastes from these cells to organs for removal. Cells in blood help fight infection and heal wounds. You can understand why blood is sometimes called the tissue of life.

Section Assessment

1. What are the four functions of blood in the body?
2. Compare blood cells, plasma, and platelets.
3. Why is blood type checked before a transfusion?
4. Describe a disease and a disorder of blood.
5. **Think Critically:** Think about the main job of your red blood cells. If red blood cells couldn't pick up carbon dioxide and wastes from your cells, what would be the condition of your tissues?
6. **Skill Builder**
   Making and Using Tables Look at the data in **Table 20-2** about blood group interactions. To which group(s) can type AB donate blood? If you need help, refer to Making and Using Tables in the **Skill Handbook** on page 700.

Using Math

Calculate the ratio of the number of red blood cells to the number of white blood cells and to the number of platelets in a cubic millimeter of blood. What are the percentages of each kind of solid?

Comparing Blood Cells

Blood is an important tissue for all vertebrates. How do human blood cells compare with those of other vertebrates?

What You'll Investigate

How does human blood compare with the blood of other vertebrates?

Goals

- **Observe** the characteristics of red blood cells, white blood cells, and platelets.
- **Compare** human blood cells with those of other vertebrates.

Procedures

1. Under low power, **examine** the prepared slide of human blood. **Locate** the red blood cells.
2. **Examine** the red blood cells under high power.
3. Make a data table. Draw, count, and **describe** the red blood cells.
4. Move the slide to another position. Find one or two white blood cells. They will be blue or purple due to the stain.
5. Draw, count, and **describe** the white cells in a data table.

Materials

- Prepared slides of human blood
  photos of human blood
- Prepared slides of two other vertebrates' (fish, frog, reptile, bird) blood
  photos of two other vertebrates' blood
- Microscope

  Alternate Materials

6. **Examine** the slide for small fragments that appear blue. These are platelets.
7. Draw, count, and **describe** the platelets on your data table.
8. Follow steps 1 to 7 for each of the other vertebrate cells.

Conclude and Apply

1. Does each vertebrate studied have all three cell types?
2. What might you infer about the ability of the different red blood cells to carry oxygen?
3. What is the function of each of the three types of blood cells?

Human blood

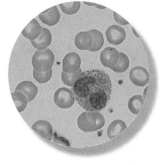

Frog blood

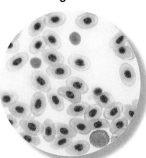

Snake blood

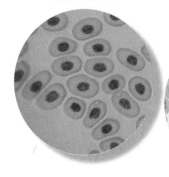

Bird blood

Fantastic Voyage
by Isaac Asimov

In the science fiction novel *Fantastic Voyage*, later made into a movie (see scene below), a scientist defecting from his native country develops a blood clot in his brain and lapses into a coma. Valuable information that governments are competing for is now beyond reach. A traditional operation won't work, but luckily for science fiction fans, an alternative is available. This new method uses miniaturization to operate on the blood clot from inside the body. A small submarine, *Proteus*, and its five passengers—one of whom is a brain surgeon—are reduced to one millionth their former size. They make their way through the patient's circulatory system (see blood vessel at right) to the blood clot. The operation must be done quickly because the ship and its crew will return to their normal size in 60 minutes. Here is Asimov's description of their fantastic voyage in the bloodstream:

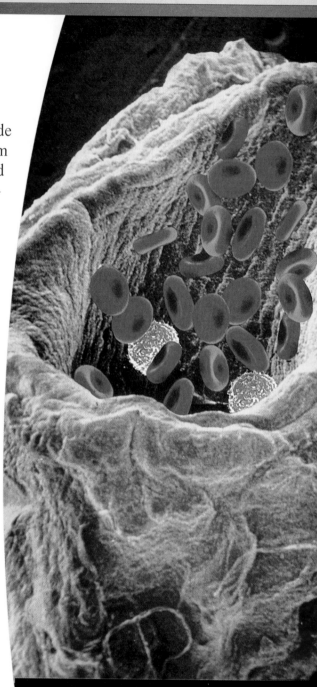

> *It was a vast, exotic aquarium they faced, one in which not fish but far stranger objects filled their vision.* Large rubber tires, the centers depressed but not pierced through, were the most numerous objects. Each was twice the diameter of the ship, each an orange-straw color, each sparkling and blazing intermittently, as though faceted with slivers of diamonds.

What are the objects described in the paragraph above? What color did you expect these objects to be?

Science JOURNAL

In your Science Journal, describe the inside of your mouth as it might have looked to the crew of the *Proteus*. If you could undergo miniaturization, what part of your body would you most like to see and explore? Why?

Your Lymphatic System

Functions of Your Lymphatic System

You have learned that blood carries nutrients and oxygen to cells. Molecules of these substances pass through capillary walls to be absorbed by nearby cells. Some of the water and dissolved substances that move out of your blood become part of a tissue fluid that is found between cells. Your **lymphatic** (lihm FAT ihk) **system,** shown in **Figure 20-16,** collects this fluid from body tissue spaces and returns it to the blood through a system of lymph capillaries and larger lymph vessels. This system also contains cells that help your body defend itself against disease-causing organisms.

What You'll Learn

▶ The functions of the lymphatic system
▶ Where lymph comes from
▶ The role of lymph organs in fighting infections

Vocabulary
lymphatic system
lymph
lymphocyte
lymph node

Why It's Important

▶ The lymphatic system plays a vital role in protecting the body against infections and diseases.

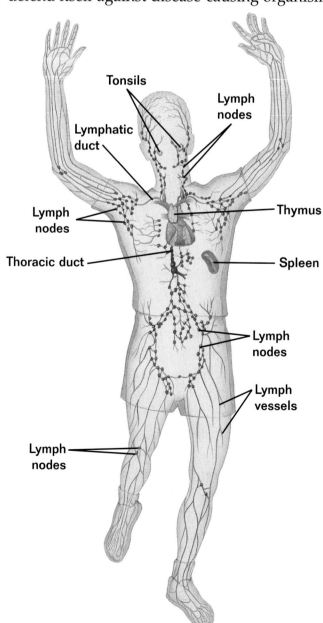

Tonsils
Lymph nodes
Lymphatic duct
Lymph nodes
Thoracic duct
Thymus
Spleen
Lymph nodes
Lymph vessels
Lymph nodes

Figure 20-16 Like the circulatory system, the lymphatic system is connected by a vast network of vessels, but does not have a pump or heart. **How do muscles help move lymph?**

Figure 20-17 Lymph is fluid that has moved from around cells into lymph vessels.

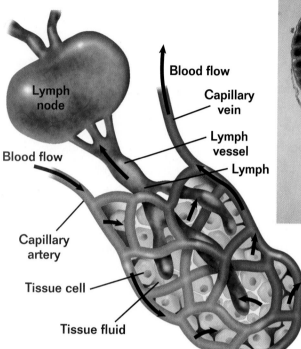

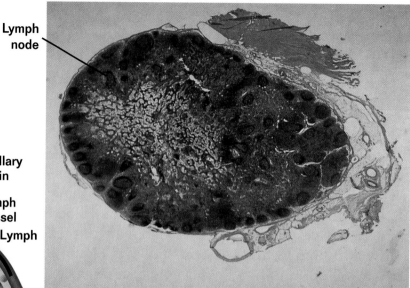

Lymphatic Organs

Once tissue fluid moves from around body tissues and into lymphatic capillaries, shown in **Figure 20-17,** it is known as lymph. It enters the capillaries by absorption and diffusion. **Lymph** consists mostly of water, dissolved substances such as nutrients and small proteins, and **lymphocytes** (LIHM fuh sites), a type of white blood cell. The lymphatic capillaries join with larger vessels that eventually drain the lymph into large veins near the heart. No heartlike structure pumps the lymph through the lymphatic system. The movement of lymph is due to contraction of skeletal muscles and the smooth muscles in lymph vessels. Like veins, lymphatic vessels have valves that prevent the backward flow of lymph. ☑

Reading Check ☑

What makes up lymph?

Lymph Nodes

Before lymph enters blood, it passes through bean-shaped structures throughout the body known as lymph nodes. **Lymph nodes** filter out microorganisms and foreign materials that have been engulfed by lymphocytes. When your body fights an infection, lymphocytes fill the nodes. They become inflamed and tender to the touch.

Tonsils are lymphatic organs in the back of the throat. They provide protection to the mouth and nose against pathogens. The thymus is a soft mass of tissue located behind the sternum. It produces lymphocytes that travel to other lymph organs. The spleen is the largest organ of the lymphatic system and is located behind the upper-left part of the stomach. Blood flowing through the spleen gets filtered. Here, worn out and damaged red blood cells are broken down. Specialized cells in the spleen engulf and destroy bacteria and other foreign substances.

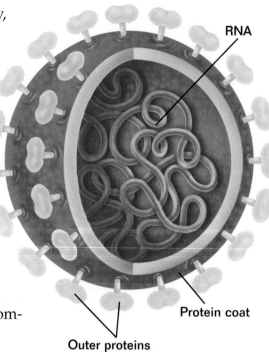

Figure 20-18 HIV, shown below, is a virus that attacks helper T cells. This makes it harder for the body to fight infections.

A Disease of the Lymphatic System

As you have probably learned, HIV is a deadly virus. As shown in **Figure 20-18,** when HIV enters a person's body, it attacks and destroys a particular kind of lymphocyte called helper T cells. Normally, helper T cells help produce antibodies to fight infections. With fewer helper T cells, a person infected with HIV is less able to fight pathogens. The infections become difficult to treat and often lead to death.

The lymphatic system collects extra fluid from body tissue spaces. It also produces lymphocytes that fight infections and foreign materials that enter your body. This system works to keep your body healthy. This system is critical in defending your body against disease. Through a network of vessels, lymph nodes, and other organs, your lymphatic system is a strong defense against invasion. However, if the system is not working properly, even a common cold can become a serious threat.

RNA

Protein coat

Outer proteins

Section Assessment

1. Describe the role of your lymphatic system.
2. Where does lymph come from and how does it get into the lymphatic capillaries?
3. List the major organs of the lymphatic system.
4. What happens when HIV enters the body?
5. **Think Critically:** When the amount of fluid in the spaces between cells increases, so does the pressure in these spaces. What do you infer will happen?
6. 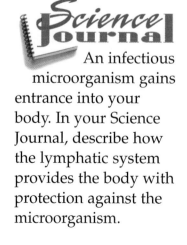 **Skill Builder**
   Concept Mapping The circulatory system and the lymphatic system are separate systems, yet they work together in several ways. Do the **Chapter 20 Skill Activity** on page 745 to make a concept map comparing the two systems.

Science Journal
An infectious microorganism gains entrance into your body. In your Science Journal, describe how the lymphatic system provides the body with protection against the microorganism.

For a **preview** of this chapter, study this Reviewing Main Ideas before you read the chapter. After you have studied this chapter, you can use the Reviewing Main Ideas to **review** the chapter.

The Glencoe MindJogger, Audiocassettes, and CD-ROM provide additional opportunities for review.

20-1 TRANSPORTATION SYSTEM

The main function of the circulatory system is to transport materials through the body. It carries food, oxygen, carbon dioxide, and a variety of other chemicals. The blood circulates in a closed system. The heart is a four-chambered pump that circulates the blood throughout the body. Through a series of coordinated muscular contractions, the heart provides the pressure that pushes blood through the vessels. *What component of blood carries oxygen to the cells of the body?*

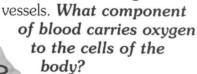

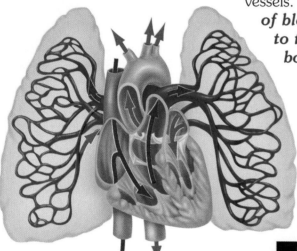

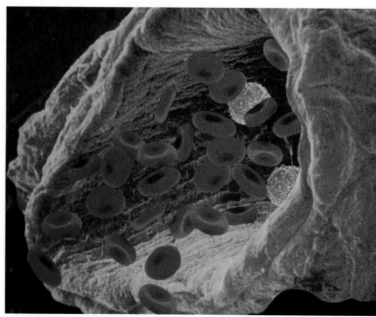

CIRCULATION

Arteries carry blood from the heart. **Capillaries** exchange food, oxygen, and wastes in cells. **Veins** return blood to the heart. Blood enters the heart through the right **atrium,** moves to the right **ventricle,** and goes to the lungs through the pulmonary artery. Blood rich in oxygen returns to the left atrium of the heart and passes through a valve into the left ventricle. Blood leaves the heart through the aorta and travels to all parts of the body. *What is the pathway of blood in the pulmonary circulation system?*

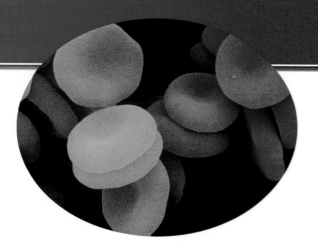

Reading Check ☑

Compare and contrast the three types of vessels. Explain why all three are necessary for circulation.

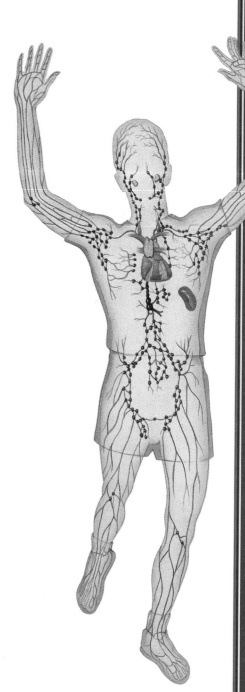

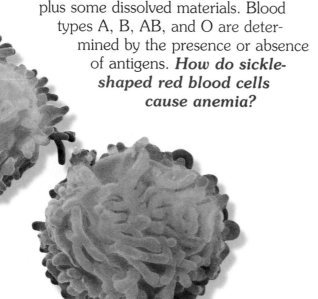

Section
20-2 BLOOD

Blood is a tissue consisting of cells, cell fragments, and liquid. Each of the solid components of blood has a specific function: the red blood cells carry oxygen and carbon dioxide, **platelets** form clots, and white blood cells fight infection. Blood also contains a liquid portion called **plasma.** The plasma consists mostly of water plus some dissolved materials. Blood types A, B, AB, and O are determined by the presence or absence of antigens. *How do sickle-shaped red blood cells cause anemia?*

Section
20-3 THE LYMPHATIC SYSTEM

Fluid found in body tissue is collected by the vessels in the **lymphatic system** and returned to the blood system. Structures in the lymphatic system filter the blood and produce white blood cells that destroy microorganisms and foreign materials. *How is an inflamed lymph node a sign that the body is fighting an infection?*

Chapter 20 Assessment

Using Vocabulary

a. artery
b. atherosclerosis
c. atria
d. blood pressure
e. capillary
f. coronary circulation
g. hemoglobin
h. hypertension
i. lymph
j. lymph node
k. lymphatic system
l. lymphocyte
m. plasma
n. platelet
o. pulmonary circulation
p. systemic circulation
q. vein
r. ventricle

Each phrase below describes a science term from the list. Write the term that matches the phrase describing it.

1. filters microorganisms
2. upper heart chambers
3. vessel connected to the heart ventricle
4. fatty deposit on artery walls
5. blood vessel that connects arteries to veins

Checking Concepts

Choose the word or phrase that best answers the question.

6. Where does the exchange of food, oxygen, and wastes occur?
   A) arteries
   B) capillaries
   C) veins
   D) lymph vessels

7. Where does oxygen-rich blood enter first?
   A) right atrium
   B) left atrium
   C) left ventricle
   D) right ventricle

8. What is circulation to all body organs?
   A) coronary
   B) pulmonary
   C) systemic
   D) organic

9. Where is blood under great pressure?
   A) arteries
   B) capillaries
   C) veins
   D) lymph vessels

10. What is blood's function?
    A) digest food
    B) produce CO_2
    C) dissolve bone
    D) carry oxygen

11. Which cells fight off infection?
    A) red blood
    B) bone
    C) white blood
    D) nerve

12. In blood, what carries oxygen?
    A) red blood cells
    B) platelets
    C) white blood cells
    D) lymph

13. To clot blood, what is required?
    A) plasma
    B) oxygen
    C) platelets
    D) carbon dioxide

14. What kind of antigen does type O blood have?
    A) A
    B) B
    C) A and B
    D) no antigen

15. What is the largest filtering lymph organ?
    A) spleen
    B) thymus
    C) tonsil
    D) node

Thinking Critically

16. Identify the following as having oxygen-rich or carbon dioxide-full blood: *aorta, coronary arteries, coronary veins, inferior vena cava, left atrium, left ventricle, right atrium, right ventricle,* and *superior vena cava.*

17. Compare and contrast the three types of blood vessels.

18. Explain how the lymphatic system works with the cardiovascular system.

19. Why is cancer of the blood or lymph hard to control?

20. Arteries are distributed throughout the body, yet a pulse is usually taken at the neck or wrist. Why do you think this is so?

Developing Skills

If you need help, refer to the **Skill Handbook.**

21. **Concept Mapping:** Complete the events chain concept map showing how lymph moves in your body.

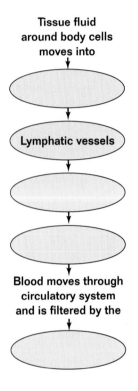

Tissue fluid
around body cells
moves into

Lymphatic vessels

Blood moves through
circulatory system
and is filtered by the

22. **Comparing and Contrasting:** Compare the life span of the different types of blood cells.

23. **Interpreting Data:** Interpret the data listed below. Find the average heartbeat rate of four males and four females and compare the two averages.
Males: 72, 64, 65, 72
Females: 67, 84, 74, 67

24. **Designing an Experiment:** Design an experiment to compare the heartbeat rate at rest and after exercising.

25. **Hypothesizing:** Make a hypothesis to suggest the effects of smoking on heartbeat rate.

THE PRINCETON REVIEW

Test-Taking Tip

Investigate Ask what kinds of questions to expect on the test. Ask for practice tests so that you can become familiar with the test-taking materials.

Test Practice

Use these questions to test your Science Proficiency.

1. The veins in the blood circulatory system and the vessels of the lymphatic system have valves. What is the major function of these structures?
    A) Valves help filter out microorganisms and foreign matter.
    B) Valves keep the fluids from moving too rapidly in the vessels.
    C) Valves permit the fluids to flow in only one direction.
    D) Valves connect arteries, veins, and lymphatic vessels.

2. Veins never carry oxygen-rich blood. Which statement below **BEST** defends or refutes the above statement?
    A) The pulmonary vein carries blood to the left atrium.
    B) The vena cava carries blood to the right atrium.
    C) The pulmonary artery carries blood to the lungs.
    D) The aorta carries blood from the heart to the body.

Respiration and Excretion

Skills Preview

Skill Builder
- Sequence
- Map Concepts

Activities
- Design an Experiment
- Observe and Infer

MiniLabs
- Measure
- Model

Reading Check ✓

As you read this chapter, look for clues that can help you understand unfamiliar terms. These clues can include nearby words and sentences, as well as illustrations.

Explore Activity

Have you ever played basketball or run so hard that it felt like your lungs would burst? How long did it take your breathing rate to return to normal? You can live more than a week without food. You might live several days without water. But, you can live only several minutes without oxygen. Your body has the ability to store food and water. It cannot store much oxygen. It needs a continuous supply to keep your body cells functioning. Sometimes, your body needs a lot of oxygen. In the following activity, find out about one factor that can change your breathing rate.

Observe Breathing Rate

1. Put your hand on your chest. Take a deep breath. Feel your chest move up and down slightly. Notice how your rib cage moves out and upward when you inhale.

2. Count your breathing rate for 15 s. Multiply this number by four to figure your breathing rate for one minute. Repeat this activity and calculate your average breathing rate.

3. Jog in place for one minute and count your breathing rate again.

4. How long does it take for your breathing rate to return to normal?

Science Journal

In your Science Journal, record your breathing rate before and after physical activity. Also, write down how long it took for your breathing rate to return to normal. Describe any changes you observed. Write an explanation of how breathing rate appears to be related to physical activity.

21·1 The Respiratory System

What You'll Learn

▶ The functions of the respiratory system
▶ How oxygen and carbon dioxide are exchanged in the lungs and in tissues
▶ The pathway of air in and out of the lungs
▶ Three effects of smoking on the respiratory system

Vocabulary

pharynx	diaphragm
larynx	chronic
trachea	bronchitis
bronchi	emphysema
alveoli	asthma

Why It's Important

▶ Your respiratory system supplies oxygen and removes carbon dioxide from your body.

Functions of the Respiratory System

People have always known that air and food are needed for life. However, until about 225 years ago, no one knew why air was so important. At that time, a British chemist discovered that a mouse couldn't live in a container in which a candle had previously been burned. He reasoned that a gas in the air of the container had been destroyed when the candle burned. He also discovered that if he put a plant into the container, whatever was necessary for life returned in eight or nine days, and a mouse again could live in the container. What do you think the plant produced when it was in the container? Think about photosynthesis. It had produced the gas needed for life that was later named oxygen.

Breathing and Respiration

People often get the terms *breathing* and *respiration* confused. Breathing is the process whereby fresh air moves into and stale air moves out of lungs. Fresh air contains oxygen, which passes from the lungs into your circulatory system. Blood then carries the oxygen to your individual cells. At the same time, your digestive system has prepared a supply of

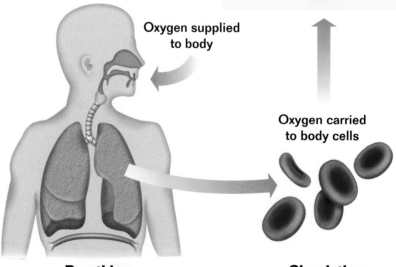

Figure 21-1 Several processes are involved in how the body obtains, transports, and utilizes oxygen.

Oxygen used in chemical reaction to release energy from glucose

Respiration

Oxygen supplied to body

Oxygen carried to body cells

Breathing
(inhale)

Circulation

Figure 21-2 Mount Everest is the highest place on Earth. Mountain climbers experience headaches, nausea, and shortness of breath while ascending to the top of high mountains.

glucose in your cells from digested food. Now, the oxygen plays a key role in the chemical reaction that releases energy from glucose. This chemical reaction, shown in the equation in **Figure 21-1,** is called respiration. Carbon dioxide is a waste product of respiration. At the end of this reaction, carbon dioxide wastes are carried back to your lungs in your blood. There, it is expelled from your body with the stale air. ☑

Figure 21-2 shows a place where there is decreased air pressure. The air is less dense at extreme heights, so there are fewer oxygen molecules in every breath you take. Why would it be harder to breathe on top of mountains?

$$C_6H_{12}O_6 + 6O_2 \rightarrow 6CO_2 + 6H_2O + Energy$$

(Glucose) + (Oxygen) → (Carbon dioxide) + (Water) + (Energy)

Respiration

Reading Check ☑

What is the difference between breathing and respiration?

Carbon dioxide exhaled

Carbon dioxide waste expelled

Carbon dioxide removed from cells to lungs

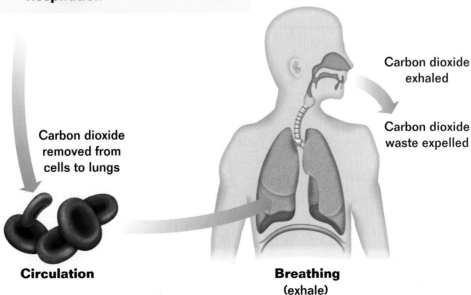

Circulation

Breathing
(exhale)

Compare the composition of the air you inhale and the air you exhale by making two circle graphs. Inhaled air is made up of 78.62 percent nitrogen, 0.5 percent water vapor, 0.04 percent carbon dioxide, and 20.84 percent oxygen. Exhaled air is made up of 74.5 percent nitrogen, 6.2 percent water vapor, 3.6 percent carbon dioxide, and 15.7 percent oxygen.

Organs of the Respiratory System

Your respiratory system is made up of body parts that help move oxygen into your body and carbon dioxide out of your body. The major structures and organs of your respiratory system are shown in **Figure 21-3.** These include your nasal cavity, pharynx (FER ingks), larynx (LER ingks), trachea (TRAY kee uh), bronchi (BRAHN ki), bronchioles (BRAHN kee ohlz), lungs, and alveoli. Air enters your body through two openings in your nose called nostrils or through your mouth. Once inside the nostrils, hair traps dust from the air. From your nostrils, air passes through your nasal cavity, where it gets moistened and warmed. Glands that produce sticky mucus line the nasal cavity. The mucus traps dust, pollen, and other materials that were not trapped by the nasal hair. This helps filter and clean the air you breathe. Tiny hair-like structures, called cilia, move mucus and trapped material to the back of the throat where it can be swallowed.

Figure 21-3 Air can enter the body through both the nostrils and the mouth. **What is the advantage of having air enter through the nostrils?**

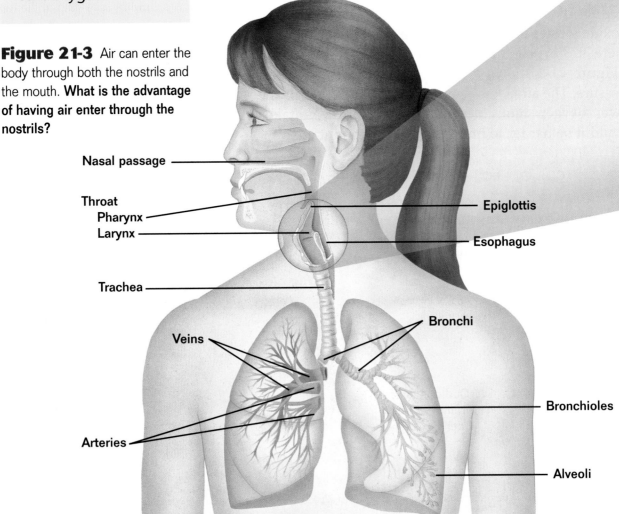

Nasal passage

Throat
Pharynx
Larynx

Epiglottis

Esophagus

Trachea

Bronchi

Veins

Bronchioles

Arteries

Alveoli

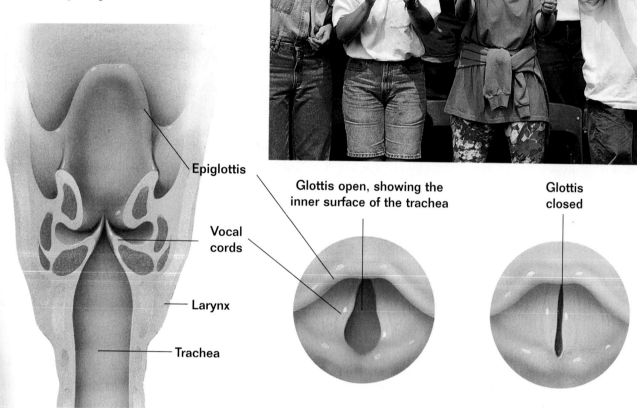

Figure 21-4 Sound made by your vocal cords gets louder with increased air pressure. Pitch gets higher as muscles pull your vocal cords tighter, thus causing the glottis to close.

Epiglottis

Vocal cords

Larynx

Trachea

Glottis open, showing the inner surface of the trachea

Glottis closed

Pharynx, Larynx, and Trachea

Warm, moist air now moves to the **pharynx,** a tubelike passageway for both food and air. At the lower end of the pharynx is a flap of tissue called the epiglottis. When you swallow, the epiglottis folds down over the glottis, the opening between your vocal cords. By doing this, food or liquid is prevented from entering your larynx. The food goes into your esophagus instead. What do you think could happen if you talk or laugh while eating?

The **larynx** is the airway to which your vocal cords are attached. Look at **Figure 21-4.** When you speak, muscles tighten or loosen your vocal cords. Sound is produced when air moves past, causing them to vibrate.

Below the larynx is the **trachea,** a tube about 12 cm in length. C-shaped rings of cartilage keep the trachea open and prevent it from collapsing. The trachea is lined with mucous membranes and cilia to trap dust, bacteria, and pollen. Why is it necessary for the trachea to stay open all the time?

Mini Lab

Measuring Surface Area

Procedure

1. Make a cylinder out of a large sheet of paper. Tape it together.

2. Make cylinders out of small sheets of paper. Place as many as will fit inside the large cylinder without crushing the cylinders.

3. Unroll each cylinder. Place the small sheets next to each other in a rectangle. Lay the large sheet on top.

Analysis

1. Compare the surface area of the large sheet with all the small sheets put together.

2. What do the large sheet and small sheets represent?

3. How does this make gas exchange more efficient?

The Bronchi and the Lungs

At the lower end of the trachea are two short branches, called **bronchi** (singular, *bronchus*), that carry air into the lungs. Your lungs take up most of the space in your chest cavity. Within the lungs, the bronchi branch into smaller and smaller tubes. The smallest tubes are the bronchioles. At the end of each bronchiole are clusters of tiny, thin-walled sacs called **alveoli** (al VE uh li). As shown in **Figure 21-5,** lungs are actually masses of alveoli arranged in grapelike clusters. Capillaries surround the alveoli. The exchange of oxygen and carbon dioxide takes place between the alveoli and capillaries. This happens easily because the walls of the alveoli and the walls of the capillaries are only one cell thick. Oxygen diffuses through the walls of the alveoli and then through the walls of the capillaries into the blood. There the oxygen is picked up by hemoglobin in red blood cells and carried to all body cells. Hemoglobin is a chemical that can carry oxygen and carbon dioxide. As this takes place, carbon dioxide is transported back from body cells in the blood. It diffuses through the walls of the capillaries and through the walls of the alveoli. Carbon dioxide then leaves your body when you breathe out, or exhale.

Figure 21-5 About 300 million alveoli are in each lung. The exchange of oxygen and carbon dioxide with the environment takes place between the alveoli and the surrounding capillaries. **What is the name for the energy-releasing process that is fueled by oxygen?**

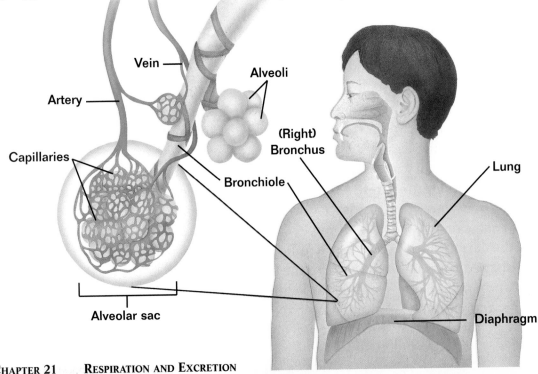

Vein

Alveoli

Artery

(Right) Bronchus

Capillaries

Bronchiole

Lung

Alveolar sac

Diaphragm

How You Breathe

Breathing is partly the result of changes in air pressure. Under normal conditions, a gas moves from an area of high pressure to an area of low pressure. When you squeeze an empty plastic bottle, air rushes out. This happens because pressure outside the top of the bottle is less than inside the bottle while your hand is gripping it. As you release your grip on the bottle, the pressure inside the bottle becomes less than outside the bottle. Air rushes back in, and the bottle resumes its shape.

Inhale and Exhale

Your lungs work in a similar way to the squeezed bottle. Your **diaphragm** (DI uh fram) is a muscle beneath your lungs that helps move air in and out of your body. It contracts and relaxes when you breathe. Like your hands on the plastic bottle, the diaphragm exerts pressure or relieves pressure on your lungs. **Figure 21-6** illustrates breathing.

Figure 21-6 Your lungs inhale and exhale about 500 mL of air with an average breath. This may increase to 2000 mL of air per breath when you do strenuous physical activity.

VISUALIZING Breathing

A When you inhale, your diaphragm contracts and moves down. The upward movement of your rib cage and the downward movement of your diaphragm cause the volume of your chest cavity to increase. Air pressure is reduced in your chest cavity. Air under pressure outside the body pushes into your air passageways and lungs. Your lungs expand as the air rushes into them.

B When you exhale, your diaphragm relaxes and moves up to return to its dome shape. Your rib cage moves downward. These two actions reduce the size of your chest cavity. Your lungs also return to their original position. Pressure on your lungs is increased by these two actions. The gases inside your lungs are pushed out through the air passages.

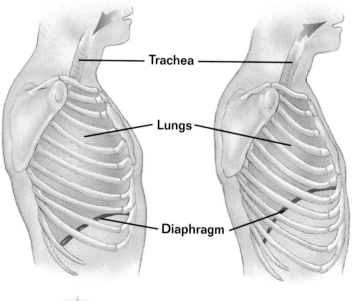

Inhale

Exhale

Trachea

Lungs

Diaphragm

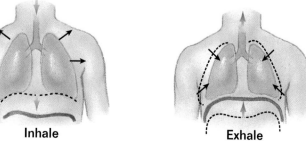

Inhale

Exhale

A Life-Saving Maneuver

The epiglottis closes over your larynx to stop food from entering the trachea. Sometimes, this process does not happen quickly enough. Each year, thousands of people die because food or other objects become lodged in the trachea. Air flow between the lungs and the mouth and nasal cavity is blocked. Death can occur in a matter of minutes.

Pressure Dislodges the Food

Rescuers use abdominal thrusts (also called the Heimlich maneuver), **Figure 21-7,** to save the life of a choking victim. **CAUTION:** *This maneuver can cause harm and should be done only if necessary.* The theory behind this maneuver is to use pressure to force out the food or object. When the diaphragm is forced up, the volume of the chest cavity quickly decreases. Pressure is suddenly increased. Air is forced up in the trachea. There may be enough force to dislodge food or an object. The victim is able to breathe again.

Figure 21-7 Abdominal thrusts are used to save a person from choking.

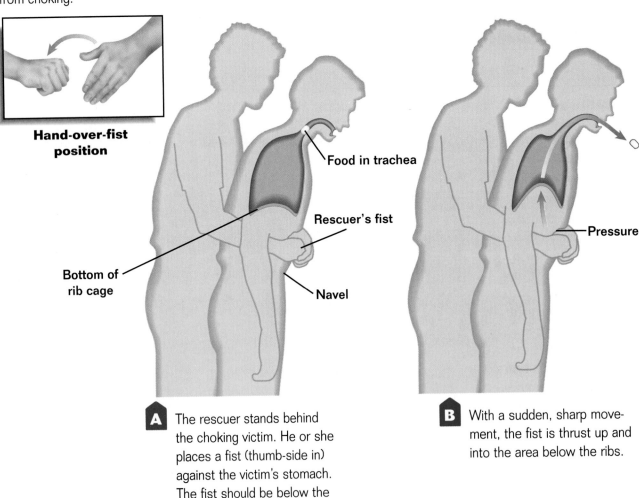

Hand-over-fist position

Food in trachea

Rescuer's fist

Bottom of rib cage

Navel

Pressure

A The rescuer stands behind the choking victim. He or she places a fist (thumb-side in) against the victim's stomach. The fist should be below the ribs and above the navel.

B With a sudden, sharp movement, the fist is thrust up and into the area below the ribs.

Diseases and Disorders

If you were asked to list some of the things that can harm your respiratory system, you would probably put smoking at the top. Many serious diseases are related to smoking. Being around others who smoke also can harm your respiratory system. Smoking, polluted air, and coal dust have been related to respiratory problems such as bronchitis, emphysema, cancer, and asthma.

Chronic Bronchitis

Bronchitis is a disease in which the bronchial tubes are irritated and too much mucus is produced. Many cases of bronchitis clear up within a few weeks, but sometimes the disease will last for a long time. When bronchitis persists for a long time, it is called **chronic bronchitis.** Many cases of chronic bronchitis result from smoking. People who have chronic bronchitis cough often to try to clear the mucus from the airway, as **Figure 21-8** shows. However, the more a person coughs, the more the cilia and bronchial tubes can be harmed. When cilia are damaged, their ability to move mucus, bacteria, and dirt particles out of the lungs is impaired. If this happens, harmful substances, such as sticky tar from burning tobacco, build up in the airways. Sometimes, scar tissue forms, impairing the ability of the respiratory system to function.

*inter***NET**
CONNECTION

Visit the Glencoe Science Web Site at **www.glencoe.com/ sec/science** for more information about lung disease.

Figure 21-8 Cilia help trap and move foreign matter that enters your respiratory passageways.

A Coughing is a reflex that moves unwanted matter from respiratory passages.

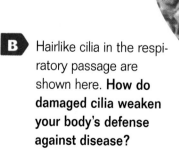

B Hairlike cilia in the respiratory passage are shown here. **How do damaged cilia weaken your body's defense against disease?**

Magnification: 3500 ×

Figure 21-9 Lung diseases can have major effects on breathing.

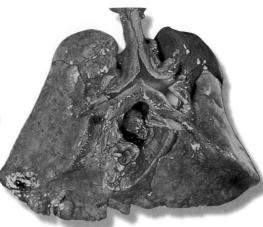

A A normal, healthy lung can exchange oxygen and carbon dioxide effectively.

B A diseased lung cuts down on the amount of oxygen that can be delivered to body cells.

C Emphysema may take 20 to 30 years to develop.

Using Math

At the beginning of this chapter, you determined your breathing rate for one minute. Use that number to calculate how many breaths you take in a day. If every two breaths filled a liter bottle, how many bottles would you fill in a day?

Emphysema

A disease in which the alveoli in the lungs lose their ability to expand and contract is called **emphysema** (em fuh SEE muh). Most cases of emphysema result from smoking. In fact, many smokers who are afflicted with chronic bronchitis eventually progress to emphysema. When a person has emphysema, cells in the bronchi become inflamed. An enzyme released by the cells causes the alveoli to stretch and lose their elasticity. As a result, alveoli can't push air out of the lungs. Less oxygen moves into the bloodstream from the alveoli. Blood becomes low in oxygen and high in carbon dioxide. This condition results in shortness of breath. As shown in **Figure 21-9,** some people with emphysema can't blow out a match or walk up a flight of stairs. Because the heart works harder to supply oxygen to body cells, people who have emphysema often develop heart problems, as well.

Lung Cancer

Lung cancer is the third leading cause of death in men and women in the United States. Inhaling the tar in cigarette smoke is the greatest contributing factor to lung cancer. Once in the body, tar and other ingredients found in smoke are changed into carcinogens (kar SIHN uh junz). These carcinogens trigger lung cancer by causing uncontrolled growth of cells in lung tissue. Smoking also is believed to be a factor in the development of cancer of the mouth, esophagus, larynx, and pancreas. **Figure 21-10** shows one way people are encouraged not to smoke.

Asthma

Some lung disorders are common in nonsmokers. **Asthma** (AZ muh) is a disorder of the lungs in which there may be shortness of breath, wheezing, or coughing. When a person has an asthma attack, the bronchial tubes contract quickly. Asthma attacks are generally treated by inhaling drugs that enlarge the bronchial tubes. Asthma is often an allergic reaction. An asthma attack can result from a reaction to breathing certain substances, such as cigarette smoke or plant pollen. Eating certain foods or stress also have been related to the onset of asthma attacks.

Except for certain bacteria, all living things would die without oxygen. Your respiratory system takes in oxygen and gets rid of carbon dioxide. This system also helps get rid of some pathogens. You can help keep your respiratory system healthy by avoiding smoking and breathing polluted air. Regular exercise helps increase your body's ability to use oxygen.

Figure 21-10 More than 85 percent of all lung cancer is related to smoking.

Section Assessment

1. What is the main function of the respiratory system?
2. How are oxygen and carbon dioxide gases exchanged in the lungs and in body tissues?
3. What causes air to move in and out of the lungs?
4. How does emphysema affect a person's alveoli?
5. **Think Critically:** How is the work of the digestive and circulatory systems related to the respiratory system?
6.  **Skill Builder**
   Making Models Lungs are important organs used in the process of respiration. Do the **Chapter 21 Skill Activity** on page 746 and make a model of how lungs function.

Science Journal
Use library references to find out about a lung disease common among coal miners, stonecutters, and sandblasters. In your Science Journal, write a paragraph about the symptoms of this disease. Research what safety measures are now required when working with coal and rock.

The Effects of Exercise on Respiration

Breathing rate increases with an increase in physical activity. A bromothymol blue solution changes color when carbon dioxide is bubbled into it. Can you predict whether there will be a difference in the time it takes for the solution to change color before and after exercise?

Possible Materials

- Clock or watch with second hand
- Drinking straws
- Bromothymol blue solution (200 mL)
- Glass cups (12 oz) (2)
  * *beakers (400 mL) (2)*
- Metric measuring cup
  * *graduated cylinder (100 mL)*
  * *Alternate Materials*

Recognize the Problem

How will an increase in physical activity affect the amount of carbon dioxide exhaled?

Form a Hypothesis

State a hypothesis about how exercise will affect the amount of carbon dioxide exhaled by the lungs.

Goals

- **Observe** the effects of the amount of carbon dioxide on the bromothymol blue solution.

- **Design an experiment** that tests the effects of a variable, such as the amount of carbon dioxide exhaled before and after exercise, on the rate at which the solution changes color.

Safety Precautions

Protect clothing from the solution. Wash hands after using the solution. **CAUTION:** *Do not inhale the solution through the straw.*

Test Your Hypothesis

Plan

1. As a group, agree upon and **write out** the hypothesis statement.

2. As a group, **list** the steps that you will need to take to test your hypothesis. Consider each of the following factors. How will you introduce the exhaled air into the bromothymol blue solution? How will you collect data on exhaled air before and after physical activity? What kind of activity is involved? How long will it go?

3. **List** your materials. Your teacher will provide instruction on safe procedures for using bromothymol blue.

4. **Design** a data table and **record** it in your Science Journal so that it is ready to use as your group collects data.

5. **Read** over your entire experiment to make sure that all the steps are in logical order.

6. **Identify** any constants, variables, and controls of the experiment.

Do

1. Make sure your teacher approves your plan before you proceed.

2. Carry out the experiment as planned.

3. While the experiment is going on, write down any observations that you make and complete the data table in your Science Journal.

Analyze Your Data

1. What caused the bromothymol blue solution to change color? What color was it at the conclusion of each test?

2. What was the control? What was the constant(s)? What was the variable(s)?

3. **Compare** the time it took the bromothymol blue solution to change color before exercise and after exercise. Explain any difference.

4. Prepare a table of your data and **graph** the results.

Draw Conclusions

1. Did exercise affect your rate of respiration? Explain your answer using data from your experiment.

2. Using your graph, **estimate** the time of color change if the time of your physical activity were twice as long.

Scuba

For humans, having a constant supply of oxygen is a matter of life or death. People get the oxygen they need from the air they breathe. This means swimmers can stay underwater only for as long as they can hold their breath. Those who want to dive deeper and stay underwater longer must use scuba equipment. Scuba stands for Self-Contained Underwater Breathing Apparatus.

GEARED FOR THE DEPTHS

Three pieces of equipment (on the diver, right) enable divers to spend a longer period of time underwater: (1) a buoyancy-control device, or BCD, (2) a scuba tank, and (3) a regulator.

1 **BCD** Before the dive, the BCD—an inflatable vest or jacket—is partially filled with air. The diver descends by letting air out of the BCD. The diver maintains his or her position at different depths by controlling the amount of air in the BCD.

2 **Scuba tank** Worn on the diver's back, the tank holds a large amount of compressed air—air that has been squeezed into a smaller space under high pressure. The diver breathes the air in this tank while underwater. The compressed air in the scuba tank also is used to add air to the BCD to increase a diver's buoyancy (make a diver rise in the water).

3 **Regulator** On the water's surface, air pressure in the lungs is equal to outside air pressure, measured as atmospheres (atm). Pressure increases at a rate of 1 atm for each 10 m underwater. As a diver descends, the regulator automatically compensates for the increase in depth (and thus, pressure). So, the regulator supplies air from the tank to the diver at the same pressure as the surrounding water. The diver never feels squeezed by the increased pressure of the deeper water.

Think Critically

1. The volume of air increases as pressure decreases. Relate this to the fact that divers should never hold their breath as they ascend.
2. Why does a diver use a weight belt in addition to a BCD when diving?

Career
CONNECTION

Professional scuba divers are paid to dive for specific purposes. Professional divers work for the military, the government, and commercial agencies. A military diver may look for a hidden bomb under the sea. A commercial diver may work on an oil platform. Law enforcement agencies often hire divers to look for missing bodies or weapons.

The Excretory System

Functions of the Excretory System

Just as wastes, in the form of sewage or garbage, are removed from your home, your body also eliminates wastes by means of your excretory system. Undigested material is eliminated by your digestive system. The waste gas, carbon dioxide, is eliminated through the combined efforts of your circulatory and respiratory systems. Some salts are eliminated when you sweat. Together, these systems function as a part of your excretory system. If wastes aren't eliminated, you can become sick. Toxic substances build up and damage organs. If not corrected, serious illness or death occurs.

Figure 21-11 shows how the urinary system functions as a part of the excretory system. The organs of your urinary system are excretory organs. Your **urinary system** is made up of organs that rid your blood of wastes produced by the metabolism of nutrients. This system also controls blood volume by removing excess water produced by body cells. A specific amount of water in blood is important to maintain normal blood pressure, the movement of gases, and excretion of solid wastes. Your urinary system also balances specific concentrations of certain salts and water that must be present for cell activities to take place.

What You'll Learn

- ► How to distinguish between the excretory and urinary systems
- ► How to describe how your kidneys work
- ► What happens when urinary organs don't work

Vocabulary

urinary system	urine
kidney	ureter
nephron	bladder
	urethra

Why It's Important

- ► The urinary system helps clean your blood.

Figure 21-11 The urinary system is linked with the digestive, circulatory, and respiratory systems, as well as skin to make up the excretory system.

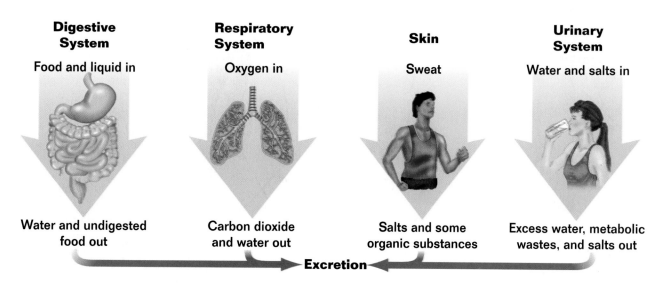

Digestive System	Respiratory System	Skin	Urinary System
Food and liquid in	Oxygen in	Sweat	Water and salts in
Water and undigested food out	Carbon dioxide and water out	Salts and some organic substances	Excess water, metabolic wastes, and salts out

Excretion

Organs of the Urinary System

The major organs of your urinary system, as shown in **Figure 21-12,** are two bean-shaped kidneys. Kidneys are located on the back wall of the abdomen at about waist level. The **kidneys** filter blood that has collected wastes from cells. All of your blood passes through your kidneys many times a day. In **Figure 21-12,** you can see that blood enters the kidneys through a large artery and leaves through a large vein.

The Filtering Unit

Each kidney is made up of about 1 million **nephrons** (NEF rahnz), the tiny filtering units of the kidney. Each nephron has a cuplike structure and a duct. Blood moves from the renal artery to capillaries in the cuplike structure. Water, sugar, salt, and wastes from your blood pass into the cuplike structure. From there, the liquid is squeezed into a narrow tubule. Capillaries that surround the tubule reabsorb most of the water, sugar, and salt and return it to the blood. These capillaries merge to form small veins. The small veins merge to form the renal veins, which return purified blood to your main circulatory system. The liquid left behind flows into collecting tubules in each kidney. This waste liquid, or **urine,** contains excess water, salts, and other wastes not reabsorbed by the body. The average adult produces about 1 L of urine per day.

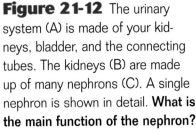

*inter*NET
CONNECTION

Visit the Glencoe Science Web Site at **www.glencoe.com/ sec/science** for more information about how kidneys work.

Figure 21-12 The urinary system (A) is made of your kidneys, bladder, and the connecting tubes. The kidneys (B) are made up of many nephrons (C). A single nephron is shown in detail. **What is the main function of the nephron?**

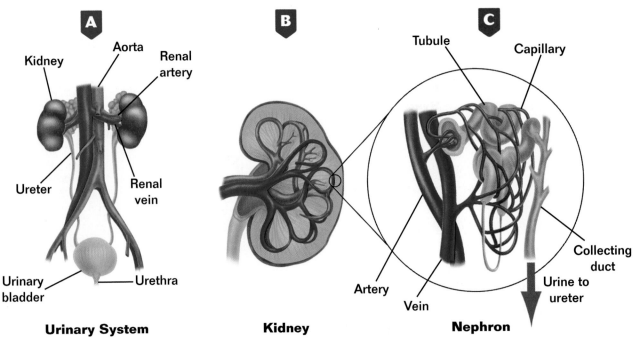

A

Kidney Aorta Renal artery

Ureter

Renal vein

Urinary bladder Urethra

Urinary System

B

Kidney

C

Tubule Capillary

Artery Vein Collecting duct Urine to ureter

Nephron

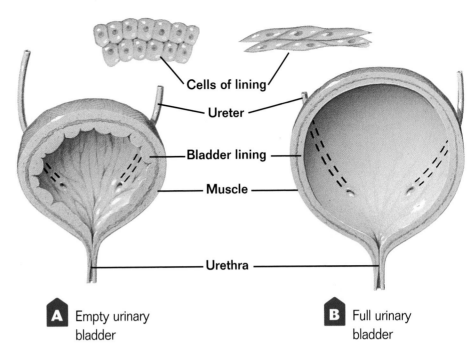

Figure 21-13 The elastic walls of the bladder can stretch to hold up to 500 mL of urine. When empty, the bladder looks wrinkled (A). The cells of the lining are thick. When full, the bladder looks similar to an inflated balloon (B). The cells of the lining are stretched and thin.

Cells of lining

Ureter

Bladder lining

Muscle

Urethra

A Empty urinary bladder

B Full urinary bladder

Urine Collection and Release

The urine in each collecting tubule drains into a funnel-shaped area of each kidney that leads to the ureters (YER ut urz). **Ureters** are tubes that lead from each kidney to the bladder. The **bladder** is an elastic, muscular organ that holds urine until it leaves the body. **Figure 21-13** shows how the shape of the cells that make up the lining of the bladder changes with the amount of urine stored in it. A tube called the **urethra** (yoo REE thruh) carries urine from the bladder to the outside of the body.

Other Water Loss

Other parts of the excretory system also help your body maintain proper fluid levels. In addition to losing salt, an adult loses about 0.5 L of water each day through perspiration. When air is exhaled, you also lose water. When you see your breath on a cold day or breathe on a cold windowpane and notice water vapor, you see this moisture. Each day, about 350 mL of water are removed from your body through your respiratory system. A small amount of water also is expelled with the undigested material that passes out of your digestive system.

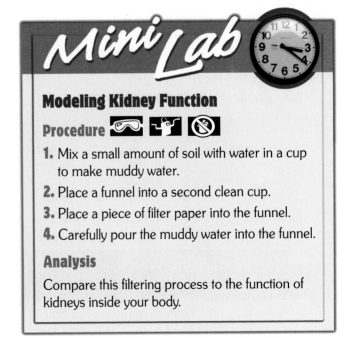

Mini Lab

Modeling Kidney Function

Procedure

1. Mix a small amount of soil with water in a cup to make muddy water.
2. Place a funnel into a second clean cup.
3. Place a piece of filter paper into the funnel.
4. Carefully pour the muddy water into the funnel.

Analysis

Compare this filtering process to the function of kidneys inside your body.

Figure 21-14 The amount of urine that you eliminate each day is determined by the level of a hormone. This hormone is produced by your hypothalamus.

Balancing Fluid Levels

To maintain good health, the fluid levels within your body must be balanced and your blood pressure must be maintained. This happens because an area of your brain, the hypothalamus, is involved in controlling your body's homeostasis (hoh mee oh STAY sus). The hypothalamus produces a hormone that regulates how much urine is produced. **Figure 21-14** shows what happens when there is too much water in your blood.

Increased level of liquid in blood

Hypothalamus

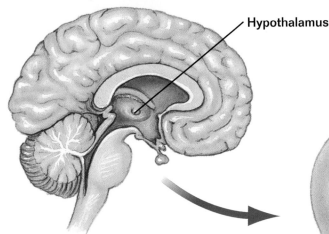

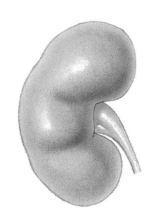

B This release signals the kidneys to return less water to the blood and increase the amount of urine excreted.

A Your brain detects too much water in your blood. Your hypothalamus then releases a lesser amount of hormone.

Problem Solving

Analyzing Water Gain and Loss

Cell activity and body functions depend on water. The balance of water must be maintained. Table A shows the major sources by which body water is gained.

Table B lists the major sources by which body water is lost.

Construct tables and calculate the percentages of sources of gain and loss of water. Complete your table with these data.

Think Critically

1. What is the greatest source of liquids gained by your body?

2. How would the percentages of water gained and lost change in a person who was working in extremely warm temperatures? What organ of the body would be the greatest contributor to water loss?

Table A

Major Sources by Which Body Water Is Gained		
Source	Amount (mL)	Percent
Oxidation of nutrients	250	
Foods	750	
Liquids	1500	
Total	**2500**	

Table B

Major Sources by Which Body Water Is Lost		
Source	Amount (mL)	Percent
Urine	1500	
Skin	500	
Lungs	350	
Feces	150	
Total	**2500**	

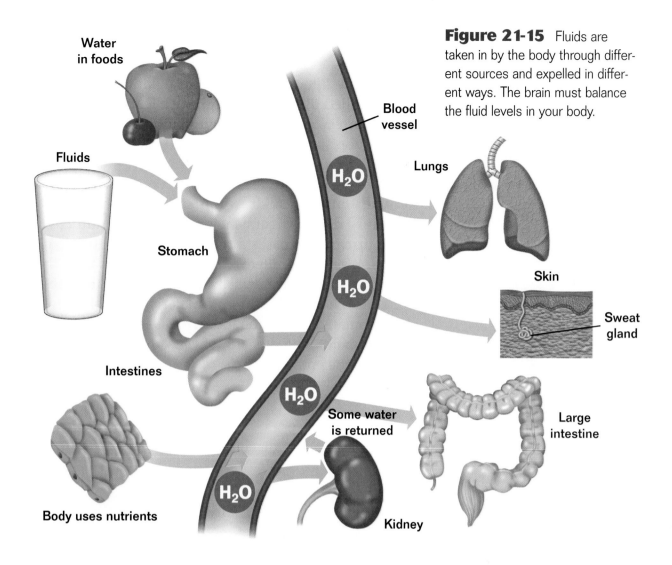

Water in foods

Fluids

Stomach

Intestines

Body uses nutrients

Blood vessel

H_2O

H_2O

H_2O

Some water is returned

H_2O

Kidney

Lungs

Skin

Sweat gland

Large intestine

Figure 21-15 Fluids are taken in by the body through different sources and expelled in different ways. The brain must balance the fluid levels in your body.

If too little water is in the blood, more of the hormone is released by your hypothalamus and more water is returned to the blood. The amount of urine excreted decreases. At the same time, your brain sends a signal that causes you to feel thirsty. You drink liquids to quench this thirst. **Figure 21-15** illustrates the different sources of fluid intake and output within your body.

Diseases and Disorders

What happens when someone's urinary organs don't work properly? Waste products that are not removed build up and act as poisons in body cells. Water that normally is removed from body tissues accumulates and causes swelling of the ankles and feet. Sometimes, fluids also can build up around the heart. The heart must work harder to move less blood to the lungs. Without excretion, an imbalance of salts may occur. The body responds by trying to restore this balance. If the balance is not restored, the kidneys and other organs can be damaged.

PHYSICS
INTEGRATION

Kidney Stones
Small, solid particles may form in the kidneys. If these stones pass into the ureter, severe pain results. One method of kidney stone removal involves the use of a lithotripter. This machine produces sound waves that cause the stones to break into small pieces. These pieces are carried out of the body in urine.

Dialysis

Persons who have damaged kidneys may need to have their blood filtered by an artificial kidney machine in a process called dialysis (di AL uh sus). During dialysis, blood from an artery is pumped through tubing that is bathed in a salt solution similar to blood plasma. Waste materials diffuse from the tube containing blood and are washed away by the salt solution. The cleaned blood is returned to a vein. A person with only one kidney can still function normally. An alternative dialysis treatment is pictured in **Figure 21-16**. ☑

The urinary system is a purifying unit for the circulatory system. Wastes are filtered from blood as it passes through the kidneys. Some water, salts, and nutrients are reabsorbed to maintain homeostasis. Waste materials, dissolved in water, are eliminated from the body. This system helps to maintain the health of cells and, therefore, the entire body.

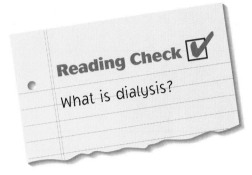

Reading Check ☑

What is dialysis?

Figure 21-16 Peritoneal hemodialysis is a procedure that can be done at home for many dialysis patients. Dialysis fluid is pumped into the stomach cavity. Waste products then move from the blood vessels into the fluid, which is then drained from the patient.

Section Assessment

1. Describe the functions of the urinary system.

2. Explain how the kidneys remove wastes and keep fluids and salts in balance.

3. Compare the excretory and urinary systems.

4. **Think Critically:** Explain why reabsorption of certain materials in the kidneys is important.

5. **Skill Builder**
   Concept Mapping Using a network tree concept map, compare the excretory functions of the kidneys and the lungs. If you need help, refer to Concept Mapping in the **Skill Handbook** on page 698.

Using Math

All 5 L of blood in the body pass through the kidneys in approximately five minutes. Calculate the average rate of flow through the kidneys in liters per minute.

Kidney Structure

Materials

- Large animal kidney
- Scalpel
- Hand lens

As your body uses nutrients, wastes are created. One role of kidneys is to filter waste products out of the bloodstream and excrete this waste outside the body.

What You'll Investigate

How does the structure of the kidney relate to its function?

Goals

- **Observe** the external and internal structures of a kidney.

Procedure

1. **Examine** the kidney supplied by your teacher.
2. If the kidney is still encased in fat, **peel** the fat off carefully.
3. Using a scalpel, carefully **cut** the tissue lengthwise in half around the outline of the kidney. This cut should result in a section similar to the illustration on this page.
4. **Observe** the internal features of the kidney using a hand lens, or view the features in a model.
5. **Compare** the specimen or model with the kidneys in the illustration.
6. **Draw** the kidney in your Science Journal and **label** the structures.

Conclude and Apply

1. What part makes up the cortex of the kidney? Why is this part red?
2. What is the main function of nephrons?
3. The medulla of the kidney is made up of a network of tubules that come together to form the ureter. What is the function of this network of tubules?
4. How can the kidney be compared to a portable water-purifying system?

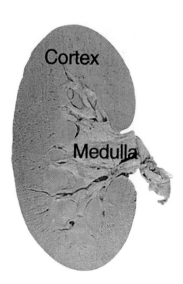

Cortex

Medulla

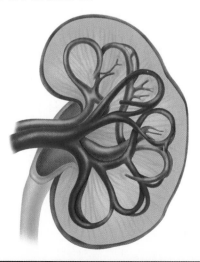

For a **preview** of this chapter, study this Reviewing Main Ideas before you read the chapter. After you have studied this chapter, you can use the Reviewing Main Ideas to **review** the chapter.

The Glencoe MindJogger, Audiocassettes, and CD-ROM provide additional opportunities for review.

Section

21-1 THE RESPIRATORY SYSTEM

Your respiratory system helps take oxygen into your lungs and body cells and helps you remove carbon dioxide. Inhaled air passes through the nasal cavity, **pharynx, larynx, trachea, bronchi,** and bronchioles and into the **alveoli** of the lungs. The mechanism of breathing results in part from the **diaphragm's** movement, which changes the pressure within the lungs. *Why does the trachea have cartilage but the esophagus does not?*

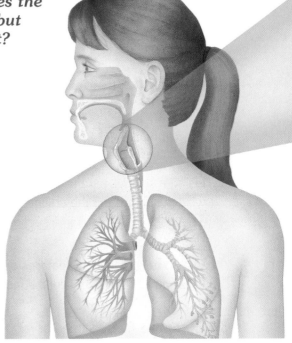

DISEASES AND DISORDERS

Many serious respiratory problems are related to smoking. In addition to smoking, polluted air and coal dust also have been associated with diseases such as **chronic bronchitis, emphysema,** lung cancer, and **asthma.** *Which respiratory disease is the third leading cause of death in men and women in the United States?*

21-2 THE EXCRETORY SYSTEM

Reading Check ✔

What probable outcome could you predict for a young person who begins smoking? What is the basis for your prediction?

Your **urinary system** is made up of organs that rid your blood of wastes produced by the metabolism of nutrients. It also controls blood volume by removing excess water produced by body cells. **Kidneys** are the major organs of the urinary system. They filter wastes from your body and keep sodium, water, and other chemicals in balance. When kidneys fail to work, dialysis may be used. In addition to the urinary system, parts of the digestive, circulatory, and respiratory systems work together as the excretory system. *How do the kidneys maintain homeostasis?*

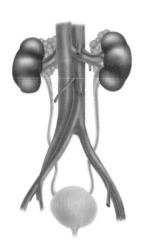
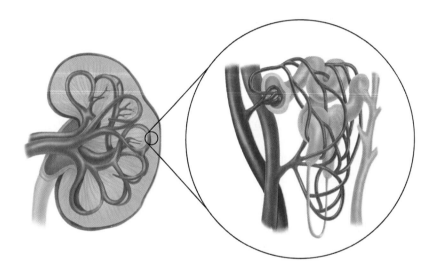

Career
CONNECTION

DR. BENJAMIN CARSON, SURGEON

Dr. Benjamin Carson is a surgeon at Johns Hopkins Hospital. Dr. Carson says that operating on a patient is like if you were a tightrope walker: If you are experienced, walking the rope isn't frightening, but if you haven't done it before, it can be scary. Dr. Carson admits that operating is sometimes taxing—especially when you do it for 16 hours at a stretch. Dr. Carson encourages young people to ask themselves, "What have I always been good at?" and to ask other people what they see that you're good at. *What problems of the respiratory system and excretory system could require surgery?*

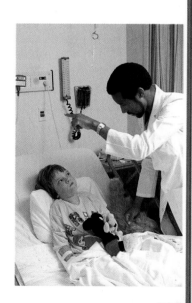

Chapter 21 Assessment

Using Vocabulary

a. alveoli
b. asthma
c. bladder
d. bronchi
e. chronic bronchitis
f. diaphragm
g. emphysema
h. kidney
i. larynx
j. nephron
k. pharynx
l. trachea
m. ureter
n. urethra
o. urinary system
p. urine

Using the list above, replace the underlined words with the correct Vocabulary term.

1. At the lower end of the <u>tubelike passageway for both food and air</u> is a flap of tissue called the epiglottis.
2. At the lower end of the trachea are two <u>short branches that carry air into the lungs.</u>
3. Each kidney is made up of about 1 million <u>tiny filtering units.</u>
4. <u>An elastic, muscular organ</u> holds urine until it leaves the body.
5. <u>A tube</u> carries urine from the bladder to the outside of the body.

Checking Concepts

Choose the word or phrase that best answers the question.

6. When you inhale, which of the following contracts and moves down?
   A) bronchioles   C) nephrons
   B) diaphragm   D) kidneys
7. Air is moistened, filtered, and warmed in which of the following structures?
   A) larynx   C) nasal cavity
   B) pharynx   D) trachea
8. Exchange of gases occurs between capillaries and which of the following structures?
   A) alveoli   C) bronchioles
   B) bronchi   D) trachea

9. When you exhale, which way does the rib cage move?
   A) It moves up.   C) It moves out.
   B) It moves down.   D) It stays the same.
10. Which of the following is a lung disorder that may occur as an allergic reaction?
    A) asthma   C) emphysema
    B) chronic bronchitis D) cancer
11. Which of the following conditions does smoking worsen?
    A) arthritis   C) excretion
    B) respiration   D) emphysema
12. Which of the following are filtering units of the kidneys?
    A) nephrons   C) neurons
    B) ureters   D) alveoli
13. Urine is temporarily held in which of the following structures?
    A) kidneys   C) ureter
    B) bladder   D) urethra
14. Through which of the following is approximately 1 L of water lost per day?
    A) sweat   C) urine
    B) lungs   D) none of these
15. Which of the following substances is **NOT** reabsorbed by blood after it passes through the kidneys?
    A) salt   C) wastes
    B) sugar   D) water

Thinking Critically

16. Compare air pressure in the lungs during inhalation and exhalation.
17. What is the advantage of the lungs having many air sacs instead of being just two large sacs, like balloons?
18. Explain the damage smoking does to cilia, alveoli, and lungs.
19. What would happen to the blood if the kidneys stopped working?
20. Explain why a large kidney stone is often painful.

Developing Skills

If you need help, refer to the **Skill Handbook.**

21. **Making and Using Graphs:** Make a circle graph of total lung capacity.
    - Tidal volume (inhaled or exhaled during a normal breath) = 500 mL
    - Inspiratory reserve volume (air that can be inhaled forcefully after a normal inhalation) = 3000 mL
    - Expiratory reserve volume (air that can be exhaled forcefully after a normal expiration) = 1100 mL
    - Residual volume (air left in the lungs after forceful exhalation) = 1200 mL

22. **Interpreting Data:** Interpret the data below. How much of each substance is reabsorbed into the blood in the kidneys? What substance is totally excreted in the urine?

Materials Filtered by the Kidneys

Substance	Amount moving through kidney to be filtered	Amount excreted in urine
water	125 L	1 L
salt	350 g	10 g
urea	1 g	1 g
glucose	50 g	0 g

23. **Recognizing Cause and Effect:** Discuss how lack of oxygen is related to lack of energy.

24. **Hypothesizing:** Hypothesize the number of breaths you would expect a person to take per minute in each situation and give a reason for each hypothesis.
    - while sleeping
    - while exercising
    - while on top of Mount Everest

THE PRINCETON REVIEW

Test-Taking Tip

Survey the Surroundings Find out what the conditions will be for taking the test. Will the test be timed? Will you be allowed to take a break? Know these things in advance so that you can practice taking tests under the same conditions.

Test Practice

Use these questions to test your Science Proficiency.

1. Air inhaled through the nose is filtered, warmed, and moistened. What are some benefits of these actions?
   A) The process prevents nitrogen and carbon dioxide from reaching the lungs.
   B) The process prevents bad odors from reaching the trachea and bronchi.
   C) The process prevents drying out of passageways and traps foreign materials.
   D) The process prevents the formation of mucus and cilia in the nasal cavity.

2. Blood flowing through the kidneys is filtered to remove excess materials and wastes. Which of the following are the major substances removed?
   A) salts, sugar, water, and wastes
   B) water, salt, sugar, and urine
   C) carbon dioxide, salt, sugar, and wastes
   D) water, salts, oxygen, and wastes

The Nervous and Endocrine Systems

Chapter Preview

Skills Preview

Skill Builders
- Map Concepts
- Make and Use a Table

Activities
- Compare and Contrast
- Design an Experiment

MiniLabs
- Interpret Data

Reading Check ✓

Before beginning Section 22-1, make a chart that will allow you to compare and contrast the central nervous system and the peripheral nervous system. Fill it in as you read.

Explore Activity

Who's in front of you? What note do we start on? Where's the conductor? Am I marching in rhythm? There's a lot to be aware of when you're part of a marching band. You must be sensitive to your surroundings and aware when changes take place. All organisms must be able to detect what is happening around them. Sights or sounds can warn of danger. Odors can help find food. Sensations of hot and cold can protect from fire or extreme temperatures. In this chapter, you will learn how your body's nervous system interprets all of the sensations it receives to produce a picture of its surroundings. In the following activity, find out whether your eyes can interpret objects correctly.

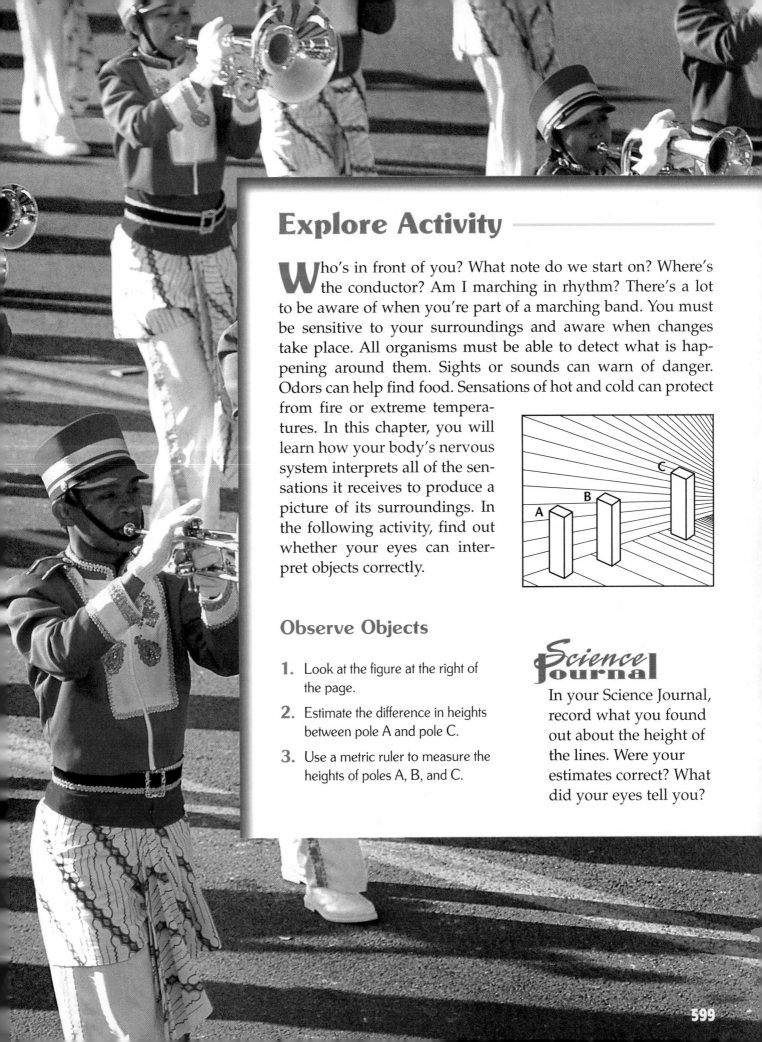

Observe Objects

1. Look at the figure at the right of the page.

2. Estimate the difference in heights between pole A and pole C.

3. Use a metric ruler to measure the heights of poles A, B, and C.

Science Journal

In your Science Journal, record what you found out about the height of the lines. Were your estimates correct? What did your eyes tell you?

The Nervous System

What You'll Learn

► The basic structure of a neuron and how an impulse moves
► Information about the central and peripheral nervous systems
► How drugs affect the body

Vocabulary

neuron
dendrite
axon
synapse
central nervous system
peripheral nervous system
cerebrum
cerebellum
brain stem
reflex

Why It's Important

► Your body can react to your environment because of your nervous system.

The Nervous System at Work

After doing the dishes and finishing your homework, you settle down in your favorite chair and pick up that mystery novel you've been trying to finish. Only three pages to go . . . Who did it? Why did she do it? Then, "CRASH!" You scream and throw your book in the air. What made that unearthly noise? You turn around to find that your dog's wagging tail just swept the lamp off the table beside you. Suddenly, you're aware that your heart is racing and your hands are shaking. But, then, after a few minutes, your breathing returns to normal and your heartbeat is back to its regular rate. What's going on?

Response to Stimuli

The scene described above is an example of how your body responds to changes in its environment and adjusts itself. Your body makes these adjustments with the help of your nervous system. Any change inside or outside your body that brings about a response is called a stimulus. Each day, you're bombarded by thousands of stimuli. Noise, light, the smell of food, and the temperature of the air are all stimuli from outside your body. A growling stomach is an example of an internal stimulus.

How can your body handle all these stimuli? Your body has internal control systems that maintain steady conditions, no matter what's going on outside the body. This is called homeostasis. Breathing rate, heartbeat rate, and digestion are just a few of the activities that are constantly checked and regulated. Your nervous system and the endocrine system, a chemical control system described later in this chapter, are the main ways your body maintains homeostasis.

Figure 22-1 A neuron is made up of a cell body, dendrites, and an axon. **How does the branching of the dendrites allow for more impulses to be picked up by the neuron?**

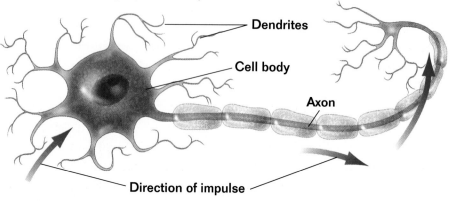

Dendrites

Cell body

Axon

Direction of impulse

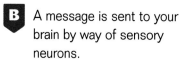

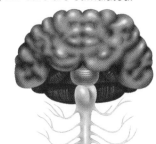

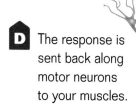

A When you hear the lamp break, sensory receptors in your ears are stimulated.

Figure 22-2 In your nervous system, impulses travel a pathway. Together, the three types of neurons act like a relay team, moving impulses through your body from stimulus to response.

B A message is sent to your brain by way of sensory neurons.

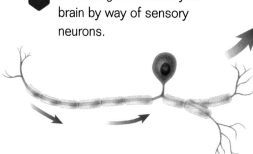

C Your brain sorts the information and determines a response.

D The response is sent back along motor neurons to your muscles.

Neurons

The working unit of the nervous system is the nerve cell, or **neuron** (NOO rahn). The single neuron in **Figure 22-1** is made up of a cell body and branches called dendrites and axons. **Dendrites** receive messages and send them to the cell body. An **axon** (AK sahn) carries messages away from the cell body. Any message carried by a neuron is called an impulse. Notice that the end of the axon branches. This allows the impulses to move to many other muscles, neurons, or glands.

Types of Neurons

Your skin and other sense organs are equipped with structures called receptors that respond to various stimuli. Three types of neurons—sensory neurons, motor neurons, and interneurons—then become involved with transporting impulses about the stimuli. As illustrated in **Figure 22-2,** sensory neurons (B) receive information and send impulses to the brain or spinal cord. Once the impulses reach your brain or spinal cord, interneurons relay the impulses from the sensory to motor neurons. You have more interneurons in your body than either of the other two types of neurons. Motor neurons (D) then conduct impulses from the brain or spinal cord to muscles or glands throughout your body.

E Your heart immediately starts to pound and your breathing rate increases. You throw the book.

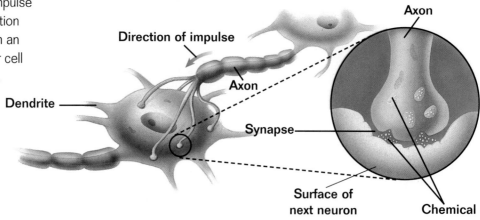

Figure 22-3 An impulse moves in only one direction across a synapse—from an axon to the dendrites or cell body of another neuron.

Direction of impulse

Dendrite

Axon

Axon

Synapse

Surface of next neuron

Chemical

Synapse

Neurons don't touch each other. How does an impulse move from one neuron to another? To get from one neuron to the next, an impulse moves across a small space called a **synapse** (SIHN aps). In **Figure 22-3,** you can see that when an impulse reaches the end of an axon, a chemical is released by the axon. This chemical diffuses across the synapse and starts an impulse in the dendrite or cell body of the next neuron. In this way, an impulse moves from one neuron to another.

The Central Nervous System

Figure 22-4 shows how organs of the nervous system are grouped into two major divisions: the central nervous system (CNS) and the peripheral nervous system (PNS). The **central nervous system** is made up of the brain and spinal cord. The **peripheral** (puh RIHF rul) **nervous system** is made up of all the nerves outside the CNS, including cranial nerves and spinal nerves. These nerves connect the brain and spinal cord to other body parts.

The brain coordinates all your body activities. If someone pokes you in the ribs, your whole body reacts. Your neurons are adapted in such a way that impulses move in only one direction. Sensory neurons send impulses that move from a receptor to the brain or spinal cord.

Figure 22-4 The brain and spinal cord (yellow) form the central nervous system, which sorts and interprets information from stimuli. All other nerves are part of the peripheral nervous system (green).

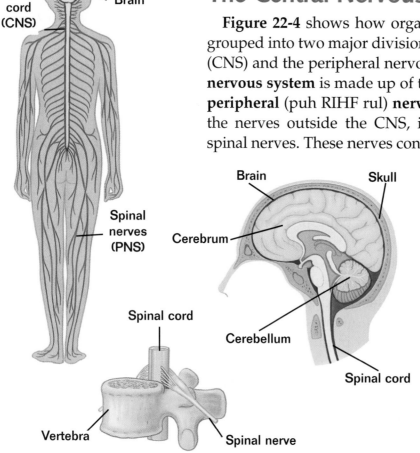

Spinal cord (CNS)

Brain

Spinal nerves (PNS)

Brain

Skull

Cerebrum

Cerebellum

Spinal cord

Spinal cord

Vertebra

Spinal nerve

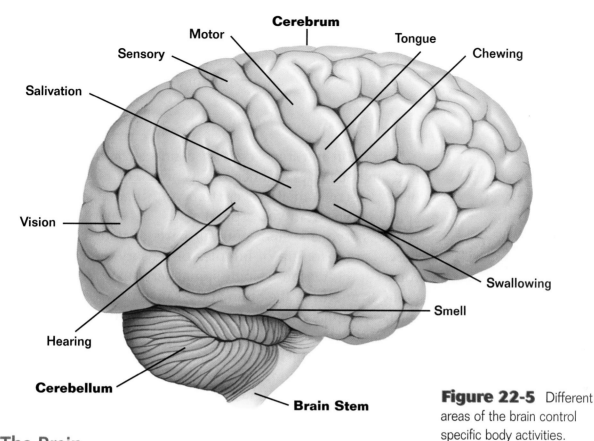

Motor
Cerebrum
Sensory
Tongue
Chewing
Salivation

Vision

Swallowing

Smell

Hearing

Cerebellum

Brain Stem

Figure 22-5 Different areas of the brain control specific body activities.

The Brain

The brain is made up of approximately 100 billion neurons. You can see in **Figure 22-5** that the brain is divided into three major parts: cerebrum, cerebellum, and brain stem. The largest part of the brain, the **cerebrum** (suh REE brum), is divided into two large sections called hemispheres. Here, impulses from the senses are interpreted, memory is stored, and the work of voluntary muscles is controlled. The outer layer of the cerebrum, the cortex, is marked by many ridges and grooves. The diagram also shows some of the tasks that sections of the cortex control.

A second part of the brain, the **cerebellum** (ser uh BEL um), is behind and under the cerebrum. It coordinates voluntary muscle movements and maintains balance and muscle tone.

The **brain stem** extends from the cerebrum and connects the brain to the spinal cord. It is made up of the midbrain, the pons, and the medulla. The brain stem controls your heartbeat, breathing, and blood pressure by coordinating the involuntary muscle movements of these functions.

The Spinal Cord

Your spinal cord is an extension of the brain stem. It is made up of bundles of neurons that carry impulses from all parts of the body to the brain and from the brain to all parts of your body. The spinal cord, illustrated in **Figure 22-4,** is about as big around as an adult thumb and it is about 43 cm long.

PHYSICS
INTEGRATION

Watching the Brain
Scientists use positron emission tomography (PET) to learn more about the brain. Brain cells that are active take up radioactive glucose, which causes an image to appear on a color monitor. Different colors indicate which areas of the brain are being stimulated. By comparing different PET images, researchers have located the areas of the brain used for seeing, reading, hearing, speaking, and thinking.

The CNS is protected by a bony cap called the skull, by vertebrae, and by three layers of membranes. Between some of these membranes is a fluid called cerebrospinal (suh ree broh SPINE ul) fluid. What purpose might this fluid serve?

The Peripheral Nervous System

Your brain and spinal cord are connected to the rest of your body by the peripheral nervous system. The PNS is made up of 12 pairs of cranial nerves from your brain and 31 pairs of spinal nerves from your spinal cord. These nerves link your central nervous system with all parts of your body. Spinal nerves are made up of bundles of sensory and motor neurons. For this reason, a single spinal nerve may have impulses going to and from the brain at the same time.

The peripheral nervous system has two divisions. The *somatic system* consists of the cranial and spinal nerves that go from the central nervous system to your skeletal muscles. The second division, the *autonomic system*, controls your heartbeat rate, breathing, digestion, and gland functions. When your salivary glands release saliva, your autonomic system is at work. Use **Figure 22-6** to help you remember these two divisions.

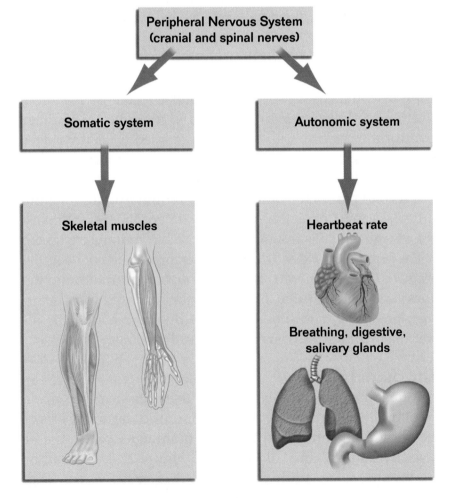

Using Math

One of the longest spinal nerves extends from the spinal cord to muscles in the foot. Estimate the length of this nerve. If the rate of travel of a nerve pulse is approximately 120 m per second, what is the length of time for an impulse to travel from the spinal cord to the foot?

Figure 22-6 The divisions of the peripheral nervous system are shown. **What part of the PNS controls your breathing while you sleep?**

Figure 22-7 Your response in a reflex is controlled in your spinal cord, not in your brain.

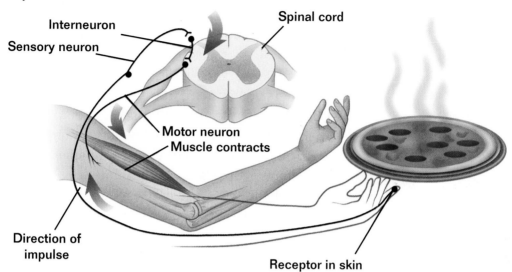

Interneuron
Sensory neuron
Spinal cord
Motor neuron
Muscle contracts
Direction of impulse
Receptor in skin

Reflexes

Have you ever moved quickly from something hot or sharp? Then you've experienced a reflex. A **reflex** is an involuntary and automatic response to a stimulus. Usually, you can't control reflexes because they occur before you know what has happened. A reflex involves a simple nerve pathway called a reflex arc. **Figure 22-7** shows a reflex arc. As you reach for the pizza, some hot cheese falls on your finger. Sensory receptors in your finger respond to the hot cheese, and an impulse is sent to the spinal cord. The impulse passes to an interneuron in the spinal cord that immediately relays the impulse to motor neurons. Motor neurons transmit the impulse to muscles in your arm. Instantly, without thinking, you pull your arm back in response to the burning food. This is a withdrawal reflex. A reflex allows the body to respond without having to think about what action to take. Reflex responses are controlled in your spinal cord, not in your brain. Your brain acts after the reflex to help you figure out what to do to make the pain stop. ☑

Remember in **Figure 22-2** how the girl was frightened after the lamp was broken? What would have happened if her breathing and heartbeat rate didn't calm down within a few minutes? Your body system can't be kept in a state of continual excitement. The organs of your nervous system control and coordinate responses to maintain homeostasis within your body.

Reading Check ☑

Why are reflexes important?

Drugs and the Nervous System

Many drugs, such as alcohol and caffeine, have a direct effect on your nervous system. When swallowed, alcohol passes directly through the walls of the stomach and small intestine into the circulatory system. Alcohol is classified as a depressant drug. A depressant slows down the activities of the central nervous system. Judgment, reasoning, memory, and concentration are impaired. Muscle functions also are affected. Heavy use of alcohol destroys brain and liver cells.

Caffeine is a stimulant, a drug that speeds up the activity of the central nervous system. Too much caffeine can increase heartbeat rate and cause restlessness, tremors, and insomnia. It also can stimulate the kidneys to produce more urine. Caffeine can cause physical dependence. When people stop taking caffeine, they can have headaches and nausea. Caffeine is found in coffee, tea, cocoa, and many soft drinks, as seen in **Figure 22-8.**

Figure 22-8 Caffeine, a substance found in cola, coffee, and other types of food and drink, can cause excitability and sleeplessness.

Think again about a scare from the loud noise. The organs of your nervous system control and coordinate responses to maintain homeostasis within your body. This task is more difficult when your body must cope with the effects of drugs.

Section Assessment

1. Draw and label the parts of a neuron.
2. Compare the central and peripheral nervous systems.
3. Compare sensory and motor neurons.
4. **Think Critically:** During a cold winter evening, you have several cups of hot cocoa. Explain why you have trouble falling asleep.
5.  **Skill Builder**
   Concept Mapping Prepare an events chain concept map of the different kinds of neurons an impulse moves along from a stimulus to a response. If you need help, refer to Concept Mapping in the **Skill Handbook** on page 698.

Using Computers

Word Processing Create a flowchart showing the reflex pathway of a nerve impulse when you step on a sharp object. Label the body parts involved in each step of the process. If you need help, refer to page 716.

Activity
22•1

Reaction Time

Materials
• Metric ruler

Your body responds quickly to some kinds of stimuli, and reflexes allow you to react quickly without even thinking. Sometimes you can improve how quickly you react. Complete this activity to see if you can improve your reaction time.

What You'll Investigate

How can reaction time be improved?

Goals

• **Observe** reflexes.
• **Identify** stimuli and responses.

Procedure

1. Make a data table in your Science Journal to record where the ruler is caught during this activity. Possible column heads are *Trial, Right Hand*, and *Left Hand*.

2. Have a partner hold the ruler at the top end.

3. Hold the thumb and finger of your right hand apart at the bottom of the ruler. Do not touch the ruler.

4. Your partner must let go of the ruler without warning you.

5. Try to catch the ruler by bringing your thumb and finger together quickly.

6. Repeat this activity several times and **record** where the ruler was caught in a data table.

7. Repeat this activity with your left hand. **Record** your results.

Conclude and Apply

1. **Identify** the stimulus in this activity.

2. **Identify** the response in this activity.

3. **Identify** the variable in this activity.

4. Use the table on this page to find your reaction time.

5. What was your average reaction time for your right hand? For your left hand?

6. **Compare** the response of your writing hand and your other hand for this activity.

7. **Draw a conclusion** about how practice relates to stimulus-response time.

Reaction Time	
Where Caught (cm)	**Reaction Time (s)**
5	0.10
10	0.14
15	0.17
20	0.20
25	0.23
30	0.25

22•2 The Senses

In Touch with Your Environment

Science fiction stories about space often describe energy force fields around spaceships. When some form of energy tries to enter the ship's force field, the ship is put on alert. Your body has an alert system as well, in the form of sense organs. Your senses enable you to see, hear, smell, taste, touch, and feel whatever comes into your personal territory. The energy that stimulates your sense organs may be in the form of light rays, heat, sound waves, chemicals, or pressure. Sense organs are adapted for capturing and transmitting these different forms of energy.

Hearing

Sound energy is to hearing as light energy is to vision. As illustrated in **Figure 22-9,** when an object vibrates, it causes the air around it to vibrate, thus producing energy in the form of sound waves. When sound waves reach your ears, they stimulate nerve cells deep in your ear. Impulses are sent to the brain. The brain responds, and you hear a sound.

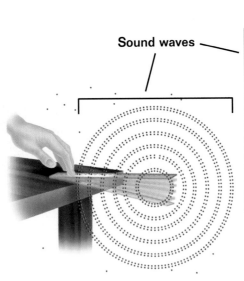

What You'll Learn

▶ The sensory receptors in each sense organ
▶ What type of stimulus each sense organ responds to and how
▶ Why healthy senses are needed

Vocabulary

cochlea   olfactory cell
retina   taste bud

Why It's Important

▶ Your senses make you aware of your environment, which helps keep you safe.

Figure 22-9 A vibrating object produces sound waves that are heard by your ears.

A When the ruler vibrates upward or downward, it pushes the particles of air in front of its movement closer together.

Sound waves

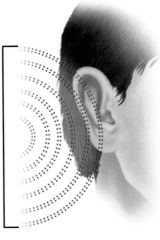

B At the same time, the air particles on the opposite side of the ruler spread farther apart.

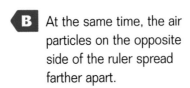

C As the ruler vibrates up and down, it creates a wave-pattern of alternating particles of air that are compressed and spread out. This wave of sound travels to your eardrum, where the sound is received.

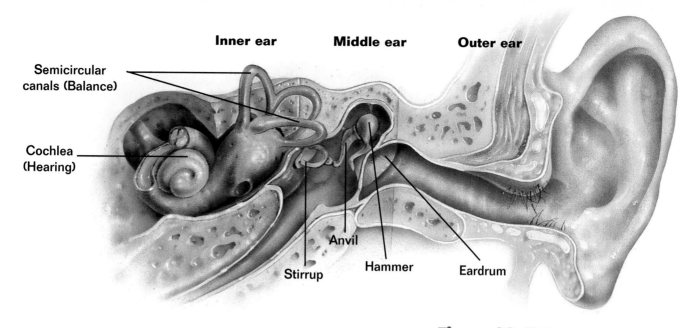

Inner ear   Middle ear   Outer ear

Semicircular canals (Balance)

Cochlea (Hearing)

Anvil

Stirrup

Hammer

Eardrum

Figure 22-10 Your ear responds to sound waves and to changes in the position of your head. **Why does spinning around make you dizzy?**

Figure 22-10 shows that your ear is divided into three sections: the outer, middle, and inner ear. Your outer ear traps sound waves and funnels them down the ear canal to the middle ear. The sound waves cause the eardrum to vibrate much like the membrane on a drum. These vibrations then move through three little bones called the hammer, anvil, and stirrup. The stirrup bone rests against a second membrane on an opening to the inner ear.

The Inner Ear

The **cochlea** (KOH klee uh) is a fluid-filled structure shaped like a snail's shell, in the inner ear. When the stirrup vibrates, fluids in the cochlea also begin to vibrate. These vibrations stimulate nerve endings in the cochlea, and impulses are sent to the brain by the auditory nerve. Depending on how the nerve endings are stimulated, you hear a different type of sound. High-pitched sounds make the endings move differently than lower, deeper sounds.

Balance also is controlled in the inner ear. Special structures and fluids in the inner ear constantly adjust to the position of your head. This stimulates impulses to the brain, which interprets the impulses and helps you make the necessary adjustments to maintain your balance.

Try at Home

Mini Lab

Observing Balance Control

Procedure

1. Place two narrow strips of paper on the wall to form two parallel vertical lines. Have a student stand between them, as still and straight as possible without leaning on the wall, for three minutes.

2. Observe how well balance is maintained.

3. Have the student close his or her eyes and repeat standing within the lines for three minutes.

Analysis

1. When was balance more difficult to maintain? Why?

2. What other factors might cause a person to lose the sense of balance?

Vision

Think about the different kinds of objects you look at every day. It's amazing that, at one glance, you can see the words on this page, the color illustrations, and your classmate sitting next to you.

Light travels in a straight line unless something bends or refracts it. Your eyes are equipped with structures that bend light. As light enters the eye, its waves are first bent by the cornea and then a lens, as illustrated in **Figure 22-11.** The lens directs the rays onto the retina (RET nuh). The **retina** is a tissue at the back of the eye that is sensitive to light energy. Two types of cells called rods and cones are found in the retina. Cones respond to bright light and color. Rods respond to dim light. They are used to help you detect shape and movement. Light energy stimulates impulses in these cells. The impulses pass to the optic nerve, which carries them to the brain. There, the impulses are interpreted, and you see what you are looking at.

Figure 22-11 Light moves through several structures—the cornea and the lens—before striking the retina.

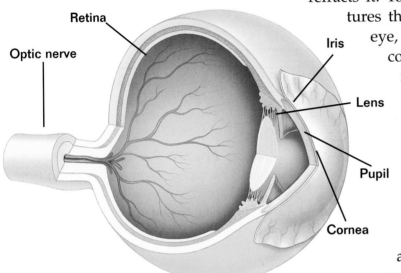

Retina
Optic nerve
Iris
Lens
Pupil
Cornea

PHYSICS
INTEGRATION ➤

Lenses—Refraction and Focus

Light is refracted, or bent, when it passes through a lens. Just how it bends depends on the type of lens it passes through. A lens that is thicker in the middle and thinner on the edges is called a convex lens. The lens in your eye is convex. If you follow the light rays in **Figure 22-12,** you'll see that the lens causes parallel light rays to come together at a focus point. Convex lenses can be used to magnify objects. The light rays enter the eyes in such a way through a convex lens that the object appears enlarged. Magnifying lenses, hand lenses, microscopes, and telescopes all have convex lenses.

A lens that has thicker edges than the middle is called a concave lens. Follow the light rays in **Figure 22-12** as they pass through a concave lens. You'll see that this kind of lens causes the parallel light to spread out. A concave lens is used along with convex lenses in telescopes to allow distant objects to be seen clearly.

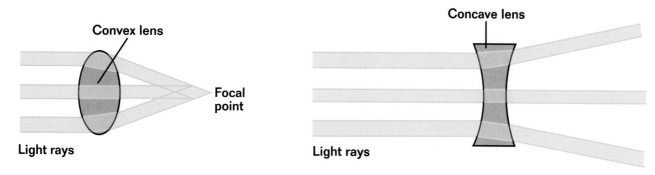

Convex lens

Focal point

Light rays

Concave lens

Light rays

Correcting Vision

In an eye with normal vision, light rays are focused by the cornea and lens onto the retina. A sharp image is formed on the retina, and the brain interprets the signal as being clear. However, if the eyeball is too long from front to back, light from distant objects is focused in front of the retina. A blurred image is formed. This condition is called nearsightedness because near objects are seen clearly. To correct nearsightedness, eyeglasses with concave lenses are used. Concave lenses focus these images sharply on the retina. If the eyeball is too short from front to back, light from nearby objects is focused behind the retina. Again, the image appears blurred. Convex lenses correct this condition known as farsightedness. **Figure 22-13** shows how lenses are used to correct these vision problems. ☑

Figure 22-12 Light rays passing through a convex lens are bent toward the center and meet at a focal point. Light rays that pass through a concave lens are bent outward. They do not meet.

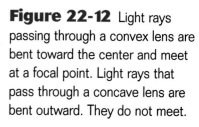

Reading Check ☑

What causes nearsightedness?

Figure 22-13 Glasses and contact lenses use concave or convex lenses to sharpen your vision.

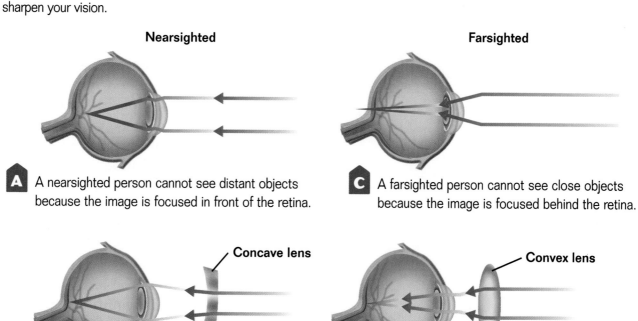

Nearsighted

A A nearsighted person cannot see distant objects because the image is focused in front of the retina.

B A concave lens corrects nearsightedness.

Concave lens

Farsighted

C A farsighted person cannot see close objects because the image is focused behind the retina.

D A convex lens corrects farsightedness.

Convex lens

Mini Lab

Comparing Sense of Smell

Procedure

1. Design an experiment to test your classmates' abilities to recognize the odors of different foods, colognes, or household products.
2. Record their responses in a data table according to the gender of the individuals tested.

Analysis

1. Compare the numbers of correctly identified odors for both males and females.
2. What can you conclude about the differences between males and females in their ability to recognize odors?

Figure 22-14 Although your taste buds distinguish four separate taste sensations (A), scientists cannot determine differences among individual taste buds (B).

B

A

Bitter

Sour

Sour/salty

Salty

Sweet

Smell

A bloodhound is able to track a particular scent through fields and forest. Even though your ability to detect odors is not as sharp, your sense of smell is still important.

You can smell food because it gives off molecules into the air. Nasal passages contain sensitive nerve cells called **olfactory cells** that are stimulated by gas molecules. The cells are kept moist by mucous glands. When gas molecules in the air dissolve in this moisture, the cells become stimulated. If enough gas molecules are present, an impulse starts in these cells and travels to the brain. The brain interprets the stimulus. If it is recognized from previous experience, you can identify the odor. If you can't recognize a particular odor, it is remembered and can be identified the next time, especially if it's a bad one.

Taste

Have you ever tasted a new food with the tip of your tongue and found that it tasted sweet? Then when you swallowed it, you were surprised to find that it tasted bitter. **Taste buds** on your tongue are the major sensory receptors for taste. About 10 000 taste buds are found all over your tongue, enabling you to tell one taste from another.

Taste buds respond to chemical stimuli. When you think of food, your mouth begins to water with saliva. This adaptation is helpful because in order to taste something, it has to be dissolved in water. Saliva begins this process. The solution washes over the taste buds, and an impulse is sent to your brain. The brain interprets the impulse, and you identify the taste.

Most taste buds respond to several taste sensations. However, certain areas of the tongue seem more receptive to one taste than another. The four basic taste sensations are sweet, salty, sour, and bitter. **Figure 22-14** shows where these tastes are commonly stimulated on your tongue.

Smell and taste are related. When you have a head cold with a stuffy nose, food seems tasteless because it is blocked from contacting the moist membranes in your nasal passages.

Touch, Pressure, Pain, and Temperature

How important is it to be able to feel pain inside your body? Several kinds of sensory receptors in your internal organs, as well as throughout your skin, respond to touch, pressure, pain, and temperature, as illustrated in **Figure 22-15.** These receptors pick up changes in touch, pressure, and temperature and transmit impulses to the brain or spinal cord. The body responds to protect itself or maintain homeostasis.

Your fingertips have many different types of receptors for touch. As a result, you can tell whether an object is rough or smooth, hot or cold, light or heavy. Your lips are sensitive to heat and prevent you from drinking something so hot that it would burn you. Pressure-sensitive cells in the skin give warning of danger to a body part and enable you to move to avoid injury.

Your senses are adaptations that help you enjoy or avoid things around you. You constantly react to your environment because of information received by your senses.

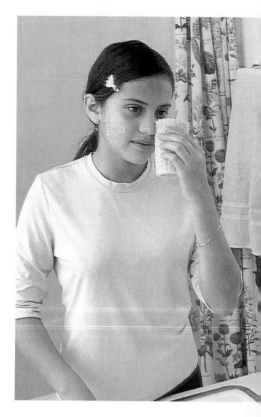

Figure 22-15 Many of the sensations picked up by receptors in the skin are stimulated by mechanical energy. Pressure, motion, and touch are examples.

Section Assessment

1. What type of stimulus do your ears respond to?
2. What are the sensory receptors for the eyes and nose?
3. Why is it important to have receptors for pain and pressure in your internal organs?
4. **Think Critically:** The brain is insensitive to pain. What is the advantage of this?
5.  **Skill Builder**
   Observing and Inferring How can you tell the direction of a sound? Do the **Chapter 22 Skill Activity** on page 747 to explore how your ears detect sound.

Science Journal Write a paragraph in your Science Journal to describe what each of the following objects would feel like.

1. coarse sand from a beach
2. ice cube
3. silk blouse
4. snake
5. smooth rock

Investigating Skin Sensitivity

Possible Materials

- Index card
  (3 inches × 5 inches)
- Toothpicks
- Tape or glue
- Metric ruler

Your body responds to touch, pressure, and temperature. Not all parts of your body are equally sensitive to stimuli. Some areas are more sensitive than others. For example, your lips are sensitive to heat. This protects you from burning your mouth. Now think about touch. How sensitive is the skin on various parts of your body to touch? Which areas can distinguish the smallest amount of distance between stimuli?

Recognize the Problem

What areas of the body are most sensitive to touch?

Form a Hypothesis

Based on your experiences, state a hypothesis about which of the following five areas of the body you believe to be most sensitive—fingertip, forearm, back of the neck, palm, and back of the hand. Rank the areas from 5 (the most sensitive) to 1 (the least sensitive).

Goals

- **Observe** the sensitivity to touch on specific areas of the body.

- **Design an experiment** that tests the effects of a variable, such as the closeness of contact points, to determine which body areas can distinguish between the closest stimuli.

Safety Precautions

Do not apply heavy pressure when using the toothpicks.

Test Your Hypothesis

Plan

1. As a group, agree upon and write out the hypothesis statement.

2. As a group, **list** the steps you need to take to test your hypothesis. Be specific, describing exactly what you will do at each step. Consider the following factors as you list the steps. How will you know that sight is not a factor? How will you use the card shown on the right to **determine** sensitivity to touch? How will you **determine** and **record** that one or both points of touch are felt? List your materials.

3. Design a data table to use in your Science Journal.

4. Read over your entire experiment to make sure that all steps are in order.

5. Identify any constants, variables, and controls of the experiment.

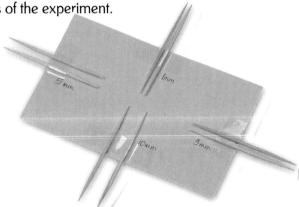

Do

1. Make sure your teacher approves your plan and your data table before you proceed.

2. **Carry out** the experiment as planned.

3. While the experiment is going on, **write down** any observations that you make and complete the data table in your Science Journal.

Analyze Your Data

1. **Compare** your results with those of other groups.

2. **Identify** which part of the body tested can distinguish between the closest stimuli.

3. **Identify** which part of the body is least sensitive.

4. **Rank** body parts tested from most to least sensitive. How did your results **compare** with your hypothesis?

Draw Conclusions

1. Based on the results of your investigation, what can you **infer** about the distribution of touch receptors on the skin?

2. What other parts of your body would you **predict** to be less sensitive? Explain your predictions.

The Endocrine System

Functions of the Endocrine System

"The tallest man in the world!" and "the shortest woman on Earth!" used to be common attractions in circuses. These people became attractions because of their extraordinary and unusual height. In most cases, their sizes were the result of a malfunction in their endocrine systems.

The endocrine system is the second control system of your body. Whereas impulses are control mechanisms of your nervous system, chemicals are the control mechanisms of your endocrine system. Endocrine chemicals called **hormones** are produced in several tissues called glands throughout your body. As the hormones are produced, they move directly into your bloodstream. Hormones affect specific tissues called **target tissues**. Target tissues are frequently located in another part of the body at a distance from the gland that affects them. Thus, the endocrine system doesn't react as quickly as the nervous system. **Table 22-1** shows the position of eight endocrine glands and what they regulate.

Table 22-1

Endocrine Glands		
	Gland	**Regulates**
	Pituitary	Endocrine glands, which produce hormones; milk production; growth
	Thyroid	Carbohydrate use
	Parathyroids	Calcium
	Adrenal	Blood sugar; salt and water balance; metabolism
	Pancreas	Blood sugar
	Ovaries	Egg production; sex organ development in females
	Testes	Sperm production; sex organ development in males

The Pancreas—Playing Two Roles

The pancreas produces a digestive enzyme. This enzyme is released into the small intestine through tubelike vessels called ducts. The pancreas is also part of your endocrine system because other groups of cells in the pancreas secrete hormones. One of these hormones, insulin, enables cells to take in glucose. Recall that glucose is the main source of energy for respiration in cells. Normally, insulin enables glucose to pass from the bloodstream through cell membranes. Persons who can't make insulin are diabetic because insulin isn't there to enable glucose to get into cells.

A Negative-Feedback System

To control the amount of hormone an endocrine gland produces, the endocrine system sends chemical information back and forth to itself. This is a negative-feedback system. It works much the way a thermostat works. When the temperature in a room drops below a certain level, a thermostat signals the furnace to turn on. Once the furnace has raised the temperature to the level set on the thermostat, the furnace shuts off. It will stay off until the thermostat signals again. In your body, once a target tissue responds to its

Visit the Glencoe Science Web Site at **www.glencoe.com/ sec/science** for more information about endocrine diseases.

Problem Solving

Interpreting Blood Sugar Levels

Diabetes results when the pancreas does not produce enough insulin. Insulin is a hormone that enables cells to take in glucose. Glucose is a sugar needed for energy. Extra glucose is not stored, so the glucose is carried in the blood unless insulin enables the cells to take it in. Patients with diabetes have high amounts of sugar in the blood. Normal levels of sugar in the morning are between 60 and 100 milligrams per deciliter (mg/dL). Eating a meal increases glucose in the blood.

The graph shows the sugar in the blood from morning to afternoon. Notice the difference in blood sugars between a diabetic and a nondiabetic person.

Think Critically: Approximately how much difference is there in blood sugar levels between the two persons first thing in the morning? What might

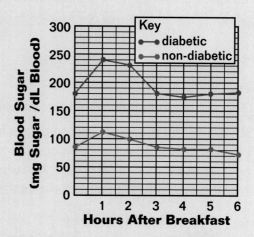

the diabetic person do to prevent such high readings one and two hours after breakfast? What might account for the increased level in blood sugar after the fourth hour?

hormone, the tissue sends a chemical signal back to the gland. This signal causes the gland to stop or slow down production of the hormone. When the level of the hormone in the bloodstream drops below a certain level, the endocrine gland is signaled to begin secreting the hormone again. In this way, the concentration of the hormone in the bloodstream is kept at the needed level. **Figure 22-16** illustrates how a negative-feedback system works.

Hormones produced by endocrine glands go directly into the bloodstream and affect target tissues. The level of the hormone is controlled by a negative-feedback system. In this way, many chemicals in the blood and body functions are controlled.

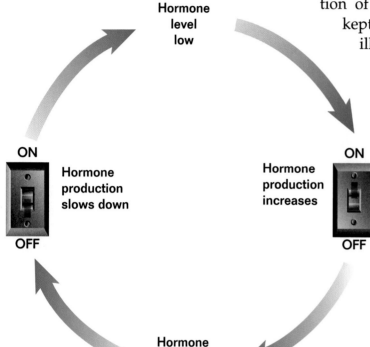

Figure 22-16 Many internal body conditions, such as hormone level and body temperature, are controlled by negative-feedback systems.

Section Assessment

1. What is the function of hormones?

2. What is a negative-feedback system?

3. Choose one hormone and explain how it works.

4. **Think Critically:** Glucose passes from the bloodstream through cell membranes and into the cells. Glucose is required for respiration within cells. How would lack of insulin affect this process?

5. 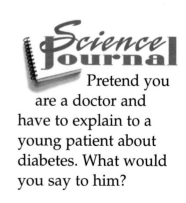 **Skill Builder**
   Comparing and Contrasting In what ways are the nervous system and endocrine system alike? If you need help, refer to Comparing and Contrasting in the **Skill Handbook** on page 704.

Science **Journal** Pretend you are a doctor and have to explain to a young patient about diabetes. What would you say to him?

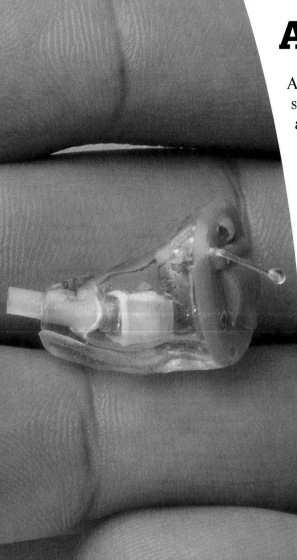

A Hearing Aid

A hearing aid is a small, electronic instrument (left) that makes sounds louder and easier to understand. A hearing aid fits around the outside of the ear or inside the ear canal. Some hearing aids are so small that they are hardly noticeable.

PARTS OF A HEARING AID

1 The tiny **microphone** built into the hearing aid picks up sounds. It changes sound waves into electrical signals.

2 The **amplifier** makes the electrical signals stronger. A hearing aid user can control the degree to which sounds are amplified, or made stronger.

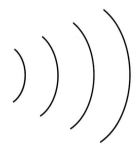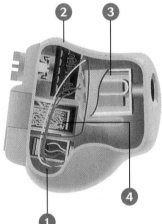

3 The **receiver** changes the amplified electrical signals back into sound signals and sends them to the eardrum.

4 The **battery** is the power source that makes the hearing aid work. Like batteries in portable tape or CD players, batteries in a hearing aid must be changed when they lose power.

Think Critically

1. Why must a person be able to hear at some level in order for a hearing aid to work?

2. How might background noise cause problems for people with hearing aids?

Career CONNECTION

An audiologist evaluates and treats people with hearing loss. He or she conducts tests to determine specific hearing problems. Most audiologists have a master's degree in audiology (hearing) or speech, language, and pathology (study of diseases). Pretend that you are an audiologist. Create an advertisement about services you can provide and hearing aids that you recommend for people who have trouble hearing.

For a **preview** of this chapter, study this Reviewing Main Ideas before you read the chapter. After you have studied this chapter, you can use the Reviewing Main Ideas to **review** the chapter.

The Glencoe MindJogger, Audiocassettes, and CD-ROM provide additional opportunities for review.

22-1 BODY REGULATION

Your body is constantly receiving a variety of stimuli from inside and outside the body. The nervous and endocrine systems respond to these stimuli to maintain homeostasis. *What are some body functions that are constantly being checked and regulated?*

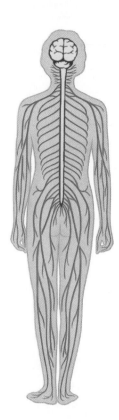

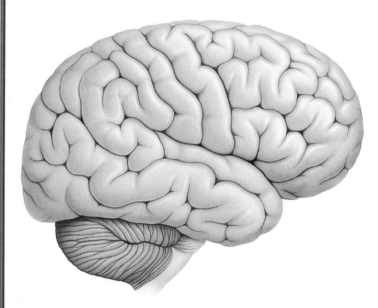

THE NERVOUS SYSTEM

The basic unit of the nervous system is the **neuron.** Stimuli are detected by sensory neurons, and the impulse is carried to an interneuron and then transmitted to a motor neuron. The result is the movement of a body part. Some responses are automatic and are called **reflexes.** *What are the two major divisions of the nervous system?*

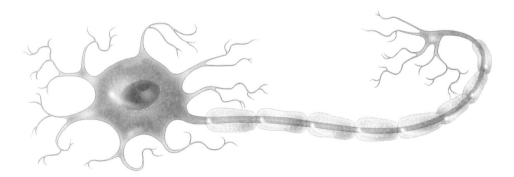

Reading Check ☑

List two or three generalizations about the nervous and endocrine systems. Exchange lists and determine if they are accurate.

Section
22-2 THE SENSES

Your senses respond to energy. The eyes respond to light, and the ears respond to sound waves. The **olfactory cells** of the nose and the **taste buds** of the tongue are stimulated by chemicals. *What senses are involved as you pick up and eat a freshly baked chocolate chip cookie?*

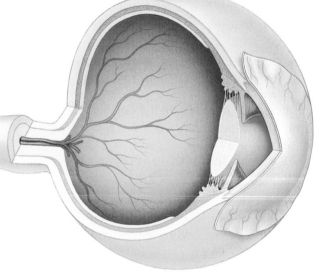

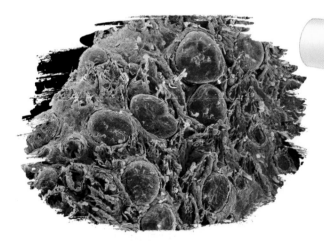

Section
22-3 THE ENDOCRINE SYSTEM

Endocrine glands secrete **hormones** directly into your bloodstream. Hormones affect specific tissues throughout the body and regulate their activities. A feedback system regulates the hormone levels in your blood. *How can a gland that is near your head control the rate of chemical activities throughout your entire body?*

Chapter 22 Assessment

Using Vocabulary

a. axon
b. brain stem
c. central nervous system
d. cerebellum
e. cerebrum
f. cochlea
g. dendrite
h. hormone
i. neuron
j. olfactory cell
k. peripheral nervous system
l. reflex
m. retina
n. synapse
o. target tissue
p. taste bud

Match each phrase with the correct term from the list of Vocabulary words.

1. a small space between neurons
2. basic unit of nervous system
3. division containing brain and spinal cord
4. an automatic response to stimuli
5. center for coordination of voluntary muscle action

Checking Concepts

Choose the word or phrase that best answers the question.

6. How do impulses cross synapses?
   A) by osmosis
   B) through interneurons
   C) through a cell body
   D) by a chemical

7. What are the neuron structures that carry impulses to the cell body?
   A) axons   C) synapses
   B) dendrites   D) nuclei

8. What are neurons detecting stimuli in the skin and eyes called?
   A) interneurons   C) sensory neurons
   B) motor neurons   D) synapses

9. What is the largest part of the brain?
   A) cerebellum   C) cerebrum
   B) brain stem   D) pons

10. What part of the brain controls voluntary muscle?
    A) cerebellum   C) cerebrum
    B) brain stem   D) pons

11. What is the part of the brain that is divided into two hemispheres?
    A) pons   C) cerebrum
    B) brain stem   D) spinal cord

12. What is controlled by the somatic division of the PNS?
    A) skeletal muscles
    B) heart
    C) glands
    D) salivary glands

13. Which of the following are endocrine chemicals produced in glands?
    A) enzymes   C) hormones
    B) target tissues D) saliva

14. Which gland controls many other endocrine glands throughout the body?
    A) adrenal   C) pituitary
    B) thyroid   D) pancreas

15. Which of the following does the inner ear contain?
    A) anvil   C) eardrum
    B) hammer   D) cochlea

Thinking Critically

16. Why is it helpful to have impulses move in only one direction in a neuron?

17. How are reflexes protective?

18. You have had your blood tested for sugar, and the doctor says you have a problem. How might your doctor determine which gland is responsible for this regulation problem?

19. Describe an example of a problem that results from improper gland functioning.

20. If a fly were to land on your face and another one on your back, which might you feel first? Explain how you would test your choice.

Developing Skills

If you need help, refer to the **Skill Handbook.**

21. **Classifying:** Classify the types of neurons as to their location and direction of impulse.

22. **Comparing and Contrasting:** Compare and contrast the structures and functions of the cerebrum, cerebellum, and brain stem. Include in your discussion the following functions: balance, involuntary muscle movements, muscle tone, memory, voluntary muscles, thinking, and senses.

23. **Concept Mapping:** Prepare a concept map showing the correct sequence of the structures through which light passes in the eye.

24. **Interpreting Scientific Illustrations:** Using the following diagram of the synapse, explain how an impulse moves from one neuron to another.

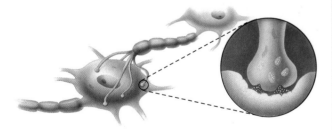

25. **Observing and Inferring:** If an impulse traveled down one neuron, but failed to move on to the next neuron, what might you infer about the first neuron?

26. **Predicting:** Refer to the Try at Home MiniLab in Section 22-2 and predict ways to improve your balance. Test your prediction.

THE PRINCETON REVIEW

Test-Taking Tip

What does the test expect of me?
Find out what concepts, objectives, or standards are being tested before the test. Keep those concepts in mind as you answer the questions.

Test Practice

Use these questions to test your Science Proficiency.

1. What happens to an endocrine gland when the blood level of its hormone is increased?
   A) The gland stops producing hormones until the hormone level in the blood falls below a certain point.
   B) The gland continues producing hormones until the blood can't hold any more hormones.
   C) All endocrine glands keep producing their hormones until all hormone levels in the blood are equal.
   D) All endocrine glands stop producing hormones until all hormone levels in the blood are balanced.

2. Which statement below is the correct pathway from the stimulus to the response in a reflex response?
   A) receptor—interneuron—brain—motor neuron—muscle
   B) sensory neuron—brain—spinal cord—motor neuron
   C) muscle—receptor—sensory neuron—interneuron—motor neuron
   D) receptor—sensory neuron—interneuron—motor neuron—muscle

Chapter Preview

Skills Preview

Skill Builders

• Sequence and
  Outline Data

Activities

• Interpret and
  Graph Data

MiniLabs

• Interpret Data

Reading Check ✓

As you meet new vocabulary terms, help yourself remember their meanings by identifying related words. One example would be menopause and menstruation.

Explore Activity

Y ou or some of your friends may come from families with both brothers and sisters. Some may come from families that have only boys or only girls. What do you think are the odds of a small family having all boys or all girls? Do the odds change as the family grows larger? What do you think is the proportion of boys to girls among children born in the general population?

Observe the Proportion of Boys to Girls

1. Take a penny and toss it in the air. The chance is equal that it will land heads or tails.

2. Toss the penny a hundred times.

3. Keep a record of the number of times it lands heads up and the number of times it lands tails up.

4. Keep a record of the order in which the penny lands.

Science Journal

In your Science Journal, record the results of your trials. Analyze your record for any patterns that occurred. Write your observations about sequences of five or more heads before a tails fell. Relate this to families that have five girls or five boys. Infer the chances that a girl would be born if there were a sixth child.

Human Reproduction

The Reproductive System

Reproduction is the process that continues life on Earth. Organisms that carry out sexual reproduction form eggs and sperm that transfer genetic information from one generation to the next. The number of offspring an organism has varies with the species. Humans and other mammals have fewer offspring than most other animals. If you baby-sit, you know that babies and young children require almost constant attention. For this reason, most humans have only one or two babies at a time. However, in rare cases, mothers have given birth to as many as eight babies. Organisms such as spiders can lay thousands of eggs, which results in thousands of offspring at one time, as shown in **Figure 23-1.**

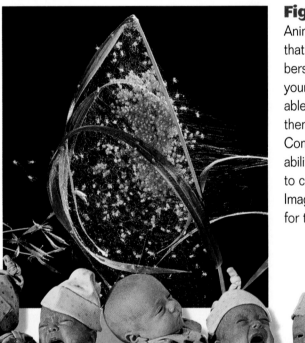

Figure 23-1
Animals such as spiders that produce large numbers of eggs have young that are usually able to take care of themselves from birth. Compare this to the ability of a human baby to care for itself. Imagine trying to care for these septuplets.

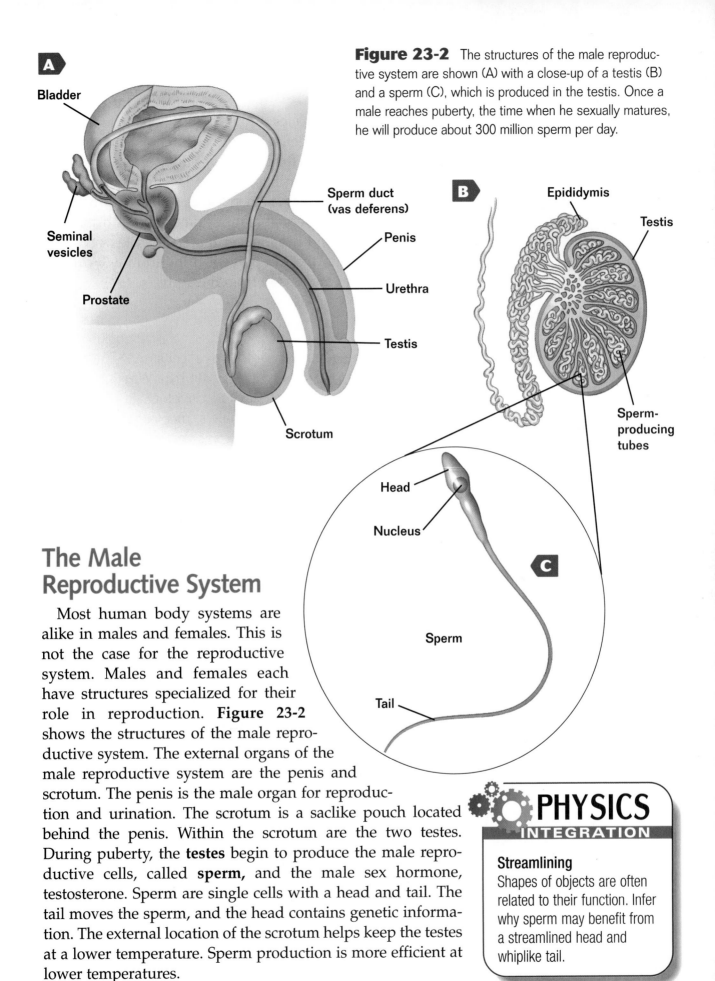

Figure 23-2 The structures of the male reproductive system are shown (A) with a close-up of a testis (B) and a sperm (C), which is produced in the testis. Once a male reaches puberty, the time when he sexually matures, he will produce about 300 million sperm per day.

Bladder

Seminal vesicles

Prostate

Sperm duct (vas deferens)

Penis

Urethra

Testis

Scrotum

B

Epididymis

Testis

Sperm-producing tubes

Head

Nucleus

C

Sperm

Tail

The Male Reproductive System

Most human body systems are alike in males and females. This is not the case for the reproductive system. Males and females each have structures specialized for their role in reproduction. **Figure 23-2** shows the structures of the male reproductive system. The external organs of the male reproductive system are the penis and scrotum. The penis is the male organ for reproduction and urination. The scrotum is a saclike pouch located behind the penis. Within the scrotum are the two testes. During puberty, the **testes** begin to produce the male reproductive cells, called **sperm,** and the male sex hormone, testosterone. Sperm are single cells with a head and tail. The tail moves the sperm, and the head contains genetic information. The external location of the scrotum helps keep the testes at a lower temperature. Sperm production is more efficient at lower temperatures.

PHYSICS
INTEGRATION

Streamlining
Shapes of objects are often related to their function. Infer why sperm may benefit from a streamlined head and whiplike tail.

Sperm Movement

Many organs help in the production, transport, and storage of sperm inside the male body. After sperm are produced, they travel from the testes through tubes that circle the bladder. Behind the bladder, a gland called the seminal vesicle provides sperm with a fluid that gives them energy and helps them move as shown in **Figure 23-3.** This mixture of sperm and fluid is called **semen.** Semen leaves the body through the urethra, the same tube that at other times carries urine from the body. Semen and urine never mix. A muscle at the back of the bladder contracts to prevent urine from entering the urethra as sperm are ejected from the body.

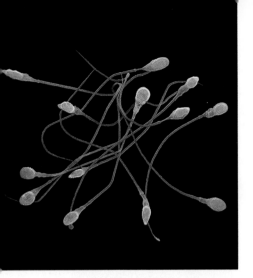

Magnification: 4500×

Figure 23-3 The photograph shows sperm swimming in fluid. A mixture of sperm and fluid is called semen.

Figure 23-4 The structures of the female reproductive system are shown from the side. **Where in the female reproductive system do the eggs develop?**

The Female Reproductive System

Eggs are the female reproductive cells. A female baby already has her total supply of eggs at birth. When the female reaches puberty, her eggs start to develop in **ovaries,** the female sex organs. Unlike the male's, most of the reproductive organs of the female are internal. The ovaries are located in the lower part of the body cavity. Each of the two ovaries is about the size and shape of an almond. **Figure 23-4** shows the structures of the female reproductive system.

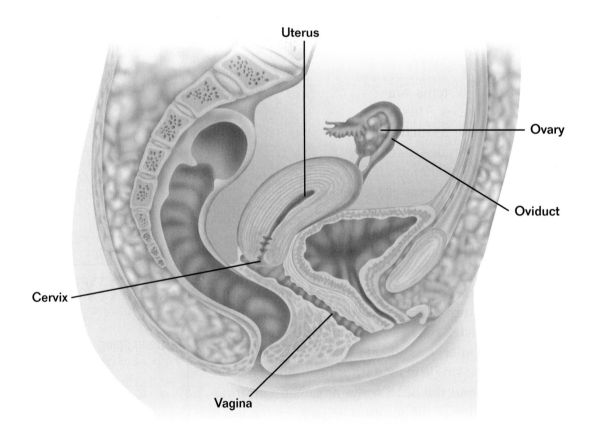

Uterus

Ovary

Oviduct

Cervix

Vagina

Egg Movement

About once a month, an egg is released from an ovary, as in **Figure 23-5.** This process is called **ovulation** (ahv yuh LAY shun). The two ovaries take turns releasing an egg. One month, the first ovary releases an egg. Next month, the other ovary releases an egg and so on. When the egg is released, it enters the oviduct, as shown in **Figure 23-6.** Sometimes, the egg is fertilized by a sperm. If fertilization occurs, it will happen in an oviduct. Short, hairlike structures called cilia help sweep the egg through the oviduct to the uterus. The **uterus** is a hollow, pear-shaped, muscular organ with thick walls in which a fertilized egg develops. The lower end of the uterus is connected to the outside of the body by a muscular tube called the **vagina.** The vagina also is called the birth canal because a baby travels through this passageway during birth.

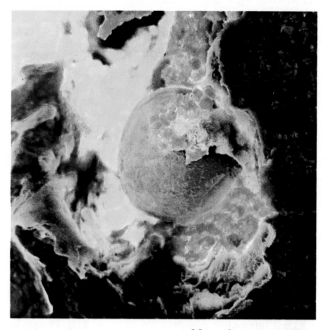

Magnification: 1850×

Figure 23-5 The egg in the photograph has just been released from the ovary.

The Menstrual Cycle

The **menstrual cycle** is the monthly cycle of changes in the female reproductive system. Before and after an egg is released from an ovary, the uterus undergoes certain changes. The menstrual cycle of a human female averages 28 days. However, the cycle can vary in some individuals from 20 to 40 days. The changes include the maturing of an egg,

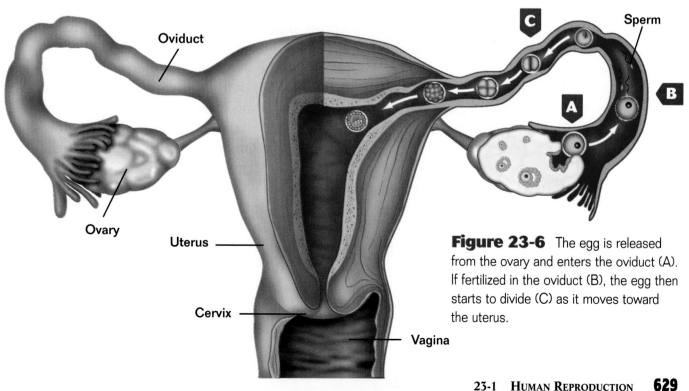

Figure 23-6 The egg is released from the ovary and enters the oviduct (A). If fertilized in the oviduct (B), the egg then starts to divide (C) as it moves toward the uterus.

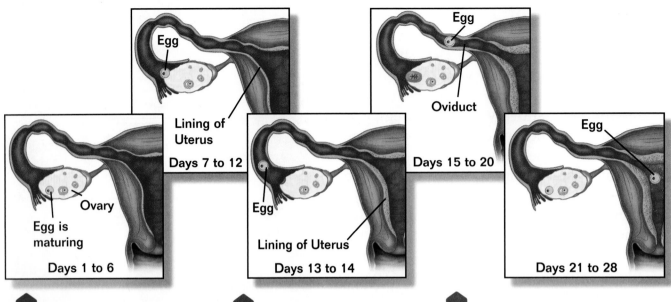

A **Phase One** The first day of the cycle starts when the menstrual flow begins.

B **Phase Two** After menstruation, the wall of the uterus begins to thicken again. Ovulation occurs on about day 14.

C **Phase Three** The wall of the uterus continues to thicken due to the action of hormones. If a fertilized egg arrives, the uterus is ready to support it.

Figure 23-7 A regular menstrual cycle is approximately 28 days long. Notice how the thickness of the uterine lining changes during the cycle. **On what day does ovulation occur?**

Visit the Glencoe Science Web Site at **www.glencoe.com/ sec/science** for more information about the menstrual cycle.

Reading Check

What causes the uterine wall to thicken again after menstruation?

the secretion of female sex hormones, and the preparation of the uterus to receive a fertilized egg, as shown in **Figure 23-7**. When an egg inside an ovary matures, the lining of the uterus thickens and prepares to receive a fertilized egg.

Three Phases

You can see in **Figure 23-7** that the first day of phase one starts when menstrual flow begins. Menstrual flow consists of blood and tissue cells from the thickened lining of the uterus. This monthly discharge is called **menstruation.** Menstruation usually lasts from four to six days.

In the second phase, hormones cause the uterine lining to thicken again. One egg in the ovary develops and matures until ovulation occurs. Ovulation occurs on about day 14 of the cycle. Once the egg is released, it can be fertilized for the next 24 to 48 hours as it moves through the oviduct. Pregnancy can occur if live sperm are in the oviduct 48 hours before or after ovulation.

During the third phase, hormones continue to increase the thickness of the uterine lining. In this way, the uterus is prepared for the arrival of a fertilized egg. If a fertilized egg does arrive, the uterus is ready to help support and nourish the developing embryo. If the egg is not fertilized, hormone levels decrease and the uterine lining deteriorates. Menstruation begins again. Another egg begins to mature and the cycle repeats itself. ✓

Menopause

Menstruation begins when a girl reaches puberty and her reproductive organs have matured. For most females, the first menstrual period happens between ages eight and 13 and continues until age 45 to 55. Then, there is a gradual reduction of ovulation and menstruation. **Menopause** occurs when the menstrual cycle becomes irregular and eventually stops.

When the reproductive systems of males and females mature, sperm are produced in the male testes, while eggs mature in the female ovaries. The reproductive process allows for the species to continue.

Figure 23-8 For most women, the menstrual cycle continues normally until around age 45 to 55. After that, the cycle becomes irregular and finally stops.

Section Assessment

1. What is the major function of a reproductive system?
2. Explain the movement of sperm through the male reproductive system.
3. List the organs of the female reproductive system and describe their functions.
4. Explain the cause of menstrual flow.
5. **Think Critically:** Adolescent females often require additional amounts of iron in their diet. Explain why.
6. **Skill Builder**
   Sequencing Sequence the movement of an egg through the female reproductive system and the movement of a sperm through the male reproductive system. If you need help, refer to Sequencing in the **Skill Handbook** on page 698.

Using Math

Usually, one egg is released each month during the reproductive years of a female. For a woman whose first menstruation starts at age 12 and ends at age 50, calculate the number of eggs released. In males, about 300 million sperm are produced in a day. Relate this number to the number of eggs released by a woman during her entire life.

Materials

- Paper and pencil

Interpreting Diagrams

Starting in adolescence, the hormone estrogen causes changes in the uterus. These changes prepare the uterus to accept a fertilized egg that may embed itself in the uterine wall.

What You'll Investigate

What happens to the uterus during a female's monthly cycle?

Goals

- **Observe** the stages in a diagram of the menstrual cycle.
- **Relate** the process of ovulation to the cycle.

Procedure

1. The diagram below shows what is explained in Section 23-1 on the menstrual cycle.
2. **Study** the diagram and labels.
3. **Use** the information in Section 23-1 and the diagram below to complete a table like the one shown.
4. How are the diagrams different?
5. On approximately what day in a 28-day cycle is the egg released from the ovary?

Conclude and Apply

1. How long is the average menstrual cycle?
2. How many days does menstruation usually last?
3. On what days does the lining of the uterus build up?
4. **Infer** why this process is called a cycle.
5. **Calculate** how many days before menstruation ovulation usually occurs.
6. **Interpret** the diagram to explain the menstrual cycle.

Menstruation Cycle		
Days	Condition of Uterus	What Happens
1–6		
7–12		
13–14		
15–28		

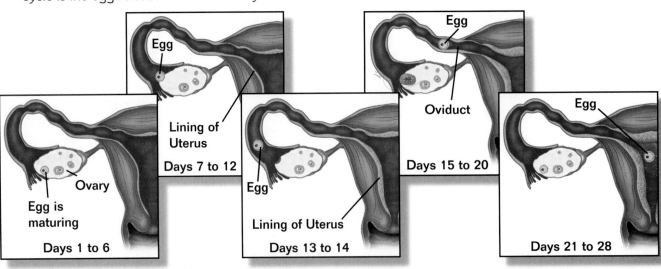

Egg

Egg

Lining of Uterus

Days 7 to 12

Oviduct

Days 15 to 20

Egg

Ovary

Egg is maturing

Days 1 to 6

Egg

Lining of Uterus

Days 13 to 14

Egg

Days 21 to 28

Fertilization to Birth

Fertilization

Before the invention of powerful microscopes, some people imagined a sperm to be a miniature person that grew in the uterus of a female. Others thought the egg contained a miniature individual that started to grow when stimulated by semen. In the latter part of the 1700s, experiments using amphibians showed that contact between an egg and sperm is necessary for life to begin development. With the development of the cell theory in 1839, scientists recognized that a human develops from a single egg that has been fertilized by a sperm. The uniting of a sperm with an egg is known as fertilization.

As you see in **Figure 23-9,** the process begins when sperm, deposited into the vagina, move through the uterus into the oviducts. Whereas only one egg is usually present, nearly 200 to 300 million sperm are deposited. Of that number, only one sperm will fertilize the egg. The nucleus of the sperm and the nucleus of the egg have 23 chromosomes each. When the egg and sperm unite, a zygote with 46 chromosomes is formed. Most fertilization occurs in an oviduct.

What You'll Learn

► How an egg becomes fertilized
► The major events in the stages of development of an embryo and fetus
► The difference between fraternal and identical twins

Vocabulary

pregnancy   amniotic sac
embryo   fetus

Why It's Important

► Fertilization begins the entire process of human growth and development.

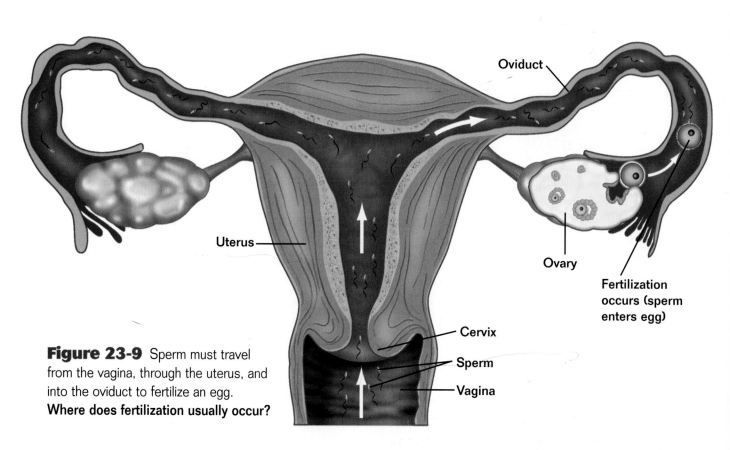

Figure 23-9 Sperm must travel from the vagina, through the uterus, and into the oviduct to fertilize an egg. **Where does fertilization usually occur?**

Labels: Oviduct, Uterus, Ovary, Fertilization occurs (sperm enters egg), Cervix, Sperm, Vagina

Figure 23-10 The sperm releases enzymes that disrupt the membrane on the surface of the egg. The sperm head can now penetrate the egg.

Magnification: 2700×

A Biochemical Event

Several hundred million sperm may be deposited in the vagina, but only several thousand actually reach the egg in the oviduct. During their travels, the sperm come in contact with chemical secretions in the vagina. It appears that this contact causes a change in the membrane of the sperm. The sperm then become capable of fertilizing eggs.

Although many sperm may actually reach the egg, only one will fertilize it, as shown in **Figure 23-10.** The one sperm that makes successful contact with the egg releases an enzyme from the saclike structure on its head. Enzymes help speed up chemical reactions. The enzyme has a direct effect on the protective egg-surface membranes. The structure of the membrane is disrupted, and the sperm head is now able to penetrate the egg.

Response of the Egg

Once a sperm has penetrated the egg, another series of chemical actions take place. These actions prevent further penetration by other sperm. Special chemical secretions are released onto the egg's surface. These secretions prevent other sperm from binding. Other chemicals cause changes on the surface of the egg itself that prevent penetration. At this point, the nucleus of the successful sperm fuses with the nucleus of the egg. This fusion creates a new cell, called a zygote, that undergoes mitosis, as shown in **Figure 23-11.**

CHEMISTRY
◄ **INTEGRATION**

Figure 23-11 Fertilization results from the fusion of an egg nucleus and a sperm (A). The resulting zygote undergoes mitosis as shown in (B) and (C) to form a hollow ball of cells (D).

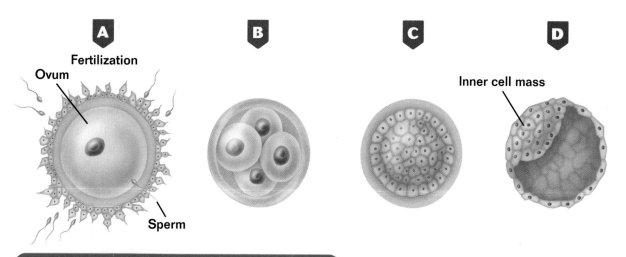

Ovum
Fertilization
Sperm
Inner cell mass

Problem Solving

When to Test?

Expectant mothers want to know, "Will my baby be healthy?" Several tests to check for birth defects can be done before a baby is born. One test is known as amniocentesis (am nee oh sen TEE sus). In this test, the doctor extracts a small amount of fluid from the amniotic sac that surrounds the fetus. Examination of the fluid can reveal certain abnormalities. A similar test takes a tissue sample of the placenta, the tissue that connects mother and child. Analysis of the tissue can show evidence of certain diseases.

One of the most frequently used tests is an ultrasound. A device generates sound waves that are transmitted through the mother's body. The sound waves produce photographic images of the fetus. Doctors observe the images to detect not only deformities, but also the size, sex, and rate of development of the fetus.

While each procedure has a benefit, each also has a risk. Some risks are to the mother, and some are to the unborn fetus. Some doctors also think that too many tests may have an adverse effect on the development of the fetus.

Think Critically: Under what conditions might parents want to know the sex of their unborn child? Study the ultrasound photo and infer what information could be obtained from these types of photos and how a doctor might make use of that information.

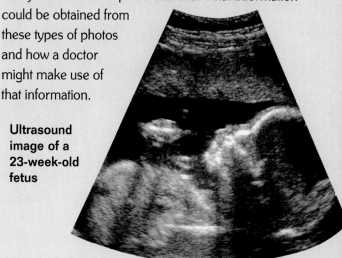

Ultrasound image of a 23-week-old fetus

Development Before Birth

The zygote moves along the oviduct to the uterus. During this time, the zygote is dividing and forming a ball of cells. After about seven days, the ball of cells is implanted in the wall of the uterus. The uterine wall has been thickening in preparation to receive a fertilized egg. Here the fertilized egg will develop for nine months until the birth of the baby. This period of time is known as **pregnancy.**

The Embryo

During the first two months of pregnancy, the unborn child is known as an **embryo.** In **Figure 23-12,** you can see how the embryo receives nutrients and removes wastes. Nutrients from the wall of the uterus are received by the embryo through villi. Blood vessels develop from the villi and form the placenta. The umbilical cord is attached to the embryo's navel and connects with the placenta. The umbilical cord transports nutrients and oxygen from the mother to the baby through a vein. Carbon dioxide and other wastes are carried through arteries in the umbilical cord back to the mother's blood. Other substances in the mother's blood can pass to the embryo, as well. These include drugs, toxins, and

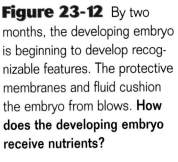

*inter*NET CONNECTION

Visit the Glencoe Science Web Site at **www.glencoe.com/ sec/science** for more information about development before birth.

Figure 23-12 By two months, the developing embryo is beginning to develop recognizable features. The protective membranes and fluid cushion the embryo from blows. **How does the developing embryo receive nutrients?**

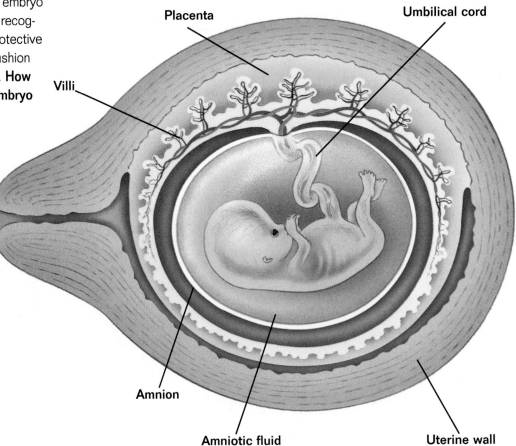

Placenta

Umbilical cord

Villi

Amnion

Amniotic fluid

Uterine wall

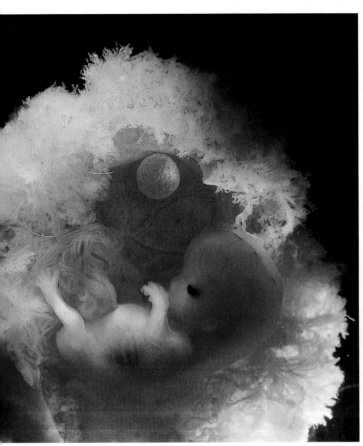

Magnification: 3×

Figure 23-13 The photograph shows an enlarged view of a two-month-old embryo. The actual size is approximately 2 cm. You can see the head with eyes and nose. Tiny arms, legs, and toes are developing. The soft looking tissue behind the embryo is the placenta.

disease organisms. Because these substances can harm the embryo, a mother needs to avoid harmful drugs, alcohol, and tobacco during pregnancy.

During the third week of pregnancy, a thin membrane begins to form around the embryo. This is called the amnion or the **amniotic** (am nee AH tihk) **sac.** It is filled with a clear liquid called amniotic fluid. The amniotic fluid in the amniotic sac helps cushion the embryo against blows and can store nutrients and wastes. This sac attaches to the placenta.

During the first three months of development, as shown in **Figure 23-13,** all of an embryo's major organs form. A heart structure begins to beat and move blood through the embryo's blood vessels. At five weeks, the embryo is only as large as a single grain of rice, but there is a head with recognizable eye, nose, and mouth features. During the sixth and seventh weeks, tiny arms and legs develop fingers and toes.

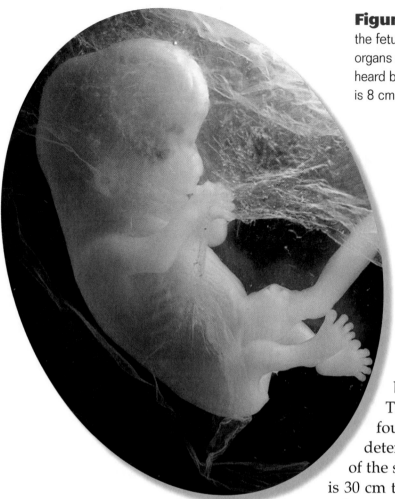

Figure 23-14 The photograph shows the fetus at about three months. The body organs are present, and the heart can be heard beating using a stethoscope. The fetus is 8 cm to 10 cm long.

The Fetus

After the first two months of pregnancy, as shown in **Figure 23-14,** the developing baby is called a **fetus.** At this time, body organs are present. Around the third month, the fetus is 8 cm to 10 cm long, the heart can be heard beating using a stethoscope, and the mother may feel the baby's movements within her uterus. The fetus may suck its thumb. By the fourth month, an ultrasound test can determine the sex of the fetus. By the end of the seventh month of pregnancy, the fetus is 30 cm to 38 cm in length. Fatty tissue builds up under the skin, and the fetus looks less wrinkled. By the ninth month, the fetus usually has shifted to a head-down position within the uterus. The head usually is in contact with the opening of the uterus to the vagina. The fetus is about 50 cm in length and weighs from 2.5 kg to 3.5 kg. The baby is ready for birth. ☑

Reading Check ☑

At what stage in pregnancy does the embryo become a fetus?

Multiple Births

Sometimes, two eggs leave the ovary at the same time. If both eggs are fertilized and both develop, fraternal twins are born. Fraternal twins may be two girls, two boys, or a boy and a girl. Fraternal twins do not always look alike. Not all twins are fraternal. Sometimes, a single egg splits apart shortly after it is fertilized. Each part of the egg then develops and forms an embryo. Because both children developed from the same egg and sperm, they are identical twins. Each has the same set of genes. Identical twins must be either two girls or two boys. **Figure 23-15** illustrates both identical and fraternal twin development. Triplets and other multiple births may occur when either three or more eggs are produced at one time or an egg splits into three or more parts.

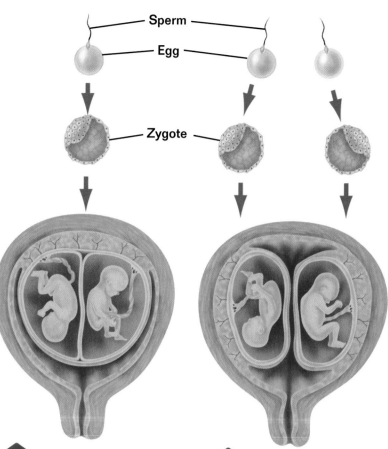

Sperm

Egg

Zygote

Figure 23-15 The development of fraternal and identical twins is quite different.

A Identical twins develop from a single egg that has been fertilized by a single sperm. The resulting zygote later splits.

B Fraternal twins develop from two different eggs that have been fertilized by two different sperm.

Section Assessment

1. What happens when an egg is fertilized?

2. What is one major event that occurs during the embryo and fetal stages?

3. At what stage in the pregnancy does the embryo become a fetus?

4. **Think Critically:** If a mother is taking drugs during pregnancy, how can these harmful substances pass into the blood system of the embryo?

5. **Skill Builder**
   Interpreting Data A human fetus grows at different rates during its development. Do the **Chapter 23 Skill Activity** on page 748 in the **Skill Handbook** and interpret data about fetal development.

Science Journal

Use different references to look up information on multiple births. In your Science Journal, describe how twins and triplets develop. Describe the differences in origin and appearance of fraternal and identical twins.

23·3 Development After Birth

What You'll Learn

▶ The sequence of events of childbirth

▶ The stages of infancy and childhood

▶ Adolescent development and preparation for adulthood

Vocabulary

infancy	adolescence
childhood	adulthood

Why It's Important

▶ During adolescence, your body and mind change from a child to an adult.

Childbirth

After developing for nine months within the mother, the baby is ready to be born. Like all newborn, living things, the baby finds itself suddenly pushed out into the world. Within the uterus and amniotic sac, the baby was in a warm, watery, dark, and protected environment. In contrast, the new environment is cooler, drier, brighter, and not as protective.

Labor

The process of childbirth as shown in **Figure 23-16** begins with labor, which is the muscular contractions of the uterus. As the contractions increase in strength and frequency, the amniotic sac usually breaks and releases its fluid. Over a period of hours, the contractions cause the opening of the uterus to widen to allow the baby to pass through. More powerful and frequent contractions push the baby out through the vagina into its new environment.

VISUALIZING Childbirth

Figure 23-16 Childbirth begins with labor. The opening to the uterus widens, and the baby passes through.

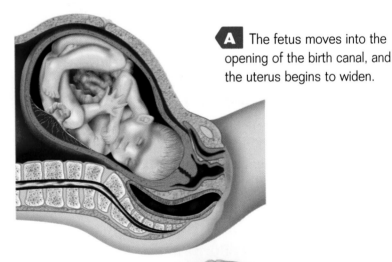

A The fetus moves into the opening of the birth canal, and the uterus begins to widen.

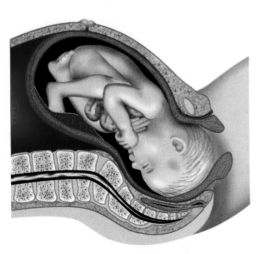

B The base of the uterus is completely dilated.

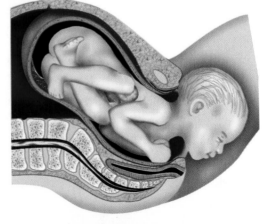

C The fetus is pushed out through the birth canal.

Figure 23-17 Infancy is a period of rapid growth and development. An early skill is the ability to smile. **What are some of the developments that occur during infancy?**

Sometimes, the mother's pelvis is too small for the baby to fit through or the baby is in the wrong position for birth. In cases like this, the baby is delivered through an incision in the mother's uterus and abdomen. This surgery is called cesarean section.

Post Labor

At birth, the baby is still attached to the umbilical cord and placenta. The person assisting with the birth of the baby ties the cord and then cuts it. The baby may cry. Crying forces air into its lungs. The scar that later forms where the cord was attached is the navel. Soon after the baby's delivery, contractions expel the placenta from the mother's body.

Infancy and Childhood

The first four weeks after birth are known as the neonatal period. *Neonatal* means "newborn." During this time, the baby adjusts to life outside of the uterus. Body functions such as respiration, digestion, and excretion are now performed by the baby rather than through the placenta. Unlike some other living things, the human baby depends on others to survive. The human baby needs to be fed and have its diaper changed. In contrast, a newborn colt begins walking a few hours after its birth.

Using Math

Cotton diapers can be reused up to 100 times before having to be replaced. Calculate how many diapers you would need for a year if an average of six were used each day. If a package of 12 cloth diapers costs $18, how much would be spent on the diapers for one year? Infer what other costs are involved.

Investigate Immunizations

Procedure

1. Find out what immunizations are usually given to babies and young children.

2. Compare these to what vaccines are required for children to enter your school.

Analysis

1. What booster shots are given to school children?

2. Investigate what immunizations are required for travel to foreign countries.

Infancy

The next stage of development is **infancy,** the period from the neonatal stage to one year. It is a period of rapid growth and development for both mental and physical skills. At around six weeks of age, babies are able to smile. At four months, most babies can laugh, sit up when propped, and recognize their mother's face. At eight months, the infant is usually able to say a few simple words. One of the major events within the first year is the ability to stand unsupported for a few seconds. Some children walk before age one.

Childhood

After infancy is **childhood,** which lasts until age 12. The physical growth rate for height and weight is not as rapid as in infancy. However, muscular coordination and mental abilities develop. By 18 months, the child is able to walk without help. Between two and three years, the child learns to control his or her bladder and bowel. At age three, the child can speak in simple sentences. By age five, many children can read a limited number of words. Throughout this stage, children develop their abilities to speak, read, write, and reason. At the same time, children also mature emotionally and learn how to get along with other people, as shown in **Figure 23-18.** Find out how old you were when you began to talk. What were your first words?

Adolescence

The next stage of development is adolescence. You are in this stage. **Adolescence** begins around ages 12 to 13. A part of adolescence is puberty. As you read earlier, puberty is the time of development when a person becomes physically able to reproduce. For girls, puberty occurs between ages eight and 13. For boys, puberty occurs between ages 13 and 15.

Figure 23-18 Childhood begins around the age of one and continues until age 12. Muscular coordination and mental abilities develop. Children also learn how to interact socially with others.

Figure 23-19 During puberty, hormones cause changes in the bodies of adolescents.

During puberty, hormones that cause changes in the body are produced by the pituitary gland. The hormone FSH helps produce reproductive cells. LH helps with the production of sex hormones. As a result of the secretion of these hormones, secondary sex characteristics, some of which are evident in **Figure 23-19,** result. In females, the breasts develop, pubic and underarm hair appears, and fatty tissue is added to the buttocks and thighs. In males, the hormones cause the growth of facial, pubic, and underarm hair; a deepened voice; and an increase in muscle size. Many young adults begin to feel sexual attraction, as well. ✔

Reading Check ✔

List three changes that occur in the female body during puberty.

The Growth Spurt

Adolescence is the time of your final growth spurt. Are you shorter or taller than your classmates? Because of differences in the time hormones begin functioning among individuals

Figure 23-20 You can compare body proportions of newborns, young children, and adults with this chart. **How does the proportion of the head compared to the rest of the body change from baby to adult?**

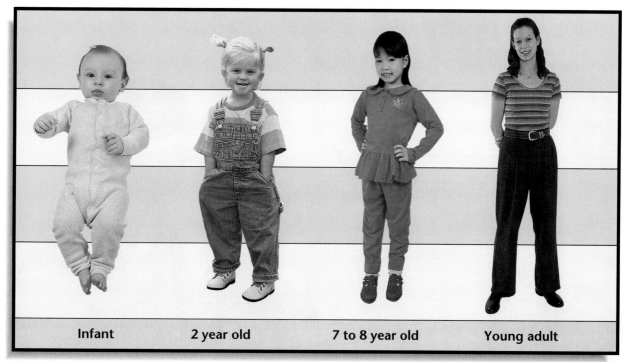

| Infant | 2 year old | 7 to 8 year old | Young adult |

and between males and females, boys' and girls' growth rates differ. Girls often begin their final growth phase between the ages of 11 and 13 and end at ages 15 to 16. Boys usually start their growth spurt at ages 13 to 15 and end at 17 to 18 years of age. Hormonal changes also cause underarm sweating and acne, requiring extra cleanliness and care. All of these physical changes can cause you to feel different or uncomfortable. This is normal. As you move through the period of adolescence, you will find that you will become more coordinated, be better able to handle problems, and gain improved reasoning abilities.

Adulthood

The final stage of development is that of **adulthood.** It begins with the end of adolescence and extends to old age. Young adults are people in their twenties. Many young adults are completing an education, finding employment, and possibly marrying and beginning a family. This is when the growth of the muscular and skeletal system stops. You can see in **Figure 23-20** how body proportions change as you grow from infancy to adulthood.

People from age 30 to age 60 are in the stage of middle adulthood. During these years, physical strength begins to decline. Blood circulation and respiration become less efficient. Bones become more brittle, and the skin's elastic tissues are lost, causing the skin to become wrinkled. People in this group are busy with family and work commitments. They often care for aging parents, as well as children.

Figure 23-21 Adulthood is the final stage of development. This is when the growth of the muscular and skeletal system stops. **What is the approximate age range for a person in middle adulthood?**

Senior Citizens

Think about someone you know over age 60. How is that person like or different from you? Around this age, many people retire. They take up hobbies, travel, or volunteer at hospitals and community organizations. Many continue to work. They are an active part of society. People over 75 years are placed in the oldest age group. While many in this group are mentally and physically active, others may need assistance in meeting their needs.

After birth, the stages of development of the human body begin with a baby making adjustments to a new environment. From infancy to adolescence, the body's systems mature, enabling the person to be physically and mentally ready for adulthood. During the next 50 years or longer, people live their lives making contributions to family, community, and society. Throughout the life cycle, people who care for their health enjoy a higher quality of life.

Figure 23-22 In 1998, former astronaut and senator John Glenn, a senior citizen, took part in a space shuttle mission. This helped to change people's views of what many senior citizens are capable of.

Section Assessment

1. What are major events during childbirth?
2. Compare infancy with childhood.
3. How does the period of adolescence prepare you for the stage of adulthood?
4. **Think Critically:** Why is it hard to compare the growth and development of different adolescents?
5. **Skill Builder**
   Concept Mapping Prepare a concept map of the various life stages of human development from the neonatal period to adulthood. If you need help, refer to Concept Mapping in the **Skill Handbook** on page 698.

Using Computers

Spreadsheet Using your text and other resources, make a spreadsheet for the stages of human development from a zygote to a fetus. Title one column *zygote*, another *embryo*, and a third *fetus*. Complete the information for all three columns. If you need help, refer to page 722.

New View of the Old

Imagine that you are 90 years old. How would you describe yourself? Some young people think that the elderly are forgetful and physically impaired. They associate certain conditions with aging—loss of hearing and sight, arthritis, osteoporosis, diabetes, and Alzheimer's disease, for example. They assume that older people have less physical energy and mental ability than younger people.

New Findings

The traditional view of the elderly has changed in light of recent studies. Researchers who studied people over age 90 discovered that the majority were mentally alert and physically active. Those over 90 suffered fewer health problems than those in their 70s and 80s. Centenarians, people 100 years old and over, participated in golf, tennis, bowling, swimming, and other physical activities. Some also were active in writing, art, reading, and business.

Longevity Genes

Why do some people remain in good health to an advanced age? Researchers think that certain genes control the aging process. Genes also may be responsible for a person's physical and mental ability to deal with disease or injury. Scientists think that genes also may determine how much functional reserve a person's organs have. For example, a centenarian may have extensive areas of damaged brain cells, but healthy cells in reserve allow these people to function normally. Obviously, good health habits also contribute to a long, healthy life.

A New View

This new image of the physical and mental wellness of the very old has had an effect on health care. Traditionally, health care programs have assumed that more and more resources would be needed as a person grows older. However, the overall good health of people over 90 may keep their health maintenance costs lower than predicted.

*inter*NET
CONNECTION

The American Association of Retired Persons is a nonprofit organization dedicated to helping older Americans. Visit the Glencoe Science Web Site at **www.glencoe.com/sec/ science** to learn more about AARP and its activities.

Average Growth Rate in Humans

Materials
• Graph paper
• Red and blue pencils

An individual's growth is dependent upon both the effects of hormones and his or her genetic makeup.

What You'll Investigate

Is average growth rate the same in males and females?

Goals

• **Analyze** the average growth rate of young males and females.

• **Compare and contrast** their growth rates.

Procedure

1. **Construct** a graph. **Label** mass on the vertical axis and age on the horizontal axis.

2. **Plot** the data in the table below for the average female growth in mass from ages eight to 18. **Connect** the points with a red line.

3. On the same graph, **plot** the data for the average male growth in mass from ages eight to 18. **Connect** the points with a blue line.

4. **Construct** a separate graph. **Label** height on the vertical axis and age on the horizontal axis.

5. **Plot** the data for the average female growth in height from ages eight to 18. **Connect** the points with a red line. **Plot** the data for the average male growth in height from ages eight to 18. **Connect** the points with a blue line.

Conclude and Apply

1. Up to what age is average growth rate in mass similar in males and females?

2. Up to what age is average growth rate in height similar in males and females?

3. When does the mass of females generally change the most?

4. How can you explain the differences in growth between males and females?

5. **Interpret** the data to determine whether the average growth rate is the same in males and females.

Average Growth and Mass in Humans				
Averages for Growth in Humans				
Age	Mass (kg)		Height (cm)	
	Female	Male	Female	Male
8	25	25	123	124
9	28	28	129	130
10	31	31	135	135
11	35	37	140	140
12	40	38	147	145
13	47	43	155	152
14	50	50	159	161
15	54	57	160	167
16	57	62	163	172
17	58	65	163	174
18	58	68	163	178

For a **preview** of this chapter, study this Reviewing Main Ideas before you read the chapter. After you have studied this chapter, you can use the Reviewing Main Ideas to **review** the chapter.

The Glencoe MindJogger, Audiocassettes, and CD-ROM provide additional opportunities for review.

Section 23-1 HUMAN REPRODUCTION

Reproduction is a means to continue life. The union of an egg and **sperm** starts the process of development from a zygote to a complete human being. The reproductive system allows new organisms to be created. **Testes** in males produce sperm. Sperm are single cells with a head and a tail. The tail allows the sperm to move as it travels through the uterus and along the oviduct to the egg. Eggs are produced by the **ovaries** in females. An egg is released from one of the ovaries on about the fourteenth day of the menstrual cycle. The egg is drawn into the oviduct, where fertilization can occur. The fertilization of an egg by a sperm forms new life. Eggs that are not fertilized disintegrate, and the lining of the **uterus** is shed. *What are the differences in the structure of the egg and sperm?*

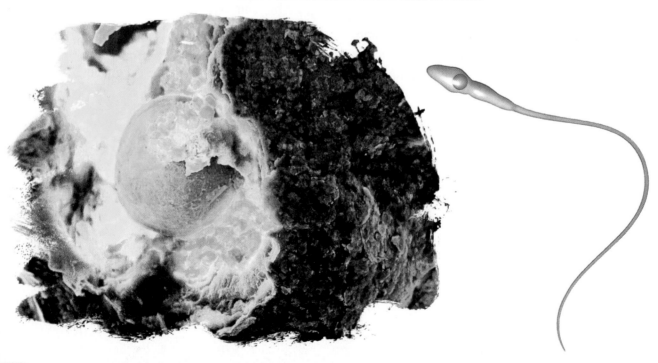

Reading Check ☑

Review a child's development. What signal words indicate the sequence of development? (An example includes words such as *next*.)

Section
23-2 FERTILIZATION TO BIRTH

When fertilized, the egg forms a zygote. The zygote moves through the oviduct and implants in the wall of the uterus. During the first two months of pregnancy, the unborn child is known as an **embryo.** A placenta forms, and the umbilical cord supplies nutrients and oxygen from the mother to the baby. Wastes are carried away through the umbilical cord. After two months, the body organs have formed and the developing baby is called a **fetus.** After nine months, the developed baby is pushed out of the mother by contractions of the uterus. Twins occur when two eggs are fertilized or when a single egg splits after fertilization. *Why are so many sperm released if only one is needed to fertilize the egg?*

Section
23-3 DEVELOPMENT AFTER BIRTH

Infancy is the stage of development from the neonatal period to one year. This stage is followed by **childhood,** which lasts to age 12 and is marked by development of muscular coordination and mental abilities. **Adolescence** is when a person becomes physically able to reproduce. The final stage of development is **adulthood.** A number of conditions are associated with aging. Certain genes are believed to be responsible for aging and for a person's adaptive ability and functional reserve. *How are the characteristics of the stages of infancy and childhood alike?*

Chapter 23 Assessment

Using Vocabulary

a. adolescence
b. adulthood
c. amniotic sac
d. childhood
e. embryo
f. fetus
g. infancy
h. menopause
i. menstrual cycle
j. menstruation
k. ovary
l. ovulation
m. pregnancy
n. reproduction
o. semen
p. sperm
q. testis
r. uterus
s. vagina

Which science term describes each of the following?

1. birth canal
2. egg-producing organ
3. release of egg from the ovary
4. place where a fertilized egg develops into a baby
5. membrane that protects the unborn baby

Checking Concepts

Choose the word or phrase that best answers the question.

6. Where does the embryo develop?
   A) oviduct
   B) ovary
   C) uterus
   D) vagina

7. What is the monthly process of egg release called?
   A) fertilization
   B) ovulation
   C) menstruation
   D) puberty

8. What is the union of an egg and sperm?
   A) fertilization
   B) ovulation
   C) menstruation
   D) puberty

9. Where is the egg fertilized?
   A) oviduct
   B) uterus
   C) vagina
   D) ovary

10. During which period do mental and physical skills rapidly develop?
    A) the neonatal period
    B) infancy
    C) adulthood
    D) adolescence

11. During which period does puberty occur?
    A) childhood
    B) adulthood
    C) adolescence
    D) infancy

12. What are sex characteristics common to both males and females?
    A) breasts
    B) increased muscles
    C) increased fat
    D) pubic hair

13. During which period does growth stop?
    A) childhood
    B) adolescence
    C) adulthood
    D) infancy

14. What is the period of development with three stages?
    A) infancy
    B) adulthood
    C) adolescence
    D) childhood

15. During which period does the ability to reproduce begin?
    A) adolescence
    B) adulthood
    C) childhood
    D) infancy

Thinking Critically

16. Explain the similar functions of the ovaries and testes.

17. Identify the structure in which each process occurs: ovulation, fertilization, and implantation.

18. When does menopause occur?

19. What kind of cell division occurs as the zygote develops?

20. Describe one major change in each stage of human development.

Developing Skills

If you need help, refer to the **Skill Handbook.**

21. **Classifying:** Classify each of the following structures of the male and female reproductive systems as female or male and internal or external: ovary, penis, scrotum, testes, uterus, and vagina.

22. **Concept Map:** Construct a concept map of egg release using the following terms: *ovary, ovulation, oviduct, uterus,* and *zygote.*

23. **Hypothesizing:** Make a hypothesis about the effects of raising identical twins apart from each other.

24. **Making and Using Graphs:** The growth of an embryo does not occur at the same rate throught development. Use the data below to make a graph showing the week of development versus size of the embryo. When is the fastest period of growth?

Embryo Size During Development

Week After Fertilization	Size
3	3 mm
4	6 mm
6	12 mm
7	2 cm
8	4 cm
9	5 cm

25. **Sequencing:** Sequence the steps involved in the birth process.

THE PRINCETON REVIEW

Test-Taking Tip

Maximize Your Score Ask how your test will be scored. In order to do your best, you need to know if there is a penalty for guessing, and if so, how much of one. If there is no penalty at all, you should always fill in what you think is the best answer.

Test Practice

Use these questions to test your Science Proficiency.

1. During the menstrual cycle, the lining of the uterus thickens. Which statement **BEST** explains the need for this phase?
   A) to prepare the uterus for sperm to fertilize an egg
   B) to prepare the uterus for discharging excess eggs from the body
   C) to prepare the uterus for supporting and nourishing the developing embryo
   D) to prepare the uterus for hormones that fight infections

2. Sperm travel a long pathway before being discharged from the body. Which statement is the correct sequence of structures through which the sperm pass?
   A) testis—sperm duct—prostate—urethra
   B) testis—sperm duct—ureter—prostate
   C) testis—seminal vesicles—sperm duct—urethra
   D) testis—urethra—prostate—sperm duct

Chapter Preview

Skills Preview

Skill Builders
- Compare and Contrast

Activities
- Experiment and Analyze

MiniLabs
- Test and Observe
- Calculate and Graph

Reading Check ✓

As you read this chapter, complete a chart with three columns: the name of the disease, its cause, and its effects.

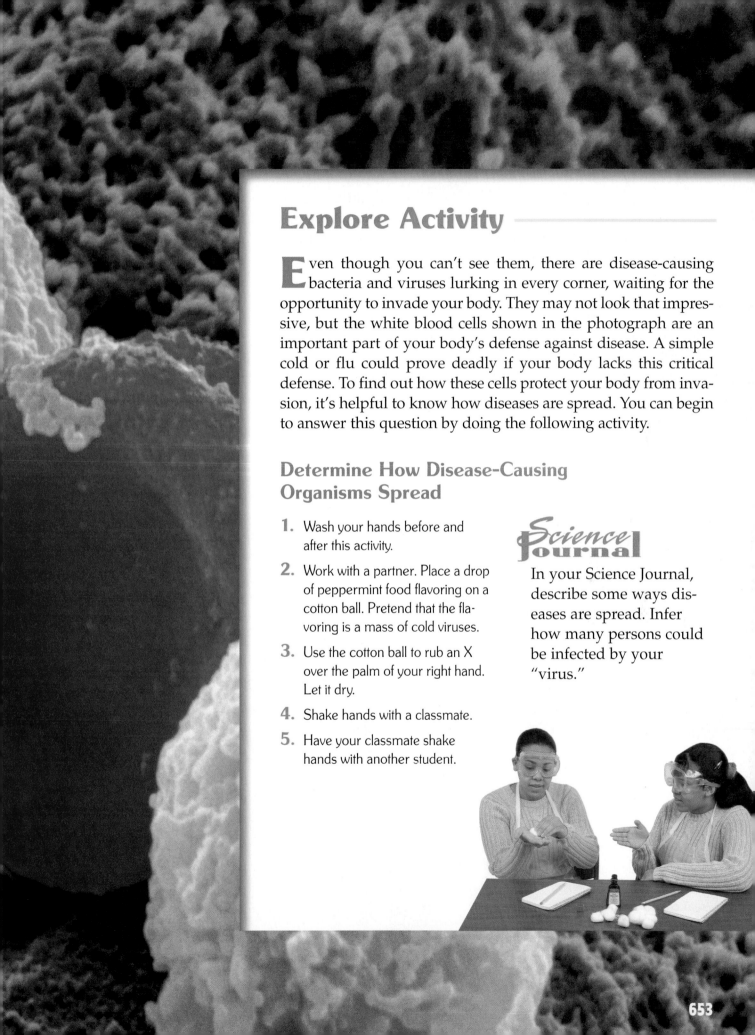

Explore Activity

Even though you can't see them, there are disease-causing bacteria and viruses lurking in every corner, waiting for the opportunity to invade your body. They may not look that impressive, but the white blood cells shown in the photograph are an important part of your body's defense against disease. A simple cold or flu could prove deadly if your body lacks this critical defense. To find out how these cells protect your body from invasion, it's helpful to know how diseases are spread. You can begin to answer this question by doing the following activity.

Determine How Disease-Causing Organisms Spread

1. Wash your hands before and after this activity.

2. Work with a partner. Place a drop of peppermint food flavoring on a cotton ball. Pretend that the flavoring is a mass of cold viruses.

3. Use the cotton ball to rub an X over the palm of your right hand. Let it dry.

4. Shake hands with a classmate.

5. Have your classmate shake hands with another student.

Science Journal

In your Science Journal, describe some ways diseases are spread. Infer how many persons could be infected by your "virus."

653

Communicable Diseases

What You'll Learn

▶ The work of Pasteur, Koch, and Lister in the discovery and prevention of disease
▶ Diseases caused by viruses and bacteria
▶ Sexually transmitted diseases (STDs), their causes, and treatments

Vocabulary
pasteurization
disinfectant
antiseptic
communicable disease
sexually transmitted disease (STD)

Why It's Important

▶ You can help prevent certain illnesses if you know what causes disease and how disease spreads.

Discovering Disease

"Ring around the rosie, A pocket full of posies, Ashes, Ashes, We all fall down."

You may not know that this rhyme is more than 600 years old. Some think this rhyme is about a disease called the Black Death, or the Plague. As shown in **Figure 24-1,** several times during the fourteenth century, the Plague spread through Europe. "Ring around the rosie" was a symptom of the disease—a ring around a red spot on the skin. People carried a pocket full of flower petals, "posies," and spices to keep away the stench of dead bodies. In spite of these efforts, 25 million people "all fell down" and died from this terrible disease.

Causes of Disease

No one knew what caused the Plague or how to stop it as it swept through Europe. It wasn't until about 150 years ago that scientists began to find out how some diseases are caused. Today, we know that diseases are caused by viruses, protozoans, and harmful bacteria. These are known as pathogens.

The French chemist Louis Pasteur proved that harmful bacteria could cause disease. He developed a method of using heat to kill pathogens. **Pasteurization** (pas chuh ruh ZAY shun), named for him, is the process of heating food to a temperature that kills most bacteria. Pasteur's work began the science of bacteriology.

Figure 24-1 Plague is caused by a bacterium that reproduces in fleas that live on rats. **What conditions in the towns of the fourteenth century encouraged the spread of this disease?**

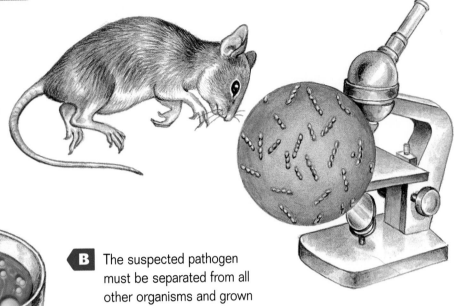

Figure 24-2 The steps used to identify an organism as the cause of a specific disease are known as Koch's rules.

A In every case of a particular disease, the organism thought to cause the disease must be present.

B The suspected pathogen must be separated from all other organisms and grown in a culture with no other organisms present.

C When the suspected pathogen from the pure culture is placed in a healthy host, it must become sick with the original disease.

D Finally, when the suspected pathogen is removed from the host and grown on agar gel again, it must be compared with the original organism to see whether they are the same. When they match, that organism is the pathogen that causes that disease.

Koch's Rules

Pasteur may have shown that bacteria caused disease, but he didn't know how to tell which specific organism caused a specific disease. It was a German doctor, Robert Koch, who first developed a way to isolate and grow, or culture, one type of bacterium at a time. Koch developed a set of rules to figure out which organism caused a particular disease. These rules are illustrated in **Figure 24-2.**

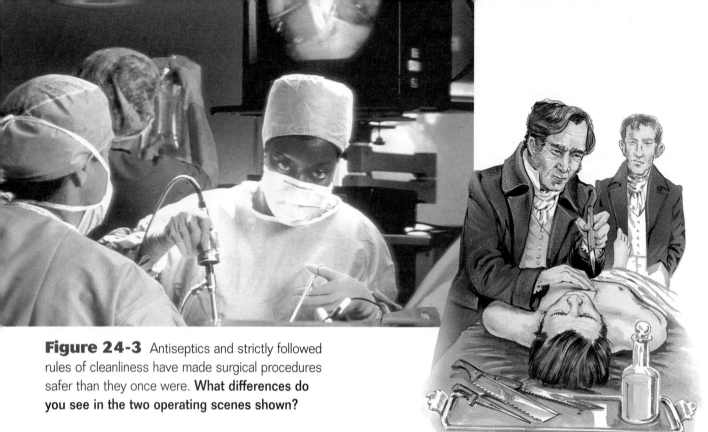

Figure 24-3 Antiseptics and strictly followed rules of cleanliness have made surgical procedures safer than they once were. **What differences do you see in the two operating scenes shown?**

Reading Check ☑

Outline the work done by Pasteur, Koch, and Lister in the discovery and prevention of disease.

PHYSICS
INTEGRATION

Surface Tension
Many chemical disinfectants lower the surface tension of bacteria, allowing the chemical to be more easily absorbed. Find out what surface tension is. Infer what makes a disinfectant effective.

Keeping Clean

Washing your hands before or after certain activities is an accepted part of your daily routine. This was not always true, even for doctors. Into the late 1800s, doctors, such as those in **Figure 24-3,** regularly operated in their street clothes and with bare hands. More patients died in surgery than survived surgery. Joseph Lister, an English surgeon, was horrified. He recognized the relationship between the infection rate and cleanliness in surgery. Lister dramatically reduced deaths among his surgical patients by washing their skin and his hands before surgery. ☑

Disinfectants and Antiseptics

Lister used a disinfectant to reduce surgical infections. A **disinfectant** kills pathogens on objects such as instruments, floors, and bathtubs. Today, antiseptics also are used. An **antiseptic** kills pathogens on skin and continues to prevent them from growing for some time after. Doctors now wash their hands often with antiseptic soaps. They also wear sterile gloves to keep from spreading pathogens from person to person.

While the role of bacteria in causing disease was better understood and the use of disinfectants and antiseptics reduced the spread of disease, doctors did not understand why some diseases could not be controlled. Not until the late 1800s and early 1900s did scientists make a connection between viruses and disease transmission.

How Diseases Are Spread

A disease that is spread to an organism from an infected organism or the environment is a **communicable disease.** Communicable diseases are caused by agents such as viruses, some bacteria, protists, and fungi. Some diseases caused by these agents are listed in **Table 24-1.**

Communicable diseases are spread through water and air, on food, by contact with contaminated objects, and by biological vectors. A biological vector is a carrier of a disease. Examples of vectors that spread disease are rats, flies, birds, cats, dogs, and mosquitos as in **Figure 24-4.** To prevent the spread of disease, city water systems add chlorine to drinking water and swimming pools. When you have influenza and sneeze, you hurl thousands of virus particles through the air. Colds and many other diseases are spread through contact. Each time you turn a doorknob or press the button on a water fountain at school, your skin comes in contact with bacteria and viruses. Some dangerous communicable diseases are transmitted by sexual contact.

In the United States, the Centers for Disease Control and Prevention (CDC) in Atlanta, Georgia, monitors the spread of diseases throughout the country. The CDC also watches for diseases brought into the country.

Mini Lab

Detecting Bacteria
Procedure

1. Methylene blue is used to detect bacteria. The faster the color fades, the more bacteria are present.
2. Use the food samples provided by your teacher. Label four test tubes 1, 2, 3, and 4.
3. Fill three test tubes half full of the food samples.
4. Fill all four tubes with water.
5. Add 20 drops of methylene blue and 2 drops of mineral oil to each tube.
6. Place the tubes into a warm-water bath for 20 minutes.
7. Record the time and your observations.

Analysis

1. Compare how long it takes each tube to lose its color.
2. What was the purpose of tube 4?
3. Why is it important to eat and drink only the freshest food?

Figure 24-4
Pathogenic organisms include bacteria, protists, fungi, and viruses. **How does the mosquito transport pathogens from infected people or objects to new hosts?**

Table 24-1

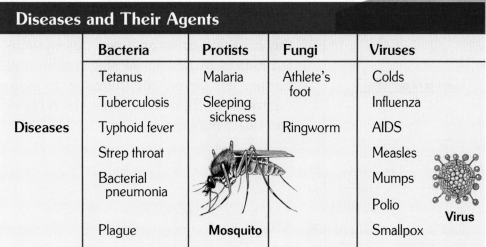

Diseases and Their Agents				
	Bacteria	**Protists**	**Fungi**	**Viruses**
Diseases	Tetanus	Malaria	Athlete's foot	Colds
	Tuberculosis	Sleeping sickness		Influenza
	Typhoid fever		Ringworm	AIDS
	Strep throat			Measles
	Bacterial pneumonia			Mumps
				Polio
	Plague	**Mosquito**		Smallpox

Virus

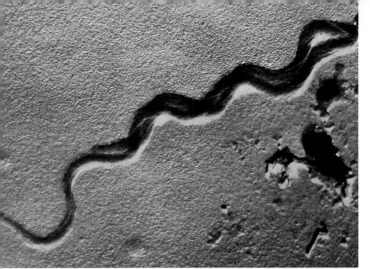

Figure 24-5 The bacterium that causes syphilis can be seen in this electron micrograph.

Magnification: 19 000×

Sexually Transmitted Diseases

Diseases transmitted from person to person during sexual contact are called **sexually transmitted diseases (STDs).** You can become infected with an STD by engaging in sexual activity with an infected person. STDs are caused by both viruses and bacteria.

Genital herpes causes painful blisters on the sex organs. Herpes can be transmitted during sexual contact or by an infected mother to her child during birth. The herpes virus hides in the body for long periods and then reappears suddenly. Herpes has no cure, and no vaccine can prevent it.

Gonorrhea and chlamydial infections are STDs caused by bacteria that may not produce any symptoms. When symptoms do appear, they can include painful urination, genital discharge, and sores. Antibiotics are used to treat these diseases. If left untreated, both diseases can cause sterility, which is the inability to reproduce.

The strangely shaped bacterium that causes syphilis is seen in **Figure 24-5.** Syphilis has several stages. In stage 1, a sore that lasts ten to 14 days appears on the mouth or genitals. Stage 2 may involve a rash, a fever, and swollen lymph glands. Within weeks to a year, these symptoms usually disappear. The victim often believes that the disease has gone away, but it hasn't. In Stage 3, syphilis may infect the cardiovascular and nervous systems. Syphilis is treated in all stages with antibiotics. However, the damage to body organs in the third stage cannot be reversed and death may result.

HIV and AIDS

HIV, shown in **Figure 24-6,** is a latent virus that can exist in blood and body fluids. A latent virus is one that hides in body cells. You can contract HIV by having sex with an HIV-infected person, or by sharing an HIV-contaminated needle used to inject drugs. The risk of contracting HIV through blood transfusion is small. Donated blood is tested for the presence of HIV. A pregnant female with HIV may infect her child when the virus passes through the placenta, when blood contacts the child during birth, or when nursing after birth. An HIV infection can lead to AIDS, a disease that attacks the body's immune system and eventually kills its victims. AIDS stands for Acquired Immune Deficiency Syndrome. No vaccine prevents AIDS, and no medication cures it. In the next section, more information will be given on how HIV breaks down the immune system.

Some communicable diseases are chronic. A chronic disease lasts a long time. AIDS is a chronic disease that, as yet, cannot be cured. Some chronic diseases can be cured. Lyme disease, carried by ticks, is a bacterial infection that can become chronic if not treated. The bacteria can affect the nervous system, heart, and joints for weeks to years. Antibiotics will kill the bacteria, but any permanent damage cannot be reversed. In Section 24-3, you will learn about chronic diseases that are not caused by pathogens.

Figure 24-6 HIV is a latent virus that can exist in blood and body fluids. It attacks the helper T cells.

Section Assessment

1. How did the discoveries of Pasteur, Koch, and Lister help in the battle against disease?

2. List a communicable disease caused by a virus, a bacterium, a protist, and a fungus.

3. What are STDs? How are they contracted and treated?

4. **Think Critically:** In what ways does Koch's procedure reflect the use of scientific methods?

5.  **Skill Builder**
   Recognizing Cause and Effect How is not washing your hands related to the spread of disease? Do the **Chapter 24 Skill Activity** on page 749 to analyze the effects of certain health habits.

Science Journal Research the history of the building of the Panama Canal. Write a report in your Science Journal about the relationship between the diseases of malaria and yellow fever and the building of the canal.

Microorganisms and Disease

Materials

- Fresh apples (6)
- Rotting apple
- Alcohol (5 mL)
- Self-sealing plastic bags (6)
- Labels and pencil
- Paper towels
- Sandpaper
- Cotton ball
- Soap and water

Microorganisms are all around us. They are on the surfaces of everything we touch. Try this experiment to see how microorganisms are involved in spreading infections.

What You'll Investigate

How do microorganisms cause infection?

Goals

- **Observe** the transmission of microorganisms.
- **Relate** microorganisms to infections.

Procedure

1. **Label** the plastic bags 1 through 6. **Put** a fresh apple in bag 1 and **seal** it.

2. **Rub** the rotting apple over the entire surface of the remaining five apples. This is your source of microorganisms. **CAUTION:** *Always wash your hands after handling microorganisms.* **Put** one apple in bag 2.

3. **Hold** one apple 1.5 m above the floor and drop it. **Put** this apple into bag number 3.

4. **Rub** one apple with sandpaper. **Place** this apple in bag number 4.

5. **Wash** one apple with soap and water. **Dry** it well. **Put** this apple in bag number 5.

6. **Use** a cotton ball to spread alcohol over the last apple. Let it air dry. **Place** it in bag 6.

7. **Place** all of the apples in a dark place for three days. Then, **wash** your hands.

8. **Write a hypothesis** to explain what you think will happen to each apple.

9. At the end of day 3 and again on day 7, **compare** all of the apples. **Record** your observations in a data table like the one shown. **CAUTION:** *Give all apples to your teacher for proper disposal.*

Conclude and Apply

1. Did you **observe** changes in apple numbers 5 and 6?

2. Why is it important to clean a wound?

3. Were your hypotheses supported?

4. **Relate** microorganisms to infections on your skin.

Apple Data			
Apple	**Condition of the apple**	**Observations**	
		Day 3	**Day 7**
1	Fresh apple		
2	Untreated apple		
3	Dropped apple		
4	Apple rubbed with sandpaper		
5	Apple washed with soap and water		
6	Apple covered with alcohol		

Your Immune System

Lines of Defense

Most microorganisms do not cause disease. Your body has many ways to defend itself against the ones that do. First-line defenses are general and work against all types of pathogens. Second-line defenses are specific and work against particular pathogens.

Your **immune system** is a complex group of defenses that your body has to fight disease. It is made up of cells, tissues, organs, and body systems that fight pathogens, harmful chemicals, and cancer cells.

General Defenses

Several body systems are involved in defending your body from pathogens. Your skin is a barrier that prevents many pathogens from entering your body. Your respiratory system contains cilia and mucus that trap pathogens. When you cough, you expel trapped bacteria. In the digestive system, enzymes in the stomach, pancreas, and liver destroy pathogens. Pathogens are disease-causing organisms. Hydrochloric acid in your stomach kills bacteria that enter your body on food.

Your circulatory system contains white blood cells that engulf and digest foreign organisms and chemicals. These white blood cells constantly patrol the body, sweeping up and digesting bacteria that manage to get into the body. As you see in **Figure 24-7,** they slip between cells in the walls of capillaries to destroy bacteria. When the white blood cells cannot destroy the bacteria fast enough, a fever may develop. A fever helps fight pathogens by slowing their growth and speeding up your body's reactions.

All of these processes are general defenses that work to keep you disease-free. If pathogens get past these general defenses, your body has another line of defense in the form of specific immunity.

Figure 24-7 White blood cells leave capillaries (A) and engulf harmful bacteria (B) in surrounding tissues. **What are harmful bacteria called?**

What You'll Learn

► The natural defenses your body has against disease
► Differences between active and passive immunity
► How HIV affects the immune system

Vocabulary
immune system
antigen
antibody
active immunity
passive immunity
vaccination
helper T cells

Why It's Important

► Your body's defenses fight the pathogens you are exposed to every day.

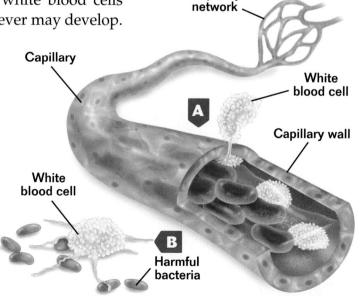

Capillary network

Capillary

White blood cell

A

White blood cell

Capillary wall

B

Harmful bacteria

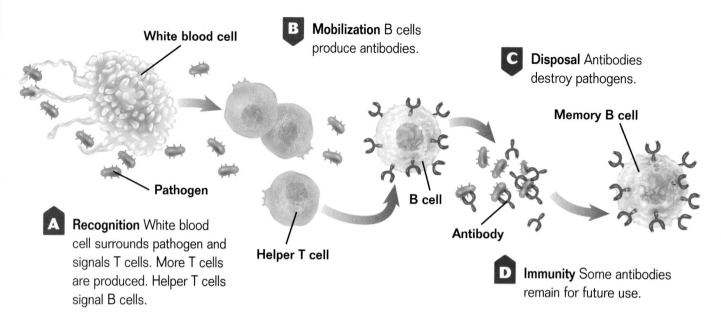

B **Mobilization** B cells produce antibodies.

C **Disposal** Antibodies destroy pathogens.

White blood cell

Pathogen

Memory B cell

B cell

Antibody

Helper T cell

A **Recognition** White blood cell surrounds pathogen and signals T cells. More T cells are produced. Helper T cells signal B cells.

D **Immunity** Some antibodies remain for future use.

Figure 24-8 The response of your immune system to disease-causing organisms can be divided into four steps: recognition, mobilization, disposal, and immunity. **What is the function of B cells?**

Visit the Glencoe Science Web Site at **www.glencoe.com/ sec/science** for more information about your lines of defense.

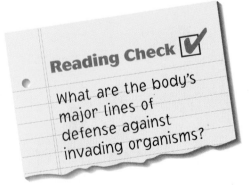
Specific Defenses

When your body fights disease, it is really battling proteins or chemicals that don't belong there. Proteins and chemicals that are foreign to your body are called **antigens** (AN tih junz). Antigens are located on the surfaces of pathogens. When your immune system recognizes a foreign protein or chemical, as in **Figure 24-8,** it forms specific antibodies. An **antibody** is a protein made by an animal in response to a specific antigen. The antibody binds up the antigen, making it harmless. Antibodies help your body build defenses in two ways, actively and passively. **Active immunity** occurs when your body makes its own antibodies in response to an antigen. **Passive immunity** occurs when antibodies that have been produced in another animal are introduced into the body.

Active Immunity

When your body is invaded by a pathogen, it immediately starts to make antibodies to inactivate the antigen. Once enough antibodies form, you get better. Some antibodies stay on duty in your blood, and more are rapidly produced if the pathogen enters your body again. This is why you do not get some diseases more than once. ✔

Another way to develop active immunity to a particular disease is to be inoculated with a vaccine. The process of giving a vaccine by injection or orally is called **vaccination.** A vaccine is a noninfectious form of the antigen and gives you active immunity against a disease without you actually getting the disease first. For example, suppose a vaccine for measles is injected into your body. Your body forms antibodies against the measles antigen. If you later encounter the virus, antibodies necessary to fight that virus are already in your bloodstream ready to destroy the pathogen. Antibodies that immunize you against one virus may not guard against a different virus. As you grow older, you will be exposed to many more types of pathogens and will build a separate immunity to each one.

Passive Immunity

How is passive immunity different from active immunity? Recall that passive immunity is the transfer of antibodies into your body. For example, you were born with all the antibodies that your mother had in her blood. However, these antibodies stayed with you for only a few months. Passive immunity does not last as long as active immunity. Because newborn babies lose their passive immunity in a few months, they need to be vaccinated to develop their own immunity.

Tetanus is a toxin produced by a bacterium in soil. The toxin paralyzes muscles. As a child, you received active vaccines that stimulated antibody production to tetanus toxin. As shown in **Figure 24-9,** you should continue to get active vaccines or "boosters" every ten years to maintain active protection. Suppose a person who has never been vaccinated against tetanus toxin gets a puncture wound. The person would be given passive immunity—antibodies to the toxin. These antibodies usually are from humans but can be from horses or cattle if human antibodies are not available.

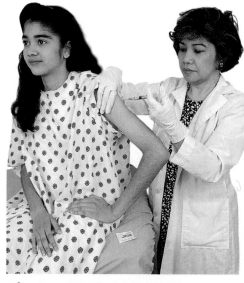

Figure 24-9 Tetanus is a toxin produced by a bacterium that lives in the soil. An active vaccine or "booster" every ten years will maintain active protection against the toxin.

Problem Solving

Interpreting Data

Each year, many people die from diseases. Medical science has found many ways to treat and cure disease. New drugs, improved surgery techniques, and healthier lifestyles have contributed to the decrease in deaths from disease. The chart shown here indicates the percent of total deaths due to six major diseases for a 45-year span. Study the statistics for each disease.

Think Critically: Which diseases have had a steady decline in deaths through the 45 years? Have any diseases shown an increase in deaths? What factors may have contributed to this increase?

Percentage of Deaths Due to Major Diseases

Disease	Year			
	1950	1980	1990	1995
Heart	37.1	38.3	33.5	32.0
Cancer	14.6	20.9	23.5	23.3
Stroke	10.8	8.6	6.7	6.8
Diabetes	1.7	1.8	2.2	2.6
Pneumonia and Flu	3.3	2.7	3.7	3.6
Tuberculosis	2.3	0.10	0.08	0.06

Figure 24-10 A person can be infected with HIV and not show any symptoms of the infection for several years. **Why does this characteristic make the spread of AIDS more likely?**

HIV and Your Immune System

HIV, as shown in **Figure 24-10,** is different from other viruses. It attacks cells in the immune system called helper T cells. A **helper T cell** is a type of white blood cell that helps other types of white blood cells produce antibodies.

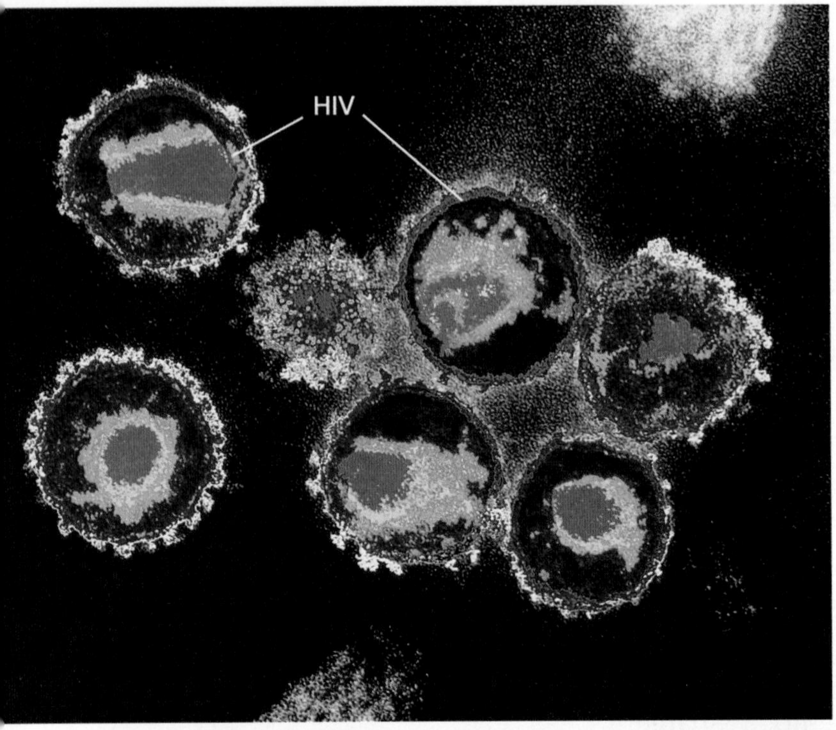

Because HIV destroys helper T cells, the body is left with no way to fight invading antigens. The immune system breaks down. The body is unable to fight HIV, many other pathogens, and certain types of cancer. For this reason, people with AIDS die from other diseases such as pneumonia, cancer, or tuberculosis. The victim's body becomes defenseless.

When a microbe enters your body, it must get past all of your general defenses. If it gets past these defenses, it encounters your specific defenses—your second line of defense.

HIV

Magnification: 130 000×

Section Assessment

1. List natural defenses your body has against disease.

2. How does an active vaccine work in the human body?

3. Explain how HIV attacks your immune system.

4. **Think Critically:** Several diseases have the same symptoms as measles. Why doesn't the measles vaccine protect you from all of these diseases?

5. **Skill Builder**
Developing Multimedia Presentations Prepare a presentation for the class on the history of immunization for a specific disease. If you need help, refer to Developing Multimedia Presentations in the **Technology Skills Handbook** on page 720.

Using Computers

Graphics Use the information in this section to create a flowchart that compares active and passive immunity. If you need help, refer to page 718.

AIDS Vaccine

Moving Target

One of the most intensive efforts in the history of medicine is currently under way—to develop a vaccine against the human immunodeficiency virus, or HIV (round virus particles, inset). Because HIV mutates, or changes, rapidly, it is difficult to develop a single vaccine that can stimulate the human immune system to mount a successful attack on the virus and its many variations. Researchers are trying different vaccine strategies to try to solve this problem. The HIV researcher, left, is working in sterile clothing, his hands placed under a protective hood. Some of the vaccine strategies being tested are discussed below.

Subunit

The subunit method involves using a piece of the HIV's outer surface that contains certain proteins. The human immune system produces antibodies that recognize this subunit on complete HIV viruses.

Viruslike Particles

Another experimental vaccine uses a noninfectious HIV look-alike. The look-alike causes the body to produce antibodies against actual HIV.

Live Attenuated Virus

The live attenuated virus method uses actual HIV virus particles that have been weakened by the removal of one or more of their disease-causing genes. This type of vaccine seems to offer the broadest protection of all the experimental HIV vaccines tested so far.

Whole Inactivated Virus

Another strategy involves using an HIV virus that is inactivated by chemicals, irradiation, or other means. The resulting virus is not infectious, and it can cause the immune system to produce antibodies against HIV.

Only with thorough research will scientists find a vaccine powerful enough to solve the unique problems that HIV presents.

interNET CONNECTION

AIDS research is such a massive effort that information is updated constantly. Visit the Glencoe Science Web Site at **www.glencoe.com/sec/ science** to find links that will help you locate the latest information available. Prepare and present a report on the progress of AIDS vaccine research.

Microorganism Growth

Possible Materials

- Sterile petri dishes with agar (5)
- Filter paper (2-cm squares)
- Test chemicals (disinfectant, hydrogen peroxide, mouthwash, alcohol)
- Transparent tape
- Pencil and labels
- Scissors
- Metric ruler
- Forceps
- Small jars for chemicals (4)
- Cotton balls

Infections are caused by microorganisms. Without cleanliness, the risk of getting an infection from a wound is high. Disinfectants are chemicals that kill or remove disease organisms from objects. Antiseptics are chemicals that kill or prevent growth of disease organisms on living tissues. You will test the effect of these chemicals by growing microorganisms in petri dishes filled with agar. Agar is a gel that provides the ideal nutrients for growing microorganisms.

Recognize the Problem

What conditions do microorganisms need to grow? How can they be prevented from growing?

Form a Hypothesis

Based on your knowledge of disinfectants and antiseptics, **state a hypothesis** about methods that will prevent the growth of microorganisms.

Goals

- **Observe** the effects of antiseptics and disinfectants on microorganism growth in petri dishes.
- **Design** an experiment that will test the effects of chemicals on microorganisms growing in contaminated petri dishes.

Safety Precautions

Handle the forceps carefully. When you complete the experiment, give your sealed petri dishes to your teacher for proper disposal.

Test Your Hypothesis

Plan

1. As a group, agree upon and write out a hypothesis statement.

2. To test disinfectants, first introduce microorganisms to the agar by rubbing your finger gently over each dish. Then, soak a different square of filter paper in each of the disinfectants. Place each square on the agar and seal the dishes with tape. Never break the seal. Look for bacteria growth under and around each square.

3. As a group, list the steps that you will need to take to test your hypothesis. Consider what you learned about how infections are stopped. **List** your materials.

4. **Design** a data table and record it in your Science Journal so that it is ready to use as your group collects data.

5. Read over your entire experiment to make sure that all steps are in logical order.

6. **Identify** any **constants, variables,** and the **control** of the experiment.

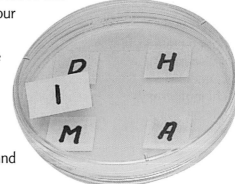

Do

1. Make sure your teacher approves your plan before you proceed.

2. Carry out the experiment as planned.

3. While the experiment is going on, write down any **observations** that you make and complete the **data table** in your Science Journal.

Analyze Your Data

1. **Compare** your results with those of other groups.

2. How did you **compare** growth beneath and around each chemical-soaked square in the petri dishes?

3. **Interpret the data** to determine what substances appeared to be most effective in preventing microorganism growth and what substances appeared to be least effective.

Draw Conclusions

1. What methods prevented the growth of microorganisms?

2. How does the growth of microorganisms on the control compare with their growth on the variables?

24·3 Noncommunicable Disease

Chronic Disease

Diseases and disorders such as diabetes, allergies, asthma, cancer, and heart disease are noncommunicable diseases. These diseases are called **noncommunicable diseases** because they are not spread from one person to another. You can't "catch" them. Allergies, genetic disorders, lifestyle diseases, or chemical imbalances such as diabetes are not spread by sneezes or handshakes.

Some communicable diseases can be chronic (KRAH nihk). Some noncommunicable diseases also are chronic. A chronic disease is one that lingers. Some chronic diseases can be cured. Others cannot. These diseases may result from improperly functioning organs, contact with harmful chemicals, or an unhealthy lifestyle. For example, your pancreas produces the hormone insulin. Diabetes is a chronic disease in which the pancreas cannot produce the amount of insulin the body needs.

Rheumatoid arthritis is a chronic disease that results from a faulty immune system. The immune system begins to treat the body's own normal proteins as if they were antigens. The faulty immune system forms antibodies against the normal proteins in joints. You can see in **Figure 24-11** that the joints become distorted and movement becomes difficult and painful.

Figure 24-11 Rheumatoid arthritis turns the body's immune system against itself. Healthy joints (A) may become severely deformed (B) as these X rays show.

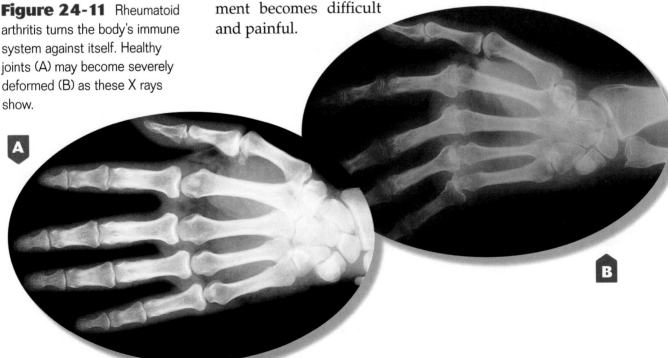

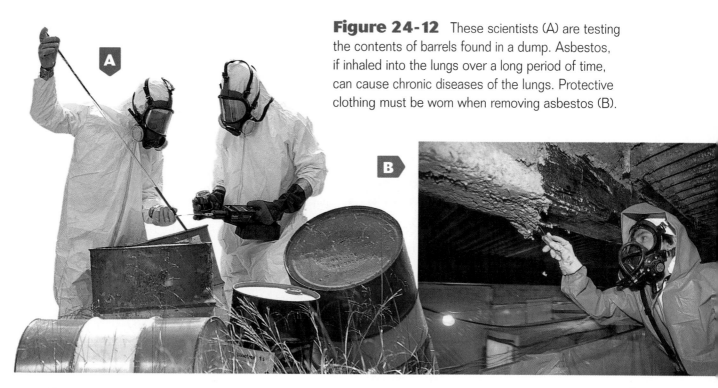

Figure 24-12 These scientists (A) are testing the contents of barrels found in a dump. Asbestos, if inhaled into the lungs over a long period of time, can cause chronic diseases of the lungs. Protective clothing must be worn when removing asbestos (B).

Chemicals and Disease

We are surrounded by chemicals. They are found in foods, cosmetics, cleaning products, pesticides, fertilizers, and building materials. Of the thousands of chemical substances used by consumers, less than two percent are harmful. Those chemicals that are harmful to living things are called toxins. Some chronic diseases are caused by toxins.

CHEMISTRY
◄ INTEGRATION

The Effects

The effects of a chemical toxin are determined by the amount that is taken into the body and how long the body is in contact with it. For example, a toxin taken into the body at low levels might cause cardiac or respiratory problems. Higher levels might even cause death. Some chemicals, such as asbestos shown in **Figure 24-12B,** may be inhaled into the lungs over a long period of time. Eventually, the asbestos can cause chronic diseases of the lungs. Lead-based paints are chemical toxins. If ingested, they can cause damage to the central nervous system. ☑

Manufacturing, mining, transportation, and farming produce waste products. These chemical substances may adversely affect the ability of the soil, water, and air to support life. Pollution, such as that caused by harmful chemicals, sometimes produces chronic diseases in humans. For example, the long-time exposure to carbon monoxide, sulfur oxides, and nitrogen oxides in the air may cause a number of diseases, including bronchitis, emphysema, and lung cancer.

Reading Check ☑

What determines the effect of a chemical toxin on the human body?

Cancer

Cancer is a major chronic disease. **Cancer** results from uncontrolled cell growth. There are many different types of cancer, but most of them have the characteristics shown in **Table 24-2.**

Table 24-2

Characteristics of Cancer Cells
• Cell growth is uncontrolled.
• These cells do not function as part of the body.
• The cells take up space and interfere with normal bodily functions.
• The cells travel throughout the body.
• The cells produce tumors and abnormal growths anywhere in the body.

Treatment

Treatment for cancer includes surgery to remove cancerous tissue, radiation with X rays to kill cancer cells, and chemotherapy. **Chemotherapy** (kee moh THAYR uh pee) is the use of chemicals to destroy cancer cells.

Cancers are complicated, and no one fully understands how cancers form. Some scientists hypothesize that cancer cells form regularly in the body. However, the immune system destroys them. Only if the immune system fails or becomes overwhelmed does the cancer begin to expand. Still, warnings, such as that in **Figure 24-13,** emphasize that tobacco products and exposure to harmful chemicals stimulate some cancers to form.

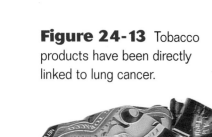

Figure 24-13 Tobacco products have been directly linked to lung cancer.

Allergies

Have you ever broken out in an itchy rash after eating a certain food? An **allergy** is an overly strong reaction of the immune system to a foreign substance. Many people have allergic reactions to cosmetics, shrimp, strawberries, peanuts, and bee stings. Allergic reactions to some things such as antibiotics can even be fatal.

Allergens

Substances that cause the allergic response are called **allergens.** These are substances that the body would normally respond to as a mild antigen. Chemicals, dust, food, pollen, molds, and some antibiotics are allergens for some sensitive people. When you come in contact with an allergen, your immune system forms antibodies and your body may react. When the body responds to an allergen, chemicals called histamines are released. Histamines promote red, swollen tissues. Allergic reactions are sometimes treated with antihistamines. Pollen is an allergen that causes a stuffy nose, breathing difficulties, watery eyes, and a tired feeling in some people. Some foods cause blotchy rashes such as hives, shown in **Figure 24-14,** or stomach cramps and diarrhea. Most allergic reactions are minor. But, severe allergic reactions can occur, causing shock and even death if not treated promptly. Some severe allergies are treated with repeated injections of small doses of the allergen. This allows the body to become less sensitive to the allergen.

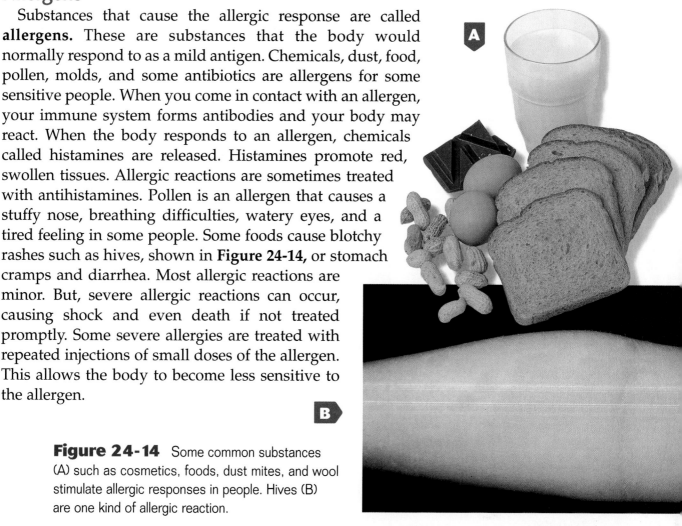

Figure 24-14 Some common substances (A) such as cosmetics, foods, dust mites, and wool stimulate allergic responses in people. Hives (B) are one kind of allergic reaction.

Section Assessment

1. What are two noncommunicable diseases?
2. What are the basic characteristics of cancer cells?
3. **Think Critically:** Joel has an ear infection. The doctor prescribes an antibiotic. After taking the antibiotic, Joel breaks out in a rash and has difficulty breathing. What is happening to him? What should he do immediately?
4. 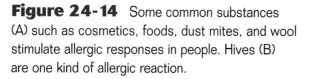 **Skill Builder**
   Making and Using Tables Make a table that lists some chronic diseases and their treatments. Use the information in this section. If you need help, refer to Making and Using Tables in the **Skill Handbook** on page 700.

Using Computers

Database Use references to find information on different allergens. Group the allergens into chemical, food, mold, pollen, and antibiotic. Use your computer to make a database. Note which group has the most allergens. If you need help, refer to page 717.

FIELD GUIDE *to First Aid*

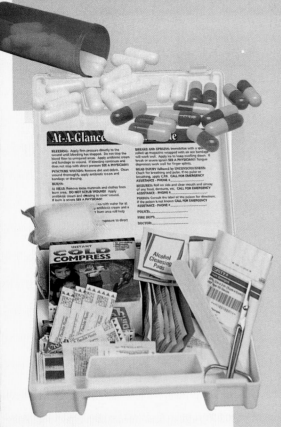

FIELD *ACTIVITY*

In the cafeteria at school, or in a place permitted by your principal, set up a display of first-aid information pamphlets and different types of first-aid kits. From the local Red Cross, find out the five most frequent types of emergencies that occur and set up posters at school showing how to treat each of these emergencies.

Have you ever found yourself in an emergency situation and wondered if you were the person who needed to help? Emergencies happen every day and everywhere. At the moment an emergency starts, you may not know how to react, but it is good to be well prepared. Learning ahead of time how to react can prevent disaster.

When and Where?

Emergencies come in all sorts of situations. It may be an auto accident or a fire. Maybe someone has slipped and twisted an ankle or perhaps cut a finger. Such things can happen at school, in the grocery store, at the movies, or at home. Regardless of where it happens or how big or small it is, what kinds of things might call your attention to an emergency situation?

Noises
- screaming or calls for help
- breaking glass
- sudden or loud noises made by things or a person falling
- screeching tires

Sights
- a stalled vehicle or a vehicle off the road
- spilled medicine or an opened, empty medicine container
- smoke or fire
- a person lying on the ground

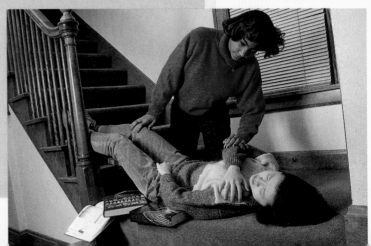

Odors
- different or strange odors
- odors that are stronger than usual

Appearance or Behavior of Another Person
- difficulty breathing
- grabbing his or her own throat
- unexplained confusion or drowsiness
- sudden change in skin color

To Act or Not to Act?

Someone must act in an emergency. Why not you? What things should you consider if you see an emergency? There are three basic steps to follow in an emergency. The steps are: Check, Call, and Care.

CHECK

Examine the scene
- Is it safe for you and any victims?
- Is there traffic, a chemical spill, extreme weather, or odors?
- If it's a dangerous situation, get help. **Remember, if you become injured, you can't help.**

Find out what happened
- Look for clues that may help to explain what caused the emergency.

Find all the victims
- Carefully account for everyone involved. Sometimes, a quiet victim may be overlooked if another is screaming.
- **Do not move victims unless they are in danger** from an explosion, fire, or poisonous gas.

Get help from others
- Anyone nearby may be able to provide more information about what happened, know where the nearest phone is, help with first aid, or comfort victims.

CALL

The most effective first-aid tool at your disposal is the telephone. In an emergency, call 911 or your local emergency number. Take the time now to find out your local emergency number. It will be valuable information if you find yourself in an emergency. Most importantly, don't hesitate to call for help, especially if you find yourself in the situations listed below. Emergency operators are trained to help you through emergency situations.

If the victim is:
- unconscious
- bleeding severely
- vomiting or passing blood

or has:
- chest pains or pressure
- trouble breathing or is making unusual noises as he or she breathes
- unexplained abdominal pressure or pain
- seizures, a severe headache, or slurred speech
- injuries to the head, neck, or back
- possible broken bones

Situations that require an immediate call are fire or explosion, downed electrical wires, flood conditions, presence of a poisonous gas, vehicle collisions, and victims who cannot be moved easily.

When calling the emergency service, **remember not to hang up first.** The emergency operator asks many questions, so it's important that you stay on the line until he or she has all the required information.

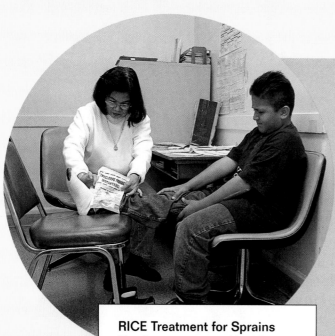

CARE

Before helping an ill or injured person, get his or her permission. Tell who you are, what training you have, and what you plan to do. If the person refuses permission, do not insist. Only a child's parent or guardian can give permission for that child. General guidelines for care are as follows:

- treat life-threatening emergencies first
- keep victims comfortable, talk to them, and be reassuring
- prevent the victim from becoming chilled or overheated
- talk with victims to identify location, type, and duration of pain
- if trained in first aid, follow standard procedures
- stay with victims until help arrives

If you remember and follow the 3 Cs, someone who is injured or ill may have a better chance to recover.

At some time in your life, you may be part of an emergency. What can you do to prepare should anything ever happen?

> **RICE Treatment for Sprains**
> The basic treatment for all types of sprains is the same. Use the term *RICE* to remember how to treat a sprain.
> **Rest**—Rest the joint when there is swelling.
> **Ice**—Apply ice for five to 15 minutes every hour.
> **Compression**—Use an elastic bandage to gently wrap the entire sprained joint.
> **Elevation**—Try to keep the joint straight and higher than the heart.

Emergency Checklist

- Learn first aid techniques.
- Learn when and how to use CPR (cardiopulmonary resuscitation) and the abdominal thrust for choking victims.
- Post emergency numbers by all phones and tape them to the first-aid kit. Teach young children how to telephone for help. Find out if your city has a 911 system.
- Place first-aid kits in your home, car, garage, and recreation areas.
- Put easy-to-read street numbers on your home or apartment. Numerals are easier to read than numbers that have been written out.
- If you have special medical needs, wear a medical alert tag.

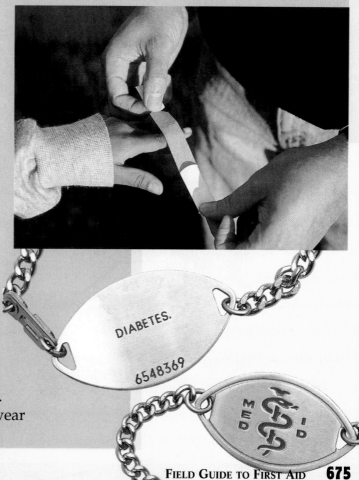

For a **preview** of this chapter, study this Reviewing Main Ideas before you read the chapter. After you have studied this chapter, you can use the Reviewing Main Ideas to **review** the chapter.

The Glencoe MindJogger, Audiocassettes, and CD-ROM provide additional opportunities for review.

Section 24-1 COMMUNICABLE DISEASES

Medical researchers Pasteur and Koch discovered that diseases are caused by microbes. **Communicable diseases** are caused by pathogenic bacteria, viruses, fungi, and protists and can be passed on through human contact, air, water, food, and animal contact. *How did people in the past believe diseases were spread?*

ANTISEPTICS AND DISINFECTANTS

One way to reduce the spread of disease is through the use of **antiseptics** and **disinfectants.** These kill pathogens on surfaces where they can be spread, such as skin, medical instruments, floors, and bathtubs. Doctors are careful to make sure their equipment is sterile and to prevent the spread of pathogens. *Why is washing your hands an effective way to lower your chances of getting a communicable disease?*

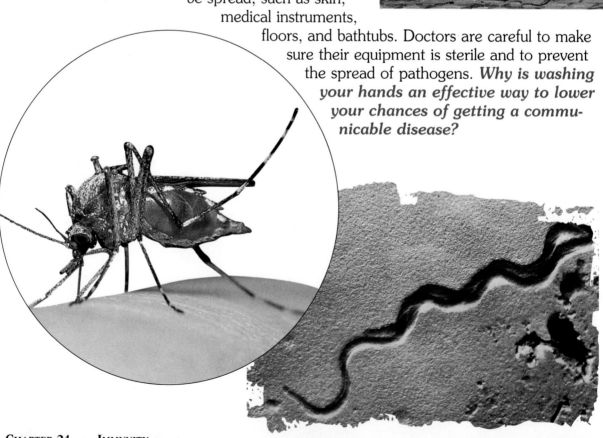

Reading Check ✓

Choose a topic in this chapter that interests you. Look it up in a reference book or on encyclopedia software. Think of a way to share what you learn with others.

Section
24-2 YOUR IMMUNE SYSTEM

One of the body's defenses against disease is the **immune system. Antibodies** are produced by the lymphocytes. These react with **antigens** and make them harmless. Vaccines can provide immunity. **Active immunity** is long lasting. **Passive immunity** does not last. As people grow and develop from childhood to adulthood, their bodies are usually more successful in fighting diseases. The immune system becomes better adapted. It can recognize foreign proteins and chemicals and destroy them. The body's naturally acquired immunity can be aided by vaccines. *How can diseases be prevented from spreading?*

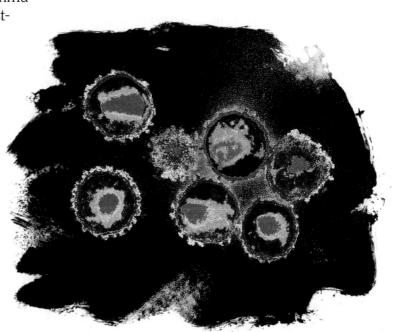

Section
24-3 NONCOMMUNICABLE DISEASES

Causes of **noncommunicable disease** include genetics, chemicals, poor diet, and uncontrolled cell growth. Chronic noncommunicable diseases include diabetes, cancer, arthritis, and allergies. *How do cancer cells move from one part of the body to another?*

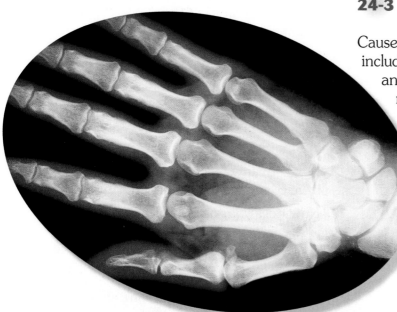

Using Vocabulary

a. active immunity
b. allergen
c. allergy
d. antibody
e. antigen
f. antiseptic
g. cancer
h. chemotherapy
i. communicable disease
j. disinfectant
k. helper T cell
l. immune system
m. noncommunicable disease
n. passive immunity
o. pasteurization
p. sexually transmitted disease (STD)
q. vaccination

Each phrase below describes a science term from the list. Write the term that matches the phrase describing it.

1. causes an allergic reaction
2. foreign protein attacked by the body
3. chemicals used to destroy cancer cells
4. uncontrolled cell division
5. introduces antigens for long-term immunity

Checking Concepts

Choose the word or phrase that best answers the question.

6. How do scientists know if a pathogen causes a specific disease?
   A) It is present in all cases of the disease.
   B) It does not infect other animals.
   C) It causes other diseases.
   D) It is treated with heat.

7. How can communicable diseases be caused?
   A) heredity   C) chemicals
   B) allergies   D) organisms

8. What organism carries the bacterium that causes Lyme disease?
   A) bird   C) rabbit
   B) tick   D) worm

9. Which of the following does a virus cause?
   A) AIDS   C) chlamydia
   B) gonorrhea   D) syphilis

10. Which of the following is NOT one of your body's defenses against pathogens?
    A) stomach enzymes   C) white blood cells
    B) skin   D) hormones

11. Which of the following is a communicable disease?
    A) allergies   C) asthma
    B) syphilis   D) diabetes

12. White blood cells are attacked by the virus that causes what?
    A) AIDS   C) flu
    B) chlamydia   D) polio

13. Which of the following is a chronic joint disease?
    A) asthma   C) diabetes
    B) arthritis   D) muscular dystrophy

14. What is formed in the blood to fight invading antigens?
    A) hormones   C) pathogens
    B) allergens   D) antibodies

15. How are cancer cells destroyed?
    A) chemotherapy   C) vaccines
    B) antigens   D) viruses

Thinking Critically

16. Which is better—to vaccinate people or to wait until they build their own immunity?

17. What advantage might a breast-fed baby have compared to a bottle-fed baby?

18. How does your body protect itself from antigens?

19. How do helper T cells eliminate antigens?

20. Describe the differences among antibodies, antigens, and antibiotics.

Developing Skills

If you need help, refer to the **Skill Handbook.**

21. **Making and Using Tables:** Make a chart comparing the following diseases and their prevention: cancer, diabetes, tetanus, and measles.

22. **Concept Mapping:** Make a network tree concept map comparing the defenses your body has against disease. Compare general defenses, active immunity, and passive immunity.

23. **Classifying:** Classify the following diseases as communicable or noncommunicable: diabetes, gonorrhea, herpes, strep throat, syphilis, cancer, and flu.

24. **Recognizing Cause and Effect:** Use a library reference to identify the cause of each disease as bacteria, virus, fungus, or protist: athlete's foot, AIDS, cold, dysentery, flu, pinkeye, pneumonia, strep throat, and ringworm.

25. **Making and Using Graphs:** Interpret the graph below showing the rate of polio cases. Explain the rate of cases between 1950 and 1965. What conclusions can you draw about the effectiveness of the polio vaccines?

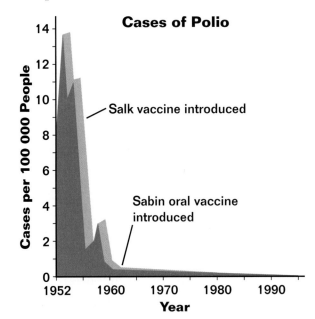

Cases of Polio

Salk vaccine introduced

Sabin oral vaccine introduced

THE PRINCETON REVIEW

Test-Taking Tip

Ignore Everyone While you take a test, pay no attention to anyone else in the room. Don't worry if friends finish a test before you do. If someone tries to talk with you during a test, don't answer. You run the risk of the teacher thinking you are cheating—even if you aren't.

Test Practice

Use these questions to test your Science Proficiency.

1. Communicable diseases are spread from one organism to another. Which statement is **NOT** true about these types of diseases?
   A) Communicable diseases can be transmitted by flies and mosquitoes.
   B) Communicable diseases can be transmitted by unclean food utensils.
   C) Communicable diseases can be transmitted by genes.
   D) Communicable diseases can be transmitted by fungi.

2. The human body has a complex group of defenses to fight disease organisms. Which statement describes a general body defense against infection?
   A) A natural body defense is the use of herbs.
   B) A natural body defense is getting a vaccination.
   C) A natural body defense is taking an antibiotic medicine.
   D) A natural body defense is the action of stomach acid.

Appendices

Appendix A

Safety in the Science Classroom

1. Always obtain your teacher's permission to begin an investigation.

2. Study the procedure. If you have questions, ask your teacher. Be sure you understand any safety symbols shown on the page.

3. Use the safety equipment provided for you. Goggles and a safety apron should be worn during an investigation.

4. Always slant test tubes away from yourself and others when heating them.

5. Never eat or drink in the lab, and never use lab glassware as food or drink containers. Never inhale chemicals. Do not taste any substances or draw any material into a tube with your mouth.

6. If you spill any chemical, wash it off immediately with water. Report the spill immediately to your teacher.

7. Know the location and proper use of the fire extinguisher, safety shower, fire blanket, first aid kit, and fire alarm.

8. Keep all materials away from open flames. Tie back long hair and loose clothing.

9. If a fire should break out in the classroom, or if your clothing should catch fire, smother it with the fire blanket or a coat, or get under a safety shower. NEVER RUN.

10. Report any accident or injury, no matter how small, to your teacher.

Follow these procedures as you clean up your work area.

1. Turn off the water and gas. Disconnect electrical devices.

2. Return all materials to their proper places.

3. Dispose of chemicals and other materials as directed by your teacher. Place broken glass and solid substances in the proper containers. Never discard materials in the sink.

4. Clean your work area.

5. Wash your hands thoroughly after working in the laboratory.

Table A-1

First Aid	
Injury	**Safe Response**
Burns	Apply cold water. Call your teacher immediately.
Cuts and bruises	Stop any bleeding by applying direct pressure. Cover cuts with a clean dressing. Apply cold compresses to bruises. Call your teacher immediately.
Fainting	Leave the person lying down. Loosen any tight clothing and keep crowds away. Call your teacher immediately.
Foreign matter in eye	Flush with plenty of water. Use eyewash bottle or fountain.
Poisoning	Note the suspected poisoning agent and call your teacher immediately.
Any spills on skin	Flush with large amounts of water or use safety shower. Call your teacher immediately.

Appendix
B

SI/Metric to English Conversions

	When you want to convert:	To:	Multiply by:
Length	inches	centimeters	2.54
	centimeters	inches	0.39
	feet	meters	0.30
	meters	feet	3.28
	yards	meters	0.91
	meters	yards	1.09
	miles	kilometers	1.61
	kilometers	miles	0.62
Mass and Weight*	ounces	grams	28.35
	grams	ounces	0.04
	pounds	kilograms	0.45
	kilograms	pounds	2.2
	tons (short)	tonnes (metric tons)	0.91
	tonnes (metric tons)	tons (short)	1.10
	pounds	newtons	4.45
	newtons	pounds	0.23
Volume	cubic inches	cubic centimeters	16.39
	cubic centimeters	cubic inches	0.06
	cubic feet	cubic meters	0.03
	cubic meters	cubic feet	35.30
	liters	quarts	1.06
	liters	gallons	0.26
	gallons	liters	3.78
Area	square inches	square centimeters	6.45
	square centimeters	square inches	0.16
	square feet	square meters	0.09
	square meters	square feet	10.76
	square miles	square kilometers	2.59
	square kilometers	square miles	0.39
	hectares	acres	2.47
	acres	hectares	0.40
Temperature	Fahrenheit	$5/9 \,(°F - 32) \; = \;$ Celsius	
	Celsius	$9/5 \,(°C) + 32 \; = \;$ Fahrenheit	

*Weight as measured in standard Earth gravity

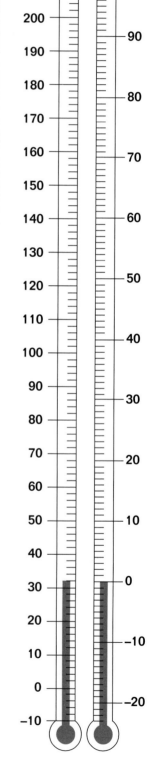

Appendix
C

SI Units of Measurement

Table C-1

SI Base Units					
Measurement	**Unit**	**Symbol**	**Measurement**	**Unit**	**Symbol**
length	meter	m	temperature	kelvin	K
mass	kilogram	kg	amount of substance	mole	mol
time	second	s			

Table C-2

Units Derived from SI Base Units		
Measurement	**Unit**	**Symbol**
energy	joule	J
force	newton	N
frequency	hertz	Hz
potential difference	volt	V
power	watt	W
pressure	pascal	Pa

Table C-3

Common SI Prefixes					
Prefix	**Symbol**	**Multiplier**	**Prefix**	**Symbol**	**Multiplier**
Greater than 1			Less than 1		
mega-	M	1 000 000	*deci-*	d	0.1
kilo-	k	1 000	*centi-*	c	0.01
hecto-	h	100	*milli-*	m	0.001
deka-	da	10	*micro-*	μ	0.000 001

Care and Use of a Microscope

Eyepiece Contains a magnifying lens you look through

Body tube Connects the eyepiece to the revolving nosepiece

Arm Supports the body tube

Revolving nosepiece Holds and turns the objectives into viewing position

Low-power objective Contains the lens with low-power magnification

High-power objective Contains the lens with the highest magnification

Stage clips Hold the microscope slide in place

Stage Supports the microscope slide

Coarse adjustment Focuses the image under low power

Light source Allows light to reflect upward through the diaphragm, the specimen, and the lenses

Fine adjustment Sharpens the image under high and low magnification

Base Provides support for the microscope

Care of a Microscope

1. Always carry the microscope holding the arm with one hand and supporting the base with the other hand.

2. Don't touch the lenses with your fingers.

3. Never lower the coarse adjustment knob when looking through the eyepiece lens.

4. Always focus first with the low-power objective.

5. Don't use the coarse adjustment knob when the high-power objective is in place.

6. Store the microscope covered.

Using a Microscope

1. Place the microscope on a flat surface that is clear of objects. The arm should be toward you.

2. Look through the eyepiece. Adjust the diaphragm so that light comes through the opening in the stage.

3. Place a slide on the stage so that the specimen is in the field of view. Hold it firmly in place by using the stage clips.

4. Always focus first with the coarse adjustment and the low-power objective lens. Once the object is in focus on low power, turn the nosepiece until the high-power objective is in place. Use ONLY the fine adjustment to focus with the high-power objective lens.

Making a Wet-Mount Slide

1. Carefully place the item you want to look at in the center of a clean, glass slide. Make sure the sample is thin enough for light to pass through.

2. Use a dropper to place one or two drops of water on the sample.

3. Hold a clean coverslip by the edges and place it at one edge of the drop of water. Slowly lower the coverslip onto the drop of water until it lies flat.

4. If you have too much water or a lot of air bubbles, touch the edge of a paper towel to the edge of the coverslip to draw off extra water and force out air.

Diversity of Life: Classification of Living Organisms

Scientists use a six-kingdom system of classification of organisms. In this system, there are two kingdoms of organisms, Kingdoms Archaebacteria and Eubacteria, which contain organisms that do not have a nucleus and lack membrane-bound structures in the cytoplasm of their cells. The members of the other four kingdoms have cells which contain a nucleus and structures in the cytoplasm that are surrounded by membranes. These kingdoms are Kingdom Protista, Kingdom Fungi, the Kingdom Plantae, and the Kingdom Animalia.

Kingdom Archaebacteria

One-celled prokaryotes; absorb food from surroundings or make their own food by chemosynthesis; found in extremely harsh environments including salt ponds, hot springs, swamps, and deep-sea hydrothermal vents.

Kingdom Eubacteria

Cyanobacteria one-celled prokaryotes; make their own food; contain chlorophyll; some species form colonies; most are blue-green

Bacteria one-celled prokaryotes; most absorb food from their surroundings; some are photosynthetic; many are parasites; round, spiral, or rod-shaped

Kingdom Protista

Phylum Euglenophyta one-celled; can photosynthesize or take in food; most have one flagellum; euglenoids

Phylum Bacillariophyta one-celled; make their own food through photosynthesis; have unique double shells made of silica; diatoms

Phylum Dinoflagellata one-celled; make their own food through photosynthesis; contain red pigments; have two flagella; dinoflagellates

Phylum Chlorophyta one-celled, many-celled, or colonies; contain chlorophyll; make their own food; live on land, in fresh water, or salt water; green algae

Phylum Rhodophyta most are many-celled; photosynthetic; contain red pigments; most live in deep saltwater environments; red algae

Phylum Phaeophyta most are many-celled; photosynthetic; contain brown pigments; most live in saltwater environments; brown algae

Phylum Foraminifera many-celled; take in food; primarily marine; shells constructed of calcium carbonate, or made from grains of sand; forams

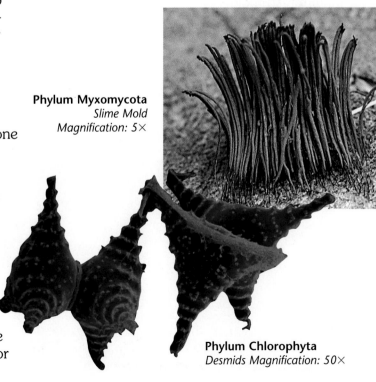

Phylum Myxomycota
Slime Mold
Magnification: 5×

Phylum Chlorophyta
Desmids Magnification: 50×

Phylum Rhizopoda one-celled; take in food; move by means of pseudopods; free-living or parasitic; amoebas

Phylum Zoomastigina one-celled; take in food; have one or more flagella; free-living or parasitic; zoomastigotes

Phylum Ciliophora one-celled; take in food; have large numbers of cilia; ciliates

Phylum Sporozoa one-celled; take in food; no means of movement; parasites in animals; sporozoans

Phylum Myxomycota and Acrasiomycota: one- or many-celled; absorb food; change form during life cycle; cellular and plasmodial slime molds

Phylum Oomycota many-celled; live in fresh or salt water; are either parasites or decomposers; water molds, rusts and downy mildews

Kingdom Fungi

Phylum Zygomycota many-celled; absorb food; spores are produced in sporangia; zygote fungi; bread mold

Phylum Ascomycota one- and many-celled; absorb food; spores produced in asci; sac fungi; yeast

Phylum Basidiomycota many-celled; absorb food; spores produced in basidia; club fungi; mushrooms

Phylum Deuteromycota: members with unknown reproductive structures; imperfect fungi; penicillin

Lichens organisms formed by symbiotic relationship between an ascomycote or a basidiomycote and green alga or cyanobacterium

Kingdom Plantae
Non-seed Plants

Division Bryophyta nonvascular plants; reproduce by spores produced in capsules; many-celled; green; grow in moist land environments; mosses and liverworts

Division Lycophyta many-celled vascular plants; spores produced in conelike structures; live on land; are photosynthetic; club mosses

Division Sphenophyta vascular plants; ribbed and jointed stems; scalelike leaves; spores produced in conelike structures; horsetails

Division Pterophyta vascular plants; leaves called fronds; spores produced in clusters of sporangia called sori; live on land or in water; ferns

Division Bryophyta
Liverwort

Lichens
British soldier lichen × 3

Appendix E

Seed Plants

Division Ginkgophyta: deciduous gymnosperms; only one living species; fan-shaped leaves with branching veins; reproduces with seeds; ginkgos

Division Cycadophyta: palmlike gymnosperms; large featherlike leaves; produce seeds in cones; cycads

Division Coniferophyta: deciduous or evergreen gymnosperms; trees or shrubs; needlelike or scalelike leaves; seeds produced in cones; conifers

Division Gnetophyta: shrubs or woody vines; seeds produced in cones; division contains only three genera; gnetum

Division Anthophyta: dominant group of plants; ovules protected in an ovary; sperm carried to ovules by pollen tube; produce flowers and seeds in fruits; flowering plants

Kingdom Animalia

Phylum Porifera: aquatic organisms that lack true tissues and organs; they are asymmetrical and sessile; sponges

Phylum Cnidaria: radially symmetrical organisms; have a digestive cavity with one opening; most have tentacles armed with stinging cells; live in aquatic environments singly or in colonies; includes jellyfish, corals, hydra, and sea anemones

Phylum Platyhelminthes: bilaterally symmetrical worms; have flattened bodies; digestive system has one opening; parasitic and free-living species; flatworms

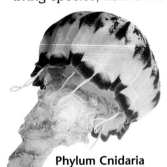

Phylum Cnidaria
Jellyfish

Phylum Arthropoda
Orb Weaver Spider

Phylum Arthropoda
Hermit Crab

Division Coniferophyta
Pine cone

Division Anthophyta
Strawberry Blossoms

Division Anthophyta
Strawberries

Phylum Mollusca
Florida Fighting Conch

Phylum Annelida
Sabellid Worms Feather Duster

Appendix E

Phylum Nematoda: round, bilaterally symmetrical body; digestive system with two openings; some free-living forms but mostly parasitic; roundworms

Phylum Mollusca: soft-bodied animals, many with a hard shell; a mantle covers the soft body; aquatic and terrestrial species; includes clams, snails, squid, and octopuses

Phylum Annelida: bilaterally symmetrical worms; have round, segmented bodies; terrestrial and aquatic species; includes earthworms, leeches, and marine polychaetes

Phylum Arthropoda: largest phylum of organisms; have segmented bodies; pairs of jointed appendages; have hard exoskeletons; terrestrial and aquatic species; includes insects, crustaceans, spiders, and horseshoe crabs

Phylum Echinodermata: marine organisms; have spiny or leathery skin; water-vascular system with tube feet; radial symmetry; includes sea stars, sand dollars, and sea urchins

Phylum Chordata: organisms with internal skeletons; specialized body systems; paired appendages; all at some time have a notochord, dorsal nerve cord, gill slits, and a tail; include fish, amphibians, reptiles, birds, and mammals

Phylum Arthropoda
Giant Swallowtail Butterfly

Phylum Echinodermata
Blood Sea Star and Red Sea Urchin

Phylum Chordata
Eastern Box Turtle

Phylum Chordata
Lemon Butterfly fish

Phylum Chordata
Great Horned Owl

Appendix F

Minerals

Mineral (formula)	Color	Streak	Hardness	Breakage pattern	Uses and other properties
graphite (C)	black to gray	black to gray	1–1.5	basal cleavage (scales)	pencil lead, lubricants for locks, rods to control some small nuclear reactions, battery poles
galena (PbS)	gray	gray to black	2.5	cubic cleavage perfect	source of lead, used in pipes, shields for X rays, fishing equipment sinkers
hematite (Fe_2O_3)	black or reddish brown	reddish brown	5.5–6.5	irregular fracture	source of iron; converted to "pig" iron, made into steel
magnetite (Fe_3O_4)	black	black	6	conchoidal fracture	source of iron, naturally magnetic, called lodestone
pyrite (FeS_2)	light, brassy, yellow	greenish black	6–6.5	uneven fracture	source of iron, "fool's gold"
talc ($Mg_3Si_4O_{10}(OH)_2$)	white greenish	white	1	cleavage in one direction	used for talcum powder, sculptures, paper, and tabletops
gypsum ($CaSO_4 \cdot 2H_2O$)	colorless, gray, white brown	white	2	basal cleavage	used in plaster of paris and dry wall for building construction
sphalerite (ZnS)	brown, reddish brown, greenish	light to dark brown	3.5–4	cleavage in six directions	main ore of zinc; used in paints, dyes and medicine
muscovite ($KAl_3Si_3O_{10}(OH)_2$)	white, light gray, yellow, rose, green	colorless	2–2.5	basal cleavage	occurs in large flexible plates; used as an insulator in electrical equipment, lubricant
biotite ($K(Mg, Fe)_3(AlSi_3O_{10})(OH)_2$)	black to dark brown	colorless	2.5–3	basal cleavage	occurs in large flexible plates
halite (NaCl)	colorless, red, white, blue	colorless	2.5	cubic cleavage	salt; soluble in water; a preservative

Appendix
F

Minerals

Mineral (formula)	Color	Streak	Hardness	Breakage pattern	Uses and other properties
calcite ($CaCO_3$)	colorless, white, pale blue	colorless, white	3	cleavage in three directions	fizzes when HCl is added; used in cements and other building materials
dolomite ($CaMg$ $(CO_3)_2$)	colorless, white, pink green, gray black	white	3.5–4	cleavage in three directions	concrete and cement; used as an ornamental building stone
fluorite (CaF_2)	colorless, white, blue green, red yellow, purple	colorless	4	cleavage in four directions	used in the manufacture of optical equipment; glows under ultraviolet light
hornblende ($(CaNa)_{2-3}(Mg,$ $Al,Fe)_5(Al,Si)_2$ $Si_6O_{22}(OH)_2)$	green to black	gray to white	5–6	cleavage in two directions	will transmit light on thin edges; 6-sided cross section
feldspar ($KAlSi_3O_8$) ($NaAlSi_3O_8$) ($CaAl_2Si_2O_8$)	colorless, white to gray, green	colorless	6	two cleavage planes meet at ~90° angle	used in the manufacture of ceramics
augite ((Ca, Na) (Mg, Fe, Al) (Al, Si)$_2O_6$)	black	colorless	6	cleavage in two directions	square or 8-sided cross section
olivine ((Mg, Fe)$_2$ SiO_4)	olive, green	none	6.5–7	conchoidal fracture	gemstones, refractory sand
quartz (SiO_2)	colorless, various color	none	7	conchoidal fracture	used in glass manufacture, electronic equipment, radios, computers, watches, gemstones

Appendix
G

Rocks

Rock Type	Rock Name	Characteristics
Igneous (intrusive)	Granite	Large mineral grains of quartz, feldspar, hornblende, and mica. Usually light in color.
	Diorite	Large mineral grains of feldspar, hornblende, mica. Less quartz than granite. Intermediate in color.
	Gabbro	Large mineral grains of feldspar, hornblende, augite, olivine, and mica. No quartz. Dark in color.
Igneous (extrusive)	Rhyolite	Small mineral grains of quartz, feldspar, hornblende, and mica or no visible grains. Light in color.
	Andesite	Small mineral grains of feldspar, hornblende, mica or no visible grains. Less quartz than rhyolite. Intermediate in color.
	Basalt	Small mineral grains of feldspar, hornblende, augite, olivine, mica or no visible grains. No quartz. Dark in color.
	Obsidian	Glassy texture. No visible grains. Volcanic glass. Fracture looks like broken glass.
	Pumice	Frothy texture. Floats. Usually light in color.
Sedimentary (detrital)	Conglomerate	Coarse-grained. Gravel or pebble-sized grains.
	Sandstone	Sand-sized grains 1/16 to 2 mm in size.
	Siltstone	Grains are smaller than sand but larger than clay.
	Shale	Smallest grains. Usually dark in color.
Sedimentary (chemical or biochemical)	Limestone	Major mineral is calcite. Usually forms in oceans, lakes, rivers, and caves. Often contains fossils.
	Coal	Occurs in swampy. low-lying areas. Compacted layers of organic material, mainly plant remains.
Sedimentary (chemical)	Rock Salt	Commonly forms by the evaporation of seawater.
Metamorphic (foliated)	Gneiss	Well-developed banding because of alternating layers of different minerals, usually of different colors. Common parent rock is granite.
	Schist	Well-defined parallel arrangement of flat, sheet-like minerals, mainly micas. Common parent rocks are shale, phyllite.
	Phyllite	Shiny or silky appearance. May look wrinkled. Common parent rocks are shale, slate.
	Slate	Harder, denser, and shinier than shale. Common parent rock is shale.
Metamorphic (non-foliated)	Marble	Interlocking calcite or dolomite crystals. Common parent rock is limestone.
	Soapstone	Composed mainly of the mineral talc. Soft with a greasy feel.
	Quartzite	Hard and well cemented with interlocking quartz crystals. Common parent rock is sandstone.

Appendix H

Topographic Map Symbols

Primary highway, hard surface

Secondary highway, hard surface

Light-duty road, hard or
Improved surface

Unimproved road

Railroad: single track and
multiple track

Railroads in juxtaposition

Buildings

Schools, church, and cemetery

Buildings (barn, warehouse, etc)

Wells other than water
(labeled as to type)

Tanks: oil, water, etc.
(labeled only if water)

Located or landmark object;
windmill

Open pit, mine, or quarry;
prospect

Marsh (swamp)

Wooded marsh

Woods or brushwood

Vineyard
Land subject to controlled
inundation

Submerged marsh

Mangrove

Orchard

Scrub

Urban area

Spot elevation   ×7369

Water elevation   670

Index contour

Supplementary contour

Intermediate contour

Depression contours

Boundaries: National
    State
    County, parish, municipal
    Civil township, precinct,
    town, barrio
    Incorporated city, village,
    town, hamlet
    Reservation, National or State
    Small park, cemetery,
    airport, etc.
    Land grant
Township or range line,
United States land survey
Township or range line,
approximate location

Perennial streams

Elevated aqueduct

Water well and spring

Small rapids

Large rapids

Intermittent lake

Intermittent streams

Aqueduct tunnel

Glacier
Small falls

Large falls

Dry lake bed

Weather Map Symbols

Sample Plotted Report at Each Station

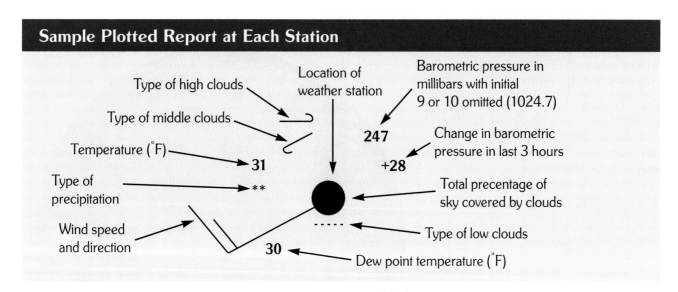

Sample Plotted Report at Each Station

Precipitation	Wind Speed and direction		Sky coverage		Some types of high clouds	
☰ Fog	○	0 calm	○	No cover	⌐	Scattered cirrus
★ Snow	╱	1-2 knots	◔	1/10 or less	⌐⌐	Dense cirrus in patches
● Rain	↘	3-7 knots	◔	2/10 to 3/10		
⊤ Thunder-storm	↘	8-12 knots	◔	4/10	⌐	Veil of cirrus covering entire sky
	↘	13-17 knots	◑	1/2		
	↘	18-22 knots	◕	6/10	⌐	Cirrus not covering entire sky
, Drizzle	↘	23-27 knots	◕	7/10		
▽ Showers	↘	48-52 knots	◕	Overcast with openings		
	1 knot = 1.852 km/h		●	Complete overcast		

Some types of middle clouds		Some types of low clouds		Fronts and pressure systems	
╱	Thin altostratus layer	⌒	Cumulus of fair weather	(H) or High	Center of high-or
╱╱	Thick altostratus layer	⌣	Stratocumulus	(L) or Low	low-pressure system
╱	Thin altostratus in patches	-----	Fractocumulus of bad weather	▲▲▲▲	Cold front
				●●●	Warm Front
╱	Thin altostratus in bands	—	Stratus of fair weather	▲●▲●	Occluded front
				●▼●▼	Stationary front

Star Charts

Shown here are star charts for viewing stars in the Northern Hemisphere during the four different seasons. These charts are drawn from the night sky at about 35° North Latitude, but they can be used for most locations in the Northern Hemisphere. The lines on the charts outline major constellations. The dense band of stars is the milky Way. To use, hold the chart vertically, with the direction you are facing at the bottom of the map.

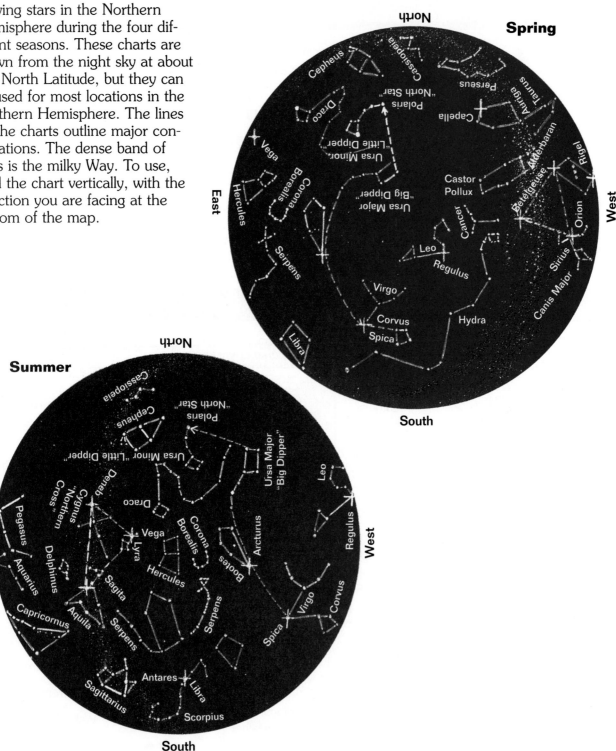

Appendix
J

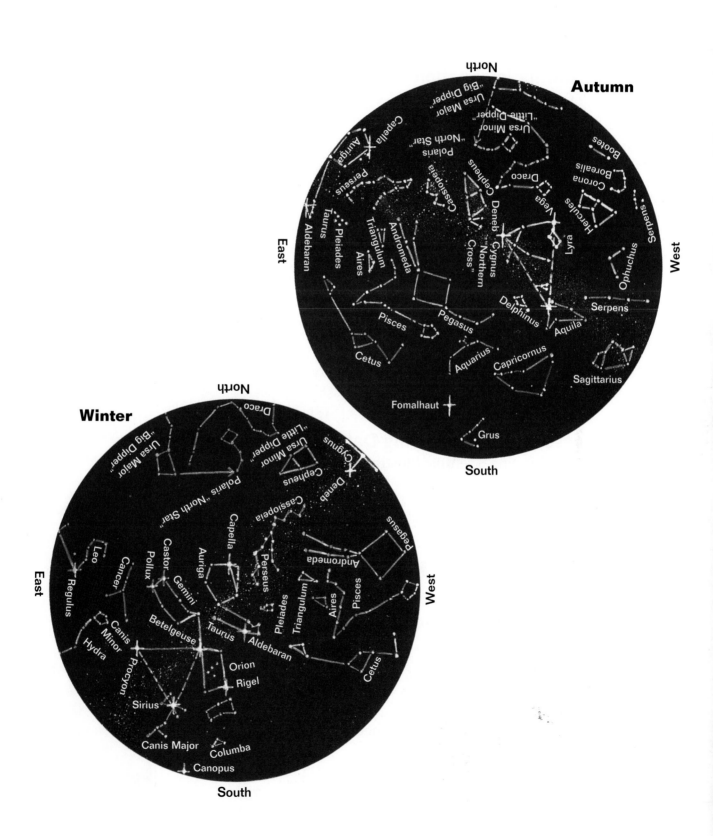

Skill Handbook

Table of Contents

Science Skill Handbook

Organizing Information

Communicating

The communication of ideas is an important part of our everyday lives. Whether reading a book, writing a letter, or watching a television program, people everywhere are expressing opinions and sharing information with one another. Writing in your Science Journal allows you to express your opinions and demonstrate your knowledge of the information presented on a subject. When writing, keep in mind the purpose of the assignment and the audience with which you are communicating.

Examples Science Journal assignments vary greatly. They may ask you to take a viewpoint other than your own; perhaps you will be a scientist, a TV reporter, or a committee member of a local environmental group. Maybe you will be expressing your opinions to a member of Congress, a doctor, or to the editor of your local newspaper, as shown in **Figure 1**. Sometimes, Science Journal writing may allow you to summarize information in the form of an outline, a letter, or in a paragraph.

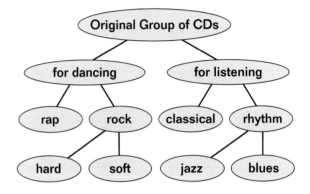

Figure 2 Classifying CDs

Classifying

You may not realize it, but you make things orderly in the world around you. If you hang your shirts together in the closet or if your favorite CDs are stacked together, you have used the skill of classifying.

Classifying is the process of sorting objects or events into groups based on common features. When classifying, first observe the objects or events to be classified. Then, select one feature that is shared by some members in the group, but not by all. Place those members that share that feature into a subgroup. You can classify members into smaller and smaller subgroups based on characteristics.

Remember, when you classify, you are grouping objects or events for a purpose. Keep your purpose in mind as you select the features to form groups and subgroups.

Example How would you classify a collection of CDs? As shown in **Figure 2**, you might classify those you like to dance to in one subgroup and CDs you like to listen to in the next subgroup. The CDs you like to dance to could be subdivided

Figure 1 A Science Journal entry

into a rap subgroup and a rock subgroup. Note that for each feature selected, each CD fits into only one subgroup. You would keep selecting features until all the CDs are classified. **Figure 2** shows one possible classification.

Figure 3 A recipe for bread contains sequenced instructions

Sequencing

A sequence is an arrangement of things or events in a particular order. When you are asked to sequence objects or events within a group, figure out what comes first, then think about what should come second. Continue to choose objects or events until all of the objects you started out with are in order. Then, go back over the sequence to make sure each thing or event in your sequence logically leads to the next.

Example A sequence with which you are most familiar is the use of alphabetical order. Another example of sequence would be the steps in a recipe, as shown in **Figure 3.** Think about baking bread. Steps in the recipe have to be followed in order for the bread to turn out right.

Concept Mapping

If you were taking an automobile trip, you would probably take along a road map. The road map shows your location, your destination, and other places along the way. By looking at the map and finding where you are, you can begin to understand where you are in relation to other locations on the map.

A concept map is similar to a road map. But, a concept map shows relationships among ideas (or concepts) rather than places. A concept map is a diagram that visually shows how concepts are related. Because the concept map shows relationships among ideas, it can make the meanings of ideas and terms clear, and help you understand better what you are studying.

There is usually not one correct way to create a concept map. As you construct one type of map, you may discover other ways to construct the map that show the

Figure 4 Network tree describing U.S. currency

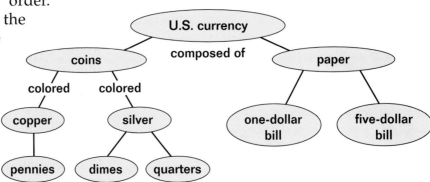

relationships between concepts in a better way. If you do discover what you think is a better way to create a concept map, go ahead and use the new one. Overall, concept maps are useful for breaking a big concept down into smaller parts, making learning easier.

Examples

Network Tree Look at the concept map about U.S. currency in **Figure 4.** This is called a network tree. Notice how some words are in ovals while others are written across connecting lines. The words inside the ovals are science concepts. The lines in the map show related concepts. The words written on the lines describe the relationships between concepts.

When you are asked to construct a network tree, write down the topic and list the major concepts related to that topic on a piece of paper. Then look at your list and begin to put them in order from general to specific. Branch the related concepts from the major concept and describe the relationships on the lines. Continue to write the more specific concepts. Write the relationships between the concepts on the lines until all concepts are mapped. Examine the concept map for relationships that cross branches, and add them to the concept map.

Events Chain An events chain is another type of concept map. An events chain map, such as the one describing a typical morning routine in **Figure 5,** is used to describe ideas in order. In science, an events chain can be used to describe a sequence of events, the steps in a procedure, or the stages of a process.

When making an events chain, first find the one event that starts the chain. This

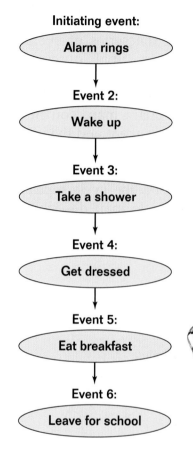

Initiating event:
Alarm rings

Event 2:
Wake up

Event 3:
Take a shower

Event 4:
Get dressed

Event 5:
Eat breakfast

Event 6:
Leave for school

Figure 5 Events chain of a typical morning routine

event is called the initiating event. Then, find the next event in the chain and continue until you reach an outcome. Suppose you are asked to describe what happens when your alarm rings. An events chain map describing the steps might look like **Figure 5.** Notice that connecting words are not necessary in an events chain.

Cycle Map   A cycle concept map is a special type of events chain map. In a cycle concept map, the series of events does not produce a final outcome. Instead, the last event in the chain relates back to the initiating event.

As in the events chain map, you first decide on an initiating event and then list each event in order. Because there is no outcome and the last event relates back to the initiating event, the cycle repeats itself. Look at the cycle map describing the relationship between day and night in **Figure 6.**

Figure 6   Cycle map of day and night.

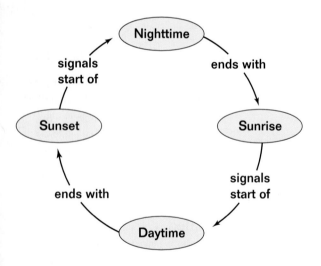

Spider Map   A fourth type of concept map is the spider map. This is a map that you can use for brainstorming. Once you have a central idea, you may find you have a jumble of ideas that relate to it, but are not necessarily clearly related to each other. As illustrated by the homework spider map in **Figure 7,** by writing these ideas outside the main concept, you may begin to separate and group unrelated terms so that they become more useful.

Figure 7   Spider map about homework.

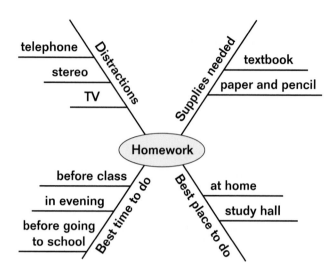

Making and Using Tables

Browse through your textbook and you will notice tables in the text and in the activities. In a table, data or information is arranged in a way that makes it easier for you to understand. Activity tables help organize the data you collect during an activity so that results can be interpreted.

Examples   Most tables have a title. At a glance, the title tells you what the table is about. A table is divided into columns and rows. The first column lists items to be compared. In **Figure 8,** the collection of recyclable materials is being compared in a table. The row across the top lists the specific characteristics being compared. Within the grid of the table, the collected data are recorded.

What is the title of the table in **Figure 8?** The title is "Recycled Materials." What is being compared? The different materials being recycled and on which days they are recycled.

Making Tables   To make a table, list the items to be compared down in columns and the characteristics to be compared across in rows. The table in

Science Skill Handbook

Figure 8 Table of recycled materials

Recycled Materials			
Day of Week	Paper (kg)	Aluminum (kg)	Plastic (kg)
Mon.	4.0	2.0	0.5
Wed.	43.5	1.5	0.5
Fri.	3.0	1.0	1.5

Figure 8 compares the mass of recycled materials collected by a class. On Monday, students turned in 4.0 kg of paper, 2.0 kg of aluminum, and 0.5 kg of plastic. On Wednesday, they turned in 3.5 kg of paper, 1.5 kg of aluminum, and 0.5 kg of plastic. On Friday, the totals were 3.0 kg of paper, 1.0 kg of aluminum, and 1.5 kg of plastic.

Using Tables How much plastic, in kilograms, is being recycled on Wednesday? Locate the column labeled "Plastic (kg)" and the row "Wed." The data in the box where the column and row intersect is the answer. Did you answer "0.5"? How much aluminum, in kilograms, is being recycled on Friday? If you answered "1.0," you understand how to use the parts of the table.

Making and Using Graphs

After scientists organize data in tables, they may display the data in a graph. A graph is a diagram that shows the relationship of one variable to another. A graph makes interpretation and analysis of data easier. There are three basic types of graphs used in science—the line graph, the bar graph, and the circle graph.

Examples

Line Graphs A line graph is used to show the relationship between two variables. The variables being compared go on two axes of the graph. The independent variable always goes on the horizontal axis, called the x-axis. The dependent variable always goes on the vertical axis, called the y-axis.

Suppose your class started to record the amount of materials they collected in one week for their school to recycle. The collected information is shown in **Figure 9.**

You could make a graph of the materials collected over the three days of the school week. The three weekdays are the independent variables and are placed on the x-axis of your graph. The amount of materials collected is the dependent variable and would go on the y-axis.

After drawing your axes, label each with a scale. The x-axis lists the three weekdays. To make a scale of the amount of materials collected on the y-axis, look at the data values. Because the lowest amount collected was 1.0 and the highest was 5.0, you will have to start numbering at least at 1.0 and go through 5.0. You decide to start numbering at 0 and number by ones through 6.0, as shown in **Figure 10.**

Next, plot the data points for collected paper. The first pair of data you want to plot is Monday and 5.0 kg of paper.

Figure 9 Amount of recyclable materials collected during one week

Materials Collected During Week		
Day of Week	Paper (kg)	Aluminum (kg)
Mon.	5.0	4.0
Wed.	4.0	1.0
Fri.	2.5	2.0

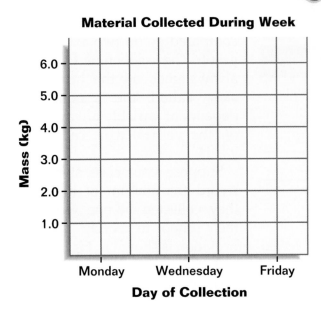

Figure 10 Graph outline for material collected during week

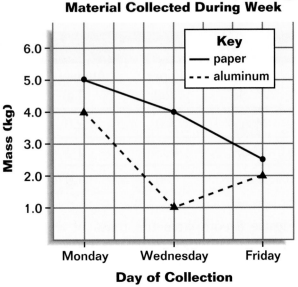

Figure 11 Line graph of materials collected during week

Locate "Monday" on the *x*-axis and locate "5.0" on the *y*-axis. Where an imaginary vertical line from the *x*-axis and an imaginary horizontal line from the *y*-axis would meet, place the first data point. Place the other data points the same way. After all the points are plotted, connect them with the best smooth curve. Repeat this procedure for the data points for aluminum. Use continuous and dashed lines to distinguish the two line graphs. The resulting graph should look like **Figure 11.**

Bar Graphs Bar graphs are similar to line graphs. They compare data that do not continuously change. In a bar graph, vertical bars show the relationships among data.

To make a bar graph, set up the *x*-axis and *y*-axis as you did for the line graph. The data is plotted by drawing vertical bars from the *x*-axis up to a point where the *y*-axis would meet the bar if it were extended.

Look at the bar graph in **Figure 12** comparing the mass of aluminum collected

over three weekdays. The *x*-axis is the days on which the aluminum was collected. The *y*-axis is the mass of aluminum collected, in kilograms.

Circle Graphs A circle graph uses a circle divided into sections to display data. Each section represents part of the whole. All the sections together equal 100 percent.

Suppose you wanted to make a circle graph to show the number of seeds that germinated in a package. You would count the total number of seeds. You find that there are 143 seeds in the package. This represents 100 percent, the whole circle.

You plant the seeds, and 129 seeds germinate. The seeds that germinated will make up one section of the circle graph, and the seeds that did not germinate will make up the remaining section.

To find out how much of the circle each section should take, divide the number of seeds in each section by the total number of seeds. Then, multiply your answer by 360, the number of degrees in a circle, and round to the nearest whole number. The

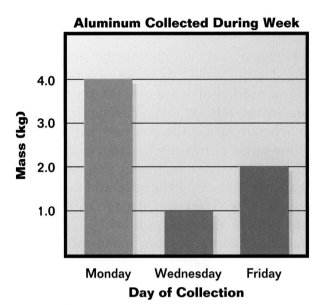

Aluminum Collected During Week

Mass (kg)

Monday   Wednesday   Friday
Day of Collection

Figure 12 Bar graph of aluminum collected during week

section of the circle graph in degrees that represents the seeds germinated is figured below.

$$\frac{129}{143} \times 360 = 324.75 \text{ or } 325 \text{ degrees (or } 325°)$$

Plot this group on the circle graph using a compass and a protractor. Use the compass to draw a circle. It will be easier to

measure the part of the circle representing the non-germinating seeds, so subtract 325° from 360° to get 35°. Draw a straight line from the center to the edge of the circle. Place your protractor on this line and use it to mark a point at 325°. Use this point to draw a straight line from the center of the circle to the edge. This is the section for the group of seeds that did not germinate. The other section represents the group of 129 seeds that did germinate. Label the sections of your graph and title the graph as shown in **Figure 13.**

Figure 13 Circle graph of germinated seeds

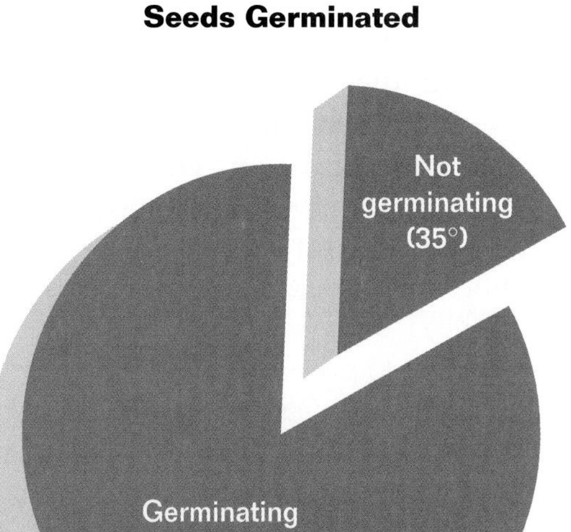

Seeds Germinated

Not germinating (35°)

Germinating (325°)

Thinking Critically

Observing and Inferring

Observing Scientists try to make careful and accurate observations. When possible, they use instruments such as microscopes, thermometers, and balances to make observations. Measurements with a balance or thermometer provide numerical data that can be checked and repeated.

When you make observations in science, you'll find it helpful to examine the entire object or situation first. Then, look carefully for details. Write down everything you observe.

Example Imagine that you have just finished a volleyball game. At home, you open the refrigerator and see a jug of orange juice on the back of the top shelf. The jug, shown in **Figure 14,** feels cold as you grasp it. Then, you drink the juice, smell the oranges, and enjoy the tart taste in your mouth.

Figure 14 Why is this jug of orange juice cold?

As you imagined yourself in the story, you used your senses to make observations. You used your sense of sight to find the jug in the refrigerator, your sense of touch when you felt the coldness of the jug, your sense of hearing to listen as the liquid filled the glass, and your senses of smell and taste to enjoy the odor and tartness of the juice. The basis of all scientific investigation is observation.

Inferring Scientists often make inferences based on their observations. An inference is an attempt to explain or interpret observations or to say what caused what you observed.

When making an inference, be certain to use accurate data and observations. Analyze all of the data that you've collected. Then, based on everything you know, explain or interpret what you've observed.

Example When you drank a glass of orange juice after the volleyball game, you observed that the orange juice was cold as well as refreshing. You might infer that the juice was cold because it had been made much earlier in the day and had been kept in the refrigerator, or you might infer that it had just been made, using both cold water and ice. The only way to be sure which inference is correct is to investigate further.

Comparing and Contrasting

Observations can be analyzed by noting the similarities and differences between two or more objects or events that you observe. When you look at objects or events to see how they are similar, you are comparing them. Contrasting is looking for differences in similar objects or events.

Figure 15 Table comparing the nutritional value of *Cereal A* and *Cereal B*

Nutritional Value

	Cereal A	Cereal B
Serving size	103 g	105 g
Calories	220	160
Total Fat	10 g	10 g
Protein	2.5 g	2.6 g
Total Carbohydrate	30 g	15 g

Example Suppose you were asked to compare and contrast the nutritional value of two kinds of cereal, *Cereal A* and *Cereal B*. You would start by looking at what is known about these cereals. Arrange this information in a table, like the one in **Figure 15.**

Similarities you might point out are that both cereals have similar serving sizes, amounts of total fat, and protein. Differences include *Cereal A* having a higher calorie value and containing more total carbohydrates than *Cereal B*.

Recognizing Cause and Effect

Have you ever watched something happen and then made suggestions about why it happened? If so, you have observed an effect and inferred a cause. The event is an effect, and the reason for the event is the cause.

Example Suppose that every time your teacher fed the fish in a classroom aquarium, she or he tapped the food container on the edge of the aquarium. Then, one day your teacher just happened to tap the edge of the aquarium with a pencil while making a point. You observed the fish swim to the surface of the aquarium to feed, as shown in **Figure 16.** What is the effect, and what would you infer to be the cause? The effect is the fish swimming to the surface of the aquarium. You might infer the cause to be the teacher tapping on the edge of the aquarium. In determining cause and effect, you have made a logical inference based on your observations.

Perhaps the fish swam to the surface because they reacted to the teacher's waving hand or for some other reason. When scientists are unsure of the cause of a certain event, the design controlled experiments to determine what causes the event. Although you have made a logical conclusion about the behavior of the fish, you would have to perform an experiment to be certain that it was the tapping that caused the effect you observed.

Figure 16 What cause-and-effect situations are occurring in this aquarium?

Practicing Scientific Processes

You might say that the work of a scientist is to solve problems. But when you decide how to dress on a particular day, you are doing problem solving, too. You may observe what the weather looks like through a window. You may go outside and see whether what you are wearing is heavy or light enough.

Scientists use an orderly approach to learn new information and to solve problems. The methods scientists may use include observing to form a hypothesis, designing an experiment to test a hypothesis, separating and controlling variables, and interpreting data.

Forming Operational Definitions

Operational definitions define an object by showing how it functions, works, or behaves. Such definitions are written in terms of how an object works or how it can be used; that is, what is its job or purpose?

Figure 17 What observations can be made about this dog?

Example Some operational definitions explain how an object can be used.
- A ruler is a tool that measures the size of an object.
- An automobile can move things from one place to another.

Or such a definition may explain how an object works.
- A ruler contains a series of marks that can be used as a standard when measuring.
- An automobile is a vehicle that can move from place to place.

Forming a Hypothesis

Observations You observe all the time. Scientists try to observe as much as possible about the things and events they study so they know that what they say about their observations is reliable.

Some observations describe something using only words. These observations are called qualitative observations. Other observations describe how much of something there is. These are quantitative observations and use numbers, as well as words, in the description. Tools or equipment are used to measure the characteristic being described.

Example If you were making qualitative observations of the dog in **Figure 17,** you might use words such as *furry, yellow,* and *short-haired.* Quantitative observations of this dog might include a mass of 14 kg, a height of 46 cm, ear length of 10 cm, and an age of 150 days.

Hypotheses Hypotheses are tested to help explain observations that have been made. They are often stated as *if* and *then* statements.

Science Skill Handbook

Examples Suppose you want to make a perfect score on a spelling test. Begin by thinking of several ways to accomplish this. Base these possibilities on past observations. If you put each of these possibilities into sentence form, using the words *if* and *then*, you can form a hypothesis. All of the following are hypotheses you might consider to explain how you could score 100 percent on your test:

If the test is easy, then I will get a perfect score.

If I am intelligent, then I will get a perfect score.

If I study hard, then I will get a perfect score.

Perhaps a scientist has observed that plants that receive fertilizer grow taller than plants that do not. A scientist may form a hypothesis that says: If plants are fertilized, then their growth will increase.

Designing an Experiment to Test a Hypothesis

In order to test a hypothesis, it's best to write out a procedure. A procedure is the plan that you follow in your experiment. A procedure tells you what materials to use and how to use them. After following the procedure, data are generated. From this generated data, you can then draw a conclusion and make a statement about your results.

If the conclusion you draw from the data supports your hypothesis, then you can say that your hypothesis is reliable. *Reliable* means that you can trust your conclusion. If it did not support your hypothesis, then you would have to make new observations and state a new hypothesis—just make sure that it is one that you can test.

Example Super premium gasoline costs more than regular gasoline. Does super premium gasoline increase the efficiency or fuel mileage of your family car? Let's figure out how to conduct an experiment to test the hypothesis, "*if* premium gas is more efficient, *then* it should increase the fuel mileage of our family car." Then a procedure similar to **Figure 18** must be written to generate data presented in **Figure 19** on the next page.

These data show that premium gasoline is less efficient than regular gasoline. It took more gasoline to travel one mile (0.064) using premium gasoline than it does to travel one mile using regular gasoline (0.059). This conclusion does not support the original hypothesis made.

Figure 18 Possible procedural steps

PROCEDURE

1. Use regular gasoline for two weeks.

2. Record the number of miles between fill-ups and the amount of gasoline used.

3. Switch to premium gasoline for two weeks.

4. Record the number of miles between fill-ups and the amount of gasoline used.

Figure 19 Data generated from procedure steps

Gasoline Data			
	Miles traveled	Gallons used	Gallons per mile
Regular gasoline	762	45.34	0.059
Premium gasoline	661	42.30	0.064

Separating and Controlling Variables

In any experiment, it is important to keep everything the same except for the item you are testing. The one factor that you change is called the *independent variable*. The factor that changes as a result of the independent variable is called the *dependent variable*. Always make sure that there is only one independent variable. If you allow more than one, you will not know what causes the changes you observe in the independent variable. Many experiments have *controls*—a treatment or an experiment that you can compare with the results of your test groups.

Example In the experiment with the gasoline, you made everything the same except the type of gasoline being used. The driver, the type of automobile, and the weather conditions should remain the same throughout. The gasoline should also be purchased from the same service station. By doing so, you made sure that at the end of the experiment, any differences were the result of the type of fuel being used—regular or premium. The type of gasoline was the *independent factor* and the gas mileage achieved was the *dependent factor*. The use of regular gasoline was the *control*.

Interpreting Data

The word *interpret* means "to explain the meaning of something." Look at the problem originally being explored in the gasoline experiment and find out what the data show. Identify the control group and the test group so you can see whether or not the variable has had an effect. Then, you need to check differences between the control and test groups.

Figure 20 Which gasoline type is most efficient?

These differences may be qualitative or quantitative. A qualitative difference would be a difference that you could observe and describe, while a quantitative difference would be a difference you can measure using numbers. If there are differences, the variable being tested may have had an effect. If there is no difference between the control and the test groups, the variable being tested apparently has had no effect.

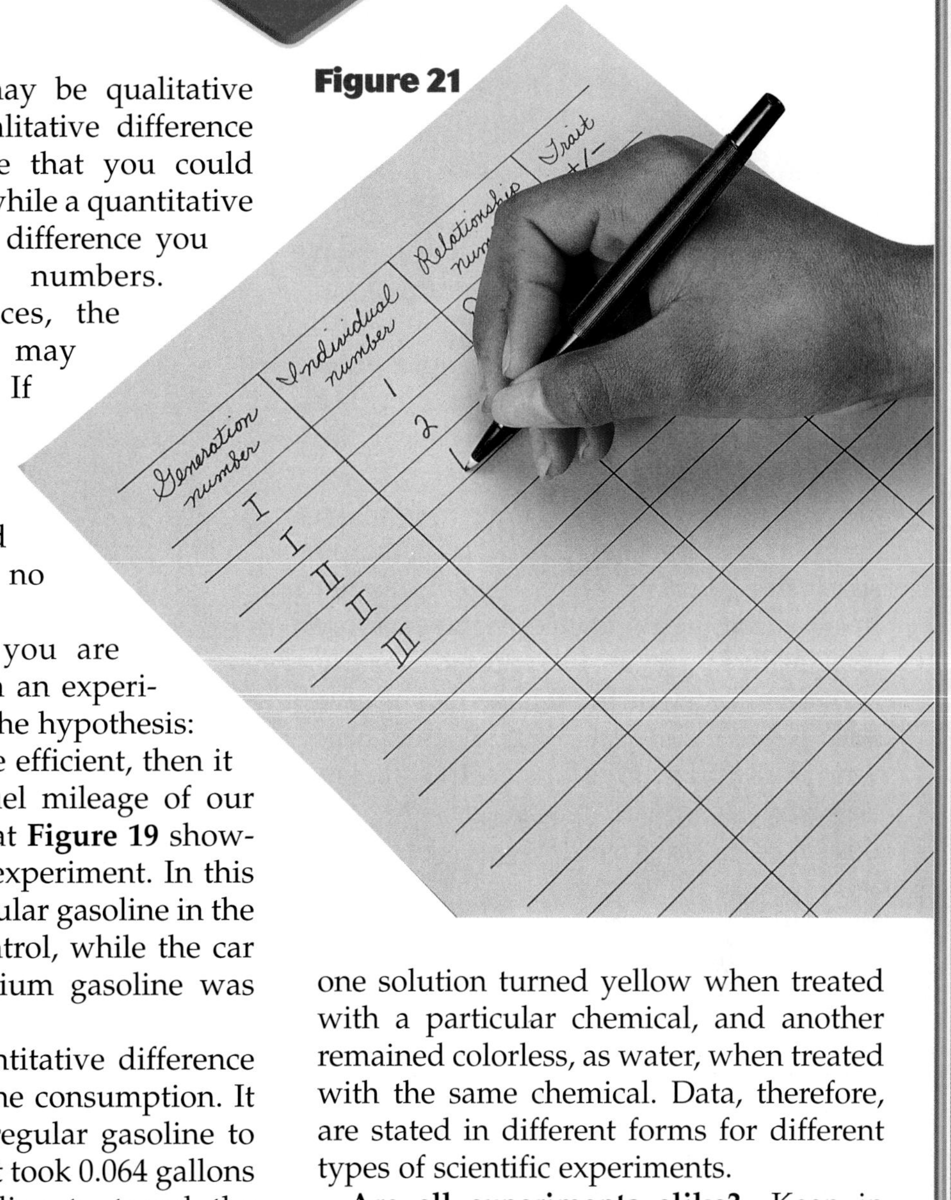

Example Perhaps you are looking at a table from an experiment designed to test the hypothesis: If premium gas is more efficient, then it should increase the fuel mileage of our family car. Look back at **Figure 19** showing the results of this experiment. In this example, the use of regular gasoline in the family car was the control, while the car being fueled by premium gasoline was the test group.

Data showed a quantitative difference in efficiency for gasoline consumption. It took 0.059 gallons of regular gasoline to travel one mile, while it took 0.064 gallons of the premium gasoline to travel the same distance. The regular gasoline was more efficient; it increased the fuel mileage of the family car.

What are data? In the experiment described on these pages, measurements were taken so that at the end of the experiment, you had something concrete to interpret. You had numbers to work with. Not every experiment that you do will give you data in the form of numbers. Sometimes, data will be in the form of a description. At the end of a chemistry experiment, you might have noted that

Figure 21

one solution turned yellow when treated with a particular chemical, and another remained colorless, as water, when treated with the same chemical. Data, therefore, are stated in different forms for different types of scientific experiments.

Are all experiments alike? Keep in mind as you perform experiments in science that not every experiment makes use of all of the parts that have been described on these pages. For some, it may be difficult to design an experiment that will always have a control. Other experiments are complex enough that it may be hard to have only one dependent variable. Real scientists encounter many variations in the methods that they use when they perform experiments. The skills in this handbook are here for you to use and practice. In real situations, their uses will vary.

Representing and Applying Data

Interpreting Scientific Illustrations

As you read a science textbook, you will see many drawings, diagrams, and photographs. Illustrations help you to understand what you read. Some illustrations are included to help you understand an idea that you can't see easily by yourself. For instance, we can't see atoms, but we can look at a diagram of an atom and that helps us to understand some things about atoms. Seeing something often helps you remember more easily. Illustrations also provide examples that clarify difficult concepts or give additional information about the topic you are studying. Maps, for example, help you to locate places that may be described in the text.

Examples

Captions and Labels Most illustrations have captions. A caption is a comment that identifies or explains the illustration. Diagrams, such as **Figure 22,** often have

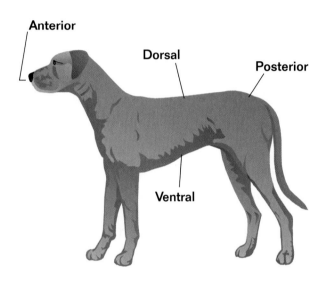

Figure 23 The orientation of a dog is shown here.

labels that identify parts of the organism or the order of steps in a process.

Learning with Illustrations An illustration of an organism shows that organism from a particular view or orientation. In order to understand the illustration, you may need to identify the front (anterior) end, tail (posterior) end, the underside (ventral), and the back (dorsal) side, as shown in **Figure 23.**

You might also check for symmetry. A shark in **Figure 24** has bilateral symmetry. This means that drawing an imaginary line through the center of the animal from the anterior to posterior end forms two mirror images.

Radial symmetry is the arrangement of similar parts around a central point. An object or organism, such as a hydra, can be divided anywhere through the center into similar parts.

Some organisms and objects cannot be divided into two similar parts. If an

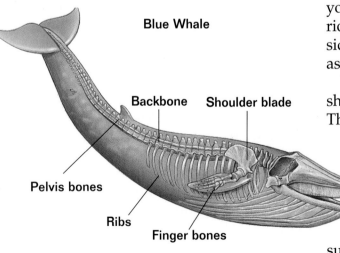

Figure 22 A labeled diagram of a blue whale

Figure 24 A shark (A) illustrating bilateral symmetry and a pear (B) illustrating a longitudinal section and a cross section

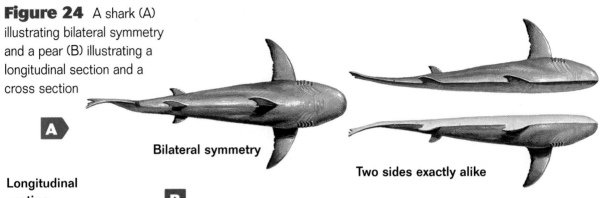

A

Bilateral symmetry

Two sides exactly alike

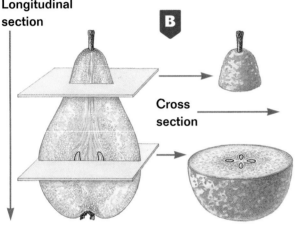

Longitudinal section

B

Cross section

organism or object cannot be divided, it is asymmetrical. Regardless of how you try to divide a natural sponge, you cannot divide it into two parts that look alike.

Some illustrations enable you to see the inside of an organism or object. These illustrations are called sections. **Figure 24** also illustrates some common sections.

Look at all illustrations carefully. Read captions and labels so that you understand exactly what the illustration is showing you.

Making Models

Have you ever worked on a model car, plane, or rocket? These models look, and sometimes work, much like the real thing, but they are often on a different scale than the real thing. In science, models are used to help simplify large or small processes or structures that otherwise would be dif-

ficult to see and understand. Your understanding of a structure or process is enhanced when you work with materials to make a model that shows the basic features of the structure or process.

Example In order to make a model, you first have to get a basic idea about the structure or process involved. You decide to make a model to show the differences in size of arteries, veins, and capillaries. First, read about these structures. All three are hollow tubes. Arteries are round and thick. Veins are flat and have thinner walls than arteries. Capillaries are small.

Now, decide what you can use for your model. Common materials are often most useful and cheapest to work with when making models. As illustrated in **Figure 25** on the next page, different kinds and sizes of pasta might work for these models. Different sizes of rubber tubing might do just as well. Cut and glue the different noodles or tubing onto thick paper so the openings can be seen. Then label each. Now you have a simple, easy-to-understand model showing the differences in size of arteries, veins, and capillaries.

What other scientific ideas might a model help you to understand? A model of a molecule can be made from balls of modeling clay (using different colors for the different elements present) and toothpicks (to show different chemical bonds).

Science Skill Handbook

from larger units to smaller, multiply by 10. For example, to convert millimeters to centimeters, divide the millimeters by 10. To convert 30 millimeters to centimeters, divide 30 by 10 (30 millimeters equal 3 centimeters).

Prefixes are used to name units. Look at **Figure 26** for some common metric prefixes and their meanings. Do you see how the prefix *kilo-* attached to the unit *gram* is *kilogram,* or 1000 grams? The prefix *deci-* attached to the unit *meter* is *decimeter,* or one-tenth (0.1) of a meter.

Examples

Length   You have probably measured lengths or distances many times. The meter is the SI unit used to measure length. A baseball bat is about one meter long. When measuring smaller lengths, the meter is divided into smaller units called centimeters and millimeters. A centimeter is one-hundredth (0.01) of a meter, which is about the size of the width of the fingernail on your ring finger. A millimeter is one-thousandth of a meter (0.001), about the thickness of a dime.

Most metric rulers have lines indicating centimeters and millimeters, as shown in

Figure 25 Different types of pasta may be used to model blood vessels

A working model of a volcano can be made from clay, a small amount of baking soda, vinegar, and a bottle cap. Other models can be devised on a computer. Some models are mathematical and are represented by equations.

Measuring in SI

The metric system is a system of measurement developed by a group of scientists in 1795. It helps scientists avoid problems by providing standard measurements that all scientists around the world can understand. A modern form of the metric system, called the International System, or SI, was adopted for worldwide use in 1960.

The metric system is convenient because unit sizes vary by multiples of 10. When changing from smaller units to larger units, divide by 10. When changing

Figure 26 Common metric prefixes

Metric Prefixes			
Prefix	Symbol	Meaning	
kilo-	k	1000	thousand
hecto-	h	200	hundred
deka-	da	10	ten
deci-	d	0.1	tenth
centi-	c	0.01	hundredth
milli-	m	0.001	thousandth

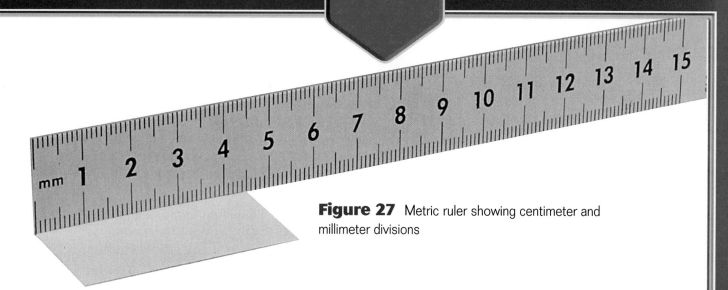

Figure 27 Metric ruler showing centimeter and millimeter divisions

Figure 27. The centimeter lines are the longer, numbered lines; the shorter lines are millimeter lines. When using a metric ruler, line up the 0-centimeter mark with the end of the object being measured, and read the number of the unit where the object ends, in this instance 4.5 cm.

Surface Area Units of length are also used to measure surface area. The standard unit of area is the square meter (m^2). A square that's one meter long on each side has a surface area of one square meter. Similarly, a square centimeter, (cm^2), shown in **Figure 28,** is one centimeter long on each side. The surface area of an object is determined by multiplying the length times the width.

Volume The volume of a rectangular solid is also calculated using units of length. The cubic meter (m^3) is the standard SI unit of volume. A cubic meter is a cube one meter on each side. You can determine the volume of rectangular solids by multiplying length times width times height.

Liquid Volume During science activities, you will measure liquids using beakers and graduated cylinders marked in milliliters, as illustrated in **Figure 29.** A graduated cylinder is a cylindrical container marked with lines from bottom to top.

Liquid volume is measured using a unit called a liter. A liter has the volume of 1000 cubic centimeters. Because the prefix *milli-* means thousandth (0.001), a milliliter equals one cubic centimeter. One milliliter of liquid would completely fill a cube measuring one centimeter on each side.

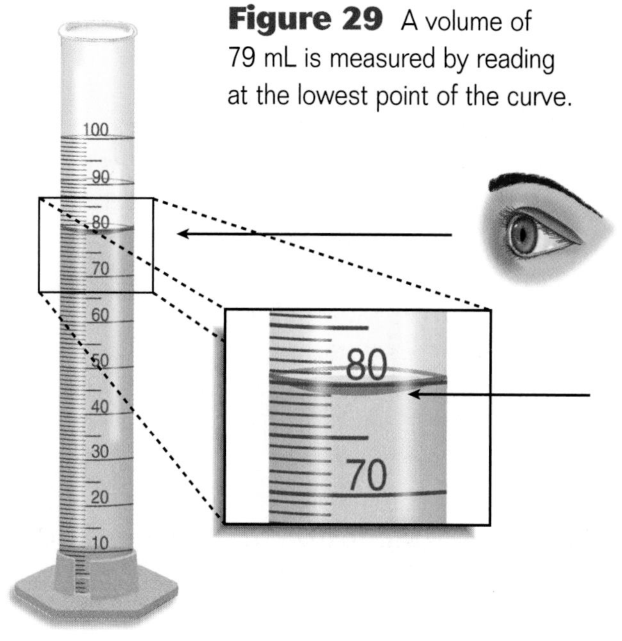

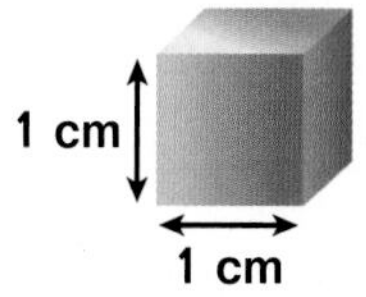

Figure 29 A volume of 79 mL is measured by reading at the lowest point of the curve.

Figure 28 A square centimeter

1 cm
1 cm

Mass Scientists use balances to find the mass of objects in grams. You might use a beam balance similar to **Figure 30.** Notice that on one side of the balance is a pan and on the other side is a set of beams. Each beam has an object of a known mass called a *rider* that slides on the beam.

Before you find the mass of an object, set the balance to zero by sliding all the riders back to the zero point. Check the pointer on the right to make sure it swings an equal distance above and below the zero point on the scale. If the swing is unequal, find and turn the adjusting screw until you have an equal swing.

Place an object on the pan. Slide the rider with the largest mass along its beam until the pointer drops below zero. Then move it back one notch. Repeat the process on each beam until the pointer swings an equal distance above and below the zero point. Add the masses on each beam to find the mass of the object.

You should never place a hot object or pour chemicals directly onto the pan. Instead, find the mass of a clean beaker or a glass jar. Place the dry or liquid chemicals in the container. Then find the combined mass of the container and the chemicals. Calculate the mass of the chemicals by subtracting the mass of the empty container from the combined mass.

Predicting

When you apply a hypothesis, or general explanation, to a specific situation, you predict something about that situation. First, you must identify which hypothesis fits the situation you are considering.

Examples People use prediction to make everyday decisions. Based on previous observations and experiences, you may form a hypothesis that if it is wintertime, then temperatures will be lower. From past experience in your area, temperatures are lowest in February. You may then use this hypothesis to predict specific temperatures and weather for the month of February in advance. Someone could use these predictions to plan to set aside more money for heating bills during that month.

Figure 30 A beam balance is used to measure mass.

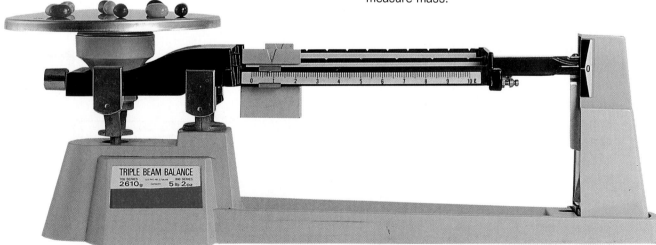

Using Numbers

When working with large populations of organisms, scientists usually cannot observe or study every organism in the population. Instead, they use a sample or a portion of the population. To sample is to take a small representative portion of organisms of a population for research. By making careful observations or manipulating variables within a portion of a group, information is discovered and conclusions are drawn that might then be applied to the whole population.

Scientific work also involves estimating. To estimate is to make a judgment about the size of something or the number of something without actually measuring or counting every member of a population.

Examples Suppose you are trying to determine the effect of a specific nutrient on the growth of black-eyed Susans. It would be impossible to test the entire population of black-eyed Susans, so you would select part of the population for your experiment. Through careful experimentation and observation on a sample of the population, you could generalize the effect of the chemical on the entire population.

Here is a more familiar example. Have you ever tried to guess how many beans were in a sealed jar? If you

did, you were estimating. What if you knew the jar of beans held one liter (1000 mL)? If you knew that 30 beans would fit in a 100-milliliter jar, how many beans would you estimate to be in the one-liter jar? If you said about 300 beans, your estimate would be close to the actual number of beans. Can you estimate how many jelly beans are on the cookie sheet in **Figure 31?**

Scientists use a similar process to estimate populations of organisms from bacteria to buffalo. Scientists count the actual number of organisms in a small sample and then estimate the number of organisms in a larger area. For example, if a scientist wanted to count the number of bacterial colonies in a petri dish, a microscope could be used to count the number of organisms in a one-square-centimeter sample. To determine the total population of the culture, the number of organisms in the square-centimeter sample is multiplied by the total number of square centimeters in the culture.

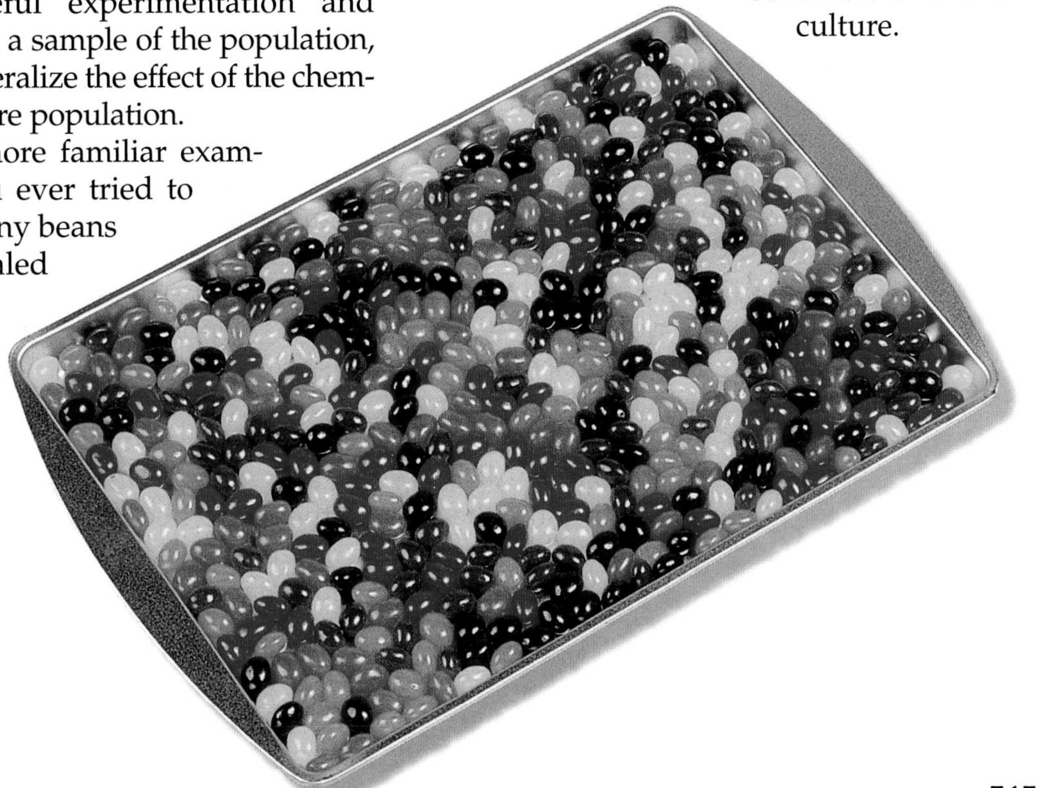

Figure 31
Sampling a group of jelly beans allows for an estimation of the total number of jelly beans in the group.

Technology Skill Handbook

Using a Word Processor

Suppose your teacher has assigned you to write a report. After you've done your research and decided how you want to write the information, you need to put all that information on paper. The easiest way to do this is with a word processor.

A word processor is a computer program in which you can write your information, change it as many times as you need to, and then print it out so that it looks neat and clean. You can also use a word processor to create tables and columns, add bullets or cartoon art, include page numbers, and even check your spelling.

Example Last week in Science class, your teacher assigned a report on the history of the atom. It has to be double spaced and include at least one table. You've collected all the facts, and you're ready to write your report. Sitting down at your computer, you decide you want to begin by explaining early scientific ideas about the atom and then talk about what scientists think about the atom now.

After you've written the two parts of your report, you decide to put a heading or subtitle above each part and add a title to the paper. To make each of these look different from the rest of your report, you can use a word processor to make the words bigger and bolder. The word processor also can double space your entire report, so that you don't have to add an extra space between each line.

You decide to include a table that lists each scientist that contributed to the theory of the atom along with his or her contribution. Using your word processor, you can create a table with as many rows and columns as you need. And, if you forget to include a scientist in the middle, you can go back and insert a row in the middle of your table without redoing the entire table.

When you've finished with your report, you can tell the word processor to check your spelling. If it finds misspelled words, it often will suggest a word you can use to replace the misspelled word. But, remember that the word processor may not know how to spell all the words in your report. Scan your report and double check your spelling with a dictionary if you're not sure if a word is spelled correctly.

After you've made sure that your report looks just the way you want it on the screen, the word processor will print your report on a printer. With a word processor, your report can look like it was written by a real scientist.

Helpful Hints

- If you aren't sure how to do something using your word processor, look under the help menu. You can look up how to do something, and the word processor will tell you how to do it. Just follow the instructions that the word processor puts on your screen.

- Just because you've spelled checked your report doesn't mean that the spelling is perfect. The spell check can't catch misspelled words that look like other words. So, if you've accidentally typed *mind* instead of *mine,* the spell checker won't know the difference. Always reread your report to make sure you didn't miss any mistakes.

Technology Skill Handbook

Using a Database

Imagine you're in the middle of research project. You are busily gathering facts and information. But, soon you realize that its becoming harder and harder to organize and keep track of all the information. The tool to solve "information overload" is a database. A database is exactly what it sounds like—a base on which to organize data. Similar to how a file cabinet organizes records, a database also organizes records. However, a database is more powerful than a simple file cabinet because at the click of a mouse, the entire contents can be reshuffled and reorganized. At computer-quick speeds, databases can sort information by any characteristic and filter data into multiple categories. Once you use a database, you will be amazed at how quickly all those facts and bits of information become manageable.

Example For the past few weeks, you have been gathering information on living and extinct primates. A database would be ideal to organize your information. An entry for gorillas might contain fields (categories) for fossil locations, brain size, average height, earliest fossil, and so on. Later on, if you wanted to know which primates have been found in Asia, you could quickly filter all entries using Asia in the field that listed locations. The database will scan all the entries and select the entries containing Asia. If you wanted to rank all the primates by arm length, you would sort all the entries by arm length. By using different combinations of sorting and filtering, you can discover relationships between the data that otherwise might remain hidden.

Helpful Hints

- Before setting up your own database, it's easier to learn the features of your database software by practicing with an established database.
- Entering the data into a database can be time consuming. Learn shortcuts such as tabbing between entry fields and automatic formatting of data that your software may provide.
- Get in the habit of periodically saving your database as you are entering data. That way, if something happens and your computer locks up or the power goes out, you won't lose all of your work.

Most databases have specific words you can use to narrow your search.

- AND: If you place an AND between two words in your search, the database will look for any entries that have both the words. For example, "blood AND cell" would give you information about both blood and cells.
- OR: If you place an OR between two words, the database will show entries that have at least one of the words. For example, "bird OR fish" would show you information on either birds or fish.
- NOT: If you place a NOT between two words, the database will look for entries that have the first word but do not have the second word. For example, "reproduction NOT plant" would show you information about reproduction but not about plant reproduction.

Using Graphics Software

Having trouble finding that exact piece of art you're looking for? Do you have a picture in your mind of what you want but can't seem to find the right graphic to represent your ideas? To solve these problems, you can use graphics software. Graphics software allows you to change and create images and diagrams in almost unlimited ways. Typical uses for graphics software include arranging clip-art, changing scanned images, and constructing pictures from scratch. Most graphics-software applications work in similar ways. They use the same basic tools and functions. Once you master one graphics application, you can use any other graphics application relatively easily.

Example For your report on bird adaptations, you want to make a poster displaying a variety of beak and foot types. You have acquired many photos of birds, scanned from magazines and downloaded off the Internet. Using graphics software, you separate the beaks and feet from the birds and enlarge them. Then, you use arrows and text to diagram the particular features that you want to highlight. You also highlight the key features in color, keeping the rest of the graphic in black and white. With graphics software, the possibilities are endless. For the final layout, you place the picture of the bird next to enlarged graphics of the feet and beak. Graphics software allows you to integrate text into your diagrams, which makes your bird poster look clean and professional.

Helpful Hints

- As with any method of drawing, the more you practice using the graphic software, the better your results.

- Start by using the software to manipulate existing drawings. Once you master this, making your own illustrations will be easier.
- Clip art is available on CD-ROMs, and on the Internet. With these resources, finding a piece of clip art to suit your purposes is simple.
- As you work on a drawing, save it often.
- Often you can learn a lot from studying other people's art. Look at other computer illustrations and try to figure out how the artist created it.

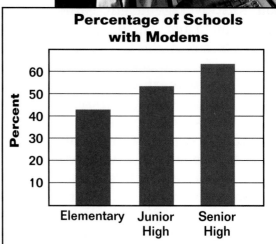

Percentage of Schools with Modems

Technology Skill Handbook

Using a Computerized Card Catalog

When you have a report or paper to research, you go to the library. To find the information, skill is needed in using a computerized card catalog. You use the computerized card catalog by typing in a subject, the title of a book, or an author's name. The computer will list on the screen all the holdings the library has on the subject, title, or author requested.

A library's holdings include books, magazines, databases, videos, and audio materials. When you have chosen something from this list, the computer will show whether an item is available and where in the library to find it.

Example You have a report due on dinosaurs, and you need to find three books on the subject. In the library, follow the instructions on the computer screen to select the "Subject" heading. You could start by typing in the word *dinosaurs*. This will give you a list of books on that subject. Now you need to narrow your search to the kind of dinosaur you are interested in, for example, *Tyrannosaurus rex*. You can type in *Tyrannosaurus rex* or just look through the list to find titles that you think would have information you need. Once you have selected a short list of books, click on each selection to find out if the library has the books. Then, check on where they are located in the library.

Helpful Hints

- Remember that you can use the computer to search by subject, author, or title. If you know a book's author, but not the title, you can search for all the books the library has by that author.
- When searching by subject, it's often most helpful to narrow your search by using specific search terms. If you don't find enough, you can then broaden your search.
- Pay attention to the type of materials found in your search. If you need a book, you can eliminate any videos or other resources that come up in your search.
- Knowing how your library is arranged can save a lot of time. The librarian will show you where certain types of material are kept and how to find something.

Technology Skill Handbook

Developing Multimedia Presentations

It's your turn—you have to present your science report to the entire class. How do you do it? You can use many different sources of information to get the class excited about your presentation. Posters, videos, photographs, sound, computers, and the Internet can help show our ideas. First, decide the most important points you want your presentation to make. Then, sketch out what materials and types of media would be best to illustrate those points. Maybe you could start with an outline on an overhead projector, then show a video, followed by something from the Internet or a slide show accompanied by music or recorded voices. Make sure you don't make the presentation too complicated, or you will confuse yourself and the class. Practice your presentation a few times for your parents or brothers and sisters before you present it to the class.

Example Your assignment is to give a presentation on bird-watching. You could have a poster that shows what features you use to identify birds, with a sketch of your favorite bird. A tape of the calls of your favorite bird or a video of birds in your area would work well with the poster. If possible, include an Internet site with illustrations of birds that the class can look at.

Helpful Hints
- Carefully consider what media will best communicate the point you are trying to make.
- Keep your topic and your presentation simple.
- Make sure you learn how to use any equipment you will be using in your presentation.
- Practice the presentation several times.
- If possible, set up all of the equipment ahead of time. Make sure everything is working correctly.

Technology Skill Handbook

Using E-Mail

It's science fair time and you want to ask a scientist a question about your project, but he or she lives far away. You could write a letter or make a phone call. But you can also use the computer to communicate. You can do this using electronic mail (E-mail). You will need a computer that is connected to an E-mail network. The computer is usually hooked up to the network by a device called a *modem*. A modem works through the telephone lines. Finally, you need an address for the person you want to talk with. The E-mail address works just like a street address to send mail to that person.

Example There are just a few steps needed to send a message to a friend on an E-mail network. First, select Message from the E-mail software menu. Then, enter the E-mail address of your friend. Next, type your message. Make sure you check it for spelling and other errors. Finally, click the Send button to mail your message and off it goes! You will get a reply back in your electronic mailbox. To read your reply, just click on the message and the reply will appear on the screen.

Helpful Hints
- Make sure that you have entered the correct address of the person you're sending the message to.
- Reread your message to make sure it says what you want to say, and check for spelling and grammar.
- If you receive an E-mail message, respond to it as soon as possible.
- If you receive frequent email messages, keep them organized by either deleting them, or saving them in folders according to the subject or sender.

Technology Skill Handbook

Using an Electronic Spreadsheet

Your science fair experiment has produced lots of numbers. How do you keep track of all the data, and how can you easily work out all the calculations needed? You can use a computer program called a *spreadsheet* to keep track of data that involve numbers. A spreadsheet is an electronic worksheet. Type in your data in rows and columns, just as in a data table on a sheet of paper. A spreadsheet uses some simple math to do calculations on the data. For example, you could add, subtract, divide, or multiply any of the values in the spreadsheet by another number. Or you can set up a series of math steps you want to apply to the data. If you want to add 12 to all the numbers and then multiply all the numbers by 10, the computer does all the calculations for you in the spreadsheet. Below is an example of a spreadsheet that is a schedule.

Example Let's say that to complete your project, you need to calculate the speed of the model cars in your experiment. Enter the distance traveled by each car in the rows of the spreadsheet. Then enter the time you recorded for each car to travel the measured distance in the column across from each car. To make the formula, just type in the equation you want the computer to calculate; in this case, *speed = distance ÷ time.* You must make sure the computer knows what data are in the rows and what data are in the

	A	B	C	D
	Test Runs	Time	Distance	Speed
1	Car 1	5 mins.	5 miles	60 mph
2	Car 2	10 mins.	4 miles	24 mph
3	Car 3	6 mins.	3 miles	30 mph

Test Run Data

columns so the calculation will be correct. Once all the distance and time data and the formula have been entered into the spreadsheet program, the computer will calculate the speed for all the trials you ran. You can even make graphs of the results.

Helpful Hints

- Before you set up the spreadsheet, sketch out how you want to organize the data. Include any formulas you will need to use.
- Make sure you have entered the correct data into the correct rows and columns.
- As you experiment with your particular spreadsheet program you will learn more of its features.
- You can also display your results in a graph. Pick the style of graph that best represents the data you are working with.

Technology Skill Handbook

Using a CD-ROM

What's your favorite music? You probably listen to your favorite music on compact discs (CDs). But, there is another use for compact discs, called CD-ROM. CD-ROM means Compact Disc-Read Only Memory. CD-ROMs hold information. Whole encyclopedias and dictionaries can be stored on CD-ROM discs. This kind of CD-ROM and others are used to research information for reports and papers. The information is accessed by putting the disc in your computer's CD-ROM drive and following the computer's installation instructions. The CD-ROM will have words, pictures, photographs, and maybe even sound and video on a range of topics.

Example Load the CD-ROM into the computer. Find the topic you are interested in by clicking on the Search button. If there is no Search button, try the Help button. Most CD-ROMs are easy to use, but refer to the Help instructions if you have problems. Use the arrow keys to move down through the list of titles on your topic. When you double-click on a title, the article will appear on the screen. You can print the article by clicking on the Print button. Each CD-ROM is different. Click the Help menu to see how to find what you want.

Helpful Hints

- Always open and close the CD-ROM drive on your computer by pushing the button next to the drive. Pushing on the tray to close it will stress the opening mechanism over time.
- Place the disc in the tray so the side with no printing is facing down.
- Read through the installation instructions that come with the CD-ROM.
- Remember to remove the CD-ROM before you shut your computer down.

Using Probeware

Data collecting in an experiment sometimes requires that you take the same measurement over and over again. With probeware, you can hook a probe directly to a computer and have the computer collect the data about temperature, pressure, motion, or pH. Probeware is a combination sensor and software that makes the process of collecting data easier. With probes hooked to computers, you can make many measurements quickly, and you can collect data over a long period of time without needing to be present. Not only will the software record the data, most software will graph the data.

Example Suppose you want to monitor the health of an enclosed ecosystem. You might use an oxygen and a carbon dioxide sensor to monitor the gas concentrations or humidity or temperature. If the gas concentrations remain stable, you could predict that the ecosystem is healthy. After all the data is collected, you can use the software to graph the data and analyze it. With probeware, experimenting is made efficient and precise.

Helpful Hints

- Find out how to properly use each probe before using it.
- Make sure all cables are solidly connected. A loose cable can interrupt the data collection and give you inaccurate results.
- Because probeware makes data collection so easy, do as many trials as possible to strengthen your data.

Technology Skill Handbook

Using a Graphing Calculator

Science can be thought of as a means to predict the future and explain the past. In other language, if x happens, can we predict y? Can we explain the reason y happened? Simply, is their a relationship between x and y? In nature, relationship between two events or two quantities, x and y, often occur. However, the relationship is often complicated and can only be readily seen by making a graph. And, to analyze a graph, there is no quicker tool than a graphing calculator. The graphing calculator shows the mathematical relationship between two quantities.

Example If you have collected data on the position and time for a migrating whale, you can use the calculator to graph the data. Using the linear regression function on the calculator, you can determine the average migration speed of the whale. The more you use the graphing calculator to solve problems, the more you will discover its power and efficiency.

Graphing calculators have some keys that other calculators do not have. The keys on the bottom half of the calculator are those found on all scientific calculators. The keys located just below the screen are the graphing keys. You will also notice the up, down, left, and right arrow keys. These allow you to move the cursor around on the screen, to "trace" graphs that have been plotted, and to choose items from the menus. The other keys located on the top of the calculator access the special features such as statistical computations and programming features.

A few of the keystrokes that can save you time when using the graphing calculator are listed below.

- The commands above the calculator keys are accessed with the [2nd] or [ALPHA] key. The [2nd] key and its commands are yellow and the [ALPHA] and its commands are green.
- [2nd] [ENTRY] copies the previous calculation so you can edit and use it again.
- Pressing [ON] while the calculator is graphing stops the calculator from completing the graph.
- [2nd] [QUIT] will return you to the home (or text) screen.
- [2nd] [A-LOCK] locks the [ALPHA] key, which is like pressing "shift lock" or "caps lock" on a typewriter or computer. The result is that all letters will be typed and you do not have to repeatedly press the [ALPHA] key. (This is handy for programming.) Stop typing letters by pressing [ALPHA] again.
- [2nd] [OFF] turns the calculator off.

Helpful Hints

- Mastering the graphing calculator takes practice. Don't expect to learn it all in an afternoon.
- Programming a graphing calculator takes a plan. Write out all of the steps before entering them.
- It's easiest to learn how to program the calculator by first using programs that have already been written. As you enter them, figure out what each step is telling the calculator to do.

Skill Activities

Table of Contents

Measuring Length

Background

We have many different units for measuring sizes and distances. It is important to know how to select the most useful unit for measuring the length of a particular object or distance. Units that are used for measuring the distance an animal can run would not be useful for measuring the length of the animal's tooth. Read this problem and answer the questions below.

What units are most useful for measuring various lengths?

Procedure 👓

1. Using a meter stick or ruler, measure the length of your classroom in meters (m), centimeters (cm), and millimeters (mm). Record the measurements in a table like the one shown below.

2. Measure the length of this book and a pencil eraser in meters, centimeters, and millimeters. Record the measurements in your table.

3. Choose more items to measure. Record your measurements in your table.

Practicing the SKILL

1. What difficulties did you encounter while making your measurements?

2. Which unit would you select if you were to measure the length of the school parking lot?

3. Which unit would you select if you were to measure the length of an insect? Why?

For more skill practice, do the Chapter 1 Interactive Exploration on the **Science Voyages Level Green CD-ROM.**

GLENCOE TECHNOLOGY

Lengths of Items			
	Length in Meters	**Length in Centimeters**	**Length in Millimeters**
Classroom			
Textbook			
Pencil Eraser			

Interpreting Scientific Illustrations

Background

You may have heard the saying "A picture is worth a thousand words." A good scientific diagram often can explain an idea better than several paragraphs of words. In order to get the most from diagrams, do the following.

- Study the entire diagram. Review the part of the text that the diagram illustrates.

- If there is a caption, read it carefully.

- Read all the labels and identify the parts.

- Visualize the dimensions. Arrows often indicate distances and direction. Distances often are indicated between arrows. The heads of the arrows show where the measurements start and end.

Use these guidelines to interpret the diagram at right.

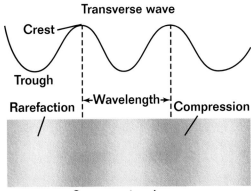

Transverse wave

Crest

Trough

Rarefaction ←Wavelength→ Compression

Compressional wave

Procedure

(1) What is the purpose of this diagram?

(2) Identify the text in Chapter 2 to which the diagram relates. Locate the discussions about types of waves.

(3) What does the crest of a transverse wave correspond to on a compressional wave?

(4) What does the trough of a transverse wave correspond to on a compressional wave?

(5) What is another way you can diagram the wavelength of a transverse wave?

Practicing the SKILL

(1) What do the darker areas of the compressional wave represent?

(2) What are the white areas?

(3) How would you measure one wavelength of a compressional wave?

For more skill practice, do the Chapter 2 Interactive Exploration on the **Science Voyages Level Green CD-ROM.**

GLENCOE TECHNOLOGY

Communicating

Background

Have you ever wanted to learn more about a topic? Writing a report is one way you can explore new topics. You can learn about anything from the galaxy Andromeda to the element zirconium.

Scientists also write reports. Their reports give them the chance to communicate their work to other scientists in their field and to exchange ideas.

Procedure

1. Select a topic for your paper that interests you.

2. Once you have chosen a topic, go to the library to find information. Start with *The Reader's Guide to Periodical Literature.* It lists magazine articles by subject. To find books on your topic, look in the card catalog. Using technology also can help you find good sources of information.

3. Write down the author and title of each reference. For books, record the publisher and date of publication. For magazine articles, include the name and date of the magazine, the volume, and the issue number. Also indicate the page numbers where the reference is located.

4. As you read your references, decide what is important. In your own words, write down the information and where you found it. Keep your notes brief.

5. After you have read all your material, pick out the main ideas and the subtopics. Use them to make a detailed outline. Once this is done, you are ready to write. At the end of the paper, list the references you used.

Practicing the SKILL

1. Research the Hubble Space Telescope.

2. Communicate the information you find by writing a report.

For more skill practice, do the Chapter 3 Interactive Exploration on the **Science Voyages Level Green CD-ROM.**

GLENCOE TECHNOLOGY

Comparing and Contrasting

Background

Scientists often have more than one object or event to look at. For example, they often carry out experiments that have many similarities and a single difference. When scientists look at objects or events to see how they are similar, they are comparing them. Contrasting involves looking for differences in similar objects or events. In this activity, you will compare and contrast the results from the experiment you will perform.

Procedure

PART 1

1. Take a tissue and loosely wad it up.

2. Tape it inside the bottom of a 12-ounce paper or foam cup.

3. Fill a bowl or sink with water.

4. Push the cup straight down into the water with the open end downward.

5. Pull the cup straight up from the water and examine the tissue.

PART 2

6. Punch a small hole in the bottom of the cup.

7. Push the cup straight down into the water with the open end downward, nearly—but not quite—immersing the bottom of the cup.

8. Pull the cup straight up from the water and examine the tissue.

Practicing the SKILL

1. Compare and contrast the results from parts 1 and 2 of your experiment.

2. What conclusions can you draw from performing your experiment?

For more skill practice, do the Chapter 4 Interactive Exploration on the **Science Voyages Level Green CD-ROM.**

GLENCOE TECHNOLOGY

Variables and Controls

Background

Suppose you disagree with a friend about which sports drink contains the most flavoring, sweetener, and other dissolved materials. You cannot accurately find out by tasting each sports drink because every individual's sense of taste is slightly different. To settle the matter, you try to find some method of testing the sports drinks that is fair, or unbiased. You don't want any personal preferences to influence the test results. You devise a test involving three brands of sports drink.

You label and weigh three identical, heat-resistant jars. You measure 100 mL of each drink into the appropriate jar. You set the jars on a hot plate and heat the drinks. Being careful to avoid burning the dry material that remains, you remove each jar when all the liquid has boiled away. You let the jars cool to room temperature, then weigh each jar. To find the mass of dry material from each drink, you subtract the mass of the empty jar from the total mass.

Scientists design experiments in much the same way. They take great care to make sure only one factor in the experiment, the independent variable, is changed. The independent variable in your experiment is the brand of sports drink. The factor that changes as a result of the independent variable is called the dependent variable. The dependent variable in your experiment is the mass of dry material. Controls are factors that are kept the same, providing a basis for comparison. Controls in your experiment are the identical jars, amounts of drink, and the temperature of the hot plate. See if you can identify the controls and variables in the following Skill Activity.

Procedure

1. Pour the same amount of water into two beakers.
2. Take the temperature of the water in each beaker to make sure the temperatures are the same.
3. Add salt to one beaker and stir the water in both beakers until all the salt has dissolved.
4. Take the temperature of the water and of the salt solution.
5. How did dissolving salt in one beaker affect the water temperature?
6. What were the controls? Variables?

Practicing the SKILL

1. Ten grams of sugar dissolves more quickly in a liter of pure, hot, tap water than it does in a liter of pure, cold, tap water. List the controls, the independent variable, and the dependent variable.
2. Identify the dependent variable from testing the following hypothesis: If premium gasoline is more efficient, then it should increase the fuel mileage of our family car.

For more skill practice, do the Chapter 5 Interactive Exploration on the **Science Voyages Level Green CD-ROM.**

Sequencing

Background

Every day you do things in a certain order. For example, you may have a schedule that tells the order of your classes. Language arts may be taught first, followed by science, math, and so on. When you go to your classes in a certain order, you follow a sequence. A sequence is a series of things or events arranged in a specific order.

For scientists, knowing the sequence of a set of events can be very important. Sequencing helps scientists better understand a process that is under study or predict what may happen next.

To help themselves outline a particular sequence, many scientists make a *flow chart,* which is a detailed description of the operations and decisions needed to solve a problem. A flow chart breaks a process down into its most basic steps.

Procedure

To understand flow charts, think about when you make a telephone call. What steps do you take?

Figure A shows the sequence of steps taken for the above activity in the form of a flow chart. Each step is written in a special kind of box. A circle (○) begins and ends a chart. A diamond (◇) shows that a question is being asked. A square (□) indicates something you do. A parallelogram (▱) represents a result. Whenever you ask a question, you must provide two paths. One path shows what to do if the answer is yes. The other path shows what to do if the answer is no.

A

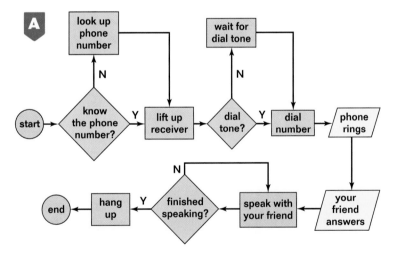

B

Practicing the SKILL

Make a flow chart to show the path electric current in **Figure B** might take in going through a circuit.

For more skill practice, do the Chapter 6 Interactive Exploration on the **Science Voyages Level Green CD-ROM.**

GLENCOE TECHNOLOGY

Concept Mapping

Background

In science, it often helps to visualize an event in order to determine how many steps it took to reach the final outcome. An events chain concept map is a helpful tool to use to describe the sequence of events, or stages of a process.

Suppose you are having a hard time understanding a drawing of the production of electricity from a generator to your home. An events chain may help you organize the information in a way you can remember.

Procedure

1. Look at the figure below.

2. Use one or two words to describe each step of the process.

3. Construct an events chain concept map that shows how electricity eventually ends up at your house.

Practicing the SKILL

1. Is your events chain easier to understand than a drawing? Explain.

2. What other processes could be explained in an events chain?

For more skill practice, do the Chapter 7 Interactive Exploration on the **Science Voyages Level Green CD-ROM.**

GLENCOE TECHNOLOGY

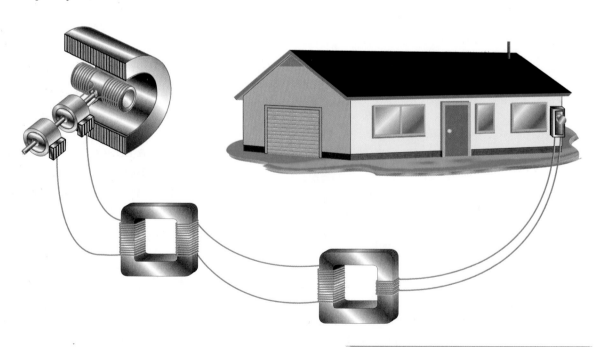

Observing and Inferring

Background

You have learned that mechanical weathering occurs when rocks break apart without changing their chemical composition. Two common mechanisms of mechanical weathering are ice wedging and growing plants.

Mechanical weathering from plants can cause problems with human-made structures such as sidewalks, driveways, walls, and house foundations. These structures usually are made of concrete, a rocklike material made of sand, crushed rock, and cement. People often plant trees near sidewalks, driveways, and houses, or there may be preexisting trees in the area. Tree roots will grow beneath the concrete slabs. As the roots grow in diameter, they generate a force that is often great enough to lift and crack the concrete. A broken sidewalk is a relatively minor problem to replace, but if tree roots lift and break a house foundation, it can lead to expensive repairs.

Procedure

① Carefully observe the outside environment where you live. Look for evidence of mechanical weathering caused by plant roots. Some good places to look might be sidewalks, driveways, and walls near large trees. In addition, you might also look for areas where plant roots have cracked large rocks.

② Once you have found a good example, write a description and draw a sketch of the mechanical weathering you observe.

③ Use a ruler to measure in centimeters how wide a crack is, or how much the structure has been lifted by the plant. This is called displacement. Note this distance in your written description.

④ Do some research to find out when the sidewalk, driveway, or wall was built or when the tree was planted. Use this information to determine the age of the crack.

Practicing the SKILL

① Share your observations with the class. How many different examples of mechanical weathering were observed?

② What was the greatest amount of displacement that was observed?

③ If you were able to determine how old your structure is, divide the displacement by the age to calculate how many centimeters per year the crack moves.

For more skill practice, do the Chapter 8 Interactive Exploration on the **Science Voyages Level Green CD-ROM.**

Concept Mapping

Background

You have learned that erosion is the process by which surface materials are transported between locations by the agents of gravity, wind, water, and glaciers. Erosional agents can be divided into two main groups: erosion caused by moving or flowing water, such as rivers and ocean waves; and erosion caused by other agents like glaciers, gravity, and wind. All of these erosional forces have similarities and differences. A concept map of erosional forces can help you understand these relationships.

Procedure

A list of terms related to erosion by glaciers, gravity, and wind is written above. Study the list and create separate tree concept maps for these three agents of erosion. Select terms for each specific tree from the list. Some of the terms may not be used. Wind has been done for you.

Erosion Terms	
gravity	glacial deposits
glaciers	slow movement
mass movement	glacial erosion features
till	fast movement
moraine	creep
outwash plains	rock slide
leaning trees and telephone poles	material moved by ice
mudflow	piles of broken rock
curved scars	thick mix of sediment and water
cirque	slump
arête	U-shaped valleys

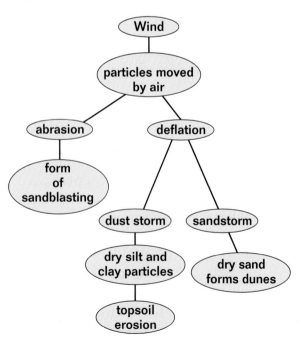

Practicing the SKILL

1. Describe two characteristics that glaciers, gravity, and wind, as erosional agents, have in common.

2. For each erosional agent, describe one characteristic that is not shared by the other two agents.

3. How do concept maps help you learn about erosional forces?

For more skill practice, do the Chapter 9 Interactive Exploration on the **Science Voyages Level Green CD-ROM.**

Interpreting Scientific Illustrations

Background

A drainage basin is the land area from which a stream or river gets its water. A drainage basin can be as small as a backyard or cover thousands of square miles. The size of drainage basins can be interpreted from a topographic map.

Procedure

1. Use a sheet of tracing paper and a pencil to trace the streams on the map at right or from another topographic map your teacher has provided.

2. Use the map scale to determine the approximate size of 4 km² on this map. Study your stream tracings and use a colored pencil to outline the drainage basins that are larger than 4 km².

Practicing the SKILL

1. How many different drainage basins can you identify?

2. Can a stream belong to more than one drainage basin? Explain your answer.

For more skill practice, do the Chapter 10 Interactive Exploration on the **Science Voyages Level Green CD-ROM.**

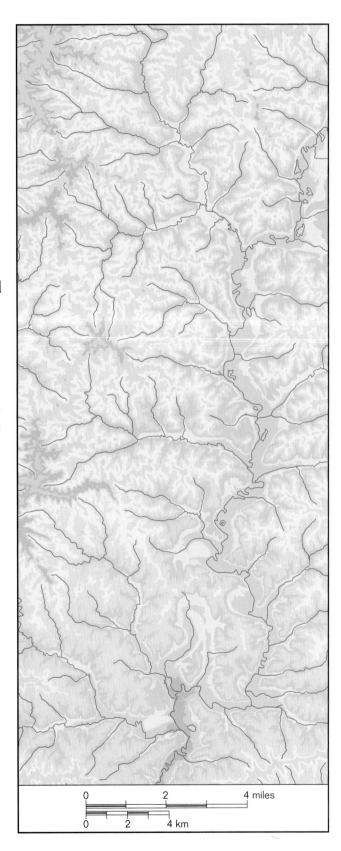

0   2   4 miles

0   2   4 km

Comparing and Contrasting

Background

You have learned that ocean tides are caused by the gravitational interactions of the sun, moon, and Earth. Most coastal locations experience two high and two low tides each day. However, the amplitude, or overall height, of these tides varies a great deal from place to place. The size of the ocean basin, the shape of the coastline, and the depth of the water are local factors affecting tides.

Procedure

(1) Study the tide graphs for Charleston, South Carolina, and Bellingham, Washington. Compare and contrast their patterns.

(2) Use a United States map to find these two coastal cities that are represented by the tide graphs.

Practicing the SKILL

(1) What are the similarities between the locations of Charleston and Bellingham? What are the differences?

(2) Describe the similarities and differences between the two tide graphs.

(3) What is the maximum tidal range for each city and when did it occur?

(4) When did neap tide conditions occur? Draw a diagram showing the positions of the sun, moon, and Earth during this time period.

For more skill practice, do the Chapter 11 Interactive Exploration on the **Science Voyages Level Green CD-ROM.**

GLENCOE TECHNOLOGY

Charleston, South Carolina
August, 1998

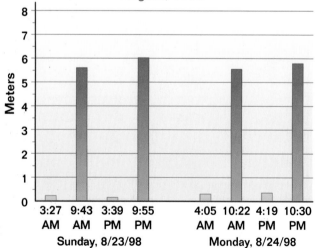

Meters

3:27 AM | 9:43 AM | 3:39 PM | 9:55 PM | 4:05 AM | 10:22 AM | 4:19 PM | 10:30 PM

Sunday, 8/23/98   Monday, 8/24/98

Date and time

Bellingham, Washington
August, 1998

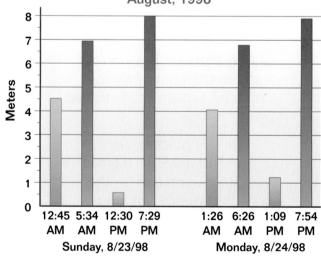

Meters

12:45 AM | 5:34 AM | 12:30 PM | 7:29 PM | 1:26 AM | 6:26 AM | 1:09 PM | 7:54 PM

Sunday, 8/23/98   Monday, 8/24/98

Date and time

Interpreting Data

Background

Early oceanographers had a difficult time obtaining ocean-depth information. The only method available was to lower a weight on a wire or rope until it hit bottom. It takes a very long time to lower and raise a weight 10 000 meters! Imagine the difficulty in figuring out when the weight touched bottom.

Today, oceanographers use sound waves to map ocean depths. A ship sends out a "ping" and listens for the echo from the bottom. The greater the echo time, the greater the water depth. By recording a series of echo times as the ship moves, scientists are able to create a profile showing the depth to the ocean floor. This is much faster than the old method and oceanographers are finally able to get enough data points to create good maps of the ocean floor.

"ping" "echo"

ocean floor

Echo Time							
Station	1	2	3	4	5	6	7
time (s)	1	0.5	1	2	4	4.5	5
Station	8	9	10	11	12	13	14
time (s)	5.5	6.5	6	5	4	2.5	2

Procedure

1. A ship recorded a series of echo times. These 14 times are listed in the Echo Time table.

2. The average speed of sound in water is 1500 m/s. To calculate the water depth from an echo time, multiply the time by the speed of sound in water and divide by two. Depth=(time × 1500)/2

3. Calculate the water depth at each point.

4. On a piece of graph paper, use the depth information to draw a profile of the ocean floor. Hint: Draw an upside-down graph with zero meters depth at the top and the depth increasing down along the y-axis.

Practicing the SKILL

1. What is the shallowest depth on the profile? What station is it?

2. What is the deepest part of the profile? What station is it?

3. Why is it necessary to divide by two when calculating the water depth?

For more skill practice, do the Chapter 12 Interactive Exploration on the **Science Voyages Level Green CD-ROM.**

GLENCOE TECHNOLOGY

Communicating

Background

Not all of the information that we read is presented honestly or accurately. In order to make informed decisions, you must be able to evaluate critically the information you read to make sure that the information is not only accurate but also that it is not biased or slanted to one particular view. Use the following guidelines to determine if the scientific information you read is reliable.

Procedure

1. Check the background of the author. Most articles written in journals or magazines give a brief biographical sketch of the author. Is the author a professional in the field about which he or she is writing, or is the author trained in another, unrelated field? Has the author earned awards in that field or awards from any of the major scientific societies?

2. Check the source of the article. Has the article been written for a scientific journal or has the article appeared in a popular magazine or local newspaper?

3. Evaluate the emotional level of the information. Scientific information is generally written in a straightforward style. When you read an article, consider the question: Does the headline or title make you angry, sad, or happy?

4. Read the article for how the content is presented. Check to see that concepts are clearly explained and supported by research. Be wary if many conclusions are drawn from only one, limited experiment. Also watch for overuse of such comments as "I think," or "In my opinion."

5. Determine whether the information has been taken out of context. Is the scientist writing the article or has someone reinterpreted the scientist's comments? Is it possible that only parts of the quoted comments are reported?

Practicing the SKILL

1. Read the following headlines. Which one do you think would contain more reliable information?

   - **Strange Fish Kill Has Public Upset**
   - **Scientists Investigate the Death of Fish in Plum River**

2. Which of the following three periodicals would be the best source of information for the situations below?

   - *An environmental periodical*
   - *A consumer periodical*
   - *An encyclopedia*

   a. Which detergent will clean your clothes the best?

   b. What new compounds are being used in making detergents?

   c. What effect do phosphate detergents have on the environment?

For more skill practice, do the Chapter 13 Interactive Exploration on the **Science Voyages Level Green CD-ROM.**

GLENCOE TECHNOLOGY

Interpreting Scientific Illustrations and Data

Background

Over the last ten years, people have begun to build houses around Maple Lake. Forty percent of the shoreline now has been developed. Recently, the residents have begun to complain about excessive algae growth and poor fishing. A scientific study indicates high levels of phosphates and nitrates in the lake. In an effort to locate the source of these chemicals, scientists collected and analyzed water samples. The sample locations are shown and the analyses are listed in the table below.

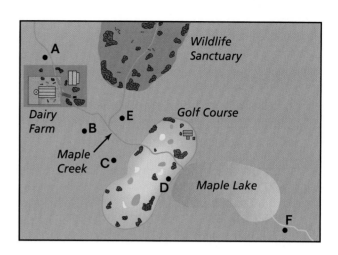

Procedure

1. Study the map of the Maple Lake area.

2. Study the table that lists location by letter and the amount of nitrates and phosphates at each location.

3. Use the map and the table to answer the questions in Practicing the Skill.

Location of Chemicals in Maple Lake		
Location	**Nitrates**	**Phosphates**
A	2 ppm*	1 ppm
B	16 ppm	2 ppm
C	8 ppm	1 ppm
D	25 ppm	12 ppm
E	<1 ppm	<1 ppm
F	30 ppm	15 ppm

*The abbreviation "ppm" means parts per million. For example, 2 ppm here means 2 parts nitrates per million parts water in Maple Lake.

Practicing the SKILL

1. What might be the source of pollution at B?

2. Why do you think the level of chemicals dropped from B to C?

3. How do you explain the data at D?

4. The level of chemicals at F are higher than D. Where do you think the extra nitrates and phosphates are coming from?

5. A scientist has proposed to create a large water hyacinth pond on the creek between the golf course and Maple Lake. Do you think this will help with the algae problem in the lake? Why or why not?

For more skill practice, do the Chapter 14 Interactive Exploration on the **Science Voyages Level Green CD-ROM**

GLENCOE TECHNOLOGY

Using Numbers

Background

H_2O and $C_6H_{12}O_6$ are chemical formulas for water and sugar, respectively. Each represents one molecule of the compound.

What do the numbers in chemical formulas tell us?

The letters are the symbols for elements. Each element symbol is written as one upper case letter or an upper case letter followed by a lower case letter. Numbers in formulas are called subscripts. A subscript is written below and after an element's symbol. It tells how many atoms of the element before it, are in the molecule. If there is no subscript, it means that there is just one atom of that element. Sometimes two or more elements are inside a set of parentheses followed by a subscript. This means that the number of atoms of each element inside the parentheses is multiplied by the subscript. For example, $(H_2O)_3$ is six atoms of hydrogen and three atoms of oxygen.

Procedure

Complete the table below. Look at the Periodic Table of Elements in the back of your book to identify the element symbols.

Practicing the SKILL

1. What do numbers as subscripts mean?

2. Which substance(s) have the most elements?

3. Which substance(s) have the most atoms?

For more skill practice, do the Chapter 15 Interactive Exploration on the **Science Voyages Level Green CD-ROM.**

GLENCOE TECHNOLOGY

Chemical Formulas					
Formula	Element/ number of atoms	Element/ number of atoms	Element/ number of atoms	Element/ number of atoms	Total number of atoms
CO_2					
$CaCO_3$					
$NaC_2H_3O_2$					
C_3H_7OH					
$C_{12}H_{22}O_{11}$					
$Al(OH)_3$					
$Ba_3(PO_4)_2$					

Designing an Experiment to Test a Hypothesis

Background

Sam's teacher has a sweet potato vine growing on a windowsill in the classroom. The sweet potato is submerged halfway in water in a glass jar. The sweet potato has toothpicks inserted around its middle to support it. Stems and leaves grow from the part of the sweet potato above the water. Roots grow from the part of the sweet potato that is under water. Sam's teacher tells the class that the sweet potato is a root. Sam thinks that if a root can grow a new plant, maybe other plant parts can grow new plants. He decides to test this idea. How does Sam begin? He may start by asking others about how to grow plants without using seeds. Then, he may read about different ways to grow new plants. Finally, Sam decides to do an experiment to see what plant parts can be used to grow new plants.

Do this activity to design an experiment that could test Sam's idea.

Procedure

1. Form a hypothesis about which parts of a plant might grow into a new plant when planted in soil.

2. Design an experiment to test your hypothesis. Be sure to include a control and identify the variable.

3. List the steps needed to complete the experiment. Be as specific as possible.

4. Make a list of materials needed to do the experiment.

5. Decide what data and observations will be taken and how they will be recorded.

6. Decide how results will be analyzed and presented.

7. Have your teacher check your design.

Practicing the SKILL

1. Compare your design to those of your classmates.

2. What is the variable in your experiment.

3. What could be sources of error?

For more skill practice, do the Chapter 16 Interactive Exploration on the **Science Voyages Level Green CD-ROM.**

GLENCOE TECHNOLOGY

Making and Using Graphs

Background

A graph is a diagram that shows the relationship of one variable to another. Graphs are a useful tool for scientists because they have many practical uses. Graphs can be used to organize a large amount of data into a more manageable format. When data is put into a graph, it is easier to see patterns that develop. This helps the scientist with the interpretation and analysis of the data. It also helps scientists determine if the original hypothesis is correct. Graphs are also helpful when presenting your conclusions to others. It presents the data in an already organized, easily understood format.

Procedure

1. Using a metric ruler, measure the length between the tip of your thumb and the tip of your little finger (excluding your fingernails) to the nearest centimeter. This is your handspan.

2. Record your handspan measurement and those of your classmates on the board.

3. Make a table like the one shown. Count the number of students with each handspan for the different measurements given. Record these numbers in your table.

4. Sets of variable data, such as handspan, can be plotted on a graph. Line graphs are used to show variation. Draw a graph on a sheet of paper. Label the horizontal (x) axis *Handspan Length*. Label the vertical (y) axis *Number of Students*.

5. Plot the number of students with each handspan measurement. Draw a curved line to connect the dots.

6. The *range* of a set of data is the difference between the greatest and the least number. The *median* is the middle number when the data are placed in order. The *mean* is the sum of the numbers divided by the number of measurements taken. The *mode* is the number that appears most often. Using the graph you have just made, find all of these numbers.

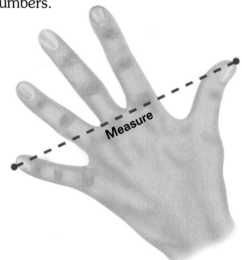

Measure

Handspan Measurements									
Handspan (cm)	12	13	14	15	16	17	18	19	20
Numbers									

Practicing the SKILL

1. What does the graph tell you about the amount of genetic variation in the population you sampled?

For more skill practice, do the Chapter 17 Interactive Exploration on the **Science Voyages Level Green CD-ROM.**

GLENCOE TECHNOLOGY

Interpreting Scientific Illustrations

Background

Using textbook illustrations is a helpful way to learn new information. Drawings in textbooks often have labeled, cutaway views of organs to show the internal structures of the organ. The cutaway view is called a sectional cut. A horizontal cut through an object is called a cross section. A vertical cut through an object is called a longitudinal, or long, section.

What does a sectional view of a bone show?

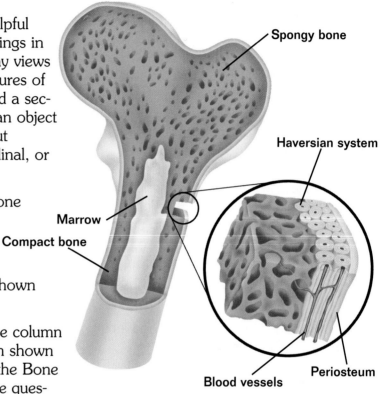

Spongy bone

Haversian system

Marrow

Compact bone

Blood vessels

Periosteum

Procedure

1 Make a data table like the one shown below.

2 Study the sections pictured in the column to the right. Use the information shown to complete the information in the Bone Parts table below and answer the questions in the Practicing the Skill box.

Bone Parts		
Bone Part	Description	Location in the Bone
periosteum		
compact bone		
spongy bone		
marrow		
blood supply		

Practicing the SKILL

1 How does the compact bone differ from the spongy bone in appearance?

2 What does a sectional view of a bone show that a solid uncut view does not show?

For more skill practice, do the Chapter 18 Interactive Exploration on the **Science Voyages Level Green CD-ROM.**

GLENCOE TECHNOLOGY

Interpreting Data

Background

Reading food labels can help a person make informed decisions about which product to buy. The United States Food and Drug Administration requires that all food labels list the name and net weight of the product. The name and address of the manufacturer, a list of ingredients, and the nutritional information per serving also are often listed. Nutrients must be listed in order of the amount by weight that the product contains. Often a column with the head RDA (recommended dietary allowance) is included on a label. The RDA is the amount of each vitamin and mineral a person needs each day for good health. RDAs listed on the labels are usually in percents and indicate what percentage of each vitamin or mineral that food provides.

How can the information on a food label be used?

Cereal A

Serving Size	2 oz.
Servings per container	2
Calories	100
Total Fat	1 g
Sodium	310 mg
Total Carbohydrates	0 g
Protein	12 g

Cereal B

Serving Size	2 oz.
Servings per container	2
Calories	230
Total Fat	8 g
Sodium	35 mg
Total Carbohydrates	28 g
Protein	15 g

Cereal C

Serving Size	2 oz.
Servings per container	2
Calories	140
Total Fat	4 g
Sodium	180 mg
Total Carbohydrates	32 g
Protein	7 g

Procedure

1. Read the food labels of Cereal A, B, and C.

2. Make a table like the Labels table below. Complete the table with the information from the food labels.

Labels			
2 oz serving	Cereal A	Cereal B	Cereal C
Calories			
Protein			
Carbohydrates			
Fat			
Sodium			

Practicing the SKILL

1. Which nutrient is in the largest amount in each of the products shown?

2. What are RDAs?

3. Bill must limit sodium intake. Which product should he buy? Why?

For more skill practice, do the Chapter 19 Interactive Exploration on the **Science Voyages Level Green CD-ROM.**

GLENCOE TECHNOLOGY

Concept Mapping

Background

The circulatory system consists of many parts with a wide variety of functions. Blood flows through the circulatory system. Some of the fluid from the blood moves into the body tissues and is returned to the circulatory system by the lymphatic system. Try the following activity to determine how concept maps help us organize information.

Procedure

1. Read Chapter 20. Pay special attention to the differences between and similarities of the cardiovascular and lymphatic systems.

2. Look at the concept map shown below. How is the information organized?

3. Using the concept map and the text, answer the questions in the Practicing the Skill box.

Practicing the SKILL

1. Compare and contrast the parts of the cardiovascular and lymphatic systems.

2. Compare the functions of the cardiovascular and lymphatic systems.

3. Compare the way blood and lymph are pumped through their vessels.

4. Lymph has little color. Blood is red. Explain the difference.

For more skill practice, do the Chpater 20 Interactive Exploration on the **Science Voyages Level Green CD-ROM.**

GLENCOE TECHNOLOGY

Making Models

Background

Sometimes it is useful to make a model of a system in order to understand it. It is difficult to see inside a human chest while a person is breathing, so you can make a model that works in a similar way.

How can you make a model of the human breathing mechanism?

Procedure

1. Look at the illustration on this page of a model of the lungs and diaphragm. This is a model on paper. In this skill, you will construct a physical model of the illustration.

2. Cut the bottom from a clear, 2-liter plastic bottle using scissors. **CAUTION:** *Always be careful when using scissors. Be careful of the sharp edges of the cut plastic as well.*

3. With your teacher's assistance, insert a y-shaped plastic tube upside down into the hole in a rubber stopper. Use a twist tie to fasten a balloon to each branch of the y-shaped tube.

4. Insert the rubber stopper into the top opening of the plastic bottle. The balloons should be inside the bottle.

5. Use a thick rubber band to tightly fasten the rubber sheet over the bottom opening of the bottle.

6. Push up gently on the rubber sheet. Observe the balloons inside the bottle. Record your observations in your Breathing Data table.

7. Pull down gently on the rubber sheet. Observe the balloons inside the bottle. Record your observations in your table.

Breathing Data		
Rubber Sheet	Balloons Empty/Filled	Person Breathing Exhale/Inhale
Pushed Up		
Pulled Down		

Practicing the SKILL

1. What happens when you push up and pull down on the rubber sheet?

2. When does air enter and leave the balloons? Why?

3. Draw the human respiratory system and compare it to the model. Label both.

For more skill practice, do the Chapter 21 Interactive Exploration on the **Science Voyages Level Green CD-ROM.**

GLENCOE TECHNOLOGY

Observing and Inferring

Background

People enjoy listening to music on a stereo that has multiple speakers placed in different areas. Dogs tilt their heads when they hear a strange sound. People turn their heads in various directions when they wonder where a sound is coming from. These actions occur while our brains are receiving information about the sounds. Two ears seem to be better than one. And, two ears on a moving head may be better than two held still.

Infer how humans can tell the direction of a sound.

Procedure

1. Put one person (the subject) in the center of the room with a blindfold on. Have eight people each sit in a circle three meters from the subject.

2. Have one of the eight people clap once. The subject is to point toward the source of the sound. If the subject points closer to the source of the sound than to any other person, count this as correct. Mark an X for each correct or incorrect response in a table like the one shown below.

3. Repeat the procedure until each of the eight people has clapped, in random order, two times.

4. Have the subject cover one ear with a small pillow or other sound-absorbing object. Repeat steps 1 through 3.

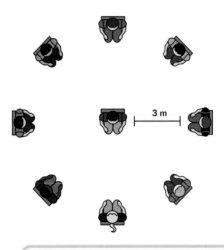

Practicing the SKILL

1. What differences in accuracy did you notice between listening with one ear and two?

2. Infer how this experiment helps you to understand the function of two ears.

3. Did the subject make any wrong guesses when listening with two ears? How do you explain this?

For more practice, do the Chapter 22 Interactive Exploration on the **Science Voyages Level Green CD-ROM.**

GLENCOE TECHNOLOGY

Hearing Chart

	Mark an X for Each Correct or Incorrect															
Two Ears	Correct															
	Incorrect															
One Ear	Correct															
	Incorrect															

Interpreting Data

Background

Graphs present data in a way that is easier to interpret.

A human fetus grows at different rates during its development. In this activity, you will learn about rapid fetal growth and at which times during pregnancy it occurs.

When do the most changes in length and mass occur in a fetus?

Procedure

(1) Construct a graph similar to that shown in Graph A. Put time in weeks on the horizontal x-axis and length in millimeters on the vertical y-axis.

(2) On the graph, plot the data shown in the first two columns of the table. The first four points have been plotted for you.

(3) Construct a second graph similar to Graph B. Put time in weeks on the horizontal axis and mass in grams on the vertical axis.

(4) On the graph, plot the data shown in the first and third columns of the table. The first few points have been plotted for you.

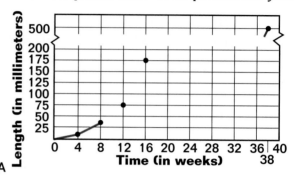

A

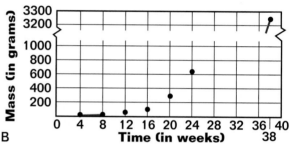

B

Practicing the SKILL

(1) How long is the average fetus at 15 weeks?

(2) How long is the average fetus at 34 weeks?

(3) At what week does the fetus reach half its full length?

(4) At what week does the fetus reach half its full mass?

For more skill practice, do the Chapter 23 Interactive Exploration on the **Science Voyages Level Green CD-ROM.**

Change in Size of Average Developing Fetus		
Time (weeks)	Length (mm)	Mass (g)
4	7	0.5
8	30	1
12	75	28
16	180	110
20	250	300
24	300	650
28	350	1200
32	410	2000
36	450	2200
38	500	3300

Recognizing Cause and Effect

Background

As you have learned in this chapter, many diseases are caused by microorganisms. One way to prevent disease is through immunization. Another way to prevent disease is to monitor and evaluate our daily habits.

Personal Health		
	Health Habit	**✓ or —**
a	take a shower or bath each day	
b	wash hands before meals	
c	wash hands after going to bathroom	
d	wash hair three times each week	
e	brush hair each day	
f	brush teeth after meals	
g	floss teeth daily	
h	change socks and underclothes each day	
i	cut toenails each week	
j	trim fingernails each week	
k	exercise for 30 minutes three or four times each week	
l	eat three well-balanced meals each day	
m	eat breakfast each day	
n	eat high-fiber foods each day	
o	do not drink alcohol	
p	have a dental checkup twice a year	
q	have regular medical checkups	
r	sleep seven to eight hours each night	
s	maintain good posture at all times	
t	keep up to date with vaccinations	
u	wear a seat belt	

The following activity will help you recognize your responsibility.

Procedure

1. There are many steps you can follow to maintain personal health. Good habits can keep you healthy for many years. Examine the list of health habits in the chart.

2. Find those habits that you have developed.

3. From the list of health habits on the left, find the habits that you sometimes or never carry out and need to develop.

4. Make a table of habits like the one shown and make a checkmark next to those habits you have developed. Make a dash next to those habits that you need to develop.

Practicing the SKILL

1. Which habits involve exercise and diet?

2. Which habits are related to preventive health practices?

3. Which of the personal health habits do you need to improve?

4. What is one way to plan for good health?

5. How will having good health habits now benefit your future health?

For more skill practice, do the Chapter 24 Interactive Exploration on the **Science Voyages Level Green CD-ROM.**

GLENCOE TECHNOLOGY

English Glossary

This glossary defines each key term that appears in **bold type** in the text. It also shows the page number where you can find the word used.

A

abrasion: erosion that occurs when wind-blown sediments strike rock, scraping the surface and wearing it away. (ch. 9, p. 261)

abyssal (uh BIHS ul) **plains:** flattest features of the ocean floor, created when currents deposited sediments on the seafloor and filled in valleys. (ch. 12, p. 335)

acid rain: rain, snow, sleet, or hail with a pH below 5.6 that is created when sulfur dioxide or nitrogen oxides combine with moisture in the air; can kill plants, trees, and fish, and damage the surfaces of cars and buildings. (ch. 14, p. 390)

acids: substances that contain hydrogen and produce positively charged hydronium ions when they dissolve in water, forming acidic solutions (ch. 5, p. 140); substances with a pH lower than 7. (ch. 14, p. 390)

active immunity: long-lasting immunity that occurs when the body makes its own antibodies to inactivate an antigen. (ch. 24, p. 662)

active transport: energy-requiring movement of substances through a cell membrane. (ch. 15, p. 424)

adolescence: stage of development when a person becomes physically able to reproduce, beginning around ages 12 to 13. (ch. 23, p. 642)

adulthood: final stage in a person's development, extending from the end of adolescence to old age. (ch. 23, p. 644)

alleles (uh LEELZ): different forms a gene may have for a trait. (ch. 17, p. 466)

allergen: substance that causes an allergic reaction. (ch. 24, p. 671)

allergy: overly strong reaction of the immune system to a foreign substance (an allergen). (ch. 24, p. 670)

alluvial (uh LEW vee ul) **fan:** triangular deposit of sediments that is formed when a river empties from a mountain valley out onto a flat, open plain. (ch. 10, p. 287)

alveoli (al VE uh li): in the lungs, the tiny, thin-walled sacs arranged in grapelike clusters at the end of each bronchiole; oxygen and carbon dioxide exchange takes place between the alveoli and capillaries. (ch. 21, p. 578)

amino acid: building block of protein. (ch. 19, p. 520)

amniotic (am nee AH tihk) **sac:** thin membrane that begins to form around the embryo during the third week of pregnancy; helps cushion and protect the unborn baby and can store nutrients and wastes. (ch. 23, p. 637)

amplitude: measure of the energy a wave carries; one-half the distance between a crest and a trough of a transverse wave. (ch. 2, p. 45)

antibody: protein made by the body in response to a specific antigen and that reacts with the antigen to make it harmless. (ch. 24, p. 662)

antigens: proteins and chemicals that are foreign to the body. (ch. 24, p. 662)

antiseptic: agent that is applied to the skin to kill pathogens and prevent their regrowth. (ch. 24, p. 656)

aqueous (AH kwee us): solution in which

water is the solvent. (ch. 5, p. 133)

aquifer (AK wuh fur): layer of permeable rock that allows water to move freely. (ch. 10, p. 291)

Archimedes' principle: states that when a object is placed in a fluid, the object weighs less by an amount equal to the weight of the displaced fluid. (ch. 4, p. 117)

artery: blood vessel with a thick elastic wall made of smooth muscle that moves blood away from the heart. (ch. 20, p. 550)

asexual reproduction: process by which a new organism is produced that has DNA identical to the DNA of the parent organism. (ch. 16, p. 445)

asthma (AZ muh): lung disorder in which there may be shortness of breath, wheezing, or coughing and that may occur as an allergic reaction. (ch. 21, p. 583)

atherosclerosis (ah thur oh skluh ROH sus): cardiovascular condition resulting from fatty deposits on arterial walls, which can clog blood vessels and interfere with blood flow. (ch. 20, p. 554)

atria (AY tree uh): two upper chambers of the heart. (ch. 20, p. 547)

axon (AK sahn): branch of neuron that carries messages, or impulses, away from the cell body. (ch. 22, p. 601)

B

barrier islands: sand deposits that run parallel to the shore but are separated from the mainland and whose size and shape change constantly due to wave action. (ch. 10, p. 299)

bases: substances that produce negatively charged hydroxide ions when they dissolve in water, forming basic solutions (ch. 5, p. 142); substances with a pH above 7. (ch. 14, p. 390)

basin: low area on Earth that contains an ocean. (ch. 11, p. 311)

beaches: deposits of sediment that run parallel to the shore and stretch inland as far as the tides and waves can deposit sediment. (ch. 10, p. 298)

benthos: plants, animals, and algae that live on or near the ocean floor and are either mobile or permanently attached to the bottom. (ch. 12, p. 344)

bladder: muscular, elastic organ that holds urine until it leaves the body. (ch. 21, p. 589)

blood pressure: force exerted on vessel walls by blood when the heart pumps it through the cardiovascular system; normally 120 over 80 for a young adult. (ch. 20, p. 551)

boiling point: temperature at which added heat energy causes the molecules of a liquid to move faster and the liquid's particles to enter the gaseous state in large numbers. (ch. 4, p. 107)

brain stem: part of the brain that controls heartbeat, breathing, and blood pressure by coordinating the involuntary movements of these functions; extends from the cerebrum and connects the brain to the spinal cord. (ch. 22, p. 603)

breaker: ocean wave that collapses forward and breaks onto the shore because its top outruns its bottom. (ch. 11, p. 322)

bronchi: two short branches at the lower end of the trachea that carry air into the lungs. (ch. 21, p. 578)

buoyancy: decrease in weight of an object in a fluid due to the net upward force caused by the displaced fluid. (ch. 4, p. 117)

C

cancer: chronic, noncommunicable disease that results from uncontrolled cell division. (ch. 24, p. 670)

capillary: microscopic blood vessel that connects arteries and veins; nutrients, oxygen, waste materials, and carbon dioxide diffuse through its walls. (ch. 20, p. 551)

carbohydrates (kar boh HI drayts): class of organic nutrients that supplies the body with its major energy sources—sugar, starch, and cellulose; contain carbon, hydrogen, and oxygen atoms. (ch. 19, p. 519)

cardiac muscle: striated, involuntary muscle that is found only in the heart. (ch. 18, p. 505)

carrying capacity: maximum number of individuals of a particular species that the planet will support. (ch. 13, p. 358)

cartilage: thick, slippery tissue layer covering the ends of bones; absorbs shock and helps make joint movements easier by reducing friction. (ch. 18, p. 496)

cave: underground opening that is formed when acidic groundwater moves through cracks in limestone and dissolves the rock. (ch. 10, p. 294)

central nervous system: division of the nervous system, containing the brain and spinal cord, which sorts and interprets information from stimuli. (ch. 22, p. 602)

cerebellum (ser uh BEL um): part of the brain that coordinates voluntary muscle movements and maintains balance and muscle tone; located behind and under the cerebrum. (ch. 22, p. 603)

cerebrum (suh REE brum): largest part of the brain; is divided into two hemispheres; controls the work of voluntary muscles, interprets impulses from the senses, and stores memory. (ch. 22, p. 603)

chemical digestion: process that breaks down large molecules of food into different, smaller molecules that can be absorbed by the body's cells; takes place in the mouth, stomach, and small intestine. (ch. 19, p. 532)

chemical weathering: type of weathering that occurs when air, water, and other substances react with minerals in rocks. (ch. 8, p. 221)

chemosynthesis: food-making process of certain deep-dwelling, ocean bacteria that use elements such as sulfur, iron, or nitrogen to produce food. (ch. 12, p. 342)

chemotherapy: use of chemicals to destroy cancer cells. (ch. 24, p. 670)

childhood: period from the end of infancy to age 12 that is marked by development of muscular coordination and mental abilities. (ch. 23, p. 642)

chromosomes: structures in the cell nucleus that contain hereditary material. (ch. 16, p. 443)

chronic bronchitis: long-lasting respiratory disease in which the bronchial tubes are irritated and too much mucus is produced. (ch. 21, p. 581)

chyme (KIME): thin, watery product that is the result of digestion. (ch. 19, p. 534)

circuit: closed, unbroken path through which an electric current can flow. (ch. 6, p. 169)

Clean Air Act: protects air quality by regulating car manufacturers, coal technologies, and other industries. (ch. 14, p. 392)

Clean Water Act: provides money to states for building sewage and wastewater-treatment facilities and for controlling runoff; also requires states to develop quality standards for their streams. (ch. 14, p. 401)

climate: pattern of weather that occurs in a particular area over many years. (ch. 8, p. 222)

cochlea (KOH klee uh): structure of the inner ear that is shaped like a snail's shell and contains fluids that vibrate, sending impulses to the brain by the auditory nerve. (ch. 22, p. 609)

communicable disease: disease that spreads from an infected organism or the environment through agents such as viruses, fungi, protists, and some bacteria. (ch. 24, p. 657)

compass: magnetic needle suspended so that it is free to turn; aligns itself with the nearest strong magnet and can be used to find and map magnetic fields. (ch. 7, p. 197)

composting: piling yard wastes where they can gradually decompose. (ch. 13, p. 372)

compressional wave: wave in which matter in the medium moves forward and backward in the same direction the wave travels. (ch. 2, p. 43)

concave lens: lens whose edges are thicker than its middle; causes light waves to diverge. (ch. 3, p. 83)

concentrated: solution that contains a large amount of solute per given amount of solvent. (ch. 5, p. 137)

concentration: measure of the amount of solute in a solution compared to the amount of solvent. (ch. 5, p. 137)

condensation: process where particles in a cooling gas slow down and come together to form droplets of liquid. (ch. 4, p. 109)

conductor: material, such as copper, silver, and iron, through which electrons can move easily. (ch. 6, p. 165)

conservation: careful use of resources to reduce damage to the environment by means such as reducing our use of materials, reusing items, and recycling materials. (ch. 13, p. 371)

constant: variable that stays the same in an experiment. (ch. 1, p. 19)

consumer: organism that can't make its own food. (ch. 15, p. 427)

continental shelf: gradually sloping end of a continent that extends out under the ocean for varying distances. (ch. 12, p. 334)

continental slope: sharp drop-off that extends from the outer edge of the continental shelf down to the ocean floor. (ch. 12, p. 335)

control: sample that is treated like other experimental groups except that the variable is not applied. (ch. 1, p. 19)

convex lens: lens whose center is thicker than its edges; causes light waves to converge. (ch. 3, p. 82)

coronary (KOR uh ner ee) **circulation:** flow of blood to the tissues of the heart. (ch. 20, p. 549)

creep: mass movement that occurs when sediments slowly inch their way down a hill and that is common in areas of freezing and thawing. (ch. 9, p. 247)

crest: highest point of a wave. (ch. 11, p. 321)

D

deflation: erosion caused by wind blowing across loose sediments, eroding only fine-grained particles such as clay and sand, and leaving behind coarse sediments. (ch. 9, p. 261)

delta: triangular or fan-shaped deposit of sediments that is formed when a stream or river slows and empties into an ocean, gulf, or lake. (ch. 10, p. 287)

dendrite: branch of neuron that receives messages and sends them to the cell body. (ch. 22, p. 601)

density: mass of an object divided by its volume. (ch. 4, p. 116)

density current: ocean current that forms when more dense seawater sinks beneath less dense seawater. (ch. 11, p. 318)

dependent variable: factor that is being measured in an experiment. (ch. 1, p. 19)

deposition: dropping of sediments that occurs when an agent of erosion loses its energy of motion and is no longer able to carry its load. (ch. 9, p. 245)

dermis: layer of tissue beneath the dermis; contains blood vessels, nerves, and oil and sweat glands. (ch. 18, p. 510)

diaphragm (DI uh fram): muscle beneath the lungs that contracts and relaxes with breathing and that helps move air in and out of the body. (ch. 21, p. 579)

diffraction: bending of waves around a barrier. (ch. 2, p. 52)

diffusion: mixing of particles in a gas or a liquid. (ch. 4, p. 111) movement of molecules from areas where there are more of them to areas where there are fewer of them. (ch. 15, p. 421)

digestion: mechanical and chemical process that breaks down food into small molecules so they can be used by the body's cells. (ch. 19, p. 530)

dilute: solution that contains a small amount of solute per given amount of solvent. (ch. 5, p. 137)

disinfectant: agent that is used to kill disease-causing organisms on objects such as surgical instruments. (ch. 24, p. 656)

DNA (deoxyribonucleic [dee AHK sih ri boh noo klay ihk] acid): chemical that contains an organism's information code and is found in the cell nucleus; is made up of two twisted strands of sugar-phosphate molecules and nitrogen bases. (ch. 16, p. 454)

dominant (DAHM uh nunt): describes a trait that covers up, or dominates, another form of the trait. (ch. 17, p. 468)

drainage basin: land area from which a stream gets its water. (ch. 10, p. 281)

E

egg: sex cell that is formed in the reproductive organs of a female and has only half the number of chromosomes of a body cell. (ch. 16, p. 448)

electric current: continuous flow of electrons through a conductor; measured in units of amperes (A). (ch. 6, p. 169)

electric discharge: rapid movement of excess electrons from one place to another. (ch. 6, p. 166)

electric generator: device that uses induction to produce electric power by spinning a wire coil in a strong magnetic field. (ch. 7, p. 204)

electric motor: device that uses a magnetic field to transform electrical energy into mechanical energy. (ch. 7, p. 202)

electrical power: rate at which an appliance converts electrical energy to another form of energy; unit is the watt (W). (ch. 6, p. 180)

electromagnet: strong magnet that can be turned on and off and that is created by wrapping a current-carrying wire around an iron core. (ch. 7, p. 199)

electromagnetic wave: type of wave, such as a light wave or a radio wave, that can travel in a vacuum as well as in various materials. (ch. 2, p. 42); (ch. 3, p. 66)

electromagnetism: force with two aspects—electricity and magnetism; occurs when a current-carrying wire produces a magnetic field. (ch. 7, p. 199)

embryo: unborn child during the first two months of pregnancy. (ch. 23, p. 636)

emphysema (em fuh SEE muh): respiratory disease in which the alveoli in the lungs lose their ability to expand and contract. (ch. 21, p. 582)

endocytosis: process in which substances too large to cross the cell membrane enter the cell; occurs when the cell membrane folds in on itself and encloses the large particles in a sphere, which pinches off, allowing the vacuole to enter the cytoplasm. (ch. 15, p. 425)

enzymes: specific proteins that regulate almost all chemical reactions in cells without being changed themselves (ch. 15, p. 419); molecules that speed up the rate of chemical reactions in the body. (ch. 19, p. 531)

epidermis: outer layer of the skin; constantly produces new cells to replace those that are rubbed off. (ch. 18, p. 509)

equilibrium: state in which the molecules of a substance are evenly distributed throughout another substance. (ch. 15, p. 422)

erosion: process that wears away surface materials and moves them from one place to another by agents such as gravity, glaciers, wind, and water. (ch. 9, p. 244)

evaporation: process by which the fastest-moving molecules of a liquid escape from the surface and form a gas. (ch. 4, p. 108)

exocytosis: process in which large particles leave the cell; occurs when vesicles and vacuoles fuse with the cell membrane and release their contents outside the cell. (ch. 15, p. 425)

F

fats: class of organic nutrients that provides energy and helps the body absorb some vitamins; may be saturated or unsaturated. (ch. 19, p. 522)

fermentation: form of respiration without oxygen; releases only part of the energy in food. (ch. 15, p. 428)

fertilization: joining of an egg and a sperm, generally from two different organisms. (ch. 16, p. 448)

fetus: developing baby after the first two months of pregnancy until birth. (ch. 23, p. 638)

floodplain: broad, flat valley floor carved by a meandering stream; often becomes covered by water when a stream floods. (ch. 10, p. 284)

focal length: distance of the focal point from the center of the mirror or lens. (ch. 3, p. 76)

focal point: single point on the optical axis of a mirror or lens. (ch. 3, p. 76)

food group: foods that contain the same nutrients; for example, the milk, yogurt, and cheese group. (ch. 19, p. 527)

freezing point: temperature at which attractive forces trap particles in a cooling liquid and form crystals. (ch. 4, p. 103)

frequency: number of waves that pass a given point in one second; measured in waves per second, or hertz (Hz). (ch. 2, p. 47); (ch. 3, p. 69)

G

gene: section of DNA on a chromosome that directs the making of a specific protein. (ch. 16, p. 456)

genetic engineering: changing of a gene's DNA sequence by biological and chemical methods. (ch. 17, p. 484)

genetics (juh NET ihks): study of how traits are inherited through the actions of alleles. (ch. 17, p. 467)

genotype (JEE nuh tipe): genetic makeup of an organism. (ch. 17, p. 470)

geyser: a hot spring that erupts periodically and shoots steam and water into the air. (ch. 10, p. 294)

glaciers: moving masses of ice and snow that are responsible for creating many landforms on Earth through erosion and deposition. (ch. 9, p. 252)

groundwater: water that soaks into the ground and collects in the small spaces between bits of rock and soil. (ch. 10, p. 290)

gully erosion: type of surface water erosion due to runoff that occurs when a rill channel becomes broader and deeper. (ch. 10, p. 279)

H

hazardous wastes: poisonous, cancer-causing, or radioactive wastes that are dangerous to living things. (ch. 13, p. 367)

heat of fusion: heat required to melt one kilogram of a solid at its melting point. (ch. 4, p. 102)

heat of vaporization: amount of energy required to change one kilogram of a liquid to a gas. (ch 4, p. 107)

helper T cell: type of white blood cell that helps other types of white blood cells produce antibodies. (ch. 24, p. 664)

hemoglobin: chemical in red blood cells that can carry oxygen and carbon dioxide. (ch. 20, p. 557)

heredity (huh RED ut ee): passing of traits from parent to offspring. (ch. 17, p. 466)

heterozygous (het uh roh ZI gus): organism that has two different alleles for a single trait. (ch. 17, p. 470)

homozygous (hoh muh ZI gus): organism that has two identical alleles for a single trait. (ch. 17, p. 470)

horizon: a soil layer in the soil profile; most areas have three—the A horizon (top soil layer), the B horizon (middle layer), and the C horizon (bottom layer). (ch. 8, p. 228)

hormones: endocrine chemicals that are produced from glands directly into the bloodstream and that affect target tissues. (ch. 22, p. 616)

humus (HYEW mus): dark-colored, decayed organic matter in soil that serves as a nutrient source for plants, promotes good soil structure, and helps soil hold water. (ch. 8, p. 227)

hypertension: cardiovascular disorder, also called high blood pressure, that can be caused by atherosclerosis. (ch. 20, p. 554)

hypothesis: prediction or statement that can be tested; may be formed by using prior knowledge, new information, and previous observations. (ch. 1, p. 18)

I

ice wedging: mechanical weathering process that occurs when water freezes in the cracks of rocks and expands, breaking the rock apart. (ch. 8, p. 220)

immovable joint: type of joint that allows little or no movement. (ch. 18, p. 498)

immune system: complex group of defenses that work to fight disease in the body. (ch. 24, p. 661)

impermeable: material through which water cannot pass. (ch. 10, p. 291)

incomplete dominance: production of a phenotype that is intermediate to those of the two homozygous parents. (ch. 17, p. 474)

independent variable: factor that is changed in an experiment. (ch. 1, p. 19)

indicator: compound that reacts with acidic and basic solutions and changes color at different pH values. (ch. 5, p. 144)

induction: process by which a changing magnetic field causes an electric current in a wire loop. (ch. 7, p. 204)

infancy: period of rapid growth and development of both mental and physical skills that extends from the neonatal period to one year. (ch. 23, p. 642)

inorganic compounds: most compounds made from elements other than carbon; for example, water, which makes up a large part of living matter. (ch. 15, p. 420)

insulator: material, such as rubber or glass, through which electrons cannot move easily. (ch. 6, p. 165)

interference: ability of two or more waves to combine and form a new wave when they overlap; can be constructive, forming a larger wave, or destructive, forming a smaller wave. (ch. 2, p. 54)

involuntary muscles: muscles, such as cardiac muscles, that can't be consciously controlled. (ch. 18, p. 502)

joint: place where two or more bones meet; may be immovable, such as in the skull, or movable, such as in the hip. (ch. 18, p. 497)

kidney: bean-shaped organ of the urinary system that is made up of about one million nephrons and that filters blood to produce waste liquid (urine). (ch. 21, p. 588)

kinetic theory of matter: states that the particles of all matter are in constant, random motion. (ch. 4, p. 99)

L

landfill: area where waste is deposited; the majority of U.S. garbage goes into landfills. (ch. 13, p. 367)

larynx: airway to which the vocal chords are attached. (ch. 21, p. 577)

law of reflection: states that the angle of incidence is equal to the angle of reflection. (ch. 3, p. 73)

leaching: removal of minerals that have been dissolved in water. (ch. 8, p. 229)

lens: transparent object that has at least one curved side that causes light to bend. (ch. 3, p. 81)

ligament: tough band of tissue that holds bones together at joints. (ch. 18, p. 497)

light ray: narrow beam of light traveling in a straight line. (ch. 3, p. 66)

litter: leaves, twigs, and other organic matter in the A horizon that changes to humus when it is exposed to decomposing organisms. (ch. 8, p. 229)

loess (LUSS): wind deposits of fine-grained, tightly packed sediments. (ch. 9, p. 265)

longshore current: ocean current that runs along the shore, moves sediment along shorelines, and is caused by waves colliding with the shore at slight angles. (ch. 10, p. 297)

lymph: tissue fluid that has moved from around cells and into lymph vessels; consists mostly of water, dissolved substances, and lymphocytes. (ch. 20, p. 566)

lymphatic (lihm FAT ihk) **system:** collects fluid from body tissue spaces and returns it to the blood through lymph capillaries and lymph vessels; plays a vital role in protecting against infection. (ch. 20, p. 565)

lymph nodes: bean-shaped structures found throughout the body that filter out microorganisms and foreign materials engulfed by lymphocytes. (ch. 20, p. 566)

lymphocyte (LIHM fuh site): type of white blood cell produced by the lymphatic system that fights infections and foreign materials that enter the body. (ch. 20, p. 566)

M

magnetic domain: group of atoms with their magnetic poles pointing in the same direction. (ch. 7, p. 193)

magnetic field: area around a magnet where magnetic forces act and that exists in three dimensions, all around a magnet. (ch. 7, p. 194)

magnetism: force that can attract or repel an object without the need to touch the object. (ch. 7, p. 194)

marrow: fatty, soft tissue in the center of long bones and the spaces of spongy bones; produces red blood cells and white blood cells. (ch. 18, p. 494)

mass movement: type of erosion in which gravity alone causes loose materials to move downslope and that can happen quickly or slowly. (ch. 9, p. 246)

matter: anything that has mass and takes up space and whose particles are in constant motion. (ch. 4, p. 98)

meander (mee AN dur): curve in the side of a stream formed by a fast-moving channel of deep water. (ch. 10, p. 284)

mechanical digestion: process that occurs when food is chewed and mixed in the mouth and churned in the stomach. (ch. 19, p. 532)

mechanical waves: waves that can travel only through matter; can be either transverse or compressional waves. (ch. 2, p. 41)

mechanical weathering: physical process that breaks rocks apart without changing their chemical composition; can be caused by growing plants, lightning, expanding ice, and expansion and contraction that occurs when an area heats and cools. (ch. 8, p. 219)

medium: material in which a light wave travels. (ch. 3, p. 66)

meiosis (my OH sus): process by which sex cells are created in the reproductive organs, producing four haploid sex cells from one diploid cell. (ch. 16, p. 448)

melanin (MEL uh nun): pigment that gives skin its color. (ch. 18, p. 509)

melting point: temperature at which a solid becomes a liquid. (ch. 4, p. 102)

menopause: occurs for most women between the ages of 45 and 60 when the menstrual cycle becomes irregular and eventually stops. (ch. 23, p. 631)

menstrual cycle: monthly cycle of changes in the female reproductive system. (ch. 23, p. 629)

menstruation: monthly discharge of blood and tissue cells from the thickened lining of the uterus that begins when a girl reaches puberty and her reproductive organs have matured. (ch. 23, p. 630)

metabolism: total of all chemical reactions in a living thing. (ch. 15, p. 427)

mid-ocean ridge: place where new ocean floor forms as a result of volcanic eruptions and molten lava moving up through rifts. (ch. 12, p. 336)

minerals: inorganic nutrients that regulate many chemical reactions in the body. (ch. 19, p. 524)

mitosis (mi TOH sus): series of continuous steps (prophase, metaphase, anaphase, and telophase) in which the cell nucleus divides to form two identical nuclei. (ch. 16, p. 442)

mixture: combination of substances that can be separated by physical means and can be either the same throughout (homogeneous) or have different parts with different compositions (heterogeneous). (ch. 5, p. 126); combination of substances in which each substance retains its own properties. (ch. 15, p. 417)

model: mathematical equation or object that saves time and money by testing ideas that may be too large or too small, take too long to build, happen too quickly, or are too dangerous to observe directly. (ch. 1, p. 16)

moraine: ridge of material deposited in the middle and along the sides of a glacier. (ch. 9, p. 256)

movable joint: type of joint (pivot, ball-and-socket, hinge, gliding) that allows a wide range of movements. (ch. 18, p. 498)

multiple alleles: term used when a trait is controlled by more than two alleles. (ch. 17, p. 474)

muscle: organ that relaxes and contracts to

allow movement of bones and body parts. (ch. 18, p. 501)

mutation: any permanent change in a gene or chromosome of a cell. (ch. 16, p. 458)

N

nekton: all organisms that actively swim throughout the ocean. (ch. 12, p. 344)

nephron: tiny filtering unit of the kidney. (ch. 21, p. 588)

neuron (NOO rahn): working unit of the nervous system, made up of a cell body and branches called dendrites and axons. (ch. 22, p. 601)

neutralization (new truh luh ZAY shun): the interaction between acids and bases in which the properties of each are canceled out by the other and a neutral solution is produced. (ch. 5, p. 145)

noncommunicable disease: disease that is not spread from one person to another but may result from factors such as poor diet or uncontrolled cell growth. (ch. 24, p. 668)

nutrients (NEW tree unts): substances in foods that provide energy and materials for cell development, growth, and repair; carbohydrates, proteins, fats, vitamins, minerals, and water. (ch. 19, p. 518)

O

Ohm's law: relationship between voltage, current, and resistance in an electric circuit; $V = IR$, where V represents the voltage, I represents the electrical current, and R the resistance. (ch. 6, p. 177)

olfactory cells: nerve cells in the nasal passages that respond to gas molecules in the air and send impulses to the brain for the interpretation of odors. (ch. 22, p. 612)

organic compounds: most compounds that contain carbon; four groups make up living things: carbohydrates, lipids, proteins, and nucleic acids. (ch. 15, p. 418)

osmosis: diffusion of water through a cell membrane. (ch. 15, p. 423)

ovary: in humans, the female reproductive organ that produces eggs. (ch. 23, p. 628)

ovulation (AHV yuh LAY shun): process in which an egg is released about once a month from an ovary. (ch. 23, p. 629)

oxidation (ahk sih DAY shun): chemical weathering process that occurs when a material such as iron is exposed to oxygen and water; causes the iron in rock to rust and turn reddish. (ch. 8, p. 222)

P

parallel circuit: circuit that has more than one path for the electric current to follow. (ch. 6, p. 178)

Pascal's principle: states that the pressure exerted on any point of a confined fluid is transmitted unchanged throughout the fluid. (ch. 4, p. 113)

passive immunity: shorter-term immunity that occurs when antibodies produced in another animal are transferred into the body. (ch. 24, p. 662)

passive transport: movement of substances through a cell membrane without the use of cellular energy. (ch. 15, p. 424)

pasteurization: process of heating food to a temperature that kills most bacteria. (ch. 24, p. 654)

pedigree: tool that shows the occurrence of a trait in a family. (ch. 17, p. 483)

periosteum (per ee AHS tee um): tough, tight-fitting membrane that covers the surface of bones. (ch. 18, p. 495)

peripheral (puh RIHF rul) **nervous system:** division of the nervous system, made up of all the nerves outside the central nervous system; connects the brain and spinal cord to other parts of the body. (ch. 22, p. 602)

peristalsis (per uh STAHL sus): wavelike, muscular contractions that move food through the digestive system. (ch. 19, p. 533)

permeable (PUR mee uh bul): describes rock and soil that have connecting pore spaces through which water can pass. (ch. 10, p. 291)

pH: measure of how acidic or basic a solution is, related to its concentration of hydronium ions and hydroxide ions; solutions with a pH below 7 are acidic; solutions with a pH above 7 are basic; solutions with a pH of 7 are neutral. (ch. 5, p. 143)

pH scale: scale used to describe how acidic or basic a substance is; ranges from 0 to 14, with 0 being the most acidic and 14 being the most basic. (ch. 14, p. 390)

pharynx: tubelike passageway for both food and air through which inhaled air passes after it is warmed and moistened in the nasal cavity. (ch. 21, p. 577)

phenotype (FEE nuh tipe): physical expression of a particular genotype. (ch. 17, p. 470)

photochemical smog: hazy, brown smog that is created when sunlight reacts with pollutants in the air; contains ozone near Earth's surface. (ch. 14, p. 388)

photosynthesis: process by which chlorophyll-containing land plants and chlorophyll-containing ocean organisms use energy, carbon dioxide, and water to produce food. (ch. 12, p. 340)

plankton: tiny marine algae and animals that drift with ocean currents. (ch. 12, p. 343)

plasma: liquid part of blood, consisting mostly of water plus dissolved nutrients, minerals, and oxygen; makes up more than half the volume of blood. (ch. 20, p. 557)

platelet: irregularly shaped cell fragment that circulates with red and white blood cells and helps to clot blood. (ch. 20, p. 558)

plucking: process that adds boulders, gravel, and sand to a glacier's bottom and sides as water freezes and thaws and breaks off pieces of surrounding rocks. (ch. 9, p. 254)

polygenic (pahl ih JEHN ihk) **inheritance:** occurs when a group of gene pairs acts together to produce a single trait. (ch. 17, p. 475)

population: total number of individuals of a particular species in a specific area. (ch. 13, p. 359)

population explosion: rapidly increasing number of humans on Earth due to factors such as modern medicine, better sanitation, better nutrition, and more people surviving to the age when they can have children. (ch. 13, p. 359)

pregnancy: nine-month period of development during which the fertilized egg grows into a baby within the uterus. (ch. 23, p. 636)

pressure: amount of force applied per unit of area; the SI unit is the pascal (Pa). (ch. 4, p. 112)

producer: organism, such as a green plant, that makes its own food. (ch. 15, p. 427)

proteins: large, organic molecules that are made up of amino acids and that are needed for growth and repair of body cells. (ch. 19, p. 520)

pulmonary (PUL muh ner ee) **circulation:** flow of blood through the heart, to the lungs, and back to the heart. (ch. 20, p. 548)

Punnett square: tool used to predict results in Mendelian genetics; shows all the ways in which alleles can combine. (ch. 17, p. 470)

R

recessive (rih SES ihv): describes a trait that is covered up, or dominated, by another form of the trait. (ch. 17, p. 468)

recyclable: any item that can be processed and used again in order to conserve natural resources and reduce solid waste. (ch. 13, p. 373)

reef: rigid, wave-resistant structure built from skeletal materials and calcium carbonate. (ch. 12, p. 346)

reflection: occurs when a wave strikes an object or surface and bounces off. (ch. 2, p. 50; ch. 3, p. 67)

reflex: involuntary and automatic response to a stimulus that allows the body to respond without having to think about what action to take. (ch. 22, p. 605)

refraction: bending of a light wave when it changes speed in moving from one material to another. (ch. 2, p. 51; ch. 3, p. 81)

reproduction: the process through which organisms produce more individuals. (ch. 23, p. 626)

resistance: measure of how difficult it is for electrons to flow through a material; unit is the ohm. (ch. 6, p. 172)

retina: light-sensitive tissue at the back of the eye; contains rods and cones; impulses stimulated here pass to the optic nerve, which carries them to the brain. (ch. 22, p. 610)

rill erosion: type of surface water erosion caused by runoff, in which a small stream forms during a heavy rain, carries away plants and soil, and leaves a scar or channel on the side of the slope. (ch. 10, p. 279)

RNA (ribonucleic acid): nucleic acid that carries codes for making proteins from the nucleus to the ribosomes. (ch. 16, p. 457)

runoff: water that doesn't soak into the ground or evaporate but instead flows across Earth's surface. (ch. 10, p. 276)

S

Safe Drinking Water Act: strengthens health standards for drinking water; protects rivers, lakes, and streams; gives the public a right to know about contaminants that might be in their tap water. (ch. 14, p. 401)

salinity (say LIHN uh tee): measure of the amount of salts dissolved in seawater, which is usually measured in grams of salt per kilogram of water. (ch. 11, p. 312)

saliva (suh LI vuh): watery, enzyme-containing fluid in the mouth that is mixed with food during digestion. (ch. 19, p. 533)

saturated: solution that contains the total amount of solute that it can hold under specific conditions. (ch. 5, p. 136)

science: process used to solve problems or answer questions about what is happening in the world; can provide information that people use to make decisions. (ch. 1, p. 6)

scientific methods: approaches taken to solve a problem in science; steps can include recognize the problem, form a hypothesis, test the hypothesis, do the experiment, analyze the data, and draw conclusions. (ch. 1, p. 14)

scrubber: device used in coal-burning power plants that allows the gases in the smoke to dissolve in water until the pH of the smoke increases to a safe level. (ch. 14, p. 393)

semen: mixture of sperm and fluid that leaves the body through the urethra. (ch. 23, p. 628)

series circuit: circuit that has only one path for the electric current to follow. (ch. 6, p. 178)

sex-linked gene: allele inherited on a sex chromosome. (ch. 17, p. 482)

sexual reproduction: process by which a new, unique organism is created when two sex cells, an egg and a sperm, come together. (ch. 16, p. 448)

sexually transmitted diseases (STDs): diseases that are transmitted from one person to another during sexual contact and that are caused by both viruses and bacteria. (ch. 24, p. 658)

sheet erosion: type of surface water erosion due to runoff, in which rainwater flowing into lower elevations loses energy and leaves behind sediments that cover the soil like a sheet. (ch. 10, p. 279)

skeletal muscles: striated, voluntary muscles that move bones. (ch. 18, p. 504)

skeletal system: all the bones in the body; gives the body shape and support, protects internal organs, forms blood cells, stores minerals for later use, and provides for muscle attachment. (ch. 18, p. 494)

slump: mass movement that happens when loose materials or rock layers slip down a slope, and a curved scar is left where the slumped materials originally rested. (ch. 9, p. 246)

smooth muscles: nonstriated, involuntary muscles that move many internal organs. (ch. 18, p. 504)

soil: material that supports vegetation and is a mixture of weathered rock, mineral fragments, organic matter, water, and air; may take thousands of years to form. (ch. 8, p. 226)

soil profile: vertical section of soil layers. (ch. 8, p. 228)

solubility: maximum amount of a solute that can be dissolved in a given amount of solvent; can be affected by temperature and pressure. (ch. 5, p. 134)

solute: in a solution, the substance that dis

solves into another substance. (ch. 5, p. 128)

solution: homogeneous mixture made up of two or more materials where one material seems to disappear into the other; can be unsaturated, saturated, or supersaturated and can be classified as gaseous, liquid, or solid. (ch. 5, p. 127)

solvent: in a solution, the substance that dissolves the solute. (ch. 5, p. 128)

sperm: sex cell produced in the reproductive organs of a male and that has only half the number of chromosomes of a body cell; has a whiplike tail that provides motion and a head that contains genetic information. (ch. 16, p. 448; ch. 23, p. 627)

spring: point where the water table meets Earth's surface and water flows out. (ch. 10, p. 293)

state of matter: physical state of a material, whether a solid, a liquid, or a gas, which depends mostly on how the material's atoms and molecules are arranged and how they move. (ch. 4, p. 98)

static charge: buildup of electric charges in one place. (ch. 6, p. 163)

sulfurous smog: smog formed when burning fuel releases sulfur compounds in the air; may collect in an area where there's little or no wind. (ch. 14, p. 389)

surface currents: ocean currents that move water horizontally, parallel to Earth's surface, are powered by wind, and distribute heat from equatorial regions to other regions of Earth. (ch. 11, p. 315)

synapse (SIHN aps): small space between neurons, across which an impulse moves by means of a chemical released by the axon. (ch. 22, p. 602)

systemic circulation: most extensive part of the circulatory system in which blood moves to and from all body organs and tissues except the heart and lungs. (ch. 20, p. 548)

T

target tissue: specific tissue affected by hormones; often is located in a part of the body distant from the gland that affects it. (ch. 22, p. 616)

taste buds: major sensory receptors for taste that are located on the tongue and respond to chemical stimuli. (ch. 22, p. 612)

technology: application of science to make products or tools. (ch. 1, p. 10)

tendon: thick band of tissue that attaches muscle to bone. (ch. 18, p. 504)

testes: male reproductive organs that produce sperm and the male sex hormone, testosterone. (ch. 23, p. 627)

tidal range: difference between the level of the ocean at high tide and low tide. (ch. 11, p. 324)

tide: daily rise and fall in sea level that is caused by a giant wave that is only 1 m or 2 m high but is thousands of kilometers long. (ch. 11, p. 324)

till: mixture of different-sized sediments dropped from the base of a slowing glacier and that can cover huge areas of land. (ch. 9, p. 256)

trachea: cartilage-reinforced tube that remains open and connects with the bronchi; is lined with mucous membranes and cilia to trap dust, bacteria, and pollen. (ch. 21, p. 577)

transformer: device used to increase or decrease the voltage of an alternating current. (ch. 7, p. 205)

transverse wave: wave in which matter moves back and forth at right angles to the direction the wave travels. (ch. 2, p. 42)

trenches: long, narrow, steep-sided depressions in the ocean floor formed where one crustal plate is forced under another; the deepest and most geologically active places on Earth. (ch. 12, p. 331)

trough (TROF): lowest point of a wave. (ch. 11, p. 321)

U

upwelling: circulation in the ocean that brings deep, cold water to the ocean surface. (ch. 11, p. 318)

ureter: tube that leads from the kidney to the bladder. (ch. 21, p. 589)

urethra (yoo REE thruh): tube that carries urine from the bladder to the outside of the body. (ch. 21, p. 589)

urinary system: system of excretory organs that rids the blood of wastes produced by the metabolism of nutrients, controls blood volume by removing excess water produced by body cells, and balances concentrations of certain salts and water. (ch. 21, p. 587)

urine: waste liquid of the urinary system, containing excess water, salts, and other wastes. (ch. 21, p. 588)

uterus: hollow, pear-shaped, thick-walled muscular organ where a fertilized egg develops into a baby. (ch. 23, p. 629)

V

vaccination: process of giving a vaccine either orally or by injection. (ch. 24, p. 662)

vagina: female muscular tube connecting the lower end of the uterus with the outside of the body; also called the birth canal. (ch. 23, p. 629)

vein: blood vessel that moves blood to the heart and has valves to prevent backward movement of the blood. (ch. 20, p. 550)

ventricles (VEN trih kulz): two lower chambers of the heart. (ch. 20, p. 547)

villi: fingerlike projections in the small intestine where nutrients are absorbed into the bloodstream. (ch. 19, p. 536)

vitamins: water-soluble or fat-soluble essential, organic nutrients that are needed in small quantities to help regulate body functions. (ch. 19, p. 523)

voltage: measure of electric potential energy; measured in units of volts (V). (ch. 6, p. 171)

voluntary muscles: muscles, such as face muscles, that can be consciously controlled. (ch. 18, p. 502)

W

water table: upper surface of the zone of saturation, which is the area where all the pores in the rock are filled with water. (ch. 10, p. 291)

wavelength: distance between a point on one wave and an identical point on the next wave, measured from crest to crest or trough to trough; in compressional waves, is measured from one compression or rarefaction to the next. (ch. 2, p. 46; ch. 3, p. 69)

waves: in the ocean, waves move through seawater and occur as sea waves or long waves. (ch. 11, p. 321)

weathering: mechanical or chemical process that breaks down rocks into smaller and smaller fragments. (ch. 8, p. 218)

Z

zygote: new diploid cell that is formed when a sperm fertilizes an egg. (ch. 16, p. 449)

Glossary/Glosario

Este glossario define cada término clave que aparece en **negrillas** en el texto. También muestra el número de página donde se usa dicho término.

abrasion/abrasión: Tipo de erosión que ocurre cuando los sedimentos arrastrados por el viento golpean las rocas. (Cap. 9, pág. 261)

abyssal plains/llanuras abisales: El relieve más llano del suelo formado cuando las corrientes depositan sedimentos en el suelo marino y rellenan los valles. (Cap. 12, pág. 335)

acid/ácido: Sustancia con un pH menor de 7 en la escala de pH. (Cap. 14, pág. 390)

acid rain/lluvia ácida: Lluvia o nieve con un pH menor de 5.6; resulta de la mezcla de vapor de agua y contaminantes del aire en la atmósfera. (Cap. 14, pág. 390)

acids/ácidos: Sustancias que contienen hidrógeno y que producen iones hidronio positivos cuando se disuelven en agua, formando soluciones ácidas. (Cap. 5, pág. 140)

active immunity/inmunidad activa: Ocurre cuando el cuerpo, por sí solo, produce anticuerpos en respuesta a un patógeno. (Cap. 24, pág. 662)

active transport/transporte activo: Movimiento de sustancias a través de la membrana celular que requiere energía. (Cap. 15, pág. 424)

adolescence/adolescencia: Etapa de desarrollo que comienza alrededor de los 12 a 13 años, cuando una persona es capaz de producir progenie. (Cap. 23, pág. 642)

adulthood/edad adulta: Etapa final de desarrollo que comienza al terminar la adolescencia y se extiende hasta la vejez. (Cap. 23, pág. 644)

alleles/alelos: Las diferentes formas que puede tener un gene para cierto rasgo. (Cap. 17, pág. 466)

allergen/alérgeno: Sustancia que causa una respuesta alérgica en el cuerpo. (Cap. 24, pág. 671)

allergy /alergia: Reacción potente del sistema inmunológico a una sustancia extraña. (Cap. 24, pág. 670)

alluvial fan/abanico aluvial: Depósito que se forma cuando las aguas de un río que descienden por un valle montañoso desembocan en una llanura plana abierta. (Cap. 10, pág. 287)

alveoli/alvéolos: Manojos de sacos pequeños de paredes delgadas ubicados en el extremo de cada bronquiolo. (Cap. 21, pág. 578)

amino acid/aminoácido: Subunidad de la cual están compuestas las proteínas. (Cap. 19, pág. 520)

amniotic sac/bolsa amniótica: Bolsa pegada a la placenta que contiene el fluido amniótico que ayuda a proteger al embrión contra golpes y que puede almacenar nutrientes y desperdicios. (Cap. 23, pág. 637)

amplitude/amplitud: La mitad de la distancia entre una cresta y un valle de una onda transversal; una medida de la energía que transporta una onda. (Cap. 2, pág. 45)

antibody/anticuerpo: Proteína que fabrica un animal en respuesta a un antígeno específico. (Cap. 24, pág. 662)

antigens/antígenos: Proteínas y químicos extraños para el cuerpo. (Cap. 24, pág. 662)

antiseptic/antiséptico: Sustancia química que destruye los patógenos sobre la piel y previene su nuevo crecimiento durante algún tiempo. (Cap. 24, pág. 656)

aqueous/acuosa: Solución en la cual el agua es el disolvente. Cap. 5, pág. 133)

aquifer/aquífero: Capa de roca permeable que deja pasar el agua libremente. (Cap. 10, pág. 291)

Archimedes' principle/principio de Arquímedes: Enuncia que cuando un objeto se sumerge en un fluido, el objeto pesa menos de acuerdo con una cantidad igual al peso del fluido desplazado. (Cap. 4, pág. 117)

artery/arteria: Vaso sanguíneo de paredes gruesas y elásticas, hechas de músculo liso, que transporta sangre fuera del corazón. (Cap. 20, pág. 550)

asexual reproduction/reproducción asexual: Tipo de reproducción en que se produce un nuevo organismo con DNA idéntico al del organismo progenitor. (Cap. 16, pág. 445)

asthma/asma: Trastorno pulmonar en que la persona puede sentirse corta de aliento, sufrir resollos asmáticos o tos; puede ocurrir como una reacción alérgica. (Cap. 21, pág. 583)

atherosclerosis/aterosclerosis: Acumulación de depósitos grasos en las paredes arteriales. Es una de las causas principales de las enfermedades cardíacas. (Cap. 20, pág. 554)

atria/aurículas: Las dos cavidades superiores del corazón. (Cap. 20, pág. 547)

axon/axón: Parte de la neurona que transmite mensajes, llamados impulsos, desde el cuerpo celular. (Cap. 22, pág. 601)

B

barrier islands/crestas prelitorales: Depósitos de arena paralelos a la costa pero separados del continente. (Cap. 10, pág. 299)

bases/bases: Sustancias que producen iones hidroxilos negativos cuando se disuelven en agua, formando soluciones básicas (Cap. 5, pág. 142); sustancia con un pH mayor que siete. (Cap. 14, pág. 390)

basin/cuenca: Área baja sobre la cual se formaron los océanos. (Cap. 11, pág. 311)

beaches/playas: Depósitos de sedimentos que corren paralelos a la costa. (Cap. 10, pág. 298)

benthos/bentos: Plantas, algas y animales que habitan los niveles más profundos del océano. (Cap. 12, pág. 344)

bladder/vejiga: Órgano muscular elástico que almacena la orina hasta que sale del cuerpo. (Cap. 21, pág. 589)

blood pressure/presión sanguínea: Fuerza que ejerce la sangre sobre las paredes de los vasos sanguíneos a medida que el corazón la bombea a través del sistema cardiovascular. (Cap. 20, pág. 551)

boiling point/punto de ebullición: Temperatura a la cual se forman burbujas de vapor en el fondo de un líquido y se elevan hasta la superficie, haciendo que el líquido entre en estado gaseoso. (Cap. 4, pág. 107)

brain stem/bulbo raquídeo: Parte del encéfalo que se extiende desde el cerebro y conecta el encéfalo con la médula espinal; controla los latidos del corazón, la respiración y la presión sanguínea, al coordinar los movimientos involuntarios de estas funciones. (Cap. 22, pág. 603)

breaker/cachón: Ola marina que rompe en la playa debido a que su parte superior viaja más rápido que su parte inferior. (Cap. 11, pág. 322)

bronchi/bronquios: Dos ramificaciones cortas en el extremo bajo de la tráquea que llevan aire a los pulmones. (Cap. 21, pág. 578)

buoyancy/flotabilidad: Disminución de peso que causa la fuerza flotante. (Cap. 4, pág. 117)

C

cancer/cáncer: Enfermedad crónica grave que resulta de un crecimiento celular descontrolado. (Cap. 24, pág. 670)

capillary/capilar: Vaso sanguíneo microscópico, con paredes de una sola célula, que conecta las arterias y las venas. (Cap. 20, pág. 551)

carbohydrates/carbohidratos: Nutrientes orgánicos que le proveen al cuerpo sus principales fuentes de energía: azúcares, almidones y celulosa; contienen átomos de carbono, hidrógeno y oxígeno. (Cap. 19, pág. 519)

cardiac muscle/músculo cardíaco: Músculo involuntario estriado que solo se encuentra en el corazón y que se contrae 70 veces por minuto cada día en la vida de una persona. (Cap. 18, pág. 505)

carrying capacity/capacidad de carga: El mayor número de individuos, de una especie en particular, que el planeta puede soportar y mantener. (Cap. 13, pág. 358)

cartilage/cartílago: Gruesa capa de tejido suave y resbaloso que cubre los extremos de los huesos. Es flexible e importante en las articulaciones en donde absorbe los choques y facilita el movimiento al reducir la fricción. (Cap. 18, pág. 496)

cave/caverna: Abertura subterránea que se forma cuando el agua subterránea ácida corre por las resquebrajaduras naturales de la piedra caliza y la disuelve. (Cap. 10, pág. 294)

central nervous system/sistema nervioso central: Uno de los dos sistemas principales en que se divide el sistema nervioso. Está compuesto por el encéfalo y la médula espinal. (Cap. 22, pág. 602)

cerebellum/cerebelo: La segunda parte del encéfalo, ubicado detrás y debajo del cerebro. Coordina los movimientos de los músculos voluntarios, mantiene el equilibrio y el tono muscular. (Cap. 22, pág. 603)

cerebrum/cerebro: La parte más grande del encéfalo; está dividida en dos hemisferios; controla el trabajo de los músculos voluntarios, interpreta los impulsos provenientes de los sentidos y almacena la memoria. (Cap. 22, pág. 603)

chemical digestion/digestión química: Proceso que rompe las moléculas grandes de alimentos en diferentes moléculas más pequeñas que pueden ser absorbidas por las células; tiene lugar en la boca, el estómago y el intestino delgado. (Cap. 19, pág. 532)

chemical weathering/meteorización química: Meteorización que ocurre cuando el agua, el aire y otras sustancias reaccionan con los minerales presentes en las rocas. (Cap. 8, pág. 221)

chemosynthesis/quimiosíntesis: Proceso en que las bacterias de las dorsales oceánicas fabrican alimento mediante la descomposición de compuestos que contienen elementos como azufre, hierro o nitrógeno, en lugar de carbono y oxígeno. (Cap. 12, pág. 342)

chemotherapy/quimioterapia: Uso de sustancias químicas para destruir células cancerosas. (Cap. 24, pág. 670)

childhood/niñez: Etapa que le sigue a la lactancia y que dura hasta los 12 años. (Cap. 23, pág. 642)

chromosomes/cromosomas: Estructuras dentro del núcleo que contienen el material hereditario. (Cap. 16, pág. 443)

chronic bronchitis/bronquitis crónica: Tipo de bronquitis que persiste por un largo período de tiempo, la cual puede ser el resultado de fumar. (Cap. 21, pág. 581)

chyme/quimo: Producto acuoso y delgado que resulta de la digestión. (Cap. 19, pág. 534)

circuit/circuito: Trayectoria cerrada a través de la cual puede fluir una corriente eléctrica. (Cap. 6, pág. 169)

Clean Air Act/Ley para el Control de la Contaminación del Aire: Protege la calidad del aire al regular la industria automotriz, las tecnologías del carbón y otras industrias. (Cap. 14, pág. 392)

Clean Water Act/Ley para el Control de la Contaminación del Agua: Otorga fondos a los estados para la construcción de instalaciones de tratamiento de aguas negras y residuales y para el control de las aguas de desagüe. También requiere que los estados desarrollen estándares de calidad para sus corrientes de agua. (Cap. 14, pág. 401)

climate/clima: Patrón de tiempo que ocurre en una región en particular, a lo largo de muchos años. (Cap. 8, pág. 222)

cochlea/cóclea: Estructura en forma de caracol llena de líquido ubicada dentro del oído interno. (Cap. 22, pág. 609)

communicable disease/enfermedad comunicable: Enfermedad causada por agentes tales como virus, bacterias patógenas, protistas y hongos, y la cual se puede difundir de una persona a otra. (Cap. 24, pág. 657)

compass/brújula: Aguja magnética que se mueve libremente y la cual se alinea a lo largo de las líneas del campo magnético más fuerte en su cercanía. (Cap. 7, pág. 197)

composting/abono orgánico: Desechos vegetales que se apilan para que se descompongan paulatinamente. (Cap. 13, pág. 372)

compressional wave/onda de compresión: Onda en la cual la materia en el medio se mueve de un lado a otro en la misma dirección en que viaja la onda. (Cap. 2, pág. 43)

concave lens/lente cóncava: Lente que es más gruesa en las orillas que en el centro y que desvía las ondas luminosas. (Cap. 3, pág. 83)

concentrated/concentrada: Solución que contiene una gran cantidad de soluto por cantidad dada de disolvente. (Cap. 5, pág. 137)

concentration/concentración: Indica la cantidad de soluto que contiene una solución, comparada con la cantidad de disolvente. (Cap. 5, pág. 137)

condensation/condensación: Proceso de enfriamiento en que las partículas de un gas se vuelven más lentas y la atracción entre ellas aumenta, haciendo que se formen gotas de líquido. (Cap. 4, pág. 109)

conductor/conductor: Material como el cobre, la plata y el hierro a través del cual los electrones se mueven con facilidad. (Cap. 6, pág. 165)

conservation/conservación: Uso cuidadoso de los recursos, lo cual disminuye el daño al ambiente. (Cap. 13, pág. 371)

constant /constante: Variable que permanece igual. (Cap. 1, pág. 19)

consumer/consumidor: Organismo que no puede elaborar su propio alimento. (Cap. 15, pág. 427)

continental shelf/plataforma continental: Extremo, inclinado paulatinamente, de un continente que se extiende bajo el océano. (Cap. 12, pág. 334)

continental slope/talud continental: Extremo de la plataforma continental que se extiende desde el borde exterior de la plataforma continental hacia abajo del suelo oceánico. (Cap. 12, pág. 335)

control/control: Es una muestra que se trata exactamente como los otros grupos experimentales, excepto que no se le aplica la variable. (Cap. 1, pág. 19)

convex lens/lente convexa: Lente que es más gruesa en el centro que en las orillas; hace que las ondas luminosas converjan. (Cap. 3, pág. 82)

coronary circulation/circulación coronaria: Flujo de sangre hacia los tejidos del corazón. (Cap. 20, pág. 549)

creep/corrimiento: Movimiento que recibe su nombre por la manera en que los sedimentos lentamente se deslizan cuesta abajo, pulgada a pulgada. Es común en áreas que se congelan y descongelan. (Cap. 9, pág. 247)

crest/cresta: El punto más alto de una ola. (Cap. 11, pág. 321)

D

deflation/deflacción: Erosión causada cuando el viento sopla los sedimentos sueltos, extrayendo pequeñas partículas tales como la arcilla, el cieno y la arena, y dejando atrás materiales más gruesos. (Cap. 9, pág. 261)

delta/delta: Depósito, en forma de abanico o triángulo, formado por los sedimentos arrastrados por un río, cuando este desemboca en un océano, golfo o lago. (Cap. 10, pág. 287)

dendrite/dendrita: Parte de la neurona que recibe mensajes y los transmite al cuerpo celular. (Cap. 22, pág. 601)

density/densidad: Masa dividida entre volumen. (Cap. 4, pág. 116)

density current/corriente de densidad: Corriente que se forma cuando el agua marina más densa se hunde bajo el agua marina menos densa, empujando el agua oceánica de la superficie hacia las profundidades del océano. (Cap. 11, pág. 318)

dependent variable/variable dependiente: Es el factor que se mide. (Cap. 1, pág. 19)

deposition/depositación: Etapa final del proceso de erosión. Ocurre cuando los agentes erosivos disminuyen su energía erosiva y depositan los sedimentos y las rocas que transportaban. (Cap. 9, pág. 245)

dermis/dermis: Capa de la piel debajo de la epidermis. Es más gruesa que la epidermis y contiene muchos vasos sanguíneos, nervios y glándulas sebáceas y sudoríparas. (Cap. 18, pág. 510)

diaphragm/diafragma: Músculo ubicado debajo de los pulmones, el cual se contrae y se relaja y, además, ayuda a mover el aire dentro y fuera del cuerpo. (Cap. 21, pág. 579)

diffraction/difracción: Doblamiento de una onda alrededor de una barrera. (Cap. 2, pág. 52)

diffusion/difusión: Libre propagación de las partículas de un gas (Cap. 4, pág. 111); proceso que tiene lugar cuando las moléculas se mueven desde un área donde hay más moléculas hasta un área con menos moléculas. (Cap. 15, pág. 421)

digestion/digestión: Proceso químico y mecánico que descompone los alimentos en moléculas más pequeñas, de modo que puedan ser utilizadas por las células corporales. (Cap. 19, pág. 530)

dilute/diluida: Solución que contiene una cantidad pequeña de soluto por cantidad dada de disolvente. (Cap. 5, pág. 137)

disinfectant/desinfectante: Sustancia química que destruye los patógenos en objetos como los instrumentos quirúrgicos. (Cap. 24, pág. 656)

DNA/DNA: Código de la información de un organismo, o ácido desoxirribonucleico, que contienen los cromosomas dentro del núcleo celular. (Cap. 16, pág. 454)

dominant/dominante: Factor que domina o cubre a un rasgo recesivo en la progenie. (Cap. 17, pág. 468)

drainage basin/cuenca hidrográfica: Extensión territorial de donde obtiene agua una corriente de agua. (Cap. 10, pág. 281)

E

egg/óvulo: Tipo de célula sexual que se forma en los órganos reproductores de la hembra y la cual contiene un gran número de moléculas alimenticias y otras partes celulares. (Cap. 16, pág. 448)

electric current/corriente eléctrica: Fuente de energía eléctrica que consiste en un flujo continuo de electrones a través de un conductor. Se mide en amperios (A). (Cap. 6, pág. 169)

electric discharge/descarga eléctrica: Movimiento rápido del exceso de electrones de un lugar a otro. (Cap. 6, pág. 166)

electric generator/generador eléctrico: Dispositivo que utiliza la inducción para producir potencia eléctrica. (Cap. 7, pág. 204)

electric motor/motor eléctrico: Motor que convierte la energía eléctrica en energía de movimiento. (Cap. 7, pág. 202)

electrical power/potencia eléctrica: La razón a la cual un artefacto convierte energía eléctrica en otra forma de energía; se mide en vatios (W). (Cap. 6, pág. 180)

electromagnet/electroimán: Alambre enrollado alrededor de un núcleo de hierro y el cual transporta electricidad. (Cap. 7, pág. 199)

electromagnetic wave/onda electromagnética: Onda que no necesita un medio a través del cual pueda viajar. Este tipo de onda puede viajar en el vacío, y también a través del aire, del agua y del vidrio (Cap. 3, pág. 66)

electromagnetism/electromagnetismo: Dos aspectos de la misma fuerza que combina la electricidad y el magnetismo. (Cap. 7, pág. 199)

embryo/embrión: Nombre que se le da al bebé nonato durante los dos primeros meses de desarrollo en el vientre materno. (Cap. 23, pág. 636)

emphysema/enfisema: Enfermedad en la cual los alvéolos pulmonares pierden su capacidad de expandirse y contraerse. La mayoría de los casos de enfisema son el resultado de fumar. (Cap. 21, pág. 582)

endocytosis/endocitosis: Proceso mediante el cual las moléculas grandes de proteínas y bacterias pueden entrar a una célula cuando se encuentran rodeadas por la membrana celular. La membrana celular se dobla sobre sí misma y encierra la sustancia en una esfera, la cual se desprende resultando en una vacuola que entra al citoplasma. (Cap. 15, pág. 425)

enzymes/enzimas: Proteínas específicas que regulan casi todas las reacciones químicas en las células, sin ser alteradas (Cap. 15, pág. 419); moléculas que aceleran el ritmo de las reacciones químicas en el cuerpo. (Cap. 19, pág. 531)

epidermis/epidermis: Capa superficial de la piel cuyas células más externas están muertas. (Cap. 18, pág. 509)

equilibrium/equilibrio: Estado en que las moléculas de una sustancia se encuentran esparcidas equitativamente en otra sustancia. (Cap. 15, pág. 422)

erosion/erosión: Proceso que agota los materiales de la superficie y los transporta de un lugar a otro. Los principales agentes de la erosión son la gravedad, los glaciares, el viento y el agua. (Cap. 9, pág. 244)

evaporation/evaporación: Proceso mediante el cual las partículas individuales de un líquido se escapan de la superficie y forman un gas. (Cap. 4, pág. 108)

exocytosis/exocitosis: Proceso mediante el cual las vesículas y las vacuolas liberan su contenido fuera de la célula. Lo opuesto de la endocitosis. En este proceso la membrana de la vesícula o vacuola se fusiona con la membrana celular liberando así su contenido. (Cap. 15, pág. 425)

F

fats/grasas: Sustancias orgánicas que proveen energía al cuerpo y que le ayudan a absorber ciertas vitaminas, además de amortiguar los órganos internos. Las grasas se clasifican en saturadas y no saturadas. (Cap. 19, pág. 522)

fermentation/fermentación: Forma de respiración sin oxígeno que libera solo parte de la energía de los alimentos. (Cap. 15, pág. 428)

fertilization/fecundación: La unión de un óvulo y un espermatozoide. (Cap. 16, pág. 448)

fetus/feto: Nombre con que se conoce al bebé nonato después de los dos primeros meses de embarazo. (Cap. 23, pág. 638)

floodplain/llanura aluvial: Piso de un valle ancho y llano tallado por una corriente de agua serpenteante. (Cap. 10, pág. 284)

focal length/longitud focal: Distancia a lo largo del eje óptico desde el centro del espejo hasta el punto focal. (Cap. 3, pág. 76)

focal point/punto focal: Para un espejo cóncavo, es el punto único a través del cual se reflejan y pasan los rayos de luz que viajan paralelos al eje óptico y que chocan contra el espejo. (Cap. 3, pág. 76)

food group/grupo de alimentos: Alimentos que contienen los mismos nutrientes. Los grupos de alimentos se organizan en una pirámide que presenta los grupos básicos y las porciones diarias sugeridas para que el cuerpo reciba los nutrientes necesarios. (Cap. 19, pág. 527)

freezing point/punto de congelación: Temperatura a la cual una sustancia pasa de líquido a sólido. Es la misma temperatura que el punto de fusión de un sólido. (Cap. 4, pág. 103)

frequency/frecuencia: Número de longitudes de onda que pasan por un punto en un segundo; se mide en ondas por segundo o hertz (Hz) (Cap. 2, pág. 47); (Cap. 3, pág. 69)

G

gene/gene: Segmento del DNA en un cromosoma que dirige la fabricación de cierta proteína. Los genes controlan las proteínas que fabrican células y tejidos o que funcionan como enzimas. (Cap. 16, pág. 456)

genetic engineering/ingeniería genética: Ciencia a través de la cual los científicos experimentan con métodos biológicos y químicos para cambiar la secuencia del DNA que forma un gene. (Cap. 17, pág. 484)

genetics/genética: El estudio de cómo se heredan los rasgos a través de las acciones de los alelos. (Cap. 17, pág. 467)

genotype/genotipo: Forma de taquigrafía que usa letras para mostrar la composición genética de un organismo. (Cap. 17, pág. 470)

geyser/géiser: Fuente termal que hace erupción periódicamente disparando agua y vapor en el aire. (Cap. 10, pág. 294)

glaciers/glaciares: Masas móviles de hielo y nieve. (Cap. 9, pág. 252)

groundwater/agua subterránea: Agua que se filtra en el suelo y que se junta en los poros subterráneos. (Cap. 10, pág. 290)

gully erosion/erosión en barrancos: Surco o zanja que se ensancha y profundiza formando un barranco. (Cap. 10, pág. 279)

H

hazardous wastes/desechos peligrosos: Desechos venenosos, cancerígenos o radiactivos que causan daño a los seres vivos. (Cap. 13, pág. 367)

heat of fusion/calor de fusión: Cantidad de calor necesario para derretir un kilogramo de un sólido hasta su punto de fusión. (Cap. 4, pág. 102)

heat of vaporization/calor de vaporización: Cantidad de energía necesaria para cambiar un kilogramo de un líquido en un gas. (Cap. 4, pág. 107)

helper T cell/célula T ayudante: Glóbulo blanco que ayuda a otros tipos de glóbulos blancos a producir anticuerpos. (Cap. 24, pág. 664)

hemoglobin/hemoglobina: Sustancia química que contienen los glóbulos rojos, la cual puede transportar oxígeno y dióxido de carbono. (Cap. 20, pág. 557)

heredity/herencia: Transferencia de rasgos del progenitor a la progenie. (Cap. 17, pág. 466)

770 GLOSSARY/GLOSARIO

heterozygous/heterocigoto: Organismo que posee dos alelos diferentes para cierto rasgo. (Cap. 17, pág. 470)

homozygous/homocigoto: Organismo con dos alelos exactamente iguales para cierto rasgo. (Cap. 17, pág. 470)

horizon/horizonte: Nombre que recibe cada capa del perfil del suelo. (Cap. 8, pág. 228)

hormones/hormonas: Sustancias químicas endocrinas producidas en varias glándulas sin conductos a través de todo el cuerpo. (Cap. 22, pág. 616)

humus/humus: Materia de color oscuro que se forma de la descomposición de la materia orgánica, como las plantas. (Cap. 8, pág. 227)

hypertension/hipertensión: Trastorno cardiovascular que puede ser causado por la aterosclerosis. (Cap. 20, pág. 554)

hypothesis/hipótesis: Predicción o enunciado que se puede probar. (Cap. 1, pág. 18)

ice wedging/grietas debido al hielo: Meteorización mecánica que se produce en áreas frías cuando las bajas temperaturas congelan el agua, la cual luego se descongela. A la larga, el ciclo de congelación y derretimiento hace que las rocas se rompan. (Cap. 8, pág. 220)

immovable joint/articulación fija: Tipo de articulación que permite poco o ningún movimiento; por ejemplo: las articulaciones del cráneo y de la pelvis. (Cap. 18, pág. 498)

immune system/sistema inmunológico: Complejo de defensas que posee el cuerpo para combatir enfermedades. (Cap. 24, pág. 661)

impermeable/impermeable: Material que no se deja atravesar por el agua. (Cap. 10, pág. 291)

incomplete dominance/dominancia incompleta: Producción de un fenotipo intermedio a los de dos progenitores homocigotos. (Cap. 17, pág. 474)

independent variable/variable independiente: Es la variable o factor que se cambia. (Cap. 1, pág. 19)

indicator/indicador: Compuesto que reacciona con soluciones ácidas o básicas para producir ciertos colores. Sirve para averiguar el grado de acidez o basicidad de una solución. (Cap. 5, pág. 144)

induction/inducción: Proceso que cambia un campo magnético para transformar energía eléctrica en energía mecánica. (Cap. 7, pág. 204)

infancy/lactancia: Período de rápido crecimiento y desarrollo mental y físico del bebé desde el nacimiento hasta que cumple un año. (Cap. 23, pág. 642)

inorganic compounds/compuestos inorgánicos: Compuestos hechos de otros elementos menos el carbono; por ejemplo, el agua, la cual compone la mayor parte de la materia viva. (Cap. 15, pág. 420)

insulator/aislador: Material en el cual los electrones no pueden moverse de un lugar a otro; por ejemplo: el plástico, la madera, el vidrio y el caucho. (Cap. 6, pág. 165)

interference/interferencia: La capacidad de dos o más ondas de combinarse y formar una nueva onda cuando se sobreponen una sobre la otra. (Cap. 2, pág. 54)

involuntary muscles/músculos involuntarios: Músculos que se pueden controlar conscientemente. (Cap. 18, pág. 502)

joint/articulación: Cualquier lugar en donde se unen dos o más huesos. (Cap. 18, pág. 497)

kidney/riñón: Órgano con forma de frijol, compuesto de aproximadamente 1 millón de nefrones que filtra la sangre y produce un desecho líquido (orina). (Cap. 21, pág. 588)

kinetic theory of matter/teoría cinética de la materia: Idea que dice que las partículas de materia se encuentran en movimiento constante y aleatorio. (Cap. 4, pág. 99)

landfill/vertedero controlado: Área en donde se depositan los residuos. (Cap. 13, pág. 367)

larynx/laringe: Vía aérea a la cual están adheridas las cuerdas vocales (Cap. 21, pág. 577)

law of reflection/ley de reflexión: Enuncia que el ángulo de incidencia es igual al ángulo de reflexión. (Cap. 3, pág. 73)

leaching/lixiviación: Extracción de materiales, al ser disueltos en agua. (Cap. 8, pág. 229)

lens/lente: Objeto transparente con por lo menos un lado encorvado que hace que la luz se doble. (Cap. 3, pág. 81)

ligament/ligamento: Banda dura de tejido que mantiene unidos los huesos en las articulaciones. (Cap. 18, pág. 497)

light ray/rayo de luz: Trayectoria muy estrecha de luz que viaja en línea recta. (Cap. 3, pág. 66)

litter/lecho superficial: Capa compuesta de hojas, ramas y otros materiales orgánicos, la cual se convierte en humus. (Cap. 8, pág. 229)

loess/loes: Depósitos de grano fino arrastrados por el viento. (Cap. 9, pág. 265)

longshore current/corriente costera: La que corre a lo largo de la costa. (Cap. 10, pág. 297)

lymph/linfa: Fluido corporal que consiste principalmente en agua, sustancias disueltas, tales como nutrientes y pequeñas cantidades de proteínas y linfocitos. (Cap. 20, pág. 566)

lymphatic system/sistema linfático: Sistema que recoge el fluido entre los tejidos corporales y lo devuelve a la sangre a través de un sistema de capilares y vasos linfáticos más grandes. (Cap. 20, pág. 565)

lymph nodes/ganglios linfáticos: Estructuras que filtran los microorganismos y los materiales extraños que han sido engullidos por los linfocitos. (Cap. 20, pág. 566)

lymphocyte/linfocito: Un tipo de glóbulo blanco. (Cap. 20, pág. 566)

magnetic domain/dominio magnético: Grupo de átomos cuyos polos magnéticos apuntan en la misma dirección. (Cap. 7, pág. 193)

magnetic field/campo magnético: Región en donde actúa una fuerza magnética. (Cap. 7, pág. 194)

magnetism/magnetismo: Fuerza que puede atraer o repeler objetos. (Cap. 7, pág. 194)

marrow/médula: Tejido grasoso suave que se halla en el centro de muchos huesos, en donde se producen glóbulos rojos al increíble ritmo de 2 millones de glóbulos rojos por segundo y glóbulos blancos, pero no con la misma rapidez. (Cap. 18, pág. 494)

mass movement/movimiento de masa: Movimiento de materiales cuesta abajo debido solo a la gravedad. Algunos movimientos de masa pueden ocurrir lentamente, pero otros sin embargo ocurren rápidamente. (Cap. 9, pág. 246)

matter/materia: Cualquier cosa que ocupa espacio y posee masa; es decir, cualquier cosa que puedes ver, tocar, oler o saborear. (Cap. 4, pág. 98)

meander/meandro: Curva que se forma en una corriente de agua cuando el agua que se mueve rápidamente erosiona el costado de la corriente donde el agua es más fuerte. (Cap. 10, pág. 284)

mechanical digestion/digestión mecánica: Proceso que ocurre cuando los alimentos se mastican y se mezclan en la boca y se revuelven en el estómago. (Cap. 19, pág. 532)

mechanical waves/ondas mecánicas: Ondas que solo pueden viajar a través de un medio: la materia. (Cap. 2, pág. 41)

mechanical weathering/meteorización mecánica: Proceso que parte las rocas, pero sin cambiar su composición química. (Cap. 8, pág. 219)

medium/medio: Cualquier material por el cual viaja una onda. (Cap. 3, pág. 66)

meiosis/meiosis: Proceso de creación de células sexuales en los órganos reproductores, y en el cual se producen cuatro células sexuales haploides a partir de dos células diploides. (Cap. 16, pág. 448)

melanin/melanina: Pigmento que da color a la piel y el cual aumenta con la exposición a los rayos ultravioleta del sol. Entre más melanina posea una persona, más oscuro es el color de su piel. (Cap. 18, pág. 509)

melting point/punto de fusión: Temperatura a la cual una sustancia pasa de sólido a líquido. (Cap. 4, pág. 102)

menopause/menopausia: Ocurre cuando el ciclo menstrual se vuelve irregular y, a la larga, cesa. (Cap. 23, pág. 631)

menstrual cycle/ciclo menstrual: Ciclo mensual de cambios en el sistema reproductor femenino. (Cap. 23, pág. 629)

menstruation/menstruación: Descarga mensual que consiste en células sanguíneas y tejidos de la cubierta interior gruesa del útero. (Cap. 23, pág. 630)

metabolism/metabolismo: La suma total de todas las reacciones químicas de un organismo. (Cap. 15, pág. 427)

mid-ocean ridge/dorsal medieooceánica: Lugar donde se forma nuevo suelo oceánico. (Cap. 12, pág. 336)

minerals/minerales: Nutrientes inorgánicos que regulan muchas reacciones químicas en el cuerpo. (Cap. 19, pág. 524)

mitosis/mitosis: Serie de pasos continuos (profase, metafase, anafase y telofase) en que el núcleo celular se divide para formar dos núcleos idénticos. (Cap. 16, pág. 442)

mixture/mezcla: Combinación de sustancias que puede ser separada por medios físicos y que puede ser homogénea o heterogénea (Cap. 5, pág. 126); combinación de sustancias en la cual las sustancias individuales retienen sus propiedades. (Cap. 15, pág. 417)

model/modelo: Algo que se usa para pensar acerca de cosas que suceden muy lenta o muy rápidamente, que son muy grandes o muy pequeñas, o que son muy peligrosas o costosas para ser observadas directamente. (Cap. 1, pág. 16)

moraine/morena frontal o terminal: Tipo de depósito parecido a un cerro que se forma de tierra y piedras arrastradas por un glaciar. Este tipo de depósito no cubre un área muy amplia de terreno. (Cap. 9, pág. 256)

movable joint/articulación móvil: Tipo de articulación que permite que el cuerpo realice una amplia gama de movimientos. Existen varios tipos de articulaciones móviles: de charnela, de bola y receptáculo, en bisagra y deslizante. (Cap. 18, pág. 498)

multiple alleles/alelos múltiples: Dos o más alelos que controlan un rasgo específico en un organismo. (Cap. 17, pág. 474)

muscle/músculo: Órgano que puede relajarse y contraerse para permitir el movimiento. (Cap. 18, pág. 501)

mutation/mutación: Cualquier cambio permanente en un gene o cromosoma celular. Las mutaciones añaden variedad a una especie, cuando el organismo afectado se reproduce, pero muchas son dañinas para los organismos. (Cap. 16, pág. 458)

nekton/necton: Animales que nadan activamente en lugar de estar a la deriva con las corrientes. (Cap. 12, pág. 344)

nephron/nefrón: Unidad diminuta de filtración de los riñones. (Cap. 21, pág. 588)

neuron/neurona: Elemento estructural del sistema nervioso, compuesto de un cuerpo celular, dendritas y axones. (Cap. 22, pág. 601)

neutralization/neutralización: Interacción entre ácidos y bases, en que las propiedades de cada uno de estos se cancelan mutuamente. (Cap. 5, pág. 145)

noncommunicable disease/enfermedad no comunicable: Enfermedad o trastorno que no se disemina de una persona a otra, pero que puede resultar de factores tales como una dieta deficiente o el crecimiento descontrolado de las células. (Cap. 24, pág. 668)

nutrients/nutrientes: Sustancias provenientes de los alimentos que proveen energía y materiales para el desarrollo, el crecimiento y la reparación de las células; carbohidratos, proteínas, grasas, vitaminas, minerales y agua. (Cap. 19, pág. 518)

Ohm's law/ley de Ohm: Relación entre el voltaje, la corriente y la resistencia en un circuito eléctrico; $V = IR$, donde V representa el voltaje, I representa la corriente y R representa la resistencia. (Cap. 6, pág. 177)

olfactory cells/células olfativas: Células nerviosas nasales las cuales son estimuladas por las moléculas de gas. (Cap. 22, pág. 612)

organic compounds/compuestos orgánicos: Compuestos que contienen carbono. Existen cuatro grupos de compuestos orgánicos que componen a todos los seres vivos: carbohidratos, lípidos, proteínas y ácidos nucleicos. (Cap. 15, pág. 418)

osmosis/osmosis: Difusión de agua a través de la membrana celular. Es importante para las células porque estas contienen moléculas de agua y la mayoría está rodeada de moléculas de agua. (Cap. 15, pág. 423)

ovary/ovario: En los seres humanos, es el órgano sexual femenino donde se producen los óvulos. (Cap. 23, pág. 628)

ovulation/ovulación: Proceso en que se libera un óvulo cada mes de uno de los ovarios. (Cap. 23, pág. 629)

oxidation/oxidación: Ocurre cuando un material, como el hierro, se expone al oxígeno y al agua. La oxidación causa la herrumbre. (Cap. 8, pág. 222)

P

parallel circuit/circuito en paralelo: El que posee más de una ruta para que fluya la corriente. Si una de las rutas se interrumpe, la corriente continúa fluyendo a lo largo de las otras rutas. (Cap. 6, pág. 178)

Pascal's principle/principio de Pascal: Dice que la presión que se le aplica a un fluido confinado, en cualquiera de los puntos, es transmitida sin cambio a través del fluido. (Cap. 4, pág. 113)

passive immunity/inmunidad pasiva: La que ocurre cuando se introducen en el cuerpo los anticuerpos producidos en otros animales. (Cap. 24, pág. 662)

passive transport/transporte pasivo: Movimiento de sustancias a través de la membrana celular, que no usa energía celular. (Cap. 15, pág. 424)

pasteurization/pasteurización: Proceso que consiste en calentar los alimentos hasta una temperatura que destruye la mayoría de las bacterias. (Cap. 24, pág. 654)

pedigree/árbol genealógico: Herramienta para rastrear la ocurrencia de un rasgo en cierta familia, en la cual los varones se representan con cuadrados y las mujeres con círculos. (Cap. 17, pág. 483)

periosteum/periósteo: Membrana dura que cubre ajustadamente la superficie de los hue-sos. (Cap. 18, pág. 495)

peripheral nervous system/sistema nervioso periférico: Uno de los dos sistemas principales en que se divide el sistema nervioso. Está compuesto de todos los nervios por fuera del sistema nervioso central, incluyendo los nervios craneales y los nervios espinales. (Cap. 22, pág. 602)

peristalsis/peristalsis: Ondas o contracciones que mueven los alimentos a lo largo del sistema digestivo. (Cap. 19, pág. 533)

permeable/permeable: Cuando los espacios entre poros de suelo y roca están conectados de manera que el agua pueda pasar a través de ellos. (Cap. 10, pág. 291)

pH/pH: Medida del grado de acidez o basicidad de una solución, en relación con su concentración de iones hidronio y iones hidroxilo; las soluciones con un pH menor que 7 son ácidas, las soluciones con un pH mayor que 7 son básicas y las soluciones con un pH de 7 son neutras. (Cap. 5, pág. 143)

pH scale/escala de pH: Escala que describe la acidez o basicidad de una sustancia; varía de 0 a 14, siendo 0 el rango más ácido y 14 el más básico. (Cap. 14, pág. 390)

pharynx/faringe: Pasaje en forma de tubo por donde pasan el aire húmedo y cálido y los alimentos (Cap. 21, pág. 577)

phenotype/fenotipo: Expresión física de un genotipo en particular. (Cap. 17, pág. 470)

photochemical smog/smog fotoquímico: Smog color café que se forma cuando la luz solar reacciona con los contaminantes del aire. (Cap. 14, pág. 388)

photosynthesis/fotosíntesis: Proceso en que las plantas usan energía luminosa, dióxido de carbono y agua para producir alimentos. (Cap. 12, pág. 340)

plankton/plancton: Algas marinas y animales minúsculos a la deriva con las corrientes oceánicas. (Cap. 12, pág. 343)

plasma/plasma: Parte líquida de la sangre, la cual consiste principalmente en agua y comprende más de la mitad del volumen de la sangre. (Cap. 20, pág. 557)

platelet/plaqueta: Fragmentos celulares de formas irregulares que ayudan en la coagulación de la sangre. (Cap. 20, pág. 558)

plucking/ablación: Proceso en que un glaciar rompe las rocas mediante la acción del agrietamiento debido al hielo; resulta en piedras grandes, grava y arena. (Cap. 9, pág. 254)

polygenic inheritance/herencia polígena: Ocurre cuando un grupo de pares de genes actúa en conjunto para producir un solo rasgo. (Cap. 17, pág. 475)

population/población: Número total de individuos de una especie en particular en un área particular. (Cap. 13, pág. 359)

population explosion/explosión demográfica: Rápido crecimiento de la población humana. (Cap. 13, pág. 359)

pregnancy/embarazo: Período de nueve meses de desarrollo, en el útero, del óvulo fecundado hasta el nacimiento del bebé. (Cap. 23, pág. 636)

pressure/presión: Cantidad de fuerza ejercida por unidad de área. (Cap. 4, pág. 112)

producer/productor: Organismo que elabora su propio alimento. (Cap. 15, pág. 427)

proteins/proteínas: Moléculas orgánicas grandes compuestas principalmente de aminoácidos y las cuales se necesitan para el crecimiento y reparación de las células corporales. (Cap. 19, pág. 520)

pulmonary circulation/circulación pulmonar: Flujo de sangre a través del corazón, hasta los pulmones y de regreso al corazón. (Cap. 20, pág. 548)

Punnett square/cuadrado de Punnett: Instrumento que se utiliza para predecir resultados en la genética mendeliana; muestra todas las formas en que se pueden combinar los alelos. (Cap. 17, pág. 470)

R

recessive/recesivo: Factor que parece desaparecer debido a un rasgo dominante en la progenie. (Cap. 17, pág. 468)

recyclable/reciclable: Cualquier artículo que se puede procesar y volver a usar, para así conservar los recursos naturales y disminuir los desechos sólidos. (Cap. 13, pág. 373)

reef/arrecife: Estructura rígida y resistente a las olas que se desarrolla a partir de materiales óseos y carbonato cálcico. (Cap. 12, pág. 346)

reflection/reflexión: Ocurre cuando una onda choca contra un objeto o superficie y luego rebota. (Cap. 2, pág. 50; Cap. 3, pág. 67)

reflex/reflejo: Respuesta involuntaria y automática a un estímulo. (Cap. 22, pág. 605)

refraction/refracción: Cambio en la dirección de propagación de una onda luminosa debido a un cambio en velocidad, al moverse la onda de un medio a otro. (Cap. 2, pág. 51; Cap. 3, pág. 81)

reproduction/reproducción: Proceso mediante el cual los organismos producen más individuos. (Cap. 23, pág. 626)

resistance/resistencia: Medida del grado de dificultad que tienen los electrones para fluir a través de un material. La unidad de resistencia es el ohmio. (Cap. 6, pág. 172)

retina/retina: Tejido sensible a la energía luminosa ubicado en la parte posterior del ojo. (Cap. 22, pág. 610)

rill erosion/erosión en regueras: Tipo de erosión causada por el agua de desagüe, en que una pequeña corriente de agua, durante una lluvia intensa, arrastra plantas y tierra, dejando una cicatriz o canal en el lado de la ladera. (Cap. 10, pág. 279)

RNA/RNA: Ácido nucleico que transporta los códigos para la fabricación de proteínas desde el núcleo hasta los ribosomas. (Cap. 16, pág. 457)

runoff/agua de desagüe: Agua que no se filtra en el suelo o que no se evapora y, por consiguiente, corre sobre la superficie de la Tierra. (Cap. 10, pág. 276)

S

Safe Drinking Water Act/Ley sobre la Seguridad del Agua Potable: Fortalece los estándares de salud para el agua potable, protege los ríos, lagos y corrientes de agua y otorga a los ciudadanos el derecho de saber acerca de los contaminantes que pueda contener el agua potable. (Cap. 14, pág. 401)

salinity/salinidad: Una medida de la cantidad de sales disueltas en agua marina; generalmente se mide en gramos de sal por kilogramo de agua. (Cap. 11, pág. 312)

saliva/saliva: Sustancia producida por tres grupos de glándulas cerca de la boca. Contiene principalmente agua, pero también contiene mucosidad y la enzima salival amilasa. (Cap. 19, pág. 533)

saturated/saturada: Solución que contiene todo el soluto que es capaz de retener bajo ciertas condiciones dadas. (Cap. 5, pág. 136)

science/ciencia: Manera o proceso que se usa para investigar lo que sucede a nuestro alrededor y el cual nos provee algunas posibles respuestas. (Cap. 1, pág. 6)

scientific methods/métodos científicos: Métodos que se usan para tratar de resolver un problema. (Cap. 1, pág. 14)

scrubber/depurador: Dispositivo que hace que los gases en el humo se disuelvan en agua, así como sucedería en la naturaleza, hasta aumentar el pH del humo a un nivel seguro. (Cap. 14, pág. 393)

semen/semen: Mezcla de espermatozoides y fluido producida en la vesícula seminal, la cual sale del cuerpo a través de la uretra. (Cap. 23, pág. 628)

series circuit/circuito en serie: El que posee solo una ruta para que fluya la corriente. Si dicha ruta se interrumpe, la corriente cesa de fluir y todos los artefactos en el circuito dejan de funcionar. (Cap. 6, pág. 178)

sex-linked gene/gene ligado al sexo: Alelo heredado en un cromosoma que determina el sexo. (Cap. 17, pág. 482)

sexual reproduction/reproducción sexual: Manera de crear un nuevo organismo de la unión de dos células sexuales—un óvulo y un espermatozoide—que por lo general provienen de diferentes organismos. (Cap. 16, pág. 448)

sexually transmitted diseases (STDs)/enfermedades transmitidas sexualmente (ETS): enfermedades transmitidas de una persona a otra mediante el contacto sexual. Causadas por virus o bacterias. (Cap. 24, pág. 658)

sheet erosion/erosión laminar o en capas: Erosión que ocurre cuando el agua de lluvia fluye hacia elevaciones más bajas, arrastrando consigo sedimentos. (Cap. 10, pág. 279)

skeletal muscles/músculos esqueléticos: Músculos que mueven los huesos y que cuando se observan bajo el microscopio se ven estriados. (Cap. 18, pág. 504)

skeletal system/sistema esquelético: Sistema compuesto de todos los huesos del cuerpo, el cual forma el marco que da apoyo y forma al cuerpo, protege los órganos internos, provee el lugar para que se adhieran los músculos, algunos huesos producen la médula ósea y en los huesos se almacenan grandes cantidades de compuestos de calcio y fósforo. (Cap. 18, pág. 494)

slump/derrumbe: Movimiento de masa que ocurre cuando materiales sueltos o capas rocosas se deslizan cuesta abajo. (Cap. 9, pág. 246)

smooth muscles/músculos lisos: Músculos involuntarios no estriados que mueven muchos de los órganos internos. Los intestinos, la vejiga y los vasos sanguíneos están hechos de una o más capas de músculo liso. (Cap. 18, pág. 504)

soil/suelo: Mezcla de roca meteorizada, materia orgánica, fragmentos minerales, agua y aire. (Cap. 8, pág. 226)

soil profile/perfil del suelo: Capas diferentes de suelo. (Cap. 8, pág. 228)

solubility/solubilidad: Término que se usa para describir la cantidad de soluto que se disuelve en una cantidad dada de disolvente. (Cap. 5, pág. 134)

solute/soluto: Sustancia que parece desaparecer o que se disuelve en el disolvente. (Cap. 5, pág. 128)

solution/solución: Otro nombre para una mezcla homogénea. (Cap. 5, pág. 127)

solvent/disolvente: Sustancia que disuelve el soluto. (Cap. 5, pág. 128)

sperm/espermatozoide: Célula masculina producida en los órganos reproductores de los hombres y la cual contiene solo la mitad del número de cromosomas de las células corporales. Consta de una cola que provee movimiento y una cabeza que posee información genética. (Cap. 16, pág. 448; Cap. 23, pág. 627)

spring/manantial: Agua que fluye en lugares donde la superficie terrestre se junta con la capa freática. (Cap. 10, pág. 293)

state of matter/estado de la materia: Te indica si un material es un sólido, un líquido o un gas. (Cap. 4, pág. 98)

static charge/carga estática: Acumulación de cargas eléctricas en un objeto. (Cap. 6, pág. 163)

sulfurous smog/smog sulfuroso: Tipo de smog que se forma debido a que la quema de combustibles libera compuestos de azufre en el aire; se puede acumular en un área donde no sopla el viento o este sopla muy poco. (Cap. 14, pág. 389)

surface currents/corrientes de superficie: Corrientes que mueven el agua horizontalmente–paralela a la superficie terrestre. Estas corrientes son accionadas por el viento. (Cap. 11, pág. 315)

synapse/sinapsis: Espacio pequeño a través del cual se mueven los impulsos al ser transmitidos de una neurona a la siguiente. (Cap. 22, pág. 602)

systemic circulation/circulación sistémica: Flujo de sangre rica en oxígeno a todos los órganos y tejidos del cuerpo, excepto el corazón y los pulmones . (Cap. 20, pág. 548)

T

target tissue/tejido asignado: Tipo de tejido específico que se ve afectado por las hormonas. (Cap. 22, pág. 616)

taste buds/papilas gustativas: Receptores principales en la lengua para el sentido del gusto. (Cap. 22, pág. 612)

technology/tecnología: La aplicación de la ciencia para fabricar productos o instrumentos que la gente puede usar. (Cap. 1, pág. 10)

tendon/tendón: Bandas gruesas de tejido que unen los músculos esqueléticos a los huesos. (Cap. 18, pág. 504)

testes/testículos: Órganos sexuales masculinos donde se empiezan a producir las células reproductoras masculinas, los espermatozoides, y la hormona sexual masculina, testosterona, durante la pubertad. (Cap. 23, pág. 627)

tidal range/alcance de la marea: La diferencia entre el nivel del océano durante la marea alta y la marea baja. (Cap. 11, pág. 324)

tide/marea: Ascenso y descenso del nivel del mar. (Cap. 11, pág. 324)

till/morena: Mezcla de sedimentos de diferentes tamaños: piedras grandes, arena, arcilla y cieno que deposita la base un glaciar, cuando este disminuye su velocidad. Este tipo de depósito puede cubrir grandes extensiones de terreno. (Cap. 9, pág. 256)

trachea/tráquea: Tubo de unos 12 cm de largo ubicado debajo de la laringe y forrado con membranas mucosas y cilios para atrapar el polvo, las bacterias y el polen. (Cap. 21, pág. 577)

transformer/transformador: Dispositivo que cambia el voltaje de una corriente eléctrica. (Cap. 7, pág. 205)

transverse wave/onda transversal: Tipo de onda mecánica en la cual la materia se mueve de un lado a otro formando ángulos rectos con la dirección en que viaja la onda. (Cap. 2, pág. 42)

trenches/fosas submarinas: Depresiones largas, estrechas y con laderas empinadas en el suelo oceánico donde una placa de la corteza terrestre es forzada a penetrar debajo de otra; son los lugares más geológicamente activos y hondos del planeta. (Cap. 12, pág. 337)

trough /valle: El punto más bajo de una ola. (Cap. 11, pág. 321)

U

upwelling/corriente de aguas resurgentes: Circulación en el océano que lleva agua profunda y fría hacia la superficie. (Cap. 11, pág. 318)

ureter/uréter: Conducto que une cada riñón con la vejiga. (Cap. 21, pág. 589)

urethra/uretra: Conducto por donde sale la orina de la vejiga. (Cap. 21, pág. 589)

urinary system/sistema urinario: Compuesto por los órganos que limpian la sangre de los desechos producidos por el metabolismo de los nutrientes. También controlan el volumen sanguíneo eliminando el exceso de agua que producen las células. (Cap. 21, pág. 587)

urine/orina: Desecho líquido que contiene exceso de agua, sales y otros residuos que no fueron absorbidos por el cuerpo. (Cap. 21, pág. 588)

uterus/útero: Órgano muscular hueco con forma de pera y paredes gruesas en donde se desarrolla el óvulo fecundado. (Cap. 23, pág. 629)

vaccination/vacunación: Proceso de administrar una vacuna por inyección o por vía oral. (Cap. 24, pág. 662)

vagina/vagina: Tubo muscular en el extremo inferior del útero que lo conecta al exterior del cuerpo. También se le denomina canal de nacimiento. (Cap. 23, pág. 629)

vein/vena: Vaso sanguíneo que transporta sangre hacia el corazón y que tiene válvulas que facilitan el regreso de la sangre al corazón. (Cap. 20, pág. 550)

ventricles/ventrículos: Las dos cavidades inferiores del corazón. (Cap. 20, pág. 547)

villi/microvellosidades: Proyecciones pequeñísimas en forma de dedos que cubren los pliegues del intestino delgado. (Cap. 19, pág. 536)

vitamins/vitaminas: Nutrientes orgánicos esenciales necesarios en pequeñas cantidades para que el cuerpo pueda utilizar otros nutrientes. (Cap. 19, pág. 523)

voltage/voltaje: Medida del potencial de energía eléctrica. Se mide en unidades de voltios (V). (Cap. 6, pág. 171)

voluntary muscles/músculos voluntarios: Músculos que no se pueden controlar conscientemente. (Cap. 18, pág. 502)

water table/nivel hidrostático o capa freática: Superficie superior de la zona de saturación o zona donde todos los poros rocosos están llenos de agua. (Cap. 10, pág. 291)

wavelength/longitud de onda: Distancia entre un punto de una onda y otro punto idéntico en la siguiente onda; como por ejemplo, de una cresta a la siguiente o de un valle al siguiente. (Cap. 2, pág. 46; Cap. 3, pág. 69)

waves/ondas: Movimientos rítmicos que transportan energía a través de la materia o del espacio. En el océano se denominan olas, las cuales se mueven a través del agua marina. (Cap. 11, pág. 321)

weathering/meteorización: Proceso que parte las rocas en fragmentos más y más pequeños. (Cap. 8, pág. 218)

zygote/cigoto: La nueva célula que se forma a raíz de la fecundación. (Cap. 16, pág. 449)

Index

The index for *Science Voyages* will help you locate major topics in the book quickly and easily. Each entry in the index is followed by the numbers of the pages on which the entry is discussed. A page number given in **boldface type** indicates the page on which that entry is defined. A page number given in *italic type* indicates a page on which the entry is used in an illustration or photograph. The abbreviation *act.* indicates a page on which the entry is used in an activity.

A

Abdominal thrusts, 580, *580*
ABO system, 560
Abrasion, **261**-262, *262*, 271
Absolute zero, 100
Acid(s), **140**-142, 155, **390**
  chemical weathering and, 221
  neutralization of, 145–146, *146*, 155, *155*
  strengths of, 144–145
  uses of, 141–142
Acid rain, 141, *141*, 145, **390**, *390*, 392
Active immunity, **662**, 662–663
Active transport, **424**, 435
Adolescence, **642**, 649
Adulthood, **644**, 649
AIDS, 659
  HIV and, 659
  vaccine for, 665
Air pollution, *386*, *act.* 387, 388–397
  causes of, 388, *388*, 389, *389*, 406, *406*
  health effects of, 391–392
  particulate, 392, *392*, *act.* 396–397
  reducing, 392–394, *392*
  smog, 388–389, *389*, 391
Alleles, **466**, 470, 486
  multiple, 474–475, 487
  separation in meiosis, *466*

Allergens, **671**
Allergies, **670**
Alloys, 131–132, *131*
Alluvial fan, *286*, **287**
Alveoli, **578**, 594
Amino acids, **520**–521
Amnion, *636*, **637**
Amniotic sac, **637**
Amperes, **169**
Amphibians, 401
Amplitude, **45**-46, *45*, 57, *57*, 60
Anaphase I, 442, *443*, 450–451
Anaphase II, 451
Angle of incidence, **73**
Angle of reflection, **73**
Antibody, 560–561, **662**
Antigens, 560–561, **662**, 673
Antiseptics, **656**
Aorta, *548*, 548, 568
Aqueous solutions, **133**
Aquifer, **291**, 293, *293*, 370
Archimedes' Principle, **117**, 121
Arteries, **550**, 568
Artesian wells, 292–293, *293*
Asexual reproduction, **445**–446, 460
Asthma, **583**
Atherosclerosis, 553, **554**
Atmosphere
  of Earth, 109, 129
Atmospheric pressure, 114–115, *115*, 552

Atom(s) 162, **414**, 415, 434
  states of matter and, 98–99
Atria, **547**, *548*, 568
Automobiles
  air pollution and, 388, *388, 389*, 392, *406*
  solar, 394
Axon, **601**–602

B

Bacteria
  genetically engineered, *484*
  role in digestion, 537
  in water, 400, 402–403
Ball-and-socket joint, *498*
Barrier islands, **299**, *299*
Bases, **142**-143, *142*, 155, **390**
  neutralization of, 145–146, *146*, 155, *155*
  strengths of, 144–145
  uses of, 142–143, *142*
Basins, **311**
  drainage, **281**, *281*, 285
Batteries, 142, 170–172
Beaches, **298**-299, 303
Biological vector, 657
Bioremediation, **402**-403, *402*
Bladder, **589**, *589*
Blood, 556–563, 569
  cell types, 563
  clotting of, 558–559

F

G

H

Haploid cells, 449

Art Credits

Photo Credits

Associates; **486** Pond & Giles; **489** Glencoe/McGraw-Hill.

Chapter 18 - **494** Molly Babich; **495** (t) Felipe Passalacqua, (b) Chris Forsey; **496** Morgan-Cain & Associates; **498** Dave Fischer/Morgan-Cain & Associates; **500** Morgan-Cain & Associates; **501** Molly Babich; **503** Molly Babich/Morgan-Cain & Associates; **504** Rolin Graphics; **505** Dave Fischer; **509** Morgan-Cain & Associates; **512** (l) Felipe Passalacqua, (tr) Molly Babich, (br) Chris Forsey; **513** (t) Rolin Graphics, (b) Morgan-Cain & Associates.

Chapter 19 - **520, 521** Morgan-Cain & Associates; **523** Michael Woods, (fish) Pond & Giles; **524** Michael Woods; **526** Glencoe-McGraw-Hill; **527** Michael Woods; **530** Molly Babich; **531** Morgan-Cain & Associates; **532** Dave Fischer; **533, 534** Morgan-Cain & Associates; **535** Tonya Hines; **536** Morgan-Cain & Associates; **540** Michael Woods; **541** Morgan-Cain & Associates.

Chapter 20 - **546** Molly Babich; **547, 548** Morgan-Cain & Associates; **549** (l) Morgan-Cain & Associates, (r) Molly Babich; **550, 552, 553, 556, 557, 558, 559, 560** Morgan-Cain & Associates; **565** Molly Babich; **566, 567** Morgan-Cain & Associates; **568** (l) Morgan-Cain & Associates, (r) Molly Babich; **569** Molly Babich; **571** Glencoe/McGraw-Hill.

Chapter 21 - **574-575** Morgan-Cain & Associates; **576** Molly Babich; **577** Dave Fischer; **578** Molly Babich; **579** Laurie O'Keefe; **580, 587, 588** Morgan-Cain & Associates; **589** Dave Fischer; **590** Laurie O'Keefe; **591, 593** Morgan-Cain & Associates; **594** Molly Babich; **595** Morgan-Cain & Associates.

Chapter 22 - **599, 600** Morgan-Cain & Associates; **601** (tl, br) Molly Babich, (c) Morgan-Cain & Associates; **602** (t) Gina Lapurga, (b) Michael Courtney; **603** Michael Courtney; **604** Morgan-Cain & Associates; **605** Michael Courtney/Morgan-Cain & Associates; **608** Morgan-Cain & Associates; **609** Jim Jobst; **610** Michael Courtney; **611** Morgan-Cain & Associates; **612** Michael Courtney; **616** Morgan-Cain & Associates; **617** Glencoe/McGraw-Hill; **618** Morgan-Cain & Associates; **620** (t, c) Michael Courtney, (b) Morgan-Cain & Associates; **621** (t) Michael Courtney, (b) Morgan-Cain & Associates; **623** Gina Lapurga.

Chapter 23 - **627** Sarah Woodward; **628, 629, 630, 632, 633, 635** Morgan-Cain & Associates; **636** Sarah Woodward; **639, 640** Morgan-Cain & Associates.

Chapter 24 - **654** Chris Forsey; **655** Cende Hill; **656** Chris Forsey; **657** Felipe Passalacqua; **661, 662** Morgan-Cain & Associates; **676** Chris Forsey; **679** Glencoe/McGraw-Hill.

VISUALIZING
The Periodic Table

PERIODIC TABLE OF THE ELEMENTS

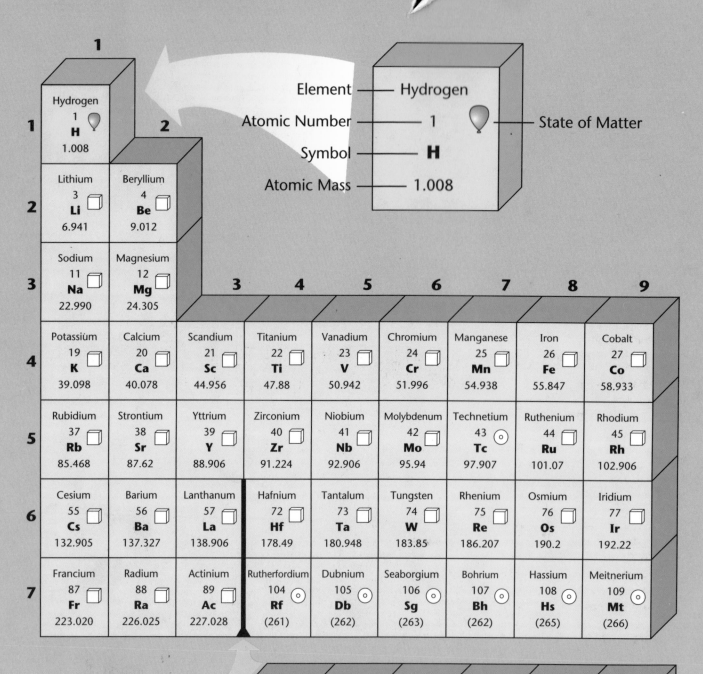

	1	2	3	4	5	6	7	8	9
1	Hydrogen 1 **H** 1.008								
2	Lithium 3 **Li** 6.941	Beryllium 4 **Be** 9.012							
3	Sodium 11 **Na** 22.990	Magnesium 12 **Mg** 24.305							
4	Potassium 19 **K** 39.098	Calcium 20 **Ca** 40.078	Scandium 21 **Sc** 44.956	Titanium 22 **Ti** 47.88	Vanadium 23 **V** 50.942	Chromium 24 **Cr** 51.996	Manganese 25 **Mn** 54.938	Iron 26 **Fe** 55.847	Cobalt 27 **Co** 58.933
5	Rubidium 37 **Rb** 85.468	Strontium 38 **Sr** 87.62	Yttrium 39 **Y** 88.906	Zirconium 40 **Zr** 91.224	Niobium 41 **Nb** 92.906	Molybdenum 42 **Mo** 95.94	Technetium 43 **Tc** 97.907	Ruthenium 44 **Ru** 101.07	Rhodium 45 **Rh** 102.906
6	Cesium 55 **Cs** 132.905	Barium 56 **Ba** 137.327	Lanthanum 57 **La** 138.906	Hafnium 72 **Hf** 178.49	Tantalum 73 **Ta** 180.948	Tungsten 74 **W** 183.85	Rhenium 75 **Re** 186.207	Osmium 76 **Os** 190.2	Iridium 77 **Ir** 192.22
7	Francium 87 **Fr** 223.020	Radium 88 **Ra** 226.025	Actinium 89 **Ac** 227.028	Rutherfordium 104 **Rf** (261)	Dubnium 105 **Db** (262)	Seaborgium 106 **Sg** (263)	Bohrium 107 **Bh** (262)	Hassium 108 **Hs** (265)	Meitnerium 109 **Mt** (266)

Element —— Hydrogen
Atomic Number —— 1 —— State of Matter
Symbol —— H
Atomic Mass —— 1.008

Lanthanide Series	Cerium 58 **Ce** 140.115	Praseodymium 59 **Pr** 140.908	Neodymium 60 **Nd** 144.24	Promethium 61 **Pm** 144.913	Samarium 62 **Sm** 150.36	Europium 63 **Eu** 151.965
Actinide Series	Thorium 90 **Th** 232.038	Protactinium 91 **Pa** 231.036	Uranium 92 **U** 238.029	Neptunium 93 **Np** 237.048	Plutonium 94 **Pu** 244.064	Americium 95 **Am** 243.061